☆☆☆ Forbes

TRAVEL GUIDE

Formerly Mobil Travel Guide

MID-ATLANTIC

ACKNOWLEDGMENTS

We gratefully acknowledge the help of our representatives for their efficient and perceptive inspections of the lodgings listed. Forbes Travel Guide is also grateful to the talented writers who contributed to this book.

MID-ATLANTIC
★★★★

2

ISBN: 9-780841-61418-5   Manufactured in the USA

10 9 8 7 6 5 4 3 2 1

TABLE OF CONTENTS

STAR ATTRACTIONS

If you've been a reader of Mobil Travel Guide, you will have heard that this historic brand partnered with another storied media name, Forbes, in 2009 to create a new entity, Forbes Travel Guide. For more than 50 years, Mobil Travel Guide assisted travelers in making smart decisions about where to stay and dine when traveling. With this new partnership, our mission has not changed: We're committed to the same rigorous inspections of hotels, restaurants and spas—the most comprehensive in the industry with more than 500 standards tested at each property we visit—to help you cut through the clutter and make easy and informed decisions on where to spend your time and travel budget. Our team of anonymous inspectors are constantly on the road, sleeping in hotels, eating in restaurants and making spa appointments, evaluating those exacting standards to determine a property's rating.

What kind of standards are we looking for when we visit a proprety? We're looking for more than just high-thread count sheets, pristine spa treatment rooms and white linen-topped tables. We look for service that's attentive, individualized and unforgettable. We note how long it takes to be greeted when you sit down at your table, or to be served when you order room service, or whether the hotel staff can confidently help you when you've forgotten that one essential item that will make or break your trip. Unlike other travel ratings entities, we visit the places we rate, testing hundreds of attributes to compile our ratings, and our ratings cannot be bought or influenced. The Forbes Five Star rating is the most prestigious achievement in hospitality—while we rate more than 8,000 properties in the U.S., Canada, Hong Kong, Macau and Beijing, for 2010, we have awarded Five Star designations to only 53 hotels, 21 restaurants and 18 spas. When you travel with Forbes, you can travel with confidence, knowing that you'll get the very best experience, no matter who you are.

We understand the importance of making the most of your time. That's why the most trusted name in travel is now Forbes Travel Guide.

STAR RATED HOTELS

Whether you're looking for the ultimate in luxury or the best value for your travel budget, we have a hotel recommendation for you. To help you pinpoint properties that meet your needs, Forbes Travel Guide classifies each lodging by type according to the following characteristics:

★★★★★These exceptional properties provide a memorable experience through virtually flawless service and the finest of amenities. Staff are intuitive, engaging and passionate, and eagerly deliver service above and beyond the guests' expectations. The hotel was designed with the guest's comfort in mind, with particular attention paid to craftsmanship and quality of product. A Five Star property is a destination unto itself.

★★★★These properties provide a distinctive setting, and a guest will find many interesting and inviting elements to enjoy throughout the property. Attention to detail is prominent throughout the property, from design concept to quality of products provided. Staff are accommodating and take pride in catering to the guest's specific needs throughout their stay.

★★★These well-appointed establishments have enhanced amenities that provide travelers with a strong sense of location, whether for style or function. They may have a distinguishing style and ambience in both the public spaces and guest rooms; or they may be more focused on functionality, providing guests with easy access to local events, meetings or tourism highlights.

★★The Two Star hotel is considered a clean, comfortable and reliable establishment that has expanded amenities, such as a full-service restaurant.

★The One Star lodging is a limited-service hotel or inn that is considered a clean, comfortable and reliable establishment.

For every property, we also provide pricing information. All prices quoted are accurate at the time of publication; however, prices cannot be guaranteed.

STAR RATED RESTAURANTS

Every restaurant in this book comes highly recommended as an outstanding dining experience.

★★★★★Forbes Five Star restaurants deliver a truly unique and distinctive dining experience. A Five Star restaurant consistently provides exceptional food, superlative service and elegant décor. An emphasis is placed on originality and personalized, attentive and discreet service. Every detail that surrounds the experience is attended to by a warm and gracious dining room team.

★★★★These are exciting restaurants with often well-known chefs that feature creative and complex foods and emphasize various culinary techniques and a focus on seasonality. A highly-trained dining room staff provides refined personal service and attention.

★★★Three Star restaurants offer skillfully-prepared food with a focus on a specific style or cuisine. The dining room staff provides warm and professional service in a comfortable atmosphere. The décor is well-coordinated with quality fixtures and decorative items, and promotes a comfortable ambience.

★★The Two Star restaurant serves fresh food in a clean setting with efficient service. Value is considered in this category, as is family friendliness.

★The One Star restaurant provides a distinctive experience through culinary specialty, local flair or individual atmosphere.

Because menu prices can fluctuate, we list a pricing range rather than specific prices. The pricing ranges are per diner, and assume that you order an appetizer or dessert, an entrée and one drink.

STAR RATED SPAS

Forbes Travel Guide's spa ratings are based on objective evaluations of more than 450 attributes. About half of these criteria assess basic expectations, such as staff courtesy, the technical proficiency and skill of the employees and whether the facility is clean and maintained properly. Several standards address issues that impact a guest's physical comfort and convenience, as well as the staff's ability to impart a sense of personalized service. Additional criteria measure the spa's ability to create a completely calming ambience.

★★★★★Stepping foot in a Five Star spa will result in an exceptional experience with no detail overlooked. These properties wow their guests with extraordinary design and facilities, and uncompromising service. Expert staff cater to your every whim and pamper you with the most advanced treatments and skin care lines available. These spas often offer exclusive treatments and may emphasize local elements.

★★★★Four Star spas provide a wonderful experience in an inviting and serene environment. A sense of personalized service is evident from the moment you check in and receive your robe and slippers. The guest's comfort is always of utmost concern to the well-trained staff.

★★★These spas offer well-appointed facilities with a full complement of staff to ensure that guests' needs are met. The spa facilities include clean and appealing treatment rooms, changing areas and a welcoming reception desk.

DELAWARE

DELAWARE "IS LIKE A DIAMOND, DIMINUTIVE, BUT HAVING WITHIN IT INHERENT VALUE," wrote John Lofland, the eccentric "Bard of Milford," in 1847. Only 96 miles long and from nine to 35 miles wide, the state is a corporate and agricultural superpower. Soybeans, corn, tomatoes, strawberries, asparagus, fruit and other crops bring in about $170 million each year. And favorable state policies have persuaded more than 183,000 corporations to base their headquarters in the "corporate capital of the world."

Within just 2,489 square miles, Delaware boasts rolling, forested hills in the north, stretches of bare sand dunes in the south and miles of marshland along the coast.

Visitors can tour a modern agricultural or chemical research center in the morning and search for buried pirate treasures in the afternoon. In fact, Coin Beach in Rehoboth gets its name from the mysterious coins that frequently wash ashore, most likely from the *Faithful Steward*, a passenger vessel lost in 1785. The *deBraak*, another doomed ship that foundered off Lewes in 1798, was raised in 1986 because of the belief that it may have had a fortune in captured Spanish coins or bullion aboard. No such luck, but the artifacts themselves are a treasure.

Despite Delaware's current riches, the state's history started on a grim note. The first 28 colonists landed in the spring of 1631, and after an argument with a Lenni-Lenape chief, their bones were found mingled with those of cattle and strewn over their burned fields. In 1638, a group of Swedes established the first permanent settlement in the state—and the first permanent settlement of Swedes in North America—at Fort Christina, in what is now Wilmington.

Henry Hudson, in Dutch service, first discovered Delaware Bay in 1609. A year later, Thomas Argall reported it to English navigators and named it for his superior, Lord de la Warr, governor of Virginia. Ownership changed rapidly from Swedish to Dutch to English hands. The Maryland-Delaware boundary was set by a British court order in 1750 and surveyed as part of the Mason-Dixon Line in 1763-1767. The boundary with New Jersey, also long disputed, was confirmed by the Supreme Court in 1935.

The "First State" (first to adopt the Constitution, on December 7, 1787) is proud of its history of sturdy independence, both military and political. During the Revolution, the "Delaware line" was a crack regiment of the Continental Army. The men would "fight all day and dance all night," according to a dispatch by General Greene. How well they danced is open to question, but they fought with such gallantry that they received regular praise in the general's dispatches.

Delaware statesman John Dickinson, "penman of the Revolution" and one of the state's five delegates to the Constitutional Convention, was instrumental in the decision to write a new federal constitution rather than to simply patch up the Articles of Confederation.

Along with Lofland and Dickinson, Delaware has produced many literary figures, including the 19th-century playwright and novelist Robert Montgomery Bird, writer and illustrator Howard Pyle, Henry Seidel Canby, founder of the *Saturday Review* and novelist John P. Marquand.

BETHANY BEACH

See also Fenwick Island, Lewes, Rehoboth Beach

As Bethany Beach was founded by members of the Christian Church, it was originally a site for revival camp meetings and eventually, it became the town of Bethany Beach. This quiet beach town on the Atlantic Ocean offers excellent surfing, fishing and swimming.

WHAT TO SEE
HOLTS LANDING STATE PARK

Road 346, Millville, 302-227-2800; www.destateparks.com

This 203-acre park located along the Indian River Bay offers fishing, crabbing, clamming, sailing, boating (launch ramp providing access to bay) and picnicking, as well as playground and ball fields. The park contains a beach, fields of grass and forests. There are also picnic areas with tables and grills set up for the public to use.

Daily 8 a.m.-dusk.

SPECIAL EVENTS
BETHANY BEACH FARMERS' MARKET

Garfield Parkway and Pennslyvania Avenue, Bethany Beach, 800-962-7873;
www.bbfm.us

This farmers' market takes place on Sunday mornings during the summertime. You can purchase fresh local fruits, cheeses, vegetables, breads and other baked goods, as well as flowers such as lavender and sunflowers.

June-September.

SEASIDE CRAFT SHOW

The Boardwalk, Garfield Parkway, Bethany Beach, 800-962-7873;
www.bethanybeachartsfestival

This juried craft show features original handmade works set up in booths along the boardwalk, the bandstand and on the street. You can find pottery, jewelry, paintings, photography and more.

Early June.

WHERE TO STAY
★HOLIDAY INN EXPRESS BETHANY BEACH

39642 Jefferson Bridge Road, Bethany Beach, 302-541-9200, 877-863-4780;
www.hiexpress.com

100 rooms. Complimentary breakfast. Business center. Fitness center. Pool. $61-150

WHERE TO EAT
★MANGO'S

97 Garfield Parkway, Bethany Beach, 302-537-6621; www.mangomikes.com

Caribbean. Lunch, dinner (Friday-Saturday). Closed Monday-Thursday; December-March. Children's menu. Outdoor seating. Bar. $16-35

DOVER

See also Lewes

Dover, Delaware's capital since 1777, was designed around the city's lovely green by William Penn who founded Dover in 1683. Lovely 18th- and 19th-century houses still line State Street. Because of Delaware's favorable corporation laws, more than 60,000 U.S. firms pay taxes in Dover. At Dover Air Force Base, the Military Airlift Command operates one of the biggest air cargo terminals in the world. The city is also home to Delaware State College, Wesley College and the Terry campus of Delaware Technical and Community College.

WHAT TO SEE

AIR MOBILITY COMMAND MUSEUM

1301 Heritage Road, Dover, 302-677-5938; www.amcmuseum.org

Located in a historic hangar on Dover Air Force Base, the museum houses a collection of more than two dozen aircraft and historical artifacts dating back to World War II. There are flight simulators and a junior pilot's plane for kid's to check out. There's also a museum store to purchase souvenirs.
Admission: Free. Tuesday-Sunday 9 a.m.-4 p.m.

DELAWARE AGRICULTURAL MUSEUM AND VILLAGE

866 N. DuPont Highway, Dover, 302-734-1618; www.agriculturalmuseum.org

This museum features displays of farm life from an early settlement to 1960. The main exhibition hall and historic structures representing a late-19th-century farming community includes a gristmill, blacksmith and wheelwright shop, farmhouse, a one-room schoolhouse, store and train station. This museum and village provide education about what life was like when people had to grow food for themselves to survive.
Admission: adults $5, seniors and students $3, children under 4 free.
Tuesday-Saturday 10 a.m.-3 p.m.

DELAWARE STATE VISITOR CENTER AND GALLERIES

The Green, 406 Federal St., Dover, 302-739-4266; www.delaware.gov

Administered by the Delaware State Museums, the center offers information on attractions. Galleries have exhibits of the state's history and culture.
Admission: Free. Tuesday-Saturday 9 a.m.-4:30 p.m., Sunday 1:30-4:30 p.m.

DOVER DOWNS HOTEL, CASINO & INTERNATIONAL SPEEDWAY

1131 N. DuPont Highway, Dover, 302-674-4600, 800-711-5882; www.doverdowns.com

This hotel, casino and speedway is a great way to get your gambling fix. Head to the casino that is open 24 hours a day and features almost 3,200 slot machines. The Colonnade offers restaurants and shopping. Dover Downs also provides plenty of entertainment in the Rollins Center which has 1,600 seats and hosts acts such as Wayne Newton, Bill Cosby, Kenny Rogers, Tom Jones, Gladys Knight and others. And if that's not enough, Dover Downs also has live harness horse racing at the Dover International Speedway where you can also catch racing events including NASCAR Winston Cup auto racing.
Casino: Daily 24 hours. Horse Racing: Late-October-mid-August. Auto Racing: June, September.

FIRST STATE HERITAGE PARK

152 S. State St., Dover, 302-739-9194; www.destateparks.com/heritagepark
This park actually connects historical and cultural sites, inlcluding the Briggs Museum of American Art, the Delaware Public Archives, Legislative Hall, Museum Square, the State House Museum, Delaware Visitor Center and Woodburn House. You can take a guided walking tour of this park. Every first Saturday of the month is First Saturdays in the First State, where each site hosts special programs designed for the specific month and you can get a tour of Legislative Hall.
Monday-Saturday 9 a.m.-3 p.m., Sunday 1:30-3 p.m. First Saturday of the month: 9 a.m.-5 p.m.

JOHN DICKINSON PLANTATION

340 Kitts Hummrock Road, Dover, 302-739-3277; www.history.delaware.gov/museums
This is the restored 1740 boyhood residence of John Dickinson, the "penman of the Revolution." Here, you can learn about Dickinson's life and background on his plantation. Take a tour led by historic interpreters dressed in period costumes, depicting characters from the early 1700s and 1800s.
Admission: Free. Tuesday-Saturday 10 a.m.-3:30 p.m., Sunday 1:30-4:30 p.m.; closed Sundays, January-February.

JOHNSON VICTROLA MUSEUM

Museum Square, 375 S. New St., Dover, 302-739-4266; www.dovermuseums.org
This museum was created as a tribute to Eldridge Reeves Johnson, founder of the Victor Talking Machine Company. Johnson retired in 1827 and the company was sold to RCA in 1930. (You might recognize the image of a terrier dog looking into a phonograph which was the logo for Victor.) Johnson received a Grammy Award posthumously in 1985, which is on display here. The museum holds a collection of talking machines, Victrolas, early recordings and equipment.
Admission: Free. Tuesday-Saturday 9 a.m.-4:30 p.m., Sunday 1:30-4:30 p.m.

MUSEUM OF SMALL TOWN LIFE

316 S. Governors Ave., Dover, 302-739-3261;www.dovermuseums.org
Housed in a building of the Old Presbyterian Church of Dover, this museum recreates life in the late 19th century. Exhibits showcase a turn-of-the-century drugstore, printing press, pharmacy, carpenter shop, general store, post office, shoemaker's shop and printer's shop. There are also changing exhibits which take a look at life in the small towns of Delaware. The building has beautiful stained glass windows that were designed in the late 19th century.
Admission: Free. Tuesday-Saturday 9 a.m.-4:30 p.m., Sunday 1:30-4:30 p.m.

THE OLD STATE HOUSE

The Green, 406 Federal St., Dover, 302-739-4266; www.history.delaware.gov
Delaware's seat of government since 1791, the State House, restored in 1976, contains a courtroom, ceremonial governor's office, legislative chambers and county offices. A portrait of George Washington in the Senate Chamber was commissioned in 1802 by the legislature as a memorial to the nation's first president. Although Delaware's General Assembly moved to nearby Legisla-

tive Hall in 1933, the 1792 State House remains the state's symbolic capital. Admission: Free. Tuesday-Saturday 9 a.m.-4:30 p.m., Sunday 1:30-4:30 p.m.

SPECIAL EVENTS
OLD DOVER DAYS
Dover, 800-233-5368; www.visitdover.com
For 76 years, Dover has celebrated its status as the capital of the first state with an old fashioned parade, dancing around the maypole, walking tours, arts and crafts, food and drinks and plenty more. This event is completely free and all the museums and public building are open for tours as well as historic houses and gardens that are not usually open to the public. There's a kick-off concert on Friday evening and a barbecue dinner and a showcase of antique and vintage cars. Plenty of activites keep children occupied, from games to arts, a scavenger hunt and carnival rides.
First weekend in May.

WHERE TO STAY
★COMFORT INN
222 S. DuPont Highway, Dover, 302-674-3300, 877-424-6423; www.choicehotels.com
94 rooms. Restaurant, bar. Complimentary breakfast. Fitness center. Pool. Pets accepted. $61-150

★★★SHERATON DOVER HOTEL
1570 N. DuPont Highway, Dover, 302-678-8500, 888-625-5144; www.sheratondover.com
This hotel is conveniently located just a few minutes from shopping and local attractions in historic Dover. Guest rooms are spacious and subdued with neutral colors and traditional furniture. Bring your dog along and they'll be treated to the Sheraton Sweet Sleeper bed. After a day of relaxing in the heated pool, head to Chops Grille for an intimate dinner in a romantic setting.
152 rooms. Business center. Fitness center. Pool. Pets accepted. $151-250

FENWICK ISLAND
See also Bethany Beach, Lewes, Rehoboth Beach; also see Ocean City, MD
Fenwick Island, at the southeast corner of Delaware, was named after Thomas Fenwick, a wealthy landowner from England who purchased the land in 1686. Once known for its "salt making"—after residents James and Jacob Brasure began extracting salt from the ocean in 1775—the island has become a popular summer resort.

WHAT TO SEE
DISCOVERSEA SHIPWRECK MUSEUM
708 Ocean Highway, Fenwick Island, 302-539-9366, 888-743-5524; www.discoversea.com
Opened in 1995, this museum contains changing exhibits of shipwreck artifacts recovered on the Delmarva Peninsula. They have around 10,000 artifacts along with rotating exhibits that have been found after years of research.
June-August, daily 11 a.m.-8 p.m.; September-May, Saturday-Sunday 11 a.m.-4 p.m.

FENWICK ISLAND LIGHTHOUSE
146th Street and Lighthouse Lane, Fenwick Island, 302-539-4115;
www.fenwickislandlighthouse.org
Built in 1858, this popular attraction is 89 feet tall and houses a mini-museum in its base. While the tower is closed, you can still explore the grounds and the museum. There's also a gift shop nearby.
May-June, Friday-Monday 10 a.m.-2 p.m.; July-September, Thursday-Tuesday 10 a.m.-2 p.m.; October, Friday-Monday 10 a.m.-2 p.m.

FENWICK ISLAND STATE PARK
Fenwick Island, 302-227-6991; www.destateparks.com/park/fenwick-island
This 344-acre seashore park is located between the Atlantic Ocean and Little Assawoman Bay. The white sandy beaches provide a popular spot for sunbathing, swimming, surfing, surf fishing and sailing. There's a bathhouse which is equipped with showers and changing rooms and a concession area and gift shop. You can also go horseback riding along the beach from November to April.
Daily 8 a.m.-dusk.

SPECIAL EVENT
DELAWARE SEASHORE FALL SURF FISHING CLASSIC
Fenwick Island State Park, Fenwick Island, 302-539-6243; www.oldinlet.com
The fishing areas for this competition are located within Delaware Seashore State Park and Fenwick Island State Park. More than $15,000 in cash and prizes are awarded in the tournament.
Early October.

WHERE TO STAY
★ATLANTIC COAST INN
37558 Lighthouse Road, Fenwick Island, 302-539-7673, 800-432-8038;
www.atlanticcoastinn.com
48 rooms. Pool. Closed October-mid-April. $61-150

LEWES
See also Bethany Beach, Fenwick Island, Rehoboth Beach
Lewes has been home base to Delaware Bay pilots for 300 years. Weather-beaten, cypress-shingled houses still line the streets where pirates plundered and Captain Kidd bargained away his loot. The treacherous sandbars outside the harbor have claimed their share of ships, and stories of sunken treasures have circulated for centuries. Some buildings show scars from cannonballs that hit their mark when the British bombarded Lewes in the War of 1812.

WHAT TO SEE
BURTON-INGRAM HOUSE
110 Shipcarpenter St., Lewes, 302-564-7670; www.historiclewes.org
This Federal-style house is made from hand-hewn timbers and cypress shingles. There is a three-story staircase open through the floors from which you can see the entire house. It is home to beautiful antiques, artifacts and impressive artwork.

DUTCH HERITAGE IN LEWES

As an Atlantic beach destination, historic Lewes is an offbeat choice. Lewes is Delaware's oldest community, which began as a Dutch attempt at establishing a whaling station in 1631. The neighborhood adjacent to the pleasure-boat harbor on the Lewes and Rehoboth Canal is dotted with beautifully restored 18th- and 19th-century cottages and mansions that once housed ship pilots working Delaware Bay.

For a one-mile stroll through the Historic District, begin at the Zwaanendael Museum. Built in 1931, it was adapted from the 17th-century town hall of Hoorn in the Netherlands, where Lewes's first colonists came from. The museum details the town's history and explains that all 28 (some sources say 32) original colonists were killed in a dispute with the local Native Americans. Behind the museum, the gambrel-roofed Fisher-Martin House acts as a visitor center.

From the museum, head up Second Street in the shade of a canopy of giant, old trees. At 218 Second Street, Lewes's oldest home, the little red- and yellow-shingled Ryves Holt House, is believed to have been built around 1665. Once a colonial inn, it also housed the Officer of the Port. A few steps to the right at 118 Front Street, which parallels the canal, a cannonball fired by a British vessel in the War of 1812 still juts from the brick foundation of the Cannonball House Marine Museum. Inside are nautical exhibits. Many of the town's Victorian homes are richly adorned with gingerbread trim, and several are brightly painted. Just off Second Street, the Ann Eliza Baker House is a dazzler in yellow, gold, purple and orange. Head north up Third Street to Shipcarpenter Street, where the Lewes Historical Society maintains an outdoor museum of early Delaware architecture. Several are scooter houses—homes relocated following local custom. Conclude this tour at Shipcarpenter Square, an attractive development of restored 18th- and 19th-century scooter homes, all private residences, set around a nicely landscaped mall.

May-early June, Saturday 11 a.m.-4 p.m.; Mid-June-mid-September, Monday-Saturday 11 a.m.-4 p.m.; mid-September-early October, Saturday 11 a.m.-4 p.m.

CANNONBALL HOUSE & MARINE MUSEUM

118 Front St., Lewes, 302-645-7670; www.historiclewes.org

Built in the late 18th century, this house was originally called the David Rowland Home. It was hit by a cannonball during the War of 1812 and renamed. (Don't miss the marker which shows where the cannon hit the house.) Over time, it has been used for many things from the mayor's office to a laundry store to a restaurant.

Admission: adults $2, children 12 and under free. May-early June, Saturday 11 a.m.-4 p.m.; Mid-June-mid-September, Monday-Saturday 11 a.m.-4 p.m.; mid-September-early October, Monday-Saturday 11 a.m.-4 p.m.

CAPE HENLOPEN STATE PARK

42 Cape Henlopen Drive, Lewes, 302-645-8983; www.destateparks.com

The park has more than 3,000 acres at the confluence of Delaware Bay and the Atlantic Ocean with six miles of beach to enjoy. There are two swimming beaches, a bath house and a concession area. There's also an 18-hole disc golf course, basketball courts, three-miles of paved trails for hiking and biking and more. The park sits on the site of decommissioned Fort Miles, part of the U.S. coastal defense system during World War II. For amazing vistas, climb up to the top of an old military bunker.

Daily 8 a.m.-dusk.

CAPE MAY-LEWES FERRY

43 Henlopen Drive, Lewes, 302-644-6030, 800-643-3779;
www.capemaylewesferry.com

This ferry is the sole connection between Highway 13 (Ocean Highway) on the Delmarva Peninsula and southern terminus of the Garden State Parkway (NJ). The trip across the Delaware Bay (17 miles) from Lewes to Cape May, New Jersey is 80 minutes one-way.

Fares and schedules vary; check Web site for information.

EARLY PLANK HOUSE

110 Shipcarpenter St., Lewes, 302-564-7670; www.historiclewes.org

This small Swedish log cabin was restored to reflect the home of an early settler. The design for the house was brought when some Swedish pioneers settled near New Castle. The house may have been used as a home for slaves.

May-early June, Saturday 11 a.m.-4 p.m.; Mid-June-mid-September, Monday-Saturday 11 a.m.-4 p.m.; mid-September-early October, Saturday 11 a.m.-4 p.m.

HIRAM R. BURTON HOUSE

Second and Shipcarpenter streets, Lewes, 302-564-7670; www.historiclewes.org

Named after a prominent Lewes physician and congressman, Hiram Rodney Burton, this house dating back to 1720 features antique furnishings and an 18th-century kitchen. There's also a reading room with materials dedicated to Delaware history and a beautiful garden.

May-early June, Saturday 11 a.m.-4 p.m.; Mid-June-mid-September, Monday-Saturday 11 a.m.-4 p.m.; mid-September-early October, Saturday 11 a.m.-4 p.m.

LEWES HISTORICAL SOCIETY COMPLEX

110 Shipcarpenter St., Lewes, 302-564-7670; www.historiclewes.org

Restored buildings were moved to this site to create a feel for Lewes' early days. The Historical Society owns 12 properties, nine of which are part of this complex.

Admission: adults $5, children 12 and under free. May-early June, Saturday 11 a.m.-4 p.m.; Mid-June-mid-September, Monday-Saturday 11 a.m.-4 p.m.; mid-September-early October, Saturday 11 a.m.-4 p.m.

OLD DOCTOR'S OFFICE

Third Street, Lewes, 302-564-7670; www.historiclewes.org/museums/odo.html

This Greek Revival building was once a doctor's office and now serves as a medical and dental museum, stocked with 19th century doctor's equipment. Over the years, the building was moved numerous times, which was typical of the time period.

May-early June, Saturday 11 a.m.-4 p.m.; Mid-June-mid-September, Monday-Saturday 11 a.m.-4 p.m.; mid-September-early October, Saturday 11 a.m.-4 p.m.

RABBIT'S FERRY HOUSE
Third Street, Lewes, 302-564-7670; www.historiclewes.org/museums/rfh.html
This traditional farmhouse was built around 1741 and contains original paneling and period pieces. It provides a good example of how a traditional farmhouse was organized.
May-early June, Saturday 11 a.m.-4 p.m.; Mid-June-mid-September, Monday-Saturday 11 a.m.-4 p.m.; mid-September-early October, Saturday 11 a.m.-4 p.m.

THOMPSON COUNTRY STORE
Third Street, Lewes, 302-564-7670; www.historiclewes.org/about/history.html
This country store was moved from its original location in Thompsonville to Lewes. The Thompson family ran it as a store until 1962. It also functioned as a post office for a time.
May-early June, Saturday 11 a.m.-4 p.m.; Mid-June-mid-September, Monday-Saturday 11 a.m.-4 p.m.; mid-September-early October, Saturday 11 a.m.-4 p.m.

ZWAANENDAEL MUSEUM
102 Kings Highway, Lewes, 302-645-1148; www.history.delaware.gov/
This adaptation of the Hoorn town hall in Holland was built in 1931 as a memorial to the original 1631 Dutch founders of Lewes. It highlights the town's maritime heritage with colonial, Native American and Dutch exhibits.
Admission: Free. Tuesday-Saturday 10 a.m.-4:30 p.m., Sunday 1:30-4:30 p.m.

SPECIAL EVENTS
COAST DAY
University of Delaware Marine Studies Complex, 700 Pilottown Road, Lewes,
302-831-8083; www.ocean.udel.edu/coastday

If you're fascinated by the sea, this event is perfect for you to explore Delaware's marine resources. Started more than a quarter century ago, this event opens their research facilities and research vessels to the public. You can meet with scientists and learn about their research in hands-on marine exhibits, demonstrations and nautical films. There are also crab races, a crab cake cook-off, a boat show and more.
First Sunday in October.

GREAT DELAWARE KITE FESTIVAL
Cape Henlopen State Park, 42 Henlopen Drive, Lewes, 302-645-8983;
www.leweschamber.com
This annual festival heralds the beginning of spring on the Friday before Easter. It's surprising how this festival began; in 1968, the Maharajah of Bharatpur in India challenged the Governor of Delaware to a kite flying contest. Because the event was so popular, it continued over the years. The day begins with an opening ceremony before the three categories of competition and ends with an awards ceremony.
Early April.

WHERE TO STAY
★★★HOTEL RODNEY

142 Second St., Lewes, 302-645-6466, 800-824-8754; www.hotelrodneydelaware.com
Built in 1926, this stylish boutique hotel is located in historic downtown Lewes, minutes from Rehoboth Beach as well as shopping and dining options. Rooms are simple and chic with neutral décor. Recently renovated, they have flat-screen TVs, iPod clock radios, hardwood floors and comfortable bedding. Room service is available from the onsite restaurant, Beseme. 20 rooms. Restaurant. Fitness center. Pets accepted. $151-250

★★★INN AT CANAL SQUARE

122 Market St., Lewes, 302-644-3377, 888-644-1911; www.theinnatcanalsquare.com
Adjacent to the beautiful historic district, this charming "Nantucket-style" bed and breakfast offers private waterfront porches in many of the rooms, along with mini-refrigerators, coffee makers, robes and flat-screen TVs. A popular vacation headquarters in summer, it's only a mile from Cape Henlopen State Park's beaches. Guests are served a large European-style breakfast each morning.
24 rooms. Complimentary breakfast. Fitness center. $151-250

WHERE TO EAT
★★★THE BUTTERY RESTAURANT AND BAR

102 Second St., Lewes, 302-645-7755; www.butteryrestaurant.com
This charming Victorian restaurant located in the restored Trader Mansion offers a variety of entrées, from Maryland crab cakes to sea scallops and Maine lobster tail. Sunday's brunch features a fruit plate and fresh pastries along with an array of tasty options, including eggs Benedict, Belgian waffles, omelets or crepes. To spice things up, opt for a glass of champagne, a mimosa or a bloody mary.
American. Lunch, dinner, Sunday brunch. $36-85

MONTCHANIN
See also Wilmington
Located in the Northeastern part of Delaware and near Wilmington, Montchanin is a small village on about 20 acres with only about 21 buildings and foundations of other buildings that are no longer standing. Most of the bulidings were built around 1840 and vary in architectural styles. The village was named after Alexandrine de Montchanin, the grandmother of Pierre Samuel duPont de Nemours, the founder of DuPont Gunpowder Company.

WHERE TO STAY
★★★INN AT MONTCHANIN VILLAGE

Route 100 and Kirk Road, Montchanin, 302-888-2133, 800-269-2473;
www.montchanin.com
Once part of the Winterthur Estate and listed on the National Register of Historic Places, this inn's white picket fence, winding walkways and country sensibilities create a relaxing retreat. Guests can stay in one of several carefully restored houses featuring lavish guest rooms with four-poster beds and modern marble bathrooms. The onsite spa has a full menu of spa treatments from massages to facials, as well as treatments just for men. Nearby activities

include antiquing, scenic country drives and the Longwood Gardens.
28 rooms. Fitness center. Spa. $151-250

WHERE TO EAT
★★★KRAZY KAT'S
Route 100 and Kirk Road, Montchanin, 302-888-2133, 800-269-2473;
www.montchanin.com

Krazy Kat's is set in a 19th-century blacksmith's shop neighboring the charming and historic Inn at Montchanin Village. Seats covered in animal prints and critter portraits adorning the walls set the stage for a menu of meaty signatures like barrel cut bison ribeye with an espresso rub, roasted fennel, fingerling potatoes, chanterelles and smoked tomato jus. At dinner, a prix fixe menu is also available. Sunday brunch features delicious favorites like eggs Benedict, Belgian waffles, and brioche French toast. The wine list is extensive and features international varietals.

French. Breakfast, lunch (Monday-Friday), dinner, Sunday brunch. Reservations recommended. Outdoor seating. $36-85

NEW CASTLE
See aslo Newark, Wilmington

Established in 1651, New Castle is one of Delaware's first settlements. Earning many accolades, it served as a meeting place for the Colonial assemblies, was the first capital of the state, and became an early center of culture and communication. Its harbor made it a busy port in the 18th century until Wilmington, a closer neighbor to Philadelphia, took over its commerce. Today, New Castle attracts historians and architects alike. It lies at the foot of the Delaware Memorial Bridge, which connects with the southern end of the New Jersey Turnpike.

WHAT TO SEE

AMSTEL HOUSE MUSEUM
2 E. Fourth St., New Castle, 302-322-2794; www.newcastlehistory.org

This 1730 restored brick mansion was built by Dr. John Finney, a wealthy landowner. The seventh governor of Delaware lived here and even George Washington attended a wedding at the home. It now houses colonial furnishings, arts and a complete colonial kitchen. You can also walk the grounds of the beautiful garden.

Admission: adults $3, children 6-12 $1.50. Wednesday-Saturday 11 a.m.-4 p.m., Sunday 1-4 p.m. Garden: Daily dawn-dusk.

FORT DELAWARE STATE PARK
Pea Patch Island, 302-834-7941; www.destateparks.com/fdsp

This grim, gray fort was built as a coastal defense in 1860 on Pea Patch Island, which is only a mile from Delaware City. The fort was used as a prisoner-of-war depot for three years, housing up to 12,500 Confederate prisoners at a time. Its damp, low-lying terrain and poor conditions encouraged epidemics that led to some 2,400 deaths. The fort was modernized in 1896 and remained in commission until 1943. There are overlooks of heronry, picnicking and living-history programs available for visitors. The museum has a scale model of the fort, model Civil War relics and an orientation video.

The only way to gain access to the Fort is by taking a ferry (see Web site for the schedule).
Ferry: adults $11, seniors $10, children 3-12 $6, children under 2 free.

GEORGE READ II HOUSE

42 The Strand, New Castle, 302-322-8411; www.hsd.org/read.htm
This is a Federal-style house with elegant interior details: gilded fanlights, silver door-hardware, carved woodwork and relief plasterwork. It's furnished with period antiques and the garden design dates back to 1847.
Admission: adults $5, seniors, students and military personnel $4, children 6-12 $2, children under 6 free. March-December, Wednesday-Friday 11 a.m.-4 p.m., Saturday 10 a.m.-4 p.m., Sunday 11 a.m.-4 p.m.; January-February, Saturday 10 a.m.-4 p.m., Sunday 11 a.m.-4 p.m.; weekdays by appointment.

THE GREEN

Delaware and Third streets, New Castle
Laid out under the direction of Peter Stuyvesant in 1651, this public square is surrounded by dozens of historically important buildings.

OLD DUTCH HOUSE

32 E. Third St., New Castle, 302-322-2794; www.newcastlehistory.org
The Old Dutch House was thought to be Delaware's oldest dwelling in its original late 17th-century form. It's filled with Dutch colonial furnishings, artifacts and decorative arts.
Admission: adults $4, children 6-12 $1.50. April-December, Wenesday-Saturday 11 a.m.-4 p.m., Sunday 1-4 p.m.

OLD NEW CASTLE COURT HOUSE MUSEUM

211 Delaware St., New Castle, 302-323-4453; www.history.delaware.gov/museums
This is the original 1732 colonial capital and oldest surviving courthouse in the state. There are furnishings and exhibits on display. The cupola is the center of a 12-mile circle that delineates the Delaware-Pennsylvania border.
Admission: Free. Tuesday-Saturday 10 a.m.-3:30 p.m., Sunday 1:30-4:30 p.m.

SPECIAL EVENT
SEPARATION DAY

220 Delaware St., New Castle, 302-322-9802
This free celebration is an observance of Delaware's declaration of independence from Great Britain. There's a regatta, parade, reenactments, bands, concerts and fireworks.
June.

WHERE TO STAY
★CLARION HOTEL THE BELLE

1612 N. DuPont Highway, New Castle, 302-428-1000; www.clarionhotel.com
125 rooms. Restaurant, bar. Business center. Fitness center. Pets accepted. $61-150

WHERE TO EAT
★★THE ARSENAL AT OLD NEW CASTLE
30 Market St., New Castle, 302-323-1812; www.arsenal1812.com
American. Lunch, dinner. Closed Sunday-Monday. $36-85

NEWARK
See also New Castle, Wilmington
Newark was established at the crossroads of two well-traveled Native American trails. Nearby, Cooch's bridge was the site of the only Revolutionary War battle on Delaware soil. And according to tradition, Betsy Ross's flag was first raised in battle at the bridge on September 3, 1777.

WHAT TO SEE
UNIVERSITY OF DELAWARE
196 S. College Ave., Newark, 302-831-2792; www.udel.edu
Now with a student population of almost 16,000 undergraduates, the University of Delaware was founded as a small private academy in 1743. The central campus sits amidst stately elm trees, finely manicured lawns and Georgian-style brick buildings.
Tours: Monday-Friday, 10 a.m., noon, 2 p.m., Saturday 10 a.m., noon.

WHERE TO STAY
★★★HILTON WILMINGTON/CHRISTIANA
100 Continental Drive, Newark, 302-454-1500, 800-445-8667; www.hilton.com
This family- and business-friendly hotel is situated on a sprawling country estate. For an afternoon respite, take advantage of the hotel's high tea. Enjoy a meal in one of two restaurants—the casual Hunt Club Lounge and the more upscale Brasserie Grille—or explore shopping and dining nearby.
266 rooms. Restaurant, bar. Business center. Fitness center. Pool. Pets accepted. $151-250

WHERE TO EAT
★KLONDIKE KATE'S
158 E. Main St., Newark, 302-737-6100; www.klondikekates.com
American, Southwestern. Lunch, dinner. Bar. Children's menu. Outdoor seating. $16-35

REHOBOTH BEACH
See also Bethany Beach, Fenwick Island, Lewes
The "nation's summer capital" got its nickname because it was a favorite of Washington diplomats and legislators. A 2 1/2-hour drive from Washington, D.C., the largest summer resort in Delaware began as a spot for camp meetings amid sweet-smelling pine groves. In the 1920s real estate boomed, triggering Rehoboth Beach's rebirth as a resort town with a variety of accommodations, shopping areas and eateries. The town's deep sea and freshwater fishing, sailing, swimming, biking and strolling along cherry tree-lined Rehoboth Avenue make it a preferred retreat from Washington's summer heat.

WHAT TO SEE
DELAWARE SEASHORE STATE PARK
850 Inlet Road, Rehoboth Beach, 302-227-2800; www.destateparks.com
This 7-mile strip of land separates the Rehoboth and Indian River bays from the Atlantic. There are two swimming areas, fishing, surfing and boating to keep you occupied. Picnic pavilions, a concession area and a bathhouse equipped with showers and changing room ar also onsite.
Daily 8 a.m.-dusk.

JUNGLE JIM'S
8 Country Club Road, Rehoboth Beach, 302-227-8444; www.funatjunglejims.com
Jungle Jim's is fifteen acres of family fun, including go-karts, batting cages, two miniature golf courses, bumper boats, rock climbing and a water park. Admission prices vary. Mid-June-Labor Day, daily; late May, early June, late-September, limited hours.

MIDWAY SPEEDWAY
18645 Coastal Highway, Rehoboth Beach, 302-644-2042; www.midwayspeedwaypark.com
This recreational racing park features four tracks, including a Super 8 Track and Family Track, eight different styles of go-karts, a kiddie raceway and bumper boats.
Hours and prices vary.

SPECIAL EVENT
SUMMER CONCERT SERIES AT REHOBOTH BEACH BANDSTAND
501 Rehoboth Ave., Rehoboth Beach, 302-227-6181; www.rehobothbandstand.com
These free open-air concerts take place at Rehoboth Beach's bandstand Fridays and Saturdays at 8 p.m. and have featured peformers such as Liverpool Beat, a Beatles tribute band; and bluegrass band Annapolis Bluegrass, among many others.
June-September.

WHERE TO STAY
★★★BOARDWALK PLAZA HOTEL
Olive Avenue and the Boardwalk, Rehoboth Beach, 302-227-7169, 800-332-3224; www.boardwalkplaza.com
This Victorian-style hotel on Rehoboth Beach offers state-of-the-art comfort with high-speed Internet access and whirlpool tubs. Enjoy the scenic ocean views at Victoria's restaurant. Or enjoy tea and sandwiches by the ocean at the afternoon tea.
84 rooms. Restaurant, bar. Business center. Fitness center. Pool. $251-350

WHERE TO EAT
★★BLUE MOON
35 Baltimore Ave., Rehoboth Beach, 302-227-6515; www.bluemoonrehoboth.com
American. Dinner, Sunday brunch. Bar. $36-85

★★LA LA LAND
22 Wilmington Ave., Rehoboth Beach, 302-227-3887; www.lalalandrestaurant.com
American. Dinner. Closed Monday-Wednesday; mid-November-late April.
Bar. Reservations recommended. Outdoor seating. $16-35

WILMINGTON
See also New Castle, Newark
Wilmington, the "chemical capital of the world" and an international hub of
industry and shipping, is the largest city in Delaware. The Swedish, Dutch
and British have left their marks on the city. The Swedes settled first, seeking their fortunes and founding the colony of New Sweden. In 1655, Dutch
soldiers under Peter Stuyvesant, governor of New Amsterdam, captured the
little colony without bloodshed. Nine years later the English arrived, and
the town grew into a market and shipping center aided by wealthy Quakers.
Wilmington has flourished as an industrial port because of its abundant water
power and proximity to other eastern ports. From here come vulcanized fiber,
glazed leathers, dyed cotton, rubber hoses, autos and many other products.
And we can't forget that Vice President Joe Biden was a Wilmington resident.

WHAT TO SEE
BELLEVUE STATE PARK
800 Carr Road, Wilmington, 302-761-6963; www.destateparks.com
Bellevue State Park takes up 328 acres with tennis courts, a pond and gardens
amongst woods and fields. The pond allows for catch and release fishing.
There are nature, hiking and horseback-riding trails, as well as eight outdoor
tennis courts. Picnicking is popular as there are a few picnic facilities and
concerts and performances run in the summer months at the bandstand.
Daily 8 a.m.-dusk.

BRANDYWINE CREEK STATE PARK
Routes 92 and 100, Wilmington, 302-577-3534; www.destateparks.com
Brandywine features 933 acres of what used to be a dairy farm in the late
1800s. Now there are miles of nature and hiking trails to enjoy, fishing, ca-
noeing, tubing, cross-country skiing and disc golf.
Daily 8 a.m.-dusk.

BRANDYWINE SPRINGS PARK
800 N. French St., Wilmington, 302-395-5652; www.nccde.org
From 1827 to 1845, this was the site of a once-famous resort hotel for Southern planters and politicos. Here, Lafayette met Washington under the Council Oak before the Battle of Brandywine in 1777. There are picnicking areas,
fireplaces, pavilions, baseball fields and more.
Daily.

BRANDYWINE ZOO AND PARK
1001 N. Park Drive, Wilmington, 302-571-7788; www.destateparks.com/wilmsp/zoo
Designed by Frederick Law Olmsted, the park includes the Josephine Garden
with a fountain, roses and stands of Japanese cherry trees. The zoo, along

North Park Drive, features animals from both North and South America. There are picnicking areas and playgrounds to enjoy.

Admission: October-May, adults $4, children 3-11 and seniors $2, children under 3 free; June-September, adults $5, children 3-11 $3, seniors $4, children under 3 free. Daily 10 a.m.-4 p.m.

DELAWARE ART MUSEUM

2301 Kentmere Parkway, Wilmington, 302-571-9590; www.delart.org

This museum features the Howard Pyle Collection of American Illustrations, with works by Pyle, N.C. Wyeth and Maxfield Parrish; an American painting collection with works by West, Homer, Church, Glackens and Hopper; the Bancroft Collection of English Pre-Raphaelite art including works by Rossetti and Burne-Jones; and the Phelps Collection of Andrew Wyeth works. There are also changing exhibits and children's participatory gallery.

Admission: adults $12, seniors $10, students and children 7-18 $6, children 6 and under free. Free Sunday. Wenesday-Saturday 10 a.m.-4 p.m., Sunday noon-4 p.m.

DELAWARE HISTORY MUSEUM

504 Market St., Wilmington, 302-656-0637; www.hsd.org/dhm.htm

This museum is located in an old Woolworth store that has since been remodeled. There are three different galleries which feature changing exhibits on the history of Delaware such as costumes, paintings and decorative arts.

Admission: adults $4, seniors, students and military personnel $3, children 3-18 $2, children under 3 free. Wednesday-Friday 11 a.m.-4 p.m., Saturday 10 a.m.-4 p.m.

DELAWARE MUSEUM OF NATURAL HISTORY

4840 Kennett Pike, Wilmington, 302-658-9111; www.delmnh.org

This museum features exhibits of shells, dinosaurs, birds and mammals. Also on display is the largest bird egg and a 500-pound clam. There are hands-on activities for young children to enjoy along with a butterfly garden and a nature trail.

Admission: adults $6, children $5, seniors $4, children under 3 free. Monday-Saturday 9:30 a.m.-4:30 p.m., Sunday noon-4:30 p.m.

GRAND OPERA HOUSE

818 Market St., Mall, Wilmington, 302-658-7898; www.grandopera.org

This historic 1871 Victorian landmark was built by Masons. Since then, it has been restored and now serves as Delaware's Center for the Performing Arts, home of Opera Delaware, the First State Ballet Theatre and the Delaware Symphony. The façade is a fine example of Second Empire style interpreted in cast iron.

Box Office: Monday-Friday 10 a.m.-7 p.m., Saturday-Sunday noon-5 p.m.

HAGLEY MUSEUM AND LIBRARY

298 Buck Road, Wilmington, 302-658-2400; www.hagley.lib.de.us

This museum consists of old riverside stone mill buildings, a one-room schoolhouse and a millwright shop highlighting 19th-century explosive manufacturing and community life. A 240-acre historic site of E.I. du Pont's original black-powder mills includes an exhibit building, an operating waterwheel, a stationary steam engine and a fully operable 1875 machine shop. Admission includes a bus ride along the river for a tour of 1803 Eleutherian Mills, a residence with antiques reflecting five generations of du Ponts, a 19th-century garden and a barn with a collection of antique wagons. Admission: adults $11, students and seniors $9, children 4-14 $4, children under 6 free. Museum: January-mid-March, Monday-Friday 1:30 p.m. (tour), Saturday-Sunday 9:30 a.m.-4:30 p.m.; mid-March-December, daily 9:30 a.m.-4:30 p.m. Library: Monday-Friday 8:30 a.m.-4:30 p.m., second Saturday of the month 9 a.m.-4:30 p.m.

HOLY TRINITY (OLD SWEDES) CHURCH AND HENDRICKSON HOUSE

606 Church St., Wilmington, 302-652-5629; www.oldswedes.org
Founded by Swedish settlers in 1698, the church stands as originally built and still holds regular services. The house, a Swedish farmhouse built in 1690, is now a museum containing 17th- and 18th-century artifacts. Admission: $2. Services: Sunday 9:30 a.m. Tours: Wednesday-Saturday 10 a.m.-4 p.m.

NEMOURS MANSION AND GARDENS

1600 Rockland Road, Wilmington, 302-651-6912, 800-651-6912; www.nemours.org/mansion.html
This is the country estate of Alfred I. du Pont. The mansion, built in 1910, is in modified Louis XVI style by Carre and Hastings, with 102 rooms of rare antique furniture, Asian rugs, tapestries and paintings dating from the 12th century. There are formal French gardens with terraces, statuaries and pools. It is also the site of the Alfred I. duPont Hospital for Children. Admission: $15. Tours: May-December, Tuesday-Saturday 9 a.m., 11 a.m., 1 p.m., 3 p.m., Sunday 11 a.m., 1 p.m., 3 p.m.

ROCKWOOD CENTER PARK MUSEUM

610 Shipley Road, Wilmington, 302-761-4340; www.rockwood.org
This museum and park is located on a 19th-century Gothic Revival estate with gardens in English Romantic style. On the grounds are a manor house, conservatory, and porter's lodge. The museum is furnished with English, European and American decorative arts of the 17th to 19th centuries. Admission: adults $5, children 2-12 $2, children under 2 free. Tours: Wednesday-Sunday, 10 a.m.-3 p.m. (on the hour). Gardens and park: Daily 6 a.m.-10 p.m.

WILMINGTON & WESTERN RAILROAD

Greenbank Station, 2201 Newport Gap Pike, Wilmington,302-998-1930; www.wwrr.com
This railroad line transported passengers through numerous communities in 1867. Now, its serves as a tourist railroad offering round-trip steam-train rides to and from Mount Cuba picnic grove.
Schedules and prices vary; see Web site for information.

SPECIAL EVENTS
HORSE RACING, DELAWARE PARK
777 Delaware Park Blvd., Wilmington, 302-994-2521, 800-417-5687; www.delpark.com
Head out to Delaware Park for thoroughbred horse racing. There is also a slot facility, golf and restaurants here to make a full day out of your visit.
Late April-mid-November.

VICTORIAN ICE CREAM FESTIVAL
Rockwood Museum, 610 Shipley Road, Wilmington, 302-761-4340;
www.coatesville.org/events/icecream.asp
This Victorian festival features high-wheeled bicycles, hot-air balloons, marionettes, an old-fashioned medicine show, a baby parade, crafts and the main event, lots of homemade ice cream.
Mid-July.

WILMINGTON GARDEN DAY
Wilmington, 302-428-6172; www.gardenday.org
This annual event features Wilmington's famous gardens and houses. There are 22 gardens to visit and 13 homes open for you to peruse.
First Saturday in May.

WINTERTHUR POINT-TO-POINT RACES
Highway 52, Wilmington, 302-888-4600, 888-448-3883; www.winterthur.org
These old-fashioned country horse races take you back to a different time. There are five races along with picnicking, old carriages and antique cars. There are also raffles, a silent auction, pony races and more.
May.

WHERE TO STAY
★★★HOTEL DU PONT

11th and Market streets, Wilmington, 302-594-3100, 800-441-9019;
www.hoteldupont.com
The Hotel du Pont has been a Delaware institution since 1913. Constructed to rival the grand hotels of Europe with ornate plasterwork and gleaming brass, this palatial hotel enjoys proximity to the city's attractions while remaining in the heart of the scenic Brandywine Valley. The guest rooms are classically decorated with mahogany furnishings, cream tones and imported linens. Patrons can dine on French cuisine at the onsite restaurant, Green Room.
217 rooms. Restaurant, bar. Business center. Fitness center. $251-350

★★★SHERATON SUITES WILMINGTON
422 Delaware Ave., Wilmington, 302-654-8300, 800-325-3535; www.sheraton.com
Located in the heart of downtown Wilmington, this all-suite hotel offers spacious rooms and conference facilities just a short drive from a number of museums, within walking distance from headquarters of several Fortune 500 companies and a few miles from major shopping malls. The contemporary guest rooms are decorated in navy and taupe and feature comfortable Sweet Sleeper mattresses.
223 rooms. Restaurant, bar. Fitness center. Pool. Pets accepted. $151-250

WHERE TO EAT
★★★GREEN ROOM
Hotel du Pont, 11th and Market streets, Wilmington, 302-594-3155,
800-441-9019; www.hoteldupont.com

Located inside the historic Hotel du Pont, this restaurant's sophisticated décor is perfect for a romantic night out or special celebration. In season, feast on a meal of crispy soft shell crabs with crab, caper rouille, heirloom tomato, chorizo quinoa, baby arugula and chorizo dust. Live music enhances the dining experience nightly.

French. Breakfast (Monday-Saturday), lunch (Monday-Saturday), dinner (Monday-Saturday), Sunday brunch. Bar. $36-85

★★★HARRY'S SAVOY GRILL
2020 Naaman's Road, Wilmington, 302-475-3000; www.harrys-savoy.com

A Brandywine Valley staple since 1988, Harry's Savoy Grill serves up the classics in an upscale English pub atmosphere. The bar and grill is known for its prime rib, its wine list and its "famous eight-shake martinis."

American. Lunch (Monday-Friday), dinner, late night, Sunday brunch. Bar. Outdoor seating. $36-85

★KID SHELLEENS CHARCOAL HOUSE & SALOON
1801 W. 14th St., Wilmington, 302-658-4600; www.kidshelleens.com

American. Lunch, dinner, late night, Saturday-Sunday brunch. Bar. Children's menu. Outdoor seating. $16-35

★★TOSCANA KITCHEN + BAR
1412 N. DuPont St., Wilmington, 302-654-8001; www.toscanakitchen.com

Northern Italian. Lunch (Monday-Friday), dinner. Bar. Reservations recommended. Outdoor seating. $16-35

MARYLAND

sports heroes and crabs are regular fixtures at the dinner table. The seventh state owns a celebrated sports history, producing superstars such as Babe Ruth and Cal Ripken, Jr., and building the Orioles' Camden Yards, lauded for its classic design. Several noteworthy colleges and universities call Maryland home, including Johns Hopkins University and the University of Maryland, home of the Terrapins. And Maryland's Chesapeake Bay keeps restaurants across the nation well stocked with crabs, producing more than 50 percent of the United States' harvest of hard-shell crabs.

Maryland prides itself on its varied terrain and diverse economy. Metropolitan areas around Baltimore and Washington, D.C. contrast with life in the rural areas in central and southern Maryland and on the Eastern Shore, across the Chesapeake Bay. Green mountains in the western counties offset the east's white Atlantic beaches. The state's prosperity stems from a flourishing travel industry, central Maryland's agricultural and dairy wealth, the seafood industry, manufacturing and commerce, and federal government and defense contracts.

Named in honor of Henrietta Maria, wife of Charles I, King of England, Maryland was established in 1634 by Leonard Calvert, Lord Baltimore's brother. Calvert and 222 passengers aboard his ships purchased a Native American village and named it "Saint Maries Citty" (now St. Mary's City). The land was cleared, tobacco was planted, and over the years profits built elegant mansions, many of which still stand.

Maryland has played a pivotal role in every war waged on U.S. soil. In 1755, British General Edward Braddock, assisted by Lieutenant Colonel George Washington, trained his army at Cumberland for the fight against the French and Indians. In the War of 1812, Baltimore's Fort McHenry withstood attacks by land and sea. The action was later immortalized in the national anthem by Francis Scott Key, a Frederick lawyer. And in the Civil War, Maryland was a major battleground at Antietam.

ANNAPOLIS

See also Baltimore, Baltimore/Washington International Airport Area

The capital of Maryland, Annapolis was the first peacetime capital of the United States. Congress met here from November 26, 1783 to August 13, 1784. In 1845, the U.S. Naval Academy was established here at the Army's Fort Severn. Every May at commencement time, thousands of visitors throng the narrow, brick streets.

WHAT TO SEE
BOAT TRIPS
980 Awald Road, No. 202, at the City Dock Annapolis, 410-268-7600; www.watermarkcruises.com

Take one of a few different sightseeing cruises and learn about the culture of Annapolis. Choose between a 40-minute narrated tour of Annapolis Harbor and the U.S. Naval Academy aboard the Harbor Queen or tour the Old An-

napolis neighborhood and Spa Creek and the U.S. Naval Academy aboard Miss Anne. There's a 90-minute cruise to the Severn River, the Annapolis Harbor, the U.S. Naval Academy, the Chesapeake Bay Bridge or the Thomas Point Lighthouse. There are other cruises to choose from including the Pirate Cruise on Chesapeake Bay, which includes a theatre performance.
Schedule and prices vary; see Web site for information.

CHESAPEAKE BAY BRIDGE

357 Pier 1 Road, Annapolis
The Chesapeake Bay Bridge is a 7 1/4-mile link of Highway 50 across the Bay to Baltimore, Annapolis and Washington D.C. There is one toll, which is charged eastbound only.

CHESAPEAKE SAILING SCHOOL

7080 Bembe Beach Road, Annapolis, 410-295-0555, 800-966-0032;
www.sailingclasses.com
This school offers everything from weekend sailing classes for beginners to live-aboard, five-day cruises on gorgeous Chesapeake Bay, with basic and advanced instruction for individuals, families and corporate groups. You can also rent sailboats and go out on your own.
April-October.

GOVERNMENT HOUSE

State Circle, Annapolis, 410-260-3930; www.mdarchives.state.md.us
This 1868 Victorian structure was remodeled in 1935 into a Georgian country house with furnishings that reflect Maryland's history and culture. It is the home of the governor of Maryland, Governor Martin O'Malley, and is located across the street from the Maryland State House. It has been the residence of every governor since 1870. Tours are available by appointment only.
Tours: Monday, Wednesday, Friday 10:30 a.m.-2:30 p.m.

HAMMOND-HARWOOD HOUSE

19 Maryland Ave., Annapolis, 410-263-4683; www.hammondharwoodhouse.org
A 1774 Georgian house designed by William Buckland, it is filled with antique furnishings and has a beautiful garden. Matthias Hammond, a Revolutionary patriot, was its first owner.
Admission: adults $6, children $3, students $5.50. April-October, Tuesday-Sunday noon-5 p.m.

HISTORIC ANNAPOLIS FOUNDATION

18 Pinkney St., Annapolis, 410-267-7619, 800-603-4020; www.annapolis.org
This foundation offers self-guided digital audio walking tours along with guided walking and carriage tours. Depending on what you want to see, certain tours include the Historic District, State House, Old Treasury, U.S. Naval Academy and William Paca House.
Audio Tours: $10. Schedule and prices vary; see Web site for information.

HISTORIC ANNAPOLIS FOUNDATION WELCOME CENTER AND MUSEUM STORE

77 Main St., Annapolis, 410-268-5576, 800-639-9153; www.annapolis.org

This 1815 building stands on the site of a storehouse for Revolutionary War troops that burned in 1790. Self-guided digital access audio walking tours can be purchases here. The store features products reflecting Annapolis history including books, jewelry, gifts and more.

Monday-Thursday 10 a.m.-5 p.m., Friday-Saturday 10 a.m.-6 p.m., Sunday 11 a.m.-5 p.m.

SAILING TOURS

80 Compromise St., Annapolis, 410-263-7837; www.schooner-woodwind.com

If you want to set sail in Chesapeake Bay, these two-hour narrated trips aboard the 74-foot sailing yacht Woodwind are the way to go. While on board, you can actually help raise the sails or steer the boat. There are certain cruises that include a themed dinner or wine tastings. It departs from Pusser's Landing Restaurant at the Annapolis Marriott Waterfront Hotel.

Admission: Monday-Friday, adults $34, seniors $32, children under 13 $22; Sunset and Saturday-Sunday, adults $37, seniors $35, children under 13 $22. May-September: Tuesday-Sunday four trips daily, Monday sunset sail only; schedule varies rest of year.

SANDY POINT STATE PARK

1100 E. College Parkway, Annapolis, 410-974-2149, 888-432-2267; www.dnr.state.md.us

The park's location on the Atlantic Flyway makes it a fine area for watching birds and other wildlife. It offers a great view of the Bay Bridge and oceangoing vessels. Swimming is available in the bay at two guarded beaches where there are two bathhouses, a marina facility with 22 launching ramps, a store and picnic areas. You can also go surf fishing, crabbing, boating, kayaking, and wind surfing.

Admission: Mid-April-November, residents $5, non-residents $6; Mid-May-early September, residents $4, non-residents $5. January-March, Daily 8 a.m.-5 p.m.; March-April 5, Daily 8 a.m.-sunset; April 6-mid-November, Daily 6 a.m.-sunset.

ST. JOHN'S COLLEGE

60 College Ave., Annapolis, 410-263-2371, 800-727-9238; www.sjca.edu

This nonsectarian liberal arts college has a campus in Annapolis as well as in Santa Fe, New Mexico; each has only 475 students. The 36-acre campus is one of the oldest in the country and is a National Historic Landmark. The college succeeded King William's School, founded in 1696. George Washington's two nephews and step-grandson studied here; and Francis Scott Key was an alumnus.

STATE HOUSE

350 Rowe Blvd., State Circle, Annapolis, 410-974-3400, 800-235-4045; www.msa.md.gov

As the oldest state house in continuous legislative use in United States, this was the first peacetime capitol of the nation. Here in 1784, a few weeks after receiving George Washington's resignation as commander-in-chief, Congress ratified the Treaty of Paris, which officially ended the Revolutionary War. Monday-Friday 9 a.m.-5 p.m., Saturday-Sunday 10 a.m.-4 p.m.

WATERMARK TOURS

26 West St., Annapolis, 410-268-7601, 800-569-9622; www.annapolis-tours.com
These are walking tours of the U.S. Naval Academy and Historic District conducted by guides in colonial attire. The tour includes historic Maryland State House, St. John's College, Naval Academy Chapel, the crypt of John Paul Jones, Bancroft Hall dormitory and Armel-Leftwich visitor center. Tours depart from the visitor center or the information booth (located at 1 Dock Street).
Late-March-October, daily 10:30 a.m.; November-March, Saturday 1:30 p.m.

WILLIAM PACA GARDEN

186 Prince George St., Annapolis, 410-990-4538, 800-603-4020; www.annapolis.org
This restored two-acre pleasure garden was originally developed in 1765 by William Paca, a signer of the Declaration of Independence and governor of Maryland during the Revolutionary War. The property includes waterways, formal parterres and a garden wilderness.
Daily.

WILLIAM PACA HOUSE

186 Prince George St., Annapolis, 410-990-4538, 800-603-4020; www.annapolis.org
William Paca, a signer of the Declaration of Independence and one of Maryland's Governors, built this five-part Georgian mansion in 1765. It's filled with furnishings from the period along with antiques from the Paca family. Admission: adult $8, senior $7, children 6-17 $5, children under 6 free. Tours: Monday-Saturday 10 a.m.-5p.m., Sunday noon-5 p.m.

UNITED STATES NAVAL ACADEMY

121 Blake Road, Annapolis, 410-263-6933; www.usna.edu
Opened in 1845, the U.S. Naval Academy sits at the edge of the Chesapeake Bay and Severn River, occupying 338 acres. Tours of the campus are available through the academy's Armel-Leftwich visitor center. You will see the tomb of John Paul Jones, the chapel, the midshipmen's living quarters and the naval museum. The center also exhibits the original wooden figurehead of the Tecumseh from the *USS Delaware* and displays the *Freedom 7* space capsule. If you time your visit right, you can witness the Noon Formation, during which all present midshipmen line up and march in for the noon meal with military precision. Access to the Academy grounds is limited so check the current security restrictions before planning a visit. All visitors over the age of 16 must have a valid picture ID.
Daily 9 a.m.-5 p.m.

SPECIAL EVENTS
ANNAPOLIS BY CANDLELIGHT
18 Pinkney St., Annapolis, 410-267-7619, 800-603-4020; www.annapolis.org
This self-guided, candlelight walking tour leads visitors through private homes in the historic district. Curator-led tours are also available.
Early November.

MARYLAND RENAISSANCE FESTIVAL
1821 Crownsville Road, Annapolis, 410-266-7304, 800-296-7304; www.rennfest.com
Transport yourself to the medieval times at this festival featuring food, crafters, minstrels and dramatic productions in a 25-acre simulated English Tudor village. Enjoy jousting events, magic shows and many other Renaissance activities. Come in costume to fit in with those who run the festival or rent some from a booth there.
Late August-October.

MARYLAND SEAFOOD FESTIVAL
Sandy Point State Park, 1100 E. College Parkway, Annapolis, 410-266-3113; www.mdseafoodfestival.com
This family-friendly event offers up hearty portions of Maryland's favorite seafood dishes, including crab cakes, flounder, oysters, clams, trout and shrimp salad. Visitors will enjoy the beauty of the Chesapeake Bay, more than 50 quality arts and crafts exhibitors, and live musical entertainment.
Weekend after Labor Day.

U.S. POWERBOAT SHOW & U.S. SAILBOAT SHOW
980 Awald Road, Annapolis, 410-268-8828; www.usboat.com
This events take place two weekends in a row in October. The Powerboat show has an extensive in-water display of powerboats. The Sailboat show has the world's largest in-water display of sailboats and both also have exhibits of related marine products.
Mid-October.

WHERE TO STAY
★BEST WESTERN ANNAPOLIS
2520 Riva Road, Annapolis, 410-224-2800, 800-780-7234; www.bestwesternannapolis.com
151 rooms. Complimentary breakfast.Fitness center. Pool. $61-150

★GIBSON'S LODGINGS
110 Prince George St., Annapolis, 410-268-5555, 877-330-0057; www.gibsonslodgings.com
21 rooms. Children over 5 years only. Complimentary breakfast. $151-250

★★★LOEWS ANNAPOLIS HOTEL
126 W. St., Annapolis, 410-263-7777, 800-235-6397; www.loewshotels.com
The Loews Annapolis Hotel is located in the heart of downtown Annapolis within walking distance of the city's historic sites. It offers newly renovated rooms—18 of which are suites—with onsite laundry service, a fitness center

and a day spa. With plenty of meeting rooms, the hotel is a great spot for business or special events.
217 rooms. Restaurant, bar. Fitness center. Spa. $151-250

★★★MARRIOTT ANNAPOLIS WATERFRONT
80 Compromise St., Annapolis, 410-268-7555, 888-773-0786;
www.annapolismarriott.com
True to its name, many of the rooms in the Marriott Annapolis Waterfront offer views of the Chesapeake Bay or Annapolis Harbor. Guest rooms are decorated in a nautical theme with sea blue tones and comfortable furnishings. Convenience is top priority and rooms have Internet access, terry cloth robes and come with complimentary newspaper delivery each morning. You can rent bicycles to check out the town.
150 rooms. Restaurant, bar. Business center. Fitness center. $251-350

★★★O'CALLAGHAN ANNAPOLIS HOTEL
174 W. St., Annapolis, 410-263-7700, 800-569-9983; www.ocallaghanhotels.com
This intimate boutique hotel welcomes guests with an air of Irish hospitality and comfortable elegance. Black leather sofas, pale yellow walls and large brass chandeliers give the space a cozy, European feel, making it perfect for couples looking for a weekend getaway.
120 rooms. Restaurant, bar. Business center. Fitness center. $61-150

★★★SHERATON ANNAPOLIS HOTEL
173 Jennifer Road, Annapolis, 410-266-3131, 800-325-3535;
www.sheraton.com/annapolis
This warm, contemporary and newly renovated Sheraton hotel is located just outside the downtown area of Annapolis. Guest rooms feature luxurious bedding, microwave, cordless phones, voicemail and bathrobes. Guests can take advantage of the hotel's transportation to go downtown.
196 rooms. Restaurant, bar. Business center. Fitness center. Pool. Pets accepted. $61-150

WHERE TO EAT
★★BREEZE
126 W. St., Annapolis, 410-295-3232; www.loewshotels.com
Seafood, steak. Breakfast, lunch (Monday-Friday), dinner. Bar. $36-85

★★CAFÉ NORMANDIE
185 Main St., Annapolis, 410-263-3382
French. Breakfast, lunch, dinner. Bar. Children's menu. $36-85

★CHICK & RUTH'S DELLY
165 Main St., Annapolis, 410-269-6737; www.chickandruths.com
American. Breakfast, lunch, dinner. Children's menu. $16-35

★★FEDERAL HOUSE BAR AND GRILLE
22 Market Space, Annapolis, 410-268-2576; www.federalhouserestaurant.com
Seafood, steak. Lunch, dinner, Sunday brunch. Bar. $36-85

★★HARRY BROWNE'S
66 State Circle, Annapolis, 410-263-4332; www.harrybrownes.com
American. Lunch (Monday-Saturday), dinner, Sunday brunch. Bar. Outdoor seating. $36-85

★JIMMY CANTLER'S RIVERSIDE INN
458 Forest Beach Road, Annapolis, 410-757-1311; www.cantlers.com
Seafood. Lunch, dinner. Bar. Children's menu. Outdoor seating. $16-35

★★LEWNES' STEAKHOUSE
401 Fourth St., Annapolis, 410-263-1617; www.lewnessteakhouse.com
Seafood, steak. Dinner. Bar. Reservations recommended. $36-85

★★MIDDLETON TAVERN
Second, Market Space, Annapolis, 410-263-3323; www.middletontavern.com
Seafood. Lunch, dinner. Bar. Children's menu. Outdoor seating. $36-85

★★O'LEARY'S SEAFOOD
310 Third St., Annapolis, 410-263-0884; www.olearysseafood.com
Seafood. Dinner. Bar. $36-85

★★TREATY OF PARIS
58 State Circle, Annapolis, 410-263-2641; www.historicinnsofannapolis.com
French, American. Lunch (Saturday-Sunday), dinner (Thursday-Saturday), Saturday-Sunday brunch. Closed Monday-Wednesday. Reservations recommended. Bar. $16-35

BALTIMORE
See also Annapolis
Baltimore, a city of neighborhoods built on strong ethnic foundations, has achieved an incredible downtown renaissance in the past 20 years. New and renovated sports and entertainment venues have reinvigorated the city. Baseball fans flock to red brick Camden Yards, while football fans come out in force to support the Baltimore Ravens at M&T Bank Stadium. And residents and visitors alike crowd Baltimore's historic Inner Harbor to enjoy its museums, restaurants and nightlife.

Lying midway between the North and South—and enjoying a rich cultural mixture of both—Baltimore is one of the nation's oldest cities. When British troops threatened Philadelphia during the Revolutionary War, the Continental Congress fled to Baltimore, which served as the nation's capital for a little more than two months.

In October 1814, a British fleet attacked the city by land and sea. The defenders of Fort McHenry withstood the naval bombardment for 25 hours until the British gave up. Francis Scott Key saw the huge American flag still flying above the fort and was inspired to pen "The Star-Spangled Banner."

Politics was a preoccupation in the early 19th century, and the city hosted many national party conventions. At least seven presidents and three losing candidates were nominated here. Edgar Allan Poe's mysterious death in the city is rumored to have been at the hands of shady electioneers.

A disastrous fire in 1904 destroyed 140 acres of the business district, but the city recovered rapidly and during the two World Wars it was a major shipbuilding and naval repair center.

In the 1950s and early 1960s, Baltimore was a victim of the apathy and general urban decay that struck the industrial Northeast. But the city fought back, replacing hundreds of acres of slums, rotting wharves and warehouses with gleaming new office plazas, parks and public buildings. The Inner Harbor was transformed into a huge public area with shops, museums, restaurants and frequent concerts and festivals. Millions of tourists and proud Baltimoreans flock downtown to enjoy the sights and activities.

Famous residents and native sons and daughters include Babe Ruth, Edgar Allan Poe, H.L. Mencken, St. Elizabeth Ann Seton, Ogden Nash, Thurgood Marshall, and sports legends Brooks Robinson, Johnny Unitas, Jim Palmer and Cal Ripken, Jr.

WHAT TO SEE
AMERICAN VISIONARY ART MUSEUM
800 Key Highway, Baltimore, 410-244-1900; www.avam.org
This museum defines visionary art as works produced by untrained individuals whose art stems from an inner vision. Opened in 1995, the museum displays more than 4,000 pieces. The main building holds seven indoor galleries. There's also a wildflower garden, a wedding chapel and altar built out of tree limbs and flowers, and a tall sculpture barn, which once showcased psychic Uri Geller's art, including a car he covered with 5,000 forks and spoons that were allegedly bent psychically.
Admission: adults 14, seniors $10, students and children 7-18 $8, children under 7 free. Tuesday-Sunday 10 a.m.-6 p.m.

ANTIQUE ROW
North Howard and West Read streets, Baltimore; www.shopantiquerow.com
Antique Row, a Baltimore fixture for more than a century, hosts more than 20 dealers and shops, along with restoration services. Shops specialize in items such as European furniture, Tiffany lamps, china and rare books.

THE AVENUE IN HAMPDEN
36th Street, Baltimore; www.hampdenmerchants.com
Novelty shops, vintage clothing stores, casual restaurants and art galleries line Hampden's main drag, with treasures both kitschy and sublime.

BABE RUTH BIRTHPLACE AND MUSEUM
301 W. Camden St., Baltimore, 410-727-1539; www.baberuthmuseum.com
Although Babe Ruth played for the New York Yankees, Baltimore calls him one of its native sons. The house where this legend was born has been transformed into a museum that showcases his life and career. Visitors can see rare family photographs as well as a complete record of his home runs. The museum also features exhibits about the Baltimore Colts and Orioles. Every February 6th, the museum commemorates Babe Ruth's birthday by offering free admission to all visitors.
April-September, daily 10 a.m.-5 p.m., 10 a.m.-7 p.m. on baseball game days; October-March, daily 10 a.m.-5 p.m.

BALTIMORE & OHIO RAILROAD MUSEUM

901 W. Pratt St., Baltimore, 410-752-2490; www.borail.org

This museum, affiliated with the Smithsonian, celebrates the birthplace of railroading in America and depicts the industry's economic and cultural influences. Encompassing 40 acres, the museum's collection of locomotives is the oldest and most comprehensive in the country. In the Roundhouse, visitors can board and explore more than a dozen of the iron horses, which include a rail post office car and the Tom Thumb train. The second floor of the Annex building has an impressive display of working miniature-scale trains. The Mount Clair Station, exhibiting the story of the B&O Railroad, was built in 1851 to replace the 1829 original, which was the first rail depot in the country. Outside, the museum features more trains, such as the "Chessie," the largest steam locomotive. On certain days, visitors can take a train ride. Admission: adults $14, seniors $12, children 2-12 $8. Monday-Saturday 10 a.m.-4 p.m., Sunday 11 a.m.-4 p.m.

BALTIMORE MARITIME MUSEUM

301 E. Pratt St., Baltimore, 410-396-3453; www.baltomaritimemuseum.org

This museum's featured ships include the *USS Torsk*, a World War II submarine; the Coast Guard cutter *Taney* and the lightship *Chesapeake*. All the ships have been designated National Historic Landmarks. Also here is the Seven Foot Knoll Lighthouse that was built in 1855.
March-October, daily 10 a.m.-5:30 p.m.; November-February, daily 10 a.m.-4:30 p.m.

BALTIMORE MUSEUM OF ART

10 Art Museum Drive, Baltimore, 410-573-1700; www.artbma.org

Located near Johns Hopkins University, this museum opened in 1923 and was designed by John Russell Pope, the architect of the National Gallery in Washington, D.C. The museum has eight permanent exhibits featuring works from the periods of Impressionism to modern art. It boasts the second largest collection of works by Andy Warhol. However, its jewel is the Cone collection, which includes more than 3,000 pieces by artists such as Picasso, Van Gogh, Renoir, Cézanne and Matisse. The Matisse collection is the largest in the Western Hemisphere. Visitors will also want to see the three-acre sculpture garden, which contains art by Alexander Calder and Henry Moore. Admission: Free. Wednesday-Friday 11 a.m.-5 p.m., Saturday-Sunday 11 a.m.-6 p.m.

BALTIMORE MUSEUM OF INDUSTRY

Inner Harbor South, 1415 Key Highway, Baltimore, 410-727-4808; www.thebmi.org

This museum educates visitors about the vital role that industry and manufacturing played in Baltimore's economic and cultural development. Located in a renovated oyster cannery on the west side of the Inner Harbor, the museum opened in 1977. Its exhibits showcase trades such as printing, garment making, canning and metalworking. Guests will learn about the invention of Noxema, the disposable bottle cap and even the first umbrella. Admission: adults $10, seniors, students and children 4-18 $6, children under 4 free. Tuesday-Saturday 10 a.m.-4 p.m., Sunday 11 a.m.-4 p.m.

BALTIMORE ORIOLES (MLB)

Oriole Park at Camden Yards, 333 W. Camden St., Baltimore, 410-685-9800,
888-848-2479; www.orioles.mlb.com

The Orioles are Baltimore's professional baseball team in the American League. Fans call them the Birds or the O's. They were actually moved to New York in 1903 to become the New York Yankees. Babe Ruth began his career playing with the Orioles for just five months.

BALTIMORE PUBLIC WORKS MUSEUM

Pier 7, 751 Eastern Ave., Baltimore, 410-396-5565;
www.baltimorepublicworksmuseum.org

This museum exhibits the history and artifacts of public works. It is located in a historic sewage pumping station. The streetscape sculpture outside depicts the various utility lines and ducts under a typical city street, in a walk-through model.

Admission: adults $3, seniors, students and military personnel $2.50, children under 6 free. Tuesday-Sunday 10 a.m.-4 p.m.

BALTIMORE RAVENS (NFL)

M&T Bank Stadium, 1101 Russell St., Baltimore, 410-261-7283;
www.baltimoreravens.com

The Ravens are Baltimore's professional football team, named after the poem written by Edgar Allan Poe which was supposedly written in Baltimore.

BALTIMORE STREETCAR MUSEUM

1901 Falls Road, Baltimore, 410-547-0264; www.baltimoremd.com/streetcar

This museum holds eleven electric streetcars and two horse cars used in the city between 1859 and 1963. The admission price includes unlimted rides on the original streetcars.

Admission: adults $6, seniors $5 and children 4-11 $5, children under 4 free. Sunday noon-5 p.m.; June-October, Saturday noon-5 p.m.

THE BATTLE MONUMENT

Calvert and Fayette streets, Baltimore

This an 1815 Memorial is dedicated to those who fell defending the city in the War of 1812. Climb the 228 steps to the top of the monument for a breathtaking view of the city.

CHARLES CENTER

36 S. Charles St., Baltimore

Bounded by Charles, Liberty, Saratoga and Lombard streets, this business area is packed with European-style plazas, shops, restaurants and outdoor activities. A prize-winning building by Mies van der Rohe borders center plaza.

CHURCH HOME AND HOSPITAL

Broadway and Fairmount avenues, East Baltimore

Edgar Allan Poe died here at Church Hospital in 1849. There have been plenty of stories surrounding this hospital about body snatching from grave sites nearby and it has been almost burned down many times by residents.

CITY COURT HOUSE

100 N. Calvert St., Baltimore

On the steps is a statue of Cecil Calvert, brother of Leonard and founder of Maryland as the second Lord Baltimore.

CITY OF BALTIMORE CONSERVATORY

Druid Hill Park, 2600 Madison Ave., Baltimore, 410-396-0180;
www.baltimoreconservatory.org

This graceful building dating back to 1885 houses a variety of tropical plants. There are special shows during Easter, November and the holidays.

CITY HALL

100 N. Holiday St., Baltimore, 410-396-3100; www.baltimorecity.gov

City Hall features post-Civil War architecture, restored to its original detail.

CLYBURN ARBORETUM

4915 Greenspring Ave., Baltimore, 410-367-2217; www.cylburnassociation.org

This arboretum is located at Cylburn Mansion. You'll find marked nature trails among the 207 acres of the park filled with maples, confiers, oaks and other trees and landscaped gardens.

Grounds: Daily. Mansion: Monday-Friday 7:30 a.m.-3:30 p.m.

EDGAR ALLAN POE GRAVE

Westminster Hall and Burial Grounds, 519 W. Fayette St., Baltimore, 410-706-2072;
www.ci.baltimore.md.us

Baltimore's oldest cemeteries also contain the graves of many prominent early Marylanders including Edgar Allan Poe. There are tours of the Westminster Burying Ground and Catacombs by appointment.

Daily 8 a.m.-dusk. Tours: April-July, first and third Friday of each month.

EDGAR ALLAN POE HOUSE AND MUSEUM

203 N. Amity St., Baltimore, 410-396-7932; www.ci.baltimore.md.usl

The famed author and father of the macabre lived in this house from 1832 to 1835. Haunted or not, the house and museum have scared up many Poe artifacts such as period furniture, a desk and telescope owned by Poe, and Gustave Dore's illustrations of "The Raven." Around January 19, the museum hosts a birthday celebration that includes readings and theatrical performances of Poe's work.

April-early December, Wednesday-Saturday noon-3:45 p.m.

ENOCH PRATT FREE LIBRARY

400 Cathedral St., Baltimore, 410-396-5430; www.pratt.lib.md.us

Since 1886, this library has served literature lovers of Baltimore. It includes collections of H.L. Mencken's and Edgar Allan Poe's work.

October-May, Monday-Wednesday 10 a.m.-8 p.m., Thursday 10 a.m.-5:30 p.m., Friday-Saturday 10 a.m.-5 p.m., Sunday 1-5 p.m.

FEDERAL HILL

Charles and Cross streets, Baltimore

Bordered by Hughes Street, Key Highway, Hanover Street and Cross Street Inner Harbor area, Federal Hill offers views of the city harbor and skyline. Named after a celebration that occurred here in 1788 to mark Maryland's ratification of the Constitution, Federal Hill is filled with shops, restaurants and pubs on tree-lined streets.

FELL'S POINT

Visitors Center, 812 S. Ann St., Baltimore, 410-675-6750; www.fellspoint.us

A shipbuilding and maritime center, this neighborhood dates back to 1730 and has approximately 350 original residential structures. Working tugboats and tankers can be observed from the docks. Its cobblestone streets are lined with plenty of shops restaurants, clubs and pubs. Locals flock here for the vibrant nightlife.

FLAG HOUSE & STAR-SPANGLED BANNER MUSEUM

844 E. Pratt St., Baltimore, 410-837-1793; www.flaghouse.org

Open to the public for more than 75 years, this museum was the home of Mary Pickersgill, who sewed the flag that Francis Scott Key memorialized in America's national anthem. Although the flag now hangs in the Smithsonian's National Museum of American History, visitors can tour the house to learn about its origins and Pickersgill's life. The house has an adjoining War of 1812 museum, which exhibits military and domestic artifacts and presents an award-winning video.

Admission: adults $7, seniors and military personnel $5, students $5, children under 6 free. Tuesday-Saturday 10 a.m.-4 p.m. Tours: 10:30 a.m.-2:30 (every half hours), 3:15 p.m.

FORT MCHENRY NATIONAL MONUMENT AND HISTORIC SHRINE

End of East Fort Avenue, Baltimore, 410-962-4290; www.nps.gov/fomc

Fort McHenry boasts a stunning view of the harbor, authentic re-created structures and a wealth of living history. Not only was it the site of the battle that inspired Francis Scott Key to pen the national anthem in 1814, but the fort was also a defensive position during the Revolutionary War, a P.O.W. camp for Confederate prisoners during the Civil War and an army hospital during World War I. Summer weekends feature precision drills and music performed by volunteers in Revolutionary War uniforms.

Grounds: Labor Day-Memorial Day, daily 8 a.m.-5 p.m.; Memorial Day-Labor Day, daily 8 a.m.-8 p.m. Fort: Labor Day-Memorial Day, daily 8 a.m.-4:45 p.m.; Memorial Day-Labor Day, daily 8 a.m.-6:30 p.m.

HARBORPLACE

200 E. Pratt St., Baltimore, 410-332-4191; www.harborplace.com

This shopping mecca boasts more than 130 stores and restaurants. Visitors who want to take a break can go outside and walk on the brick-paved promenade that runs along the water's edge. Harborplace also has a small outdoor amphitheater, where in good weather, guests are treated to free performances.

Monday-Saturday 10 a.m.-9 p.m., Sunday noon-6 p.m.

HOLOCAUST MEMORIAL AND SCULPTURE

Water, Gay and Lombard streets, Baltimore

Located in the Inner Harbor, this large marble slab memorializes the victims of the Holocaust. There is also the Joseph Sheppard Holocaust sculpture that symbolizes the horror of the Holocaust with bodies entwined in flames. The center plaza forms a triangle similar to the badges holocaust victims wore.

JEWISH MUSEUM OF MARYLAND

15 Lloyd St., Baltimore, 410-732-6400; www.jhsm.org

The museum includes three buildings: Lloyd St. Synagogue, which is the oldest in Maryland; B'nai Israel Synagogue and the Jewish Museum of Maryland. The museum features rotating exhibits, galleries, a research library (available by appointment only), shop, and programs.

Admission: adults $8, students $4, children 11 and under $3. Tuesday-Thursday, Sunday noon-4 p.m.

JOHNS HOPKINS UNIVERSITY

3400 N. Charles St., Baltimore, 410-516-8000; www.jhu.edu

Founded in 1876 and located in northern Baltimore, Johns Hopkins enrolls 18,000 students and is renowned for the Bloomberg School of Public Health, the Peabody Institute (a music conservatory) and its Applied Physics Laboratory located 30 minutes outside of Baltimore. *US News & World Report* continuously ranks its affiliated hospital, which has its own separate campus in eastern Baltimore, as one of the top medical facilities in the country.

JOSEPH MEYERHOFF SYMPHONY HALL

1212 Cathedral St., Baltimore, 410-783-8000, 877-276-1444;
www.baltimoresymphony.org

This is the permanent residence of the Baltimore Symphony Orchestra. The striking modern circular facade was constructed of glass, brick and wood. Box Office: Monday-Friday 10 a.m.-6 p.m., Saturday-Sunday noon-5 p.m. (also open 60 minutes before performances and during intermission).

LACROSSE HALL OF FAME MUSEUM

113 W. University Parkway, Baltimore, 410-235-6882; www.lacrosse.org/museum

This Lacrosse Museum and Hall of Fame holds steam trophies, lacrosse artifacts and memorabilia, including rare photographs and art, vintage equipment and uniforms. There is also a historical video documentary.

Admission: adults $3, children 5-15 $2, children under 5 free. February-May, Tuesday-Saturday 10 a.m.-3 p.m.; June-January, Monday-Friday 10 a.m.-3 p.m.

LEXINGTON MARKET

400 W. Lexington St., Baltimore, 410-685-6169; www.lexingtonmarket.com

This roofed market is more than two centuries old. Covering two blocks, it has more than 130 stalls offering fresh vegetables, seafood, meats, baked goods and prepared foods. Vendors outside the market sell clothing, jewelry, T-shirts and other items. Throughout the year, the market hosts several events, such as the Chocolate Festival in October, which boasts free samples

and a chocolate-eating contest. But the most anticipated event at the market is Lunch with the Elephants. Every March, Ringling Bros. and Barnum & Bailey Circus elephants parade up Eutaw Street accompanied by fanfare, live music and clowns. When they finally reach the market, they are served lunch, consisting of 1,100 oranges, 1,000 apples, 500 heads of lettuce, 700 bananas, 400 pears and 500 carrots.
Monday-Saturday 8:30 a.m.-6 p.m.

LOVELY LANE MUSEUM & ARCHIVES
The Lovely Lane United Methodist Church, 2200 St. Paul St., Baltimore, 410-889-4458; www.lovelylanemuseum.com
Located on the main floor of the Lovely Lane United Methodist Church, this museum holds permanent and changing exhibits of items of Methodist church history since 1760.
Thursday-Friday 10 a.m.-4 p.m., Sunday noon.

MARYLAND HISTORICAL SOCIETY
201 W. Monument St., Baltimore, 410-685-3750; www.mdhs.org
The state's oldest cultural institution includes a library, a museum and even a small press that promotes scholarship about Maryland's history and material culture. The library has more than 5.4 million works and is a valuable resource for genealogists. The society's collection of historical artifacts includes the original draft of "The Star Spangled Banner."
Admission: Museum, adults $4, seniors, students and children 13-17 $3, children under 13 free; Library, $6. First Thursday of the month free. Museum: Wednesday-Sunday 10 a.m.-5 p.m. Library: Wednesday-Saturday 10 a.m.-4:30 p.m.

MARYLAND SCIENCE CENTER & DAVIS PLANETARIUM
601 Light St., Baltimore, 410-685-5225; www.mdsci.org
Located in the Inner Harbor, the three-story building contains hundreds of exhibits guaranteed to spark young (and old) minds. In the Chesapeake Bay exhibit, you can learn about the bay's delicate ecosystem or you can explore the mysteries of the human body in BodyLink. The Kids Room, for guests eight and younger, gives children the chance to operate a fish camera or dress up like turtles. Don't miss the Hubble Space Telescope National Visitor Center, a 4,000-square-foot interactive space gallery with 120 high-resolution images that allow guests to see space through the Hubble's eye.
Late-March-mid-June, Monday-Friday 10 a.m.-5 p.m., Saturday 10 a.m.-6 p.m., Sunday 11 a.m.-5 p.m.; Mid-June-Labor Day, Sunday-Thursday 10 a.m.-6 p.m., Friday-Saturday 10 a.m.-8 p.m. Kid's Room: Late-March-mid-June, Monday-Friday 10 a.m.-4 p.m., Saturday 10 a.m.-5 p.m., Sunday 11 a.m.-4 p.m.

MARYLAND ZOO
Druid Hill Park Lake Drive, Baltimore, 410-366-5466; www.marylandzoo.org
Located in Druid Hill Park, the third-oldest zoo in the United States covers 180 acres and features more than 2,250 animals. Children can visit the giraffes and elephants in the African Safari exhibit, as well as ride the carousel

or try out the climbing wall. The zoo also hosts special events during Halloween and Christmas.

Admission: Monday-Frida, adults $11, seniors $10, children $9; Saturday-Sunday, adults $15, seniors $12, children $11. Daily 10 a.m.-4 p.m. Closed mid-December-mid-March.

MOTHER SETON HOUSE

600 N. Paca St., Baltimore, 410-523-3443; www.nps.gov/history

This was the home of Saint Elizabeth Ann Bayley Seton from 1808 to 1809. Here she established the forerunner of the parochial school system, as well as an order of nuns that eventually became the Daughters & Sisters of Charity in the U.S. and Canada. She was the first native born American Saint of the Catholic Church.

Saturday-Sunday 1-3 p.m., also by appointment.

MOUNT CLARE MUSEUM HOUSE

1500 Washington Blvd., Baltimore, 410-837-3262; www.mountclare.org

A National Historic Landmark, Mount Clare is the oldest mansion in Baltimore, dating back to 1760. It is the former home of barrister and senator Charles Carroll who was a relative of Charles Carroll of Carrollton who signed the Declaration of Independence. The interior has 18th- and 19th-century furnishings. Guided tours take place on the hour.

Admission: adults $6, seniors $5, students 18 and under $4. Tuesday-Saturday 10 a.m.-4 p.m.

MOUNT VERNON PLACE UNITED METHODIST CHURCH

10 E. Mount Vernon Place, Baltimore, 410-685-5290;
www.gbgm-umc.org/mtvernonplumc

Circa 1850, this church is a brownstone with balcony and grillwork extending the entire width of the house. The interior features a spiral staircase suspended from three floors, a library with century-old painting on the ceiling and a drawing room.

Services: Sunday 9 a.m.

NATIONAL AQUARIUM BALTIMORE

501 E. Pratt St., Baltimore, 410-576-3800; www.aqua.org

The National Aquarium introduces guests to stingrays, sharks, puffins, seals and a giant Pacific octopus. Visitors can explore the danger and mystery of a South American tropical rainforest complete with poisonous frogs, exotic birds, piranha and swinging tamarin monkeys, or delight in the underwater beauty of the replicated Atlantic coral reef. The Children's Cove, a touch pool, provides an interactive experience for kids. Feeding schedules are posted in the lobby. The Marine Mammal Pavilion features a a 1,300-seat amphitheater surrounding a 1.2-million-gallon pool that houses Atlantic bottlenose dolphins underwater viewing areas enable visitors to observe the mammals from below the surface. There is also a dolphin show and 4-D Immersion Theater.

Admission: adults $24.95, seniors $23.95, children 3-11 $14.95. Daily; hours vary.

PATTERSON PARK

200 S. Linwood Ave., Baltimore, 410-396-3932; www.pattersonpark.com

Defenses here helped stop the British attack in 1814. Breastworks and artillery pieces are displayed. Similar to that of Central Park in New York City, you'll find a pagoda, boat lake, a fountain, statues and plenty of walking paths. The architecture of the structures here are representative of the Victorian Age. There is also an ice skating rink here, ball fields, tennis courts, a swimming pool, playgrounds and picnic areas.

Daily.

PORT DISCOVERY

35 Market Place, Baltimore, 410-727-8120; www.portdiscovery.org

Opened in 1998 in collaboration with Walt Disney Imagineering, Port Discovery has been ranked the fourth best children's museum in the country by *Child* magazine. Kids will have a blast exploring the three-story urban tree house. In MPT Studioworks, they can become producers of their own television broadcasts. The museum also operates the HiFlyer, a giant helium balloon anchored 450 feet above the Inner Harbor. The enclosed gondola holds 20 to 25 passengers and offers a spectacular view of the city.

Admission: $11.75, children under 2 free. October-late-May, Tuesday-Friday 9:30 a.m.-4:30 p.m., Saturday 10 a.m.-5 p.m., Sunday noon-5 p.m.; Memorial Day-Labor Day, Monday-Saturday 10 a.m.-5 p.m., Sunday noon-5 p.m.

POWER PLANT

601 E. Pratt St., Baltimore, 410-752-5444; www.powerplantlive.com

This commercial complex was once a power plant owned by Baltimore Gas & Electric. The renovated plant now houses a two-story Barnes & Noble bookstore, a Hard Rock Café and the original ESPN Zone, a 35,000-square-foot sports-themed restaurant and arcade. There are also other restaurants and bars located here. From May through October, there are concerts on the Plaza stage outside featuring both regional and national acts.

SENATOR THEATRE

5904 York Road, North Baltimore, 410-435-8338; www.senator.com

Movie buffs will appreciate the charm and history of the Senator. Showing first-run, independent and classic films, the theater seats 900 and has a 40-foot-wide screen. Listed on the National Register of Historic Places, its architecture is elegant Art Deco. The theater recently added its own mini Walk of Fame outside the entrance.

SHERWOOD GARDENS

Stratford Road, and Greenway, Baltimore, 410-785-0444; www.guifordnews.com

More than 6 acres in size, the gardens reach their peak of splendor in late April and early May, when thousands of tulips, azaleas and flowering shrubs bloom. The gardens are located on property that was once part of the Guilford estate which was owned by the Baltimore Sun founder, A.S. Abell.

Admission: Free. Daily, dawn-dusk.

STONELEIGH DUCKPIN BOWLING CENTER

6703 York Road, Baltimore, 410-377-8115; www.stoneleighlanes.com
There are no ducks on the lanes, just smaller pins and balls in this game designed in Baltimore back in 1900.
Monday noon-9 p.m., Tuesday 9 a.m.-11 p.m., Wednesday noon-11 p.m., Thursday 10 a.m.-11 p.m., Friday-Saturday 10 a.m.-midnight, Sunday 10 a.m.-8 p.m.

TOP OF THE WORLD

World Trade Center, 401 E. Pratt St., Baltimore, 410-837-8439; www.viewbaltimore.org
This is the observation deck and museum on the 27th floor of the World Trade Center Baltimore, which was designed by I.M. Pei. Exhibits illustrate the city's history, famous residents and the activities of the port.
Admission: adults $5, seniors and military personnel $4, children 3-12 $3, children under 3 free. Labor Day-Memorial Day, Wednesday-Sunday 10 a.m.-6 p.m.; Memorial Day-Labor Day, Monday-Sunday, 10 a.m.-6 p.m. (Saturday until 8 p.m.)

UNIVERSITY OF MARYLAND AT BALTIMORE

520 W. Lombard St., Baltimore, 410-706-3100; www.umaryland.edu
The 32-acre downtown campus includes six professional schools, the University of Maryland Medical System and the Graduate School. Davidge Hall is the oldest medical teaching building in continuous use in the Western hemisphere dating back to 1812.

USS CONSTELLATION

301 E. Pratt St., Pier 1, Baltimore, 410-539-1797; www.constellation.org
This retired sloop, anchored at Pier 1 in the Inner Harbor, has a proud naval history that spans from the Civil War to World War II. Visitors can board the ship for a self-guided audio tour. Kids can participate in the Powder Monkey program, in which they learn what it was like to serve in President Lincoln's navy.
Admission: adults $10, seniors $8, children 6-14 $5, children under 6 and military personnel free. January-February, Monday-Thursday 10 a.m.-4:30 p.m., Friday-Sunday 10 a.m.-4:30 p.m.; March-October, Monday-Thursday 10 a.m.-5 p.m., Friday-Sunday 10 a.m.-5 p.m.; November-December, Monday-Thursday 10 a.m.-4:30 p.m., Friday-Sunday 10 a.m.-4:30 p.m.

VAGABOND PLAYERS

806 S. Broadway, Baltimore, 410-563-9135; www.vagabondplayers.org
The Vagabond Players are the oldest continuously operating "little theater" in the United States having started in 1916. The players perform recent Broadway shows, revivals and original scripts as well.
Tickets: $15; $20 musicals. Friday-Sunday.

WALTERS ART MUSEUM

600 N. Charles St., Baltimore, 410-547-9000; www.thewalters.org
This museum's collection traces the history of the world from ancient times to the present day. Father and son William and Henry Walters gave the muse-

um and its numerous holdings to Baltimore, though the New York Metropolitan Museum of Art also coveted it. With more than 30,000 pieces of art, the collection is renowned for its French paintings and Renaissance and Asian art. The museum also exhibits Imperial Fabergé eggs, paintings by Raphael and El Greco, and an impressive assortment of ivories and Art Deco jewelry. Visitors will also want to check out the unique Roman sarcophagus.
Admission: Free. Wednesday-Sunday 10 a.m.-5 p.m.

WASHINGTON MONUMENT AND MUSEUM
699 N. Charles St., Baltimore, 410-396-1049; www.baltimoremuseums.org
This was the first major monument to honor George Washington. There's a museum in the base and you can view the city from the top. Other monuments nearby honor Lafayette, Chief Justice Roger Brooke Taney, philanthropist George Peabody, lawyer Severn Teackle Wallis and Revolutionary War hero John Eager Howard.
Admission: $1. Wednesday-Friday 10 a.m.-4 p.m. Saturday-Sunday 10 a.m.-5 p.m.

SPECIAL EVENTS
ARTSCAPE
1200 block of Mount Royal Ave., Baltimore, 877-225-8466; www.artscape.org
This free festival celebrates the area's abundance of visual, literary and performing arts. The three-day event takes place in the cultural corridor of the city's Bolton Hill neighborhood. It features live music performances, poetry and fiction readings by regional writers and even a one-act opera. The Artists' Market exhibits and sells the work of more than 140 artists. There are a wide variety of activities for children, which in the past have included a youth Shakespearean performance and an interactive art tent.
Mid-July.

MARYLAND FILM FESTIVAL
107 E. Read St., Baltimore, 410-752-8083; www.mdfilmfest.com
Since 1999, this four-day festival has become a premier cinema event for Baltimore, presenting more than 120 foreign, domestic and short films throughout the city's movie houses, including the famous Senator Theatre. Most screenings are followed by a discussion with the film's director or producer. The festival has also hosted films for children, such as a silent version of *Peter Pan* accompanied by an orchestra.
Early May.

PIER 6 CONCERT PAVILION
731 Eastern Ave., Pier 6, Baltimore; www.piersixpavilion.com
Summertime outdoor concerts and plays are performed at the water's edge at this pavilion. There is some covered seating avaiable but it's more fun to sit on the lawn where you can bring your own blankets and chairs. Acts range from Joe Cocker to Heart to Robin Thicke and Jennifer Hudson.
May-September.

PREAKNESS STAKES AND CELEBRATION WEEK

Pimlico Race Course, 5201 Park Heights Ave., Baltimore, 410-542-9400,
877-206-8042; www.preakness.com

The Preakness Stakes, the second jewel in horse racing's Triple Crown, is a time-honored tradition in Baltimore. On the third Saturday in May, nearly 100,000 people from Maryland and around the world gather at the Pimlico Race Course. Celebration festivities begin one week before the race, with activities that include a parade, a hot-air balloon festival, outdoor concerts, huge infield parties, boat races as well as 5K and 10K runs. On race day, the Preakness is the second-to-last race and begins at around 5:30 p.m. Visitors looking for a good value and an eye-level view of the horses should reserve seats in the infield. Those willing to spend more money—and dress more formally—should purchase seats in the clubhouse or grandstand.
Third Saturday in May.

WHERE TO STAY

★CELIE'S WATERFRONT INN

1714 Thames St., Baltimore, 410-522-2323, 800-432-0184; www.celieswaterfront.com
9 rooms. Complimentary breakfast. $61-150

★★CLARION HOTEL PEABODY COURT

612 Cathedral St., Baltimore, 410-727-7101, 800-292-5500;
www.peabodycourthotel.com
104 rooms. Restaurant, bar. Business center. Fitness center. $61-150

★★DAYS INN INNER HARBOR HOTEL

100 Hopkins Place, Baltimore, 410-576-1000, 800-329-7466;
www.daysinnerharbor.com
250 rooms. Restaurant, bar. Business center. Fitness center. Pool. $61-150

★★EMBASSY SUITES BALTIMORE AT BWI AIRPORT

1300 Concourse Drive, Linthicum, 410-850-0747, 800-362-2779;
www.embassy-suites.com
251 rooms. Restaurant, bar. Complimentary breakfast. Business center. Fitness center. Pool. $151-250

★★★FOUR POINTS BY SHERATON BWI AIRPORT

7032 Elm Road, Baltimore, 410-859-3300, 800-368-7764; www.fourpoints.com
Whether you are homeward bound or flying off for business, let this hotel situated on the site of Baltimore's major airport be the "stepping stone" to your final destination. It includes all the thoughtful amenities you would expect—Internet access, a fitness center, and an onsite restaurant. The decor has a futuristic/contemporary airport look with leather seating, steel lighting and airport-themed artworks. City attractions, such as the Inner Harbor, Camden Yards, and Laurel Racecourse, are less than 20 minutes away.
201 rooms. Restaurant, bar. Business center. Fitness center. Pool. $151-250

★HAMPTON INN

829 Elkridge Landing Road, Linthicum, 410-850-0600, 800-426-7866;
www.hamptoninnbwiairport.com

182 rooms. Complimentary breakfast. Fitness center. $61-150

★★★HYATT REGENCY BALTIMORE ON THE INNER HARBOR

300 Light St., Baltimore, 410-528-1234, 800-233-1234; www.baltimore.hyatt.com

Conveniently located across the street from Baltimore's Inner Harbor, this hotel is linked by a skywalk to the convention center and shopping at Harborplace. It is also situated within minutes of the National Aquarium, Maryland Science Center and Oriole Park. Guest rooms are decorated with wall coverings resembling white leather, white bedding with gold accents and marble bathrooms. In addition to a rooftop pool and a huge fitness center, amenities include a basketball half-court, putting green and jogging track, along with 29,000 square feet of meeting space.

488 rooms. Restaurant, bar. Business center. Fitness center. Pool. $251-350

★INN AT HENDERSON'S WHARF

1000 Fell St., Baltimore, 410-522-7777, 800-522-2088; www.hendersonswharf.com

38 rooms. Complimentary breakfast. Fitness center. $61-150

★★INN AT THE COLONNADE

4 W. University Parkway, Baltimore, 410-235-5400, 800-222-8733;
www.colonnadebaltimore.com

125 rooms. Restaurant, bar. Fitness center. Pool. Spa. $61-150

★★★INTERCONTINENTAL HARBOR COURT BALTIMORE

550 Light St., Baltimore, 410-234-0550, 800-496-7621;
www.intercontinental.com/baltimore

The InterContinental Harbor Court Hotel, located across the street from the Inner Harbor and Harborplace, recreates the spirit of a grand English manor home. Guest rooms offer views of the harbor or the garden on the courtside. The professional staff tends to your every need, even offering hot, buttery popcorn for guests enjoying in-room movies. The hotel has a fitness center and yoga studio for athletic-minded guests.

195 rooms. Restaurant, bar. Business center. Fitness center. Pool. Spa. $61-150

★★★MARRIOTT BALTIMORE WATERFRONT

700 Aliceanna St., Baltimore, 410-385-3000, 800-228-9290; www.marriott.com

From its large rooms offering stunning views of the harbor to its amenities, this hotel puts you in the center of everythong at Baltimore's Inner Harbor. Walk (or take a water taxi) to some of the city's premier tourist destinations: Little Italy, Pier 6 Concert Pavilion or Harborplace.

754 rooms. Restaurant, bar. Business center. Fitness center. Pool. $251-350

★★★MARRIOTT BALTIMORE WASHINGTON INTERNATIONAL AIRPORT

1743 W. Nursery Road, Linthicum, 410-859-8300, 800-228-9290; www.marriott.com

This Marriott is perfect if you need to stay close to the airport. Rooms are bright and cheery with luxurious bedding, Internet access and more. Dining options onsite include Champions Sports Bar, serving American fare, and Monikers Grille which serves Continental cuisine. Enjoy the fitness center and indoor pool when you're not exploring the sites.

309 rooms. Restaurant, bar. Business center. Fitness center. Pool. $151-250

★★★RENAISSANCE BALTIMORE HARBORPLACE HOTEL
202 E. Pratt St., Baltimore, 410-547-1200, 800-535-1201;
www.renaissancehotels.com/bwish
This hotel adjoins the upscale Gallery mall, with four floors of shopping and dining. Nearby attractions include the National Aquarium, the Baltimore Convention Center and Ride the Ducks of Baltimore. Many guest rooms offer views of the harbor.

622 rooms. Restaurant, bar. Business center. Fitness center. Pool. $251-350

★★★SHERATON BALTIMORE NORTH
903 Dulaney Valley Road, Baltimore, 410-321-7400, 800-325-3535;
www.starwoodhotels.com
Located near the Towson business district, Baltimore's Inner Harbor, Camden Yard and the Timonium Fairgrounds, this hotel couldn't be more convenient. Lodgings are roomy and the heated indoor pool provides a built-in playground for the family. It's also connected by a skywalk to the Towson Town Center for all your shopping needs.

283 rooms. Restaurant, bar. Business center. Fitness center. Pool. Pets accepted. $151-250

WHERE TO EAT
★THE BAYOU CAFÉ
8133-A Honeygo Blvd., Baltimore, 410-931-2583; www.thebayoucafe.com
American, Cajun. Lunch, dinner, late-night, Sunday brunch. Bar. $16-35

★BERTHA'S
734 S. Broadway, Baltimore, 410-327-5795; www.berthas.com
Seafood. Lunch, dinner. Children's menu. Bar. $16-35

★★★BLACK OLIVE
814 S. Bond St., Baltimore, 410-276-7141; www.theblackolive.com
This Mediterranean restaurant, formerly Fells Point's General Store, has retained the building's original hardwood floors and brick archways. The restaurant serves its organic fare al fresco under a grape arbor. Fresh fish are displayed in front of the open kitchen and filleted tableside. The carrot cake is a perfect finale.
Mediterranean, seafood. Lunch, dinner, brunch. Reservations recommended. Outdoor seating. Bar. $36-85

★★BRASSERIE TATIN
105 W. 39th St., Baltimore, 443-278-9110; www.brasserietatin.com
French. Dinner, Sunday brunch. Reservations recommended. Outdoor seating. Bar. $36-85

★★★CAFÉ BRETTON
849 Baltimore-Annapolis Blvd., Severna Park, 410-647-8222
Whether or not you like French cooking, the amicable waitstaff, appealing atmosphere and classically prepared dishes will win you over. If the Chilean sea bass is on the menu, order it. Also be sure to try a glass of wine from the extensive wine list.
French. Dinner. Closed Monday. Reservations recommended. Bar. $36-85

★CAFÉ HON
1002 W. 36th St., Baltimore, 410-243-1230; www.cafehon.com
American. Breakfast, lunch, dinner, brunch. Bar. $16-35

★★★★CHARLESTON
1000 Lancaster St., Baltimore, 410-332-7373; www.charlestonrestaurant.com
Chef/owner Cindy Wolf's regional restaurant serves up dishes such as sautéed heads-on Gulf shrimp with andouille sausage and Tasso ham with creamy stone-milled grits. The restaurant also has an impressive wine program that includes several dozen sparkling wines and a selection of about 600 well-chosen whites and reds from the New World (Australia, South Africa, New Zealand and Chile) and the Old (France, Italy and Spain). Charleston also offers more than a dozen microbrews and imported beers.
American, French. Dinner. Closed Sunday. Reservations recommended. Outdoor seating. Bar. $36-85

★★★DELLA NOTTE
801 Eastern Ave., Baltimore, 410-837-5500; www.dellanotte.com
A popular spot, Della Notte's interior is replete with faux-white brick walls covered with murals and busts of Roman emperors. The menu offers a selection of antipasti, fish, meats and daily specials, along with a vast wine list of more than 1,400 selections. After dinner, settle into the Emperor's Lounge with an after-dinner drink and enjoy the live entertainment offered daily.
Italian. Lunch, dinner. Reservations recommended. Bar. $36-85

★★GERMANO'S TRATTORIA
300 S. High St., Baltimore, 410-752-4515; www.germanostrattoria.com
Italian. Lunch, dinner. Reservations recommended. $16-35

★★THE HELMAND
806 N. Charles St., Baltimore, 410-752-0311; www.helmand.com
Middle Eastern. Dinner. Reservations recommended. Bar. $16-35

★★★IXIA
518 N. Charles St., Baltimore, 410-727-1800; www.ixia-online.com
This eclectic, international restaurant serves entrées such as pan-roasted sea scallops with mole sauce, blood orange, avocado relish and lobster tamale; sauerbraten-braised lamb shank with brown butter brussel sprouts and herbed potato dumpling; and lump crab cake with sweet corn and fingerling potato salad with dill, lemon and caper beure blanc. There are tasting menus, flights and a happy hour Tuesday through Saturday with special prices on drinks.
Dinner. Closed Sunday-Monday. Reservations recommended. Bar. $36-85

★★JOHN STEVEN, LTD.
1800 Thames St., Baltimore, 410-327-0489; www.johnstevenltd.com
Seafood. Lunch, dinner. Reservations recommended. Outdoor seating. Children's menu. Bar. $36-85

★★LA SCALA
1012 Eastern Ave., Baltimore, 410-783-9209; www.lascaladining.com
Italian. Dinner. Reservations recommended. Outdoor seating. Bar. $16-35

★★★LINWOOD'S
25 Crossroads Drive, Owings Mills, 410-356-3030; www.linwoods.com
This sophisticated restaurant is one of Baltimore's most popular and for good reason. The dining room is formal but not stuffy and the menu is inventive and enticing. Dishes have included crab cakes with corn pudding and fried tomatoes and grilled veal porterhouse with sautéed spinach, grilled onions and fingerling potatoes. They also have wood-burning oven pizzas and comfort foods like hamburgers and mac and cheese.
American. Lunch, dinner. Bar. Reservations recommended. Outdoor seating. Bar. $36-85

★★★THE MILTON INN
14833 York Road, Sparks, 410-771-4366; www.miltoninn.com
This old stone house has been restored for use as a country inn that serves exceptional food in an authentic colonial atmosphere. This cozy spot serves tasty dishes including roast Hudson Valley duck and cinnamon-crusted Atlantic salmon.
American. Lunch (Monday-Friday), dinner. Reservations recommended. Outdoor seating. Bar. $36-85

★★MT. WASHINGTON TAVERN
5700 Newbury St., Baltimore, 410-367-6903; www.mtwashingtontavern.com
American. Lunch, dinner, Sunday brunch. Outdoor seating. Bar. $36-85

★★OBRYCKI'S CRAB HOUSE
1727 E. Pratt St., Baltimore, 410-732-6399; www.obryckis.com
Seafood. Lunch, dinner. Closed December-February. Reservations recommended. Bar. $16-35

★★★THE OCEANAIRE SEAFOOD ROOM
801 Aliceanna St., Baltimore, 443-872-0000; www.theoceanaire.com
The restaurant's upscale décor features hardwood floors, rich cherry wood accents, wood blinds and leather. The menu changes daily, since seafood is the specialty and the restaurant has it flown and trucked in every morning. Diners choose their fish preparation—grilled, broiled, sautéed, steamed or fried.
Seafood. Dinner. Reservations recommended. Bar. $36-85

★★★PAZO
1425 Aliceanna, Baltimore, 410-534-7296; www.pazorestaurant.com
Pazo gives diners a taste of Spain without having to travel overseas. The

tapas dishes here are delicious and feature Mediterranean cuisine (vegetarian dishes are also available). Group dining is popular, with diners ordering multiple tapas entrees and sharing with their dining companions. The restaurant is also a popular romantic spot, with soft lighting, wood tables, soaring ceilings, and wrought-iron accents. After dinner, guests can stroll on the famed Inner Harbor where they'll find shops, activities and attractions.
Mediterranean, Tapas. Dinner. Reservations recommended. Bar. $36-85

★★PIERPOINT
1822 Aliceanna St., Baltimore, 410-675-2080; www.pierpointrestaurant.com
American. Dinner, Sunday brunch. Closed Monday. Reservations recommended. Bar. $16-35

★★★THE PRIME RIB
1101 N. Calvert St., Baltimore, 410-539-1804; www.theprimerib.com
The Prime Rib has been serving consistently good steaks, chops and seafood since 1965. With black walls, candlelit tables and tuxedoed waitstaff, it's known as "the civilized steakhouse." They also have an extensive wine list so you can be sure to find something to complement your meal.
American. Dinner. Bar. Reservations recommended. $36-85

★★★RUTH'S CHRIS STEAK HOUSE
600 Water St., Baltimore, 410-783-0033; www.ruthschris.com
Born from a single New Orleans restaurant that Ruth Fertel bought in 1965 for $22,000, the Ruth's Chris Steak House chain has made it to the top of every steak lover's list. Aged prime Midwestern beef is broiled to your liking and served on a heated plate, sizzling in butter. Sides such as creamed spinach and fresh asparagus with hollandaise are not to be missed. You can also choose from seven different potato preparations, like a one-pound baked potato with everything to au gratin potatoes covered with cheese.
Steak. Dinner. Reservations recommended. Bar. $36-85

★★SOTTO SOPRA
405 N. Charles St., Baltimore, 410-625-0534; www.sottosoprainc.com
Italian. Lunch (Monday-Saturday), dinner. Reservations recommended. Outdoor seating. Bar. $16-35

★★TAPAS TEATRO
1711 N. Charles St., Baltimore, 410-332-0110; www.tapasteatro.net
Mediterranean, Tapas. Dinner. Closed Monday. Outdoor seating. Bar. $16-35

BETHESDA
See also Washington, D.C.
A suburb of Washington, D.C., Bethesda is home to both the National Institutes of Health, the National Library of Medicine and the Bethesda National Naval Hospital. There are plenty of restuarants and shops to enjoy in the downtown area along with plenty of events and activities.

WHAT TO SEE
BETHESDA THEATRE
7719 Wisconsin Avenue, Bethesda, 301-657-7827; www.bethesdatheatre.com
This 650-seat Art Deco theatre hosts off-Broadway plays and musicals. On the National Register of Historic Places, the Bethesda Theatre opened in 1938.

NATIONAL LIBRARY OF MEDICINE
8600 Rockville Pike, Bethesda, 301-594-5983, 888-346-3656; www.nlm.nih.gov
This is the world's largest biomedical library filled with rare books, manuscripts, prints and medical art displays.
Reading Room: Monday-Friday 8:30 a.m.-5 p.m., Saturday 8:30 a.m.-2 p.m. Tours: Monday-Friday 1:30 p.m.

SPECIAL EVENT
BETHESDA FINE ARTS FESTIVAL
Woodmont Triangle,Bethesda; www.bethesda.org
This arts festival features fine arts and crafts by more than 150 artists from all over the country. Featured art includes furniture, glass, ceramics, jewelry, painting, photography and more. There is also live musical entertainment and food from a variety of Bethesda's many restaurants.
Early May.

WHERE TO STAY
★★★HYATT REGENCY BETHESDA
1 Bethesda Metro Center, Bethesda, 301-657-1234; www.bethesda.hyatt.com
Located at Metro Center and within steps to restaurants, theaters and shopping, this hotel is perfect for both the business and leisure traveler. The rooms offer Hyatt Grand beds, iPod docking stations and deluxe bathrooms with Portico products. Their onsite restaurant, Morton's, The Steakhouse, provides delicious steaks and seafood and great cocktails.
390 rooms. Restaurant, bar. Business center. Fitness center. Pool. $61-150

★★MARRIOTT SUITES BETHESDA
6711 Democracy Blvd., Bethesda, 301-897-5600, 800-228-9290;
www.marriotthotels.com
274 rooms. Restaurant, bar. Business center. Fitness center. Pool. $61-150

WHERE TO EAT
★★AUSTIN GRILL
7278 Woodmont Ave., Bethesda, 301-656-1366; www.austingrill.com
Southwestern, Mexican. Lunch, dinner, late-night, Saturday-Sunday brunch. Outdoor seating. Children's menu. Bar. $16-35

★★BACCHUS OF LEBANON
7945 Norfolk Ave., Bethesda, 301-657-1722; www.bacchusoflebanon.com
Middle Eastern. Lunch (Tuesday-Friday), dinner. Outdoor seating. $16-35

★BETHESDA CRAB HOUSE

4958 Bethesda Ave., Bethesda, 301-652-3382; www.bethesdabigcrabs.com

Seafood. Lunch, dinner, late-night. Outdoor seating. $16-35

★★★CESCO TRATTORIA

4871 Cordell Ave., Bethesda, 301-654-8333

This intimate Italian restaurant features breads that are baked fresh daily in a wood-burning oven, which is visible to diners. You can't go wrong choosing any of the pasta dishes.

Italian. Lunch (Tuesday-Friday), dinner. Outdoor seating. Bar. $36-85

★★FOONG LIN

7710 Norfolk Ave., Bethesda, 301-656-3427; www.foonglin.com

Chinese. Lunch, dinner. Bar. $16-35

★★FRASCATI

4806 Rugby Ave., Bethesda, 301-652-9514

Italian. Lunch, dinner. Closed Monday. Outdoor seating. $16-35

★★JEAN-MICHEL

10223 Old Georgetown Road, Bethesda, 301-564-4910; www.jeanmichelrestaurant.com

French. Lunch (Monday-Friday), dinner. $36-85

★★★LE VIEUX LOGIS

7925 Old Georgetown Road, 301-652-6816; www.levieuxlogisrestaurant.com

Mixing American and Scandinavian techniques with their classic French menu, Le Vieux Logis creates dishes that are innovative and delicious. The menu includes dishes like pan-seared tilapia with tomatoes, garlic and saffron as well as rack of grilled lamb chops with tarragon sauce. The exterior of the restaurant is painted with murals of a French countryside town; on the interior, the ambience is romantic with dim lighting and warm color tones.

French. Dinner. Closed Sunday-Monday. Outdoor seating. $36-85

★★★RUTH'S CHRIS STEAK HOUSE

7315 Wisconsin Ave., Bethesda, 301-652-7877; www.ruthschris.com

Thick, juicy USDA Prime steaks slathered with butter as well as market fresh seafood are the hallmarks of Ruth's Chris, and the Bethesda outpost is no exception. Found on the ground floor of the Air Rights building, the dining room features a relaxed, informal atmosphere with dark wood accents, a large lobster tank, and a cigar lounge. In addition to hearty cuts of meat like the filet, rib eye, and T-bone, and seafood items such as fresh lobster and seared ahi tuna, Ruth's Chris offers a number of tasty sides.

American, steak. Dinner. Bar. $36-85

★★★TRAGARA

4935 Cordell Ave., Bethesda, 301-951-4935; www.tragara.com

Tragara is one of Bethesda's most elegant and romantic restaurants, offering delightful Italian cuisine and impeccable service. Bathed in soft light, with fresh roses on every linen-topped table, Tragara is serene and relaxing—a lovely place to dine and then linger. Tables fill up quickly at lunch and dinner with smartly dressed business executives and stylish quartets of 30-something couples. The impressive Italian kitchen draws them all in with a tempting menu of pastas, fish, meat, and antipasti, but be sure to save room to indulge in the house-made gelato before saying, "Ciao."

Italian. Lunch (Monday-Friday), dinner. Reservations recommended. Bar. $36-85

CHESAPEAKE BAY BRIDGE AREA

The majestic twin spans of the Chesapeake Bay Bridge carry visitors to the Eastern Shore, a patchwork of small picturesque towns, lighthouses and fishing villages tucked away from the city. Scenic rivers and bays, wildlife, gardens and wildflowers fill the countryside. The main attractions of any visit, however, are the many fine inns and the restaurants specializing in local seafood.

WHAT TO SEE
WYE OAK STATE PARK

Highway 662, Wye Mills, 410-820-1668; www.dnr.state.md.us

On the Eastern Shore in Talbot County, approximately one mile from the junction of Routes 50 and 404. The official state tree of Maryland is in this 29-acre park; it is the largest white oak in the United States (108 feet high, 28 feet around) and is believed to be more than 460 years old. A new tree has even been started from one of its acorns. A restored 18th-century one-room schoolhouse and the Old Wye Mill (used since the late 1600s) are nearby.

WHERE TO STAY
★COMFORT SUITES

160 Scheeler Road, Chestertown, 410-810-0555, 877-424-6423; www.comfortinn.com

53 rooms. Complimentary breakfast. Pool. $61-150

★★★KENT MANOR INN

500 Kent Manor Drive, Stevensville, 410-643-7716, 800-820-4511;
www.kentmanor.com

This historic 1820 inn sits among 220 wooded acres on picturesque Thompson Creek, a tributary to the Chesapeake Bay. Its location just 12 miles from Annapolis makes it a convenient spot for both business and leisure travelers. The luxurious and romantic guest rooms are beautifully decorated in Victorian style and feature four poster beds, Italian marble fireplaces, and stunning views of the grounds. Several rooms also have window seats and porches. There are many outdoor activities for guests to enjoy: a walk through the flower garden, an outdoor pool, and bike and paddleboat rentals. Guests can also enjoy nearby activities like golfing, shopping, antiquing, and water sports. The Restaurant at Kent Manor is the perfect choice for a quiet, intimate fine-dining meal.

24 rooms. Restaurant. Complimentary breakfast. Pool. $61-150

WHERE TO EAT

★★FISHERMAN'S INN AND CRAB DECK
3116 Main St., Kent Narrows, 410-827-8807; www.fishermansinn.com
Seafood, steak. Lunch, dinner. Closed November-March. Bar. $16-35

★HARRIS CRAB HOUSE
433 Kent Narrows Way North, Grasonville, 410-827-9500; www.harriscrabhouse.com
American, seafood. Lunch, dinner. Children's menu. Outdoor seating. Bar.
$36-85

★★★NARROWS
3023 Kent Narrows Way South, Grasonville, 410-827-8113;
www.thenarrowsrestaurant.com
This restaurant offers waterfront dining with a spectacular view of the Kent
Narrows. The crab cakes are their signature; in fact, they have become so
popular that the restaurant now ships them anywhere in the country.
American. Lunch, dinner, brunch. Children's menu. Bar. $36-85

★WATERMAN'S CRAB HOUSE
21055 Sharp St., Rick Hall, 410-639-2261; www.watermanscrabhouse.com
Seafood. Lunch, dinner. Reservations recommended. Outdoor seating. Children's menu. Bar. $16-35

CHEVY CHASE
See also Bethesda
Incorporated in 1918, this town governs itself with their town council. Located in Montgomery County, there are only about 3,000 people living here in
this quiet setting with plenty of tree-lined streets outside Washington, D.C.

WHERE TO STAY
★★COURTYARD CHEVY CHASE
5520 Wisconsin Ave., Chevy Chase, 301-656-1500, 800-315-2621;
www.holiday-inn.com
225 rooms. Restaurant, bar. Fitness center. Pool. $61-150

WHERE TO EAT
★★★LA FERME
7101 Brookville Road, Chevy Chase, 301-986-5255; www.lafermerestaurant.com
In a French country-house setting, La Ferme serves entrées such as hickory-
smoked and grilled double-cut pork chops with potato gratin, grilled vegetables and Meaux mustard sauce. In warmer weather, the outdoor terrace is
on the perfect spot to grab a quick lunch or romantic dinner. Desserts might
include chocolate and Grand Marnier mousse cake or warm brioche pudding
with rum-raisin ice cream and caramel sauce.
French. Lunch (Monday-Friday), dinner, Sunday brunch. Reservations
recommended. Outdoor seating. Bar. $16-35

COLLEGE PARK

See also Silver Springs; Washington, D.C.

College Park is the location of the flagship University of Maryland as well as the College Park Aviation Museum.

WHAT TO SEE
COLLEGE PARK AVIATION MUSEUM

1985 Corporal Frank Scott Drive, College Park, 301-864-6029;
www.collegeparkaviationmuseum.com

This museum is located on the site of the world's oldest operating airport, started by Wilbur Wright in 1909 to train two military officers in the operation of aircraft. First airplane machine gun and radio navigational aids were tested here as well as the first air mail and controlled helicopter flights. There is a museum with a gallery of historic aircrafts as well as changing exhibits. Admission: adults $4, seniors $3, students and children under 2 free. Daily 10 a.m.-5 p.m.

GREENBELT PARK

6565 Greenbelt Road, College Park, 301-344-3948; www.hikercentral.com/parks/gree

A 1,100-acre wooded park operated by the National Park Service that includes 174 sites. Nature trails, picnicking, camping and skiing keeps guest busy. Self-registration is required; patrons are first-come, first-served. Daily.

UNIVERSITY OF MARYLAND

Highway 1, College Park, 301-405-1000; www.umd.edu

This university is attended by 35,000 students. Tawes Fine Arts Theater has plays, musicals, concerts, dance, opera and music festivals. Be sure to find the statue of the University mascot, Testudo, the Diamondback terrapin and rub his nose for good luck. Also, there's a statue of 1960 alumnus Jim Henson with his alter-ego Kermit the Frog surrounded by the memorial garden.

WHERE TO STAY
★★HOLIDAY INN

10000 Baltimore Ave., College Park, 301-345-6700, 800-315-2621;
www.holidayinncollegepark.com

222 rooms. Restaurant, bar. Fitness center. Pool. $61-150

COLUMBIA

See also Baltimore

A planned city built on a tract of land larger than Manhattan Island, Columbia comprises 11 villages surrounding a central downtown service area. Located in Howard County, construction of the city began in 1966 as a model city. Since it's located in between Baltimore and Washington, D.C., Columbia is a thriving community.

WHAT TO SEE
AFRICAN ART MUSEUM OF MARYLAND

5430 Vantage Point Road, Columbia, 410-730-7106; www.africanartmuseum.org
Masks, sculptured figures, textiles, basketry, household items and musical instruments are displayed in a 19th-century manor turned museum.
Tuesday-Friday 10 a.m.-4 p.m., Sunday noon-4 p.m.

HOWARD COUNTY CENTER OF AFRICAN-AMERICAN CULTURE
5434 Vantage Point Road, Columbia, 410-715-1921; www.hccaacres.org
The center contains artifacts and memorabilia depicting images of African-Americans over the last 200 years. There is an extensive collection of spiritual, jazz and rap music as well as more than 2,000 books and periodicals. There are also hands-on exhibits for children.
Tuesday-Friday noon-5 p.m., Saturday noon-4 p.m., Sunday by appointment.

SPECIAL EVENTS
COLUMBIA FESTIVAL OF THE ARTS
5575 Sterrett Place, Columbia, 410-715-3044; www.columbiafestival.com
The festival offers music, dance, theater and lakeside entertainment.
June.

WINE IN THE WOODS
Symphony Woods, 7120 Oakland Mills Road, Columbia, 410-313-4700; www.wineinthewoods.com
Located in Symphony Woods at Merriweather Post Pavilion, this two-day celebration features Maryland wines, gourmet food, entertainment, arts and crafts. Live music features everything from blues and rock to jazz and soul. More than 25 wineries attend.
Third weekend in May.

WHERE TO STAY
★★★HILTON COLUMBIA
5485 Twin Knolls Road, Columbia, 410-997-1060, 800-445-8667;
www.columbia.hilton.com
Located in the heart of Columbia in a parklike setting, this hotel offers a very relaxing stay, with a glassed atrium and well-appointed guest rooms. A state-of-the-art fitness center and indoor pool make this a good choice for the active set.
152 rooms. Restaurant, bar. Business center. Fitness center. Pool. Pets accepted. $61-150

★★★SHERATON COLUMBIA TOWN CENTER HOTEL
10207 Wincopin Circle, Columbia, 410-730-3900, 800-638-2817;
www.sheratoncolumbia.com
Recognized for its gracious accommodations and superb service, this modern hotel is a welcome retreat for both business and leisure travelers. Guest rooms have been updated to include flat-screen TVs, high-speed Internet access and Sheraton Sweet Sleeper Beds with luxurious bedding.
290 rooms. Restaurant, bar. Fitness center. Pets accepted. $61-150

WHERE TO EAT
★★★KING'S CONTRIVANCE
10150 Shaker Drive, Columbia, 410-995-0500; www.thekingscontrivance.com
Guests can enjoy fine country dining in this circa 1900 mansion filled with
Early American décor. The menu offers selections such as crab cakes, veni-
son and rack of lamb, as well as an extensive wine list. A new outdoor patio
is the perfect spot to enjoy lunch or dinner al fresco.
American. Lunch (Monday-Friday), dinner. Children's menu. Reservations
recommended. Outdoor seating. Bar. $36-85

CUMBERLAND
See also Frederick
Cumberland is nestled between Pennsylvania and West Virginia in western
Maryland. George Washington, who once defended the town, thought the
nation's primary east-west route would eventually pass through Cumberland.
In 1833, the National Road made the town a supply terminus for overland
commerce. Today's economy includes services and recreational facilities.

WHAT TO SEE
FORT CUMBERLAND TRAIL
Cumberland
This walking trail covers several city blocks downtown around the site of
Fort Cumberland. Boundary markers with narrative plaques lead you through
sites such as Riverside Park, the Narrows, Allegany County Library, Folck's
Mill and others.

GORDON-ROBERTS HOUSE
218 Washington St., Cumberland, 301-777-8678; wwwgordonrobertshouse.com
Located in the Washington Street Historic District, this restored 18-room
Victorian house, dating back to 1867, has nine period rooms as well as a re-
search room. Tours are given by docents dressed up in period costumes who
guide you through the three floors. There is also a gift shop onsite selling
Victorian items such as teapots, tea, jewelry and more.
Tuesday-Saturday 10 a.m.-5 p.m.

THE NARROWS
Route 40, Cumberland
This picturesque 1,000-foot gap through the Alleghenies was used by pioneers on their way West. This is a great spot to photograph the surrounding
beauty. There's also an old stone bridge that goes across Wills Creek.

ROCKY GAP STATE PARK
12500 Pleasant Valley Road N.E., Cumberland, 301-722-1480, 888-432-2267;
www.dnr.state.md.us
Rocky Gap State Park covers 3,00 acres of mountain scenery around a 243-
acre lake with three swimming beaches. Tourists and locals come here for the
swimming, fishing, boating, nature and hiking trails. There's also picnicking,

camping and lodging onsite. Activities include an 18-hole Jack Nicklaus golf course, playground, tennis and volleyball courts.

WESTERN MARYLAND SCENIC RAILROAD
13 Canal St., Cumberland, 301-759-4400, 800-872-4650; www.wmsr.com
This excursion train makes a scenic trip 17 miles through the Allegheny Mountains to Frostburg where you stop for lunch then take a trip through the Thrasher Carriage Museum and back. A narrator provides information about the history of the area. Passengers sit in restored coaches that have large picture windows, a snack car and gift shop. Tickets are available on the second floor of the Western Maryland Station.
May-October: Thursday-Sunday, 11:30 a.m.; November-mid-December, Friday-Sunday, 11:30 a.m. Admission: adults $29, seniors $27, children $15.

WESTERN MARYLAND STATION CENTER
13 Canal St., Cumberland, 301-724-3655; www.nps.gov
Part of the Canal Place Heritage Area, this 1913 railroad station houses Canal Place Authority, Industrial and Transportation Museum, C&O Canal National Historical Park Visitors Center and Allegany County Visitors Center. Train rides are offered for only a portion of the year.
Daily.

SPECIAL EVENTS
AGRICULTURAL EXPO AND FAIR
Allegany County Fairgrounds, 11490 Moss Ave. Cumberland, 301-729-1200; www.alleganycofair.org
This county expo and fair features poultry and livestock shows, a carnival, and entertainment. There is a also a demolition derby, a monster truck show and races.
Late July.

DELFEST
Allegany County Fairgrounds, 11490 Moss Ave., Cumberland, 510-595-1115; www.delfest.com
This three-day festival features a blugrass band competition, food, drink, an art and craft fair, a kid's area with activities, onsite camping and more. The Del McCoury band plays along with other bluegrass bands and they also offer a DelFest Adacemy for students to perform or take classes on the banjo, mandolin, fiddle and bass.
Memorial Day weekend.

WHERE TO STAY
★★HOLIDAY INN CUMBERLAND-DOWNTOWN
100 S. George St., Cumberland, 301-724-8800, 888-465-4329; www.hicumberland.com
130 rooms. Restaurant, bar. Business center. Fitness center. Pool. $61-150

WHERE TO EAT
★★★AU PETIT PARIS

86 E. Main St., Frostburg, 301-689-8946; www.aupetitparis.com

The atmosphere at this cozy French bistro is intimate and relaxed. The à la carte menu will satisfy even the most discriminating gourmet with dishes like duck a l'orange and le coq au vin. The wine cellar boasts the most extensive collection in western Maryland.

French. Dinner. Closed Sunday-Monday. Children's menu. Bar. $36-85

EASTON

See also St. Michael's

This town might be small, but it offers quite a lot. Near Baltimore, Annapolis and Washington D.C., it's easy to escape from the city here and enjoy sailing and canoeing on the Chesapeake Bayor the charming shops and restaurants you will find here.

WHAT TO SEE
ACADEMY ART MUSEUM

106 South St., Easton, 410-822-2787; www.art-academy.org

Housed in a renovated 1820s schoolhouse, the Academy exhibits works by local and national artists in its permanent collection. It also hosts more than 250 visual and performing arts programs annually.

Admission: Free. Monday, Friday 10 a.m.-4 p.m., Tuesday-Thursday 1-a.m.-7 p.m., Saturday 10 a.m.-3 p.m.

HISTORICAL SOCIETY OF TALBOT COUNTY

25 S. Washington St., Easton, 410-822-0773; www.hstc.org

This Historical Society includes a three-gallery museum in a renovated early commercial building with changing exhibits and a museum shop. Also on-site are three historic houses including an 1810 Federal town house, a 1700s Quaker cabinetmaker's cottage, Forman's Studio as well as period gardens.

Admission: Free. Monday-Saturday 10 a.m.-4 p.m.

THIRD HAVEN FRIENDS MEETING HOUSE

405 S. Washington St., Easton, 410-822-0293; www.thirdhaven.org

This is one of the oldest frame-construction houses of worship for Quaker or the Religious Society of Friends in the U.S. In 1684, this building was used for Quaker meetings. Notable Quakers have worshipped here including William Penn.

Worship Services: Sunday 10 a.m., Wednesday 5:30 p.m.

SPECIAL EVENTS
CHESAPEAKE CHAMBER MUSIC FESTIVAL

21 S. Harrison St., Easton, 410-819-0380; www.chesapeakechambermusic.org

This festival features world-class chamber music concerts taking place in Talbot County, Queenstown and Chestertown. Performances are held at various venues during weeknight and weekend days in June.

June.

WATERFOWL FESTIVAL

40 S. Harrison St., Easton, 410-822-4567; www.waterfowlfestival.org

The Waterfowl Festival takes place downtown as well as various locations in and around town. There are exhibits featuring waterfowl, pictures, carvings, collectibles, decoy auctions, calling contests, fly fishing, kid's activities and concerts. Local vendors come out to provide food and there is also a wine tasting.

Second weekend in November.

WHERE TO STAY
★★BISHOP'S HOUSE
214 Goldsborough St., Easton, 410-820-7290, 800-223-7290; www.bishopshouse.com
5 rooms. No children under 12. Complimentary breakfast. $151-250

★HOLIDAY INN EXPRESS EASTON
8561 Ocean Gateway, Easton, 410-819-6500, 877-327-8661; www.hotel-easex.com
73 rooms. Complimentary breakfast. Fitness center. Pool. $61-150

★★★ROBERT MORRIS INN
314 N. Morris St., Oxford, 410-226-5111, 888-823-4012; www.robertmorrisinn.com
Rooms at the Robert Morris Inn include private porches with views of the Chesapeake Bay. Relax in an Adirondack chair on the inn's property, which stretches down to the water's edge. You can visit the nearby marine museum, go for a bike ride or scout for antiques in Oxford.
34 rooms. Complimentary breakfast. Closed December-March. No children under 10. Restaurant. $151-250

WHERE TO EAT
★★★RESTAURANT LOCAL
Tidewater Inn, 101 E. Dover St., Easton, 410-822-1300; www.tidewaterinn.com
Opened in 2006 as part of the Historic Tidewater Inn's renovations, Restaurant Local serves contemporary American cuisine in a modern but casual setting. Entrées include a local rockfish filet with shrimp and basil risotto, mushrooms and saffron butter, and filet mignon with roasted garlic potatoes, grilled asparagus and wild mushroom bordelaise.
American. Breakfast, lunch, dinner, Sunday brunch. Outdoor seating. Bar. $36-85

ELLICOTT CITY
See also Baltimore
Originally named Ellicott Mills, this town was founded by three Quaker brothers as the site of their gristmill. Charles Carroll of Carrollton, whose Doughoregan Manor can still be seen nearby, lent financial help to the Ellicotts, and the town eventually became the site of ironworks, rolling mills and the first railroad terminus in the United States. The famous Tom Thumb locomotive race with a horse took place near here. Many of the town's original stone houses and log cabins, on hills above the Patapsco River, have been preserved.

WHAT TO SEE
ELLICOTT CITY B&O RAILROAD STATION MUSEUM

2711 Maryland Ave., Ellicott City, 410-461-1945; www.ecborail.org

Completed by the Baltimore and Ohio Railroad in 1830, the Ellicott City Station is the oldest standing railroad station in America and the site of first 13 miles of commercial track constructed in the United States. In the 1970s the station was restored as a museum, and a second restoration in 1999 returned the building to its 1857 appearance. Today, the site interprets the story of transportation and travel in early America through seasonal exhibits, education programs and living history programs.

Admission: adults $5, seniors $4, children 2-12 $3. Wednesday-Sunday 11 a.m.-4 p.m.

PATAPSCO VALLEY STATE PARK

8020 Baltimore National Pike, Ellicott City, 410-461-5005, 888-432-2267; www.dnr.state.md.us

Spread across three counties, this great nature and recreational area runs along a 32-mile stretch of the scenic Patapsco River, spans 14,000 acres and contains five sites. Guests can hike, bike, ride horses, fish, camp, canoe, tube or picnic. The park also includes the world's largest multiple-arched stone railroad bridge, a 300-foot suspension bridge and a paved hiking trail for the disabled.

Park: Daily dawn-dusk. Information desk: Daily 8 a.m.-4:30 p.m.

WHERE TO STAY
★★★TURF VALLEY RESORT AND CONFERENCE CENTER

2700 Turf Valley Road, Ellicott City, 410-465-1500, 888-833-8873; www.turfvalley.com

This full-service resort (formerly a thoroughbred farm and country club) is convenient to Baltimore and offers well-appointed guest rooms. The resort also features a full-service European spa, two golf courses, tennis courts and a nightly hors d'oeuvres and cocktail reception.

234 rooms. Restaurant, bar. Business center. Fitness center. Pool. Spa. Golf. Tennis. $151-250

WHERE TO EAT
★★CRAB SHANTY

3410 Plumtree Drive, Ellicott City, 410-465-9660; www.crabshanty.com

Seafood. Lunch, dinner, Sunday brunch. Children's menu. Bar. $16-35

★★★TERSIGUEL'S

8293 Main St., Ellicott City, 410-465-4004; www.tersiguels.com

Tersiguel's offers fine dining in a 19th-century home with six individual dining rooms. Chef Michel Tersiguel prepares seasonal cuisine with fresh vegetables and herbs from their garden, and chèvre cheese is made daily.

French. Lunch, dinner. Reservations recommended. Bar. $36-85

FREDERICK

See also Hagerstown, Thurmont, Westminster

Home of fearless Barbara Frietschie, who reportedly spoke her mind to Stonewall Jackson and his "rebel hordes," Frederick is a town filled with history. Named for Frederick Calvert, sixth Lord Baltimore, it is the seat of one of America's richest agricultural counties. Francis Scott Key and Chief Justice Roger Brooke Taney made their homes here. Court House Square was the scene of several important events during the Revolutionary War, including the famed protest against the Stamp Act, in which an effigy of the stamp distributor was burned.

During the Civil War, Frederick was a focal point for strategic operations by both sides. In the campaign of 1862, the Confederacy's first invasions of the North were made at nearby South Mountain and Sharpsburg, at Antietam Creek. Thousands of wounded men were cared for here. In July 1864, the town was forced to pay a $200,000 ransom to Confederate General Jubal Early before he fought the Battle of Monocacy a few miles south. Frederick today is an educational center, tourist attraction, the location of Fort Detrick army installation, and home to diversified small industry. A 33-block area has been designated a Historic District.

WHAT TO SEE
BARBARA FRITCHIE HOUSE AND MUSEUM
154 W. Patrick St., 301-698-8992, Frederick; www.fredericktourism.org
This is the old home of Barbara Fritchie who was the heroine in John Greenleaf Whittier's poem about the Civil War and a friend of Francis Scott Key. The house has been reconstructed and the exterior is available to view. For a look at the interior, call for an appointment.

GAMBRILL STATE PARK
8602 Gambrill Park Road, Frederick, 301-271-7574, 888-432-2267; www.dnr.state.md.us
This park covers 1,137 acres with two developed areas in which visitors can enjoy fishing, nature and hiking trails, picnicking, and camping. There are three shelters that can be rented along with the Tea room, a stone shelter which has a stone fireplace, a kitchen and a balcony with beautiful vistas. In spring, plenty of flowers, trees and shrubs add color to the area.

HISTORICAL SOCIETY OF FREDERICK COUNTY MUSEUM
24 E. Church St., Frederick, 301-663-1188; www.hsfcinfo.org
This house, built in the early 1800s, shows both Georgian and Federal-style details in the center of downtown Frederick. Inside the house, portraits of early Frederick residents and tall case clocks are on display. The Heritage Garden features flower gardens, brick paths, trellises and grassy areas. Admission: adults $3. Monday-Saturday 10 a.m.-4 p.m., Sunday 1-4 p.m. Closed first two weeks in January.

MONOCACY NATIONAL BATTLEFIELD
4801 Urbana Pike, Frederick, 301-662-3515; www.nps.gov/mono
On July 9, 1864, Union General Lew Wallace and 5,000 men delayed General Jubal Early and his 23,000 Confederate soldiers for 24 hours, during which Grant was able to reinforce and save Washington, D.C., New Jersey, Vermont and Pennsylvania. Confederate monuments mark the area.

CIVIL WAR SITES OF FREDERICK

A well-preserved city of elegant 18th- and 19th-century structures, Frederick is a necessary stop on any tour of Civil War landmarks. It is an especially appropriate sequel to visit after nearby Antietam National Battlefield, the site of the single bloodiest day of the Civil War—September 17, 1862. At the end of the battle, thousands of Union wounded were transported to Frederick, where 29 buildings were turned into makeshift hospitals. President Lincoln later praised townsfolk for their humanity. This heritage led to Frederick's selection as the site of the National Museum of Civil War Medicine.

Begin an hour-long, one-mile walking tour of the city's historic district at the museum at 48 East Patrick St. The museum tells the story of radical improvements in medical treatment during the four-years war, as the divided nation coped with the flood of ill or wounded soldiers on both sides of the Mason-Dixon line. From the museum, walk three blocks west to the reconstructed Barbara Frietschie House & Museum at 154 West Patrick. Frietschie was immortalized in John Greenleaf Whittier's Civil War poem, "Shoot if you must, this old gray head, but spare your country's flag." According to legend, she waved a Union flag defiantly at Stonewall Jackson, who was leading a Confederate army through the city. In truth, she may have waved a flag, but to honor Union troops passing by later.

Double back on Patrick Street to Court Street and walk north one block to tour Courthouse Square. On Court Street, opposite City Hall, is the small office where Francis Scott Key, author of "The Star-Spangled Banner," practiced law. Revolutionary War General Lafayette was a guest at 103 Council St. during his ceremonial U.S. tour in 1824. At 119 Record St. Lincoln visited a wounded general and addressed a crowd from its steps after the Antietam battle. Head east on West Church Street. Conclude your tour two blocks east at the Historical Society of Fredericksburg at 24 East Church. A large 1820 home, it is maintained as a house museum furnished with local antiques—appropriately so, because nearby East Patrick Street has been dubbed "Antique Row" for its many antique shops.

Daily 8:30 a.m.-5 p.m.

MOUNT OLIVET CEMETERY
515 S. Market St., Frederick, 301-662-1164, 888-662-1164;
www.mountolivetcemeteryinc.com
This beautiful cemetary houses the marked graves of Francis Scott Key and Barbara Fritchie along with Governor Thomas Johnson who was the first governor of Maryland. A flag flies over Key's grave.

ROGER BROOKE TANEY HOME
121 S. Bentz St., Frederick, 301-663-1188; www.hsfcinfo.org
Chief Justice of the United States from 1835 to 1864, Taney was chosen by Andrew Jackson to succeed John Marshall. He swore in seven presidents, including Abraham Lincoln, and issued the famous Dred Scott Decision. He is buried in the cemetery of St. John's Catholic Church at East Third and East streets. This home features displays of what life was like in the early 19th century.
Admission: adults $3, children 17 and under free. April-mid-December,

Saturday 10 a.m.-4 p.m., Sunday 1-4 p.m.

ROSE HILL MANOR PARK & CHILDREN'S MUSEUM
1611 N. Market St., Frederick, 301-694-1646, 800-999-3613;
www.rosehillmuseum.com
This museum features hands-on exhibits of 19th-century family life with a carriage museum, colonial herb and fragrant gardens, a farm museum, blacksmith shop, and log cabin.
Park: Daily 8 a.m.-4:30 p.m. Museum: April-October, Monday-Saturday 10 a.m.-4 p.m., Sunday 1-4 p.m.; November, Saturday 10 a.m.-4 p.m., Sunday 1-4 p.m.; December-March, group reservations only.

TRINITY CHAPEL
10 West Church Street, Frederick, 301-694-2489
This graceful colonial church is where Francis Scott Key was baptized. The steeple from 1807 houses the town clock and 10-bell chimes. The chimes play every Saturday evening. The stone tower is from 1763.

SPECIAL EVENTS
BEYOND THE GARDEN GATES TOUR
19 E. Church St., Frederick, 301-394-2489; www.celebratefrederick.com
Head downtown in May to explore the beautiful gardens of Frederick's private homes. You can tour the backyard gardens where artists are working to capture the surroundings for posterity. Purchase tickets on the Web site. Mid-May.

FALL FESTIVAL
Rose Hill Manor, 1611 N. Market St., Frederick, 301-600-1650; www.co.frederick.md.us
Head to the Farm Museum at Rose Hill Manor for this fall festival featuring apple butter making, music, crafts demonstrations, tractor pull, hay rides and country cooking.
Early October.

GREAT FREDERICK FAIR
797 E. Patrick St., Frederick, 301-663-5895; www.thegreatfrederickfair.com
The Frederick county fair features plenty of fun for everyone including entertainment by such performers as Billy Ray Cyrus and Foreigner. There's a demolition derby, a FMX freestyle motocross championship, stunt car drivers, contests, carnival rides, concessions and more.
Mid-late September.

PANGAEA FREDERICK
Westridge Square Shopping Center, 1053 West Patrick St., Frederick, 301-600-2844;
www.celebratefrederick.com
This free festival brings together the different cultures of Frederick to celebrate the common origin and Pangaea which means "entire earth." Come out to enjoy food and entertainment from different cultures, including Irish, Hispanic, Asian and German music.

Second Saturday in May.

WHERE TO STAY
★FAIRFIELD INN & SUITES FREDERICK
5220 Westview Drive, Frederick, 301-631-2000, 800-228-2800; www.marriott.com
105 rooms. Complimentary breakfast. Pool. $61-150

★★HAMPTON INN
5311 Buckeystown Pike, Frederick, 301-698-2500, 800-426-7866;
www.hamptoninn.com
161 rooms. Restaurant, bar. Complimentary breakfast. Business center. Fitness center. Pool. Pets accepted. $61-150

WHERE TO EAT
★★RED HORSE STEAK HOUSE
996 W. Patrick St., Frederick, 301-663-3030; www.redhorseusa.com
Steak. Dinner. Children's menu. Reservations recommended. Bar. $151-250

GAITHERSBURG
See also Rockville
Located in Montgomery County, Gaithersburg is near Washington D.C, and Rockville, MD. It's a suburb of Washington, D.C. where many citygoers can escape the hustle and bustle. When it was formed in 1765, it was known as Log Town. With its small-town feel, Gaithersburg provides an old downtown area with plenty of shopping and dining options.

WHAT TO SEE
SENECA CREEK STATE PARK
11950 Clopper Road, Gaithersburg, 301-924-2127, 888-432-2267;
www.dnr.state.md.us
This park comprises 6,300 acres with a 90-acre lake for boating, fishing, canoeing, hunting, picnicking, disc golf, hiking, bicycle and bridle trails and winter sports. In May the Schwartz peony garden is in full bloom for visitors to admire. There are historic sites to explore including old mills, an old schoolhouse and stone quarries.

SPECIAL EVENT
MONTGOMERY COUNTY AGRICULTURAL FAIR
16 Chestnut St., Gaithersburg, 301-926-3100; www.mcagfair.com
One of the East Coast's leading county fairs, Montgomery County Agricultural Fair features entertainment such as magicians, a hynotist, a demolition derby, rodeo, monster trucks, a tractor pull, carnival rides and more. There are animal demonstrations and contests along with plenty of vendors selling food and drink.
August.

WHERE TO STAY
★COMFORT INN
16216 Frederick Road, Gaithersburg, 877-424-6423; www.choicehotels.com

127 rooms. Complimentary breakfast. Fitness center. Pool. $61-150

★★★GAITHERSBURG MARRIOTT WASHINGTONIAN CENTER

9751 Washingtonian Blvd., Gaithersburg, 301-590-0044; www.marriott.com

This newly renovated hotel offers bright and spacious guest rooms with luxurious bedding, Internet access and suites with full kitchens. It is conveniently located near top restaurants, shops and a multiplex theater. The hotel's restaurant, the Washingtonian Grille features a casual atmosphere serving delicious American fare.

284 rooms. Restaurant, bar. Business center. Fitness center. Pool. $16-35

★★★HILTON WASHINGTON D.C. NORTH/GAITHERSBURG

620 Perry Parkway, Gaithersburg, 301-977-8900, 800-445-8667; www.hilton.com

Enjoy newly renovated guest rooms with pillow-top beds, luxurious bedding, wireless Internet access and updated furnishings. The staff is friendly and accommodating and the location just outside the Nation's Capital means sightseeing opportunities abound.

301 rooms. Restaurant, bar. Business center. Fitness center. Pool. Pets accepted. $151-250

★★HOLIDAY INN GAITHERSBURG

2 Montgomery Village Ave., Gaithersburg, 301-948-8900, 800-465-4329;
www.higaithersburg.com

301 rooms. Restaurant, bar. Business center. Fitness center. Pool. Pets accepted. $61-150

★★WYNDHAM GARDEN HOTEL GAITHERSBURG

805 Russell Ave., Gaithersburg, 301-670-0008, 877-999-3223; www.wyndham.com

203 rooms. Restaurant, bar. Business center. Fitness center. Pool. Tennis. $61-150

WHERE TO EAT

★★GOLDEN BULL GRAND CAFÉ

7 Dalamar St., Gaithersburg, 301-948-3666; www.golden-bull.com

American. Lunch (Monday-Saturday), dinner. Children's menu. Reservations recommended. Bar. $16-35

★★OLD SIAM

108 E. Diamond Ave., Gaithersburg, 301-926-9199

Thai. Lunch, dinner. $15 and under.

★★PEKING CHEERS

519 Quince Orchard Road, Gaithersburg, 301-216-2090

Chinese. Lunch, dinner. Reservations recommended. $15 and under.

★ROY'S PLACE

2 E. Diamond Ave., Gaithersburg, 301-948-5548; www.roysplacerestaurant.com

American. Lunch, dinner. Outdoor seating. Bar. $16-35

GREENBELT

See also College Park

A suburb of Washington, D.C., the planned community of Greenbelt is between the Baltimore and Washington, D.C. metropolitan areas. It was modeled after 19th-century English garden cities and is surrounded by forests. NASA's Goddard Space Flight Center is located here.

WHAT TO SEE
NASA/GODDARD SPACE FLIGHT CENTER & VISITOR CENTER

Greenbelt, 301-286-3978; www.gsfc.nasa.gov/vc
The Goddard Space Flight Center's Visitor Center showcases satellites, rockets, capsules and exhibits in all phases of space research.
Admission: Free. September-May, Tuesday-Friday 10 a.m.-3 p.m., Saturday-Sunday noon-4 p.m.; June-August, Tuesday-Friday 10 a.m.-5 p.m., Saturday noon-4 p.m.

WHERE TO STAY
★★COURTYARD GREENBELT

6301 Golden Triangle Drive, Greenbelt, 301-441-3311, 800-321-2211; www.marriott.com
152 rooms. Business center. Fitness center. Pool. $61-150

★★★MARRIOTT GREENBELT

6400 Ivy Lane, Greenbelt, 301-441-3700, 800-228-9290; www.marriott.com
The close proximity to BWI airport and downtown Washington, D.C., along with laptop plug-in connections to flat-screen HDTVs, makes this a hotel ideal for business travelers. And the pillow-top beds guarantee that you'll be well rested for your morning meeting. Enjoy the fitness center, the indoor and outdoor pools and an outdoor whirlpool.
288 rooms. Restaurant, bar. Business center. Fitness center. Pool. Tennis. $151-250

WHERE TO EAT
★★SIRI'S CHEF'S SECRET

5810 Greenbelt Road, Greenbelt, 301-345-6101; www.sirichef.com
Thai. Lunch (Monday-Friday), dinner. $36-85

HAGERSTOWN

See also Frederick, Thurmont

Visitors to Hagerstown might appear lost in thought, alternately staring at their shoes and turning their gaze to the heavens as they walk. But they're actually soaking up some history on the town's walking tour—points of interest are marked on downtown sidewalks and walking paths in city parks. South Prospect Street is one of the city's oldest neighborhoods, listed on the National Register of Historic Places. The tree-lined street is graced by homes dating back to the early 1800s.

WHAT TO SEE
HAGERSTOWN ROUNDHOUSE MUSEUM
300 S. Burhans Blvd., Hagerstown, 301-739-4665; www.roundhouse.org
The museum houses photographic exhibits of the seven railroads of Hagerstown, as well as historic railroad memorabilia, tools and equipment, archives of maps, books, papers and related items. There is also a gift shop. Friday-Sunday 1-5 p.m.

JONATHAN HAGER HOUSE AND MUSEUM
Hagerstown City Park, 110 Key St., Hagerstown, 301-739-8393;
www.fortedwards.org/cwffa/hager.htm
This stone house located in Hagerstown City Park is the old home of Jonathan Hager, who is the co-founder of Hagerstown. Inside are authentic 18th-century furnishings as well as artifacts from the 18th and 19th century. Admission: adults $3, seniors $2, children 6-12 $1. April-December, Tuesday-Saturday 10 a.m.-4 p.m., Sunday 2-5 p.m. Closed January-March.

MILLER HOUSE
135 W. Washington St., Hagerstown, 301-797-8782; www.msa.md.gov
This is the site of the Washington County Historical Society headquarters. This federal townhouse circa 1820 has a three-story spiral staircase, period furnishings and Bell pottery collections. There are also Chesapeake and Ohio Canal and Civil War exhibits and a 19th-century country store display. April-December, Wednesday-Saturday 1-4 p.m., Sunday afternoons; closed first two weeks in December.

WASHINGTON COUNTY MUSEUM OF FINE ARTS
91 Key St., Hagerstown, 301-739-5727; www.wcmfa.org
Founded in 1929, this fine arts museum displays paintings, sculptures and changing exhibits. They also offer films, classes, concerts and lectures. Tuesday-Friday 9 a.m.-5 p.m., Saturday 9 a.m.-4 p.m., Sunday 1-5 p.m.

SPECIAL EVENTS
ALSATIA MUMMERS HALLOWEEN PARADE FESTIVAL
Downtown Hagerstown, 301-739-2044
Ten thousand participants enter this downtown Hagerstown parade, which includes floats, bands, organizations and mummers.
Saturday closest to Halloween.

LEITERSBURG PEACH FESTIVAL
21378 Leiters Mill Road, Hagerstown
If you love eating peaches, this is the festival for you. Come out to enjoy peach pie, preserves, peach ice cream or simply a fresh peach. There's a

farmers' market and entertainment featuring bluegrass music, a petting zoo, pony rides and more.

Second weekend in August.

WHERE TO STAY
★★CLARION HOTEL
901 Dual Highway, Hagerstown, 301-733-5100, 877-424-6423;
www.clarionhagerstown.com
144 rooms. Restaurant, bar. Business center. Fitness center. Pool. $61-150

★★PLAZA HOTEL
1718 Underpass Way, Hagerstown, 301-797-2500, 800-732-0906;
www.plazahotelhagerstown.com
159 rooms. Restaurant, bar. Fitness center. Pool. $61-150

OCEAN CITY
See also Easton, Salisbury
Deep-sea fishing is highly regarded in Maryland's only Atlantic Ocean resort town which is located on a barrier island. The white-sand beach, three-mile boardwalk, amusements, golf courses and boating draw thousands of visitors every summer.

WHAT TO SEE
ASSATEAGUE ISLAND NATIONAL SEASHORE
7206 National Seashore Lane, Berlin, 410-641-1441, 800-365-2267; www.nps.gov/asis
Visitors interested in sandy beaches and wildlife should visit Assateague Island, which is about a four-hour drive from Baltimore. Straddling Maryland and Virginia, it contains a state park and wildlife refuge with swimming, hiking, canoeing, sea kayaking, biking and camping on the beach, as well as some of the best surf-fishing on the Atlantic Coast. Guests also come to see the wild horses. According to legend, the horses swam to the island from a shipwrecked Spanish galleon. On every last Wednesday in July, the world-famous Pony Penning event occurs. During this event, the horses swim from the Maryland side of the island to the Virginia side with a crowd of spectators cheering them on. The visitor center offers more information about the horses as well as the seashore's many activities.

Daily dawn-dusk.

BAHIA MARINA
2107 Herring Way, Ocean City, 410-289-7438; www.bahiamarina.com
The Bahia Marina is the place to go for boating rentals and tackle and bait. Charter fishing fleets leave from here to go offshore to fish for bluefish, marlin, tuna and to spot sharks and dolphins. You can take scenic cruises if you're not into fishing. There's also a restaurant here, Fish Tales, on the bay.

JOLLY ROGER AMUSEMENT PARK
30th Street and Coastal Highway, Ocean City, 410-289-3477
This large amusement park features plenty of rides, games and concessions to keep both adults and children happy. Rides includes a roller coaster, bum-

per cars, ferris wheel and more. There's also an antique train, the Jolly Roger Express, to ride around the park. A second location, at the Ocean City pier has a two-level carousel, a roller coaster, bumper cars, and more.
Admission: $14.99. Hours vary according to season.

OCEAN CITY BEACH & BOARDWALK
Ocean City
Ten miles of beach bring mobs of people out during warm weather to swim, surf, fish, boogie board, sunbathe, play on the beach and just enjoy the ocean. The nearly three mile boardwalk and pier is filled with shops, restaurants and amusements. Try to stay at the boardwalk long enough to see the sunset.
Daily.

SPECIAL EVENTS
SPRINGFEST
Inlet Parking Lot, Ocean City, 800-626-2326
To celebrate the beginning of spring, this four-day free event features live music, tons of food vendors and crafts situated in large tents.
Early May.

SUNDAES IN THE PARK
Northside Park, 127th Street, Ocean City,
This fun family event features a concert series for both adults and children to enjoy. And everyone can make their own ice cream sundae to eat while listening to the music. Bring your own blanket, chairs and snacks.
July-August, Sunday night.

WHERE TO STAY
★BEST WESTERN OCEAN CITY HOTEL & SUITES
5501 Coastal Highway, Ocean City, 443-664-4001; www.bestwestern.com
72 rooms. Complimentary breakfast. Business center. Fitness center. $151-250

★★CLARION RESORT FOUNTAINEBLEAU HOTEL
10100 Coastal Highway, Ocean City, 410-524-3535, 877-424-6423;
www.clarioninn.com
250 rooms. Restaurant, bar. Business center. Fitness center. Pool. Pets accepted. $151-250

★★HOLIDAY INN
6600 Coastal Highway, Ocean City, 410-524-1600, 888-465-4329; www.holidayinn.com
216 rooms. Restaurant, bar. Fitness center. Pool. Beach. Tennis. $151-250

★★PRINCESS ROYALE OCEANFRONT RESORT
9100 Coastal Highway, Ocean City, 410-524-7777, 800-476-9253;
www.princessroyale.com
310 rooms. Restaurant, bar. Business center. Fitness center. Pool. Beach. $61-150

★★QUALITY INN BOARDWALK

5400 Coastal Highway, Ocean City, 410-524-7200, 877-424-6423;
www.choicehotels.com
179 rooms. Restaurant, bar. Fitness center. Pool. $61-150

WHERE TO EAT

★★BONFIRE
71st Street and Coastal Highway, Ocean City, 410-524-7171;
www.thebonfirerestaurant.com
American. Dinner. Bar. $36-85

★★EMBERS
24th Street and Coastal Highway,, Ocean City, 410-289-3322; www.embers.com
American. Dinner. Bar. $16-35

★★★FAGER'S ISLAND
201 60th St., Ocean City, 410-524-5500, 888-371-5400; www.fagers.com
At Fager's Island, the outdoor deck overlooking the bay is the perfect spot
to take in a glorious summer sunset. The menu excels at creative seafood
preparations as well as classics like prime rib. Choose from a wine list that
features over 500 bottles to accompany your meal. The Sunday brunch offers
inventive and delicious dishes.
Pacific-Rim/Pan-Asian, seafood. Lunch, dinner, Sunday brunch. Reservations recommended. Outdoor seating. Children's menu. Bar. $16-35

★★HARRISON'S HARBOR WATCH
806 S. Boardwalk, Ocean City, 410-289-5121; www.ocmdhotels.com
Seafood. Lunch (Saturday-Sunday), dinner. Closed Monday-Wednesday
December-mid-May. Bar. Children's menu. $16-35

★★★HOBBIT
101 81st St., Ocean City, 410-524-8100; www.thehobbitrestaurant.com
This restaurant serves many of your old favorites, as well as creative new
items. The crab cakes are outstanding. For dessert, try the decadent Chambord cake, a yellow bundt cake with the raspberry Chambord liqueur poured
over it doused in whipped cream.
American, seafood. Lunch, dinner. Reservations recommended. Bar. $16-35

★MARINA DECK RESTAURANT
306 Dorchester St., Ocean City, 410-289-4411; www.marinadeckrestaurant.com
Seafood, steak. Lunch, dinner. Closed mid-November-mid-March. Outdoor
seating. Bar. $15 and under.

★★PHILLIPS CRAB HOUSE
2004 Philadelphia Ave., Ocean City, 410-289-6821; www.phillipsoc.com
Seafood. Lunch, dinner. Closed November-March. Bar. $16-35

★★PHILLIPS SEAFOOD HOUSE
14101 Coastal Highway, Ocean City, 410-250-1200, 800-799-2788;
www.phillipscrabhouse.com

Seafood. Lunch, dinner. Closed Monday-Thursday. Closed late November-late February. Bar. $16-35

ROCKVILLE
See also Bethesda, Gaithersburg

Located at the northern edge of D.C., Rockville is the second-largest city in Maryland. Rockville offers a busy downtown area with plenty of shops and restaurants to explore and art and culture abounds. The Great Falls of the Potomac are nine miles south off Highway 189. Stone locks and levels are still visible from the Chesapeake & Ohio Canal, which was built to circumvent the falls. St. Mary's Cemetery holds the graves of famous American writer F. Scott and his wife Zelda Fitzgerald.

WHAT TO SEE
BEALL-DAWSON HOUSE
103 W. Montgomery Ave., Rockville, 301-762-1492; www.montgomeryhistory.org
The Beall-Dawson House is an example of Federal architecture with and interior that has rooms with period furnishings, changing exhibits, a library, museum shop and a 19th-century doctor's office. Tours guided by docents cover the culture of the Bealls, an upperclass family and their African American slaves who worked in the house.
Admission: adults $3, seniors and children $2. Tuesday-Sunday noon-4 p.m.

CABIN JOHN REGIONAL PARK
7700 Tuckerman Lane, Rockville, 301-299-0024; www.mcparkandplanning.org
Spend the day at this 551-acre park which has plenty to keep you busy, including playgrounds, a miniature train ride, a nature center offering educational programs, walks, films and more. Concerts are offered during the summer at the outdoor amphitheater. Indoor tennis courts, game fields, an ice skating rink, nature trails, a campground and picnicking areas are also onsite.
Daily dawn-dusk.

F. SCOTT FITZGERALD THEATRE
603 Edmonston Drive, Rockville, 240-314-8690; www.rockvillemd.gov
Rockville's theater features performances by Little Theatre peforming classics such as Eugene O'Neil's *A Long Day's Journey Into Night*. The Victorian Lyric Opera Company, Rockville Civic Ballet and others also perform here.
Box Office: Tuesday-Saturday 2-7 p.m.

ST. MARY'S CHURCH
520 Veirs Mill Road, Rockville,
Built in 1817, St. Mary's is Rockville's oldest church still in use. There is a new church onsite, but in the 1960s, this church was nearly demolished then saved. In the cemetery next to the church, you'll find the graves of the famous American writer F. Scott Fitzgerald, his wife Zelda and other family members.

SPECIAL EVENT
FIRST FRIDAYS DECK PARTY
Arts and Innovation Building, 155 Gibbs St., Rockville, 301-424-9300;

First Fridays kick off the month with live bands, food and drinks on the rooftop deck of the Arts and Innovation Building in Rockville's Town Square. It's a fun time to gather after work and enjoy the view from above.

May-September, first Friday of the month.

HOMETOWN HOLIDAYS

Rockville, 301-424-9300; www.rockvillechamber.org

Hometown Holidays is a popular and fun event for all ages. There is live entertainment, which in the past has included Rick Springfield, Pat McGee and The Wailers. There are carnival rides and games, arts and crafts, food, a skate park and more.

Memorial Day weekend.

WHERE TO STAY

★★COURTYARD ROCKVILLE

2500 Research Blvd., Rockville, 301-670-6700; www.courtyard.com

147 rooms. Business center. Fitness center. Pool. $61-150

★CROWNE PLAZA ROCKVILLE

3 Research Court, Rockville, 301-840-0200, 877-227-6963; www.cprockville.com

124 rooms. Restaurant, bar. Fitness center. Pool. $61-150

★★HILTON EXECUTIVE MEETING CENTER

1750 Rockville Pike, Rockville, 301-468-1100; www.hilton.com

315 rooms. Restaurant, bar. Business center. Pool. Pets accepted. $151-250

WHERE TO EAT

★★ADDIE'S

11120 Rockville Pike, Rockville, 301-881-0081; www.addiesrestaurant.com

American. Lunch (Monday-Saturday), dinner, brunch. Outdoor seating. Children's menu. Bar. $15-35

★★BOMBAY BISTRO

98 W. Montgomery Ave., Rockville, 301-762-8798; www.bombaybistro.com

Indian, vegetarian. Lunch, dinner. Children's menu. $16-35

★★COPELAND'S OF NEW ORLEANS

10200 Wincopin Circle, Columbia, 301-230-0968; www.copelandsofneworleans.com

Cajun/Creole, seafood. Lunch, dinner. Bar. $15 and under.

★HARD TIMES CAFÉ

1117 Nelson St., Rockville, 301-294-9720; www.hardtimes.com

American. Lunch, dinner. Bar. $15 and under.

★★IL PIZZICO

15209 Frederick Road, Rockville, 301-309-0610; www.ilpizzico.com

Italian. Lunch (Monday-Friday), dinner. Closed Sunday. Bar. $15 and under.

★★★NORMANDIE FARM
10710 Falls Road, Potomac, 301-983-8838; www.popovers.com
Normandie Farm is reminiscent of a country home, serving entrées such as fresh sea scallops with bacon, scallions, pine nuts and citrus beurre blanc or beef medallions with truffle sauce and béarnaise-filled artichoke bottoms. The atmosphere is relaxed and welcoming. Friday and Saturday nights, guests spill into Margery's Lounge next to the restaurant's lobby, for drinks by the fireplace and live entertainment. The outdoor Café Normandie is open all day, offering a lighter menu and complimentary Internet access.
French, seafood. Lunch, dinner, Sunday brunch. Closed Monday. Reservations recommended. Outdoor seating. Children's menu. Bar. $16-35

★★★OLD ANGLER'S INN
10801 MacArthur Blvd., Potomac, 301-299-9097; www.oldanglersinn.com
Located in a Tudor-style house built in 1860, the rustic dining room is a perfect spot for a cozy evening. In winter, get a table near the fireplace for a romantic meal. In summer, the terrace provides a lovely setting beneath the trees. New Point oysters are always on the menu and the wild Chesapeake rockfish with corn salad is delicious. They also have an extensive wine list to choose from along with delectable desserts such as the warm Braeburn apple tart with cinnamon ice cream.
Seafood. Lunch, dinner. Closed Monday. Reservations recommended. Outdoor seating. Children's menu. Bar. $16-35

★SEVEN SEAS
1776 E. Jefferson St., Rockville, 301-770-5020; www.sevenseasrestaurant.com
Chinese, Japanese. Lunch, dinner. Bar. $16-35

★SILVER DINER
11806 Rockville Pike, Rockville, 301-770-0333; www.silverdiner.com
American. Breakfast, lunch, dinner. Children's menu. $15 and under.

★★THAT'S AMORE
15201 Shady Grove Road, Rockville, 240-268-0682; www.thatsamore.com
Italian. Lunch (Monday-Saturday), dinner. Bar. $16-35

SALISBURY
See also Ocean City
"Central City of the Eastern Shore" and of the Delmarva Peninsula, Salisbury has a marina on the Wicomico River providing access to Chesapeake Bay. It lies within 30 miles of duck hunting and deep-sea fishing.

WHAT TO SEE
POPLAR HILL MANSION
117 Elizabeth St., Salisbury, 410-749-1776; www.poplarhillmansion.org
The Poplar Hill Mansion is an example of Georgian- and Federal-style architecture with Palladian and bull's-eye windows, large brass box locks on the doors and mantels and fireplaces. The interior is decorated with period furniture and there is a country garden to peruse.

Admission: $3 (Tuesday-Saturday). Free on Sunday.

SALISBURY ZOO

755 S. Park Drive, Salisbury, 410-548-3188; www.salisburyzoo.org
This zoo features natural habitats for almost 400 mammals, birds and reptiles. Major exhibits include bears, monkeys, jaguars, bison and waterfowl. There are also exotic plants.
Admission: Free. Memorial Day-Labor Day, daily 9 a.m.-7:30 p.m.; Labor Day-Memorial Day, daily 9 a.m.-4:30 p.m.

THE WARD MUSEUM OF WILDFOWL ART

909 S. Schumaker Drive, Salisbury, 410-742-4988; www.wardmuseum.org
This museum has displays that include the history of decoy and wildfowl carving in North America; wildfowl habitats; and contemporary wildfowl art in two galleries that have changing exhibits. There's also a gift shop where you can pick up a souvenir.
Admission: adults $7, seniors $5, children and students $3. Monday-Saturday 10 a.m.-5 p.m., Sunday noon-5 p.m.

WHERE TO STAY
★COMFORT INN

2701 N. Salisbury Blvd., Salisbury, 410-543-4666, 800-638-7949;
www.choicehotels.com
96 rooms. Complimentary breakfast. Pets accepted. $61-150

★★RAMADA INN

300 S. Salisbury Blvd., Salisbury, 410-546-4400; www.ramada.com
156 rooms. Restaurant, bar. Business center. Fitness center. Pool. Pets accepted. $61-150

SILVER SPRING

See also College Park, Laurel, Rockville; Washington, D.C.
Located between Baltimore and Washington, D.C., Silver Spring is part of Mongomery County and has a newly developed and growing commerical center in its downtown area. There are plenty of restaurants and shops to visit and it's a prime spot for art and technology businesses.

WHAT TO SEE
BROOKSIDE GARDENS

1800 Glenallan Ave., Wheaton, 301-962-1400; www.mc-mncppc.org
This 50 acre public garden features two conservatories and many different gardens including a rose garden, a children's garden, a Japanese garden and more. This is a beautiful spot to explore.
Admission: Free. Gardens: Daily, dawn-dusk. Visitor center: 9 a.m.-5 p.m. Conservatories: 10 a.m.-5 p.m.

WHERE TO EAT
★★BLAIR MANSION INN

7711 Eastern Ave., Silver Spring, 301-588-1688; www.blairmansion.com

American. Lunch (Monday-Friday), dinner. Closed Sunday. Bar. $16-35

★★MRS. K'S TOLL HOUSE
9201 Colesville Road, Silver Spring, 301-589-3500; www.mrsks.com
American. Lunch (Tuesday-Saturday), dinner, Sunday brunch. Closed Monday. Reservations recommended. Outdoor seating. $16-35

ST. MARY'S CITY
See also Chesapeake Bay Bridge Area; Washington, D.C.
Under the leadership of Leonard Calvert, Maryland's first colonists bought a Native American village on this site upon their arrival in the New World. The settlement was the capital and hub of the area until 1694, when the colonial capital was moved to Annapolis, and the town gradually disappeared. The city and county are still rich in historical attractions.

WHAT TO SEE
HISTORIC ST. MARY'S CITY
Route 5 and Rosecroft Road, St. Mary's City, 240-895-4990, 800-762-1634;
www.stmaryscity.org
This outdoor museum at the site of Maryland's first capital includes a reconstructed State House replica of the original capitol building. Other exhibits include the "Maryland Dove," a replica of a 17th-century ship and archaeological exhibits. There is a 17th-century tobacco plantation, and a reconstructed 17th-century inn, a visitor center and an outdoor café. Admission: adults $10, seniors $8, students 13-18 $6, children 6-12 $3.50, children under 6 free. Mid-March-mid-June, Tuesday-Saturday 10 a.m.-5 p.m.; Mid-June-mid-November, Wednesday-Sunday 10 a.m.-5 p.m.; December 2-20th, Wednesday-Sunday 10 a.m.-5 p.m. Closed mid-December-January.

MARGARET BRENT MEMORIAL
Trinity Churchyard, 18751 Hogaboom Lane, St. Mary's City
This Victorian gazebo overlooks the river as memorial to the woman who, being a wealthy landowner, requested the right to vote in the Maryland Assembly in 1648 to settle Leonard Calvert's affairs after his death. There is also a garden.

LEONARD CALVERT MONUMENT
Trinity Churchyard, 18751 Hogaboom Lane, St. Mary's City
This is a memorial for Maryland's first colonial governor, Leonard Calvert.

POINT LOOKOUT STATE PARK
11175 Point Lookout Road, Scotland, 301-872-5688, 888-432-2267;
www.dnr.state.md.us
Located near St. Mary's County, this park is the site of Confederate Monument, the only memorial erected by the U.S. government to honor P.O.W.s who died in Point Lookout Prison Camp during the Civil War (3,384 died here). This park features swimming, fishing, boating; hiking, picnicking and camping. There's a nature center and a Civil War musuem here as well.

April-October, daily dawn-dusk; November-March, daily 10 a.m.-4 p.m.

SPECIAL EVENTS
DUNGENESS CRAB & SEAFOOD FESTIVAL
St. Mary's County Fairgrounds, Leonardtown; ww.stmaryscrabfestival.org
This annual festival features fresh steamed crabs, crab cakes, crab soup and other dishes. There is also handmade arts and crafts, line dancing and live country music.
June.

MARYLAND DAY
Town Center, St. Mary's City; www.stmaryscity.org
This festival celebrates Maryland Day, the anniversary year of Maryland's founding. There is plenty to enjoy: music, food, free admission to musuems, a free lecture program, boat rides, American Indian dancing, a beer garden, a concert and fireworks.
Third weekend in March.

ST. MICHAELS
See also Easton
Chartered in 1804, Saint Michaels now offers visitors an abundance of shops, marinas, restaurants, bed and breakfasts and country inns, as well as many Federal- and Victorian-period buildings.

WHAT TO SEE
CHESAPEAKE BAY MARITIME MUSEUM
Mill Street and Navy Point, St. Michaels, 410-745-2916; www.cbmm.org
This waterside museum consists of nine buildings and includes a historic lighthouse, floating exhibits, boat-building shop with working exhibit, ship models, small boats and is a non-profit organization.
Admission: adults $13, seniors $10, children 6-17 $6, children under 6 free. April-May, October-mid-November, daily 10 a.m.-5 p.m.; June-September, daily 10 a.m.-6 p.m.; mid-November-mid-January, daily 10 a.m.-4 p.m.

THE FOOTBRIDGE
109 S. Talbot St., St. Michaels; www.stmichaelsmd.org
This footbridge joins Navy Point to Cherry Street and is the only bridge remaining of three. It is often called other names such as the "Sweetheart" or "Lovers'" bridge.

PATRIOT CRUISES
Chesapeake Bay Museum Dock, St. Michaels, 410-745-3100; www.patriotcruises.com
Take a one-hour narrated cruise aboard the Patriot on Miles River, which is part of the Chesapeake Bay Estuary.
Admission: adults $24.50, seniors $20.75, children 12-17 $12.50, children under 12 free. April-October, daily 11 a.m., 12:30 p.m., 2:30 p.m., 4 p.m.; March, November, Friday-Sunday 11 a.m., 12:30 p.m., 2:30 p.m., 4 p.m.

ST. MARY'S SQUARE

EASTERN SHORE OF THE CHESAPEAKE BAY

The Chesapeake Bay, North America's largest estuary, commands more than 4,500 miles of shoreline, much of it in Maryland. It is one of the Mid-Atlantic's most popular destinations, known for its rich history and savory shellfish.

A two-day driving tour covering about 250 miles makes a fine introduction to the bay. Begin your drive in Annapolis, Maryland's beautiful old capital, which doubles as the bay's sailing headquarters. In summer, catch the regular Wednesday evening races, when as many as 100 boats may compete. The finish is easily visible from City Dock at the foot of the city's colonial-era streets.

From Annapolis, take Highway 50 east across the soaring Chesapeake Bay Bridge. Just before you reach the bridge, a five-minute detour leads to Sandy Point State Park, the only stop on this drive where you can take a dip in the bay. At the eastern end of the bridge, turn north onto Highway 301 to Route 213 north to Chestertown. Founded in 1706, Chestertown is a pretty village with a collection of 18th- and 19th-century homes, several of them situated along the scenic Chester River.

After browsing the shops of High and Cross streets, take Route 213 south to Highway 50 south. In Easton, take Route 33 west to the historic sailing port of St. Michaels, an inviting place to spend the night. St. Michaels is one of the Mid-Atlantic's prettiest little towns, with lovely inns, fine restaurants, offbeat shops, expansive bay views and charming back streets lined with homes dating to the 18th and 19th centuries. Your first stop should be the Chesapeake Bay Maritime Museum. The museum's 18-acre harbor site features more than a dozen historic structures, including a fully restored 1879 lighthouse. Stop by Waterman's Wharf, where you can try your skill at crab fishing. Boat builders are often at work restoring historic bay work boats for the museum's large collection. The Patriot, a cruise ship departing from the museum's dock, takes visitors on a 60-minute tour up the Miles River, a bay tributary.

From St. Michaels, follow Route 33 to its end at Tilghman Island, a charter fishing port. Plan on having lunch at one of its waterside seafood houses. On the return trip to St. Michaels, stop about three miles east of the city and take the road south to Bellevue. There you can catch the little Bellevue-Oxford Ferry for a 10-minute ride across the Tred Avon River to Oxford, a sleepy pleasure-boat port dating back to 1694. To stretch your legs, walk along the Strand, a lovely river promenade, or rent a bicycle and ride along the quiet streets. From Oxford, return to Annapolis via Route 333 and Highway 50, stopping briefly in Easton to admire its attractive town center and to investigate its shops and galleries.

Approximately 250 miles.

This public square was laid out in 1770 by Englishman James Braddock. Several buildings date to the early 1800s, including the Cannonball House and Dr. Miller's Farmhouse. The Ship's Carpenter Bell was cast in 1842; across from the bell stand two cannons, one dating from the Revolution, the other from the War of 1812.

ST. MICHAEL'S MUSEUM AT ST. MARY'S SQUARE

409 St. Mary's Square, St. Michaels, 410-745-9561

This museum is located within a mid-19th-century home of "half-timber" construction and one of the earliest buildings in St. Michaels. Exhibits are of historical and local interest.

Admission: Free; donations accepted. May-October, Saturday-Sunday 10 a.m.-4 p.m.; also by appointment.

SPECIAL EVENT
ST. MICHAEL'S FOOD AND WINE FESTIVAL
Chesapeake Bay Maritime Museum, Mill Street at Navy Point,
St. Michaels,443-205-2185; www.stmichaelsfoodandwinefestival.com
This celebration features demonstrations by celebrity chefs, guest speakers, wine tastings, food samples, admission to the exhibits at the Maritime Museum, and live entertainment
Late April.

WHERE TO STAY
★★HARBOURTOWNE GOLF RESORT & CONFERENCE CENTER
Route 33 and Martingham Drive, St. Michaels, 410-745-9066, 800-446-9066;
www.harbourtowne.com
111 rooms. Restaurant, bar. Pool. Golf. Tennis. $61-150

★★★THE INN AT PERRY CABIN
308 Watkins Lane, St. Michaels, 410-745-2200, 866-278-9601; www.perrycabin.com
Built just after the War of 1812, the Inn at Perry Cabin looks and feels like a manor house, with mahogany sleigh beds, antiques and views of the Miles River. Cycling, golfing and sailing are popular pastimes. The inn offers high tea and scones with Devonshire cream and shortbread served at evening turndown.
78 rooms. Restaurant, bar. Fitness center. Pool. Spa. $251-350

★★★ST. MICHAELS HARBOUR INN, MARINA & SPA
101 N. Harbor Road, St. Michaels, 410-745-9001, 800-955-9001; www.harbourinn.com
From this waterfront resort, visitors can take a short stroll down the main road to shops, museums and historical sites. Rooms are spacious and many have Jacuzzi tubs, panoramic views of the harbor and private balconies. The onsite Spa at Harbour Inn offers relaxing treatments after a day of activity around the bay.
46 rooms. Restaurant, bar. Pool. Spa. $251-350

WHERE TO EAT
★★★208 TALBOT
208 N. Talbot St., St. Michaels, 410-745-3838; www.208talbot.com
Chef Brendan Keegan puts a sophisticated, soulful twist on local ingredients, serving entrées including cornflake-crusted fried mahi mahi with basil potato salad, sweet corn cream and grape tomato relish; and braised pork shoulder with peach chutney, corn tamale and salsa roja. The atmosphere is as upscale and sophisticated as the cuisine, with rich décor accents and a knowledgeable waitstaff.
American. Dinner. Closed Sunday-Tuesday. Bar. $36-85

★★BISTRO ST. MICHAELS
403 S. Talbot St., St. Michaels, 410-745-9111; www.bistrostmichaels.com

French. Dinner. Closed Tuesday-Wednesday. Bar. Outdoor seating. $36-85

★★CHESAPEAKE LANDING SEAFOOD
23713 St. Michael's Road, St. Michaels, 410-745-9600
Seafood. Lunch, dinner. Children's menu. $16-35

★★★SHERWOOD'S LANDING
308 Watkin Lane, St. Michaels, 410-745-2200, 866-278-9601; www.perrycabin.com
Located in the Inn at Perry Cabin, Sherwood Landing serves continental selections made with regional ingredients such as crab spring rolls with pink grapefruit, avocado and toasted almonds; and honey- and tarragon-glazed lamb shank with sun-dried tomato sauce.
American. Breakfast, lunch, dinner. Outdoor seating. Bar. $36-85

★★SHORE RESTAURANT & LOUNGE
101 N. Harbor Road, St. Michaels, 410-924-4769; www.shorerestaurant.net
American, International. Breakfast (Saturday), lunch (Monday-Saturday), dinner (Tuesday-Sunday), Sunday brunch. Outdoor seating. Bar. $36-85

★ST. MICHAELS CRAB HOUSE
305 Mulberry St., St. Michaels, 410-745-3737; www.stmichaelscrabhouse.com
Seafood. Lunch, dinner. Closed Wednesday. Children's menu. Outdoor seating. Bar. $16-35

THURMONT
See also Frederick
This small town is the gateway to the Catoctin Mountains. It's close to Camp David, the U.S. president's retreat home and also not far from Baltimore.

WHAT TO SEE

CATOCTIN MOUNTAIN NATIONAL PARK
Park Central Road, Thurmont, 301-663-9388; www.nps.gov/cato
Located one hour outside Baltimore, this 5,810-acre forest is an easily accessible nature retreat. The park is adjacent to two state parks and Camp David, the weekend mountain home of the U.S. president. The park offers camping, picnicking areas, fishing and playgrounds.
Daily.

CUNNINGHAM FALLS STATE PARK
14039 Catoctin Hollow Road, Thurmont, 301-271-7574, 888-432-2267;
www.dnr.state.md.us/publiclands/western/CunninghamFalls.html
This state park encompasses 4,950 acres in the Catoctin Mountains. There are two recreation areas: Houck, five miles west of town, has swimming, fishing, boating; picnicking, camping, and hiking trails that lead to 78-foot falls and scenic overlooks. And the Manor Area, three miles south of town on Route 15, has picnicking, camping, and a playground. There is also trout fishing in Big Hunting Creek and the ruins of Iron Masters Mansion and the industrial village surrounding it are also here.

SPECIAL EVENT

MAPLE SYRUP DEMONSTRATION

Cunningham Falls State Park, 14039 Catoctin Hollow Road, Thurmont, 301-271-7574
This event showcases tree tapping, sap boiling and sugaring demonstrations.
There are also carriage rides, live music, a pancake and sausage breakfast
and children's storytelling corner.
March.

WHERE TO STAY
★★COZY RESTAURANT AND COUNTRY INN

103 Frederick Road, Thurmont, 301-271-4301; www.cozyvillage.com
21 rooms. Restaurant, bar. Complimentary breakfast.$61-150

TOWSON

See also Baltimore
This suburb of Baltimore is home to Towson University, making it a popular
college town filled with shops, restaurants, live music venues and a collegiate
atmosphere.

WHAT TO SEE
HAMPTON NATIONAL HISTORIC SITE

535 Hampton Lane, Towson, 410-823-1309; www.nps.gov/hamp
This historic site includes the ornate Georgian mansion completed in 1790,
formal gardens and plantation outbuildings. A tour takes you through where
indentured servants, agricultural workers and their owners lived.
Admission: Free. January-mid-May, daily 9 a.m.-4 p.m. Mansion tours: 10
a.m., 11 a.m., 1-4 p.m. (on the hour).

TOWSON STATE UNIVERSITY

8000 York Road, Towson, 410-704-2000; www.towson.edu
This University was founded in 1866 and one of the best public universities
in the U.S. Eight miles north of Baltimore, Towson University is situated in
suburban Towson on a 328 acre campus. There are more than 21,000 students
in attendance. On campus are three art galleries, including Holtzman Art
Gallery, with an extensive collection of art media. Concerts and sporting
events are held in the Towson Center.

SPECIAL EVENTS
MARYLAND HOUSE AND GARDEN PILGRIMAGE

1105-A Providence Road, Towson, 410-821-6933; www.mhgp.org
More than 100 homes and gardens throughout the state are open for touring.
Tours begin in April and run through May.
Late April-early May.

MARYLAND STATE FAIR

Maryland Fairgrounds, 2100 York Road, Timonium, 410-252-0200;
www.marylandstatefair.com
This 11 day festival features entertainment including live bands, pig races,
thoroughbred races, bull riding, agricultural demonstrations, livestock pre-

sentations, food, drink and more.
Late August-early September.

WHERE TO STAY
★★★BALTIMORE MARRIOTT HUNT VALLEY INN
245 Shawan Road, Hunt Valley, 410-785-7000; www.marriott.com
Located on 18 acres of land 20 minutes north of Baltimore's Inner Harbor,
this hotel offers comfortable guest rooms with the amenities that business
and leisure travelers expect. Play a round of golf at one of the six nearby
golf courses. For your business needs, take advantage of Marriott's Wired for
Business program that offers high-speed Internet access and unlimited local
and long distance calls for a low daily fee.
390 rooms. Restaurant, bar. Business center. Fitness center. Pool. $151-250

WHERE TO EAT
★★★THE OREGON GRILLE
1201 Shawan Road, Hunt Valley, 410-771-0505; www.theoregongrille.com
The Oregon Grille succeeds in differentiating itself from its competitors by
offering not only a terrific selection of impeccably prepared steaks (all beef
is dry-aged USDA Prime), but also a creative selection of classic American
cuisine, including free-range poultry, fresh seafood and appetizers made with
regional ingredients. The restaurant, set in a renovated 19th-century stone
farmhouse, has four fireplaces and is filled with deep, luxurious banquettes.
American. Lunch, dinner, Sunday brunch. Reservations recommended.
Outdoor seating. Bar. $36-85

WESTMINSTER
See also Baltimore, Frederick
Westminster, a Union supply depot at the Battle of Gettysburg, saw scattered
action before the battle. It was the first town in the United States to offer
complete rural free delivery mail service (started in 1899 with four two-
horse wagons).

WHERE TO EAT
★★★ANTRIM 1844
30 Trevanion Road, Taneytown, 410-756-6812, 800-858-1844; www.antrim1844.com
The Paris-trained chef at Antrim 1844 serves a unique menu each night, with
entrées such as filet mignon with bacon and walnut, braised lamb volcano or
porcupine shrimp. On a nice night, there isn't a better seat than on the spacious verandah overlooking the formal gardens.
American, French. Breakfast, dinner. Reservations recommended. Outdoor
seating. Bar. $86 and up.

★★JOHANSSON'S DINING HOUSE
4 W. Main St., Westminster, 410-876-0101; www.johanssonsdininghouse.com
American. Dinner, Sunday brunch. Children's menu. Bar. $16-35

NEW JERSEY

FROM INDUSTRIAL CITIES TO LUSH TREE-SHADED, 18TH-CENTURY TOWNS TO SMALL SEA-SIDE communities, New Jersey is a state of contrasts. Hard-working areas such as Newark and Elizabeth might lead the unacquainted visitor to believe that the Garden State is a misnomer, but traveling deeper into New Jersey—out of the cities and off the highways—will reveal the flourishing greenery that earned the state its nickname.

The swampy meadows west of the New Jersey Turnpike have been reclaimed and transformed into commercial and industrial areas. The Meadowlands, a multimillion-dollar sports complex, offers horse racing, the New York Giants and the New York Jets NFL football teams, the New Jersey Devils NHL hockey team and the New Jersey Nets NBA basketball team. But commercial and industrial interests have reached only so far into the state's natural resources. More than 800 lakes and ponds, 100 rivers and streams and 1,400 miles of freshly stocked trout streams are scattered throughout the state's wooded, scenic northwest corner. The coastline, stretching 127 miles from Sandy Hook to Cape May, offers excellent swimming and ocean fishing.

New Jersey is also rich in history. George Washington spent a quarter of his time as commander-in-chief of the Revolutionary Army here. On Christmas night in 1776, he crossed the Delaware and surprised the Hessians at Trenton. A few days later, he marched to Princeton and defeated three British regiments. He then spent the winter in Morristown, where the memories of his campaign are preserved in a national historical park.

ALLAIRE STATE PARK

See also Asbury Park, Freehold

Allaire State Park has more than 3,000 acres and offers a fishing pond for children under 14; multiuse trails, picnic facilities, playground, camping and the opportunity to visit a historic 19th-century village.

WHAT TO SEE
HISTORIC ALLAIRE VILLAGE

524 Allaire Road, Farmingdale, 732-915-3500; www.allairevillage.org

In 1822, James Allaire bought this site as a source of bog ore for his ironworks. The furnace also produced items such as hollowware pots and kettles, stoves, sadirons and pipes for New York City's waterworks. Today, visitors can explore the bakery, general store, blacksmith and carpentry shops, worker's houses, the community church and other buildings still much as they were in 1836.

Admission (May-October, Saturday-Sunday): adults $3, children 6-12 $2. Village buildings: Memorial Day-Labor Day, Wednesday-Sunday noon-4 p.m.; Labor Day-November and May, Saturday-Sunday noon-4 p.m. Visitor center: Memorial Day-Labor Day, daily 10 a.m.-5 p.m.; Labor Day-Memorial Day, Wednesday-Sunday 10 a.m.-4 p.m.

ASBURY PARK

See also Red Bank

This popular shore resort was bought in 1871 by New York brush manufacturer James A. Bradley and named for Francis Asbury, first American Bishop of the Methodist Episcopal Church. Bradley established a town for temperance advocates and good neighbors. The beach and the three lakes proved so attractive that by 1874, Asbury Park had grown into a borough, and by 1897, a city. It is the home of the famous boardwalk, Convention Hall and the Paramount Theatre. In September 1934, the *SS Morro Castle* was grounded off this beach and burned with a loss of 122 lives. Asbury Park became the birthplace of a favorite sweet when a local confectioner introduced saltwater taffy. Today, this is a popular resort area for swimming and fishing.

WHAT TO SEE
ASBURY PARK BEACH AND BOARDWALK

Ocean Avenue, Asbury Park; www.theasburyparkboardwalk.com
Head to Asbury Park's mile of sandy beach and enjoy the sun and surf. The boardwalk just underwent a multi-million dollar renovation. You'll find shops, galleries restaurants, cafes and nightclubs here. At the end of the boardwalk, you'll find the Paramount Theatre and Convention Hall (*1300 Ocean Avenue*) where Jersey acts such as Bruce Springsteen and Jon Bon Jovi have played.
Daily; hours vary for venues.

STEPHEN CRANE HOUSE

508 Fourth Ave., Asbury Park, 732-775-5682
This is the early home of Stephen Crane, the author of *The Red Badge of Courage*. It contains photos, drawings and other artifacts.
Tours by appointment.

THE STONE PONY

913 Ocean Ave., Asbury Park, 732-502-0600; www.stoneponyonline.com
This legendary nightclub, which opened in 1974, is known for unexpected visits from Bruce Springsteen and others. This rock club has launched the careers of many legendaray musicians and continues to do so today.
See Web site for schedules and ticket information.

SPECIAL EVENTS
HORSE RACING

Monmouth Park, 175 Oceanport Ave., Oceanport, 732-222-5100;
www.monmouthpark.com
Head to Monmouth Park for thoroughbred horse racing.
Memorial Day-Labor Day.

TRI CITY ARTS TOUR

Asbury Park; www.tricityartstour.com
This three-day festival takes place in Eastern Monmouth County, including Asbury Park, Long Branch and Red Bank. Festivities take place in different areas of Asbury Park. It features a "Walk of Art" which showcases more than 70 artists' work on the boardwalk. There is an arts and crafts fair at Cookman

Avenue, a vintage flea market at the Grand Carousel, tours of the Paramount Theatre, local music and theater performances at a main stage downtown, and other programs and exhibits.
Mid-May.

WHERE TO EAT
★★MOONSTRUCK
517 Lake Ave., Asbury Park, 732-988-0123; www.moonstrucknj.com
American, Mediterranean. Dinner. Closed Monday-Tuesday. Outdoor seating. $16-35

ATLANTIC CITY
See also Ocean City
Honeymooners, conventioneers, Miss America (until it moved to Las Vegas) and some 37 million annual visitors have made Atlantic City the best-known New Jersey beach resort. Built on Absecon Island, the curve of the coast shields it from battering northeastern storms while the nearby Gulf Stream warms its waters, helping to make it a year-round resort.
A 60-foot-wide boardwalk extends along five miles of beaches. Hand-pushed wicker rolling chairs take visitors up and down the Boardwalk. Absecon Lighthouse ("Old Ab"), a well-known landmark, was first lit in 1857 and now stands in an uptown city park.

WHAT TO SEE
ABSECON LIGHTHOUSE
31 S. Rhode Island Ave., Atlantic City, 609-449-1360; www.abseconlighthouse.org
Climb the 228 steps to the top of this 1857 lighthouse, designed by Civil War general George Gordon Meade. This is the tallest lighthouse in New Jersey, and the third-tallest in the United States.
Admission: adults $7, seniors $5, children 4-12 $4, children 3 and under and military personnel free. July-August, daily 10 a.m.-5 p.m.; September-June, Thursday-Monday 11 a.m.-4 p.m.

ATLANTIC CITY BOARDWALK & BEACHES
Atlantic City; www.atlanticcitynj.com
This famous spot has everything from restaurants, shops, casinos, carnival rides and resorts to peruse. Get some famous salt water taffy from James' at the Tropicana, where you can see the taffy being pulled and chocolate being made. Head to the beach to sunbathe, swim, have some cocktails and enjoy the Jersey shore. If you want to surf, head to Crystal Beach, Delaware Avenue Beach or the Downtown Beach.
Lifeguards on duty: Memorial Day-Labor Day, daily 10 a.m-6 p.m.

ATLANTIC CITY BOARDWALK HALL
2301 Boardwalk, Atlantic City, 609-348-7000, 800-736-1420; www.boardwalkhall.com
This National Historic Landmark seats 13,800 people for special events, concerts, boxing, ice shows and sports events. It's also the site of where the annual Miss America Pageant was once held (now it takes place in Las Vegas).
Box office: Monday-Saturday 11 a.m.-5 p.m.

EDWIN B. FORSYTHE NATIONAL WILDLIFE REFUGE, BRIGANTINE DIVISION

Box 72, Great Creek Road, Oceanville, 609-652-1665; www.www.njaudubon.org

Over the years, more than 200 species of birds have been observed at this nearly 45,000-acre wildlife refuge that was established in 1939. The public-use area has an eight-mile wildlife drive through diversified wetlands and uplands habitat. It's most popular in the spring and fall, during the course of the waterbird migration and at sunset, when the birds roost for the evening. Daily.

FISHING & DIVING

Go surf and deep-sea fishing on a chartered boat. A license may be required, depending upon which company you go with. Kammerman's Atlantic City Marina features Atlantic Star Charters (*www.atlanticstarcharters.com*) offering fishing charters, party cruises and a kayaking cruise, depending on your interests. Atlantic City Fishing and Dive Center (*www.missac.com*) offers fishing and diving charters. Daily.

GARDEN PIER

Boardwalk and New Jersey Avenue, Atlantic City, 609-347-5837; www.acmuseum.org

Garden Pier features Spanish Renaissance architecture with landscaped gardens. Opened in 1913, it held the B.F. Keith's Theater and a large ballroom. The restored pier also is the home to the Atlantic City Art Center and Atlantic City Historical Museum.

Admission: Free. Daily 10 a.m.-4 p.m.

HISTORIC GARDNER'S BASIN

800 New Hampshire Ave., Atlantic City, 609-348-2880; www.gardnersbasin.com

An eight-acre, sea-oriented park featuring working lobstermen. The Ocean Life Center contains eight tanks totaling 29,800 gallons of aquariums, exhibiting more than 100 varieties of fish and marine animals. There are also 10 exhibits featuring themes on the marine and maritime environment.

Admission: adults $7, seniors $5, children 4-12 $4, children 3 and under free. Daily 10 a.m.-5 p.m.

RIPLEY'S BELIEVE IT OR NOT

1441 Boardwalk., Atlantic City, 609-347-2001; www.ripleys.com

Located on the boardwalk, Ripley's Believe It or Not museum features amazing and interesting artifacts and exhibits.

Admission: adults $14.99, students and military personnel $12.99, seniors $11.99, children 5-12 $9.99. Monday-Friday 10 a.m.-8 pm., Saturday 10 a.m.-9 p.m., Sunday 10 a.m.-8 p.m.

WHERE TO STAY

★★★BALLY'S PARK PLACE CASINO RESORT

Park Place and Boardwalk, Atlantic City, 609-340-2000, 800-225-5977;
www.ballysac.com

A geometric glass chandelier twinkles overhead at the entrance to this large, classic Boardwalk casino. There are several dining options to choose from, including some that fit into the Wild West theme of the hotel's annex casino. 1,246 rooms. Restaurant, bar. Business center. Fitness center. Pool. Spa. Casino. Golf. $151-250

★★★BORGATA CASINO HOTEL AND SPA

1 Borgata Way, Atlantic City, 609-317-1000, 866-638-6748; www.theborgata.com

The Borgata Hotel Casino and Spa is a stylish resort, where the rooms and suites are luxurious havens from traditional casino style, with cool earth tones, contemporary furnishings and advanced in-room technology. The hotel's five restaurants include Wolfgang Puck's American Grille and Bobby Flay Steak. Those who are not successful at the blackjack tables may want to ensconce themselves in the confines of Spa Toccare, where a wide variety of relaxing treatments melt tension away, or in one of the hotel's several high-end boutiques.

2,000 rooms. Restaurant, bar. Business center. Fitness center. Pool. Spa. Casino. $251-350

★BAYMONT INN AND SUITES WEST ATLANTIC CITY

7079 Black Horse Pike, West Atlantic City, 609-484-1900, 800-426-7866;
www.baymontinns.com

144 rooms. Complimentary breakfast. Fitness center. Beach. $61-150

★★★CAESARS ATLANTIC CITY HOTEL CASINO

2100 Pacific Ave., Atlantic City, 609-348-4411, 800-223-7277; www.caesarsac.com

This oceanfront hotel, dubbed "Rome on the Jersey shore," houses 26,000 square feet of meeting space and a nicely appointed business center. Enjoy an international dish at the hotel's Chinese, Japanese and American restaurants, Roman-themed eateries, casual restaurants and lounges. Head to the Pier Shops at Caesars for some shopping and then to Qua Baths and Spa for some pampering.

1,144 rooms. Restaurant, bar. Fitness center. Pool. Spa. Beach. Casino. Golf. $151-250

★★★DOLCE SEAVIEW RESORT AND SPA

401 S. New York Road, Galloway, 609-652-1800, 800-983-6523; www.seaviewgolf.com

A golfer's dream, this hotel is located on 670 secluded acres near Reeds Bay and offers two 18-hole championship golf courses. It is also only 15 minutes from the bright lights of Atlantic City. The hotel's lobby has a traditional 1912 elegance and features black-and-white antique golf pictures, mahogany furniture and bar, overstuffed brown leather chairs and large windows with views of the grounds. Guests can enjoy volleyball and basketball courts, a kids' playground and the Seaview Golf Academy.

297 rooms. Restaurant, bar. Business center. Fitness center. $251-350

★★★HILTON CASINO RESORT

Boston and the Boardwalk, Atlantic City, 609-340-7235, 800-257-8677;
www.hiltonac.com

The Hilton Casino Resort offers convenient access to everything in the area, though the luxurious hotel itself might lure guests inside. Onsite offerings include a 9,000-square-foot pool, full-service health spa, 60,000-square-foot casino with poker room and Asian gaming room, an assortment of fine dining restaurants and an entertainment venue.

800 rooms. Restaurant, bar. Fitness center. Pool. Spa. Beach. Casino. Reservations recommended. $151-250

★★★RESORTS ATLANTIC CITY

1133 Boardwalk, Atlantic City, 609-344-6000, 800-336-6378; www.resortsac.com

Opened in 1978, Resorts Atlantic City offered the first casino in the area. The hotel's charmingly beachy 480-room Ocean Tower offers views of and convenient access to the boardwalk, and the newly renovated Rendezvous Tower boasts the largest guest rooms in Atlantic City.

538 rooms. Restaurant, bar. Fitness center. Pool. Spa. Casino. $151-250

★★★SHERATON ATLANTIC CITY CONVENTION CENTER HOTEL

2 Miss America Way, Atlantic City, 609-344-3535, 800-325-3535; www.sheraton.com

This tower hotel with Art Deco accents is near Atlantic City's boardwalk as well as designer outlet shops. Guests will appreciate the Sheraton's signature "Sweet Sleeper Bed" (also available for man's best friend) and in-room movies and games, while business travelers will be able to work in comfort with oversized desks, ergonomic chairs and an in-room fax/copier/printer. During the summer, in-room massages and poolside massages are available.

502 rooms. Restaurant, bar. Business center. Fitness center. Pool. Pets accepted. $151-250

★★★TRUMP PLAZA HOTEL & CASINO

The Boardwalk and Mississippi Avenue, Atlantic City, 609-441-6000, 800-677-7378; www.trumpplaza.com

If you're looking for a little relaxation along with some Atlantic City excitement, the Trump Plaza Hotel and Casino is for you. Whether you're willing to gamble with $5 or $5,000, the casino offers games for every skill level and interest, from slots to blackjack, roulette, and Caribbean stud poker. When you've had enough casino excitement and want to unwind, head to the hotel's health spa, where you can relax in the sauna or Jacuzzi, indulge in a massage, body scrub or wrap, or take in a workout in the well-equipped fitness center.

906 rooms. Restaurant, bar. Fitness center. Pool. Spa. Beach. Casino. $151-250

★★★TRUMP TAJ MAHAL CASINO HOTEL

1000 Boardwalk, Atlantic City, 609-449-1000, 800-825-8888; www.trumptaj.com

To say that the Trump Taj Mahal Casino Resort is opulent is an understatement. After all, where else can you find a 4,500-square-foot suite named for Alexander the Great that features its own steam room, sauna, weight room, lounge, and pantry? Covering 17 acres, this resort offers comforts you wish you had at home. Rooms are spacious, feature beautiful decor, marble bathrooms, and spectacular views of the city. Treat yourself to a day in the health spa, where highly trained therapists pamper you with luxurious treatments like reflexology and Swedish massages. Hotel dining options range from upscale to casual, while the casino can keep you going all night with 4,000 slot machines, 210 gaming tables, and a baccarat pit.

1,250 rooms. Restaurant, bar. Fitness center. Pool. Spa. Casino. $151-250

★★★THE WATER CLUB AT BORGATA

1 Renaissance Way, Atlantic City, 800-800-8817; www.thewaterclubhotel.com

Soaring 43 stories above Atlantic City, Borgata's upscale sister property is large without feeling impersonal. The contemporary vibe carries from the verdant sunroom off the lobby to the naturally-inspired guest rooms, each with a stunning water view. Flat-screen TVs, iPod docking stations and 400-thread-count Egyptian sheets are just some of the pleasures awaiting boardwalk-weary guests. The five indoor and outdoor pools, state-of-the-art fitness center and top-notch Immersion Spa give little reason to leave the hotel, but if you do get antsy, the amenities of the Borgata Casino Hotel are only minutes away.

800 rooms. Fitnesse center. Pool. Spa. Business center. $151-250

WHERE TO EAT

★★CHEF VOLA'S

111 S. Albion Place, Atlantic City, 609-345-2022; www.chefvolas.com

Italian, American. Dinner. Closed Monday. Reservations required. $36-85

★★DOCK'S OYSTER HOUSE

2405 Atlantic Ave., Atlantic City, 609-345-0092; www.docksoysterhouse.com

Seafood. Dinner. Bar. Reservations recommended. $36-85

★IRISH PUB AND INN

164 St. James Place and Boardwalk, Atlantic City, 609-344-9063; www.theirishpub.com

American, Irish. Lunch, dinner, late-night. Outdoor seating. Bar. $15 and under.

★★★RAM'S HEAD INN

9 W. White Horse Pike, Galloway, 609-652-1700; www.ramsheadinn.com

Only eight miles from Atlantic City, this continental restaurant is also a busy banquet facility that can accommodate up to 350 people. Dine in a glass-enclosed veranda, ballroom or brick courtyard.

American. Lunch, dinner. Closed Monday. Children's menu. Reservations recommended. Outdoor seating. Bar. $36-85

★★★SEABLUE BY MICHAEL MINA

1 Borgata Way, Atlantic City, 609-317-1000, 866-692-6742; www.theborgata.com

Guests can enjoy an eclectic dining experience at Seablue, located in the upscale Borgata Casino Hotel & Spa. The ultramodern décor features blue deco-type lighting, terra-cotta and gold colors, and lavender suede-covered chairs (in the bar area). The restaurant features the creations of well-known executive chef Michael Mina, with many of the fresh fish options being grilled over mesquite wood in a tandoori oven. The eight-page menu includes a page for guests to design their own salad—crayons are placed on the table for filling in the blanks—and dessert consists of three different items, one always being ice cream or sherbet.

Seafood. Dinner. Closed Tuesday-Wednesday. Reservations recommended. Bar. $36-85

SPAS
★★★SPA TOCCARE
1 Borgata Way, Atlantic City, 609-317-7555, 866-692-6742; www.theborgata.com

Spa Toccare looks to nature for much of its inspiration, and its treatment menu highlights the healing properties of many botanicals. Facials employ bilberry for sensitive skin and rainforest propolis for supreme hydration. Pamper the body with a healing mud or green tea body treatment, or let the oil of Kamani restore firmness. Hot stone, deep tissue, Swedish, and reflexology massage are among the tension tamers, or retreat to the bath to soak your troubles away. One step inside the Spa Toccare and your gambling losses will quickly disappear. Its contemporary Mediterranean styling makes modern sophisticates feel instantly at home. From coifs at the Salon, circuit training at the Pump Room, and cabanas at the Pool & Gardens to bachelor bliss at the Barbershop, this spa offers a complete approach to perfecting and pampering.

IMMERSION SPA AT THE WATER CLUB AT BORGATA
1 Renaissance Way, Atlantic City, 800-800-8817; www.thewaterclubhotel.com

A view may not be the first thing that comes to mind when you think spa, but the 360-degree floor-to-ceiling water views at Immersion are hard not to notice. Located on the 32nd and 33rd floors of The Water Club, the spa is all about relaxation and rejuvenation with spacious "experience" rooms, a 25-yard infinity lap pool and spa cuisine prepared by chef Geoffrey Zakarian. The list of treatments is extensive, but whichever body part you choose to pamper, you can't go wrong. The Borgata Glow Facial incorporates an enzyme peel and tightening masks to give you that youthful look (sans Botox), while the Sea Spa Body Float lets mother nature do the work as your body is scrubbed and layered in warm algae. Be sure to visit the fitness center, which is outfitted with Techno Gym equipment and, of course, a knock-out view of the water.

BERNARDSVILLE
See also Chatham

This small town serves as a quiet respite from city life for New Yorkers who take an hour train-ride to Bernardsville set in the Somerset Hills.

WHERE TO STAY
★★★THE BERNARDS INN
27 Mine Brook Road, Bernardsville, 908-766-0002, 888-766-0002;
www.bernardsinn.com

This historic property, which opened in 1907, is a favored retreat for those looking for a relaxing getaway or quiet retreat. Guest rooms are individually decorated with antiques and reproductions. They are complete with luxurious bedding, plush bathrobes, complimentary Internet access, and a stocked mini-bar. The restaurant serves progressive American fare in an elegant and romantic setting.

20 rooms. Restaurant, bar. Business center. $251-350

WHERE TO EAT

★★★THE BERNARDS INN

27 Mine Brook Road, Bernardsville, 908-766-0002, 888-766-0002;
www.bernardsinn.com

This traditional restaurant features chef Corey Heyer's creative progressive American menu—along with a 960-bottle wine cellar and award-winning wine list—in an elegant, intimate setting that's just a short drive from New York City. Three different dining rooms each exude their own warm ambiance and a beautiful outdoor patio provides alfresco dining under the stars. Contemporary American. Breakfast, lunch (Monday-Friday), dinner. Reservations recommended. Outdoor seating. Bar. $36-85

BURLINGTON

See also Trenton; Philadelphia, PA

In 1774, like New York, Philadelphia and Boston, Burlington was a thriving port. A Quaker settlement, it was one of the first to provide public education. A 1682 Act of Assembly gave Matinicunk (now Burlington) Island in the Delaware River to the town with the stipulation that the revenue it generated would be used for public schools; that act is still upheld. Burlington was the capital of West Jersey; the legislature met here and in the East Jersey capital of Perth Amboy from 1681 until after the Revolution. In 1776, the Provincial Congress adopted the state constitution here.

WHAT TO SEE

BURLINGTON COUNTY HISTORICAL SOCIETY

451 High St., Burlington, 609-386-4773; www.tourburlington.org

The society complex holds the D.B. Pugh Library, a Revolutionary War exhibit, the James Fenimore Cooper House, birthplace of the famous author; the Bard-How House, dating back to 1740, with period furnishings; Captain James Lawrence House, birthplace of the commander of the Chesapeake during the War of 1812 and speaker of the immortal words "Don't give up the ship." Historic Society: Tuesday-Saturday 1-5 p.m. Museum and Library: First Friday of every month 6-9 p.m.

HISTORIC TOURS

City of Burlington Tourism Office, 12 Smith Alley, Burlington, 609-386-3993;
www.tourburlington.org

Costumed guides lead walking tours of 33 historic sites in Burlington. April-November, Friday-Sunday, 11 a.m.-4 p.m. Tours: 11:30 a.m., 2 p.m.

OLD ST. MARY'S CHURCH

145 W. Broad St., Burlington, 609-386-0902; www.stmarysburlington.org

Built in 1703, Old St. Mary's is the oldest Episcopal Church building in the state.

THOMAS REVELL HOUSE

213 Wood St., Burlington, 609-386-3993; www.tourburlington.org

This is the oldest building in Burlington County as it was built in 1685. It is included in the Burlington County Historical Society home tour.

SPECIAL EVENT
WOOD STREET FAIR
Burlington; www.woodstreetfair.com
This annual event brings out over 25,000 visitors who take part in this rec-reation of a colonial fair. There are more than 175 artisans selling their art, jewelry, ceramics, crafts and more. There are food vendors, baked good and a Jazz festival. You can take a tour of the Revell House for free as well.
First Saturday after Labor Day.

WHERE TO EAT
★★★CAFÉ GALLERY
219 High St., Burlington, 609-386-6150; www.cafegalleryburlington.com
Local artwork adorns the walls and large windows offer views of the Dela-ware River and the brick terrace. The well-landscaped outdoor terrace is set with umbrella-topped tables and a large fountain. The creative menu includes options such as roast Long Island duckling with orange and cognac sauce, braised pork loin in champagne with baked apples and pineapple, and sau-téed rainbow trout on crust with almond butter sauce.
Continental, French. Lunch (Monday-Saturday), dinner, Sunday brunch. Reservations recommended. Outdoor seating. Bar. $16-35

CAMDEN
See also Cherry Hill; Philadelphia, PA
Camden's growth as the leading industrial, marketing and transportation center of southern New Jersey dates from post-Civil War days. Its location across the Delaware River from Philadelphia prompted large companies such as Campbell's Soup (national headquarters) to establish plants here. Walt Whitman spent the last 20 years of his life in Camden.

WHAT TO SEE
CAMDEN COUNTY HISTORICAL SOCIETY-POMONA HALL
1900 Park Blvd., Camden, 856-964-3333; www.cchsnj.com
The Historical Society is located in this brick Georgian house that belonged to descendants of William Cooper, an early Camden settler. Museum exhibits focus on regional history and include antique glass, lamps, toys, early hand tools, fire-fighting equipment and Victor Talking Machines. The library has more than 20,000 books, as well as maps from the 17th century to the pres-ent, newspapers from the 18th to the 20th century and more.
Mansion/Museum Tours: Tuesday-Thursday, Sunday, noon-3:30 p.m.

NEW JERSEY STATE AQUARIUM
1 Riverside Drive, Camden, 856-365-0352; www.adventureaquarium.com
This home to more than 4,000 total fish of some 500 species is just minutes across the Ben Franklin Bridge in Camden, on the Delaware River water-front. Curious kids can find out how fish sleep and which fish can change from male to female and back again. You will also find exhibits of seals, penguins, sharks, turtles and tropical fish, as well as elaborate rain forest, water filtration and conservation awareness displays.
Admission: adults $19.95, chidren 2-12 $12.95. Daily 9:30 a.m.-5 p.m.

TOMB OF WALT WHITMAN

Harleigh Cemetery, 1640 Haddon Ave., Camden, 856-963-0122;
www.harleighcemetery.org

This is the final resting place of Walt Whitman. The vault of the "good gray poet," designed by the poet himself, is of rough-cut stone with a grillwork door. Monday-Saturday 8:30 a.m.-4:30 p.m.

USS NEW JERSEY

62 Battleship Place, Camden, 856-966-1652, 866-877-6262;
www.battleshipnewjersey.org

The United States Navy permanently berthed the *USS New Jersey* (or "Big J"), one of the nation's largest and most decorated battleships, at the Camden Waterfront in 2000 and has transformed it into a floating museum. First launched in 1942, the ship was commissioned for operations during World War II at Iwo Jima and Okinawa. The ship conducted its last mission, providing fire support to Marines in embattled Beirut, Lebanon, in 1983. Military history buffs will be awed by the guided two-hour tour through this 887-foot, 11-story, 212,000-horsepower, Iowa-class ship. Big J is available for special events, retreats and overnight encampments.
Tour: adults $18.50, seniors, veterans and children 6-11 $14, children under 6 and military personnel free.

WALT WHITMAN ARTS CENTER

Second and Cooper streets, Camden, 856-964-8300; www.waltwhitmancenter.org
Providing art programs to Camden, this art center features poetry readings, concerts, performances, a children's theater and gallery exhibits.
Hours and schedules vary; see Web site for information.

WALT WHITMAN HOUSE STATE HISTORIC SITE

328 Mickle Blvd., Camden, 856-964-5383; www.waltwhitman.org
The last residence of the poet and the only house he ever owned; he lived here from 1884 until his death on March 26, 1892. It contains original furnishings, including the bed in which Whitman died, as well as books and photographs, Whitman's death notice and mementos.
Admission: adults $5, seniors and students $4, children under 6 free.
Mid-June-Labor Day, Monday-Friday 11 a.m.-4 p.m., Saturday-Sunday 11 a.m.-5 p.m.; Labor Day-mid-June, Wednesday-Friday 1-4 p.m., Saturday-Sunday 11 a.m.-4 p.m.

WHERE TO EAT

★★★BRADDOCK'S TAVERN

39 S. Main St., Medford Village, 609-654-1604; www.braddocks.com
This casual restaurant features traditional American cuisine with European influences. Don't miss the cooking classes held throughout the year and other fun events like wine tastings.
American. Lunch, dinner, Sunday brunch. Bar. $16-35

CAPE MAY

See also Wildwood Crest

Cape May, the nation's oldest seashore resort, is located on the southernmost tip of the state. Popular with Philadelphia and New York society since 1766, Cape May has been host to presidents Lincoln, Grant, Pierce, Buchanan and Harrison, as well as notables such as John Wanamaker and Horace Greeley. The entire town has been proclaimed a National Historic Landmark because it has more than 600 Victorian homes and buildings, many of which have been restored. The downtown Washington Street Victorian Mall features three blocks of shops and restaurants. Four miles of beaches and a 1 1/4-mile paved promenade offer vacationers varied entertainment. "Cape May diamonds," often found on the shores of Delaware Bay by visitors, are actually pieces of pure quartz, rounded by the waves.

WHAT TO SEE
CAPE MAY MID-ATLANTIC CENTER FOR THE ARTS
TROLLEY TOURS

202 Ocean St., Cape May, 809-884-5404; www.capemaymac.org

These trolley tours feature many options depending upon what you're interested in. Interested in ghosts? Take the Ghosts of Cape May tour which takes you through the streets documenting the paranormal activity. Or if your a nature lover, take the Cape Island Nature Tour which will take you through wildlife habitats.

CAPE MAY-LEWES (DEL.) FERRY

Sandman Boulevard and Lincoln Drive, North Cape May, 609-889-7200, 800-643-3779; www.capemaylewesferry.com

The Cape May-Lewes Ferry is the sole connection between southern terminus of Garden State Parkway and Highway 13 (Ocean Highway) on the Delmarva Peninsula. It's a 17-mile, 80-minute trip across the Delaware Bay.

EMLEN PHYSICK ESTATE

1048 Washington St., Cape May, 609-884-5404; www.capemaymac.org

This authentically restored 18-room Victorian mansion, built in 1879, was designed by Frank Furness. It's said that this estate is haunted by Dr. Physick's Aunt Emilie along with a few of Physick's dogs and other ghosts. The mansion is also the headquarters for the Mid-Atlantic Center for the Arts. Daily.

HISTORIC COLD SPRING VILLAGE

720 Route 9, Cape May, 609-898-2300; www.hcsv.org

The village subsists of a restored early 1800s South Jersey farm village, including 25 restored historic buildings on 22 acres. Craft shops, spinning, blacksmithing, weaving, pottery, broom making, ship modeling demonstrations, folk art are displayed throughout the village. If you're hungry, there is a bakery, food shops and a restaurant.

Memorial Day-late June, daily 10 a.m.-4:30 p.m.; late June-Labor Day, Tuesday-Sunday 10 a.m.-4:30 p.m.

THE AMUSEMENTS OF THE JERSEY SHORE

Pennsylvania Route 40 leads to the Jersey Shore, Atlantic City, Ocean City and historic Cape May. Atlantic City offers fun activities for everyone. Children love Lucy the Margate Elephant, a six-story, elephant-shaped building with an observation deck on her back, and Storybook Land, with its rides, animals, playground and more than 50 storybook buildings. Older children will enjoy the Ripley's Believe It or Not Museum. And adults will have a great time exploring the Renault Winery, Noyes Museum and Smithville's specialty shops and restaurants. Travelers can also visit one of the many recreation areas or amusement piers along the coast, as well as the Marine Mammal Stranding Center and Museum, the Edwin B. Forsythe National Wildlife Refuge and the casinos.

Head south from Atlantic City to Ocean City, a popular family resort with eight miles of beaches. Walk along the boardwalk. Take a ride to the top of the 140-foot Ferris wheel, or take a turn at the video arcades, roller coasters and water slides. Stop for a snack at one of the outdoor cafes or fill up on ice cream and cotton candy.

Cape May, the nation's oldest seaside resort, is at New Jersey's southernmost tip. Explore historic Cold Spring Village, a restored 1870 farm village with craft shops and demonstrations. Take the ferry across Delaware Bay, or take a guided walking tour of the historic district or a one-hour Ocean Walk tour of the area's beaches and marine life.

SPECIAL EVENTS
CAPE MAY JAZZ FESTIVAL

Cape May; www.capemayjazz.org

This annual event takes place in multiple venues within Cape May. This festival features plenty of live jazz music, workshops and other performances. April.

WHERE TO STAY
★AVONDALE BY THE SEA

Beach and Gurney avenues, Cape May, 609-884-2332, 800-676-7030; www.avondalebythesea.com

46 rooms. Complimentary breakfast. Pool. $151-250

★★THE CARROLL VILLA BED AND BREAKFAST HOTEL

19 Jackson St., Cape May, 609-884-5970, 877-275-8452; www.carrollvilla.com

21 rooms. Restaurant, bar. Complimentary breakfast. $151-250

★★★CONGRESS HALL

251 Beach Ave., Cape May, 609-884-8421, 888-944-1816; www.congresshall.com

Guests feel like royalty when they step beneath the 32-foot tall colonnade and into Congress Hall's beautiful lobby, complete with the hotel's original black-and-white marble floor, 12-foot tall doors and black wicker furniture. The guest rooms feature views of the Atlantic, antiques, custom furnishings and large bathrooms with 1920s-style tubs and pedestal sinks. The Blue Pig Tavern is a great place to stop for a bite to eat or meet up with new friends, and the Grand Ballroom is not to be missed.

108 rooms. Closed mid-week January and February. Restaurant, bar. Fitness center. Pool. Beach. $151-250

★★★MAINSTAY INN

635 Columbia Ave., Cape May, 609-884-8690; www.mainstayinn.com

Guests at this beautiful Victorian-style inn near the water will find their stay in Cape May to be serene and somewhat luxurious. Rooms are spacious and decorated withoriental carpets and silk-screened wallpaper, and each morning, guests can enjoy large family-style breakfast by the fireplace or on the private porch. Guests are provided with beach towels and beach chairs with umbrellas and there's a shower and changing room for guests to use as well.
6 rooms. Complimentary breakfast. Beach. $151-250

★★MONTREAL INN

Beach at Madison Ave., Cape May, 609-884-7011, 800-525-7011;
www.montreal-inn.com

70 rooms. Restaurant, bar. Closed December-mid-March. Fitness center. Pool. Beach. $61-150

★★★THE SOUTHERN MANSION

720 Washington St., Cape May, 609-884-7171, 800-381-3888;
www.southernmansion.com

Originally built as a country estate in 1863 by Philadelphia industrialist George Allen, the Victorian décor of this painstakingly restored home has graced the covers of several magazines. Each room is meticulously decorated with antiques and vibrant colors, and features private bathrooms. The hotel's location is within walking distance of beaches, shops and restaurants.
24 rooms. Complimentary breakfast. No children under 10. Beach. $151-250

★★★VIRGINIA HOTEL

25 Jackson St., Cape May, 609-884-5700, 800-732-4236; www.virginiahotel.com

This elegant hotel, built in 1879, has been remodeled and no detail was overlooked. Bright and airy rooms feature flat-screen televisions, Italian duvet covers, Belgian linens and Bulgari bath products.
24 rooms. Restaurant, bar. Complimentary breakfast. No children under 12. Beach. $151-250

WHERE TO EAT

★★410 BANK STREET

410 Bank St., Cape May, 609-884-2127; www.410bankstreet.com

Caribbean, Seafood. Dinner. Closed October-May. Reservations recommended. Outdoor seating. $36-85

★★ALEATHEA'S

7 Ocean St., Cape May, 609-884-5555, 800-582-5933; www.aleatheas.com

American. Breakfast, lunch, dinner. Closed various days in October-March. Reservations recommended. Bar. $16-35

★★ALEXANDER'S INN

653 Washington St., Cape May, 609-884-2555, 877-484-2555; www.alexandersinn.com

French. Dinner, Sunday brunch. Reservations recommended. $36-85

★★THE BLUE PIG TAVERN
Congress Hall, 251 Beach Ave., Cape May, 609-884-8421, 888-944-1816;
www.congresshall.com
American. Breakfast, lunch, dinner. Closed mid-week January and February.
Reservations recommended. Outdoor seating. Bar. $36-85

★★★EBBITT ROOM
The Virginia Hotel, 25 Jackson St., Cape May, 609-884-5700, 800-732-4236;
www.virginiahotel.com
Nestled in an 1870s Victorian in the charming Virginia Hotel, the equally inviting Ebbitt Room reflects the quaint Cape May atmosphere. Crystal chandeliers, beautiful floral arrangements, and soft colors set an elegant and romantic mood, perfectly complementing the unique plates of contemporary
American fare. American. Dinner. Reservations recommended. Outdoor
seating. Bar. $36-85

★★THE MAD BATTER RESTAURANT AND BAR
19 Jackson St., Cape May, 609-884-5970; www.madbatter.com
American. Breakfast, lunch, dinner. Reservations recommended. Outdoor
dining. Bar. $16-35

★★MERION INN
106 Decatur St., Cape May, 609-884-8363; www.merioninn.com
Seafood, steak. Dinner, late-night. Reservations recommended. Outdoor
seating. Bar. $36-85

★★★WASHINGTON INN
801 Washington St., Cape May, 609-884-5697; www.washingtoninn.com
The Washington Inn is located in a former plantation house in the heart of
the Cape May Historic District. An impressive wine list beautifully comple-
ments the seasonal American menu, which may include appetizers like a
warm goat cheese tart and entrées such as pan-seared filet mignon and herb-
crusted rack of lamb.
American. Dinner. Reservations recommended. Outdoor seating. Bar. $36-85

CAPE MAY COURT HOUSE
See also Cape May, Stone Harbor, Wildwood
To be accurately named, this county seat would have to be called Cape May
Court Houses because there are two of them; the white 19th-century building
is now used as a meeting hall.

WHAT TO SEE
CAPE MAY COUNTY HISTORICAL MUSEUM
504 Route 9 North, Cape May Court House, 609-465-3535; www.cmcmuseum.org
This historical museum features a period dining room (predating 1820), an
18th-century kitchen, a doctor's room, a military room with Merrimac flag,
and Cape May diamonds. There are also barn exhibits, whaling implements,
Indian artifacts, pioneer tools and a lens from Cape May Point Lighthouse.
There is also a genealogical library.
Admission: Free. Library: Wednesday-Friday 10 a.m.-2 p.m.

CAPE MAY: AN ARCHITECTURAL BOUNTY

The Center for the Arts, located at the historic Emlen Physick Estate at 1048 Washington Street (609-884-5404), is a good place to begin a walking tour that explores some of more than 600 Victorian-era buildings in Cape May. Take the 45-minute house tour. Leaving the estate, turn left, go right onto Madison, and having arrived at the corner of Virginia Street, turn left and walk the grid created by Madison, Philadelphia and Reading streets as they intersect Virginia, Ohio, Cape May, Idaho, Maryland, New York and New Jersey streets. The entire neighborhood is rich in antique homes.

Return to Madison. Turn left onto Sewell, then right onto Franklin. At the corner of Columbia Avenue, note the Clivedon Inn (709 Columbia) on the right. Turn left on Columbia. Here stands the Henry Sawyer Inn (722 Columbia) with its magnificent garden; the Dormer House (800 Columbia), a Colonial Revivalist home; the Inn at Journeys End (710 Columbia) and the Mainstay Inn (635 Columbia), once a gentlemen's gambling house.

Walk toward the ocean on Howard Street. At Beach Drive is the Hotel Macomber (727 Beach Drive), built in the Shingle style. Turn right, walk three blocks to Ocean Street, turn right and look for the Queen Anne-style Columbia House (26 Ocean St.) and Twin Gables (731 Ocean St.). Go left on Hughes to Decatur, turn right and in three short blocks enter the downtown shopping district. Here, along the Washington Street Mall, Lyle Lane, Jackson Street and Perry Street are dozens of shops, restaurants and inns. Stop at the corner of the Washington Street Mall and Perry to look at Congress Hall, a gargantuan hotel. At 9 Perry, near Beach Drive, stands the Kings Cottage, built in the Mansard style with Stick-style detailing. Another excellent Queen Anne-style building, the Inn at 22 Jackson, is found on Jackson Street parallel to Perry. Nearby, the Virginia Hotel (25 Jackson) serves elegant meals in its upscale dining room. You could also enjoy a meal at the Mad Batter (19 Jackson), a Victorian bed and breakfast inn, where breakfast on the veranda is a long-standing Cape May tradition.

For a classic Jersey Shore finish, return to the beach (at Jackson and Beach Drive) and stroll along the water's edge, or shop and snack along the Promenade. On a summer's eve, another option is to take in a play performed by the professional Cape May Stage. To reach them, stroll back up Jackson (away from the ocean), past the Washington Street Mall to Lafayette Street. Turn right—the theater is in the visitor center.

CAPE MAY COUNTY PARK AND ZOO

7070 Route 9 North, Cape May Court House, 609-465-5271; www.capemayzoo.org

This zoo sits on almost 80 acres and has more than 200 different species and more than 55 animals. Besides the animals, there are jogging paths, bike trails, tennis courts, picnicking areas, and a playground.

Admission: Free. Memorial Day-Labor Day, daily 10 a.m.-4:45 p.m.; July-August, Wednesday until 6:45 p.m.; Labor Day-Memorial Day, daily 10 a.m.-3:30 p.m.

CHATHAM

See also Short Hills

This suburban, residential community is known for it's lovely and equisite homes, gardens and quality of life. It's a short commute to New York City and has a variety of excellent restaurants and shopping centers.

WHERE TO EAT
★★★RESTAURANT SERENADE
6 Roosevelt Ave., Chatham, 973-701-0303; www.restaurantserenade.com
Owned by husband-and-wife team James and Nancy Sheridan Laird, Restaurant Serenade opened in 1996. The kitchen uses seasonal local ingredients to create innovative, contemporary French cuisine with Asian flair, such as seared sea bass with cantaloupe risotto, opal basil, purslane and Romano beans, or roasted rack of lamb with grilled corn, escarole, feta cheese and spicy tomato coulis.
American. Lunch (Monday-Friday), dinner. $36-85

CHERRY HILL
See also Camden, Haddonfield; also Philadelphia, PA
Cherry Hill is a busy, family-oriented community that is home the the Garden State Park racetrack, Cherry Hill Mall, and a large commercial center. It's also only five miles from Philadelphia, Pennsylvania, making it a great commuter suburb to reside in.

WHAT TO SEE
BARCLAY FARMSTEAD
209 Barclay Lane, Cherry Hill, 856-795-6225; www.barclayfarmstead.org
This is one of the earliest properties settled in what is now Cherry Hill with origins traced to 1684. The township-owned site consists of 32 acres of open space with a restored Federal-style farmhouse and a Victorian spring house. Admission: Free. Tuesday-Friday noon-4 p.m., first Sunday each month 1-4 p.m.

CHERRY HILL MALL
2000 Route 38, Cherry Hill, 856-662-7441; www.cherryhillmall.com
Opened in 1961, Cherry Hill Mall was the first enclosed mall on the East Coast, making it quite the popular destination. Today, it's still popular as it has been redeveloped to provide the best shopping possible. Stores include Nordstrom, Crate & Barrel, Macy's, J.C. Penney, J.Crew, Urban Outfitters, and many others. There is also a new food court and Bistro row which features a handful of finer restaurants.
Monday-Saturday 10 a.m.-9:30 p.m., Sunday 11 a.m.-6 p.m.

WHERE TO STAY
★★CLARION HOTEL
1450 Route 70 E., Cherry Hill, 856-428-2300, 877-424-6423; www.choicehotels.com
197 rooms. Restaurant, bar. Fitness center. Pets accepted. $61-150

★★★CROWNE PLAZA HOTEL PHILADELPHIA/CHERRY HILL
2349 W. Marlton Pike, Cherry Hill, 856-665-6666, 877-227-6963;
www.crowneplaza.com
This suburban hotel is located only 10 minutes from Philadelphia's historic and business districts, and just a few miles from the Aquarium and the Cherry Hill Mall.
408 rooms. Restaurant, bar. Fitness center. Pool. $61-150

★★HOLIDAY INN
2175 Marlton Pike, Cherry Hill, 856-663-5300, 800-315-2621;
www.holidayinncherryhill.com
186 rooms. Restaurant, bar. Business center. Fitness center. Pool. Pets accepted. $61-150

WHERE TO EAT
★★★LA CAMPAGNE
312 Kresson Road, Cherry Hill, 856-429-7647; www.lacampagne.com
This 150-year-old restaurant and farmhouse serves country French cuisine with an emphasis on the Provençal region of southeast France. Highlights of their bistro menu includes an extensive cheese table as well as a gourmand six course tasting.
French. Dinner, Sunday brunch. Closed Monday. Reservations recommended. Outdoor seating. $36-85

★★MELANGE CAFÉ
1601 Chapel Ave., Cherry Hill, 856-663-7339; www.melangecafe.com
Cajun/Creole, Italian. Lunch, dinner. Closed Monday. Reservations recommended. Outdoor seating. $16-35

★RED HOT & BLUE
2175 Route 70, Cherry Hill, 856-665-7427; www.redhotandblue.com
American. Breakfast, lunch, dinner, late-night. Outdoor seating. Bar. $16-35

★★SIRI'S THAI FRENCH CUISINE
2117 Route 70 W., Cherry Hill, 856-663-6781; www.siris-nj.com
Thai, French. Lunch (Monday-Saturday), dinner. $16-35

EDISON
See also Elizabeth
Although Thomas A. Edison's house has been destroyed, Menlo Park and the Edison Memorial Tower stand in tribute to the great American inventor. It was here, on December 6, 1877, that Edison invented the phonograph. Two years later, he perfected the first practical incandescent light, designing and constructing electrical equipment we now take for granted. (His workshop has been moved to the Ford Museum in Dearborn, Mich.) Edison also built the first electric railway locomotive here in 1880; it ran 1 1/2 miles over the fields of Pumptown.

WHAT TO SEE
EDISON MEMORIAL TOWER AND MENLO PARK MUSEUM
37 Christie St., Edison, 732-248-7298; www.menloparkmuseum.com
A 131-foot tower topped by a 13 1/2-foot-high electric light bulb stands at the birthplace of recorded sound. Edison's other inventions are also here.
Thursday-Saturday 10 a.m.-4 p.m.

WHERE TO STAY
★★CROWNE PLAZA EDISON
2055 Lincoln Highway, Edison, 732-287-3500, 877-424-6423; www.crowneplaza.com
169 rooms. Restaurant, bar. Complimentary breakfast. Business center. Fitness center. $151-250

★★★SHERATON EDISON HOTEL RARITAN CENTER
125 Raritan Center Parkway, Edison, 732-225-8300, 800-325-3535;
www.sheraton.com/edison
Just a half-hour from New York City, the Sheraton Edison Hotel Raritan Center offers a convenient location along with elegant accommodations. Fluffy robes and Sheraton's signature Sweet Sleeper Beds with beautiful duvets and fluffy down pillows are just some of the wonderful amenities guests will find in their rooms. A large indoor pool, a well-equipped fitness facility, and a sauna offer onsite recreation, while Lily's Restaurant is the hotel's casual bistro-style dining facility.
276 rooms. Restaurant, bar. Business center. Fitness center. Pool. Pets accepted. $15-250

★★★SOMERSET HILLS HOTEL
200 Liberty Corner Road, Warren, 908-647-6700, 800-688-0700; www.shh.com
Visitors will find that this hotel, located in the Watchung Mountains, combines the service of a country inn with the facilities, entertainment and accommodations expected from a full-service hotel.
111 rooms. Restaurant, bar. Fitness center. Pool. Pets accepted. $151-250

WHERE TO EAT
★★CHARLIE BROWN'S
222 Plainfield Road, Edison, 732-494-6135; www.charliebrowns.com
American. Lunch, dinner, late-night. Children's menu. Outdoor seating. Bar. $16-35

★★MOGHUL
1665-195 Oaktree Center, Edison, 732-549-5050; www.moghul.com
Indian. Lunch, dinner. Closed Monday. Reservations recommended. $36-85

EGG HARBOR CITY
See also Atlantic City
Created by German investros from Philadelphia, Pennslyvania, Egg Harbor was incorporated in 1858. Not far from Atlantic City, Egg Harbor City is a resort town with golf courses, wineries and restaurants to visit and enjoy.

WHAT TO SEE
RENAULT WINERY
72 N. Bremen Ave., Egg Harbor City, 609-965-2111; www.renaultwinery.com
Renault Winery covers 1,500 acres including a golf course, restaurants and the Tuscany House Hotel. Take a guided tour (approximately 45 minutes) which includes a tour of the wine-aging cellars, their Antique Glass Museum and you'll learn about the history of the winery and more. At the end, you'll

also get a free wine tasting. There is also the Vineyard Golf course here to enjoy before or after you explore the winery.

Guided tours and wine tasting: Monday-Friday 10 a.m.-4 p.m., Saturday 10 a.m.-8 p.m., Sunday noon-4 p.m.

WHERE TO STAY
★DAYS INN
6708 Tilton Road, Egg Harbor City, 609-641-4500, 800-329-7466; www.daysinn.com
115 rooms. Restaurant, bar. Complimentary breakfast. Business center. Fitness center. Pool. $61-150

WHERE TO EAT
★★★RENAULT GOURMET RESTAURANT
Renault Winery, 72 N. Bremen Ave., Egg Harbor City, 609-965-2111;
www.renaultwinery.com
This gourmet restaurant offers two different dining experiences: Guests may enjoy a six-course dinner with two wine samplings (reservations are required) or try the Sunday country brunch. If you're looking for breakfast or lunch, relax at the garden café at Joseph's Restaurant for a more casual meal. American. Dinner, Sunday brunch. Closed Monday-Thursday. Reservations recommended. $36-85

ELIZABETH

See also Jersey City, Newark
More than 1,200 manufacturing industries are located in Elizabeth and Union County. Long before the Revolution, Elizabeth was not only the capital of New Jersey but also a thriving industrial town. The first Colonial Assembly met here from 1669 to 1692. Princeton University began in Elizabeth in 1746 as the College of New Jersey. More than 20 pre-Revolutionary buildings still stand. Noteworthy citizens include: William Livingston, first governor of New Jersey; Elias Boudinot, first president of the Continental Congress; Alexander Hamilton; Aaron Burr; General Winfield Scott; John Philip Holland, builder of the first successful submarine and Admiral William J. Halsey. The Elizabeth-Port Authority Marine Terminal is the largest container port in the United States.

WHAT TO SEE
BOXWOOD HALL STATE HISTORIC SITE
1073 E. Jersey St., Elizabeth, 973-648-4540
Boxwood Hall was the home of Elias Boudinot, president of the Continental Congress in 1783 and director of the U.S. Mint. It was also the home of Jonathan Dayton, who was the youngest person to sign the Constitution. Boudinot entertained George Washington here on April 23, 1789, when Washington was on his way to his inauguration. Call to make an appointment to visit. Monday-Saturday.

FIRST PRESBYTERIAN CHURCH AND GRAVEYARD
42 Broad St., Elizabeth, 908-353-1518
The first General Assembly of New Jersey convened in an earlier building in

1668. The burned-out church was rebuilt from 1785-1787 and again in 1949. The Reverend James Caldwell was an early pastor. Alexander Hamilton and Aaron Burr attended an academy where the parish house now stands.

WARINANCO PARK

Elizabethtown Town Plaza, Elizabeth, 908-527-4900; www.elizabethnj.org
Designed by Frederick Olmstead, Warinanco Park is one of the largest Union County parks. You can take part in many different activities here including fishing, boating, running on a parcourse fitness circuit, tennis, handball, horseshoes and indoor ice-skating. The Henry S. Chatfield Memorial Garden features tulip blooms, azaleas, magnolias and Japanese cherry blossoms each spring; and there are also summer and fall flower displays.
Skating rink: Tuesday-Sunday.

WATCHUNG RESERVATION

Between Routes 22 and 78, Elizabeth, 908-527-4900; www.ucnj.org
A 2,000-wooded-acre reservation in the Watchung Mountains includes the 25-acre Surprise Lake. There are nature and bridle trails, ice-skating, picnic areas, playground and a ten-acre nursery and rhododendron display garden.

WHERE TO STAY
★★★HILTON NEWARK AIRPORT

1170 Spring St., Elizabeth, 908-351-3900, 800-445-8667; www.hilton.com
With the airport at its doorstep and a fully equipped business center, the Hilton Newark Airport is an ideal choice for business travelers. But with kids' movies and games available in rooms and dining menus just for the little ones, the hotel is also great for families.
374 rooms. Restaurant, bar. Business center. Fitness center. Pool. Pets accepted. $151-250

WHERE TO EAT
★★★STAGE HOUSE INN

366 Park Ave., Scotch Plains, 908-322-4224; www.stagehouserestaurant.com
A local favorite, this establishment offers lightened versions of classic French dishes, beautifully presented and full of flavor. Guests enjoy the simple, refined atmosphere and the casual patio dining.
American. Lunch, dinner. Reservations recommended. Outdoor seating. Bar. $36-85

FORT LEE

North and south of the George Washington Bridge, Fort Lee is named for General Charles Lee, who served in the Revolutionary Army under George Washington. Its rocky bluff achieved fame as the cliff from which Pearl White hung in the early movie serial The Adventures of Pearl White. From 1907 to 1916, 21 companies and seven studios produced motion pictures in Fort Lee. Stars such as Mary Pickford, Mabel Normand, Theda Bara and Clara Kimball Young made movies here.

WHAT TO SEE
FORT LEE HISTORIC PARK
Hudson Terrace and Palisades Interstate, Fort Lee, 201-461-1776;
www.njpalisades.org/flhp.htm
This 33-acre historic park overlooks views of the George Washington Bridge, the Hudson River and the skyline of upper Manhattan. Nature trails take you through the grounds that have reproductions of 18th century life. The visitor center features information on Fort Lee and the Revolutionary War in displays on the first two floors. There is also a gift shop here.

WHERE TO STAY
★★CROWNE PLAZA HOTEL ENGLEWOOD
401 S. Van Brunt St., Englewood, 201-871-2020, 800-972-3160;
www.crowneplaza.com
194 rooms. Restaurant, bar. Business center. Fitness center. Pool. $151-250

★★★DOUBLETREE FORT LEE/GEORGE WASHINGTON BRIDGE
2117 Route 4, Fort Lee, 201-461-9000, 800-445-8667; www.doubletree.com
This hotel sits near the George Washington Bridge. Along with its convenient location, this Hilton offers its guests two restaurants, a lounge, a karaoke night club, an indoor pool and a modern fitness center. Guest rooms are spacious and feature standard rooms with either a king size bed or two double beds; suites with whirlpool baths and a separate living room; and an Executive floor with acccess to the exclusive lounge.
236 rooms. Restaurant, bar. Business center. Fitness center. Pool. $151-250

★★HOLIDAY INN GEORGE WASHINGTON BRIDGE-FORT LEE
2339 Route 4 East, Fort Lee, 201-944-5000, 800-315-2621; www.ichotelsgroup.com
184 rooms. Restaurant, bar. Business center. Fitness center. Pool. $61-150

HACKENSACK
See also Fort Lee, Paterson
Hackensack was officially known as New Barbados until 1921 when it received its charter under its present name, thought to be derived from the Native American word "Hacquinsacq." The influence of the original Dutch settlers who established a trading post here remained strong even after British conquest. A strategic place during the Revolutionary War, the city contains a number of historical sites from that era. Hackensack is the hub for industry, business and government in Bergen County. Edward Williams College is located here.

WHAT TO SEE
CHURCH ON THE GREEN
42 Court St., Hackensack, 201-342-7050
Organized in 1686, the original building was built in 1696 (13 monogrammed stones preserved in the east wall) and rebuilt in 1791 in Stone Dutch architectural style. It is the oldest church building in Bergen County. The museum contains pictures, books and colonial items. Enoch Poor, a Revolutionary War general, is buried in the cemetery.

Monday-Friday on request.

USS LING SUBMARINE

Court and River streets, Hackensack, 201-342-3268; www.njnm.com

The *USS Ling* is a restored World War II fleet submarine and this is also the site of the New Jersey Naval Museum.

Admission: Free. Tours: adults $8, children under 12 $3. Saturday-Sunday 10 a.m.-4 p.m. (last tour 3:15 p.m.)

WHERE TO STAY

★★★HILTON HASBROUCK HEIGHTS/MEADOWLANDS

650 Terrace Ave., Hasbrouck Heights, 201-288-6100, 800-445-8667; www.hilton.com

A stay at the Hilton Hasbrouck Heights puts attractions like New York City and the Meadowlands right outside your door. Along with the convenient location, the hotel provides comfortable, modern rooms packed with amenities that make your stay pleasant. Coffee makers, wireless high-speed Internet access, pillow-top mattresses, and cozy duvets are just some of the in-room comforts, while a business center, concierge service, and laundry service are a few on conveniences provided by the hotel staff. The onsite restaurant, Bistro 650, offers casual American fare for breakfast, lunch, and dinner.

355 rooms. Restaurant. Business center. Fitness center. Pool. $151-250

WHERE TO EAT

★★★STONY HILL INN

231 Polifly Road, Hackensack, 201-342-4085; www.stonyhillinn.com

Housed in a historic Dutch colonial house, this restaurant offers eight dining rooms, all decorated in 18th-century style. Some rooms are themed, such as the Pipe Room or Herb Room, while others, such as the Green Room and Apricot Room, are more sophisticated. Menu specialties include chateaubriand bouquetiere for two and a grilled double-cut loin veal chop. The cigar-friendly bar is decorated in deep, rich tones and mahogany woodwork. On Friday and Saturday evenings, guests can enjoy live entertainment performed in the Garden Room.

American. Lunch, dinner. Bar. Reservations recommended. $36-85

HADDONFIELD

See also Camden, Cherry Hill

Haddonfield is named for Elizabeth Haddon, a 20-year-old Quaker girl whose father sent her here from England in 1701 to develop 400 acres of land. This assertive young woman built a house, started a colony and proposed to a Quaker missionary who promptly married her. The Theologian's Tale in Longfellow's *Tales of a Wayside Inn* celebrates Elizabeth Haddon's romance with the missionary.

WHAT TO SEE

GREENFIELD HALL

343 Kings Highway E. (Route 41), Haddonfield, 856-429-7375;
www.historicalsocietyofhaddonfield.org

Haddonfield's Historical Society headquarters is situated in the old Gill

House and contains personal items of Elizabeth Haddon including furniture, costumes and doll collection. There is also the Boxwood garden and a library on local history here. Also on the grounds is a house once owned by Elizabeth Haddon.

Library: Tuesday, Thursday 9:30-11:30 a.m., first Sunday of each month 1-3 p.m. Museum: Wednesday-Friday 1-4 p.m., first Sunday of the month 1-3 p.m. Closed August.

INDIAN KING TAVERN MUSEUM STATE HISTORIC SITE

233 Kings Highway E., Haddonfield, 856-429-6792

Built as an inn, state legislatures met here frequently, inlcuding when they passed a bill in 1777 substituting "State" for "Colony" in all state papers. It has colonial furnishings.

Wednesday-Friday, Saturday 10 a.m.-noon, 1-4 p.m.; Sunday 1-4 p.m.

THE SITE OF THE ELIZABETH HADDON HOUSE

Wood Lane and Merion Avenue, Haddonfield

Isaac Wood built this house in 1842, on the foundation of Elizabeth Haddon's 1713 brick mansion, immediately after it was destroyed by fire. The original brew house Elizabeth built and the English yew trees she brought over from England in 1712 are in the yard. This is a private residence and is not open to the public.

WHERE TO STAY

★★★HADDONFIELD INN

44 West End Ave., Haddonfield, 856-428-2195, 800-269-0014;
www.haddonfieldinn.com

Located in a Victorian home, the Haddonfield Inn offers well-appointed rooms and suites with varying styles and themes, including the Dolley Madison Room, with an antique desk, Franklin stove and pewter light fixtures, and the Dublynn Room, with antiques and a lace-canopied, four-poster King bed. All rooms feature fireplaces and high-speed Internet access. Each morning, a gourmet breakfast is served in the dining room or on the wraparound porch and complimentary beverages, coffee, tea and snacks are available throughout the day.

9 rooms. Complimentary breakfast. $151-250

HIGH POINT STATE PARK

High Point's elevation (1,803 feet), the highest point in New Jersey, gave this 15,000-acre park its name. Marked by a 220-foot stone war memorial, the spot offers a magnificent view overlooking Tri-State—the point where New Jersey, New York and Pennsylvania meet—with the Catskill Mountains to the north, the Pocono Mountains to the west and hills, valleys and lakes all around. Elsewhere in the forests of this Kittatinny Mountain park are facilities for swimming, fishing, boating, picnicking, and camping.

HOBOKEN

See also Jersey City

In the early 19th century, beer gardens and other amusement centers dotted the Hoboken shore, enticing New Yorkers across the Hudson. John Jacob Astor, Washington Irving, William Cullen Bryant and Martin Van Buren were among the fashionable visitors. By the second half of the century, industries and shipping began to encroach on the fun. Today, Hoboken is returning to its roots, as bars, restaurants and shops do steady business there, and young commuters flock to the birthplace of Frank Sinatra for more affordable housing than New York can provide. Hoboken is connected to Manhattan by the PATH rapid-transit system and New Jersey Transit buses.

WHAT TO SEE
STEVENS INSTITUTE OF TECHNOLOGY
Hudson and Eighth streets, Hoboken, 201-216-5105; www.stevens.edu
Founded in 1870, Stevens is a leading college of engineering, science, computer science management and the humanities with 3,600 students. You'll also find the Davidson Laboratory here, which is One of the largest privately owned hydrodynamic labs of its kind in the world. It's the testing site for models of ships, hydrofoils, America's Cup participants and the Apollo command capsule. Also, the Samuel C. William Library Special collections include a set of facsimiles of every drawing by Leonardo da Vinci, a library of 3,000 volumes by and about da Vinci; an Alexander Calder mobile; and the Frederick Winslow Taylor Collection of Scientific Management.

WHERE TO EAT
★★BAJA MEXICAN CUISINE
104 14th St., Hoboken, 201-653-0610; www.bajamexicancuisine.com
Mexican. Lunch (Friday-Saturday), dinner, Sunday brunch. Reservations recommended. Bar. $16-35

★CAFÉ MICHELINA
423 Bloomfield St., Hoboken, 201-659-3663; www.cafemichelina.com
Italian. Dinner. Closed Monday. Reservations recommended. Outdoor seating. $15 and under.

★GRIMALDI'S
133 Clinton St., Hoboken, 201-792-0800; www.grimaldis.com
Italian. Lunch (Friday-Sunday), dinner. $16-35

★ODD FELLOWS
80 River St., Hoboken, 201-656-9009; www.oddfellowsrest.com
Creole, Cajun. Lunch, dinner. Outdoor seating. Bar. $16-35

JERSEY CITY
See also Elizabeth, Hoboken, Newark
Located on the Hudson River, due west of the southern end of Manhattan Island, Jersey City is now the second-largest city in New Jersey. New Yorkers across the bay tell time by the Colgate-Palmolive Clock at 105 Hudson Street; the dial is 50 feet across, and the minute hand, weighing 2,200 pounds, moves 23 inches each minute. Linking Jersey City with New York are the 8,557-foot Holland Tunnel, which is 72 feet below water level; the Port Authority Trans-Hudson (PATH) rapid-transit system; and New York

Waterways Ferries, which run between Exchange Place, the city's Financial District and the World Financial Center in lower Manhattan.

WHAT TO SEE
LIBERTY SCIENCE CENTER
Liberty State Park, 222 Jersey city Boulevard, Jersey City, 201-200-1000; www.lsc.org
This four-story structure encompasses Environment, Health and Invention areas that feature more than 250 hands-on exhibits. A geodesic dome houses IMAX Theater with a six-story screen featuring fascinating animal and nature films.
Admission: adults $15.75, children 2-12 and seniors $11.50, children under 2 free. Monday-Friday 9 a.m.-4 p.m., Saturday-Sunday 9 a.m.-5 p.m.; late June-August, Monday-Friday 9 a.m.-5 p.m., Saturday-Sunday 9 a.m.-6 p.m.

LIBERTY STATE PARK
Morris Pesin Drive, Jersey City, 201-915-3400; www.libertystatepark.org
Liberty State Park is located just off NJ Turnpike, on the New York Harbor, less than 2,000 feet from the Statue of Liberty. It offers breathtaking view of the New York City skyline; a flag display includes state, historic and U.S. flags; a boat launch; a fitness course, and a picnic area. The historic railroad terminal has been partially restored. The Interpretive Center houses an exhibit area; adjacent to the Center is a 60-acre natural area consisting mostly of salt marsh. Nature trails and observation points complement this wildlife habitat. Boat tours and ferrys to Ellis Island and Statue of Liberty are available. Daily 6 a.m.-10 p.m.

LONG BEACH ISLAND
See also Little Egg Harbor
Six miles out to sea, this island is separated from the New Jersey mainland by Barnegat and Little Egg Harbor bays. Route 72, going east from Manahawkin on the mainland, enters the island at Ship Bottom. The island is no more than three blocks wide in some places and extends 18 miles from historic Barnegat Lighthouse to the north. It includes towns such as Loveladies, Harvey Cedars, Surf City, Ship Bottom, Brant Beach and the Beach Havens at the southern tip. A popular family resort, the island offers fishing, boating, swimming in the bay and in the ocean's surf. Tales are told of pirate coins buried on the island and over the years, silver and gold pieces have occasionally turned up. Whether they are part of pirate treasure or the refuse of shipwrecks remains a mystery.

WHAT TO SEE
BARNEGAT LIGHTHOUSE STATE PARK
Long Beach Island, 609-494-2016; www.state.nj.usl
Barnegat Lighthouse, a 167-foot red and white tower, was engineered by General George G. Meade and completed in 1858; its 217-step spiral staircase leading to the lookout offers a spectacular view. You can go fishing here and there are picnic tables.
Lighthouse: Memorial Day-Labor Day, daily 9 a.m.-4:30 p.m.; May and September-October, Saturday-Sunday 9 a.m.-3:30 p.m.

FANTASY ISLAND AMUSEMENT PARK

320 W. Seventh St., Beach Haven, 609-492-4000; www.fantasyislandpark.com

This family-oriented amusement park featuring rides, games, a family casino arcade, entertainment and concessions.

Admission: Free. May-September; schedule varies.

SPECIAL EVENT
SURFLIGHT THEATRE

Beach and Engleside avenues, Beach Haven, 609-492-9477; www.surflight.org

This theater puts on Broadway musicals, like *Hairspray* and *Little Shop of Horrors* as well as concerts nightly. There is also a children's theater that runs Wednesday-Saturday.

May-mid-October.

WHERE TO STAY
★★THE ENGLESIDE INN

30 E. Engleside Ave., Beach Haven, 609-492-1251, 800-762-2214; www.engleside.com

71 rooms. Restaurant, bar. Fitness center. Pool. $61-150

★★★THE SAND CASTLE BED AND BREAKFAST

710 Bayview Ave., Barnegat Light, 609-494-6555, 800-253-0353;
www.sandcastlelbi.com

This intimate bayfront bed and breakfast features five uniquely appointed guest rooms and two spacious, luxurious suites. Each morning, guests awaken to find a full breakfast served in the dining room, while complimentary tea, coffee and soft drinks are available throughout the day. The outdoor pool is a popular spot.

7 rooms. Closed December-March. No children under 16. Complimentary breakfast. Pool. $151-250

WHERE TO EAT
★★BUCKALEW'S

101 N. Bay Ave., Beach Haven, 609-492-1065; www.buckalews.com

American. Breakfast, lunch, dinner. Reservations recommended. Bar. $16-35

★★THE LEEWARD ROOM

30 E. Engleside Ave., Beach Haven, 609-492-5116, 800-762-2214; www.engleside.com

American, sushi. Lunch, dinner. Children's menu. Outdoor seating. $16-35

MORRISTOWN

See also Bernardsville, Morristown National Historical Park

Today, Morristown is primarily residential, but the town and its surrounding area were developed thanks to the iron industry, so desperately needed during the Revolutionary War. George Washington and his army spent two winters here, operating throughout the area until the fall of 1781. Morristown was the site of the first successful experiments with the telegraph by Samuel F.B. Morse and Stephen Vail. Cartoonist Thomas Nast, writers Bret Harte and Frank Stockton, and millionaire Otto Kahn all lived here.

WHAT TO SEE
ACORN HALL
68 Morris Ave., Morristown, 973-267-3465; www.acornhall.org
This Victorian Italianate house was built in 1853 and today still has its original furnishings, and exhibit gallery, a reference library and a garden.
Admission: adults $6, seniors $5, students $3, children under 12 free. Monday, Thursday 10 a.m.-4 p.m., Sunday 1-4 p.m.

FOSTERFIELDS LIVING HISTORICAL FARM
73 Kahdena Road, Morristown, 973-326-7645
This turn-of-the-century living history farm is set on 200 acres and includes a self-guided trail in which you can see displays, audiovisual presentations, workshops, and farming demonstrations from the past. There is also a restored Gothic Revival house on the farm.
Admission: adults $6, seniors $5, children 4-16 $4, children 2-3 $2, children 1 and under free. April-October, Wednesday-Friday 1-5 p.m., Saturday 10 a.m.-5 p.m, Sunday noon-5 p.m.

FRELINGHUYSEN ARBORETUM
53 E. Hanover Ave., Morristown, 973-326-7600; www.arboretumfriends.org
Built in 1891, this arboretum features 127 acres of forest and open fields, natural and formal gardens, spring and fall bulb displays, and labeled collections of trees and shrubs.The Haggerty Education Center offers horticultural educational programs.
Education center: Daily 9 a.m.-4:30 p.m.

HISTORIC SPEEDWELL
333 Speedwell Ave., Morristown, 973-540-0211; www.morrisparks.net
This is the home and factory of Stephen Vail, iron master, who in 1818 manufactured the engine for the *S.S. Savannah*, the first steamship to cross the Atlantic. In 1838, Alfred Vail (Stephen's son) and Samuel F.B. Morse perfected the telegraph and first publicly demonstrated it here in the factory. Displays include period furnishings in the mansion, exhibit on Speedwell Iron Works, exhibits on history of the telegraph; a water wheel, carriage house and granary. There's a gift shop and picnic area.
April-June, Wednesday-Saturday 10 a.m.-5 p.m.; July-October, Wednesday-Saturday 10 a.m.-5 p.m., Sunday noon-5 p.m.

MACCULLOCH HALL HISTORICAL MUSEUM
45 Macculloch Ave., Morristown, 973-538-2404; www.macullochhall.org
This restored 1810 house and garden was the home of George P. Macculloch, initiator of the Morris Canal, and his descendants for more than 140 years. It displays American and European decorative arts from the 18th and 19th centuries as well as illustrations by Thomas Nast.
Gift shop: Monday-Friday 9 a.m.-4 p.m. Museum: Wednesday-Thursday, Sunday 1-4 p.m.

MORRIS MUSEUM

6 Normandy Heights Road, Morristown, 973-971-3700; www.morrismuseum.org

The Morris Museum features art, science and history exhibits. There are more than 48,000 items on display. They also host musical and theatrical events along with lectures and films.

Admission: adults $10, seniors and children $7, children under 3 free. Wednesday, Friday-Saturday 11 a.m.-5 p.m., Thursday 11 a.m.-8 p.m., Sunday 1-5 p.m.

MORRISTOWN NATIONAL HISTORICAL PARK

30 Washington Place, Morristown, 973-543-2016; www.nps.gov/morr

Morristown National Historic Park was created by an Act of Congress in 1933, the first national historical park to be established and maintained by the federal government. Its three units cover more than 1,600 acres, and all but Jockey Hollow and the New Jersey Brigade Area are within Morristown's limits. The Continental Army's main body stayed here in the winter of 1779-1780. While here, visit the Ford Mansion (*10 Washington Place*), one of the finest early houses in Morristown was built in 1772-1774 by Colonel Jacob Ford, Jr., who produced gunpowder for American troops during the Revolutionary War. His widow rented the house to the army for General and Mrs. Washington when the Continental Army spent the winter of 1779-1780 here. Also visit Jockey Hallow (*30 Washington Place*), the site of the Continental Army's winter quarters in 1779-1780 and the 1781 mutiny of the Pennsylvania Line.

Headquarters and museum: Daily 9 a.m.-5 p.m. Ford Mansion: Daily 9 a.m.-5 p.m. Jockey Hollow: hours vary.

WHERE TO STAY

★★★HILTON PARSIPPANY

1 Hilton Court, Parsippany, 973-267-7373, 800-445-8667; www.parsippany.hilton.com

Located in Parsippany, this Hilton is only 25 minutes from the Newark International Airport and 27 miles from New York. Spacious guest rooms are recently renovated and feature luxurious bedding and Herman Miller ergonomic chairs. The hotel has a new state-of-the-art fitness center, pool, and outdoor patio as well as two restaurants and two lounges.

354 rooms. Restaurant, bar. Business center. Fitness center. Pool. Pets accepted. $61-150

★★★THE MADISON HOTEL

1 Convent Road, Morristown, 973-285-1800, 800-526-0729;
www.themadisonhotel.com

This Georgian-style hotel has been family owned since 1951. Individually appointed guest rooms combine Victorian charm and style with modern comforts like high-speed Internet access, mini-bars, cable TV, and cordless telephones. An outdoor pool and well-equipped fitness center offer opportunities to relax and unwind, and Rod's Steak and Seafood Grille is a sophisticated spot that features elegant dining in two turn-of-the-century Pullman cars. New York City is just an hour-long train ride away via the nearby Convent Station stop of the Midtown Direct Train.

200 rooms. Restaurant, bar. Complimentary breakfast. Fitness center. Pool.
$151-250

★★★THE WESTIN GOVERNOR MORRIS, MORRISTOWN
2 Whippany Road, Morristown, 973-539-7300, 800-937-8461;
www.westin.com/morristown
Although housed in a landmark building with a colonial-style setting, The
Westin Governor Morris is thoroughly modern in every way. Its lobby is
decorated with contemporary furnishings, as are guest rooms, which also
include wireless high-speed Internet access, mini-bars, spacious work desks
with ergonomic chairs, luxurious bath amenities, and Westin's signature
Heavenly Beds and Heavenly Showers. A sparkling outdoor pool and state-
of-the-art fitness center keep guests fit with style, and the Copeland Restaurant whets appetites with a mouthwatering menu of New American cuisine.
224 rooms. Restaurant, bar. Fitness center. Pool. Pets accepted. $251-350

WHERE TO EAT
★★ROD'S STEAK AND SEAFOOD GRILLE
Highway 124, Convent Station, 973-539-6666; www.rodssteak-seafoodgrill.com
Seafood, steak. Breakfast, lunch, dinner, Sunday brunch. Children's menu.
Reservations recommended. Bar. $36-85

NEW BRUNSWICK
See also Edison
On the south bank of the Raritan River, New Brunswick is both a college
town and a diversified commercial and retail city. Rutgers University, the
eighth-oldest institution of higher learning in the country and the only state
university with a colonial charter, was founded in 1766 as Queens College
and opened in 1771 with a faculty of one—aged 18. Livingston College,
Cook College and Douglass College (for women), all part of the university,
are also located here. The headquarters for Johnson & Johnson is located
downtown. The poet Joyce Kilmer was born in New Brunswick; his house, at
17 Joyce Kilmer Avenue, is open to visitors.

WHAT TO SEE
BUCCLEUCH MANSION AND PARK
George Street and Easton Avenue, New Brunswick, 732-745-5094
This mansion was built in 1739 by Anthony White, the son-in-law of Lewis
Morris, a colonial governor of New Jersey. It features rooms with period fur-
nishings. The park offers athletic fields, a fitness trail, a playground, gardens
and a picnic area.
June-October, Sunday 2-4 p.m.

CROSSROADS THEATRE
7 Livingston Ave., New Brunswick, 732-545-8100; www.crossroadstheatrecompany.org
This professional African-American theater company offers plays, musicals,
touring programs and workshops.
October-May, Wednesday-Sunday.

GEOLOGY MUSEUM

Rutgers University, George and Somerset streets, New Brunswick, 732-932-7243

You'll find displays of New Jersey minerals, mammals, including a mastodon; Egyptian exhibit with mummy here.

Monday 1-4 p.m., Tuesday-Friday 9 a.m.-noon.

GEORGE STREET PLAYHOUSE

9 Livingston Ave., New Brunswick, 732-246-7717; www.georgestplayhouse.org

This nationally recognized regional theater offers a six-show season of plays and musicals, such as The Seafarer, and they have a touring Outreach program for students.

Tuesday-Sunday.

HUNGARIAN HERITAGE CENTER

300 Somerset St., New Brunswick, 732-846-5777; www.ahfoundation.org

This museum has changing exhibits that focus on Hungarian folk life, fine and folk art as well as a library with archives.

Admission: $5. Museum: Tuesday-Saturday 11 a.m.-4 p.m., Sunday 1-4 p.m. Library: Monday, Friday 9 a.m.-1 p.m., Tuesday-Thursday 9 a.m.-5 p.m.

JANE VOORHEES ZIMMERLI ART MUSEUM

Rutgers University, George and Hamilton streets, New Brunswick, 732-932-7237; www.zimmerlimuseum.rutgers.edu

This museum holds paintings from early 16th century through the present with changing exhibits.

Admission: $3, children under 18 free. Tuesday-Friday 10 a.m.-4:30 p.m., Saturday-Sunday noon-5 p.m.

NEW JERSEY MUSEUM OF AGRICULTURE

103 College Farm Road, New Brunswick, 732-249-2077; www.agriculturemuseum.org

This museum features a large collection of farm implements covering three centuries of farming history. They also have science and history exhibits.

Tuesday-Saturday 10 a.m.-3 p.m. Closed Saturday in February, first two weeks of March and August-mid-September.

RUTGERS-THE STATE UNIVERSITY OF NEW JERSEY

126 College Ave., New Brunswick, 732-932-1766; www.rutgers.edu

Founded in 1766, Rutgers consists of three campuses in Newark, Camden and New Brunswick, including 27 schools and colleges serving more than 50,000 students at all levels through postdoctoral studies; the main campus is on College Avenue.

THE RUTGERS GARDENS

Rutgers University, 112 Ryder's Lane (Route 1), New Brunswick, 732-932-8451; www.rutgersgardens.rutgers.edu

Here, you find extensive gardens including the largest display of American hollies, shrub collections, Rhododendron and Azaleas, evergreens and more.

Tour Admission: adults $10, seniors $8, children $5; Saturday, adults $12, seniors $10, children $5. Monday-Saturday.

SPECIAL EVENT
MIDDLESEX COUNTY FAIR
Cranbury-South River Road, East Brunswick, 732-257-8858;
www.middlesexcountyfair.org

This county fair features a lumberjack show, a magic show, the Victoria Circus, carnival rides, games, live entertainment and food and drink. August.

WHERE TO STAY
★★★CROWNE PLAZA HOTEL SOMERSET-BRIDGEWATER
110 Davidson Ave., Somerset, 732-560-0500, 877-227-6963;
www.crowneplaza.com/somersetnj

Sleep comfortably on the Crowne Plaza Hotel Somerset's 300 thread-count sheets. And if you can pull the kids away from the hotel's connecting indoor/outdoor pool, you can visit nearby attractions, including Six Flags Great Adventure, golf courses and Rutgers University. The Garden State Exhibit Center and Ukrainian Cultural Center are adjacent to the hotel.

440 rooms. Restaurant, bar. Business center. Fitness center. Pool. Pets accepted. Tennis. $151-250

★★DOUBLETREE HOTEL
200 Atrium Drive, Somerset, 732-469-2600, 800-222-8733;
www.somerset.doubletree.com

364 rooms. Restaurant, bar. Business center. Fitness center. Pool. Tennis. $151-250

★★★HILTON EAST BRUNSWICK
3 Tower Center Blvd., East Brunswick, 732-828-2000, 800-445-8667; www.hilton.com

The Hilton East Brunswick offers spacious guest rooms with high-speed Internet access and the Hilton's Serenity Collection bedding that features pillow-top mattresses and luxurious bed linens. Nearby attractions include Princeton University and Six Flags Great Adventure Theme Park.

405 rooms. Restaurant, bar. Business center. Fitness center. Pool. Pets accepted. $151-250

★★★HYATT REGENCY NEW BRUNSWICK
2 Albany St., New Brunswick, 732-873-1234, 800-233-1234; www.hyatt.com

This property is located downtown on a six-acre lot, midway between New York and Philadelphia. The central location offers easy access to shopping, restaurants and nearby attractions. Spacious guest rooms offer luxurious bedding, pillow-top mattresses, Internet access, an iPod dock, and a complimentary newspaper delivered in the morning.

288 rooms. Restaurant, bar. Business center. Fitness center. Pool. $151-250

WHERE TO EAT
★★DELTA'S
19 Dennis St., New Brunswick, 732-249-1551; www.deltasrestaurant.com
American. Dinner. Closed Monday. Reservations recommended. Bar. $16-35

★★★THE FROG AND THE PEACH

29 Dennis St., New Brunswick, 732-846-3216; www.frogandpeach.com

Housed in a converted factory, this restaurant has been in business since 1983 and features painted brick walls and exposed ductwork. Entrées include summer mushroom and local chard strudel with goat cheese and Jersey tomato emulsion; and Moroccan-spiced lamb sirloin with corn and garlic flan, popcorn shoots and pine nut yogurt sauce.

American. Lunch (Monday-Friday), dinner. Reservations recommended. Outdoor seating. Children's menu. Bar. $36-85

★★MAKEDA ETHIOPIAN RESTAURANT

338 George St., New Brunswick, 732-545-5115; www.makedas.com

Ethiopian. Lunch (Monday-Saturday), dinner, late-night. Bar. $16-35

★★THE OLD BAY

61-63 Church St., New Brunswick, 732-246-3111; www.oldbayrest.com

French Creole. Dinner, late-night. Closed Sunday. Outdoor seating. Children's menu. Bar. $16-35

★★★STAGE LEFT RESTAURANT

5 Livingston Ave., New Brunswick, 732-828-4444; www.stageleft.com

Since 1992, Stage Left has been serving up creative American cuisine in a warm setting. Selections from an extensive wine list can be paired with menu options such as pistachio-studded organic free-range chicken breast, pan-roasted cod and apple cider-braised pork belly. Wine-tasting dinners with guest speakers and festive brunches are among the special events offered.

American. Lunch (Friday), dinner. Reservations recommended. Outdoor seating. Bar. $36-85

NEWARK

See also Elizabeth, Jersey City, West Orange

Once a strict Puritan settlement, Newark has grown to become the largest city in the state and one of the country's leading manufacturing cities. Major insurance firms and banks have large offices in Newark, dominating the city's financial life. Newark was the birthplace of Stephen Crane, author of *The Red Badge of Courage*, and Mary Mapes Dodge, author of the children's book *Hans Brinker*, or the Silver Skates. Newark is also an educational center with Newark College of Rutgers University, College of Medicine and Dentistry of New Jersey, New Jersey Institute of Technology, Seton Hall Law School and Essex County College.

WHAT TO SEE
MILITARY PARK

Broad Street, Newark

Located on Broad Street between Rector Street and Raymond Boulevard, this Military Park was originally planned to be a training area for soldiers in 1667. There are a few significant sculptures here including the Wars of America monument by Gutzon Borglum and a bust of John F. Kennedy. Another relevant staute by Borglum is a statue of Abraham Lincoln at the Essex County Courthouse.

MINOR BASILICA OF THE SACRED HEART

89 Ridge St., Newark, 973-484-4600; www.cathedralbasilica.org

French Gothic in design, the Cathedral Basilica of the Sacred Heart resembles the cathedral at Rheims.

Services: Monday-Friday 7:30 a.m., 5:30 p.m., Sunday 8:45 a.m., noon.

NEW JERSEY HISTORICAL SOCIETY

52 Park Place, Newark, 973-596-8500; www.jerseyhistory.org

This museum has collections of paintings, prints, furniture and decorative arts. Also, there is a reference and research library of state and local history including manuscripts, documents and maps.

Admission: $4 (suggested donation). Society: Tuesday-Saturday 10 a.m.-5 p.m. Library: Wednesday-Thursday, Saturday noon-5 p.m.

NEW JERSEY PERFORMING ARTS CENTER

1 Center St., Newark, 973-297-5857, 888-466-5722, 973-642-8989; www.njpac.org

This is the home to New Jersey Symphony Orchestra.

See Web site for schedule and ticket information.

NEWARK MUSEUM

49 Washington St., Newark, 973-596-6550; www.newarkmuseum.org

This museum of art and science features changing exhibitions including American paintings and sculpture; American and European decorative arts; classical art; and more. Also here are the Junior Museum, Mini Zoo, Dreyfuss Planetarium and the Newark Fire Museum. There are special programs, lectures, concerts and a café serving lunch.

Admission: adults $10, children, seniors and students $6. Planetariaum: adults $3, children under 12, seniors and students $2. Wednesday-Friday noon-5 p.m.; October-June, Saturday-Sunday 10 a.m.-5 p.m.; July-September, Saturday-Sunday noon-5 p.m.

PLUME HOUSE

407 Broad St., Newark, 973-483-8202

The current rectory of the adjoining House of Prayer Episcopal Church is thought to have been standing as early as 1710, which would make it the oldest building in Newark.

SYMPHONY HALL

1020 Broad St., Newark, 973-643-4550; www.newarksymphonyhall.org

In 1925 this 2,811-seat auditorium was built by the Shriner's Salaam Temple, it is now home to the New Jersey State Opera, the New Jersey Ballet Company, the Theatre of Universal Images and the New Jersey Symphony Orchestra. Also here is the famous Terrace Ballroom, which is a large meeting space used for dance classes, weddings and more.

See Web site for schedules and ticket information.

WHERE TO STAY
★★★NEWARK LIBERTY INTERNATIONAL AIRPORT MARRIOTT
Newark International Airport, Newark, 973-623-0006, 800-882-1037; www.marriott.com
Located on the premises of Newark Airport, this Marriott features a connecting indoor/outdoor pool, complimentary coffee in the lobby, laundry, dry cleaning and babysitting services. Plush guest rooms offer convenience and luxury with high-quality, 300 thread-count linens, fluffy down duvets, and high-speed Internet access. The hotel's three restaurants—Mangiare di Casa, JW Prime Steakhouse and Chatfields English Pub—cater to all tastes. Area attractions include Ellis Island and the Statue of Liberty, the Jersey Gardens Outlet Mall and Six Flags Great Adventure.
591 rooms. Restaurant, bar. Business center. Fitness center. Pool. $151-250

OCEAN CITY
See also Atlantic City
Families from all over the country come to this popular resort year after year, as do conventions and religious conferences. In accordance with its founder's instructions, liquor cannot be sold here. Ocean City is an island that lies between the Atlantic Ocean and Great Egg Harbor. It has eight miles of beaches, more than two miles of boardwalk, an enclosed entertainment auditorium on the boardwalk and excellent swimming, fishing, boating, golf and tennis.

WHAT TO SEE
OCEAN CITY BEACH AND BOARDWALK
Ocean City; www.ocnj.us
There are 42 Ocean City beaches covering eight miles. A lot of the beaches have lifeguards from Memorial Day through Labor Day. Three of the beaches are suitable for surfing including Waverly, 7th and 16th. The Ocean City Boardwalk runs from St. James Place to 24th Street covering 2 1/2 miles of shops, restuarants, and entertainment from arcades to miniature golf. The Music Pier is also along the Boardwalk and features concerts throughout the year. Beach-goers must have a beach tag which can be purchased on the listed Web site.
Daily fee $5, weekly fee $10.

OCEAN CITY HISTORICAL MUSEUM
1735 Simpson Ave., Ocean City, 609-399-1801; www.ocnjmuseum.org
This Historical Museum features Victorian furnishings and fashions; a doll exhibit, a local shipwreck, historical tours and a research library. There is also a gift shop here.
Admission: Free. November-May, Tuesday-Friday 10 a.m.-4 p.m., Saturday 11 a.m.-2 p.m.; May-November, Monday-Friday 10 a.m.-4 p.m., Saturday 11 a.m.-2 p.m.

SPECIAL EVENTS
BOARDWALK ART SHOW
Arts Center, 1735 Simpson Ave., Ocean City, 609-399-7628;
www.oceancityartscenter.org

IRONBOUND NEWARK

Once moribund, Newark is experiencing a renaissance. The city now offers fascinating history, modern facilities and some of the finest Spanish/Portugese dining around. This walk first covers the historic Ironbound section. Named for the surrounding railroads, this area has been the settling site for immigrants since the 1830s and is now home to about 40 ethnic groups. The walk then continues into the resurgent Four Corners/Military Park section.

Start at Pennsylvania Station, built in 1933 and beautifully decorated with Art Deco wall reliefs and ceiling sculptures. Walk east on Market Street, passing diminutive Mother Cabrini Park, site of a bust of Jose Marti, liberator of Cuba. Turn right onto Union Street. In one block, at Ferry Street, Our Lady of Mount Carmel Roman Catholic Church stands opposite at McWhorter Street. Originally opened in 1848, this building is now home to the Ironbound Educational and Cultural Center. Turn left onto Ferry Street. This is the commercial heart of the Ironbound, and is filled with shops and restaurants.

Turn right onto Prospect Street. Number 76 is the Gothic Revival-style Christ Episcopal Church, completed in 1850. Destroyed by vandalism and fire, it was restored in 1978 and now serves as the Chancery Professional Center. At the corner of Lafayette Street stands St. Joseph's Roman Catholic Church, circa 1858, now called Immaculate Heart of Mary. Its basement holds hidden catacombs that are replicas of those found in Rome, complete with crypts featuring wax likenesses of Spanish saints. Turn left on Lafayette and walk six blocks to Van Duren. Turn right two blocks to Independence Park. Covering 12 1/2 acres, this was one of the city's first neighborhood parks. Turn left on New York Avenue, go one block and turn right on Pulaski Street. Pass East Side High School, and come to St. Casimir's Roman Catholic Church, built in 1919 in the Italian Renaissance style. Continue to Chestnut Street and turn right. Five blocks down the road stand the remains of the Murphy Varnish Company, once comprising six major structures; note the carving of a Roman chariot carrying a can of Murphy Varnish on the west side of the building.

Follow Chestnut under the railroad and across McCarter Highway to Broad Street. Turn right and walk through the business district to the Prudential Building at the heart of the Four Corners Historic District. Among the many historic buildings are the National Newark Building (744 Broad St.), a 34-story neoclassical structure completed in 1930, and at 1180 Raymond Blvd. another Depression-era skyscraper. In two more blocks, Military Park appears. Walk on the left side of the park to the New Jersey Historical Society (52 Park Place), which has an onsite museum and is next door to the historic Robert Treat Hotel. At the end of the park on Center Street stands the architecturally stunning New Jersey Performing Arts Center. Opened in 1997, it has become a world-renowned performance space. Return on Center Street towards Military Park, turn left on Central Street and go two blocks to the Newark Museum (49 Washington St.), site of the largest collection of Tibetan art outside Tibet, the Dreyfus Planetarium and the historic 1885 Ballantine House

This art show displays international and regional artists.
August.

CONCERTS AT MUSIC PIER

Music Pier, Highways 152 and 40, Ocean City, 732-316-1095

Head to Music Pier along the Boardwalk for concerts including music by the Ocean City Pops orchestra and dance band, along with other performers. July-October.

MISS CRUSTACEAN HERMIT CRAB BEAUTY PAGEANT

Sixth St. Beach, Ocean City, 609-525-9300; www.oceancityvacation.com

This annual contest is for the Miss Crustacean Hermit Crab Beauty contest for crustaceans. There are also hermit crab races.
Early August.

NIGHT IN VENICE

Ocean City, 609-525-9300; www.oceancityvacation.com

This decorated boat parade features many boats and runs from Longport Bridge to Tennessee Avenue.
Mid-July.

WHERE TO STAY
★★BEACH CLUB HOTEL

1280 Boardwalk, Ocean City, 609-399-8555; www.beachclubhotel.com

82 rooms. Closed mid-October-April. Restaurant. Pool. Beach. $151-250

★★PORT-O-CALL HOTEL

1510 Boardwalk, Ocean City, 609-399-8812, 800-334-4546; www.portocallhotel.com

99 rooms. Pool. Beach. $61-150

★★SERENDIPITY BED & BREAKFAST

712 E. Ninth St., Ocean City, 609-399-1554, 800-842-8544; www.serendipitynj.com

6 rooms. Complimentary breakfast. $61-150

PARAMUS

See also Hackensack, Paterson

Now a well-known shopping area with a handful of sizeable malls, Paramus was once a Dutch farm community. Beginning in the Revolutionary War, the city was an important hub of transportation and western Paramus was headquarters for the Continental Army. Paramus has grown as a residential community from 4,000 inhabitants in 1946 to more than 25,000 today.

WHAT TO SEE
NEW JERSEY CHILDREN'S MUSEUM

599 Valley Health Plaza, Paramus, 201-262-5151; www.njcm.com

This museum for children features interactive displays on aviation, firefighting as well as a TV studio, a ballet studio, grocery store and hospital.
Admission: $10, children under 1 free. Monday-Friday 10 a.m.-6 p.m., Saturday 10 a.m.-6 p.m.; May-September, Saturday-Sunday 10 a.m.-5 p.m.

VAN SAUN COUNTY PARK

216 Forest Ave., Paramus, 201-336-7275; www.co.bergen.nj.us

This county park has a fishing lake, bike trail, tennis courts, horseshoes, shuffleboard, an ice-skating rink, sledding, picnicking, concessions, playgrounds, ball fields and a soccer field. There is also a zoo here with train rides and pony rides. There is a garden surrounding historic Washington Spring.
Park: Daily dawn-dusk. Zoo: Daily10 a.m.-4:30 p.m.

WHERE TO STAY
★★CROWNE PLAZA HOTEL AT PARAMUS PARK
601 From Road, Paramus, 201-262-6900, 800-972-3160; www.crowneplaza.com
120 rooms. Restaurant, bar. Fitness center. $61-150

WHERE TO EAT
★★★THE PARK STEAKHOUSE
151 Kinderkamack Road, Park Ridge, 201-930-1300; www.theparksteakhouse.com
This classic American steakhouse is a local favorite, specializing in 21-day dry-aged sirloins (aged on premises) and a variety of fish entrées. The chef uses the freshest ingredients in the creative cuisine, and the wine list includes nearly 200 selections.
Steak. Lunch (Monday-Friday), dinner. Bar. $36-85

PATERSON
See also Hackensack, Wayne
Named after Governor William Paterson, this city owes its present and historic eminence as an industrial city to Alexander Hamilton. He was the first to realize the possibility of harnessing the Great Falls of the Passaic River for industrial purposes. As Secretary of the Treasury, he helped to form the Society for Establishment of Useful Manufactures in 1791, and a year later he was instrumental in choosing Paterson as the site of its initial ventures. Paterson was the country's major silk-producing town in the late 1800s. Today, it is a diversified industrial center. The area surrounding the Great Falls is now being restored and preserved as a historic district.

WHAT TO SEE
AMERICAN LABOR MUSEUM-BOTTO HOUSE NATIONAL LANDMARK
83 Norwood St., Haledon, 973-595-7953
The history of the working class is presented through restored period rooms, changing exhibits and ethnic gardens. Tours and workshops are offered. Admission: $3 (suggested donation). Museum: Wednesday-Saturday 1-5 p.m.

GARRET MOUNTAIN RESERVATION
Rifle Camp Road and Mountain Avenue, Paterson, 973-881-4832
A 575-acre woodland park on a 502-foot-high plateau. There is a fishing pond (stocked with trout), boat dock, rowboats and paddleboats. There are also plenty of trails and picnic groves. The Garret Mountin Equestrian Center offers horseback riding lessons and bridle paths. Also located here is Lambert Castle and its Observation Tower.
Daily.

GREAT FALLS HISTORIC DISTRICT CULTURAL CENTER
65 McBride Ave., Paterson, Location: City Hall Room 155 Market St., Paterson, NJ, 973-321-9587; www.patersonnj.gov
The Great Falls district includes 77-foot-high falls, a park and picnic area, a renovated raceway system and restored 19th-century buildings.
Monday-Friday 8:30 a.m.-4.30 p.m.

LAMBERT CASTLE

Garret Mountain Reservation, 3 Valley Road, Paterson, 973-247-0085;
www.lambertcastle.com

Built by an English immigrant who rose to wealth as a silk manufacturer, the 1893 castle of brownstone and granite houses a local history museum, restored period rooms, an art-history gallery and a library.
Grounds: Daily dawn-dusk.

RIFLE CAMP PARK

Rifle Camp Road, West Paterson, 973-881-4832

This 158-acre park is 584 feet above sea level. It includes nature and geology trails, nature center with astronomical observatory, walking paths, a fitness course and picnic areas.
Daily.

WHERE TO STAY

★★★THE INN AT MILLRACE POND

313 Johnsonberg Road, Route 519 N., Hope, 908-459-4884, 800-746-6467;
www.innatmillracepond.com

This colonial-style bed and breakfast features guest rooms in three historic buildings: the Grist Mill, built in 1769 by Moravian settlers; the Miracle House, built in the early 19th century and the Stone Cottage, the home of the mill's caretaker. Some accommodations feature fireplaces, televisions and whirlpool tubs. The onsite restaurant offers a freshly prepared, contemporary American menu for dinner, while the Colonial Tavern features casual pub fare in 18th-century surroundings.
17 rooms. Complimentary breakfast. Restaurant, bar. $151-250

★★★SHERATON MAHWAH HOTEL

1 International Blvd., Mahwah, 201-529-1660, 800-325-3535;
www.sheraton.com/crossroads

Located nearly 35 miles from Newark International Airport and not far from New York City, this hotel offers spacious rooms with a garden or a fountain view as well as an indoor heated pool, tennis courts, two restaurants and two lounges. Rooms have the Sheraton Sweet Sleeper Bed, oversized desks, Internet access, and microwaves. Golfers will enjoy the nearby courses, Central Valley Golf Club and Darlington County Course.
225 rooms. Restaurant, bar. Fitness center. Pool. Tennis. Pets accepted. $151-250

PRINCETON

See also Trenton

In 1776, the first State Legislature of New Jersey met in Princeton University's Nassau Hall. Washington and his troops surprised and defeated a superior British Army in the 1777 Battle of Princeton. From June to November 1783, Princeton was the new nation's capital. Around the same time, Washington was staying at Rockingham in nearby Rocky Hill, where he wrote and delivered his famous "Farewell Orders to the Armies."

Princeton's life is greatly influenced by the university, which opened here in 1756; at that time it was known as the College of New Jersey. In 1896, on the 150th anniversary of its charter, the institution became Princeton University. Woodrow Wilson, the first president of the university who was not a clergyman, held the office from 1902 to 1910. Princeton is also the home of the Institute for Advanced Study, where Albert Einstein spent the last years of his life.

WHAT TO SEE
BAINBRIDGE HOUSE
158 Nassau St., Princeton, 609-921-6748; www.princetonhistory.org
Circa 1766, this is the birthplace of commander of the *USS Constitution* during the War of 1812. Here, you'll find changing exhibits on Princeton history, a research library and museum shops. There is also a walking tours of historic district offered.
Tuesday-Sunday noon-4 p.m.

KUSER FARM MANSION AND PARK
390 Newkirk Ave., Princeton, 609-890-3630; www.state.nj.us
This is the farm and 1890s summer mansion of Fred Kuser. There are more than 20 rooms open, which include many original furnishings. The grounds consist of 22 acres with original buildings including coachman's house, chicken house and tennis pavilion. There is also a park with picnic areas, quoit courts, lawn bowling, walking trails, a formal garden and gazebo.
Admission: Free. Tours: May-November, Thursday-Sunday; February-April, Saturday and Sunday; limited hours, call for schedule.

MCCARTER THEATRE
91 University Place, Princeton, 608-258-2787, 888-278-7932; www.mccarter.org
This leading professional repertory company performs classical and modern drama, concerts, and ballet. There are also other special programs offered. See Web site for schedule and ticket information.

MORVEN MUSEUM & GARDEN
55 Stockton St., Princeton, 609-924-8144; www.historicmorven.org
Circa 1750 house of Richard Stockton, signer of the Declaration of Independence and the once home of the former New Jersey governor. Galleries display permanent and temporary artwork.
Admission: adults $5, seniors and students $4. April-October, Wednesday-Friday 11 a.m.-3 p.m., Saturday-Sunday noon-4 p.m. Tours: Wednesday-Friday 11:15 a.m.; 12:15, 1:15, 2:15 p.m., Saturday-Sunday 12:15, 1:15, 2:15, 3:15 p.m.

NASSAU HALL
Princeton University, Princeton, 609-258-3000; www.princeton.edu
Buily in 1756, Nassau Hall has provided all college facilities, classrooms, dormitories, library and prayer hall for about 50 years. New Jersey's first legislature met here in 1776, and the Continental Congress met here in 1783, when Princeton was the capital. During the Revolution, it served as a bar-

SKYLANDS AT RINGWOOD STATE PARK

Skylands, the official state garden of New Jersey, covers 96 acres, with Skylands Manor House at its center. The Tudor-style manor house, circa 1922, holds an outstanding collection of antique stained-glass medallions set in leaded windows. Guided house tours are offered one Sunday each month from March through December (973-962-9534).

The walking here is largely on marked dirt paths, with some paved drives and paths. Start at the Visitors Center/Carriage House and pick up a self-guided tour brochure. Walk first to the right (in the general direction of Parking Lot A), skirting the manor house counter-clockwise. The Winter Garden contains New Jersey's largest Jeffery pine, a century-old upright beech and an elegant weeping beech. The Japanese umbrella pine is distinctive for its dark green needles. Also on display here are Atlas cedars and an Algerian fir, a tree that produces seven-inch-tall, purple standing cones.

Walk around the house along the lawn to the Terrace Garden. This garden comprises five terraces, each with its own particular ambience. Continue past a pair of Sweet Bay Magnolias to the third level. Here the centerpiece is a rectangular reflecting pool that in summer displays water lilies and tropical fish. Surrounding it is a large collection of azaleas and rhododendrons that bloom in many colors. Next comes the Summer Garden, home to annuals and day lilies, followed by the final terrace level, the Peony Garden.

Walk to the left into the Lilac Garden, which peaks in mid-May. Step onto Maple Avenue, the paved lane, and walk back toward the house. On the right, you'll see the Perennial Garden. A constant flow of color is maintained here from March until November. Just beyond that stands the Annual Garden, a frequently changing formal garden centered on a 16th-century Italian marble well. Move from there to the right, turn around and walk along Crab Apple Vista, a 1,600-foot grassy corridor of 166 Carmine crab apple trees that erupts into full bloom in early- to mid-May. At the end of the Vista stands a series of sculptures known as the "Four Continents Statues" and to the left, a collection of horse chestnut trees.

Turn left at the horse chestnut trees, and another world appears, revealing woodland paths that travel past swan ponds and through a bog. The paths also travel through a cactus collection, a wildflower garden and a heather garden and end at a colorful yet formal Rhododendron Display Garden. From here, follow East Cottage Road as it winds its way back to the Carriage House.

racks and hospital for Continental and British troops.

PRINCETON BATTLE MONUMENT

Monument Drive and Stockton streets, Princeton, 609-921-0074; www.state.nj.us

The work of Frederick W. MacMonnies, this 50-foot block of Indiana limestone commemorates the famous 1777 battle when George Washington's troops defeated the British.

PRINCETON CEMETERY

Nassau Presbyterian Church, Witherspoon and Wiggens streets, Princeton,
609-924-1369; www.princetonol.com/groups/cemetery

Buried in the Presidents' Plot are 11 university Presidents, including Aaron Burr, Sr., Jonathan Edwards and John Witherspoon. There is a monument to Grover Cleveland and the grave of Paul Tulane, in whose honor Tulane University was named.

PRINCETON UNIVERSITY

1 Nassau Hall, Princeton, 609-258-3603; www.princeton.edu

Founded in 1746, this Ivy League college is the fourth oldest college in the U.S. It has 4,850 undergraduate students and 2,295 graduate students and has been coeducational since 1969. It's one of the leading research universities and has a strong financial aid program. The University provides an Orange Key campus tour guide service in which guides show the visitor points of interest on the main campus.

THE PUTNAM SCULPTURES AT PRINCETON

Princeton University, 1 Nassau Hall, Princeton; www.princton.edu

One of the largest modern outdoor sculpture showcases in the country, with 19 sculptures on display throughout the campus, including pieces by Picasso, Moore, Noguchi, Calder and Lipchitz. The collection stands as a memorial for Princeton Alumni John, Putnam Jr., who died in World War II.

WOODROW WILSON SCHOOL OF PUBLIC AND INTERNATIONAL AFFAIRS

Princeton University, Robertson Hall Princeton, 609-258-4831; wws.princeton.edu

This school was inspired by Woodrow Wilson and designed by Minoru Yamasaki, the architect of the World Trade Center. The reflecting pool and "Fountain of Freedom" is by James Fitzgerald.

WHERE TO STAY

★★DOUBLETREE HOTEL PRINCETON

4355 U.S. Route 1, Princeton, 609-452-2400; www.doubletree.com

238 rooms. Restaurant, bar. Business center. Fitness center. Pool. $151-250

★★★HYATT REGENCY PRINCETON

102 Carnegie Center, Princeton, 609-987-1234, 800-233-1234; www.hyatt.com

This hotel is nestled on 16 acres of landscaped property just one mile from the city's business center and near the Princeton Junction Train Station. Guests receive a complimentary shuttle to anywhere within a five-mile radius of the property.

347 rooms. Restaurant, bar. Business center. Fitness center. Pool. Tennis. $151-250

★★NASSAU INN

10 Palmer Square, Princeton, 609-921-7500, 800-862-7728; www.nassauinn.com

203 rooms. Restaurant, bar. Business center. Fitness center. Pets accepted. $61-150

★★★PRINCETON MARRIOTT HOTEL & CONFERENCE CENTER AT FORRESTAL

100 College Road, East, Princeton, 609-452-7800, 800-943-6709; www.marriott.com

Located on 25 wooded acres, this newly renovated hotel offers a full-service spa, The Spa at Forrestal, along with a health club, pool and jogging and recreational facilities. Spacious guest rooms are bright and cheery and feature a work desk, refrigerator, and wireless Internet access. The Revive bed features 300 thread-count linens and plush pillows and comforters. Enjoy a burger and a cold beer at Barley's Pub or opt for a heartier meal at the Fireside Grill, a casual steakhouse.

300 rooms. Restaurant, bar. Business center. Fitness center. Pool. $61-150

WHERE TO EAT
★★ALCHEMIST AND BARRISTER
28 Witherspoon, Princeton, 609-924-5555; www.alchemistandbarrister.com
American. Lunch (Monday-Saturday), dinner, late-night, Sunday brunch. Outdoor seating. Bar. $36-85

★★★TRE PIANI
120 Rockingham Row, Princeton, 609-452-1515; www.trepiani.com
In its dining room, bistro and banquet space, Tre Piani (meaning three floors in Italian) serves entrées such as grilled filet mignon with wild mushroom ragu and a crispy potato and cheese galette; prosciutto-wrapped tuna loin with white bean stew and cherry tomatoes; and breast of Muscovy duck with duck confit and walnut risotto.
Italian, Mediterranean. Lunch (Monday-Friday), dinner. Closed Sunday. Outdoor seating. Bar. $36-85

RED BANK
See also Gateway National Recreation Area (Sandy Hook Unit)
Formed in 1870, Red Bank is a historic community on the shores of the Navesink River in New Jersey's Monmouth County.

WHERE TO STAY
★★COURTYARD LINCROFT RED BANK
245 Half Mile Road, Red Bank, 732-530-5552, 800-321-2211; www.courtyard.com
146 rooms. Fitness center. Pool. $61-150

WHERE TO EAT
★★2 SENZA RISTORANTE
2 Bridge Ave., Building 5, Red Bank, 732-758-0999; www.2senza.com
Italian, Mediterranean. Lunch, dinner. Closed Monday. Outdoor seating. $16-35

★★★FROMAGERIE
26 Ridge Road, Rumson, 732-842-8088; www.fromagerierestaurant.com
This romantic French restaurant first opened in 1972. Classical French cuisine is paired with an award-winning selection of wines, some of which may be sampled during special gourmet wine dinners.
French. Lunch (Friday), dinner. Closed Monday. Lunch, dinner, Sunday Brunch. Bar. $36-85

★GAETANO'S
10 Wallace St., Red Bank, 732-741-1321; www.gaetanosredbank.com
Italian. Lunch (Monday-Saturday), dinner. Outdoor seating. $16-35

★★★MOLLY PITCHER INN

Oyster Point Hotel, 88 Riverside Ave., Red Bank, 732-747-2500, 800-221-1372;
www.mollypitcher-oysterpoint.com

Located on the waterfront in the Oyster Point Hotel on the banks of the Navensink river, this sophisticated restaurant serves up dishes like country duck with smoked bacon, roasted pearl onions and couscous or salmon with California avocado mashed potatoes and overnight tomatoes.
Lunch, dinner, Sunday brunch. Reservations recommended. $36-85

★OAK BRIDGE TAVERN

115 Oakland St., Red Bank, 732-842-4830; www.oakbridgetavern.com

German. Dinner. Closed Monday. Outdoor seating. Bar. $16-35

★★★THE RAVEN & THE PEACH

740 River Road, Fair Haven, 732-747-4666; www.ravenandthepeach.net

Guests will enjoy dining at this popular, elegant restaurant, perfect for a romantic evening. Enjoy a lighter lunch menu in the Tea Room including sandwiches, appetizers and salads. For dinner, try the macadamia nut and banana-crusted halibut with watermelon-scented basmati rice and aspiration toasted coconut, jumbo lump crab and tropical fruit chutney.
French. Lunch (Monday-Saturday), dinner. Outdoor seating. Reservations recommended. Bar. $36-85

RUTHERFORD

See also Jersey City, Paterson, Newark

Only eight miles from New York City, Rutherford is popular for commuters to and from the city. It's home to Giants Stadium, the Arena, home of the New Jersey Nets, the Meadowlands, home of the New York Jets, and Meadowlands Racetrack. Downtown Rutherford features restaurants and bars for those looking to enjoy the nightlife.

WHAT TO SEE

MEADOWLANDS RACETRACK

50 State Route 120, East Rutherford, 201-843-2446; www.thebigm.com

The suburban leafy Meadowlands complex offers fine thoroughbred racing from September through mid-December and harness racing for the remainder of the year.
Wednesday-Sunday.

NEW YORK GIANTS (NFL)

Giants Stadium, 50 Highway 120, East Rutherford, 201-935-8111; www.giants.com

New York's professional football team, the New York Giants play in East Rutherford's Giants Stadium, part of the Meadowlands.

NEW YORK JETS (NFL)

The Meadowlands, 50 Highway 120, East Rutherford, 201-583-7000, 800-469-5387;
www.newyorkjets.com

New York's other professional football team, the New York Jets will start their new 2010 season in their own home stadium, the New Jets Stadium, located in the Meadowlands, featuring top-of-the-line amenities.

NEW JERSEY NETS (NBA)

Izod Center, 50 Highway 120, East Rutherford, 201-935-3900; www.nba.com/
nets;www.nhl.com/devils

New Jersey's professional basketball team, the New Jersey Nets play at the Izod Center, which is also a concert venue with state-of-the-art acoustics.

WHERE TO STAY

★FAIRFIELD INN EAST RUTHERFORD MEADOWLANDS

850 Paterson Plank Road, East Rutherford, 201-507-5222, 800-854-7897;
www.marriott.com

141 rooms. Complimentary breakfast. Fitness center. $61-150

★★★SHERATON MEADOWLANDS HOTEL AND CONFERENCE CENTER

2 Meadowlands Plaza, East Rutherford, 201-896-0500, 800-325-3535;
www.sheraton.com

Located just across the river, this newly renovated hotel is only minutes from Manhattan. Many guest rooms offer views of the city's sparkling skyline. Grab a cup of coffee from the full-service Starbucks onsite before heading out to shop at the nearby outlets, or hunker down in the Chairman's Grill for a hearty bite before the Giants game.

427 rooms. Restaurant, bar. Business center. Fitness center. Pool. Pets accepted. $61-150

SHORT HILLS

See also Elizabeth, Morristown, West Orange

Located within the township of Millburn, Short Hills is not far from New York City making is a popular spot to live for those commuting to the city for work. It ws actually built as planned commuter suburb. This small residential community features high-end shopping in it's downtown area, along with the Mall at Short Hills which also features high-end stores.

WHAT TO SEE

CORA HARTSHORN ARBORETUM AND BIRD SANCTUARY

324 Forest Drive S., Short Hills, 973-376-3587; www.hartshornarboretum.org

A 17-acre sanctuary with nature trails and guided walks. Stone House Museum features a range of nature exhibits.

Stone House: Monday-Friday 9 a.m.-4:30 p.m., Saturday 10 a.m.-11:30 a.m. Closed Sunday; August.

THE MALL AT SHORT HILLS

1200 Morris Turnpike, Short Hills, 973-376-7350; www.shopshorthills.com

This upscale mall features high-end stores including Nordstrom, Ann Taylor, Anya Hindmarch, Bloomingdale's, Betsey Johnson, Burberry, Cartier, Crate&Barrel, D&G, Fendi, French Connection, The Gap, J.Crew, Louis Vuitton, Neiman Marcus, Saks Fifth Avenue, Tiffany & Co., and Macy's.

Monday-Friday 10 a.m.-9 p.m., Saturday 10 a.m.-7 p.m., Sunday 11 a.m.-6 p.m.

PAPER MILL PLAYHOUSE

Brookside Drive and Old Shore Hills Road, Millburn, 973-376-4343; www.papermill.org

Originally opened in 1795 as the Thistle Paper Mill, the first theater was burned down by fire. After being rebuilt, it continued on until it was purchased in 1934 by Antoinette Scudder and then opened in 1938 as the Paper Mill Playhouse. It burned down again in 1980 and was rebuilt, again. Over the years, famous actors have graced this stage including Jean Stapleton, Shelley Winters, Chita Rivera, Carol Channing, Gene Wilder, Helen Hayes, Betty White, Maureen Stapleton, Patrick Swayze, and many others. It also has a theatre school and musical theatre conservatory.

WHERE TO STAY
★★★HILTON SHORT HILLS

41 John F. Kennedy Parkway, Short Hills, 973-379-0100, 800-445-8667;
www.hiltonshorthills.com

Executives visiting the New York metropolitan area appreciate this hotel's proximity to Manhattan, New Jersey's businesses and Newark airport—yet this hotel is not just a destination for corporate travelers. Located across from the fabulous Short Hills Mall, the Hilton Short Hills is also a favorite stomping ground for shopaholics. A beauty salon keeps guests properly primped, whereas a fitness center and pool are a boon for fitness enthusiasts. You can also dine at the Hilton's Terrace restaurant featuring American fare or opt for the Retreat, a more casual spot with lighter fare.

304 rooms. Restaurant, bar. Business center. Fitness center. Pool. Tennis. $151-250

★★★HOTEL WESTMINSTER

550 W. Mount Pleasant Ave., Livingston, 973-533-0600; www.westminsterhotel.net

The Hotel Westminster provides classic, sophisticated accommodations in the heart of Livingston. Guest rooms feature Egyptian cotton sheets and marble baths. The hotel also offers a well-equipped business center, state-of-the-art fitness facility, pool, jacuzzi and spa. They also have a "green" program in place, using organic room amenities, energy saving light bulbs, a recycling program and more.

183 rooms. Restaurant, bar. Business center. Fitness center. Pool. Spa. $151-250

SPRING LAKE

See also Trenton

This small town is located on the Jersey Shore and has two miles of beaches and a boardwalk. Downtown Spring Lake has plenty of shops to explore and restaurants to enjoy. It's a fun spot for a weekend get-away, a romantic weekend or family fun.

WHERE TO STAY
★★★THE HEWITT WELLINGTON HOTEL

200 Monmouth Ave., Spring Lake, 732-974-1212; www.hewittwellington.com

Situated on Spring Lake in the town of the same name, this Victorian-style hotel offers well-appointed rooms and suites with wireless Internet access, along with a wraparound porch on which guests can relax. Those who wish

to explore the area will find golf courses and tennis courts just a short distance away as well as unique shops and restaurants. The beach is just three blocks away.
16 rooms. Restaurant. Pool. $151-250

★★SPRING LAKE INN
104 Salem Ave., Spring Lake, 732-449-2010; www.springlakeinn.com
16 rooms. Complimentary breakfast. $151-250

WHERE TO EAT
★★THE BLACK TRUMPET
7 Atlantic Ave., Spring Lake, 732-449-4700; www.theblacktrumpet.com
American. Lunch, dinner. Reservations recommended. $16-35

★★★MILL INN
Old Mill Road, Spring Lake, 732-449-1800; www.themillatslh.com
For more than 65 years, the Mill has been a popular New Jersey dining destination, serving contemporary American cuisine such as fresh seafood and prime aged steaks. On special nights, the Mill features supper club events with comedians and musicians, as well as big band nights.
American. Dinner, Sunday brunch. Closed Monday. Reservations recommended. Outdoor seating. Bar. $16-35

TRENTON
See also Princeton
The capital of New Jersey since 1790, Trenton is one of the fastest-growing business and industrial areas in the country and has been a leading rubber-manufacturing center since colonial times.

WHAT TO SEE
COLLEGE OF NEW JERSEY

Trenton, 609-771-1855; www.tcnj.edu
Founded in 1855, this 289-acre wooded campus has 5,900 students and is located within a suburban community. This highly selective liberal arts college offers seven different schools in which students can study and has gained national recognition.

JOHNSON FERRY HOUSE STATE HISTORIC SITE
Washington Crossing State Park, 355 Washington Crossing, Titusville, 609-737-2515; www.state.nj.us
Located in Washington Crossing State Park, this building sheltered General Washington and some of his men on December 25, 1776 after they had crossed the Delaware from Pennsylvania. It is believed that the strategy for the attack on Trenton was discussed here.
Monday-Sunday 9 a.m.-4 p.m.

NEW JERSEY STATE MUSEUM
205 W. State St., Trenton, 609-292-6464; www.newjerseystatemuseum.org
Adjacent to the Capitol, this museum is like having four museums in one as it

covers archaeology and ethnology; cultural history, fine art; and natural history. Check out the Planetarium with cutting-edge technology used in their Full Dome Video which feels like you're looking at the entire solar system. Admission: Free. Tuesday-Sunday, Saturday 9 a.m.-5 p.m., Sunday noon-5 p.m.

OLD BARRACKS MUSEUM

Barrack St., Trenton, 609-396-1776; www.barracks.org
One of the finest examples of colonial barracks in the United States. Built between 1758 and 1759, it housed British, Hessian and Continental troops during the Revolutionary War. The museum contains restored soldiers' squad room, antique furniture, ceramics, firearms and dioramas. Tour guides in period costumes take you around and give you an overview of everything. Admission: adults $8, seniors and children 6-18 $6, children under 6 free. Daily 10 a.m.-5 p.m.

SESAME PLACE

100 Sesame Road, Langhorne, 215-752-7070; www.sesameplace.com
If your children love Oscar, Elmo and Big Bird, this family play park featuring characters from Sesame Street is the perfect place to take them. This park has everything kids will love: a water park, shows and parades, Sesame Street characters, rides and other attractions.
Admission: adults and children 2-18 $50.95, seniors $45.95, children under 2 free. Hours vary; see Web site for information.

SIX FLAGS GREAT ADVENTURE/SIX FLAGS WILD SAFARI ANIMAL PARK

1 Six Flags Blvd., Jackson, 732-928-1821; www.sixflags.com/national
This family entertainment center includes a 350-acre drive-through safari park with more than 1,200 free-roaming animals from six continents and a 125-acre theme park featuring more than 100 rides, shows and attractions.

Admission: $49.99, children $29.99, children under 3 free. April-August, hours vary; see Web site for information.

WASHINGTON CROSSING STATE PARK

355 Washington Crossing-Pennington Road, Titusville, 609-737-0623; www.state.nj.us
This 3,126-acre park commemorates the famous crossing on Christmas night, 1776, by the Continental Army under the command of General George Washington. There are nature trails, picnicking areas, campsites, a playground, a visitor center and a nature center. There's also an open-air summer theater. The Johnson Ferry House is also located here.
Admission: $5 per vehicle. Visitor center and Museum: Monday-Sunday 9 a.m.-4 p.m.

WILLIAM TRENT HOUSE

15 Market St., Trenton, 609-989-3027; www.williamtrenthouse.org
Trenton's oldest building, the William Trent House, built in 1719, is an example of Georgian architecture. It was the home of Chief Justice William Trent, for whom the city was named. Also here is a colonial garden filled with vegetables, and programs are offered to learn about gardening methods

of the 18th century.
Admission: Free. Daily 12:30-4 p.m.

SPECIAL EVENTS
REENACTMENT OF CROSSING OF THE DELAWARE
Washington Crossing State Park, 355 Washington Crossing Road, Trenton,
609-737-9303; www.state.nj.us

Witness this annual reenactment of Genearl Washington and his troops crossing the Delaware River. Every year, on the second Sunday in December, there is a dress rehearsal (crossing is at 1 p.m.) and other activities taking place in the village including speeches, demonstrations and more. Then, on Christmas Day, the actual crossing reenactment occurs (also at 1 p.m.). Second Sunday in December; December 25.

TRENTON KENNEL CLUB DOG SHOW
Mercer County Park, Old Trenton and South Post Roads, West Windsor Township,
609-448-6247; www.trentonkennelclub.net

This all-breed dog show and obedience trial takes place at Mercer County Park. In the past, there have been over 3,000 entries and more than 150 different breeds of dogs entered.
Early May.

WHERE TO STAY
★★★TRENTON MARRIOTT AT LAFAYETTE YARD
1 W. Lafayette St., Trenton, 609-421-4000, 888-796-4662; www.marriott.com

New Jersey's capital city is home to this downtown hotel, located near a number of historical sites, family activities, and sports facilities. Like all Marriott hotels, the Lafayette Yard is created with comfort in mind; guest rooms offer luxurious linens, fluffy comforters and pillows, and a host of amenities like in-room coffee and tea and high-speed Internet access. Archives Restaurant offers a casual and comfortable setting along with an appetizing American menu for breakfast, lunch, and dinner, while the Archives Bar and Lounge features lighter fare.

197 rooms. Restaurant, bar. Business center. Fitness center. $151-250

VERNON
See also Newark

Established in 1792, Vernon Township is located in Northern Sussex County which is filled with hills, lakes and natural beauty. It's a perfect spot to escape to from the city for a long weekend filled with pampering at a spa, skiing on a mountain, and enjoying the beautiful surroundings.

WHAT TO SEE
MOUNTAIN CREEK SKI RESORT
200 NJ 94, Vernon, 973-827-2000, 888-767-0762; www.mountaincreek.com

This ski resort has open-air gondola rides; four quad, triple, double chairlifts; three surface lifts, a rope tow; a skiing school, rentals, and snowmaking. When you're not skiing, there are cafeterias, restaurants, bars, and a night club to enjoy. There are forty-three runs, the highest with a vertical drop of 1,040 feet.

Admission: ticket prices vary. December-March, hours vary; see Web site for information.

MOUNTAIN CREEK WATERPARK
200 Route 94, Vernon, 973-827-2000, 888-767-0762;
www.mountaincreekwaterpark.com
Located only an hour and a half from New York City, this is the perfect week-end spot. This waterpark includes more than 40 water rides, including river rides, waterslides, High Tide Wavepool, tubing rides, and other water rides.
Admission: 48 inches and over $34.99, under 48 inches and seniors $24.99, children under 3 free. Mid-June-Labor Day, hours vary; see Web site for information.

WHERE TO STAY
★★★MINERALS RESORT AND SPA
2 Chamonix Drive, Vernon, 973-827-5996; www.crystalgolfresort.com
Located in the Kittatinny Mountains just an hour from New York City, Minerals Resort and Spa offers luxuriously appointed guest rooms and suites, all of which include unlimited access to the sports club on site. For those looking for more privacy, they also have condominiums with multiple bedrooms and fully-equipped kitchens.
175 rooms. Restaurant, bar. Business center. Fitness center. Pool. Golf. Tennis. $151-250

WEST ORANGE
See also Newark
West Orange is only 17 miles from New York City making it a convenient commuter suburb to live in if you don't want to live in the city. Downtown West Orange has restaurants and shops and the Turtle Back Zoo is located here.

WHAT TO SEE
EAGLE ROCK RESERVATION
Prospect and Eagle Rock avenues, West Orange, 973-268-3500;
www.essex-countynj.org
This reservation covers 408 acres with a 644-foot elevation in the Orange Mountains with streams, hills and valleys. It stretches from the Passaic River Valley east to New York City. Visitors can hike along the many trails, picnic, and ride along bridle paths. There is also a September 11, 2001 commemorative memorial here. Daily.

RICHARD J. CODEY ARENA AT SOUTH MOUNTAIN
560 Northfield Ave., West Orange, 973-731-3828; www.essexcountynj.org
This indoor ice rink hosts hockey games, special events and is open to the public for ice skating. It is the offical practicing and training home of the New Jersey Devils.
Admission: adults $6, children and seniors $4. Skate rental: $4. Call for public skating schedule.

THOMAS EDISON NATIONAL HISTORICAL PARK & EDISON LABO-RATORY

Main Street and Lakeside Avenue, West Orange, 973-324-9973; www.nps.gov/edis

This park is the site of Edison's home and laboratory. Built by Thomas A. Edison in 1887, this was his laboratory for 44 years. During that time, he was granted more than half of his 1,093 patents (an all-time record). Here he perfected the phonograph, motion picture camera and electric storage battery. There is a one-hour lab tour includes the chemistry lab and library and demonstrations of early phonographs. The visitor center has exhibits and films. Admission: $3. Estate Tour: Friday-Sunday noon-4 p.m. (on the hour). Grounds: Friday-Sunday 11:30 a.m.-5 p.m.

TURTLE BACK ZOO

560 Northfield Ave., West Orange, 973-731-5800; www.turtlebackzoo.com

This 20-acre park features animals in natural surroundings. Attractions include a river otter pool, the Essex Farm with farm animals and a miniature train ride. There is also Zoo Cafe and a covered picnic area.
Admission: adults $9, children and seniors $5, children under 2 free.
Monday-Saturday 10 a.m.-4:30 p.m., Sunday 11 a.m.-5:30 p.m.

WHERE TO EAT

★★★HIGHLAWN PAVILION

Eagle Rock Reservation, West Orange, 973-731-3463; www.highlawn.com

This restaurant offers a picturesque view of the Manhattan skyline. The 1909 building was restored and opened as a restaurant in 1986. A French rotisserie and Italian brick wood-burning oven bring out the flavors of the delightful American cuisine.
American. Lunch (Monday-Friday), dinner. Reservations recommended. Outdoor seating. Bar. $36-85

★★★THE MANOR

111 Prospect Ave., West Orange, 973-731-2360; www.themanorrestaurant.com

One of the most well-known (and most formal) restaurants in New Jersey, the Manor offers dishes such as Maine lobster braised in sweet butter with wild mushrooms, and English pea risotto; and filet mignon with truffled mashed potatoes, haricots verts, baby carrots, mushrooms and perigourdine sauce. You'll also find foie gras, oysters and caviar on the menu.
American. Lunch (Wednesday), dinner, Sunday brunch. Closed Monday. Reservations recommended. Bar. $36-85

WILDWOOD CREST

See also Cape May, Cape May Court House

Wildwood's busy boardwalk extends for approximately two miles along the five miles of protected sandy beach it shares with North Wildwood and Wildwood Crest, two neighboring resorts. The area offers swimming, waterskiing, ocean and bay fishing, boating, sailing, bicycling, golf, tennis and shuffleboard.

WHERE TO STAY
★★PAN AMERICAN HOTEL
5901 Ocean Ave., Wildwood Crest, 609-522-6936; www.panamericanhotel.com
78 rooms. Pool. Closed mid-October-mid-May. $151-250

★★PORT ROYAL HOTEL
6801 Ocean Ave., Wildwood Crest, 609-729-2000; www.portroyalhotel.com
100 rooms. Pool. Closed mid-October-April. $151-250

WHERE TO EAT
★★GARFIELD'S GIARDINO RISTORANTE
3800 Pacific Ave., Wildwood, 609-729-0120; www.garfieldsnj.net
Italian, seafood. Dinner. Children's menu. Bar. $16-35

PENNSYLVANIA

FROM ITS EASTERNMOST TIP NEAR BORDENTOWN, NEW JERSEY, TO ITS STRAIGHT WESTERN
boundary with Ohio and West Virginia, Pennsylvania's 300-mile stride across
the country covers a mountain-and-farm, river-and-stream, mine-and-mill
topography. Its cities, people and resources are just as diverse. In the eastern
part of the state, Philadelphia is a treasure chest of tradition and historical
shrines; in the west, Pittsburgh is a mighty museum of our nation's industrial
heritage. Pennsylvania miners dig nearly all the anthracite coal in the United
States and still work some of the oldest iron mines in the country. Oil employees work more than 19,000 producing wells, and 55,000 farm families
make up 20 percent of the Pennsylvania workforce.

The state is a leader in cigar leaf tobacco, apples, grapes, ice cream, chocolate products, mushrooms and soft drinks, plus factory and farm machinery,
electronic equipment, scientific instruments, watches, textile machines, railroad cars, ships, assorted metal products and electrical machinery.

Pennsylvania has also been a keystone of culture. The first serious music in
the colonies was heard in Bethlehem; today, both Pittsburgh and Philadelphia
have well-known symphonies. Celebrated art galleries, museums and more
than 140 institutions of higher learning (including the oldest medical school
in the United States at the University of Pennsylvania) are based here.

Swedes made the first settlement on this fertile land in 1643 at Tinicum
Island in the Delaware River. The territory became Dutch in 1655 and British in 1664. After Charles II granted William Penn a charter that made him
proprietor of "Pennsilvania," the Quaker statesman landed here in 1682 and
invested the land with his money and leadership. Commercial, agricultural
and industrial growth came quickly.

The Declaration of Independence was signed in Pennsylvania, and the Constitution was drafted here.

ALLENTOWN
See also Bethlehem, Easton, Kutztown, Quakertown
Situated in the heart of Pennsylvania Dutch country, Allentown is conveniently accessible via a network of major highways and is only 45 minutes away
from Philadelphia. Allentown was originally incorporated as Northampton-
town. The city later took the name of its founder, William Allen, a Chief
Justice of Pennsylvania. Allentown was greatly influenced by the Pennsylvania Germans who settled the surrounding countryside and helped the city
become the business hub for a rich agricultural community.

WHAT TO SEE
DORNEY PARK AND WILDWATER KINGDOM
3830 Dorney Park Road, Allentown, 610-395-3724; www.dorneypark.com
This amusement and water park is one of the country's oldest. A former fish
hatchery, the 200-acre park is home to nearly 100 rides, 11 water slides and
four roller coasters. Little ones can discover turtle fountains and squirt guns.
Bigger kids can climb and play on a submarine. Older kids may want to
torpedo through an enclosed tube or float slowly down a 1,600-foot winding

river. Just an hour from Philadelphia, the park also features song and dance revues and 40 food locations, including two dine-in restaurants.
Admission: adults $39.99, children and seniors $19.99. Daily; hours vary. Closed November-April.

LIBERTY BELL SHRINE
622 Hamilton St., Allentown, 610-435-4232; www.libertybellmuseum.org
This reconstructed Zion's church has a shrine in basement area where the Liberty Bell was hidden in 1777. It contains a full-size replica of the original bell along with other historical exhibits and an art collection.
Admission: Free. Mid-January-March Wednesday-Saturday noon-4 p.m.; April-November, Monday-Saturday noon-4 p.m.

TROUT HALL
414 W. Walnut St., Allentown, 610-435-4664; www.lchs.museum
The Georgian Colonial Trout Hall is the oldest house in city, built in 1770 and has been restored since. It has period rooms and a museum.
Admission: adults $5, children $3. June-October, Tuesday-Sunday 1-4 p.m.; April-May, September-November, Saturday-Sunday 1-4 p.m.

SPECIAL EVENTS
GREAT ALLENTOWN FAIR
Fairgrounds, 17th and Chew streets, Allentown, 610-435-7469; www.allentownfair.com
This annual fair features farm and commercial exhibits, rides, games, food and entertainment. Past performers in the grandstand have included Chicago, Jeff Dunham, Kelly Clarkson and Brad Paisley.
Early September.

MAYFAIR FESTIVAL OF THE ARTS
Cedar Beach Park, Allentown, 610-437-6900; www.mayfairfestival.org
Over Memorial Day weekend, for five days, Cedar Beach Park hosts this family arts festival with 150 free musical performances, art exhibits and food.
Memorial Day weekend.

WHERE TO STAY
★★FOUR POINTS BY SHERATON HOTEL & SUITES ALLENTOWN AIRPORT
3400 Airport Road, Allentown, 610-266-1000; www.fourpoints.com
147 rooms. Restaurant, bar. Business center. Fitness center. Pool. $61-150

★★★THE GLASBERN INN
2141 Pack House Road, Fogelsville, 610-285-4723; www.glasbern.com
Stay in rustic luxury, amidst both antique furnishings and all of the contemporary comforts. Built in the late 1800s on 100 acres near Allentown, the inn is housed in an old farm and includes a renovated farmhouse, barn, gate house and carriage house.
38 rooms. Complimentary breakfast. Business center. Fitness center. Pool. Spa. Pets accepted. $61-150

★HAMPTON INN

7471 Keebler Way, Allentown, 610-391-1500, 800-426-7866; www.hamptoninn.com

124 rooms. Complimentary breakfast. Fitness center. $61-150

★HOLIDAY INN ALLENTOWN CITY CENTER

4 Hamilton Mall, Allentown, 610-433-2221, 888-465-4329; www.ichotelsgroup.com

224 rooms. Restaurant, bar. Business center. Fitness center. Pool. Pets accepted. $61-150

WHERE TO EAT
★★BAY LEAF

935 W. Hamilton St., Allentown, 610-433-4211; www.allentownbayleaf.com

Thai. Lunch (Monday-Friday), dinner. Closed Sunday. Reservations recommended. Bar. $16-35

★★FEDERAL GRILL

536 Hamilton St., Allentown, 610-776-7600; www.federalgrill.com

Seafood. Lunch (Tuesday-Friday), dinner. Closed Sunday-Monday. Reservations recommended. Outdoor seating. Bar. $16-35

ALTOONA

See also Johnstown, State College

The rough, high Alleghenies ring this city, which was founded by the Pennsylvania Railroad. Altoona expanded rapidly after 1852, when the difficult task of spanning the Alleghenies with track to link Philadelphia and Pittsburgh was completed. The railroad shops still offer substantial employment for residents of the city and Blair County.

WHAT TO SEE
BAKER MANSION MUSEUM

3500 Oak Lane, Altoona, 814-942-3916; www.blairhistory.org

This stone Greek Revival house of an early ironmaster was built from 1844-1848. It is now occupied by Blair County Historical Society. It is furnished with hand-carved Belgian furniture of the period and displays transportation exhibits, gun collection, clothing and housewares.

Admission: adults $6, students and seniors $4.50, children 5-12 $3. June-September, Tuesday-Friday 11 a.m.-3 p.m., Saturday-Sunday 12:30-2:15 p.m. September-May, by appointment only.

CANOE CREEK STATE PARK

Altoona, 814-695-6807; www.dcnr.state.pa.us

This 950-acre park features a 155-acre lake where visitors can enjoy the swimming beach, fishing, boating, hiking, picnicking, cross-country skiing, sledding, ice boating and ice skating. There are also modern cabins available for rental.

DELGROSSOS PARK

Altoona, 814-684-3538; www.delgrossos.com

This theme park has more than 30 rides and attractions including an antique carousel, miniature golf and pony rides. There are also arcade games, picnic pavilions and restaurants. You'll also find the Tipton Waterworks and Tipton Rapids waterparks here.

Admission: $12.95 (all-day rides), $15.95 (all-day rides, waterworks and rapids). May-September, hours vary.

FORT ROBERDEAU

Altoona, 814-946-0048; www.fortroberdeau.org

This reconstructed Revolutionary War fort built with horizontal logs, contains a blacksmith shop, barracks, a storehouse, and a powder magazine. Costumed guides perform historical skits and demonstrations. There are areas for picnicking and nature trails.

Admission: Free. May-October, Tuesday-Saturday 11 a.m.-5 p.m., Sunday-Monday 1-5 p.m.

HORSESHOE CURVE VISITORS CENTER

Altoona, 814-946-0834; www.railroadcity.com

This world-famous engineering feat carries main-line Conrail and Amtrak trains around western grade of 91 feet per mile. The curve is 2,375 feet long and has a central angle of 220 degrees. There are funicular railway runs between interpretive center and observation area.

Admission: $6, children under 3 free. May, Monday-Saturday 10 a.m.-6 p.m., Sunday 11 a.m.-6 p.m.; June-September, Monday-Saturday 10 a.m.-8 p.m., Sunday 11 a.m.-8 p.m.; September-November, Monday-Thursday 10 a.m.-6 p.m., Sunday 11 a.m.-6 p.m.

LAKEMONT PARK

700 Park Ave., Altoona, 800-434-8006; www.lakemontparkfun.com

This amusement park has more than 30 rides and attraction. It's home of the nation's oldest wooden roller coaster. There's a water park, miniature golf and other entertainment.

Admission: all day pass $9.95. May-September, closed Monday-Tuesday.

PRINCE GALLITZIN STATE PARK

Highway 53 and Beaver Valley Road, Flinton, 814-674-1000;
www.dcnr.state.pa.us/stateparks/parks

This state park covers 7,335 acres and has 26 miles of shoreline on a 1,635-acre lake. Here, you'll find a swimming beach, fishing, boating, hiking trails, horseback riding, cross-country skiing, snowmobiling, ice-skating, ice fishing, picnicking areas, a snack bar, store, laundry facilities, tent and trailer sites as well as rental cabins.

Beach: Late-May-mid-September 8 a.m.-sunset. Campgrounds: April-October.

RAILROADER'S MEMORIAL MUSEUM

1300 Nineth Ave., Altoona, 814-946-0834, 888-428-6662; www.railroadcity.com

This museum features exhibits displaying railroad artifacts and railroad rolling stock, steam and electric locomotive collections.

Admission: adults $9, seniors $7, children 4-12 $5, children 3 and under free. May-November, Monday-Saturday 10 a.m.-5 p.m., Sunday 11 a.m.-5 p.m.; November-December, Friday-Saturday, Monday 10 a.m.-5 p.m., Sunday 11 a.m.-5 p.m.

SPECIAL EVENT
BLAIR COUNTY ARTS FESTIVAL
Penn State Altoona Campus, 3000 Ivyside Park, Altoona, 814-949-2787;
www.mishlertheatre.org
This arts festival honors the arts with displays and a full lineup of performers including musicians, choirs, and dancing.
Mid-May.

WHERE TO STAY
★★RAMADA INN
I-99 Exit 31 Plank Road Route 220 and Plank Road exit Altoona, 814-946-1631,
800-311-5192; www.ramadainnaltoona.com
215 rooms. Restaurant. Complimentary breakfast. Business center. Fitness center. Pool. $61-150

WHERE TO EAT
★★ALLEGRO
3926 Broad Ave., Altoona, 814-946-5216, 800-372-5524; www.allegro-restaurant.com
American, Italian. Lunch (Thursday-Friday), dinner. Closed Sunday. Children's menu. Bar. $16-35

BEDFORD
See also Altoona, Somerset, Martinsburg
Fort Bedford was a major frontier outpost in pre-Revolutionary War days. After the war, it became an important stopover along the route of western migration. Garrett Pendergrass, the second settler here, built Pendergrass's Tavern, which figures in a number of novels by Hervey Allen.

WHAT TO SEE
FORT BEDFORD PARK AND MUSEUM
Fort Bedford Drive, North end of Juliana Street, Bedford, 814-623-8891, 800-259-4284;
www.motherbedford.com
This log blockhouse was erected during Bedford's bicentennial. The museum contains a large-scale replica of the original fort and displays of colonial antiques and Native American artifacts. The park is along Raystown River.
Admission: 4. May 15-25, Wednesday-Sunday 11 a.m.-7 p.m.; Mid-May-early September, daily 11 a.m.-7 p.m.; Early September-mid-October, Wednesday-Sunday 11 a.m.-7 p.m.

OLD BEDFORD VILLAGE
220 Sawblade Road, Bedford, 814-623-1156, 800-238-4347;
www.oldbedfordvillage.com
This village consists of more than 40 authentic log and frame structures built between 1750 and 1851. There are crafts demonstrations and operating pioneer farm. There are many special events throughout the year.
Admission: adults $10, students $5, children 5 and under free. Memorial

Day-Labor Day, Thursday-Tuesday 9 a.m.-5 p.m.; September-October, Thursday-Sunday 9 a.m.-5 p.m.

SPECIAL EVENTS
CIVIL WAR REENACTMENT
Old Bedford Village, Bedford; www.oldbedfordvillage.com
In Old Bedford Village, witness this Civil War reenactment with opposing sides setting up camp in the village with horses and cannons.
Mid-June.

FALL FOLIAGE FESTIVAL DAYS
141 S. Juliana St., Bedford; www.bedfordcounty.net/fall
This fall festival features entertainment, ethnic foods, antique cars and more than 350 arts and crafts booths. There is a kid's area with a puppet theater, a magician, pony rides and more.
Early October.

WHERE TO STAY
★★BEST WESTERN BEDFORD INN
4517 Business 220, Bedford, 814-623-9006, 800-752-8592; www.bestwestern.com
104 rooms. Complimentary breakfast. Fitness center. Pool. Pets accepted. $61-150

★★★MERCERSBURG INN
405 S. Main St., Mercersburg, 717-328-5231; www.mercersburginn.com
Located between the civil war battlefield and other historic sites, the Mercersburg Inn is a 17-room turn-of-the-century Georgian mansion. Golf courses, tennis facilities, skiing, fly fishing, mountain biking and hiking trails are all located within a short distance.
17 rooms. Restaurant, bar. Complimentary breakfast. $61-150

★★QUALITY INN
4407 Business 220, Bedford, 814-623-5188, 877-424-6423; www.choicehotels.com
65 rooms. Complimentary breakfast. Pool. Pets accepted. $61-150

WHERE TO EAT
★★ED'S STEAK HOUSE
4476 Business 220, Bedford, 814-623-8894
Seafood, steak. Breakfast, lunch, dinner. Bar. Children's menu. $16-35

★★★MERCERSBURG INN
405 S. Main St., Mercersburg, 717-328-5231; www.mercersburginn.com
Built in 1909, this Georgian-style mansion resides in a charming, 230-year-old village. With both a prix fixe and an à la carte menu, the inn's restaurant serves entrées such as sautéed skate à la meuniere with capers, preserved lemon and caramelized onion risotto or rosemary lemon Cornish hen with roasted fingerling potatoes.
French. Dinner. Closed Monday-Wednesday. Bar. $36-85

BETHLEHEM

See also Allentown, Easton

Bethlehem Steel products have put this city on the map, but Bethlehem is also known for its Bach Festival, for its historic district, and for Lehigh University and Moravian College.

Not surprisingly, Bethlehem has earned itself the nickname, "America's Christmas city." Moravians, members of a very old Protestant denomination, assembled here on Christmas Evening 1741 in a log house that was part stable, which was the only building in the area at the time. Singing a hymn that praised Bethlehem, they found a name for their village. Their private musical performance also was the first of many in Bethlehem; string quartets and symphonies were heard here before any other place in the colonies.

The Lehigh Canal's 1829 opening kicked off the area's industrialization, along with the development of the borough of South Bethlehem, which was incorporated into Bethlehem in 1917.

WHAT TO SEE
CENTRAL MORAVIAN CHURCH

73 W. Church St., Bethlehem, 610-866-5661; www.centralmoravianchurch.org
This federal-style church was built in 1806, features hand-carved detail and is considered the foremost Moravian church in the U.S. It has been noted for its music, including a trombone choir in existence since 1754.

GOD'S ACRE

Church and Market streets, Bethlehem
This is an old Moravian cemetery following Moravian tradition that all gravestones are laid flat, indicating that all are equal in the sight of God.

HILL-TO-HILL BRIDGE

Joins old and new parts of the city and provides excellent view of the historic area, river and Bethlehem Steel plant.

KEMERER MUSEUM OF DECORATIVE ARTS

427 N. New St., Bethlehem, 610-691-6055, 800-360-3687; www.historicbethlehem.org
This museum displays exhibits that include art, Bohemian glass, toys, prints, china as well as regional German folk art from 1750-1900, Federal furniture and period room settings.
Friday-Saturday 10 a.m.-1 p.m., Sunday 1-4 p.m.

MORAVIAN MUSEUM (GEMEINHAUS)

66 W. Church St., Bethlehem, 610-867-0173; www.historicbethlehem.org
This five-story log building was built in 1741 and is the oldest structure in the city; docents interpret the history and culture of early Bethlehem and the Moravians.

OLD CHAPEL

Heckewelder Place, adjacent to Moravian Museum, Bethlehem;
www.historicbethlehem.org
Once called the "Indian chapel" because so many Native Americans attended

the services, this stone structure, the second church for the Moravian congregation, was built in 1751 and is still used frequently. May be toured only in combination with Moravian Museum community walking tour.

SPECIAL EVENTS
BETHLEHEM BACH FESTIVAL
First Presbyterian Church of Bethlehem, 2344 Center St., Bethlehem, 610-867-5865;
www.bach.org
One of the country's outstanding musical events. Many famous artists and the Bach Choir of Bethlehem participate in the festival.
Mid-late May.

MUSIKFEST
25 W. Third St., Bethlehem, 610-861-0678; www.musikfest.org
This nine-day festival celebrates Bethlehem's rich musical and ethnic heritage. There are more than 600 performances (most are free) of all types of music including folk, big-band, jazz, country-western, chamber, classical, gospel, rock and swing. Past performers have included Panic at the Disco, Third Eye Blind, Pat Benetar, Blondie, The Wallflowers and Crosby, Stills and Nash.
Late July-early-August.

WHERE TO STAY
★★BEST WESTERN LEHIGH VALLEY HOTEL AND CONFERENCE CENTER
300 Gateway Drive, Bethlehem, 610-866-5800; www.bestwestern.com
192 rooms. Restaurant. Complimentary breakfast. Pool. $61-150

★COMFORT INN
3191 Highfield Drive, Bethlehem, 610-865-6300, 877-424-6423; www.choicehotels.com
112 rooms. Complimentary breakfast. Fitness center. Pets accepted. $61-150

WHERE TO EAT
★★CAFÉ
221 W. Broad St., Bethlehem, 610-866-1686
International. Lunch (Tuesday-Friday), dinner. Closed Sunday-Monday. Reservations recommended. $16-35

★★★MAIN STREET DEPOT
61 W. Lehigh St., Bethlehem, 610-868-7123; www.mainstreetdepotrestaurant.com
On the National Registry of Historic Buildings, the location out of which the Main Street Depot now operates was built in 1873 and served as a station for the Jersey Central railroad. Grab a depot burger at the bar, or sit down for dinner and enjoy an entrée like butter rum chicken with cashews, coconut and fresh pineapple over rice or filet mignon wrapped in bacon and served with asparagus and béarnaise sauce.
American. Lunch, dinner. Closed Sunday. Bar. $36-85

BLOOMSBURG

See also Scranton

On the north bank of the Susquehanna River, Bloomsburg was a center for mining, transportation and industry during the 19th and early 20th centuries. While it remains a manufacturing town, Bloomsburg retains the relaxed atmosphere of earlier days with its lush scenery and covered bridges. In nearby Orangeville, Fishing Creek offers trout, bass and pickerel.

WHAT TO SEE

BLOOMSBURG UNIVERSITY OF PENNSYLVANIA

400 Second St., Bloomsburg, 570-389-4316; www.bloomu.edu

Established in 1839, this campus of 6,000 students features Carver Hall; the Harvey A. Andruss Library; Haas Center for the Arts with 2,000-seat auditorium and art gallery; McCormick Center for Human Services; Redman Stadium and Nelson Field House.

THE CHILDREN'S MUSEUM

2 W. Seventh St., Bloomsburg, 570-389-9206; www.the-childrens-museum.org

This museum has more than 50 hands-on activities that aim to make learning about our world and the environment fun. The museum has a new theme each year, and most of the exhibits change as well.

Admission: adults and children 2-18 $5, children under 2 free. Tuesday-Saturday 10 a.m.-4 p.m.

HISTORIC DISTRICT

Bounded by West, Fifth, First, Lake streets, Bloomsburg, 570-784-7703

More than 650 structures spanning architectural styles from Georgian to Art Deco are featured in this historic district in the center of town.

SPECIAL EVENTS

BLOOMSBURG THEATRE ENSEMBLE

Alvina Krause Theatre, 226 Center St., Bloomsburg, 570-784-8181; www.bte.org

Founded in 1978, this theatre consists of a resident professional ensemble that completes three to four weeks of performances for each of six plays. Admission: adults $24, seniors $19, students and children $11. Main stage: September-May (special performances rest of year). Box office: Monday-Wednesday noon- 5 p.m., Thursday-Friday noon-7:30 p.m., Saturday 6-7:30 p.m., Sunday 1:30-3 p.m.

WHERE TO STAY

★BUDGET HOST PATRIOT INN

6305 Columbia Blvd., Bloomsburg, 570-387-1776, 800-873-1180;
www.budgethost.com

59 rooms. $61-150

★★★INN AT TURKEY HILL

991 Central Road, Bloomsburg, 570-387-1500; www.innatturkeyhill.com

This inn's 1839 brick farmhouse offers two guest bedrooms with whirlpool tubs. 16 additional rooms are available on the property. Visit the inn's gazebo,

duck pond and two resident ducks.
18 rooms. Restaurant. Complimentary breakfast. Pets accepted. $61-150

BRADFORD
See also Warren
When oil was discovered in Bradford in the late 1800s, the price of land jumped from about six cents to $1,000 an acre, and wells appeared on front lawns, in backyards and even in a cemetery. An oil exchange was established in 1877, two years after the first producing well was brought in. A Ranger District office of the Allegheny National Forest is located here.

WHAT TO SEE
CROOK FARM
476 Seaward Ave., Bradford, 814-362-3906;
The Crook Farm is the original home of Erastus and Betsy Crook and was built in 1848 and restored to reflect the 1870s period.
May-September, Tuesday-Friday, Saturday by appointment.

WHERE TO STAY
★★BEST WESTERN BRADFORD INN
100 Davis St., Bradford, 814-362-4501; www.bestwestern.com
112 rooms. Complimentary breakfast. Fitness center. Pool. Pets accepted. $61-150

★★★GLENDORN
1000 Glendorn Drive, Bradford, 814-362-6511, 800-843-8568; www.glendorn.com
Set on 1,280 acres, this one-time private estate offers a sophisticated twist on the traditional wooded retreat. A long, private drive welcomes visitors to this hideaway, where guests enjoy walks in the woods, canoe and fishing trips, hiking and biking adventures, and a host of other outdoor pursuits. The accommodations in the Big House reflect a warm, country house spirit, while the cabin suites have a rugged charm. Fine dining is a hallmark of this country lodge, with hearty country breakfasts, delicious lunches and four-course prix fixe dinners.
17 rooms. Restaurant, bar. Pool. Pets accepted. No children under 8. Tennis. $351 and up.

CARLISLE
See also Harrisburg
In the historically strategic Cumberland Valley, Carlisle was a vital point for Native American fighting during the Revolutionary and Civil wars. The Carlisle Barracks is one of the oldest military posts in America. Soldiers mounted guard here as early as 1750 to protect the frontier. In 1794 President Washington reviewed troops assembled here to march against the "Whiskey Rebels," and troops went from the Barracks to the Mexican and Civil wars. The Barracks was reopened in 1920 as the Medical Field Service School. It is now home to the U.S. Army War College. George Ross, James Wilson and James Smith, all signers of the Declaration of Independence, lived in Carlisle, as did Molly Pitcher.

WHAT TO SEE
DICKINSON COLLEGE
242 W. High St., Carlisle, 717-243-5121; www.dickinson.edu
Founded in 1773, Dickinson is the tenth college chartered in the United States. President James Buchanan was a graduate. On campus is "Old West," a building registered as a National Historic Landmark, designed by Benjamin Henry Latrobe, one of the designers of the Capitol in Washington. Tours: Monday-Friday 9, 11 a.m., 1, 2, 3 p.m.

PINE GROVE FURNACE STATE PARK
1212 Pine Grove Road, Carlisle, 717-486-7575; www.dcnr.state.pa.us
This area was used for pre-Revolutionary iron, slate and brick work. This state park takes up approximately 696 acres. There is swimming, fishing, boating; hunting, hiking, bicycling, cross-country skiing, ice skating, ice fishing and picnicking allowed. There is a snack bar, store and trailer sites.

WHERE TO STAY
★★ALLENBERRY RESORT INN
1559 Boiling Springs Road, Boiling Springs, 717-258-3211, 800-430-5468; www.allenberry.com
69 rooms. Restaurant, bar. Pool. Tennis. $61-150

★CARLISLE DAYS INN & SUITES
101 Alexander Spring Road, Carlisle, 717-258-4147, 888-271-4147; www.daysinn.com
136 rooms. Restaurant, bar. Complimentary breakfast. Business center. Fitness center. Pool. Pets accepted. $61-150

★★HOLIDAY INN HARRISBURG-CARLISLE
1450 Harrisburg Pike, Carlisle, 717-245-2400, 888-465-4329; www.holidayinn.com
100 rooms. Restaurant, bar. Fitness center. Pool. Pets accepted. $61-150

★★HOTEL CARLISLE
1700 Harrisburg Pike, Carlisle, 717-243-1717, 800-692-7315; www.hotelcarlisle.com
267 rooms. Restaurant, bar. Business center. Fitness center. Pool. Pets accepted. $61-150

★QUALITY INN
1255 Harrisburg Pike, Carlisle, 717-243-6000, 877-424-6423; www.qualityinn.com
96 rooms. Restaurant, bar. Complimentary breakfast. Fitness center. Pool. Pets accepted. $61-150

WHERE TO EAT
★★BOILING SPRINGS TAVERN
Front and First streets, Boiling Springs, 717-258-3614; www.boilingspringstavern.net
American. Lunch, dinner. Closed Sunday-Monday. Children's menu. Bar. $16-35

★★CALIFORNIA CAFÉ
38 W. Pomfret St., Carlisle, 717-249-2028; www.calcaf.com
California, French. Lunch, dinner. Reservations recommended. $16-35

CONNELLSVILLE

See also New Stanton, Uniontown

George Washington once owned land in the region, and many places are named in his honor. The restored Crawford Cabin near the river was the home of Colonel William Crawford, surveyor of these properties and Washington's surveying pupil. Northwest of town in Perryopolis, the town square is named for Washington, who some believe planned the design of the town.

WHAT TO SEE
FALLINGWATER (KAUFMANN CONSERVATION ON BEAR RUN)

Highway 381 S., Mill Run, Connellsville, 724-329-8501; www.fallingwater.org

One of the most famous structures of the 20th century, Fallingwater, designed by Frank Lloyd Wright in 1936, is cantilevered on three levels over a waterfall. The interior features Wright-designed furniture, textiles and lighting, as well as sculpture by modern masters; extensive grounds are heavily wooded and planted with rhododendron, which blooms in early July. The visitor center has a self-guided orientation program, concessions, and a gift shop. There are also guided tours.

Admission (tours): adults $18, children 6-12 $12. Admission (grounds): $8. Daily. Closed Wednesday mid-March-Thanksgiving; January-February. No children under age 6 (for regular tour). Reservations required.

DELAWARE WATER GAP NATIONAL RECREATION AREA

See also Milford, Pocono Mountains, Stroudsburg

It is difficult to believe that the quiet Delaware River could carve a path through the Kittatinny Mountains, which are nearly a quarter of a mile high at this point. Conflicting geological theories account for this natural phenomenon. The prevailing theory is that the mountains were formed after the advent of the river, rising up from the earth so slowly that the course of the Delaware was never altered.

Despite the speculation about its origin, there is no doubt about the area's recreational value. A relatively unspoiled area along the river boundary between Pennsylvania and New Jersey, stretching approximately 35 miles from Matamoras to an area just south of I-80, the site of the Delaware Water Gap is managed by the National Park Service.

Trails and overlooks offer scenic views. Also here are canoeing and boating, and hunting and fishing; camping is nearby at the Dingmans Campground within the recreation area. Swimming and picnicking are available at Smithfield and Milford beaches. Dingmans Falls and Silver Thread Falls, two of the highest waterfalls in the Poconos, are near here. Several 19th-century buildings are in the area, including Millbrook Village (several buildings open May-October) and Peters Valley. The visitor center is located off I-80 in New Jersey, at Kittatinny Point.

DOYLESTOWN

See also Philadelphia, Quakertown

A small town located in Bucks County, Doylestown is a pleasant place to visit with their historic architechture and plenty of restaurants and shops to enjoy. Stroll down Mercer Mile which is where the Fonthill Museum, Mercer Museum and Moravian Pottery and Tiles Works is located.

WHAT TO SEE
FONTHILL MUSEUM
525 E. Court St., Doylestown, 215-348-9461; www.mercermuseum.org
This concrete castle of Henry Chapman Mercer, an archaeologist, historian, a major proponent of the Arts and Crafts movement in America, displays his collection of tiles and prints from around the world.
Admission: adults $9.50, seniors $8.50, children 5-17 $4, children under 5 free. Admission to Fonthill and Mercer Museums: $14. Monday-Saturday 10 a.m.-5 p.m., Sunday noon-5 p.m.

JAMES A. MICHENER ART MUSEUM
138 S. Pine St., Doylestown, 215-340-9800; www.michenerartmuseum.org
This museum, a former prison modeled after the Eastern State Penitentiary in Philadelphia, is as large as a football field and was named for Doylestown's most famous son, the Pulitzer Prize-winning writer James Michener. He supported the arts and dreamed of a regional art museum dedicated to preserving, interpreting and exhibiting the art and cultural heritage of the Bucks County region. The museum is now home to more than 2,500 paintings, sculptures, drawings and photographs, as well as stained glass collections and an outdoor gallery paying homage to the local landscape.
Admission: adults $10, seniors $9, students $7.50, children 6-18 $5, children 5 and under free. Tuesday-Friday 10 a.m.-4:30 p.m., Saturday 10 a.m.-5 p.m., Sunday noon-5 p.m. First Friday of the month 10 a.m.-9 p.m.

MERCER MUSEUM
84 S. Pine St., Doylestown, 215-345-0210; www.mercermuseum.org
In this towering castle built in 1969, visitors will find implements, folk art and furnishings of early America before mechanization. See a Conestoga wagon, a whaling boat, carriages and an antique fire engine. Fifty thousand pieces of more than 60 early American crafts and trade tools on display.
Admission: adults $9, seniors $8, children 5-17 $4, children 4 and under free. Monday, Wednesday-Saturday 10 a.m.-5 p.m., Tuesday 10 a.m.-9 p.m., Sunday noon-5 p.m. First Tuesday of each month 5-9 p.m. free. Admission to Fonthill and Mercer Museums: $14.

147

THE MORAVIAN POTTERY AND TILE WORKS
130 Swamp Road, Doylestown, 215-345-6722; www.buckscounty.org
This historic landmark is a working history museum in which visitors can witness tiles produced by hand. Visitors may purchase tiles made onsite in the tile shop.
Admission: adults $4.50, seniors $3.50, children 7-17 $2.50. Daily 10 a.m.-4:45 p.m.

WHERE TO STAY
★★★GOLDEN PHEASANT INN
763 River Road, Erwinna, 610-294-9595, 800-830-4474; www.goldenpheasant.com

Located an hour and a half from New York City and 20 minutes outside of Philadelphia, this provincial and romantic weekend hideaway sits between the Delaware River and the Pennsylvania Canal. The guest rooms are homey and unique (if a little snug) with canopy beds and plush carpeting. Don't miss dinner at the restaurant, as it turns out spectacular French cuisine. 6 rooms. Restaurant. Complimentary breakfast. $61-150

WHERE TO EAT

★★★GOLDEN PHEASANT INN

763 River Road, Erwinna, 610-294-9595; www.goldenpheasant.com

Enjoy entrées such as roasted pheasant with apple and calvados sauce or grilled petite lamb chops with a roasted shallot and mint sauce. The interior is decorated in dark woods and beamed ceilings, and chandeliers hang throughout the dining room.

French. Dinner, Sunday brunch. Closed Monday. Bar. $36-85

EPHRATA

See also Denver/Adamstown, Reading

Located in Lancaster County, the small town of Ephrata holds on to Pennsylvania's Dutch and Amish cultures along with offering a diverse setting with plenty to see and do.

WHAT TO SEE

EPHRATA CLOISTER

632 W. Main St., Ephrata, 717-733-6600; www.ephratacloister.org

These buildings stand as a monument to an unusual religious experiment. In 1732 Conrad Beissel, a German Seventh-Day Baptist, began to lead a hermit's life here. Within a few years he established a religious community of recluses, with a Brotherhood, a Sisterhood and a group of married "householders." The members of the solitary order dressed in concealing white habits; the buildings were without adornment, the halls were narrow, the doorways were low, and board benches served as beds and wooden blocks as pillows. Their religious zeal and charity, however, proved to be their undoing. After the Battle of Brandywine, the cloistered community nursed the Revolutionary sick and wounded but contracted typhus, which decimated their numbers. Celibacy also contributed to the decline of the community, but the Society was not formally dissolved until 1934. An orientation exhibit and video prepare each visitor for their journey back through time.

Admission: adults $9, seniors $8, children 3-11 $6, children under 3 free. Monday-Saturday 9 a.m.-5 p.m., Sunday noon-5 p.m. Closed Monday-Tuesday January-Febrary.

THE HISTORICAL SOCIETY OF COCALICO VALLEY

237-249 W. Main St., Ephrata, 717-733-1616; www.cocalicovalleyhs.org

This Italianate Victorian mansion contains period displays, historical exhibits, genealogical and a historical research library on Cocalico Valley area and its residents.

Monday, Wednesday, Thursday, Saturday.

SPECIAL EVENT
THE EPHRATA FAIR

717-733-4451; www.ephratafair.org

This is one of the largest street fairs in the state. There are arts and crafts, contests, live animal contests, a livestock sale, entertainment, food, parades, carnival rides and more.

Last full week in September.

WHERE TO EAT
★★★ANITA'S AT DONECKERS

333 N. State St., Ephrata, 717-738-9501; www.anitasatdoneckers.com

Guests can opt for a formal atmosphere amidst antiques and artwork in the main dining room, or a more casual setting in the bistro. Opened in 1984 as the Restaurant at Doneckers, Anita's now continues this fine dining traditions offering American fare with a French influence.

American, French. Lunch (Tuesday-Saturday), dinner. Closed Sunday. Reservations recommended. Bar. $36-85

ERIE

See also Pittsburgh

The third-largest city in Pennsylvania, Erie is the state's only port on the Great Lakes and boasts a wealth of natural beauty and fascinating historical tales. Visitors enjoy Presque Isle State Park, with its seven miles of sandy beaches, hiking and biking trails. Downtown offers cultural and entertainment options including Broadway shows, classical ballet, philharmonic performances and comedy clubs. Explore acres of vineyards at local wineries, take in a play at the Erie Playhouse or the Roadhouse Theater, cheer for the AA Seawolves Baseball or the Otters OHL professional hockey team, splash around at northwest Pennsylvania's only indoor water park, or strap on your skis for downhill or cross-country fun.

The lake and city take their name from the Erie tribe, who were killed by the Seneca about 1654. On the south shore of Presque Isle Bay, Commodore Oliver Hazard Perry built his fleet, floated the ships across the sandbars and fought the British in the Battle of Lake Erie. Fort Presque Isle, built by the French in 1753 and destroyed by them in 1759, was rebuilt by the English, burned by Native Americans, and rebuilt again in 1794 by Americans.

WHAT TO SEE
BICENTENNIAL TOWER

7 Dobbins Landing, Erie, 814-455-6055

Commemorating Erie's 200th birthday, this 187-foot tower features two observation decks with an aerial view of the city, bay and Lake Erie.

Admission: adults $3, children 7-12 $2, children six and under free. May, daily 10 a.m.-8 p.m.; Memorial Day-Labor Day, daily 9:30 a.m.-10 p.m.; Labor Day-October 1- a.m.-6 p.m.; November-March, Saturday-Sunday noon-4 p.m.; April 10 a.m.-6 p.m. Free Sunday.

ERIE ART MUSEUM

411 State St., Erie, 814-459-5477; www.erieartmuseum.org

Temporary art exhibits in a variety of media are on display here including regional artwork and lectures in the restored Greek Revival Old Customs House. Art classes, concerts, lectures and workshops are also offered.

Admission: adults $4, seniors and students $3, children under 13 free. Tuesday-Saturday 11 a.m.-5 p.m., Sunday 1-5 p.m. Free Wednesday.

ERIE LAND LIGHTHOUSE

2 Lighthouse St., Erie, 814-870-1452; www.nps.gov

The first lighthouse on the Great Lakes was constructed on this site in 1818. Daily.

ERIE ZOO

423 W. 38th St., Erie, 814-864-4091; www.eriezoo.org

The Erie Zoo houses more than 300 animals, including gorillas, polar bears and giraffes on 15 acres. There is also a children's zoo and a one-mile tour of grounds on Safariland Express Train. There is also an indoor ice rink open during the fall and winter months.

Admission: March-November, adults $7, seniors $6, children 2-11 $4, chidlren 1 and under free. Monday-Saturday 10 a.m.-5 p.m., Sunday 10 a.m.-6 p.m. Free Sunday 3-5 p.m.

FIREFIGHTERS HISTORICAL MUSEUM

428 Chestnut St., Erie, 814-456-5969; www.firefightershistoricalmuseum.com

More than 1,300 items of firefighting memorabilia are displayed in the old #4 Firehouse. Exhibits include fire apparatus dating from 1823, alarm systems, uniforms, badges, ribbons, helmets, nozzles, fire marks and fire extinguishers; fire safety films are shown in the Hay Loft Theater.

Admission: adults $4, seniors and firefighters $2.50, children 6-12 $1. May-August, Saturday 10 a.m.-5 p.m., Sunday 1-5 p.m.; September-October, Saturday-Sunday 1-5 p.m.

MISERY BAY

N.E. corner of Presque Isle Bay, Presque Isle State Park, Erie; www.dcnr.state.pa.us

Misery Bay is the location of the Perry monument, which is named after Perry's naval squadron who defeated the British and the fleet suffered cold and privations of a bitter winter. This wetland is perfect for hiking.

PRESQUE ISLE STATE PARK

1 Peninsula Drive, Erie, 814-833-7424; www.presqueisle.org

This peninsula stretches seven miles into Lake Erie and curves back toward city. There is approximately 3,200 acres of recreation and conservation areas, in which visitors can go swimming, fishing, boating, hiking, birding, cross-country skiing, ice skating, ice fishing, ice boating and picnicking. There are also concessions available here. The Tom Ridge Environmental Center offers environmental education and interpretive programs along with exhibits, a theater, nature shop and gallery, cafe and visitor's center. There is also an observation tower. The Presque Isle Lighthouse is also located here; it's the

second lighthouse built on Lake Erie.
Envioronmental center: Daily 10 a.m.-8 p.m.

WALDAMEER PARK & WATER WORLD

220 Peninsula Drive., Erie, 814-838-3591; www.waldameer.com
At the entrance to Presque Isle State Park, you'll find Waldameer amusement
park and Water World water park. There are rides, an arcade, roller coasters,
a kiddieland, water rides, a picnic area, food stands, and a dance pavilion.
Admission to the park is free but you must purchase passes for indivdual
parks to enjoy the rides. Admission: Free. Admission to Water World:
over 48 inches tall $15.45, under 48 inches tall $10.95. Waldameer: over
48 inches $20.45, under 48 inches $12.95. Combo (both parks): over 48
inches tall $22.95, under 48 inches tall $16.95. Memorial Day-Labor Day,
Tuesday-Sunday.

WHERE TO STAY
★COMFORT INN

3041 W. 12th St., Erie, 814-835-4200, 877-424-6423; www.choicehotels.com
100 rooms. Complimentary breakfast. Business center. Pool. $61-150

★★DOWNTOWN ERIE HOTEL

18 W. 18th St., Erie, 814-456-2961, 800-832-9101; www.downtowneriehotel.com
133 rooms. Complimentary breakfast. Business center. Fitness center. Pool.
$61-150

★GLASS HOUSE INN

3202 W. 26th St., Erie, 814-833-7751, 800-956-7222; www.glasshouseinn.com
30 rooms. Complimentary breakfast. Pool. $61-150

★QUALITY INN & SUITES

8040-A Perry Highway, Erie, 814-864-4911, 877-424-6423; www.qualityinn.com
110 rooms. Complimentary breakfast. Pool. $61-150

WHERE TO EAT
★★PUFFERBELLY

414 French St., Erie, 814-454-1557; www.thepufferbelly.com
Lunch, dinner, Sunday brunch. Outdoor seating. Bar. $16-35

★★THE STONEHOUSE INN

4753 W. Lake Road, Erie, 814-838-9296; www.stonehouse-inn.com
International. Dinner. Closed Sunday-Monday. Reservations recommended.
Bar. $36-85

FARMINGTON

See also Warren
This small town is located in Pennsylvania's Laurel Highlands where nature
is at your fingertips, where you can enjoy the great outdoors and go hiking,
skiing, canoeing and more.

WHAT TO SEE
BRADDOCK'S GRAVE AT FORT NECESSITY NATIONAL BATTLEFIELD
1 Washington Parkway, Farmington, 724-329-5512; www.nps.gov/fone
A granite monument marks the burial place of British General Edward Braddock, who was wounded in battle with French and Native American forces on July 9, 1755, and died four days later.
Fort Necessity Education Center: Daily 9 a.m.-5 p.m.

LAUREL CAVERNS
200 Caverns Park Road, Farmington, 724-438-2070, 800-515-4150;
www.laurelcaverns.com
This 435 geological park holds the largest cave found in Pennsylvania with colored lighting and unusual formations. There are group tours of the caves available; see Web site for information. There is also an eighteen hole indoor miniature golf course along with repelling courses and exploring trips.
May-October, daily 9 a.m.-5 p.m.; April and November, Saturday-Sunday 9 a.m.-5 p.m. Closed December-March.

WHERE TO STAY
★★★★FALLING ROCK AT NEMACOLIN
150 Falling Rock Blvd., Farmington, 724-329-8555; www.nemacolin.com/fallingrock
Inspired by the architecture of Frank Lloyd Wright, Falling Rock extends almost organically from the Pennsylvania countryside with its natural stone exterior, fountains and seasonally open, heated outdoor infinity pool. All rooms include 24-hour butler service and 1,200-thread-count sheets. But perhaps its most indulgent quality, at least for duffers, is its location—at the 18th hole of the Mystic Rock Golf Course, within the Nemacolin Woodlands Resort, and the accompanying 50,000-square-foot clubhouse.
42 rooms. Restaurant, bar. Business center. Fitness center. Pool. Golf. Tennis. Beach. Closed December-April. $251-350

★★★★NEMACOLIN WOODLANDS RESORT & SPA
1001 Lafayette Drive, Farmington, 724-329-8555, 866-344-6957; www.nemacolin.com
Tucked away in Pennsylvania's scenic Laurel Highlands, this comprehensive resort offers a multitude of recreational opportunities, from the Hummer driving club, equestrian center and shooting academy to the adventure and activities centers, culinary classes and art museums. Two golf courses and a renowned golf academy delight players, while special activities entertain children and teenagers. Grand European style defines the guest accommodations at Chateau LaFayette, while the Lodge maintains a rustic charm. Families enjoy the spacious accommodations in the townhouses, and the luxury homes add a touch of class to group travel.
293 rooms. Restaurant, bar. Business center. Fitness center. Pool. Spa. Golf. Tennis. Beach. $251-350

★★★SUMMIT INN RESORT

101 Skyline Drive, Farmington, 724-438-8594, 800-433-8594;
www.summitinnresort.com

Located at the peak of Mount Summit, the Summit Inn Resort offers sparkling panoramic views of the surrounding counties. The 1907 inn is an architecture lover's dream: It's located near Frank Lloyd Wright's Fallingwater and
has its own spot on the National Register of Historic Places.
94 rooms. Restaurant, bar. Pool. Closed early November-mid-April. $61-150

WHERE TO EAT
★★★AQUEOUS

Falling Rock Hotel, 150 Falling Rock Blvd., Farmington, 724-329-8555;
www.nemacolin.com/aqueous

Plunge into a true farm-to-table experience with local meats and produce at
this upscale American steakhouse overlooking the Mystic Rock Golf Course.
Porterhouse, bone-in ribeye, filet mignon and New York strip are available
with a choice of delectable sauces, such as classic béarnaise and roasted red
pepper. Country-style sides "big enough for two" include creamed spinach,
creamed corn, onion rings and plenty of potatoes. Don't forget the surf and
turf with king crab, jumbo shrimp and Maine lobster tail.
American. Breakfast, lunch, dinner. $36-85

★★★★★LAUTREC

Chateau LaFayette, 1001 LaFayette Drive, Farmington, 724-329-8555;
www.nemacolin.com/lautrec

Savor a bit of fine French cuisine—the restaurant wasn't named after French
artist Henri de Toulouse-Lautrec for nothing—in Pennsylvania's Laurel
Highlands. Self-taught chef Dave Racicot achieved high accolades while in
his twenties with his frequently changing menu, driven by the availability of
the freshest ingredients. Spend an entire evening focusing on the complexi-
ties of a four-course meal plus dessert, or go all out with the Grand Tasting
Menu that includes over a dozen selections. Wine pairings are also offered.
French. Dinner. Reservations recommended. Bar. $36-85

SPAS
★★★★WOODLANDS SPA AT NEMACOLIN RESORT

1001 LaFayette Drive, Farmington, 724-329-8555, 800-422-2736; www.nemacolin.com

Famed interior designer Clodagh created the look of this spa using natural
materials and the guiding properties of feng shui, the ancient Chinese philosophy of balancing the forces of nature. Achieving inner tranquility is the
mission here, and the treatments embrace this guiding principle. An extensive massage menu includes favorites such as Swedish, sports, aromatherapy,
shiatsu and deep tissue, as well as Eastern methods such as reflexology and
reiki. From Japanese citrus and Balinese hibiscus to German chamomile and
Greek mint, the body scrubs embody international personalities. Fitness and
nutrition consultations help you gain insight into your body and its needs.
The onsite spa restaurant makes healthy eating easier.

GETTYSBURG

See also Hanover, York

Because of the many historical attractions in this town, visitors may want to stop in at the Gettysburg Convention & Visitors Bureau for complete information about bus tours, guide service (including a tape-recorded and self-guided tour) and help in planning their visit here.

WHAT TO SEE

A. LINCOLN'S PLACE

571 Steinwehr Ave., Gettysburg, 717-334-6049; www.jimgetty.com

This theatrical live portrayal of the 16th president is by well-known actor and Lincoln historian, James A. Getty. The program runs 45 minutes and can only be booked for groups; call for information.

BOYD'S BEAR COUNTRY

75 Cunningham Road, Gettysburg, 717-630-2600, 866-367-8338; www.boydsbearcountry.com

"The World's Most Humongous Teddy Bear Store" features four floors of bears (plus rabbits, moose and other furry friends) in a giant barn. At the Boyd's Teddy Bear Nursery, kids can adopt their very own baby bear; personalize your bear at the Make-N-Take-Craft Center. Live entertainment every weekend adds to the merriment.

Daily 10 a.m.-6 p.m.

EISENHOWER NATIONAL HISTORIC SITE

97 Taneytown Road, Gettysburg, 717-338-9114; www.nps.gov/eise

Farm and home of the 34th President of the United States and his wife, Mamie. Tour of grounds and home take 1 1/2-2 hours. Self-guided tours explore the farm and skeet range. Access to site is by shuttle only, from the National Park Service Visitor Center.

Admission: adults $6.50, children 6-12 $4. Daily 9 a.m.-4 p.m.

GENERAL LEE'S HEADQUARTERS

401 Buford Ave., Gettysburg, 717-334-3141; www.civilwarheadquarters.com

Robert E. Lee planned Confederate strategy for the Gettysburg battle in this house, which now contains collection of historical items from the battle.

Mid-March-November, daily 9 a.m.-5 p.m.

GETTYSBURG COLLEGE

300 N. Washington St., Gettysburg, 717-337-6300; www.gettysburg.edu

This small liberal arts college only has 2,000 students. Founded in 1832, this is the oldest Lutheran-affiliated college in the U.S. Liberal arts. Pennsylvania Hall was used as Civil War hospital and there is an Eisenhower House and statue on grounds.

GETTYSBURG NATIONAL MILITARY PARK

97 Taneytown Road, Gettysburg, 717-334-1124; www.nps.gov/gett

The hallowed battlefield of Gettysburg, the site of one of the Civil War's most decisive battles and immortalized by Lincoln's Gettysburg Address, is preserved by the National Park Service. The town itself is still a college community, as it was more than a hundred years ago on July 1-3, 1863, when General Robert E. Lee led his Confederate Army in its greatest invasion of the North. The defending Northerners, under Union General George Meade, repulsed the Southern assault after three days of fierce fighting, which left 51,000 men dead, wounded or missing. It has more than 35 miles of roads through 5,900 acres of the battlefield area. There are more than 1,300 monuments, markers and tablets of granite and bronze, as well as 400 cannons. Visitors may wish to tour the battlefield with a Battlefield Guide who is licensed by the National Park Service. The guides escort visitors to all points of interest and sketch the movement of troops and details of the battle. Admission: adults $7.50, seniors and military personnel $6.50, children 5-18 $5.50, children 5 and under free. Visitor center and Museum: April-May, daily 8 a.m.-6 p.m.; June-August, daily 8 a.m.-7 p.m.; September-October, daily 8 a.m.-6 p.m.; November-March, daily 8 a.m.-5 p.m.

GHOSTS OF GETTYSBURG CANDLELIGHT WALKING TOURS
271 Baltimore St., Gettysburg, 717-337-0445; www.ghostsofgettysburg.com
Armed with tales from Mark Nesbitt's "Ghosts of Gettysburg" books, knowledgeable guides lead 1 1/4-hour tours through sections of town that were bloody battlefields 130 years ago.
March and November, Saturday-Sunday; April-October, daily.

LAND OF LITTLE HORSES
125 Glenwood Drive, Gettysburg, 717-334-7259; www.landoflittlehorses.com
A variety of performing horses—all in miniature. Continuous entertainment is provided. There is an indoor arena and exotic animal races. There are also pony and wagon rides. There is a picnic area, a snack bar and a gift shop. Admission: adults $13.95, children 2-11 $11.95. Hours vary; see Web site for information.

LINCOLN TRAIN MUSEUM
425 Steinwehr Ave., Gettysburg, 717-334-5678; www.gettysburgbattlefieldtours.com
This museum features more than 1,000 model trains and railroad memorabilia. Lincoln Train Ride is a simulated trip of 15 minutes.
Admission: adults $7.25, children 6-12 $3.50, children under 6 free.
May-mid-May, daily 9 a.m.-5 p.m.; mid-May-August, daily 9 a.m.-7 p.m.; September-November and March-May, daily 9 a.m.-5 p.m.

SPECIAL EVENTS
APPLE BLOSSOM FESTIVAL
South Mountain Fairgrounds, 615 Narrows Road, Route 234, Biglerville, 717-677-7444; www.gettysburg.travel
This annual festival has been bringing people together for more than 55 years. The festival features wine tastings, live entertainment, wagone rides, agricultural exhibits, orchard bus tours, arts and crafts, and the presentation of the Pennsylvania Apple Queen. There are also activities for children including bobbing for apples, a petting zoo, pony rides and more.
Early May.

WHERE TO STAY
★★BEST WESTERN GETTYSBURG HOTEL
1 Lincoln Square, Gettysburg, 717-337-2000, 866-378-1797; www.hotelgettysburg.com
119 rooms. Restaurant, bar. Business center. Fitness center. Pool. $61-150

★★★THE HERR TAVERN AND PUBLICK HOUSE
900 Chambersburg Road, Gettysburg, 717-334-4332, 800-362-9849;
www.herrtavern.com
Built in 1815, this inn served as the first Confederate hospital during the Battle of Gettysburg. Guest rooms have been modernized with a light touch that has not marred their quaint, historic charm.
16 rooms. Restaurant, bar. Complimentary breakfast. Restaurant. No children under 12. $61-150

★QUALITY INN AT GENERAL LEE'S HEADQUARTERS
401 Buford Ave., Gettysburg, 717-334-3141, 877-424-6423; www.choicehotels.com
48 rooms. Restaurant, bar. Complimentary breakfast. Business center. Fitness center. Pool. $61-150

WHERE TO EAT
★★DOBBIN HOUSE TAVERN
89 Steinwehr Ave., Gettysburg, 717-334-2100; www.dobbinhouse.com
American. Lunch, dinner. Children's menu. Bar. $36-85

★★FARNSWORTH HOUSE INN
401 Baltimore St., Gettysburg, 717-334-8838; www.farnsworthhouseinn.com
American. Dinner. Children's menu. Outdoor seating. $16-35

★GETTYSBURG EDDIE'S
217 Steinwehr Ave., Gettysburg, 717-334-1100; www.thegingerbreadman.net
American. Lunch, dinner. Bar. $16-35

★★★HERR TAVERN AND PUBLICK HOUSE
900 Chambersburg Road, Gettysburg, 717-334-4332, 800-362-9849;
www.herrtavern.com
This restaurant is housed in the historic country inn of the same name, which served as the first Confederate hospital during the Battle of Gettysburg. Guests here are treated to friendly, pleasant service and an appetizing menu of American-inspired fare that includes some Mediterranean influences. Because most ingredients are obtained from local farmers, the menu frequently changes. Past dishes included shrimp and scallops in red pepper fondue with baby spinach and fettuccine; and Black Angus filet mignon with port wine demi-glace and a stuffed potato.
American. Lunch, dinner. Reservations recommended. Bar. $36-85

HARRISBURG
See also Carlisle, Hershey, York
This mid-state metropolis holds what many consider the finest capitol building in the nation. Other showplaces include the city's riverside park (known

as City Island), Italian Lake, unique museum and beautiful Forum.

Harrisburg's location was viewed in 1615 by Etienne Brul on a trip down the Susquehanna, but more than a century passed before John Harris, the first settler, opened his trading post here. His son established the town in 1785. The cornerstone of the first capitol building was laid in 1819.

WHAT TO SEE
CAPITOL
Third and State streets, Harrisburg, 717-787-6810; www.pacapitol.com
The Capitol of Pennsylvania is an Italian Renaissance building which was dedicated in 1906 and covers two acres and has 651 rooms. It has a 26,000-ton, 272-foot dome, imitating that of St. Peter's in Rome, which dominates city skyline. It includes murals by Abbey and Okley.
Tours: Monday-Friday 8:30 a.m.-4 p.m. (every half hour); Saturday-Sunday 9 a.m., 11 a.m., 1 p.m., 3 p.m.

FORT HUNTER MANSION
5300 N. Front St., Harrisburg, 717-599-5751; www.forthunter.org
Federal-style stone mansion, built in three sections. Front stone portions were built in 1786 and 1814; the rear wooden portion was built in 1870. Spacious mansion displays period furnishings, clothing, toys and other artifacts.
Admission: adults $5, seniors $4, students $3. Tours: May-December, Tuesday-Saturday 10:30 a.m.-4:30 p.m., Sunday noon-4:40 p.m.

FORT HUNTER PARK
5300 N. Front St., Harrisburg, 717-599-5751; www.forthunter.org
This historic 37-acre property is the site of British-built fort erected in 1754 to combat mounting threats prior to the French and Indian War. In 1787, the land was purchased and became a farm that eventually grew into a self-sufficient village. The Pennsylvania Canal runs through the park; on the grounds are historic buttonwood trees dating from William Penn's time, a 19th-century boxwood garden and picnic area.

JOHN HARRIS AND SIMON CAMERON MANSION
219 S. Front St., Harrisburg, 717-233-3462; www.dauphincountyhistory.org
Home of city's founder, now Historical Society of Dauphin County head-quarters. Stone house has 19th-century furnishings, library, collection of county artifacts.
Admission: adults $7.50, seniors $6.50, children 6-16 $5.50, children 5 and under free. Tours: June-October, Monday-Friday 1-4 p.m., second Saturday of the month 1-4 p.m. Closed January-March (for individual tours).

THE STATE MUSEUM OF PENNSYLVANIA
300 N. St., Harrisburg, 717-787-4980; www.statemuseumpa.org
A six-story circular building housing four stories of galleries, authentic early country store, Native American life exhibit, technological and industrial exhibits, collection of antique autos and period carriages; planetarium; natural history and geology exhibits and one of the world's largest framed paintings, Rothermel's *The Battle of Gettysburg*. The planetarium has public shows on

Saturday and Sunday.
Admission: Free. Tuesday-Saturday 9 a.m.-5 p.m., Sunday noon-5 p.m.
April-early-June, Monday.

SPECIAL EVENTS
PENNSYLVANIA NATIONAL HORSE SHOW
1509 Cedar Cliff Drive, Harrisburg, 717-770-0222; www.panational.org
For ten days in October, more than 1,200 horses and riders are part of this
equestrian competition. There are also more than 65 vendors selling gifts,
clothing, pet items and more.
Mid-October.

PENNSYLVANIA STATE FARM SHOW
State Farm Show Complex, 2300 N. Cameron St., Harrisburg, 717-787-5373;
www.farmshow.state.pa.us
The Pennsylvania agriculture and farm show is fun for the whole family. It
features plenty of competitions from apple pie contests to cow milking con-
tests and cook-offs. There are also talent competitions, a rodeo and more.
There is also a food court featuring the best food of Pennsylvania.
Mid-January.

WHERE TO STAY
★★BEST WESTERN HARRISBURG/HERSHEY HOTEL & SUITES
300 N. Mountain Road, Harrisburg, 717-652-7180; www.bestwestern.com
101 rooms. Complimentary breakfast. Business center. Fitness center. Pool.
Pets accepted. $61-150

★★★CROWNE PLAZA HOTEL HARRISBURG-HERSHEY
23 S. Second St., Harrisburg, 717-234-5021, 800-496-7621; www.crowneplaza.com
A smart choice for families and budget travelers, this full-service hotel is
near all the attractions of Harrisburg but does not leave the wallet empty.
Hershey Park is minutes away, as are Chocolate World, the Carlisle Fairgrounds, the National Civil War Museum and the Capitol Complex. Restaurant Row (a collection of more than 30 restaurants, clubs, pubs and shops) is
literally outside the front door and should not be missed. After a busy day, a
nap in one of the contemporary guest rooms is the answer.
261 rooms. Restaurant, bar. Business center. Fitness center. Pool. Pets accepted. $61-150

★DAYS INN HARRISBURG NORTH
3919 N. Front St., Harrisburg, 717-233-3100, 800-329-7466; www.daysinn.com
116 rooms. Complimentary breakfast. Business center. Fitness center. Pool.
Pets accepted. $61-150

★★FOUR POINTS BY SHERATON HARRISBURG
800 E. Park Drive, Harrisburg, 717-561-2800, 800-325-3535; www.starwoodhotels.com
174 rooms. Restaurant, bar. Business center. Fitness center. Pool. $61-150

★HAMPTON INN HARRISBURG-EAST

4230 Union Deposit Road, Harrisburg, 717-545-9595, 800-426-7866;
www.hamptoninn.com

145 rooms. Complimentary breakfast. Business center. Fitness center. Pool.
$61-150

★★★HILTON HARRISBURG

1 N. Second St., Harrisburg, 717-233-6000, 800-445-8667; www.harrisburg.hilton.com

This elegant, family-friendly hotel is located in the heart of historic Harrisburg and is connected to the Whitaker Center by an enclosed walkway. Although the standard guest rooms are well-appointed, guests who choose to upgrade to Tower Level rooms will enjoy upgraded amenities including access to a private lounge that serves complimentary continental breakfast and evening hors d'oeuvres. The hotel also features three restaurants, including a seasonal restaurant.

341 rooms. Restaurant, bar. Business center. Fitness center. Pool. Pets accepted. $151-250

★★RADISSON PENN HARRIS HOTEL & CONVENTION CENTER

1150 Camp Hill Bypass, Camp Hill, 717-763-7117, 800-395-7046; www.radisson.com

250 rooms. Restaurant, bar. Business center. Fitness center. Pool. Pets accepted. $61-150

★★★SHERATON HARRISBURG HERSHEY HOTEL

4650 Lindle Road, Harrisburg, 717-564-5511, 800-325-3535; www.sheraton.com

Minutes from downtown Harrisburg and the airport, this full-service hotel is also near many attractions such as Hershey Park, Hershey Chocolate World, historic Gettysburg, the Pennsylvania Dutch Country and the State Museum of Pennsylvania. The traditional-style guest rooms are spacious and include large work desks. The Dog and Pony Restaurant serves breakfast, lunch and dinner in a casually elegant setting, and the Dog and Pony Pub is a nice place for a nightcap.

348 rooms. Restaurant, bar. Business center. Fitness center. Pool. Pets accepted. $61-150

WHERE TO EAT

★★★ALFRED'S VICTORIAN RESTAURANT

38 N. Union St., Middletown, 717-944-5373; www.alfredsvictorian.com

Housed in a picturesque, 1888-Victorian brownstone, this 30-year-old restaurant offers five intimate dining rooms, each with authentically restored design elements and period décor. The menu has a Northern Italian influence and offers nearly 30 different entrées, such as lobster tail and filet mignon. American, Italian. Lunch (Tuesday-Friday), dinner. Closed Monday. Reservations recommended. Outdoor seating. Bar. $36-85

HAWLEY

See also Milford, Scranton

A major attraction in this Pocono resort area is man-made Lake Wallenpaupack, offering summer recreation and winter recreation nearby.

WHAT TO SEE
LAKE WALLENPAUPACK
Highway 6, Hawley, 570-226-2141; www.800poconos.com
One of the largest man-made lakes in the state, it was formed by the damming of Wallenpaupack Creek in 1927. The lake offers a swimming beach, fishing, boating, water sports, ice fishing, and camping sites. There are six public recreation areas to enjoy, each of which offer trails, wildlife and more. Daily.

WHERE TO STAY
★★★SETTLERS INN AT BINGHAM PARK
4 Main Ave., Hawley, 570-226-2993, 800-833-8527; www.thesettlersinn.com
The Settlers Inn, a Craftsmen mountain lodge, was built in 1927. Guests can request in-room massages, champagne or flowers to greet them upon their arrival. All guests receive a complimentary pass to the Woodloch Springs Health Club where you can use the fitness center, sauna, swimming pool and more. Enjoy dinner at the restaurant which features dishes made with fresh and local ingredients in a casual yet romantic setting.
21 rooms. Restaurant, bar. Business center. $61-150

WHERE TO EAT
★★THE SETTLERS INN
4 Main Ave., Hawley, 570-226-2993; www.thesettlersinn.com
American. Lunch (Wednesday-Saturday), dinner, Sunday brunch. Reservations recommended. Outdoor seating. Bar. $16-35

HERSHEY
See also Harrisburg
One of America's most fascinating success stories, this planned community takes its name from founder M.S. Hershey, who established his world-famous chocolate factory here in 1903, then built a town around it. The streets have names like Chocolate and Cocoa and streetlights are shaped like chocolate kisses. But there's more than chocolate here. Today, Hershey is known as one of the most diverse entertainment and resort areas in the eastern United States. Hershey is also known as the "golf capital of Pennsylvania" and has a number of well-known golf courses.

WHAT TO SEE
HERSHEY GARDENS
170 Hotel Road, Hershey, 717-534-3492; www.hersheygardens.org
From mid-June to first frost, 8,000 rose plants bloom on 23 acres. There is a tulip garden (mid-April-mid-May); chrysanthemums and annuals; butterfly house featuring 400-500 butterflies; and six theme gardens including the Children's Garden.
Admission: adults $10, seniors $9, children 3-12 $6, children under 3 free. March, November-December, daily 10 a.m.-4 p.m.; April-late-May, mid-September-October, daily 9 a.m.-5 p.m.; June-early-September, daily 9 a.m.-8 p.m.; January-February, Saturday-Sunday 10 a.m.-4 p.m.

HERSHEYPARK

100 W. Hershey Park Drive, Hershey, 800-437-7439; www.800hershey.com

This 110-acre theme park includes the waterpark Boardwalk at Hersheypark with 9 water rides; Pioneer Frontier, Midway America, Music Boz Way, Minetown, and Founder's Circle. There's also plenty of entertainment, more than 60 rides include 11 roller coasters, live family shows and plenty of food and beverage vendors. ZooAmerica is also located at Hersheypark.

Admission (one day): adults and children 9-18 $51.95, seniors (ages 55-69) $30.95, seniors plus (ages 70 and over) $20.95, children 3-8 $30.95, children under 3 free. Mid-May-Labor Day, daily; hours vary.

HERSHEYPARK STADIUM AND THE STAR PAVILION

100 W. Hersheypark Drive, Hershey, 717-534-3911; www.hersheyparkstadium.com

Hersheypark stadium with a grandstand of the capacity 16,000 (and can hold up to 30,000 for concerts) hosts professional hockey games, basketball games, ice skating, variety shows and concerts including the Dave Matthews Band and U2. The Star Pavilion hosts summer concerts with a seating and a lawn area. It can hold up to 8,000 people.

HERSHEY'S CHOCOLATE WORLD

251 Park Blvd., Hershey, 717-534-4900; www.hersheys.com/chocolateworld

Hershey's Chocolate World offers you everything you need to know about chocolate and how Hershey makes it. Tour via automated conveyance; simulates steps of chocolate production from cacao bean plantations through chocolate-making in Hershey. Enjoy Hershey's really big 3-D Show featuring Hershey's products' characters. There are also tropical gardens, a shopping village, restaurants, and marketplace shops.

May-December; hours vary.

ZOO AMERICA

100 W. Hershey Park Drive, Hershey, 717-534-3900; www.zooamerica.com

An 11-acre environmental zoo featuring five climatic regions of North America; home to more than 200 animals and 75 different species. If you're also visiting Hersheypark, you can visit Zoo America for free with a combined admission fee.

Admission: adults and children 9-18 $9, seniors $7.50, children 3-8 $7.50, children under 3 free. November-March, daily 10 a.m.-4:30 p.m.; April-October, daily; hours vary.

SPECIAL EVENTS

HERSHEYPARK IN THE DARK

Hersheypark, 100 W. Hershey Park Drive, Hershey, 717-534-3900;
www.hersheypark.com

This festival celebrated Halloween for three weekends in October with a Halloween-theme throughout the park including shows and attractions. There is also fall food and a trick-or-treat adventure for children where they can collect treats in a treat-themed village.

October.

WHERE TO STAY
★DAYS INN
350 W. Chocolate Ave., Hershey, 717-534-2162, 800-329-7466; www.daysinn.com
100 rooms. Restaurant. Complimentary breakfast. Business center. Fitness center. Pool. Pets accepted. $61-150

★★★HERSHEY LODGE AND CONVENTION CENTER
West Chocolate Avenue and University Drive, Hershey, 717-533-3311, 800-437-7439;
www.hersheylodge.com
The Hershey Lodge stays true to its name, with chocolate-themed décor in every guest room and special Hersheypark privileges including discounted tickets and early access to certain rides. Kids can even check themselves in at their own check-in desk and greet the friendly Hershey's product characters who might make an appearance in the lobby.
665 rooms. Restaurant, bar. Complimentary breakfast. Business center. Fitness center. Pool. $151-250

★★★★THE HOTEL HERSHEY
100 Hotel Road, Hershey, 717-533-2171, 800-437-7439; www.thehotelhershey.com
Perched atop a hill overlooking town, The Hotel Hershey sits on 300 acres of formal gardens, fountains and reflecting pools. Instead of mints, you'll find chocolate kisses on your pillow at evening turndown. With a multi-million dollar renovation completed in 2009, be sure to enjoy the new recreation campus with 72 holes of golf, six miles of nature trails, basketball, volleyball, bocce ball and tennis courts, pools, a fitness center and an ice skating rink. You'll also find 10 new luxurious cottages with multiple rooms and the new Shops at Hotel Hershey which feature seven boutiques. Rest your sweet tooth with a meal at the Fountain Cafe, or at the Circular Dining Room, Hotel Hershey's spot for fine dining. Or head to the brand new Harvest restaurant serving American cuisine in a casual environment. The Spa at Hotel Hershey is a wonderfully sinful place, with whipped cocoa baths and chocolate fondue wraps.
278 rooms. Restaurant, bar. Business center. Fitness center. Pool. Spa. Golf. Tennis. $251-350

★SPINNERS INN
845 E. Chocolate Ave., Hershey, 717-533-9157, 800-800-5845; www.spinnersinn.com
52 rooms. Restaurant, bar. Complimentary breakfast. Fitness center. Pool. $61-150

WHERE TO EAT
★★★CIRCULAR DINING ROOM
1 Hotel Road, Hershey, 717-534-8800, 800-437-7439; www.hersheypa.com
This elegant dining destination is tucked away in the Hotel Hershey. Its circular design—the idea of founder Milton S. Hershey—affords all guests, no matter where they are seated, unobstructed views of the exquisite formal gardens and reflecting pools from the room's soaring windows. The contemporary-American menu is as refined as the restaurant's surroundings, and changes seasonally to ensure only the freshest and most flavorful ingredients are used. Past

menus have included cocoa-braised beef short ribs, pulled pork shoulder with house-made sauerkraut, and grilled beef filet with truffled dauphinoise pota-toes. Decadent desserts feature many choices for chocolate lovers, like warm chocolate soufflé and the Chocolate Evolution, a tasting of chocolate. American. Breakfast, lunch (Saturday), dinner (Thursday-Saturday). Sunday brunch. Children's menu. Reservations recommended. $36-85

★★UNION CANAL HOUSE
107 S. Hanover St., Hershey, 717-566-0054, 888-566-5867;
www.unioncanalhouse.com
American. Dinner. Closed Sunday. Reservations recommended. Bar. $36-85

SPAS
★★★THE SPA AT THE HOTEL HERSHEY
100 W. Hersheypark Drive, Hershey, 717-533-2171, 800-437-7439;
www.spaathotelhershey.com
The Spa at Hotel Hershey doesn't skimp on using its signature luscious in-gredient. Chocolate reigns at this three-story spa, from the chocolate bean polish and whipped cocoa bath to the chocolate fondue wrap and the choco-late scrub. Or enjoy a Cuban-influenced mojito sugar scrub or body wrap, inspired by Mr. Hershey's love of Cuba where he owned many sugar planta-tions. The 30,000-square-foot facility includes an inhalation room, a quiet room for meditation, soaking tubs, steam rooms, saunas and signature show-ers for hydrotherapy treatments. There's also an indoor swimming pool and fitness center for guests to use along with fitness classes offered daily.

HOPEWELL FURNACE NATIONAL HISTORIC SITE
See also Reading
Hopewell, an early industrial community, was built around a charcoal-burn-ing cold-blast furnace, which made pig iron and many other iron products from 1771 to 1883. Nearby mines and forests supplied ore and charcoal for the furnace. The National Park Service has restored the buildings, and inter-pretive programs emphasize the community's role in the history of American industry. Hopewell is surrounded by French Creek State Park.

The visitor center has a museum and audiovisual program on iron-making and community life. A self-guided tour includes charcoal house, blacksmith shop, office store and more. Stove molding and casting demonstrations (late June-Labor Day). There is a vaptioned slide program for the hearing im-paired, Braille map and large-print pamphlets for the visually impaired and wheelchair access. Daily.

JOHNSTOWN
See also Altoona, Pittsburgh
On May 31, 1889, a break in the South Fork Dam that impounded an old reservoir 10 miles to the east poured a wall of water onto the city, causing the disastrous "Johnstown Flood." The death toll rose to 2,209 and property damage totaled $17 million. The city has been flooded 22 times since 1850, most recently in 1977. Founded by a Swiss Mennonite, Joseph Johns, the city is now the center of Cambria County's iron and steel industry, producing iron and steel bars, railroad cars, parts and railroad supplies.

WHAT TO SEE
CONEMAUGH GAP
Located at the West end of the city. the gorge, seven miles long and 1,700 feet deep, cuts between Laurel Hill Ridge and Chestnut Ridge.

INCLINED PLANE RAILWAY
711 Edgehill Drive, Johnstown, 814-536-1816; www.inclinedplane.com
The railway joins Johnstown and Westmont. Ride is on steep (72 percent grade) passenger incline with 500-foot ascent. Counterbalanced cable cars take 50 passengers and two automobiles each.
Admission: round trip, adults $4, children 2-12 $2.50, seniors and children under 2 free. Mid-April-September, Monday-Thursday 7:30 a.m.-10:30 p.m., Friday 7:30 a.m.-11 p.m., Saturday 9 a.m.-11 p.m., Sunday 9 a.m.-10 p.m.; October-December, Sunday-Thursday 11 a.m.-9 p.m., Friday-Saturday 11 a.m.-10 p.m.; January-March, Sunday-Thursday 11 a.m.-7p.m., Friday-Saturday 11 a.m.-10 p.m.

JOHNSTOWN FLOOD MUSEUM
304 Washington St., Johnstown, 814-539-1889; www.jaha.org
This museum depicts the history of Johnstown, with permanent exhibits on 1889 Johnstown Flood as well as an Academy Award-winning film, photographs, artifacts and memorabilia.
Admission: adults $6, seniors $5, students $4. Daily 10 a.m.-5 p.m.

JOHNSTOWN FLOOD NATIONAL MEMORIAL
733 Lake Road, Johnstown, 814-495-4643; www.nps.gov/jofl
The memorial commemorates 1889 Johnstown Flood; there are preserved remnants of the South Fork Dam. The visitor center has exhibits and a 30-minute movie.
Admission: $4. Daily 9 a.m.-5 p.m.

WHERE TO STAY
★COMFORT INN
455 Theatre Drive, Johnstown, 814-266-3678; www.choicehotels.com
115 rooms. Complimentary breakfast. Fitness center. Pool. Pets accepted. $61-150

★★HOLIDAY INN
250 Market St., Johnstown, 814-535-7777, 800-443-5663; www.holidayinn.com
159 rooms. Restaurant, bar. Fitness center. Pool. $61-150

★SLEEP INN
453 Theatre Drive, Johnstown, 814-262-9292, 877-424-6423; www.sleepinn.com
62 rooms. Complimentary breakfast. Pets accepted. $61-150

KING OF PRUSSIA

See also Norristown, Philadelphia, West Chester

Originally named Reeseville for the Welsh family that owned the land, the town renamed itself after the local inn, which is still standing.

WHAT TO SEE
KING OF PRUSSIA MALL

160 N. Gulph Road, King of Prussia, 610-265-5727; www.kingofprussiamall.com

The king of malls on the eastern seaboard is located just 18 miles west of central Philadelphia. Bloomingdales, Neiman Marcus, Nordstrom, Macy's and Lord & Taylor anchor this mall, and more than 365 specialty shops and 40 restaurants will keep you from staying in one place too long.

Monday-Saturday 10 a.m.-9 p.m., Sunday 11 a.m.-6 p.m.

WHERE TO STAY
★BEST WESTERN THE INN AT KING OF PRUSSIA

127 S. Gulph Road, King of Prussia, 610-265-4500, 800-780-7234; www.bestwestern.com

166 rooms. Complimentary breakfast. Fitness center. Pool. $61-150

★★CROWNE PLAZA VALLEY FORGE

260 Mall Blvd., King of Prussia, 610-265-7500, 800-496-7621; www.cpvalleyforge.com

225 rooms. Restaurant, bar. Business center. Fitness center. Pool. $61-150

★★DOUBLETREE HOTEL GUEST SUITES PHILADELPHIA WEST

640 W. Germantown Pike, Plymouth Meeting, 610-834-8300, 800-222-8733; www.doubletree.com

253 rooms. Restaurant, bar. Business center. Fitness center. Pool. $61-150

★HOLIDAY INN EXPRESS HOTEL & SUITES KING OF PRUSSIA

260 N. Gulph Road, King of Prussia, 610-768-9500, 800-315-2621

205 rooms. Complimentary breakfast. Business center. $61-150

★★★THE RADNOR HOTEL

591 E. Lancaster Ave., Saint Davids, 610-688-5800, 800-537-3000; www.radnorhotel.com

This beautiful hotel has formal gardens often used for weddings, and charming accomodations fit for any traveler. Take a dip in the expansive outdoor swimming pool in the summer. Enjoy a meal in the Glenmorgan Bar & Grill where you'll find contemporary American cuisine.

171 rooms. Restaurant, bar. Business center. Fitness center. Pool. $151-250

★SPRINGHILL SUITES PHILADELPHIA PLYMOUTH MEETING

430 Plymouth Road, Plymouth Meeting, 610-940-0400; www.marriott.com

199 rooms. Complimentary breakfast. Business center. Fitness center. Pool. $61-150

WHERE TO EAT
★★CREED'S
499 N. Gulph Road, King of Prussia, 610-265-2550; www.creedskop.com
American. Lunch (Monday-Friday), dinner. Closed Sunday. Bar. $16-35

LAHASKA
See also Allentown, Quakertown
Lahaska is located within Bucks County's countryside and was founded by English Quakers. It's known for it's many antique shops and Peddler's Village, which was founded more than 47 years ago and features shops, restaurants, lodging and more.

WHAT TO SEE
PEDDLER'S VILLAGE
Highways 202 and 263, Lahaska, 215-794-4000; www.peddlersvillage.com
This 18th-century-style country village with 42 acres of landscaped gardens and winding brick paths makes a great day trip from Philadelphia. Browse through a selection of more than 70 specialty shops for handicrafts, toys, accessories, leather goods, collectibles and gourmet foods. Take the kids for a ride on an antique carousel, or take advantage of the many free family events and seasonal festivals. Daily.

SPECIAL EVENTS
SCARECROW FESTIVAL
Peddler's Village, between Highways 202 and 263, Lahaska, 215-794-4000; www.peddlersvillage.com
This free festival features scarecrow making, pumpkin painting, a jack-o-lantern and gourd art contest. There is also square dancing and entertainment. September.

STRAWBERRY FESTIVAL
Peddler's Village, between Highways 202 and 263, Lahaska, 215-794-4000; www.peddlersvillage.com
The Strawberry festival features plenty of strawberry treats from chocolate-covered strawberries, jams, shortcake, pastries, fritters and pints of fresh strawberries. This annual free festival marks the beginning of spring. May.

WHERE TO STAY
★★★GOLDEN PLOUGH INN
41 Peddlersvillage, Lahaska, 215-794-4004; www.peddlersvillage.com
Scattered throughout Peddler's Village on 42 acres, this inn charms guests in every season. Many of the beautifully appointed rooms have gas-lit fireplaces and whirlpools. Guests are greeted with a snack basket upon arrival.
71 rooms. Restaurant, bar. Complimentary breakfast. Fitness center. Pool. $61-150

WHERE TO EAT
★★COCK N' BULL
Highways 202 and 263, Lahaska, 215-794-4000; www.peddlersvillage.com
American. Lunch (Monday-Saturday), dinner, Sunday brunch. Bar. Reservations recommended. $16-35

LANCASTER
See also Denver/Adamstown, Ephrata, Reading, York

Lancaster blends the industrial modern, the colonial past and the Pennsylvania Dutch present. It is in the heart of the Pennsylvania Dutch Area, one of the East's most colorful tourist attractions. To fully appreciate the area, visitors should leave the main highways and travel on country roads, which Amish buggies share with automobiles. Lancaster was an important provisioning area for the armies of the French and Indian and Revolutionary wars. Its crafters turned out fine guns, which brought the city fame as the "arsenal of the Colonies." When Congress, fleeing Philadelphia, paused here on September 27, 1777, the city was the national capital for one day. It was the state capital from 1799 to 1812.

WHAT TO SEE
AMISH FARM AND HOUSE
2395 Lincoln Highway, East Lancaster, 717-394-6185; www.amishfarmandhouse.com
This is a typical Amish farm in operation. Listen to a lecture on the Amish and tour through the early 19th-century stone buildings furnished and decorated as an old-order Amish household. Onsite there are waterwheels, a windmill, a hand-dug well, carriages, a spring wagon and sleighs.
Admission: adults $7.95, seniors $7.25, children 5-11 $5.25, children 4 and under free. January-March, November-December, daily 8:30 a.m.-4 p.m.; April-May, September-October, daily 8:30 a.m.-5 p.m.; June-August, daily 8:30 a.m.-6 p.m.

DUTCH WONDERLAND
2249 Lincoln Highway, East Lancaster, 866-386-2839; www.dutchwonderland.com
This family fun park has 30 rides, botanical gardens, diving shows, shops, and a monorail.
Admission: adults and children 3-18 $30.95, seniors $25.95, seniors 70 and over $18.95, children 2 and under free. Early June-August, daily 10 a.m.-8:30 p.m.; May, September-October; hours vary.

FRANKLIN AND MARSHALL COLLEGE
Race and College avenues, Lancaster, 717-291-3981; www.fandm.edu
This liberal arts college, founded in 1787, has 2,100 students today. Rothman Gallery showcases Pennsylvania-German artifacts including quilts, Fraktur and stoneware.
Tours: Monday-Friday 10 a.m., 11 a.m., 2 p.m., 3 p.m.

FULTON OPERA HOUSE
12 N. Prince St., Lancaster, 717-394-7133; www.thefulton.org
First opened in 1852, this is one of the oldest American theaters and many

legendary people have performed here. It is believed that more than one ghost haunts the theater's Victorian interior. This is home to professional regional theater, community theater, opera and symphony organizations.
See Web site for schedule and ticket information.

HANS HERR HOUSE

1849 Hans Herr Drive, Lancaster, 717-464-4438; www.hansherr.org
Built in 1719, this is a fine example of medieval Germanic architecture. The house served as an early Mennonite meetinghouse and colonial residence of the Herr family; there is a Mennonite rural life exhibit and blacksmith shop.
Admission: adults $5, children 7-12 $2, children 6 and under free. April-November, Monday-Saturday 9 a.m.-4 p.m.

HERITAGE CENTER MUSEUM OF LANCASTER COUNTY

13 W. King St., Lancaster, 717-299-6440; www.lancasterheritage.com
This museum houses examples of early Lancaster County arts and crafts, including furniture, tall clocks, quilts, needlework, silver, pewter and rifles.
Admission: Free. Mid-April-early January, Monday-Saturday 9 a.m.-5 p.m., Sunday 10 a.m.-3 p.m.; First Friday of the month 5-9 p.m.

HISTORIC LANCASTER WALKING TOUR

100 S. Queen St., Lancaster, 717-392-1776; www.padutchcountry.com
In a 90-minute tour of historic downtown area, costumed guide narrates 50 points of architectural or historic interest covering six square blocks.
Tours: April-October, Sunday-Monday, Wednesday-Thursday 1 p.m.; Tuesday, Friday-Saturday 10 a.m., 1 p.m.

HISTORIC ROCK FORD

881 Rockford Road, Lancaster, 717-392-7223; www.rockfordplantation.org
This is the preserved 1794 home of General Edward Hand, Revolutionary War commander and member of Continental Congress.
Admission: adults $6, seniors $5, children 6-12 $4. April-October, Wednesday-Sunday 11 a.m.-3 p.m. (last tour at 3 p.m.).

JAMES BUCHANAN'S WHEATLAND

1120 Marietta Ave., Lancaster, 717-392-8721; www.wheatland.org
Built in 1828, this building served as the residence of President James Buchanan from 1848 to 1868. Today, the restored Federal mansion with period rooms containing American Empire and Victorian furniture and decorative arts are available to tour.
Admission: adults $8, seniors $7, students $6, children 6-11 $3, children 5 and under free. April-October, Tuesday-Saturday 10 a.m.-4:30 p.m. Christmas candlelight tours early December.

LANDIS VALLEY MUSEUM

2451 Kissel Hill Road, Lancaster, 717-569-0401; www.landisvalleymuseum.org
The Landis Valley Museum interprets Pennsylvania German rural life with the largest collection of Pennsylvania-German objects in U.S. Also here, you'll find craft and living history demonstrations and country store.

Admission: adults $12, seniors $10, children 3-11 $8, children 2 and under free. Monday-Saturday noon-5 p.m.

NORTH MUSEUM OF NATURAL HISTORY AND SCIENCE

400 College Ave., Lancaster, 717-291-3941; www.northmuseum.org
This museum focuses on general science and natural history with planetarium shows, a children's Discovery Room, a film series and monthly art exhibits.
Admission: adults $7, seniors $6, children 3-17 $6, children 2 and under free. Tuesday-Saturday 10 a.m.-5 p.m., Sunday noon-5 p.m.

THE WATCH AND CLOCK MUSEUM

514 Poplar St., Columbiar, 717-684-8261; www.nawcc.org
This is the National Association of Watch and Clock Collectors living museum of timepieces, related tools and memorabilia. More than 8,000 items representing the 1600s to the present. There is also an extensive research library and special exhibitions.
Admission: adults $8, seniors $7, children 5-16 $4, children 4 and under free. April-November, Tuesday-Saturday 10 a.m.-5 p.m., Sunday noon-4 p.m.; December-March, Tuesday-March 10 a.m.-4 p.m.

SPECIAL EVENTS
HARVEST DAYS

Landis Valley Museum, 2451 Kissel Hill Road, Lancaster, 717-569-0401;
www.landisvalleymuseum.org
This festival celebrates the harvest season with demonstrations of more than 80 traditional crafts and harvest-time activities including apple butter making, open hearth cooking, horse-drawn wagon rides, music and food. You can also pick out your pumpkin from the pumpkin patch.
Columbus Day weekend.

WHERE TO STAY
★★BEST WESTERN EDEN RESORT INN & SUITES

222 Eden Road, Lancaster, 717-569-6444; www.edenresort.com
276 rooms. Restaurant, bar. Fitness center. Pool. Pets accepted. Tennis. $61-150

★THE INN AT HERSHEY FARM

240 Hartman Bridge Road, Ronks, 717-687-8635, 800-827-8635;
www.hersheyfarm.com
60 rooms. Restaurant, bar. Complimentary breakfast. Pool. $61-150

★★HILTON GARDEN INN LANCASTER

101 Granite Run Drive, Lancaster, 717-560-0880, 877-782-9444
156 rooms. Business center. Fitness center. Pool. $61-150

★★HOLIDAY INN EXPRESS LANCASTER-ROCKVALE OUTLETS

24 S. Willowdale Drive, Lancaster, 717-293-9500, 888-465-4329;
www.ichotelsgroup.com
112 rooms. Complimentary breakfast. Fitness center. Pool. $61-150

★★WILLOW VALLEY RESORT AND CONFERENCE CENTER
2416 Willow St., Pike, Lancaster, 717-464-2711, 800-444-1714; www.willowvalley.com
342 rooms. Restaurant, bar. Fitness center. Pool. Business center. Golf. Tennis. $151-250

WHERE TO EAT
★★THE BRASSERIE RESTAURANT AND BAR
1679 Lincoln Highway East, Lancaster, 717-299-1694; www.dandsbrasserie.com
American. Lunch (Monday-Friday), dinner. Outdoor seating. Reservations recommended. Bar. $36-85

★★★HAYDN ZUG'S
1987 State St., East Petersburg, 717-569-5746; www.haydnzugs.com
Owner and Chef Terry Lee hails from Petersburg and offers an award-winning wine list and exceptional cuisine.
American. Lunch, dinner. Closed Sunday. Bar. $36-85

★★OLDE GREENFIELD INN
595 Greenfield Road, Lancaster, 717-393-0668; www.theoldegreenfieldinn.com
American. Breakfast, lunch, dinner, Sunday brunch. Bar. Children's menu. Outdoor seating. Reservations recommended. $36-85

MILFORD
See also Hawley
The borough of Milford was settled by Thomas Quick, a Hollander. Noted forester and conservationist Governor Gifford Pinchot lived here. His house, Grey Towers, is near the town.

WHAT TO SEE
CANOEING, RAFTING, KAYAKING AND TUBING
Kittatinny Canoes, River Beach Campsites, 378 Routes 6 & 209, Milford, 570-828-2338, 800-356-2852; www.kittatinny.com
Kittany Canoes provides trips which travel down the Delaware River. Choose from a canoe trip, kayaking, rafting, tubing, paintball and camping. Mid-April-October, daily.

GREY TOWERS
151 Grey Tower Drive, Milford, 570-296-6401; www.fs.fed.us/gt
A 100-acre estate originally built in 1886 as summer house for philanthropist James W. Pinchot. It then became the residence of his son, Gifford Pinchot, the "father of American conservation," governor of Pennsylvania and the first chief of USDA Forest Service. Now, it's the site of the Pinchot Institute for Conservation Studies.
Admission: adults $6, seniors $5, children 12-17 $3, children 11 and under free. Tours: Memorial Day weekend-Labor Day weekend, daily 11 a.m.-4 p.m. (on the hour).

WHERE TO STAY
★★★CLIFF PARK INN

155 Cliff Park Road, Milford, 570-296-6491, 800-225-6535; www.cliffparkinn.com

The Cliff Park Inn (originally a farmhouse, built in 1820) is located on 500 acres overlooking the Delaware River. With 12 guest rooms, three restaurants, seven miles of hiking trails, a nine-hole golf course and free wireless Internet access, all this inn has to offer might encourage you to extend your stay. Nearby activities include cross-country skiing, hiking trails, swimming and more.

12 rooms. Restaurant, bar. Complimentary breakfast. Reservations recommended. Golf. $61-150

MOUNT POCONO
See also Pocono Mountains

One of the many thriving resort communities in the heart of the Pocono Mountains, Mount Pocono offers recreation year-round in nearby parks, lakes and ski areas.

WHAT TO SEE
MOUNT POCONO CAMPGROUND

30 Edgewood Road, Mount Pocono, 570-839-8950; www.mtpoconocampground.com

Enjoy 188 seasonal campsites for every need on 42 wooded acres in sunny or shaded locations. This campground is only 2 hours from Philadelphia and 90 minues from New York City. These are sites for RV, trailer and tents with either full hook-ups (with cable), water and electrical hook-ups, electrical hook-ups, or no hook-ups. There is also a convenience store, outdoor pool, a game room, volleyball court, picnic areas and a children's pool.

May-October.

POCONO KNOB

Southeast edge of town of Mount Pocono

This spot has excellent view of surrounding countryside.

SUMMIT LANES

Three Park Drive E., Pocono Summit, 570-839-9635; www.summitlanespa.com

Summit Lanes is a terrific bowling center with 36 new state-of-the-art synthetic lanes and automatic scorers with color monitors. It also has a billiards area, food court, pro shop, lounge and video game room.

Daily. Cosmic bowling: Saturday 9:30 p.m.-2 a.m.

WHERE TO STAY
★★★CAESARS PARADISE STREAM

Highway 940, Mount Pocono, 570-226-2101, 800-432-9932;
www.caesarsparadisestream.com

For that honeymoon experience the Poconos are so well known for, Caesars is the place to stay. These are all-inclusive resorts, with heart-shaped tubs, round beds and champagne glass-shaped whirlpools that offer a romantic getaway. Big-name entertainers often appear at Caesars.

164 rooms. Restaurant, bar. Pool. Spa. No children. Tennis. $251-350

★★★CRESCENT LODGE

191 Paradise Valley, Mount Pocono, 570-595-7486, 800-392-9400;
www.crescentlodge.com

Nestled in the heart of the Pocono Mountains, the Cresecnt Lodge is elegant and welcoming. Guests enjoy uniquely furnished guest rooms, with some rooms boasting sunken Jacuzzis, private patios and sundecks overlooking the well-maintained grounds.

31 rooms. Restaurant, bar. Complimentary breakfast. Pool. $61-150

★★★FRENCH MANOR

50 Huntington Road, South Sterling, 570-676-3244, 877-720-6090;
www.thefrenchmanor.com

Each guest room in this elegant inn shines with personal touches and lots of space. But don't let the antique ambience foul you; modern amenities abound in the rooms including DVD players and free high-speed Internet access. The Great Hall has two floor-to-ceiling fireplaces.

15 rooms. Restaurant, bar. Complimentary breakfast. Fitness center. Pool. Spa. No children under 12. $151-250

★★★THE INN AT POCONO MANOR

Highway 314, Pocono Manor, 570-839-7111, 800-233-8150; www.poconomanor.com

Less than two hours from New York, this "Grand Lady of the Mountains" has been in business since 1902. Its rooms are well appointed and tasteful, in keeping with its spot on the National Register of Historic Places. Golf, horseback riding, swimming and tennis are all available on the 3,000-acre estate, as are fishing, clay shooting and more. Also, pamper yourself at Laurel Spa, also onsite.

250 rooms. Restaurant, bar. Fitness center. Pool. Spa. Golf. $151-250

★★★SKYTOP LODGE

One Skytop, Mount Pocono, 570-595-7401, 800-345-7759; www.skytop.com

Skytop Lodge is the ultimate mountain getaway for outdoor enthusiasts, with an 18-hole golf course, seven tennis courts, a clay shooting range, indoor and outdoor pools and fly fishing in the natural streams found throughout the property. This retreat in the heart of the Poconos is easily accessed from New York or Philadelphia. Accommodations are offered within the historic hotel, four-bedroom cottages or the intimate golf-course inn. The American menu at the Windsor Dining Room draws a crowd, while more casual dining is available at the Lake View Dining Room and the Tap Room.

148 rooms. Restaurant, bar. Pool. Spa. Golf. Beach. $351 and up.

★★★STERLING INN

Highway 191, South Sterling, 570-676-3311, 800-523-8200; www.thesterlinginn

Built in the 1850s, this country Inn is perfect for families ready to hit the nearby ski areas or antiquers looking for a new piece of history. Guest rooms have quilts on the beds and personalized homey touches.

54 rooms. Complimentary breakfast. Tennis. $61-150

WHERE TO EAT
★★★POWERHOUSE
1 Powerhouse Road, White Haven, 570-443-4480; www.powerhouseeatery.net
This restaurant is popular for its Italian-American menu. Its brick walls and exposed pipes remind diners of when it was as a coal-fueled power plant. American, Italian. Lunch (Tuesday-Sunday), dinner. Reservations recommended. Bar. $16-35

★TOKYO TEAHOUSE
Highway 940, Pocono Summit, 570-839-8880; www.tokyoteahouse.us
Japanese. Lunch, dinner. Closed Tuesday. Reservations recommended. $16-35

NEW CASTLE
See also Beaver Falls
At the junction of the Shenango, Mahoning and Beaver rivers, New Castle was long an important Native American trading center. Today, the fireworks and plastics industries have become an integral part of the community.

WHAT TO SEE
THE HOYT INSTITUTE OF FINE ARTS
124 E. Leasure Ave., New Castle, 724-652-2882; www.hoytartcenter.org
This cultural arts center housed in two early 20th-century mansions on four acres of landscaped grounds. There's a permanent art collection, changing exhibits, period rooms, performing arts programs and classes.
Art Galleries: Tuesday-Thursday 11 a.m.-8 p.m., Wednesday, Friday-Saturday 11 a.m.-4 p.m. Admission: Free. Tours of Period House: Tuesday-Saturday 11 a.m.-4 p.m. Tours: $5. Gift Shop: Tuesday-Saturday 11 a.m.-4 p.m.

LAWRENCE COUNTY HISTORICAL SOCIETY AND MUSEUM
408 N. Jefferson, New Castle, 724-658-4022; www.lawrencechs.com
The Greer House, a turn-of-the-century restored mansion houses the Lawrence County Historical Society and Museum. The museum has extensive Shenango and Castleton china collections, a Sports "Hall of Fame," and a fireworks room. There are also archives, workshops and speakers.
Tuesday, Thursday, Saturday 11 a.m.-4 p.m.; also by appointment.

LIVING TREASURES ANIMAL PARK
Highway 422, Moraine 724-924-9571; www.ltanimalpark.com
Visitors can pet and feed over 100 species from around the world.
Adults: adults $7.50, seniors $7, children 3-11 $5.50, children 2 and under free. April-May, September-October, daily 10 a.m.-6 p.m.; Memorial Day-August, daily 10 a.m.-8 p.m.

MCCONNELL'S MILL STATE PARK
New Castle, 724-368-8091; www.dcnr.state.pa.us
This state park takes up approximately 2,500 acres with a century-old mill surrounded by beautiful landscape and scenery. Go fishing, hunting, whitewater rafting and hiking. There are picnicking areas, a historical center and interpretive programs. There is no swimming at Slippery Rock Creek how-

ever, as it has been deemed too dangerous.
Daily dawn-dusk.

SCOTTISH RITE CATHEDRAL
110 E. Lincoln Ave., New Castle, 724-654-6683; www.cathedralnewcastle.com
Located on a hillside, this cathedral's six 32-foot columns dominate the city's skyline. There is a large auditorium and ballroom. It's also the site of local Masonic headquarters. The Pittsburgh Symphony also plays here somtimes. See Web site for event information.

WHERE TO STAY
★COMFORT INN
1740 New Butler Road, New Castle, 724-658-7700, 877-424-6423;
www.choicehotels.com
79 rooms. Complimentary breakfast. Business center. Pets accepted. $61-150

WHERE TO EAT
★★THE TAVERN
108 N. Market St., New Wilmington, 724-946-2020
American. Lunch, dinner. Outdoor seating. $16-35

NEW HOPE
See also Erwinna
The river village of New Hope was originally the largest part of a 1,000-acre land grant from William Penn to Thomas Woolrich of Shalford, England. In the 20th century, the area gained fame as the home of artists and literary and theatrical personalities.

WHAT TO SEE

BOWMAN'S HILL WILDFLOWER PRESERVE
New Hope, 215-862-2924; www.bhwp.org
Pennsylvania's native plants come into focus at this 134-acre preserve located 40 miles northeast of Philadelphia. Hike or walk along woodland, a meadow, a creek or an arboretum. Botanic enthusiasts will discover 1,000 species of trees, shrubs, ferns, vines and herbaceous wildflowers. There are many contemplative places for meditation and study, scenic picnic spots and several historic sites within hiking distance. Head five miles south to Washington Crossing Historic Park (*1112 River Road, Washington Crossing; 215-493-4076*), where George Washington crossed the Delaware River in 1776. Bowman's Hill Tower, a lookout commemorating the American Revolution, offers a view of the Delaware River and rolling countryside one mile on foot or by car.
Admission: adults $5, seniors $3 and students $3, children 4-14 $2, children 3 and under free. Visitor center: Daily 9 a.m.-5 p.m. Grounds: Daily 8:30 a.m.-sunset.

CORYELL'S FERRY
22 S. Main St., New Hope, 215-862-2050
Passenger and chartered rides aboard the Major William C. Barnett, a 65-

foot Mississippi-style sternwheel riverboat, on the Delaware River. Memorial Day-Labor Day, daily 11 a.m., noon, 1 p.m. (and every 45 minutes on the hour until 7 p.m.).

NEW HOPE & IVYLAND RAILROAD
32 W. Bridge St., New Hope, 215-862-2332; www.newhoperailroad.com
A nine-mile, 50-minute narrated train ride through Bucks County. Reading Railroad passenger coaches from the 1920s depart from restored 1890 New Hope Station.
March-November; see Web site for schedule and ticket information.

PARRY MANSION MUSEUM AND BARN
South Main and Ferry streets, New Hope, 215-862-5652;
www.newhopehistoricalsociety.org
This restored stone house built in 1784 by Benjamin Parry, a prosperous merchant and mill owner. There are eleven rooms on view, restored and furnished to depict period styles from late 18th to early 20th centuries.
Admission: adults $6, seniors and children 12-18 $5, children 11 and under $2. May-October, Saturday-Sunday 1:30 p.m., 3 p.m.

WHERE TO STAY

★★★HOTEL DU VILLAGE
2535 N. River Road, New Hope, 215-862-9911; www.hotelduvillage.com
Simple and intimate, Hotel du Village offers 20 cozy guest rooms, two tennis courts, a pool and a restaurant specializing in French country cuisine. Situated just north of New Hope, the inn is only a short distance to shops, art galleries and entertainment options.
20 rooms. Restaurant, bar. Complimentary breakfast. Tennis. $61-150

★★★THE INN AT BOWMAN'S HILL
518 Lurgan Road, New Hope, 215-862-8090; www.theinnatbowmanshill.com
The Inn at Bowman's Hill consists of stone and stucco buildings sitting on five acres of well-manicured grounds. An 80-foot stream runs out front, and the property adjoins the Bowman's Hill Wildflower Preserve. The décor and furnishings are rustic but very upscale, with lots of natural wood. Guest rooms are intimate, with gas fireplaces and large whirlpool tubs. Guests can enjoy a three-course gourmet breakfast in the breakfast room or in their own rooms, and afternoon snacks are offered from 3-7 p.m.
5 rooms. Restaurant, bar. Complimentary breakfast. Pool. $251-350

★★★THE MANSION INN
Nine S. Main St., New Hope, 215-862-1231; www.themansioninn.com
This grand 1865 Baroque Victorian mansion is located along a tranquil canal in the center of downtown New Hope, within walking distance to numerous shops and restaurants, as well as the Michener Art Museum. The stately building welcomes guests with its garden, gazebo, refreshing outdoor pool and beautifully decorated Empire/French Victorian rooms.
7 rooms. Restaurant, bar. Complimentary breakfast. Pool. No children under 14. $151-250

WHERE TO EAT
★★THE CENTRE BRIDGE INN
2998 N. River Road, New Hope, 215-862-9139; www.centrebridgeinn.com
International, Fusion. Dinner. Closed Monday-Tuesday. Bar. Reservations recommended. Outdoor seating. $36-85

★★★THE MANSION INN
The Mansion Inn, Nine S. Main St., New Hope, 215-862-1231; www.themansioninn.com
Situated in the Mansion Inn, this casual yet stately restaurant offers continental cuisine in candlelit dining rooms. The restaurant serves entrées including pan-seared sea scallops with lobster ravioli, porcini mushrooms, cream sauce and sautéed organic spinach or a slow-braised lamb shank with sweet potato risotto, wilted leek fondue and minted demi-glace.
Continental. Lunch, dinner, Sunday brunch. Reservations recommended. Outdoor seating. Bar. $36-85

★★THE INN AT PHILLIPS MILL
2590 N. River Road, New Hope, 215-862-9919; www.theinnatphillipsmill.com
French. Dinner. Reservations recommended. Outdoor seating. $36-85

NORRISTOWN
See also King of Prussia, Philadelphia
William Penn, Jr., owner of the 7,600-acre tract around Norristown, sold it to Isaac Norris and William Trent for 50 cents an acre in 1704. It became a crossroads for colonial merchants and soldiers; Washington's army camped nearby. Dutch, German, Swedish, Welsh and English immigrants all left their mark on the city. Today, Norristown is still a transportation hub.

WHAT TO SEE
ELMWOOD PARK ZOO
1661 Harding Blvd., Norristown, 610-277-3825; www.elmwoodparkzoo.org
This zoo features an extensive North American waterfowl area as well as other animals including cougars, bobcats, bison and elk. There is also an outdoor aviary, a children's zoo barn and a museum with exhibit on animal senses. There are also different habitats to visit including farmland, grasslands, bayou, wetlands and more.
Admission: adults $10.75, seniors $7.75, children 2-12 $7.75, children 1 and under and military personnel free. Daily 10 a.m.-5 p.m.

WHERE TO STAY
★★★SHERATON BUCKS COUNTY HOTEL
400 Oxford Valley Road, Norristown, 215-547-4100, 800-325-3535; www.sheraton.com
Only 25 miles from Philadelphia in the foothills of Bucks County, this full-service hotel features well-appointed rooms, as well as complimentary aerobics classes and certified personal trainers in its fitness center.
186 rooms. Restaurant, bar. Business center. Fitness center. Pool. Pets accepted. Tennis. $151-250

★★★WILLIAM PENN INN

US 202 & Sumneytown Pike, Gwynedd, 215-699-9272; www.williampenninn.com

Since 1714, this inn has offered guests a luxurious stay with period furnishings and a large delicious breakfast in the morning. The restaurant, claiming more than 300 years of service and experience, is a picturesque dining spot and a popular choice for weddings and other celebratory events. The menu leans heavily on seafood with such signature dishes as snapper soup and baked Maryland crab imperial. The Sunday brunch is a hit with locals.

4 rooms. Restaurant, bar. Complimentary breakfast. $61-150

WHERE TO EAT
★★★THE JEFFERSON HOUSE

2519 DeKalb Pike, Norristown, 610-275-3407; www.jefferson-house.com

Since 1926, this casual lakefront dining spot has been pleasing locals with a craving for fresh seafood and friendly service. Try the shrimp scampi or the handmade cheeseburger with a side of perfectly browned fries.

American. Lunch, dinner, Sunday brunch. Children's menu. Bar. $36-85

★★WILLIAM PENN INN

US 202 and Sumneytown Pike, Gwynedd, 215-699-9272; www.williampenninn.com

American. Lunch, dinner, Sunday brunch. Bar. $36-85

NORTH EAST

See also Erie

When Pennsylvania bought the tract containing North East from the federal government in 1778, the state gained 46 miles of Lake Erie frontage, a fine harbor and some of the best Concord grape terrain in the nation.

WHAT TO SEE
HERITAGE WINE CELLARS

12160 E. Main Road, North East, 814-725-9495, 800-747-0083; www.heritagewine.biz

For more than 150 years the Bostwick family has owned this winery. Located in an 18th century barn, they produce more than 50 wine varieties. Stop in for a wine tasting and purchase a bottle to take home. Daily.

MAZZA VINEYARDS

11815 E. Lake Road, North East, 814-725-8695; www.mazzawines.com

Joseph Mazza brought his family vineyard to the Lake Erie region from Calabria, Italy in 1954. Since then, the winery has been producing acclaimed wine including German rieslings. Take a guided tour and a wine tasting.

July-August, Monday-Saturday 9 a.m.-8 p.m., Sunday 11 a.m.-4:30 p.m.; September-June, Monday-Saturday 9 a.m.-5:30 p.m., Sunday noon-4:30 p.m.

PENN-SHORE VINEYARDS AND WINERY

10225 E. Lake Road, North East, 814-725-8688; www.pennshore.com

Penn Shore Vineyards opened the winery in 1970 and is the largest and longest-established winery in the state. Sign up on their Web site for a tour and wine-tasting.

Daily.

SPECIAL EVENTS
WINE COUNTRY HARVEST FESTIVAL
21 S. Lake St., North East, 814-725-4262; www.nechamber.org
This wine festival features five wineries serving their varietals. There's arts and crafts on display, plenty of food and live music. There is also a free shuttle service to the different wineries.
September.

PHILADELPHIA
See also Burlington, Camden, Bristol, Chester, King of Prussia, Norristown

In the mid-18th century, it was the second largest city in the English-speaking world. Today, Philadelphia is the second largest city on the East Coast and the fifth largest in the country. Here, in William Penn's City of Brotherly Love, the Declaration of Independence was written and adopted, the Constitution was molded and signed, the Liberty Bell was rung, Betsy Ross was said to have sewn her flag and Washington served most of his years as president.

This is the city of "firsts," including the first American hospital, medical college, women's medical college, bank, paper mill, steamboat, zoo, sugar refinery, daily newspaper, U.S. mint and public school for black children.

The first Quakers, who came here in 1681, lived in caves dug into the banks of the Delaware River. During the first year, 80 houses were raised; by the following year, William Penn's "greene countrie towne" was a city of 600 buildings. The Quakers prospered in trade and commerce, and Philadelphia became the leading port in the colonies. Its leading citizen for many years was Benjamin Franklin.

The fires of colonial indignation burned hot and early in Philadelphia. Soon after the Boston Tea Party, a protest rally of 8,000 Philadelphians frightened off a British tea ship. In May 1774, when Paul Revere rode from Boston to Philadelphia to report Boston's harbor had been closed, all of Philadelphia went into mourning. The first and second Continental Congresses convened here, and Philadelphia became the headquarters of the Revolution. After the Declaration of Independence was composed and accepted by Congress, the city gave its men, factories and shipyards to the cause. But, British General Howe and 18,000 soldiers poured in on September 26, 1777, to spend a comfortable and social winter here while Washington's troops endured the bitter winter at Valley Forge. When the British evacuated the city, Congress returned. Philadelphia continued as the seat of government until 1800, except for a short period when New York City held the honor. Since those historic days, Philadelphia has figured prominently in the country's politics, economy and culture.

More than 1,400 churches and synagogues grace the city. There are more than 25 colleges, universities and professional schools in Philadelphia as well. Fine restaurants are in abundance, along with exciting nightlife. Entertainment is offered by the world-renowned Philadelphia Orchestra, theaters, college and professional sports, outstanding parks, recreation centers and playgrounds. Shoppers may browse major department stores and hundreds of specialty and antique shops.

WHAT TO SEE
ACADEMY OF MUSIC
Broad and Locust streets, Philadelphia, 215-893-1999; www.academyofmusic.org
The city's opera house and concert hall, this academy was built in 1857 and is home of the Philadelphia Orchestra, Opera Company of Philadelphia and Pennsylvania Ballet. See Web site for schedule and ticket information.

ACADEMY OF NATURAL SCIENCES MUSEUM
1900 Ben Franklin Parkway, Philadelphia, 215-299-1000; www.acnatsci.org
This museum displays dinosaurs, Egyptian mummies, animal displays in natural habitats and live animal programs. There is also a hands-on children's museum.
Admission: adults $12, seniors $10, students and military personnel $10, children 3-12 $10, children 2 and under free. Monday-Friday 10 a.m.-4:30 p.m., Saturday-Sunday 10 a.m.-5 p.m.

AFRICAN-AMERICAN MUSEUM OF PHILADELPHIA
701 Arch St., Philadelphia, 215-574-0380; www.aampmuseum.org
Built to house and interpret African-American culture, this museum has changing exhibits and lectures, workshops, films and concerts.
Admission: adults $10, seniors, students and children 4-12 $8. Tuesday-Saturday 10 a.m.-5 p.m., Sunday noon-5 p.m..

AMERICAN SWEDISH HISTORICAL MUSEUM
Franklin Delano Roosevelt Park, 1900 Pattison Ave., Philadelphia, 215-389-1776; www.americanswedish.org
From tapestries to technology, the museum celebrates Swedish influence on American life. There are special exhibits on the New Sweden Colony. There's also a research library and collections.
Admission: adults $6, seniors, students, children 12-18 $5, children 11 and under free. Tuesday-Friday 10 a.m.-4 p.m, Saturday-Sunday noon-4 p.m.

ANTIQUE ROW
From Ninth to 17th streets along Pine Street, Philadelphia; www.antique-row.org
Dozens of antique, craft and curio shops as well as restaurants, bars and cafes line this popular row.

ATHENAEUM OF PHILADELPHIA
219 S. Sixth St., Philadelphia, 215-925-2688; www.athenaonline.org
This landmark is an example of Italian Renaissance architecture. This restored building has American neoclassical-style decorative arts, paintings, sculpture; a research library; furniture and art from the collection of Joseph Bonaparte, King of Spain and older brother of Napoleon; changing exhibits of architectural drawings, photos and rare books.
Tours by appointment. Monday-Friday 9 a.m.-5 p.m., first Saturday of the month 10 a.m.-2 p.m.

ATWATER KENT MUSEUM OF PHILADELPHIA

15 S. Seventh St., Philadelphia, 215-685-4830; www.philadelphiahistory.org
Hundreds of fascinating artifacts, toys and miniatures, maps, prints, paintings and photographs reflect the city's social and cultural history.
Monday-Friday 9 a.m.-5 p.m.

BETSY ROSS HOUSE

239 Arch St., Philadelphia, 215-686-1252; www.betsyrosshouse.org
This house is where the famous seamstress is said to have made the first American flag. You can see the upholsterer's shop and memorabilia. Flag Day ceremonies take place June 14.
Admission: adults and seniors $3, students and children 12 and under $2.
Audio tour: $5 (includes admission). April-October, daily 10 a.m.-5 p.m.;
October-March, Tuesday-Sunday 10 a.m-5 p.m.

BLUE CROSS RIVER RINK

Festival Pier at Penn's Landing, Columbus Boulevard and Spring Garden Street,
Philadelphia, 215-925-7465; www.riverrink.com
Few outdoor ice-skating rinks are as well-located as this one along the Delaware River. Visitors have a great vantage point from which to view the Benjamin Franklin Bridge and the Philadelphia skyline. This Olympic-size rink, at 200 feet by 85 feet, can accommodate 500 skaters. After skating, warm up in the heated pavilion, which features a video game area and concessions.
Late November-February, daily.

THE BOURSE

111 S. Independence Mall E., Philadelphia, 215-625-0300; www.bourse-pa.com
This restored Victorian building, completed in 1895, houses shops, restaurants and more.
December-February, Monday-Saturday 10 a.m.-6 p.m.; March-November,
Monday-Saturday 10 a.m.-6 p.m., Sunday 11 a.m.-5 p.m.

CHRIST CHURCH AND BURIAL GROUND

Second and Market streets, Philadelphia, 215-922-1695; www.oldchristchurch.org
Patriots, loyalists and heroes have worshiped at this Episcopal church since 1695. Sit in pews once occupied by Washington, Franklin and Betsy Ross. The burial ground is the final resting place of Benjamin Franklin, his wife, Deborah, and six other signers of the Declaration of Independence.
Admission (burial ground): adults $2, students $1. Church: Monday-Saturday 9 a.m.-5 p.m., Sunday 1-5 p.m.; Closed Monday-Tuesday in January-February. Burial Ground: March-November, Monday-Saturday 10 a.m.-4 p.m., Sunday noon-4 p.m.; December, Sunday-Friday noon-4 p.m., Saturday 10 a.m.-4 p.m. Closed January-February.

CITY HALL

Broad and Market streets, Philadelphia, 215-686-2840; www.phila.gov
A granite statue of William Penn stands 510 feet high above the heart of the city on top of this municipal building, which is larger than the Capitol. It's known as Penn Square and was designated by Penn as the location for a

building of public concerns. It also functions as Philadelphia's City Hall and is one of the finest examples of French Second-Empire architectural style. Boasting the tallest statue (37,000 feet) in the world on its top, this building took 30 years to construct. Penn's famous hat is more than seven feet in diameter, and the brim creates a two-foot-wide track. There are more than 250 sculptures around this marble, granite and limestone structure, 20 elevators, and a four-faced, 50-ton clock. Tours start at the Tour Information Center. Tours: Monday-Friday 12:30 p.m.

CLIVEDEN
6401 Germantown Ave., Philadelphia, 215-848-1777; www.cliveden.org
A 2½-story stone Georgian house built in 1767 as a summer home by Benjamin Chew, Chief Justice of colonial Pennsylvania. On October 4, 1777, British soldiers used the house as a fortress to repulse Washington's attempt to recapture Philadelphia. Used as the Chew family residence for 200 years; it features many original furnishings. This is a National Trust for Historic Preservation property.
Admission: adults $10, students $8. April-December, Thursday-Sunday noon-4 p.m.

COLONIAL MANSIONS
Fairmount Park, 4231 N. Concourse Drive, Philadelphia, 215-683-0200; www.fairmountpark.org
Handsome 18th-century dwellings in varying architectural styles, authentically preserved and furnished are located here at Fairmount Park and include Mount Pleasant, Cedar Grove, Strawberry Mansion, Sweetbriar, Lemon Hill, Woodford and Laurel Hill. Further details and guided tours from Park House office at Philadelphia Museum of Art.
Hours and admission vary; see Web site for information.

CONGRESS HALL
Independence Park, Sixth and Chestnut streets, Philadelphia, 215-965-2305; www.nps.gov/inde
Located in Independence Park, this hall is where congress met during the last decade of the 18th century. The House of Representatives and Senate chambers are restored. The inaugurations of George Washington and John Adams took place here.
Admission: Free. Daily 9 a.m.-5 p.m.

DECLARATION HOUSE
701 Market St., Philadelphia, 215-965-2305; www.nps.gov
Reconstructed house on the site of the writing of the Declaration of Independence by Thomas Jefferson. Two rooms that Jefferson rented have been reproduced. There is a short orientation and movie about Jefferson, his philosophy on the common man, and the history of the house.
Daily; hours vary.

DESHLER-MORRIS HOUSE

5442 Germantown Ave., Philadelphia, 215-597-7130; www.nps.gov/demo

This house was the residence of President Washington in the summers of 1793 and 1794. The interior features period furnishings; the exterior has a lovely garden.

See Web site for schedule.

EDGAR ALLAN POE NATIONAL HISTORIC SITE

532 N. Seventh St., Philadelphia, 215-597-8780; www.nps.gov/edal

This is the site of where Poe lived before his move to New York in 1844. The site is the nation's memorial to the literary genius of Edgar Allan Poe. There are exhibits, a slide show, tours and special programs.

Wednesday-Sunday 9 a.m.-5 p.m.

ELECTRIC FACTORY

421 N. Seventh St., Philadelphia, 215-627-1332; www.electricfactory.info

This all ages live-music venue offers accessibility to lesser-known bands, although well-known national artists play here as well including Lady Gaga, Sonic Youth, and others. Arrive early to get a bar table in the upstairs balcony overlooking the stage.

See Web site for schedules and ticket information.

ELFRETH'S ALLEY

126 Elfreth's Alley, Philadelphia, 215-574-0560; www.elfrethsalley.org

Philadelphians still live in these Georgian- and Federal-style homes along cobblestoned Elfreth's Alley, the nation's oldest continued-use residential street. A few homes have been converted into museums, offering guided tours, a quaint gift shop and handcrafted memorabilia. Fans of culture and architecture will pick up all sorts of historical facts through the collections.

Tours: adults $5, children 6-18 $1, children 5 and under free. Tuesday-Saturday 10 a.m.-5 p.m., Sunday noon-5 p.m.

FAIRMOUNT PARK

4231 N. Concourse Drive, Philadelphia, 215-683-0200; www.phila.gov/fairpark

With more than 9,200 acres, Fairmount Park has been considered as one of the largest city parks in America. It is home to more than 215 miles of beautifully landscaped paths for walking and horseback riding. Cyclists love to bike along the Pennypack and Wissahickon trails. Walkers stroll or power-hike in Valley Green alongside the ducks. In-line skaters and rowing and sculling enthusiasts at Boathouse Row enjoy the sights along the Schuykill River on Kelly Drive. Within the park are the Philadelphia Zoo, the Shofuso Japanese House, the Philadelphia Museum of Art, the outdoor festival center Robin Hood Dell and the Philadelphia Orchestra's summer amphitheater (Mann Music Center), as well as 127 tennis courts and numerous picnic spots. The park contains America's largest collection of authentic colonial homes, features majestic outdoor sculptures, and includes Memorial Hall, the only building remaining from the 1876 Centennial Exhibition.

Daily.

FIREMAN'S HALL MUSEUM

147 N. Second St., Philadelphia, 215-923-1438; www.firemanshall.org

This museum features a collection of antique firefighting equipment along with displays and exhibits of fire department history since it began in 1736. Admission: Free. Tuesday-Saturday 10 a.m.-4:30 p.m. First Friday of every month 10 a.m-9 p.m.

FIRST BANK OF THE UNITED STATES

Third and Walnut streets, Philadelphia

The first bank was organized by Alexander Hamilton and is the country's oldest bank building. The exterior is restored. Although it's closed to the public, you can still view the façade.

FIRST PRESBYTERIAN CHURCH

201 S. 21st St., Philadelphia, 215-567-0532; www.fpcphila.org

This more than 300-year-old church was designed in the Victorian-Gothic style, combining French and English medieval Gothic cathedral motifs with massive details, flamboyant decoration and mixed materials, including granite, sand-toned brick, six types of marble, terra-cotta and stone. No plaster was used anywhere within the original building, a matter of some architectural significance toward the end of the 19th century.
Services: Sunday 11 a.m.

FORT MIFFLIN

Fort Mifflin and Hog Island roads, Philadelphia, 215-685-4167; www.fortmifflin.us

Fort Mifflin, a Revolutionary War fort strategically located in the Delaware River at the mouth of the Schuylkill, is a complex of 11 restored buildings. Here, you can climb into a bombproof enclosure used to shelter troops; witness the uniform and weapons demonstrations that take place throughout the year; explore the four-foot-thick walls of the Arsenal, soldiers' barracks, officers' quarters and blacksmith's shop; or simply enjoy the spectacular view of Philadelphia and the Delaware from the Northeast Bastion.
Wednesday-Sunday 10 a.m.-4 p.m.

FRANKLIN COURT

Independence Park, 316-322 Market St., Philadelphia, 215-965-2305; www.ushistory.org/franklin

The site of Benjamin Franklin's house has been developed as a tribute to him and just a steel structure stands outlining his house. The area includes working printing office and bindery, underground museum with multimedia exhibits, an archaeological exhibit and the B. Free Franklin Post office.
Printing office: Daily 10 a.m.-5 p.m. Post office: Monday-Saturday 9 a.m.-5 p.m.

THE FRANKLIN INSTITUTE

222 N. 20th St., Philadelphia, 215-448-1200; www2.fi.edu

This 300,000-square-foot science museum complex and memorial hall brings biology, earth science, physics, mechanics, aviation, astronomy, communications and technology to life with a variety of highly interactive exhibits honoring Philadelphia's mechanical inventor Ben Franklin. A 30-foot marble statue of Franklin sits in a Roman Pantheon-inspired chamber known as the Benjamin Franklin National Memorial. Stargazers can witness the birth of the universe, see galaxies form, or discover wondrous nebulae under the Fels Planetarium dome.

Admission: adults $14.75, seniors, students and military personnel $13.75, children under 18 $12. Daily 9:30 a.m.-5 p.m.

FRANKLIN MILLS MALL

1455 Franklin Mills Circle, Philadelphia, 215-632-1500; www.simon.com

Bargain hunters will feel like they've hit the jackpot in the more than 200 discount stores in this mega shopping complex, just 15 miles outside the city center, which touts itself as Pennsylvania's most visited attraction. Shoppers will find outlets of retailers like Kenneth Cole, Tommy Hilfiger, Neiman Marcus, Saks Fifth Avenue and Old Navy. There is no sales tax on apparel in Pennsylvania, which makes slashed prices even more appealing. If you don't want to fight for a parking spot, take advantage of the daily shuttle services from area hotels, airport and train stations.

Monday-Saturday 10 a.m.-9:30 p.m., Sunday 11 a.m.-7 p.m.

THE GALLERY AT MARKET EAST

Ninth and Market streets, Philadelphia, 215-625-4962; www.galleryatmarketeast.com

The Gallery at Market East is a concentration of 130 shops and restaurants in a four-level mall with glass elevators, trees, fountains and benches.

Monday-Thursday, Saturday 10 a.m.-7 p.m.; Friday 10 a.m.-8 p.m.; Sunday noon-5 p.m.

GLORIA DEI OLD SWEDES' EPISCOPAL CHURCH

143 S. Third St., Philadelphia, 215-389-1513; www.old-swedes.org

The state's oldest church was built in 1700 and is now a national historic site as well. A memorial to John Hanson, first president of the Continental Congress under the Articles of Confederation, is located here also.

Services: September-May, Sunday 9 a.m., 11 a.m.; Memorial Day-Labor Day, Sunday 10 a.m.

THE HISTORICAL SOCIETY OF PENNSYLVANIA

1300 Locust St., Philadelphia, 215-732-6200; www.hsp.org

The Historical Society features a first draft of the U.S. Constitution, 500 artifacts and manuscripts, plus video tours of turn-of-the-century urban and suburban neighborhoods. Research library and archives house historical and genealogical collections.

Library Admission: adults $6, students $3. Library: Tuesday, Thursday 12:30-5:30 p.m., Wednesday 12:30-8:30 p.m., Friday 10 a.m.-5:30 p.m.

INDEPENDENCE HALL

Fifth and Chestnut streets, Philadelphia, 215-965-2305; www.nps.gov/inde

Built in the mid-1700s, Independence Hall is the site of the first public reading of the Declaration of Independence. It also played host to large political rallies during the country's founding years. It is considered a fine example of Georgian architecture. Visitors often find the Hall a good first stop for their tour of Independence National Historic Park, which includes the Liberty Bell, Congress Hall, Old City Hall and Carpenters' Hall. The building is open for tours only and admission by tour only; you must get a timed ticket. Daily 9 a.m.-5 p.m.

INDEPENDENCE NATIONAL HISTORICAL PARK

Third and Chestnut streets, Philadelphia, 215-965-2305; www.nps.gov/inde
The park has been called "America's most historic square mile." The Independence Visitor Center at Sixth and Market streets has a tour map, information on all park activities and attractions, and a 30-minute film entitled "Independence." Unless otherwise indicated, all historic sites and museums in the park are free and open daily.
Admission: Free. Independence Visitor Center: Daily 8:30 a.m.-7 p.m.

INDEPENDENCE SEAPORT MUSEUM

211 S. Columbus Blvd., Philadelphia, 215-413-8655; www.phillyseaport.org
Maritime enthusiasts of all ages will appreciate the creative interactive exhibits about the science, history and art of boat building along the region's waterways at the Independence Seaport Museum. Oral histories of the men and women who have lived and worked here take visitors through immigration, commerce, defense, industry and the recreational aspects of boats.
Admission: adults $12, seniors $10, students, military personnel and children 2-18 $7. Daily 10 a.m.-5 p.m.

INDEPENDENCE VISITOR CENTER

First N. Independence Mall W., Philadelphia, 215-965-2307;
www.independencevisitorcenter.com
Head to the visitor center to plan your itinerary in Philadelphia where you can also get tickets to Independence Hall here.
October-March, daily 8:30 a.m.-5 p.m.; April-May and September, daily 8:30 a.m.-6 p.m.; Memorial Day-Labor Day, daily 8:30 a.m.-7 p.m.

JAPANESE HOUSE AND GARDEN (SHOFUSO)

Fairmount Park Horticulture Center, Philadelphia, 215-878-5097; www.shofuso.com
The Japanese House recreates a bit of Japan, complete with a garden, pond and bridge.
Admission: adults $6, seniors and students $3. May-September, Wednesday-Friday 10 a.m.-4 p.m.; Saturday-Sunday 11 a.m.-5 p.m.

JEWELER'S ROW

Seventh and Sansom streets, Philadelphia
This is the largest jewelry district in the country other than New York City. More than 300 shops, including wholesalers and diamond cutters can be found here.

JOHN HEINZ NATIONAL WILDLIFE REFUGE AT TINICUM

8601 Lindbergh Blvd., Philadelphia, 215-365-3118; www.fws.gov/northeast/heinz
This is the largest remaining freshwater tidal wetland in the state, protecting more than 1,000 acres of wildlife habitat. Area was first diked by Swedish

farmers in 1643; Dutch farmers and the colonial government added dikes during the Revolutionary War. More than 280 species of birds and 13 resident mammal species. Hiking, bicycling, nature observation, canoeing on Darby Creek. You can go fishing but a license is required.

Admission: Free. Grounds: Daily dawn-dusk. Education center: Daily 8:30 a.m.-4 p.m.

LIBERTY BELL

Liberty Bell Center, Market and Sixth streets, Philadelphia, 215-597-8974

An international icon and one of the most venerated stops in Independence Park, this mostly copper symbol of religious freedom, justice and independence is believed to hang from its original yoke. Daily.

MANAYUNK

111 Grape St., Philadelphia, 215-482-9565; www.manayunk.com

This historic district, just seven miles from Center City, makes a great destination point or place to hang out. Old rail lines, canal locks and textile mills dot this quaint town. Joggers, walkers, hikers and off-road cyclists will enjoy traveling the towpath that edges the town while their shopaholic counterparts check out the more than 70 boutiques and galleries, with 35 of them being furniture shops.

MASONIC TEMPLE

One N. Broad St., Philadelphia, 215-988-1900; www.pagrandlodge.org

Philadelphia's Masonic Temple was designed for the Fraternal Order of Freemasons, of which Benjamin Franklin and George Washington were members. The interior houses seven different halls, including the Gothic Hall, Oriental Hall and the better-known Egyptian Hall. It showcases treasures of freemasonry, including a book written by Franklin and Washington's Masonic apron.

Admission: adults $8, students $6, children 12 and under and seniors $5, military personnel and children 5 and under free. Tours: Tuesday-Friday 10 a.m., 11 a.m., 1 p.m., 2 p.m., 3 p.m., Saturday 10 a.m., 11 a.m., noon.

MORRIS ARBORETUM OF THE UNIVERSITY OF PENNSYLVANIA

100 E. Northwestern Ave., Philadelphia, 215-247-5777; www.upenn.edu/arboretum

Established in 1887, this public garden features more than 13,000 accessioned plants on 92 acres; special garden areas such as Swan Pond, Rose Garden and Japanese gardens are onsite.

Admission: adults $14, seniors $12, students and children 3-17 $7, children 2 and under free. April-October, Monday-Friday 10 a.m.-4 p.m., Saturday-Sunday 10 a.m.-5 p.m.; June-August, Monday-Wednesday, Friday 10 a.m.-4 p.m., Saturday-Sunday 10 a.m.-5 p.m., Thursday 10 a.m.-8:30 p.m.; November-March, daily 10 a.m.-4 p.m.

MUMMER'S MUSEUM

1100 S. Second St., Philadelphia, 215-336-3050; www.mummersmuseum.com

Participatory exhibits and displays highlighting the history and tradition of the Mummer's Parade. There are costumes and videotapes of past parades

and seasonal free outdoor string band concerts.
Admission: adults $3.50, students, seniors and children 12 and under $2.50. October-April, Wednesday-Saturday 9:30 a.m.-4:30 p.m., May-September, Wednesday, Friday, Saturday 9:30 a.m.-9:30 p.m., Thursday 9:30 a.m.-9:30 p.m.

MUTTER MUSEUM
19 S. 22nd St., Philadelphia, 215-563-3737; www.collphyphil.org
This collection of one-of-a-kind, hair-raising medical curiosities includes President Cleveland's jawbone; the thorax of John Wilkes Booth; a plaster cast of Siamese twins; human bones shattered by bullets; a liver in a jar; and a drawer full of buttons, coins and teeth removed from human stomachs without surgery. Located at the esteemed College of Physicians of Philadelphia, the gallery holds an internationally revered collection of creepy anatomical and pathological specimens, medical instruments and illustrations.
Admission: adults $14, children 6-17, seniors, students and military personnel $10, children 5 and under free. Monday-Sunday 10 a.m.-5 p.m.

NATIONAL MUSEUM OF AMERICAN JEWISH HISTORY
Independence Mall East, 55 N. Fifth St., Philadelphia, 215-923-3811; www.nmajh.org
The museum presents experiences and educational programs that preserve, explore, and celebrate the history of Jews in America. In the fall of 2010, the museum will move to a brand new building (which is being constructed at 101 S. Independence Mall East) on Independence Mall, with five floors and 100,000 square feet of space.
Admission: Free. Monday-Thursday 10 a.m.-5 p.m., Friday 10 a.m.-3 p.m., Sunday noon-5 p.m.

NINTH STREET ITALIAN MARKET
Ninth Street, between Wharton and Fitzwater, Philadelphia, 215-923-5637; www.9thstreetitalianmarket.com
Sip on Italian gourmet coffee, inhale imported cheeses or treat yourself to a cannoli. With more than 100 merchants selling their wares, this is the largest working outdoor market in the United States. Dining choices range from fine Italian dining to lunch counters to an outdoor snack tent.
Tuesday-Sunday, hours vary.

PENNSYLVANIA ACADEMY OF FINE ARTS
118 N. Broad St., Philadelphia, 215-972-7600; www.pafa.org
This is the nation's oldest art museum and school of fine arts. Within the Gothic-Victorian structure are paintings, works on paper and sculptures by American artists ranging from colonial masters to contemporary artists. Many of the nation's finest artists, including Charles Willson Peale, Mary Cassatt, William Merritt Chase and Maxfield Parrish, were founders, teachers or students here.
Admission: adults $10, seniors and students $8, children 5-18 $6. Tuesday-Saturday 10 a.m.-5 p.m., Sunday 11 a.m.-5 p.m.

PENNSYLVANIA BALLET

1819 JFK Blvd., Philadelphia, 215-551-7000; www.paballet.org

This company with a George Balanchine influence includes a varied repertoire of ballets ranging from classics like "The Nutcracker" to original works. Performances are held at the Academy of Music and the Merriam Theatre. See Web site for schedule and ticket information.

PENTIMENTI GALLERY

145 N. Second St., Philadelphia, 215-625-9990; www.pentimenti.com

Exhibiting works of art in all modes ranging from figurative to abstract by local, regional and international artists.

Wednesday-Friday 11 a.m.-5 p.m., Saturday noon-5 p.m. Closed August.

PHILADELPHIA 76ERS (NBA)

Wachovia Complex, 3601 S. Broad St, 215-336-3600, ,Philadelphia; www.nba.com/sixers

Philadelphia's professional basketball team plays at the Wachovia Complex which was built and opened in 1996. It's used by the Philadelphia Flyers along with serving as a host to many music concerts and more.

PHILADELPHIA CARRIAGE COMPANY

500 N. 13th St., Philadelphia, 215-922-6840; www.philacarriage.com

Guided tours via horse-drawn carriage covering Society Hill and other historic areas. Begin and end on Fifth Street at Chestnut.

Daily, weather permitting.

PHILADELPHIA EAGLES (NFL)

Lincoln Financial Field, 11th Street and Pattison Avenue, Philadelphia, 215-463-2500; www.philadelphiaeagles.com

Philadelphia's professional football team, the Eagles, play at Lincoln Financial Stadium built from 2001-2003.

PHILADELPHIA PHILLIES (MLB)

Citizens Bank Park, One Citizens Bank Way, Philadelphia, 215-463-5000; www.philadelphiaphillies.com

The Phillies are Philadelphia's professional baseball team.

PHILADELPHIA MUSEUM OF ART

26th Street and the Benjamin Franklin Parkway, Philadelphia, 215-763-8100; www.philamuseum.org

Modeled after a Greco-Roman temple, this massive museum amplifies the beauty of more than 300,000 works of art, and offers spectacular natural views. From the top of the steps outside (made famous by Sylvester Stallone in "Rocky"), visitors discover a breathtaking view of the Ben Franklin Parkway toward City Hall. Inside, the collections span 2,000 years and many more miles. There's a lavish collection of period rooms, a Japanese teahouse and a Chinese palace hall. Art lovers will also find Indian and Himalayan pieces, European decorative arts, medieval sculptures, Impressionist and Post-Impressionist paintings, and contemporary works in many media.

Admission: adults $14, seniors $12, students $10, children 13-18 $10, children 12 and under free. Tuesday-Thursday, Saturday-Sunday 10 a.m-5 p.m., Friday 10 a.m.-8:45 p.m.

THE PHILADELPHIA ORCHESTRA
260 S. Broad St. No. 1600, Philadelphia, 215-893-1900; www.philorch.org
The internationally renowned Philadelphia Orchestra has distinguished itself through a century of acclaimed performances, historic international tours and best-selling recordings. Performances are held at the Kimmel Center for the Performing Arts at Broad and Spruce streets; the Academy of Music at Broad and Locust streets; the Mann Center for the Performing Arts, 52nd Street and Parkside Avenue; Saratoga Performing Arts Center in upstate New York; and annually at New York's Carnegie Hall.
See Web site for schedule and ticket information.

PHILADELPHIA ZOO
3400 W. Girard Ave., Philadelphia, 215-243-1100; www.philadelphiazoo.org
The Philadelphia Zoo may have been America's first zoo (it was home to the nation's first white lions and witnessed its first successful chimpanzee birth), but you'll see no signs of old age here. Over the last century, the zoo has transformed itself into a preservation spot for rare and endangered animals and as a garden and wildlife destination point. The zoo is home to 1,300 animals, from red pandas to Rodrigues fruit bats. Take a pony, camel or elephant ride; feed nectar to a parrot in a walk-through aviary; or engage with a playful wallaby. Pedal a boat around Bird Lake. Or take a soaring balloon 400 feet up on the country's first passenger-carrying Zooballoon.
Admission: March-October, adults $18, children 2-11 $15, children 1 and under free; November-February, adults $12.95, children 2-11 $12.95, children 1 and under free.March-November, daily 9:30 a.m.-5 p.m.; December-February, daily 9:30 a.m.-4 p.m.

189

PHYSICK HOUSE
321 S. Fourth St., Philadelphia, 215-925-7866; www.philalandmarks.org
House of Dr. Philip Sung Physick, "father of American surgery," from 1815-1837. There is a restored Federal-style house and a garden.
Admission: adults, students and seniors $4, children 6 and under free.
Thursday-Saturday noon-4 p.m., Sunday 1-4 p.m.

PLEASE TOUCH MUSEUM FOR CHILDREN
210 N. 21st St., Philadelphia, 215-581-3181; www.pleasetouchmuseum.org
A group of artists, educators and parents conceived of this award-winning, interactive exploratory learning center for children of ages one to seven in 1976. The safe, hands-on learning laboratory has since become a model for children's museums nationwide. Story lovers will enjoy having tea with the Mad Hatter or hanging out with Max in the forest where the wild things are. Children who don't want to sit still can board the life-size bus or shop at the miniature supermarket. The ones who like to get their hands dirty can engage in science experiments. Creature lovers can interact with fuzzy human-made barnyard animals. And the entertainment-minded can see themselves on television or audition for a news anchor position.

Admission: adults and children $15, children 1 and under free. Monday-Saturday 9 a.m.-5 p.m., Sunday 11 a.m.-5 p.m.

POWEL HOUSE
244 S. Third St., Philadelphia, 215-627-0364; www.philalandmarks.org
This is the Georgian townhouse of Samuel Powel, the last colonial mayor of Philadelphia and first mayor under the new republic. There are period furnishings, silver and porcelain and garden.
Admission: adults $5, students and seniors $4, children 6 and under free. Thursday-Saturday noon-4 p.m., Sunday 1-4 p.m.

READING TERMINAL MARKET
12th and Arch streets, Philadelphia, 215-922-2317; www.readingterminalmarket.org
The nation's oldest continuously operating farmers market is alive—and thriving—in downtown Philadelphia. An indoor banquet for the senses, the market offers an exhilarating array of baked goods, meats, poultry, seafood, produce, flowers and Asian, Middle Eastern and Pennsylvania Dutch foods. Locals recommend the family-run stands, three of which are descendants of the original market. Head to Fisher's where you'll find Philadelphia soft pretzels. Aficionados claim that the Amish girls in hairnets here sell the best ones. These famous soft pretzels are hand-rolled, freshly baked, coarsely salted, buttery, golden-brown comfort food served in a paper bag.
Monday-Saturday 8 a.m.-6 p.m., Sunday 9 a.m.-5 p.m.

RITA'S WATER ICE
239 South St., Philadelphia, 215-629-3910; www.ritasice.com
The best water ice is not a solid and not quite a liquid, and visitors to Philadelphia will find it at Rita's. With locations throughout the city and surrounding area, Rita's is the city's favorite for frozen water ice, offering a changing selection of smooth, savory water ice, as well as ice cream and gelato.
Monday-Thursday noon-10 p.m., Friday noon-11 p.m., Saturday 11 a.m.-11 p.m., Sunday 11 a.m.-10 p.m.

RITTENHOUSE SQUARE
1800 Walnut St., Philadelphia; www.rittenhouserow.org
In the blocks that surround this genteel urban square in Philadelphia's most fashionable section of town are exclusive shops, restaurants and cafes. Discover what's new at chic boutiques or experience department store shopping; either way, there's something for everyone here.

RODIN MUSEUM
22nd Street and Franklin Parkway, Philadelphia, 215-568-6026; www.rodinmuseum.org
This museum, built in the Beaux Arts style, houses more than 200 sculptures created by Auguste Rodin and is considered the largest collection of his works outside his native France. "The Thinker," Rodin's most famous piece, greets visitors outside at the gateway to the museum.
Admission: $5. Tuesday-Sunday 10 a.m.-5 p.m.

SESAME PLACE

100 Sesame Road, Langhorne, 215-752-7070; www.sesameplace.com

The kids will love this wet and dry amusement park with attractions like Ernie's Bed Bounce and the Monster Maze. Elmo's World is also popular. Admission: $50.95, children under 1 free. May-October; hours vary.

SHOPS AT THE BELLEVUE

200 S. Broad St., Philadelphia, 215-875-8350; www.bellevuephiladelphia.com

Beaux Arts architecture of the former Bellevue Stratford Hotel has been preserved and transformed; it now contains offices, a hotel and a four-level shopping area centered around an atrium court.

Monday-Saturday 10 a.m.-6 p.m., Wednesday 10 a.m.-8 p.m., Sunday varies.

SOCIETY HILL AREA

Seventh and Lombard streets, Philadelphia; www.societyhillcivic.com

Secret parks, cobblestone walkways and diminutive alleys among beautifully restored brick colonial townhouses make this historic area a treasure for visitors. A popular, daily 30-minute walking tour will inspire history fans as well as architecture lovers. Highlights along the way include a courtyard designed by I.M. Pei; gardens planted by the Daughters of the American Revolution; a sculpture of Robert Morris, one of the signers of the Declaration of Independence; Greek Revival-style architecture now home to the National Portrait Gallery; and the burial ground of Revolutionary War soldiers. In the summer months, the area hosts outdoor arts festivals in Headhouse Square. It's also home to some of Philadelphia's finest restaurants.

SOUTH STREET DISTRICT

South Street, Philadelphia, 215-413-3713; www.south-street.com

On South Street, the young and hip will enjoy the search for thrift store finds and people watching of the pierced and tattooed variety. The rest can rifle through dusty rare books or cruise the art galleries. These blocks at the southern boundary of the city—as well as the numbered streets just off of it—are chock full of offbeat shops, cafés, street musicians and water ice stands, all within walking distance of Penn's Landing and Society Hill. For a Philadelphia signature treat, don't miss the cheesesteaks at Jim's Steaks (www.jimssteaks.com).

STENTON HOUSE

4601 N. 18th St., Philadelphia, 215-329-7312; www.stenton.org

This mansion was built from 1723-1730 by James Logan, secretary to William Penn. It's an excellent example of Pennsylvania colonial architecture, furnished with 18th- and 19th-century antiques. General Washington spent August 23, 1777 here and General Sir William Howe headquartered here for the Battle of Germantown. There is a colonial barn, gardens and kitchen. March-December, Tuesday-Saturday 1-4 p.m.; also by appointment.

THADDEUS KOSCIUSZKO NATIONAL MEMORIAL

301 Pine St., Philadelphia, 215-597-9618; www.nps.gov/thko

House of Polish patriot during his second visit to the United States. He was

191

one of 18th century's greatest champions of American and Polish freedom and one of the first volunteers to come to the aid of the American Revolutionary Army. The exterior and second-floor bedroom have been restored. Admission: Free. Wednesday-Sunday noon-4 p.m.

TROCADERO THEATRE
1003 Arch St., Philadelphia, 215-922-5483; www.thetroc.com
This former 1870s opera house hosted vaudeville, burlesque and Chinese movies before it became the beautiful, contemporary live music venue that it is today. The theater now hosts many well-known rock and pop artists. On Movie Mondays, the theater holds almost free ($3 for admission which goes toward a snack of your choice) screenings (on its original screen) of such classic and cult movies such as *Apocalypse Now* and *Donnie Darko*.
Box office: Monday-Friday 11:30 a.m.-6 p.m., Saturday 11:30 a.m.-5 p.m.

UNIVERSITY OF PENNSYLVANIA
32nd and Walnut streets, Philadelphia, 215-898-5000; www.upenn.edu
Founded by Benjamin Franklin, this Ivy League university has more than 24,000 students enrolled. Here, you'll find the prestigious Wharton School for business, the Annenberg School for Communication, the School of Medicine, Law School, and other top ranking schools.

UNIVERSITY OF PENNSYLVANIA MUSEUM OF ARCHAEOLOGY AND ANTHROPOLOGY
3260 South St., Philadelphia, 215-898-4000; www.museum.upenn.edu
World-famous archaeological and ethnographic collections developed from the museum's own expeditions, gifts and purchases; features Chinese, Near Eastern, Greek, ancient Egyptian, African, Pacific and North, Middle and South American materials.
Admission: adults $10, seniors $7, children 6-17 and students $6, children 5 and under free. Tuesday-Saturday 10 a.m.-4:30 p.m., Sunday 1-5 p.m.

THE U.S. MINT
151 N. Independence Mall East, Philadelphia, 215-408-0110; www.usmint.gov
Produces coins of all denominations. Gallery affords visitors an elevated view of the coinage operations. Medal-making may also be observed. Audiovisual, self-guided tours. Rittenhouse Room on the mezzanine contains historic coins, medals and other exhibits.
Tours: Free. Monday-Friday 9 a.m.-3 p.m.

WAGNER FREE INSTITUTE OF SCIENCE
1700 W. Montgomery Ave., Philadelphia, 215-763-6529; www.wagnerfreeinstitute.org
Victorian science museum with more than 50,000 specimens illustrating the various branches of the natural sciences. Dinosaur bones, fossils, reptiles and rare species are all mounted in the Victorian style. There is a reference library and research archives for scholars.
Admission: $8 donation. Tuesday-Friday 9 a.m.-4 p.m.

WALNUT STREET THEATRE

825 Walnut St., Philadelphia, 215-574-3550; www.wstonline.org
America's oldest theater, the Walnut Mainstage offers musicals, classical and cont-emporary plays. Two studio theaters provide a forum for new and avant-garde works.
See Web site for schedules and ticket information.

WASHINGTON SQUARE

Walnut and Sixth streets, Philadelphia
Site where hundreds of Revolutionary War soldiers and victims of the yellow fever epidemic are buried. The life-size statue of Washington has tomb of Revolutionary War's Unknown Soldier at its feet.

WOK N' WALK TOURS OF PHILADELPHIA CHINATOWN

1010 Cherry St., Philadelphia, 215-928-9333; www.josephpoon.com
Considered one of the best culinary tours in the country, Joseph Poon's Wok N' Walk Tour is rich with Chinese history and culture as well as calories. This two-and-a-half-hour tour begins at Poon's Asian restaurant, Chef Kitchen. Walkers are treated to a tai chi demonstration, a peek at Poon's state-of-the-art kitchen and a vegetable carving lesson. Along the tour, you visit a Chinese herbal medicine expert, a fortune cookie factory and a Chinese noodle shop and best of all, snack on free samples from a Chinese bakery in one of the city's more vibrant ethnic communities.
Admission: $45 per person. Reservations required; call for information.

SPECIAL EVENTS
ELFRETH'S ALLEY FETE DAY

126 Elfreth's Alley, Philadelphia, 215-574-0560; www.elfrethsalley.org
Residents homes are open to the public at this event with costumed guides and demonstrations of colonial crafts, food and entertainment.
June.

MANN CENTER FOR THE PERFORMING ARTS

Fairmount Park, 5201 Parkside Ave., Philadelphia, 215-546-7900; www.manncenter.org
The Philadelphia Orchestra and other popular musicians perform in this outdoor amphitheater with plenty of lawn seats to picnic and enjoy the music.
Late May-September.

MUMMER'S PARADE

Philadelphia, 215-336-3050; www.mummers.com
The Mummers Parade is Philadelphia's version of New Orleans' Mardi Gras or Spain's Carnivale. It is an annual tradition to dress in outlandish costumes and noisily parade down the streets of Philadelphia on New Year's Day (the word "mummer" comes from an old French word meaning to wear a mask).
January 1.

PENN RELAYS

Franklin Field, 235 S. 33rd St., Philadelphia, 215-898-6151; www.thepennrelays.com
These races originally served as a way to dedicate Franklin Field to the Uni-

versity of Pennsylvania. That was in 1895. Today, the Penn Relays hold the record for being the longest uninterrupted amateur track meet in the country. Thousands of men and women, ranging in age from eight to 80, have competed. More than 400 races take place, one every five minutes.
Last weekend in April.

PHILADELPHIA FLOWER SHOW
Pennsylvania Convention Center, 12th and Arch streets, Philadelphia, 215-988-8899;
www.theflowershow.com
The country's first formal flower show took place here in 1829 in the city's Masonic Hall on Chestnut Street. More than 150 years later, exotic and rare flowers are still on display in the Pennsylvania Convention Center. Flower lovers will be dazzled by more than 275,000 flowers from Africa, Germany, Japan, England, France, Holland, Italy and Belgium.
Late-February-early-March.

WHERE TO STAY
★BEST WESTERN INDEPENDENCE PARK HOTEL
235 Chestnut St., Philadelphia, 215-922-4443, 800-624-2988;
www.independenceparkinn.com
36 rooms. Complimentary breakfast. Pets accepted. $151-250

★★COURTYARD PHILADELPHIA DOWNTOWN
21 N. Juniper St., Philadelphia, 215-496-3200, 888-887-8130; www.courtyard.com
498 rooms. Restaurant, bar. Fitness center. Pool. $151-250

★★DOUBLETREE HOTEL
237 S. Broad St., Philadelphia, 215-893-1600, 800-222-8733; www.doubletree.com
432 rooms. Restaurant, bar. Business center. Fitness center. Pool. $61-150

★★EMBASSY SUITES CENTER CITY
1776 Benjamin Franklin Parkway, Philadelphia, 215-561-1776, 800-362-2779;
www.embassysuites.com
288 rooms. Restaurant, bar. Complimentary breakfast. Business center. Fitness center. $151-250

★★★★FOUR SEASONS HOTEL PHILADELPHIA
One Logan Square, Philadelphia, 215-963-1500, 866-516-1100;
www.fourseasons.com/philadelphia
Located on historic Logan Square, this hotel puts the city's museums, shops and businesses within easy reach. The eight-story Four Seasons is itself a Philadelphia institution, from its dramatic Swann Fountain to its highly rated Fountain Restaurant, considered one of the best dining establishments in town. The rooms and suites are a celebration of Federalist décor, and some accommodations incorporate deep soaking tubs. City views of the Academy of Natural Science, Logan Square and the tree-lined Ben Franklin Parkway provide a sense of place for some guests, while other rooms offer tranquil views over the inner courtyard and gardens. The Four Seasons spa focuses on nourishing treatments, while the indoor pool resembles a tropical oasis with

breezy palm trees and large skylights.
364 rooms. Restaurant, bar. Business center. Fitness center. Pool. Spa. $251-350

★★HILTON GARDEN INN PHILADELPHIA CENTER CITY

1100 Arch St., Philadelphia, 215-923-0100, 877-782-9444; www.hiltongardeninn.com
279 rooms. Restaurant, bar. Business center. Fitness center. Pool. $61-150

★★★THE HILTON INN AT PENN

3600 Sansom St., Philadelphia, 215-222-0200, 800-774-1500; www.theinnatpenn.com
Experience a distinctly collegiate environment at this hotel, located in the middle of the University of Pennsylvania's campus, not far from the city's central business district. Travelers find the Inn at Penn easily accessible from Interstate 76, Amtrak's 30th Street Station, and the Philadelphia International Airport. The Penne Restaurant and Wine Bar features regional Italian cuisine with fresh pasta made daily, while the University Club at Penn serves up breakfast and brunch favorites daily.
238 rooms. Restaurant, bar. Business center. Fitness center. $151-250

★★★HYATT REGENCY PHILADELPHIA AT PENN'S LANDING

201 S. Columbus Blvd., Philadelphia, 215-928-1234, 800-233-1234; www.hyatt.com
Located in the Penn's Landing area of Philadelphia, this Hyatt property offers unobstructed views of the Delaware River. Major historic attractions and many shops and restaurants are within walking distance. Travelers can take advantage of the indoor pool and fitness center after a busy day of work or play; or head to the restaurant for a relaxing dinner.
350 rooms. Restaurant, bar. Business center. Fitness center. Pool. $251-350

★★★THE LATHAM HOTEL

135 S. 17th St., Philadelphia, 215-563-7474, 877-528-4261; www.lathamhotel.com
This charming hotel is a favorite of guests looking for an intimate setting in downtown Philly. It is near Rittenhouse Square and close to Walnut Street, Philadelphia's main shopping area.
139 rooms. $61-150

★★★LOEWS PHILADELPHIA HOTEL

1200 Market St., Philadelphia, 215-627-1200, 800-235-6397; www.loewshotels.com
This 1930s National Historic Landmark building (formerly the Pennsylvania Savings Fund Society), is situated across from the Market East train station and the convention center. The modern, Art Deco guest rooms feel spacious with their 10-foot ceilings. Upscale amenities include 300-thread-count linens, Lather toiletries, flat-screen televisions and large work areas with ergonomic chairs. There are three floors of Concierge-level rooms, which include entry to the private library and lounge. Guests can keep up with their workouts in the nicely equipped Breathe Spa Fitness Salon—a 15,000-square-foot-space, including a full-service spa, fitness room and indoor lap pool.
581 rooms. Restaurant, bar. Business center. Fitness center. Pool. Spa. Pets accepted. Golf. $251-350

★★★MARRIOTT PHILADELPHIA WEST
111 Crawford Ave., West Conshohocken, 610-941-5600, 800-237-3639;
www.marriott.com
This hotel is located just miles from the Valley Forge National Park, Philadelphia Zoo, Museum of Art and Franklin Institute, as well as many other local points of interest. Rooms are sizeable and well-appointed.
288 rooms. Restaurant, bar. Business center. Fitness center. Pool. $151-250

★★★OMNI HOTEL AT INDEPENDENCE PARK
401 Chestnut St., Philadelphia, 215-925-0000, 888-444-6664; www.omnihotels.com
Situated in the downtown area, only 10 minutes from Philadelphia International Airport and just a stone's throw from historic sights like the Liberty Bell and Independence Hall, the Omni offers an ideal location for both business and leisure trips to Philadelphia. Each well-appointed guest room combines old-world elegance with modern day luxury. Feather pillows, comfortable bath robes, 27-inch TVs with cable, and executive desks are found in all rooms, while the ultra-plush penthouse suite features marble baths, Jacuzzi tubs and a parlor room with 20-foot cathedral ceilings, multiple sitting areas and a dining table. Kids are welcomed with the Omni Sensational Kids program.
150 rooms. Restaurant, bar. Fitness center. Spa. $251-350

★★★PARK HYATT PHILADELPHIA AT THE BELLEVUE
200 S. Broad and Walnut streets, Philadelphia, 215-893-1234, 800-464-9288;
www.parkphiladelphia.hyatt.com
This elegant hotel was built in 1904 and is listed on the National Historic Register. Beautiful, early 20th-century architecture reflects the building's history, yet guests are pampered with a number of modern amenities and comforts. Goose-down duvets are found in each guest room along with luxurious linens, large televisions, DVD players, minibars and plush bathrobes.
172 rooms. Restaurant, bar. Business center. Spa. $251-350

★★★PENN'S VIEW HOTEL
Front and Market streets, Philadelphia, 215-922-7600, 800-331-7634;
www.pennsviewhotel.com
Located in historic Old City Philadelphia, near Penn's Landing and the Delaware River, Penn's View Hotel is on the National Historic Register. The décor here is European, but guest rooms have a slightly more modern feel. Guests looking for a smaller hotel with more personal touches will find this property especially appealing.
51 rooms. Restaurant, bar. Complimentary breakfast. $151-250

★★★PHILADELPHIA AIRPORT MARRIOTT
1 Arrivals Road, Philadelphia, 215-492-9000, 800-682-4087; www.marriott.com
This well-maintained Marriott property is situated within the Philadelphia Airport. It is physically connected to Terminal B, sharing the same parking garage. Sports complexes are close by, and historic and downtown Philadelphia are just a short drive away.
419 rooms. Restaurant, bar. Business center. Fitness center. $151-250

★★★PHILADELPHIA MARRIOTT DOWNTOWN

1201 Market St., Philadelphia, 215-625-2900, 800-320-5744;
www.philadelphiamarriott.com

Guests are assured a comfortable and relaxing stay at the Marriott Philadelphia Downtown. When not outdoors exploring nearby attractions like the Liberty Bell, Independence Park, the Franklin Institute and the waterfront area, guests can work out in the hotel's fitness center or take advantage of the indoor pool, whirlpool and sauna. There are also a number of dining options, from steakhouse to sushi.

1,408 rooms. Restaurant, bar. Fitness center. Pool. Spa. $151-250

★★★THE RADISSON PLAZA WARWICK HOTEL PHILADELPHIA

1701 Locust St., Philadelphia, 215-735-6000, 800-395-7046;
www.radisson.com/philadelphia

Just one block from Rittenhouse Park, this property is close to shops, restaurants, performing arts and museums. It is also convenient to the universities. Listed on the National Register of Historic Places, the 1926 hotel has an English Renaissance theme, with guest rooms providing a more contemporary feel.

301 rooms. Restaurant, bar. Business center. Fitness center. Pets accepted. $151-250

★★★THE RITTENHOUSE HOTEL AND CONDOMINIUM RESIDENCES

210 W. Rittenhouse Square, Philadelphia, 215-546-9000, 800-635-1042;
www.rittenhousehotel.com

This intimate hotel occupies a particularly enviable address across from the leafy Rittenhouse Square and is among the prestigious townhouses of this exclusive area. The accommodations are among the most spacious in the city and are decorated with a sophisticated flair. Guests at the Rittenhouse are treated to the highest levels of personalized service. From the mood-lifting décor of the gracious Mary Cassatt Tea Room and Garden and the striking contemporary style of Lacroix, to upscale Bar 210 at Lacroix and the traditional steakhouse feel of Smith & Wollensky, the Rittenhouse Hotel also provides memorable dining experiences to match every taste.

98 rooms. Restaurant, bar. Fitness center. Pool. Spa. Pets accepted. $351 and up.

★★★THE RITZ-CARLTON, PHILADELPHIA

10 Avenue of the Arts, Philadelphia, 215-523-8000, 800-241-3333; www.ritzcarlton.com

Once occupied by both Girard Bank and Mellon Bank at some point, this building was designed in the 1900s by the architectural firm of McKim, Mead and White, and was inspired by Rome's Pantheon. Marrying historic significance with trademark Ritz-Carlton style, this Philadelphia showpiece boasts handsome decor. Impressive marble columns dominate the lobby. The rooms and suites are luxurious, while Club level accommodations offer private lounges filled with five food and beverage selections daily. Dedicated to exceeding visitors expectations, the Ritz-Carlton even offers a pillow menu, a bath butler and other unique services. Dine at well-known chef Eric Ripert's 10 Arts restaurant.

300 rooms. Restaurant, bar. Spa. Pets accepted. $251-350

★★★SHERATON GREAT VALLEY HOTEL

707 E. Lancaster Ave., Frazer, 610-524-5500, 800-325-3535; www.sheraton.com
Located in Chester County, this full-service hotel is conveniently located near area attractions and corporate offices. Historic Philadelphia is about 30 miles away, and Exton Square and King of Prussia Mall are nearby. Guests can get comfortable in the spacious guest rooms, which feature large work desks and the Sheraton Sweet Sleeper Beds (also available for dogs). The hotel offers a complimentary shuttle service to the surrounding area for guests who would like to see the sites or need a ride to the office. The White Horse Tavern, a historic 18th-century farmhouse, serves traditional American fare. Guests can also enjoy a bite to eat or a drink at the casual Chesterfields Lounge.
198 rooms. Restaurant, bar. Business center. Fitness center. Pool. Pets accepted. $151-250

★★★SHERATON SOCIETY HILL HOTEL

1 Dock St., Philadelphia, 215-238-6000, 800-325-3535; www.sheraton.com/societyhill
The Sheraton Society Hill offers affordable comfort in downtown Philadelphia, just steps from Independence Hall, Society Hill, the Liberty Bell, the Philadelphia Zoo and the Pennsylvania Convention Center.
365 rooms. Restaurant, bar. Business center. Fitness center. Pool. Pets accepted. $151-250

★★★SHERATON UNIVERSITY CITY

36th and Chestnut streets, Philadelphia, 215-387-8000, 800-596-0369;
www.philadelphiasheraton.com
Perfect for visitors to the University of Pennsylvania, this Sheraton is located in the midst of an eclectic university environment. The hotel's early American décor and lobby fireplace give it a cozy feel, and the friendly staff makes a stay here even more pleasant. A "pet suitcase," which includes a bed, bowls, mat, brush, toys and treat, is available for cats and dogs.
316 rooms. Restaurant, bar. Business center. Fitness center. Pool. Pets accepted. $151-250

★★★SOFITEL PHILADELPHIA

120 S. 17th St., Philadelphia, 215-569-8300, 800-763-4835; www.sofitel.com
Modern French style permeates the Sofitel Philadelphia. This elegant hotel sits on the former site of the Philadelphia Stock Exchange, and its downtown Center City location makes it ideal for both business and leisure travelers. Warm and inviting, the accommodations welcome with a variety of thoughtful touches, such as fresh flowers and plush towels. Comfortable chic defines the lobby bar, La Bourse, while the bistro fare and unique setting of Chez Colette recall the romance of 1920s Paris.
306 rooms. Restaurant, bar. Fitness center. Pool. Pets accepted. $251-350

ALSO RECOMMENDED
RITTENHOUSE 1715 A BOUTIQUE HOTEL

1715 Rittenhouse Square, Philadelphia, 215-546-6500, 877-791-6500;
www.rittenhouse1715.com
Formerly Rittenhouse Square Bed and Breakfast, this renovated 1900s car-

riage house affords guests a choice of 10 deluxe rooms in an ideal setting just off Rittenhouse Square, one of the city's most fashionable locations. Rooms feature marble bathrooms, telephone, cable TV and workstations with Internet access. Guests are made comfortable with 24-hour concierge service, nightly turndown service, a nightly complimentary wine and snack reception, and continental breakfast served in the café.

23 rooms. Complimentary breakfast. $151-250

WHERE TO EAT

★★★AZALEA
Omni Hotel at Independece Park, 401 Chestnut St., Philadelphia, 215-925-0000; www.omnihotels.com

Just a block from historic Independence Hall and the Liberty Bell, this restaurant at the Omni Hotel at Independence Park is a restful spot to enjoy a meal. The décor is stylishly eclectic, and the menus are rooted in classic French technique, featuring contemporary touches and international accents. Dishes range from comfortingly rich (house-made herb spaetzle baked with Gruyère and Emmental cheeses and assorted summer vegetables) to heart-healthy (mustard-glazed salmon over golden whipped potatoes with a sauce ver jus and baby bok choy). Sunday brunch is popular here, where live piano, harp or guitar music sets an elegant tone.

Continental. Breakfast, lunch, dinner, Sunday brunch. Closed Monday. Children's menu. Reservations recommended. Bar. $36-85

★★★BISTRO ROMANO
120 Lombard St., Philadelphia, 215-925-8880; www.bistroromano.com

When you walk into this cozy Italian restaurant located in the Society Hill area, one of the first things you see is the majestic oak bar from the City of Detroit III, a 1912 side-wheel passenger steamer. There is also a beautiful painting from the ship, of a sea nymph, in the stairwell that leads downstairs to the romantic dining room. Besides the beautiful décor, Bistro Romano is well known for its tableside Caesar salad, homemade ravioli and award-winning tiramisù.

Italian. Dinner. Children's menu. Reservations recommended. Bar. $16-35

★★★BUDDAKAN
325 Chestnut St., Philadelphia, 215-574-9440; www.buddakan.com

Slick, sexy and spectacular, Buddakan is one of Philadelphia's hottest spots for dining, drinking and lounging. Whether you're seated in the shadow of the restaurant's 10-foot gilded Buddha at the elevated communal table or at one of the other more intimate tables for two in chairs backed with black-and-white photo portraits, you will never guess that this den of fabulousness was once a post office. If your mail carrier were here feasting on Buddakan's brand of splashy Asian fusion fare, like lobster fried rice with Thai basil and saffron or crisp pizza topped with seared tuna and wasabi, you can be sure that the mail would never arrive on time. Entrées are meant for sharing.

Asian. Lunch (Monday-Friday), dinner. Reservations recommended. Bar. $36-85

★★CAFÉ SPICE
35 S. Second St., Philadelphia, 215-627-6273; www.cafespice.com
Indian. Dinner, Saturday-Sunday brunch. Reservations recommended. Outdoor seating. Bar. $16-35

★★★CHEZ COLETTE
Sofitel Philadelphia, 120 S. 17th St., Philadelphia, 215-569-8300; www.sofitel.com
Black-and-white photos decorate the walls in this brasserie, jazz plays in the background, and the staff and menus are both bilingual—French and English. All the pastries, breads and desserts are made on premise. For breakfast, try the fruit sushi.
French. Breakfast, lunch, dinner, Sunday brunch. Bar. $36-85

★★CITY TAVERN
138 S. Second St., Philadelphia, 215-413-1443; www.citytavern.com
American. Lunch, dinner, Sunday brunch. Children's menu. Outdoor seating. Bar. $36-85

★★DARK HORSE
421 S. Second St., Philadelphia, 215-928-9307; www.darkhorsepub.com
American. Lunch, dinner, Sunday brunch. Bar. $16-35

★★FEZ
620 S. Second St., Philadelphia, 215-925-5367; www.fezrestaurant.com
Middle Eastern. Dinner. Reservations recommended. $16-35

★★FORK
306 Market St., Philadelphia, 215-625-9425; www.forkrestaurant.com
American. Lunch (Monday-Friday), dinner, Sunday brunch. Reservations recommended. Outdoor seating. Bar. $36-85

★★★★★FOUNTAIN RESTAURANT
Four Seasons Hotel Philadelphia, 1 Logan Square, Philadelphia, 215-963-1500; www.fourseasons.com/philadelphia
The Fountain is the stunning flagship restaurant of the Four Seasons Hotel Philadelphia. The wine list, which covers all of France as well as Germany, Italy, the United States, Australia, New Zealand and South America, is just one of the highlights of dining here. The kitchen often uses ingredients from local producers and includes the farm names on the menu, so you'll know which farmer planted your baby greens and where your beets were picked. As you'll see here, the best ingredients really do make a difference. Vegetarian items are available on request, and the kitchen offers several selections that are marked as nutritionally balanced, healthier fare.
American, French. Breakfast, lunch (Monday-Saturday), dinner, Sunday brunch. Children's menu. Reservations recommended. Bar. $36-85

★GENO'S STEAKS
1219 S. Ninth St., Philadelphia, 215-389-0659; www.genossteaks.com
American. Lunch, dinner, late-night. Outdoor seating. $15 and under.

★★ITALIAN BISTRO OF CENTER CITY
211 S. Broad St., Philadelphia, 215-731-0700; www.italianbistro.com
Italian. Lunch, dinner. Reservations recommended. Bar. $16-35

★★JACK'S FIREHOUSE
2130 Fairmount Ave., Philadelphia, 215-232-9000; www.jacksfirehouse.com
American. Lunch (Monday-Friday), dinner, Saturday-Sunday brunch. Outdoor seating. Bar. $16-35

★★★JAKE'S RESTAURANT
4365 Main St., Manayunk, 215-483-0444; www.jakesrestaurant.com
Located in Manayunk, Philadelphia's funky, high-energy, artsy neighborhood, Jake's Restaurant is a lively spot to meet friends for drinks and stay for dinner. Chef/owner Bruce Cooper's chic regulars make a habit of staying all night, savoring his unique brand of stylish, regional American food. While at the bar, go for one of Jake's wild house cocktails or take a chance on a unique microbrew. The kitchen is in sync with its customers' desire for both fun and flavor in their food.
American. Lunch (Monday-Saturday), dinner, Sunday brunch. Reservations recommended. Outdoor seating. Bar. $36-85

★★★JOSEPH AMBLER INN
1005 Horsham Road, Montgomeryville, 215-362-7500; www.josephamblerinn.com
Complex combinations of local fare and International cuisine make up the innovative menu at this rustic country inn. Executive Chef Pedro Luga and his team offer entrées such as pan roasted Chilean sea bass with lump crab and English pea risotto; grilled rack of lamb with Dauphinoise potato, cauliflower puree and red wine demi-glace; and pan roasted chicken breast with potato pancake, fontina tuille, baby asparagus and rosemary pan jus.
International. Lunch (Monday-Friday), dinner. Outdoor seating. Bar. $36-85

★★★★LACROIX AT THE RITTENHOUSE
210 W. Rittenhouse Square, Philadelphia, 215-790-2533; www.rittenhousehotel.com
Set in the stately Rittenhouse Hotel, Lacroix is a restaurant of understated elegance. The kitchen plays up fresh local ingredients with a delicate French hand, while guests dine in posh, sophisticated luxury and enjoy views of charming Rittenhouse Square. While acclaimed chef Jean-Marie Lacroix has retired, the kitchen is still in able hands under the direction of chef Jason Cichonski. The flexible tasting menu is the best option here, where diners can choose three, five or eight courses, and desserts are generously provided as a gift from the chef. The Sunday brunch (where the buffet is set up in the kitchen) is a particular Philadelphia favorite.
French. Breakfast, lunch (Monday-Saturday), dinner, Sunday brunch. Reservations recommended. Bar. $36-85

★★LAS TARASCAS EN ZOCALO
3600 Lancaster Ave., Philadelphia, 215-895-0139; www.zocalophilly.com
Mexican. Lunch (Monday-Friday), dinner. Closed Sunday. Reservations recommended. Outdoor seating. Bar. $16-35

★★★LE BAR LYONNAIS
1523 Walnut St., Philadelphia, 215-567-1000; www.lebecfin.com

Since Georges Perrier added Le Bar Lyonnais to his internationally renowned Le Bec-Fin restaurant in 1990, the bar has achieved status as one of Philadelphia's best French bistros, winning kudos for its comfortable setting and accessible menu. The decor is subdued and casual, with dark wallpaper, dark woods, soft lighting and marble-topped tables. The bistro has featured dishes such as a cassolette of snails in champagne and hazelnut butter sauce, grilled Dover sole with basmati rice and veal medallions with hazelnut mashed potatoes. This lower-level bar is a great choice for diners who want to sample some of Le Bec-Fin's signature dishes without paying for a prix fixe menu. French. Lunch (Friday-Saturday), dinner. Closed Sunday. Reservations recommended. Bar. $36-85

LE BEC-FIN
1523 Walnut St., Philadelphia, 215-567-1000; www.lebecfin.com

Georges Perrier's Le Bec-Fin, which opened in 1970, remains a shining star for French cuisine, although the restaurant took a more casual turn in 2009. Perrier's talented team brings out the brilliance in classic dishes, while offering several new creations destined to be classics. Perrier's signature crab cake with French green beans and whole grain mustard sauce is divine and joins an exciting menu that leans on seasonal availability. French. Lunch (Monday-Saturday), dinner. Closed Sunday. Reservations recommended. Bar. $86 and up.

★★★LE CASTAGNE RISTORANTE
1920 Chestnut St., Philadelphia, 215-751-9913; www.lecastagne.com

This contemporary Italian restaurant offers a menu that concentrates on northern Italian dishes, and in season, a pretheater menu is offered. Everything is made in-house, including breads, pastas, sauces and desserts. Some dessert and fish selections are prepared tableside. Italian. Lunch (Monday-Friday), dinner. Closed Sunday. Reservations recommended. Outdoor seating. Bar. $36-85

★MANAYUNK BREWERY AND RESTAURANT
4120 Main St., Philadelphia, 215-482-8220; www.manayunkbrewery.com

American. Lunch (Monday-Saturday), dinner, late-night, Sunday brunch. Reservations recommended. Outdoor seating. Bar. $16-35

★MANAYUNK DINER
3720 Main St., Philadelphia, 215-483-4200

American. Breakfast, lunch, dinner. Outdoor seating. Bar. $16-35

★★★MOONSTRUCK
7955 Oxford Ave., Philadelphia, 215-725-6000; www.moonstruckrestaurant.com

Formerly known as Ristorante DiLullo, this elegantly casual northern Italian gem has been doing business for more than 20 years. Menus let customers choose among a wide range of antipasti, primi piatti (pasta appetizers), secondi piatti (second courses) and piatti tradizionale (traditional classics). The latter menu section features one special dish per night, ranging from

caciucco, a bouillabaisse of seafood and fish, to osso buco.
Italian. Dinner. Reservations recommended. Bar. $36-85

★★★MORIMOTO
723 Chestnut St., Philadelphia, 215-413-9070; www.morimotorestaurant.com
Japanese fusion cuisine from Iron Chef Masaharu Morimoto of New York's
Nobu fame (he was executive chef at Nobu Matsuhisa's restaurant for six
years) pulsates with life and creativity. His Philadelphia outpost, stunningly
shaped by local restaurant impresario Stephen Starr, is Morimoto's first restaurant in the United States. Ceilings undulate, booths change color and the
sushi bar at the back never stops bustling. The best way to challenge your
taste buds is to select one of Morimoto's omakase menus.
Japanese. Lunch (Monday-Friday), dinner. Reservations recommended.
Bar. $36-85

★★★MOSHULU RESTAURANT
401 S. Columbus Blvd., Philadelphia, 215-923-2500; www.moshulu.com
Moshulu is a stunning South Seas-inspired restaurant housed in a 100-year-
old, 394-foot, four-masted sailing ship. Its several dining rooms are elegantly
decorated with rattan chairs, cane furniture, dark mahogany and Polynesian
artwork. The kitchen, headed by executive chef Ralph Fernandez, churns out
creative, delicious dishes that will keep you coming back for more.
American. Lunch, dinner, Sunday brunch. Reservations recommended.
Outdoor seating. Bar. $36-85

★★PALOMA
6516 Castor Ave., Philadelphia, 215-533-0356; www.palomafinedining.com
French, Mexican. Dinner. Closed Sunday-Wendesday. Reservations recommended. Bar. $36-85

★★THE PLOUGH
Old City Philadelphia on Second Street, 215-733-0300; www.ploughstars.com
Continental. Lunch, dinner, Saturday-Sunday brunch, late-night. Reserva-
tions recommended. Outdoor seating. Bar. $36-85

★★★RISTORANTE PANORAMA
Penn's View Hotel, Front and Market streets, Philadelphia, 215-922-7800;
www.pennsviewhotel.com
Panorama is part of the boutique-style Penn's View Hotel. The beautiful dining room features marble floors, a wall of windows and murals throughout.
The cuisine is gutsy, old-world Italian, featuring dishes such as paillard of
beef rolled in garlic, cheese, egg and herbs, slow-cooked in tomato sauce,
and served with house-made gnocchi. But this place is known for its wine:
Daily wine lists offer 22 to 26 different flights (five wines per flight), plus
dozens of by-the-glass options. The quality, made possible by the restaurant's
cruvinet preservation and dispensing system, is exceptional, earning Panorama numerous awards.
Italian. Lunch (Monday-Friday), dinner. Reservations recommended. Bar. $36-85

★★★RUTH'S CHRIS STEAK HOUSE
260 S. Broad St., Philadelphia, 215-790-1515; www.ruthschris.com
Ruth's Chris is a top choice of many steak lovers. With a menu that highlights aged prime Midwestern beef that's broiled at 1800 degrees and drizzled with butter, carnivores can't go wrong. Dark wood accents and comfortable leather booths give the room a club-like steakhouse feel.
Steak. Dinner. Bar. $36-85

★★★THE SALOON
750 S. Seventh St., Philadelphia, 215-627-1811; www.saloonrestaurant.net
Richard Santore has been operating this venerable establishment in Philadelphia's Bellavista neighborhood, bordering Center City and South Philly, for nearly 40 years. The food is classic Italian fare, served for lunch and dinner. Appetizers include poached pear and gorgonzola salad with roasted walnuts, baby greens and red onion with pear vinaigrette. Fettuccini Lobster Amatriciana is a toss of house-made fettuccini with lobster, bacon, onion, fresh tomato and pecorino cheese in tomato sauce. Dinner specials range from beef carpaccio drizzled with truffle essence and fava beans to a double veal chop marinated in white wine, pan seared and served with Yukon gold potatoes.
Italian. Lunch, dinner. Closed Sunday. Bar. $36-85

★★SERRANO
20 S. Second St., Philadelphia, 215-928-0770; www.tinangel.com
International. Dinner. Reservations recommended. Bar. $16-35

★★★SUSANNA FOO
1512 Walnut St., Philadelphia, 215-545-8800; www.susannafoo.com
Thanks to the plethora of greasy Chinese takeout joints, Chinese food has been much maligned over the years. But at Susanna Foo, a Zen-like dining oasis, the delicious, traditional cuisine of China sheds its unfortunate reputation and gains the respect it deserves. For years, chef/owner Susanna Foo has been dressing up the dishes of her native land with sophisticated French flair and modern, global accents. Foo's dim sum can be a meal on their own. The entrées are equally mouthwatering, especially the famous tea-smoked Peking duck breast. You may never be able to order takeout again.
Chinese, French. Lunch, dinner. Reservations recommended. Bar. $$$

★★★SWANN CAFÉ
Four Seasons Hotel Philadelphia, 1 Logan Square, Philadelphia, 215-963-1500, 866-516-1100; www.fourseasons.com/philadelphia
Named for the spectacular Logan Square fountain in front of the Four Seasons Hotel Philadelphia, Swann Café is the more accessible of the hotel's exceptional restaurants. Menus range from light and lovely dishes, such as an appetizer ragout of forest mushrooms and asparagus tips, to a zesty sandwich of pulled osso buco with aged provolone and spicy pepper and onion relish on a stirato roll.
American. Lunch (Monday-Saturday), dinner, Sunday brunch. Children's menu. Reservations recommended. Bar. $36-85

★★★TANGERINE
232 Market St., Philadelphia, 215-627-5116; www.tangerinerestaurant.com
This Middle Eastern-themed restaurant in the heart of Old City Philadelphia features a menu that blends flavors from the Mediterranean, France, Spain, Italy and Africa. The appetizer of harissa-spiced barbecue lamb with rosemary socca bread and smoky vegetable salad is an inspired choice. For an entrée, try the delicious seared suck with creamy polenta, currant jus and grilled radicchio.
Mediterranean. Dinner. Reservations recommended. Bar. $36-85

★★★VETRI
1312 Spruce St., Philadelphia, 215-732-3478; www.vetriristorante.com
Chef Mark Vetri learned to prepare rustic Italian cuisine (think: rabbit loin and sweetbreads wrapped in pancetta with morels or baby goat poached in milk and then oven roasted to crispness) from Italy's best chefs and then brought his skills home to Philly. Ensconced in the tiny, 35-seat space once occupied by other pinnacle establishments (Le Bec-Fin, Chanterelle), Vetri is intent on creating likewise legendary meals. The wine list has been nationally lauded, and the service is seamless. On Saturdays, indulge in Vetri's five- or seven-course prix fixe menus (not available during the summer).
Italian. Dinner. Closed Sunday. Reservations recommended. $86 and up.

★★WHITE DOG CAFÉ
3420 Sansom St., Philadelphia, 215-386-9224; www.whitedog.com
American. Lunch, dinner, Saturday-Sunday brunch. Reservations recommended. Outdoor seating. Bar. $36-85

★★★XIX
Park Hyatt Philadelphia, 200 S. Broad St., Philadelphia, 215-790-1919; www.nineteenrestaurant.com
XIX (pronounced "nineteen") sits on the top 19th floor of the historic Bellevue Building (now the Park Hyatt), and exudes a level of opulence from a bygone era with two 36-foot-high grand rotundas, mosaic marble and a 19-foot-tall pearl chandelier. The fine dining experience is further enhanced by spectacular views of the city through floor-to-ceiling arched picture windows. The raw bar features a choice of 12 varieties of fresh oysters and a separate café offers its own menu and afternoon tea.
American, French. Breakfast, lunch, dinner, Sunday brunch, late night. $36-85

PITTSBURGH
See also Beaver Falls, New Castle
Pittsburgh has become one of the most spectacular civic redevelopments in America, with modern buildings, clean parks and community pride. The new Pittsburgh is a result of a rare combination of capital-labor cooperation, public and private support, enlightened political leadership and imaginative, venturesome community planning. Its $1 billion international airport was designed to be the most user-friendly in the country.
After massive war production, Pittsburgh labored to eliminate the 1930s image of an unsophisticated mill town. During the 1950s and 1960s, Renaissance I began, a $500-million program to clean the city's air and develop

new structures, such as Gateway Center, the Civic Arena and Point State Park. The late 1970s and early 1980s ushered in Renaissance II, a $3 billion expansion program deflecting the movement away from industry and toward high technology.

Today Pittsburgh has completed this dramatic shift from industry to a diversified base including high technology, health care, finance and education and continues its transition to a service-oriented city.

Pittsburgh's cultural personality is expressed by the Pittsburgh Symphony Orchestra, Pittsburgh Opera, Pittsburgh Ballet, Phipps Conservatory and the Carnegie Museums of Pittsburgh, which include the Museum of Natural History and the Museum of Art. The city has 25 parks, 45 "parklets," 60 recreation centers and 27 swimming pools.

Born of frontier warfare in the shadow of Fort Pitt, the city is named after the elder William Pitt, the great British statesman. Its strategic military position was an important commercial asset, and Pittsburgh soon became a busy river port and transit point for the western flow of pioneers.

Industry grew out of the West's need for manufactured goods; foundries and rolling mills were soon producing nails, axes, frying pans and shovels. The Civil War added tremendous impetus to industry, and by the end of the war, Pittsburgh was producing half the steel and one-third of the glass made in the country. Captains of industry and finance, such as Thomas Mellon, Andrew Carnegie and Henry Clay Frick, built their industrial empires in Pittsburgh. The American Federation of Labor was born here in 1881 because the city has been the scene of historic clashes between labor and management.

WHAT TO SEE
ALCOA BUILDING/REGIONAL ENTERPRISE TOWER
425 Sixth Ave., Pittsburgh, 412-391-5590; www.spcregion.org/ret/
This building was a pioneer in aluminum for skyscraper construction, as the exterior work was done from inside and no scaffolding was required. Draped in aluminum waffle, at 30 stories high it's considered to be one of the country's most daring experiments in skyscraper design. It was built in 1953 for Alcoaand; now it's known as the Regional Enterprise Tower.

ALLEGHENY COUNTY COURTHOUSE
436 Grant St., Pittsburgh; www.alleghenycounty.us/directions
One of the country's outstanding Romanesque buildings, the two-square city block structure was designed by Henry Hobson Richardson in 1884.

ALLEGHENY OBSERVATORY
159 Riverview Ave., Pittsburgh, 412-321-2400; www.pitt.edu
Tour this observatory maintained by University of Pittsburgh. Children under 12 years only allowed with adult supervision.
May-August, Thursday 8-10p.m.; April-November, Friday 8-10 p.m.

ANDY WARHOL MUSEUM
117 Sandusky St., Pittsburgh, 412-237-8300; www.warhol.org
The most comprehensive single-artist museum in the world. There are more than 500 works from Andy Warhol here.

Admission: adults $15, seniors $9, students and children 3-18 $8. Tuesday-Thursday, Saturday 10 a.m.-5 p.m., Friday 10 a.m.-10 p.m. Half-price admission Friday 5-10 p.m.

BENEDUM CENTER FOR THE PERFORMING ARTS

719 Liberty Ave., Pittsburgh, 412-456-6666; www.pgharts.org

Expansion and restoration of the Stanley Theater, a movie palace built in 1928. Gilded plasterwork, a 500,000-piece crystal chandelier and a nine-story addition to the backstage area make this an exceptional auditorium with one of the largest stages in the country. The center is home to Pittsburgh Ballet Theatre, the Pittsburgh Dance Council, the Pittsburgh Opera and Civic Light Opera. See Web site for schedules and ticket information.

CARNEGIE MELLON UNIVERSITY

5000 Forbes Ave., Pittsburgh, 412-268-2000; www.cmu.edu

Founded by Andrew Carnegie in 1900, this university is composed of seven colleges and is home to more than 1,000 students.

CARNEGIE MUSEUM OF ART

4400 Forbes Ave., Pittsburgh, 412-622-3131; www.cmoa.org

Possibly America's first modern art museum, Carnegie urged the gallery to exhibit works dated after 1896. They have a collection of Impressionist and Post-Impressionist paintings, and a hall of sculpture and architecture. Admission: adults $15, seniors $12, students and children 3-18 $11, children 2 and under free. Tuesday-Wednesday, Friday-Saturday 10 a.m.-5 p.m., Thursday 10 a.m.-8 p.m., Sunday noon-5 p.m.

CARNEGIE MUSEUM OF NATURAL HISTORY

4400 Forbes Ave., 412-622-3131; www.carnegiemnh.org

This museum houses one of the most complete collections of dinosaur fossils. Exhibits include Dinosaur Hall, Polar World, Hillman Hall of Minerals and Gems and the Walton Hall of Ancient Egypt. Admission: adults $15, seniors $12, students and children 3-18 $11. Tuesday-Saturday 10 a.m.-5 p.m., Thursday 10 a.m.-8 p.m., Sunday noon-5 p.m.

CARNEGIE MUSIC HALL

4400 Forbes Ave., Pittsburgh, 412-622-1906; www.carnegiemuseums.org

Carnegie Music Hall is home to Mendelssohn Choir, Pittsburgh Chamber Music Society and River City Brass Band. Upon entry, you're faced with an elaborate gilt and marble foyer. There are walls of French eschallion, 24 pillars made of green stone and a gold baroque ceiling.

CARNEGIE SCIENCE CENTER

1 Allegheny Ave., Pittsburgh, 412-237-3400; www.carnegiesciencecenter.org

Learning and entertainment complex has more than 40,000 square feet of exhibit galleries that demonstrate how human activities are affected by science and technology. *USS Requin*, moored in front of the center, is a World War II diesel electric submarine; 40 minute tours demonstrate the electronic, visual and voice communication devices on board. Henry Buhl Jr. Planetarium and

Observatory is a technologically sophisticated interactive planetarium with control panels at every seat. Also here are the 350-seat Rangos Omnimax Theater and the Health Sciences Amphitheater.
Admission: adults $14, seniors and children 3-12 $10. Sunday-Friday 10 a.m.-5 p.m., Saturday 10 a.m.-7 p.m.

COUNTY PARKS
Pittsburgh, 412-350-2455; www.alleghenycounty.us
The Allegheny County parks include South Park, North Park, Boyce Park, and Settler's Cabin Park. There are bicycling paths, ball fields, golf, picnicking and tennis courts.

DUQUESNE INCLINE
220 Grandview Ave., Pittsburgh, 412-381-1665; www.portauthority.org
Built 1877, this inline was restored and now run by community effort. The observation deck has great views.
Admission: one way, adults $2, children 6-11 $1, children 5 and under and seniors free; round-trip, adults $4, children 6-11 $2, children 5 and under and seniors free. Monday-Saturday 5:30 a.m.-12:45 a.m., Sunday 7 a.m.-12:45 a.m.

FORT PITT MUSEUM
101 Commonwealth Place Pittsburgh, 412-281-9284; www.fortpittmuseum.com
Built on part of original fort with exhibits on early Pittsburgh and Fort Pitt.
Admission: adults $7, seniors $6, children 3-11 $4, children 2 and under free.
Wednesday-Sunday 9 a.m.-5 p.m.

THE FRICK ART AND HISTORICAL CENTER/ART MUSEUM
7227 Reynolds St., Pittsburgh, 412-371-0600; www.frickart.org
This museum complex built on grounds of the estate once belonging to industrialist Henry Clay Frick has numerous attractions. Here, you'll find Clayton, the home of Henry Clay Frick, which is a restored four-story Victorian mansion with 23 rooms. It's the only remaining house of area in East End once known as "Millionaire's Row." There are some original décor and personal mementos of the Fricks' inside. The art musuem here has the collection of Helen Clay Frick, daughter of Henry Clay Frick, which includes Italian Renaissance, Flemish and French 18th-century paintings and decorative arts. There are also Italian and French furniture, Renaissance bronzes, tapestries, Chinese porcelains. There are also gardens, the Car and Carriage Museum, a greenhouse, café and a visitor's center.
Admission: Free. Tuesday-Sunday 10 a.m.-5 p.m.

FRICK FINE ARTS BUILDING
University of Pittsburgh, Schenley Plaza, 104 Frick Fine Arts, Pittsburgh, 412-648-2400; www.haa.pitt.edu
In this University of Pittsburgh buliding, you'll find an art gallery with collections and changing exhibits as well as a research library. There is also a glass-enclosed cloister and courtyard garden.
Hours vary; see Web site for information.

FRICK PARK

Beechwood Boulevard and English Lane, Pittsburgh, 412-422-6538;

www.pittsburghparks.org

Covering 561 acres, Frick Park is Pittsburgh's largest regional parks and it's largely in a natural state. Nature trails wind through ravines and over hills with more over 100 species of birds. There is a nature center, tennis courts, picnic areas, baseballs fields, and a popular playground.
Daily 6 a.m.-11 p.m.

HARTWOOD ACRES

200 Hartwood Acres, Pittsburgh, 412-767-9200; www.alleghenycounty.us

Located on this 629-acre recreation area is a Tudor mansion built in 1929 with many antiques, formal gardens and stables. There are also music and theater events during summer and at other times throughout the year.
Admission (to mansion): adults $6, seniors and children 13-17 $4, children 6-12 $2, children 5 and under free. Mansion and Stables: Monday-Saturday 10 a.m.-3 p.m., Sunday noon-4 p.m.

HEINZ CHAPEL

Fifth and Bellefield avenues, Pittsburgh, 412-624-4157; www.heinzchapel.pitt.edu

This chapel was donated from Henry John Heinz, of the H.J. Heinz Company, as a gift and memorial for his family. It has tall stained-glass windows and beautiful French Gothic architecture.

MELLON ARENA

66 Mario Lemieux Place, Pittsburgh, 412-642-1800; www.mellonarena.com

This all-weather amphitheater accommodates more than 17,000 people. There is a retractable roof that can fold up within 2 1/2 minutes. Many events take place here from concerts, Penguins hockey games to Disney on Ice.

MONONGAHELA INCLINE

Pittsburgh, 412-442-2000; www.portauthority.org

Take this incline to the top for panoramic views from observation deck.
Admission: adults $2, children 6-11 $1. Monday-Saturday 5:30 a.m.-12:45 a.m., Sunday 8:45 a.m.-midnight.

MUSEUM OF PHOTOGRAPHIC HISTORY

531 E. Ohio, Pittsburgh, 412-231-7881; www.photoantiquities.org

This photo gallery and museum has selections from 100,000 antique photographic images.
Admission: adults $6.50, students and seniors $5, chidlren 5-12 $3. Monday, Wednesday-Saturday 10 a.m.-4 p.m.

NATIONAL AVIARY

700 Arch St., Allegheny Commons West, Pittsburgh, 412-323-7235; www.aviary.org

The Aviary is home to one of the world's premier bird collections and is the only indoor bird facility independent of a larger zoo in North America.
Admission: adults $10, seniors $9, children 2-18 $8.50, children 1 and under free. Daily 10 a.m.-5 p.m.

PHIPPS CONSERVATORY

700 Frank Curto Drive, Pittsburgh, 412-622-6914; www.conservatory.org

This conservatory has a constantly changing array of flowers; tropical gardens; and an outstanding orchid collection. There's also a children's Discovery Garden with interactive learning opportunities and seasonal flower shows. Check Web site for schedule.

Admission: adults $10, seniors and students $9, children 2-18 $7, children 1 and under free. Saturday-Thursday 9:30 a.m.-5 p.m., Friday 9:30 a.m.-10 p.m.

PITTSBURGH CHILDREN'S MUSEUM

10 Children's Way, Pittsburgh, 412-322-5058; www.pittsburghkids.org

This museum offers hands-on exhibits, a silkscreen studio, storytelling, regularly scheduled puppet shows, and live performances for children to enjoy.

Admission: adults $11, seniors and children 2-18 $9, children 1 and under free. Monday-Saturday 10 a.m.-5 p.m., Sunday noon-5 p.m.

PITTSBURGH PIRATES (MLB)

PNC Park, 115 Federal St., Pittsburgh, 412-323-5000; www.pittsburghpirates.com

Pittsburgh's professional baseball team, the Pirates, play at PNC Park which was opened in 2001.

PITTSBURGH STEELERS (NFL)

Heinz Field, 600 Stadium Circle, Pittsburgh, 412-432-7800; www.steelers.com

The professional football team of Pittsburgh is the Steelers.

PITTSBURGH ZOO & AQUARIUM

1 Wild Place, Pittsburgh, 412-665-3640, 800-474-4966; www.pittsburghzoo.com

The zoo covers more than 70 acres containing more than 4,000 animals, children's farm, discovery pavilion, reptile house, tropical and Asian forests, and African savanna among much more. The PPG Aquarium is 45,000 square feet and has more than 40 exhibits. If animals aren't enought, there are merry-go-round and train rides.

Admission: adults $12, seniors $11, children 2-13 $10, children 1 and under free. Memorial Day-Labor Day, daily 9 a.m.-6 p.m.; Labor day-December, daily 9 a.m.-5 p.m.; January-March, daily 9 a.m.-4 p.m.; April-Memorial Day, daily 9 a.m.-5 p.m.

POINT STATE PARK

101 Commonwealth Place Fort Duquesne and Fort Pitt boulevards, Pittsburgh, 412-471-0235; www.pointstatepark.com

This is the point where the Allegheny and Monongahela rivers meet to form the Ohio and a 150-foot fountain symbolizes the joining of the rivers. The park covers 36 acres and there are military drills with fifes, drums, muskets and cannon. A huge renovation will be completed by the end of 2010, when the park will be revitalized for the community to use.

PPG PLACE

Market Square, Pittsburgh; www.ppgplace.com

Designed by Philip Johnson, this is Pittsburgh's most popular Renaissance II building. PPG Place consists of six separate buildings designed in a postmodern, Gothic skyscraper style. Shopping and a food court can be found in Two PPG Place. There is also a public ice skating rink.

Shops: Monday-Friday 10 a.m.-6 p.m. Food court: Monday-Friday 11 a.m.-3 p.m.

RODEF SHALOM BIBLICAL BOTANICAL GARDEN

4905 Fifth Ave., Pittsburgh, 412-621-6566; www.rodefshalom.org/who/garden

The natural world of ancient Israel is re-created here in settings that specialize in plants of the Bible. A waterfall, desert and stream all help simulate the areas of the Jordan, Lake Kineret and the Dead Sea. There is a garden with more than 100 tropical plants.

Admission: Free. June-mid-September, Sunday-Tuesday, Thursday 10 a.m.-2 p.m., Wednesday 10 a.m.-2 p.m., 7-9 p.m., Saturday noon-1 p.m.

SANDCASTLE WATER PARK

1000 Sandcastle Drive, Pittsburgh, 412-462-6666; www.sandcastlewaterpark.com

The city's down-by-the-riverside water park has 14 water slides, adult and kiddie pools, a lazy river, a boardwalk and food. Its fun for all without leaving the city.

See Web site for schedule and ticket information.

SCHENLEY PARK

5000 Forbes Ave., Pittsburgh, 412-687-1800; www.pittsburghparks.org

Covering 456 acres, Schenley park offers trails, woods, picnic areas, an 18-hole golf course, lighted tennis courts, a swimming pool, an ice skating rink, softball fields, a running track, nature trails and a bandstand. There is also the Schenley Cafe here.

Daily 6 a.m.-11 p.m.

SENATOR JOHN HEINZ HISTORY CENTER

1212 Smallman St., Pittsburgh, 412-454-6000; www.pghhistory.org

Associated with the Smithsonian Institution, this history center is 275,000 square feet and has exhibits which preserve nearly 300 years of the region's history with artifacts and extensive collection of archives and photos. It also houses the Western Pennsylvania Sports Museum.

Admission: adults $10, seniors $9, students and children 4-17 $5, children 3 and under free. Daily 10 a.m.-5 p.m.

SOLDIERS AND SAILORS MEMORIAL HALL AND MUSEUM

At Bigelow Boulevard, 4141 Fifth Ave., Pittsburgh, 412-621-4253;
www.soldiersandsailorshall.org

The auditorium here has Lincoln's Gettysburg Address inscribed above stage. You'll also find flags, weapons, uniforms, and more from U.S. wars.

Admission: adults $5, seniors, veterans and children 6-13 $3, children 5 and under free. Monday-Saturday 10 a.m.-4 p.m.

STATION SQUARE

125 W. Station Square, Pittsburgh, 412-471-5808, 800-859-8959;
www.stationsquare.com

This 52-acre area located along the riverfront features shopping, dining and entertainment in and among the historic buildings of the P and LE Railroad. Shopping is available in warehouses that once held loaded railroad boxcars. Monday-Saturday 10 a.m.-9 p.m., Sunday noon-5 p.m. Hours vary; see Web site for information.

TOUR-ED MINE AND MUSEUM

748 Bull Creek Road, Pittsburgh, 724-224-4720; www.tour-edmine.com

This mine and museuem gives you the experience of a complete underground coal mining operation. There's a sawmill, furnished log house, old company store, a historical mine museum and shelters.

Admission: adults $8, children 12 and under $6.50. May-Labor Day, Wednesday-Monday 10 a.m.-4 p.m.

UNIVERSITY OF PITTSBURGH

Fifth Avenue and Bigelow Boulevard, Pittsburgh, 412-624-4141; www.pitt.edu

Founded in 1787, this city university has a student body numbering 34,000. The campus located in the Oakland neighborhood covers 132 acres.

U.S. STEEL TOWER

Grant Street and Seventh Avenue, Pittsburgh

This is the tallest building in Pittsburgh, and the 35th tallest in the nation with 10 exposed triangular columns and an exterior paneling of steel.

SPECIAL EVENTS

PITTSBURGH IRISH FESTIVAL

Riverplex at Sandcastle, Pittsburgh, 412-422-1113; www.pghirishfest.org

This three day Irish celebration features Irish foods and beer, Irish dance performances and plenty of entertainment including Gaelic Storm. September.

THREE RIVERS ARTS FESTIVAL

937 Liberty Ave., Pittsburgh, 412-281-8723; www.artsfestival.net

Here you'll find a festival featuring juried, original works of local and national artists: paintings, photography, sculpture, crafts and videos. There's an artists' market in outdoor plazas. Entertainment includes music, dance and performance art. There's also a film festival, food and children's activities. June.

THREE RIVERS REGATTA

412-427-4893; www.threeriversregatta.net

This festival featers water, land and air events. There are water shows and speedboat races, freestyle motocross performances and fishing tournaments among other things. Live entertainment includes concerts by Three Dog Night and others.

Fourth of July weekend.

WHERE TO STAY

★★DOUBLETREE HOTEL

One Bigelow Square, Pittsburgh, 412-281-5800, 800-222-8733; www.doubletree.com

308 rooms. Restaurant, bar. Complimentary breakfast. Business center. Fitness center. Pool. $61-150

★★★HILTON PITTSBURGH

600 Commonwealth Place, Pittsburgh, 412-391-4600; www.hilton.com

713 rooms. Restaurant, bar. Business center. Fitness center. Pets accepted. $61-150

★★★HYATT REGENCY PITTSBURGH INTERNATIONAL AIRPORT

1111 Airport Blvd., Pittsburgh, 724-899-1234, 800-633-7313; www.hyatt.com

Whether you're in town for the day and need a place to clean up or have an early flight in the morning, this Hyatt is connected to the airport terminals and offers soundproof windows so you're guaranteed a restful night. A 24-hour business center ensures that no matter what time you arrive, you'll be able to get to work.

336 rooms. Restaurant, bar. Business center. Fitness center. Pool. $61-150

★★★MARRIOTT PITTSBURGH CITY CENTER

112 Washington Place, Pittsburgh, 412-471-4000, 888-456-6600; www.marriott.com

Located across the street from Mellon Arena and the downtown business district, you won't have to travel far to get a taste of the city. Guest rooms include luxury down comforters, TVs and VCRs and free Internet access.

402 rooms. Restaurant, bar. Business center. Fitness center. Pool. Spa. $151-250

★★★OMNI WILLIAM PENN HOTEL

530 William Penn Place, Pittsburgh, 412-281-7100, 888-444-6664;
www.omnihotels.com

This hotel, built in 1916, fuses historic charm with modern luxury in the heart of downtown Pittsburgh. The rooms and suites are tastefully and elegantly appointed with distinguished style. Executives on the go appreciate the hotel's complete business and fitness centers; families adore the Omni Kids Program; and leisure visitors enjoy the spa and salon services and proximity to the city's leading stores. The hotel offers a variety of convenient and tempting dining choices, from Starbucks to pub food at the Palm Court and Tap Room, to fine dining at the Terrace Room.

596 rooms. Restaurant, bar. Business center. Fitness center. Spa. Pets accepted. $151-250

★QUALITY SUITES

700 Mansfield Ave., Pittsburgh, 412-279-6300, 877-424-6423; www.choicehotels.com

127 rooms. Complimentary breakfast. Fitness center. Pool. $61-150

★★★RENAISSANCE PITTSBURGH HOTEL

107 Sixth St., Pittsburgh, 412-562-1200, 800-468-3571; www.renaissancehotels.com

Housed in the classic Fulton Building downtown, this hotel is an architectural stunner in the city's renowned Cultural District. Stroll across the Roberto

Clemente Bridge to reach North Shore destinations.

300 rooms. Restaurant, bar. Business center. Fitness center. Spa. $151-250

★★★SHERATON STATION SQUARE HOTEL
300 W. Station Square Drive, Pittsburgh, 412-261-2000, 800-325-3535; www.sheraton.com

In the heart of Station Square, a major nightlife destination, this riverfront hotel is convenient for sightseeing, North Shore destinations and the Gateway Clipper Fleet.

292 rooms. Restaurant, bar. Fitness center. Pool. Pets accepted. $151-250

★★★TARA COUNTRY INN
2844 Lake Road, Clark, 724-962-3535, 800-782-2803; www.tara-inn.com

Inspired by *Gone With the Wind*, this pillared inn brings Southern charm and hospitality to the northeast. All 27 rooms boast personalized décor and furnishings such as floral wallpaper, antique four-poster beds and hand-carved mantels. Ashley's Gourmet Dining Room continues the upscale vibe.

27 rooms. Restaurant, bar. $251-350

★★★THE WESTIN CONVENTION CENTER PITTSBURGH
1000 Penn Ave., Pittsburgh, 412-281-3700; www.westin.com

The Westin Convention Center is located in the heart of Pittsburgh's business and cultural districts, and connected to the new David L. Lawrence Convention Center by a skywalk.

616 rooms. Restaurant, bar. Business center. Fitness center. Pool. Pets accepted. $151-250

WHERE TO EAT

★★1902 LANDMARK TAVERN
24 Market Square, Pittsburgh, 412-471-1902

American. Lunch, dinner. Closed Sunday. Bar. $16-35

★ABRUZZI'S RESTAURANT
20 S. 10th St., Pittsburgh, 412-431-4511; www.abruzzis.net

Italian. Lunch, dinner. Bar. $16-35

★★CAFÉ AT THE FRICK
7227 Reynolds St., Pittsburgh, 412-371-0600; www.frickart.org

American. Lunch. Closed Monday. Outdoor seating. $15 and under.

★★★THE CARLTON RESTAURANT
500 Grant St., Pittsburgh, 412-391-4152; www.thecarltonrestaurant.com

American. Lunch (Monday-Friday), dinner. Closed Sunday. Bar. $36-85

★★CASBAH
229 S. Highland Ave, Pittsburgh, 412-661-5656; www.bigburrito.com/casbah

Mediterranean. Lunch (Monday-Friday), dinner, Sunday brunch. Outdoor seating. Bar. $16-35

★★THE CHURCH BREW WORKS
3525 Liberty Ave., Pittsburgh, 412-688-8200; www.churchbrew.com
American. Lunch, dinner. Outdoor seating. Bar. $16-35

★★★COMMON PLEA
310, Ross St., Pittsburgh, 412-697-3100; www.commonplea-restaurant.com
With its dark paneling, glass wall and subdued lighting, this restaurant caters to the legal crowd. Fish tends to rule the roost here, offered in a variety of appetizers and entrées.
Seafood. Lunch (Tuesday-Friday), dinner. Closed Sunday. Bar. $16-35

★★THE DAILY GRILL AT THE GEORGETOWN INN
Georgetown Inn, 1230 Grandview Ave., Pittsburgh, 412-481-4424; www.georgetowninn.com
American. Lunch, dinner. Bar. $36-85

★★★GRAND CONCOURSE
100 W. Station Square Drive, Pittsburgh, 412-261-1717; www.muer.com
This converted railroad station serves a legendary Sunday brunch.
International. Lunch (Monday-Saturday), dinner. Sunday brunch. Children's menu. Outdoor seating. Bar. $36-85

★★★HYEHOLDE
1516 Coraopolis Heights Road, Moon Township, 412-264-3116; www.hyeholde.com
Don a jacket and tie at this traditional outpost of English-country elegance 20 minutes from downtown Pittsburgh. The game and seafood menu and manor-like setting of rich tapestries, exposed wood beams and candlelight makes this a popular choice for special events.
International. Lunch, dinner. Closed Sunday. Outdoor seating. $36-85

★★INDIA GARDEN
328 Atwood St., Pittsburgh, 412-682-3000; www.indiagarden.net
Indian. Lunch, dinner. $15 and under.

★★KAYA
2000 Smallman St., Pittsburgh, 412-261-6565; www.bigburrito.com/kaya
Caribbean. Dinner. Bar. $36-85

★★LE MONT
1114 Grandview Ave., Pittsburgh, 412-431-3100; www.lemontpittsburgh.com
American. Dinner. Bar. $36-85

★★★LE POMMIER
2104 E. Carson St., Pittsburgh, 412-431-1901; www.lepommier.com
Located in the oldest storefront in the area, Le Pommier serves French-American bistro entrées such as cauliflower sautéed in brown butter with a roasted cauliflower-gruyere sauce and fresh oregano in puff pastry.
French. Dinner. Closed Sunday. Outdoor seating. Bar. $16-35

★★MAX'S ALLEGHENY TAVERN
537 Suismon St., Pittsburgh, 412-231-1899; www.maxsalleghenytavern.com
German. Lunch, dinner. Bar. $16-35

★★MONTEREY BAY FISH GROTTO
1411 Grandview Ave., Pittsburgh, 412-481-4414; www.montereybayfishgrotto.com
Seafood. Lunch (Monday-Friday), dinner. Children's menu. $36-85

★PENN BREWERY
800 Vinial St., Troy Hill, Pittsburgh, 412-237-9400; www.pennbrew.com
German. Lunch, dinner. Closed Sunday. Children's menu. Outdoor seating.
Bar. $16-35

★PRIMANTI BROTHERS
46 18th St., Pittsburgh, 412-263-2142; www.primantibros.com
American, Italian. Dinner. $15 and under.

★★RICO'S
One Rico Lane, Pittsburgh, 412-931-1989; www.ricos.biz
Italian, American. Lunch (Monday-Saturday), dinner. Closed Sunday. Bar.
$36-85

★★SEVICHE
930 Penn Ave., Pittsburgh, 412-697-3120; www.seviche.com
Tapas. Dinner. Closed Sunday. Bar. $16-35

★★★SOBA
5847 Ellsworth Ave., Pittsburgh, 412-362-5656; www.bigburrito.com/soba
A modern interior with a two-story waterfall, plush seating, tropical wood
tones and mellow lighting serves as the perfect backdrop for Soba's sophisticated Asian fusion cuisine. Recent small-plate selections have included crispy
tofu with lemongrass sauce and Vietnamese chicken spring rolls, while pad
Thai, wok-seared sea scallops with sweet chili soy sauce, and filet mignon
with chili-garlic mashed potatoes and Alaskan halibut have been featured as
large plate choices. Soups and salads round out the menu. An ambitious wine
list with selections that span the globe is also offered, along with a number of
sakes, martinis and cocktails.
Pan-Asian. Dinner. Outdoor seating. Bar. $36-85

★★SONOMA GRILLE
947 Penn Ave., Pittsburgh, 412-697-1336; www.thesonomagrille.com
American. Lunch, dinner. Bar. $16-35

★★★STEELHEAD BRASSERIE AND WINE BAR
112 Washington Place, Pittsburgh, 412-394-3474; www.thesteelhead.com
This casual American brasserie features artistically prepared cuisine that
highlights fresh seafood like Prince Edward Island mussels, seared ahi tuna
and oysters. The menu also includes certified Angus beef strip steak, filet
mignon and a porterhouse pork chop. On a daily basis, a special soup, pasta,
pizza and grilled fresh fish dish are offered, all of which can be perfectly

paired with a selection from the adventurous wine list.
American. Breakfast, lunch (Monday-Friday), dinner. Children's menu. Bar.
$36-85

★★TAMBELLINI
860 Saw Mill Run Blvd., Pittsburgh, 412-481-1118; www.eatzucchini.com
American. Lunch (Monday-Friday), dinner. Closed Sunday. Children's menu.
Bar. $16-35

★★THAI PLACE
5528 Walnut St., Pittsburgh, 412-687-8586; www.thaiplacepgh.com
Thai. Lunch, dinner. Bar. $16-35

READING
See also Denver/Adamstown, Ephrata, Lancaster, Pottstown
A city of railroads and industry famous for its superb pretzels, Reading was
the second community in the United States to vote a Socialist government
into office; however, the city has not had such a government for many years.
The characters of this unofficial capital of Pennsylvania Dutch land reflect
the love of music and the thrift and vigor of the "Dutch."

William Penn purchased the land now occupied by Reading from the Lenni-
Lenape Native Americans and settled his two sons, Thomas and Richard, on
it. They named it Reading (fern meadow) for their home in England. During
the Revolution, the citizens of Reading mustered troops for the Continental
army, forged cannons and provided a depot for military supplies and a prison
for Hessians and British. The hundreds of skilled German craftspeople, plus
canal and railroad transportation, ignited Reading's industrial development.

WHAT TO SEE
BERKS COUNTY HERITAGE CENTER
2201 Tulpehocken Road, Reading, 610-374-8839; www.countyofberks.com/parks
Here are the Gruber Wagon Works, where finely crafted wagons were produced for farm and industry; Wertz's Red Bridge, the longest single-span
covered bridge in the state; Deppen Cemetery, with graves of Irish workers
who died of "swamp fever" while building the Union Canal; C. Howard Hi-
ester Canal-Center, with its collection of canal artifacts. There are tours of
the wagon works and canal center as well as an orientation slide program.
May-October, Tuesday-Saturday 10 a.m.-4 p.m., Sunday noon-5 p.m.

CONRAD WEISER HOMESTEAD
28 Weiser Lane, Reading, 610-589-2934; www.conradweiserhomestead.org
Originally built in 1729, this house is the restored and furnished house of
colonial "ambassador" to the Iroquois nation and includes a springhouse,
gravesite, visitor center, and picnicking in the 26-acre park.
Admission: adults $5, children 3-11 $4, children 2 and under free. April-
November, Friday-Saturday 9 a.m.-5p.m., Sunday noon-5 p.m.

DANIEL BOONE HOMESTEAD

400 Daniel Boone Road, Reading, 610-582-4900; www.danielboonehomestead.org
This was the birthplace of Daniel Boone in 1734. It covers approximately 579 acres and includes Boone House, barn, blacksmith shop and sawmill. There are picnicking areas, nature trails, youth camping and a visitor center. Admission: adults $6, seniors $5.50, students $4. Tuesday-Saturday 9 a.m.-4:30 p.m., Sunday noon-4:30 p.m.

HISTORICAL SOCIETY OF BERKS COUNTY

940 Centre Ave., Reading, 610-375-4375; www.berkshistory.org
The Historical Society showcases local history exhibits, decorative arts, antiques, and transportation displays.
Admission: adults $4, seniors $3, children 5-12 $2. Tuesday-Saturday 9 a.m.-4 p.m.

MID-ATLANTIC AIR MUSEUM

11 Museum Drive, Reading, 610-372-7333; www.maam.org
This aviation museum is dedicated to the preservation of vintage aircraft; planes here are restored to flying condition by volunteers. They have a collection of 40 airplanes and helicopters; 20 on public display, including Martin 4-0-4-airliners, B-25 bomber and others.
Admission: adults $6, children 6-12 $3, children 5 and under free. Daily 9:30 a.m.-4 p.m.

PLANETARIUM

500 Museum Road, Reading, 610-371-5854; www.readingpublicmuseum.org
This planetarium features changing exhibits and star and laser light shows.
Admission: adults $7, seniors, children 4-18, students $5, children 3 and under free. Tuesday-Thursday, Saturday 11 a.m.-5 p.m., Friday 11 a.m.-8 p.m., Sunday noon-5 p.m.

THE READING PUBLIC MUSEUM AND ART GALLERY

500 Museum Road, Reading, 610-371-5850; www.readingpublicmuseum.org
This 25-acre Museum has exhibits on art and science. There are also galleries with art collections covering Asia, Ancient Civilizations, Africa and more.
Admission: adults $7, seniors, students and children 4-18 $5, children 3 and under free. Tuesday-Thursday, Saturday 11 a.m.-5 p.m., Friday 11 a.m.-8 p.m., Sunday noon-5 p.m.

WHERE TO STAY
★COMFORT INN

2200 Stacy Drive, Reading, 610-371-0500, 877-424-6423; www.choicehotels.com
60 rooms. Complimentary breakfast. Fitness center. $61-150

WHERE TO EAT
★★ALPENHOF BAVARIAN

903 Morgantown Road, Reading, 610-373-1624; www.alpenhofbnb.com
American, German. Lunch (Thurday-Friday, Sunday), dinner. Closed Monday-Wednesday. Outdoor seating. Bar. $16-35

★★★GREEN HILLS INN
2444 Morgantown Road, Reading, 610-777-9611
The owner of this small-town spot has big-city pedigree: He was a student of Georges Perrier, owner of Philadelpia's renowned La Bec-Fin. It should come as no surprise that the kitchen churns out impeccable French fare including grilled moulard duck breast and chateaubriand.
French, American. Dinner. Closed Sunday. $36-85

SCRANTON
See also Carbondale, Hawley, Pocono Mountains, Wilkes Barre
The first settlers here found a Monsey Native American village on the site. In 1840, George and Seldon Scranton built five iron furnaces using the revolutionary method of firing with anthracite coal instead of charcoal. Manufacture of iron and steel remained important industries until 1901, when the mills moved to Lake Erie to ease transportation problems.

After World War II, Scranton thoroughly revamped its economy when faced with depletion of the anthracite coal mines, which for more than a century had fired its forges. Scranton's redevelopment drew nationwide attention and served as a model for problem cities elsewhere. Today, Scranton is the home of electronic and printing industries and is host to several major trucking firm terminals. And if you're a fan of the television show *The Office*, you'll know that the show is set in Scranton.

WHAT TO SEE
ANTHRACITE HERITAGE MUSEUM
Keyser Avenue and Bald Mountain Road, Scranton, 570-963-4804;
www.anthracitemuseum.org
This museum contains displays on the history and culture of anthracite region. Other affiliated parts of the complex are the Iron Furnaces; Museum of Anthracite Mining, with emphasis on the technology of the industry, and the 19th-century miners' village of Eckley, near Hazleton.
Admission: adults 6, seniors $5.50, children 3-11 $4. Monday-Saturday 9 a.m.-5 p.m., Sunday noon-5 p.m. Closed Monday December-March.

CATLIN HOUSE
232 Monroe Ave., Scranton, 570-344-3841; www.lackawannahistory.org
Originally built in 1912, this is the headquarters of Lackawanna Historical Society. The home features period furnishings historic exhibits, antiques and a research library.
Tuesday-Friday 10 a.m.-5 p.m., Saturday noon-3 p.m.

EVERHART MUSEUM
1901 Mulberry St., Scranton, 570-346-7186; www.everhart-museum.org
Permanent collections includes 19th- and 20th-century American art; Dorflinger glass; Native American, Asian and primitive art; natural history displays including the Dinosaur Hall. There is also an on site gift shop.
Admission: adults $5, seniors and students $3, children 6-12 $2, children 5 and under free. Monday, Thursday-Friday noon-4 p.m., Saturday 10 a.m.-5 p.m., Sunday noon-5 p.m.

HOUDINI MUSEUM

1433 N. Main Ave., Scranton, 570-342-5555; www.houdini.org

This museum is devoted to the career and life of the great magician Harry Houdini. Tours, films featuring Houdini himself and a magic show (with live animals) are all included.

See Web site for schedule and ticket information.

LACKAWANNA COAL MINE TOUR

McDade Park, Keyser Ave., Scranton, 570-963-6463, 800-238-7245

The tour of this underground coal mine provides a realistic glimpse of the working lives of anthracite miners in an earlier time. A five-minute ride in a coal-mine car takes you into the cool and damp mine, and the ensuing hour-long tour will enlighten you about the hazards and harsh conditions faced by miners, as well as the unfortunate pit ponies, who lived in the mine.

Admission: adults $10, seniors $9.50, military personnel $9, children 3-12 $7.50, children 2 and under free. April-November, daily 10 a.m.-4:30 p.m.

LACKAWANNA COUNTY STADIUM

235 Montage Mountain Road, Scranton, 570-969-2255; www.lackawannacounty.org

This open-air stadium/civic arena seats 11,000. It's home of AAA baseball, high school and college football and marching band competitions.

MONTAGE MOUNTAIN SKI AREA

1000 Montage Mountain Road, Scranton, 570-969-7669; www.snomtn.com

Head to Sno Mountain to enjoy skiing and more. This ski area offers quad, double, three triple chairlifts; school, rentals, snowmaking; a bar, restaurant, and lodge. The vertical drop is 1,000 feet. Night skiing is available and there are more than 140 acres of trails set in 400 acres of mountainside. Summer activities include water slides, batting cages, and an amphitheater.

December-late March, daily; see Web site for information.

NAY AUG PARK

Arthur Avenue and Mulberry Street, Scranton, 570-348-4186

This park covers more than 35 acres with memorials to pioneer days. There are plenty of areas for picnicking, two playgrounds, two olympic-sized swimming pools, a waterslide, walking trails and refreshment stands. Enjoy a recently built tree house soaring over a gorge at 150 feet. There are also weekend concerts in the summer.

Admission to pool: adults and children 6-18 $3, seniors $1, children 5 and under free. Pool: Monday-Friday noon-6 p.m., Saturday-Sunday noon-6 p.m.

SCRANTON IRON FURNACES

159 Cedar Ave., Scranton, 570-344-4993; www.anthracitemuseum.org

The Iron Furnaces covers a partially restored site of four anthracite-fired iron furnaces built 1848-1857 and used until 1902. There is a visitor center and outdoor exhibits.

Visitor center: April-October, daily 10 a.m.-4 p.m.

STEAMTOWN NATIONAL HISTORIC SITE
Lackawanna and Cliff streets, Scranton, 570-340-5204; www.nps.gov/stea
This historic site has a large collection of steam locomotives and other memorabilia located in an authentic freight yard. Take a steam train ride through the yard.
Admission: $6. Park: May-December, daily 10 a.m.-4 p.m.; January-April, daily 10 a.m.-4 p.m.

WHERE TO STAY
★★CLARION HOTEL
300 Meadow Ave., Scranton, 570-344-9811, 800-347-1551; www.choicehotels.com
135 rooms. Restaurant, bar. Complimentary breakfast. Fitness center. Pool. Pets accepted. $61-150

★HAMPTON INN
22 Montage Mountain Road, Scranton, 570-342-7002, 800-426-7866;
www.hamptoninn.com
129 rooms. Complimentary breakfast. Business center. Pool. $61-150

★★RADISSON LACKAWANNA STATION HOTEL SCRANTON
700 Lackawanna Ave., Scranton, 570-342-8300; www.radisson.com
146 rooms. Restaurant, bar. Business center. Fitness center. $61-150

WHERE TO EAT
★COOPER'S SEAFOOD HOUSE
701 N. Washington Ave., Scranton, 570-346-6883; www.coopers-seafood.com
American. Lunch, dinner. Children's menu. Bar. $16-35

SOMERSET
See also Johnstown
James Whitcomb Riley described the countryside in his poem "Mongst the Hills of Somerset," starting the poem by saying, "Mongst the Hills of Somerset, I wish I were a 'roamin' yet." The county offers fishing, swimming, boating, hiking, biking, camping, skiing and ice skating.

WHAT TO SEE
KOOSER STATE PARK
943 Glades Pike, Somerset, 814-445-8673; www.dcnr.state.pa.us
Kooser State Park covers approximately 250 acres, and contains a four-acre lake with fishing and a swimming beach. The park also offers cross-country skiing and sledding in winter and picnicking and camping in summer. There are also tent and trailer sites as well as cabins.
Daily.

LAUREL HILL STATE PARK
1454 Laurel Hill Park Road, Somerset, 814-445-7725; www.dcnr.state.pa.us
This state park covers 3,935 acres mostly of mountain terrain. Laurel Hill Lake is 63 acres and provides a swimming beach and boating. There are also hiking trails, hunting, snowmobiling and ice fishing. There are picnicking

areas and a snack bar.

Beach: Late-May-mid-September 8 a.m.-sunset.

MOUNT DAVIS
Somerset, 724-238-1200; www.dcnr.state.pa.us

Mount Davis is the highest point in state at 3,213 feet. Take the High Point Trail to the top and on a clear day you can see parts of Maryland and the town of Salisbury.

SPECIAL EVENTS
MAPLE FESTIVAL
Festival Park, 120 Meyers Ave., 814-634-0213; Somerset, www.pamaplefestival.com

This annual festival is a weeklong celebration with a parade, quilting contests, an auto show, and tractor show, and more.

Admission: adults $4, children 6-12 $1, children 5 and under free.

March.

SEVEN SPRINGS WINE AND FOOD FESTIVAL
Seven Springs Mountain Resort, 777 Waterwheel Drive, Champion, 814-352-7777,
866-703-7625; www.7springs.com

Sample some of the best local producers have to offer and drink from the complimentary wine glass that comes with the price of admission. With easy access from the Pennsylvania turnpike, you can head to Champion to stomp grapes or simply enjoy the cuisine of the Keystone State.

Third weekend in August.

WHERE TO STAY
★★★INN AT GEORGIAN PLACE
800 Georgian Place Drive, Somerset, 814-443-1043; www.theinnatgeorgianplace.com

This bed and breakfast overlooks Lake Somerset and is packed with antiques. The restaurant offers classic dishes wish seasonal ingredients such as salmon filet with a maple mustard sauce served with asparagus and wild rice pilaf. 11 rooms. Restaurant, bar. Complimentary breakfast. $61-150

★QUALITY INN
215 Ramada Road, Somerset, 814-443-4646, 877-424-6423; www.choicehotels.com

146 rooms. Complimentary breakfast. Business center. Fitness center. Pool. Pets accepted. $61-150

★★SEVEN SPRINGS MOUNTAIN RESORT
777 Waterwheel Drive, Seven Springs, 814-352-7777, 800-452-2223;
www.7springs.com

418 rooms. Restaurant, bar. Fitness center. Pool. Spa. Golf. $61-150

WHERE TO EAT
★★★HELEN'S
Seven Springs Mountain Resort, 777 Waterwheel Drive, Seven Springs, 814-352-7777;
www.7springs.com

The formal service, complete with tableside carving and preparations, comes as a surprise considering the rural setting. Though the menu changes with the seasons, it leans towards classics with dishes such as pork osso buco with cheese risotto and grilled trout with baby beans and watercress.

American. Dinner. Closed Monday-Thursday. Reservations recommended. Bar. $36-85

★★PINE GRILL
800 N. Center Ave., Somerset, 814-445-2102; www.pinegrill.com
American. Lunch, dinner. Children's menu. Bar. $15 and under.

STATE COLLEGE
See also Harrisburg
Not surprisingly, State College is the home of Pennsylvania State University. In the beautiful Nittany Valley, the borough is surrounded by farmland famous for its production of oats and swine. Iron ore was discovered just east of town in 1790, and many iron furnaces later sprang up.

WHAT TO SEE
MOUNT NITTANY VINEYARD & WINERY
350 Houser Road, State College, 814-466-6373; www.mtnittanywinery.com
Opened in 1990, the winery is located within a stone-faced, chalet-style building nestled on the southern slopes of Mount Nittany. The tasting room offers variety of wines and view of large pond, vineyard and mountains. Tastings are free.

Tuesday-Friday 1:30-5 p.m., Saturday 10 a.m.-5 p.m., Sunday 12:30-4 p.m. Closed January.

PENNSYLVANIA STATE UNIVERSITY
College and Atherton streets, State College, 814-865-4700; www.psu.edu
Founded in 1855, today this university is home to more than 43,000 students. There are approximately 760 major buildings on this 15,984-acre campus, which is the land grant institution of Pennsylvania. The first college to be established here was the College of Agricultural Studies which is a showplace for the state's dairy industry, which includes their dairy center, which is the largest university creamery in the country. It has five herds of cows and automatic milking equipment. The creamery (in the Food Science Building) has a retail salesroom for cheeses, milk, cream and ice cream.

Creamery: Monday-Thursday 7 a.m.-10 p.m., Friday 7 a.m.-11 p.m., Saturday 8 a.m.-11 p.m., Sunday 9 a.m.-10 p.m.

WHIPPLE DAM STATE PARK
State College, 814-667-3808; www.dcnr.state.pa.us
Whipple Dam State Park covers approximately 256 acres and features a swimming beach as well as fishing and boating. You can aslo go hunting, hiking, snowmobiling, ice-skating and ice fishing. There are plenty of areas for picnicking as well as a snack bar.

Beach: Daily 8 a.m.-sunset.

SPECIAL EVENT
CENTRAL PENNSYLVANIA FESTIVAL OF THE ARTS
403 S. Allen St. 201, State College, 814-237-3682; www.arts-festival.com
This festival features an open-air display of visual and performing arts, indoor exhibits, demonstrations of arts and crafts, a sidewalk sale, sand sculptures, music, dance and theatre performances and food booths.
Mid-July.

WHERE TO STAY
★★★ATHERTON HOTEL
125 S. Atherton St., State College, 814-231-2100, 800-832-0132;
www.athertonhotel.net
This inn is located half a mile from Penn State. The Anthropology Museum, Historic Boalsburg Village and Palmer Museum of Art are also nearby. Guest lodgings are roomy with large picture windows and work desks.
150 rooms. Restaurant, bar. Fitness center. $61-150

★★AUTOPORT MOTEL & RESTAURANT
1405 S. Atherton St., State College, 814-237-7666, 800-932-7678;
www.theautoport.com
86 rooms. Restaurant, bar. $61-150

★★★CARNEGIE HOUSE
100 Cricklewood Drive, State College, 814-234-2424, 800-229-5033;
www.carnegiehouse.com
When you've conquered the links, stow your golf gear in your cozy guest room, relax in a deep library chair and have a celebratory drink. Carnegie House offers packages for golf and Penn State football weekends. Guest rooms have dormer windows and floral bedspreads.
22 rooms. Restaurant, bar. Complimentary breakfast. $61-150

★★DAYS INN
240 S. Pugh St., State College, 814-238-8454; www.daysinn.com
186 rooms. Restaurant, bar. Complimentary breakfast. Business center. Fitness center. Pool. Pets accepted. $61-150

★HAMPTON INN STATE COLLEGE
1101 E. College Ave., State College, 814-231-1590, 800-426-7866;
www.hamptoninn.com
120 rooms. Complimentary breakfast. Business center. Fitness center. Pool. $61-150

★★★THE NITTANY LION INN
200 W. Park Ave., State College, 800- 233-7505; www.pshs.psu.edu
Managed by the surrounding University, this hotel offers standard rooms with free high-speed Internet access, king-sized beds and coffee makers. It's located on the Penn State campus.
223 rooms. Restaurant, bar. Fitness center. Pool. $61-150

★★★TOFTREES RESORT AND FOUR STAR GOLF CLUB

1 Country Club Lane, State College, 814-234-8000, 800-252-3551; www.toftrees.com

This "home among the trees" sits in 1,500 wooded acres and offers private patios and balconies from which guests can enjoy the view. Enjoy the 18-hole golf course, volleyball court, tennis courts, and outdoor heated pool. 113 rooms. Restaurant, bar. Business center. Fitness center. Pool. Golf. Tennis. $61-150

WHERE TO EAT
★★TAVERN

220 E. College Ave., State College, 814-238-6116; www.thetavern.com

American. Dinner. Reservations recommended. Bar. $16-35

UNIONTOWN

See also Pittsburgh, State College

Coal and its byproducts made Uniontown prosperous, but with the decline in coal mining, the city has developed a more diverse economic base. First known as Union, this city has been the Fayette County seat since 1784. Uniontown was a hotbed of the Whiskey Rebellion, and federal troops were sent here in 1794.

WHAT TO SEE
FRIENDSHIP HILL NATIONAL HISTORIC SITE

1 Washington Parkway, Uniontown, 724-329-5512; www.nps.gov/frhi

This historic site preserves the restored home of Albert Gallatin, a Swiss immigrant who served his adopted country, in public and private life, for nearly seven decades. Gallatin made significant contributions to the young Republic in the fields of finance, politics, diplomacy and scholarship. He is best known as the Treasury Secretary under Jefferson and Madison. Here, you can visit his home as well as exhibits, audiovisual programs and an audio tour. Park: Daily dawn-dusk. Visitor center: April-October, daily 9 a.m.-5 p.m.

JUMONVILLE GLEN

Fort Necessity, 200 Caverns Park Road, Uniontown;www.nps.gov/fone

This is the site of the skirmish between the British and French forces that led to the battle at Fort Necessity.

Grounds: Daily dawn-dusk. Visitor center: Daily 9 a.m.-5 p.m.

WHITE WATER ADVENTURERS

6 Negley St., Ohiopyle, 800-992-7238; www.wwaraft.com

If you're interested in white water rafting, the Youghiogheny River has some of the wildest and most scenic in the eastern United States. Decide on a trip for you based on experience and what level of rapids you want to experience. Plenty of different trips are offered for thrill-seekers and families alike. They also offer bike and raft rentals.

Call or check Web site for information.

WILDERNESS VOYAGEURS

103 Garrett St., Ohiopyle, 800-272-4141; www.wilderness-voyageurs.com

These trips run on the lower, upper and middle Youghiogheny River. Also they rent bicycles and canoes, kayaks and offer canoe lessons. They also offer instruction for mountain biking, climbing, fly fishing and more.
Call or see Web site for more information.

WHERE TO STAY

★★HOLIDAY INN

700 W. Main St., Uniontown, 724-437-2816, 800-465-4329; www.hiuniontown.com

178 rooms. Restaurant, bar. Fitness center. Pool. Pets accepted. $61-150

WHERE TO EAT

★★★CHEZ GERARD AUTHENTIC FRENCH RESTAURANT

1187 National Pike, Highway 40 E., Hopwood, 724-437-9001; www.chezgerard.net

Chez Gerard is located in the historic Hopwood House, which dates to 1790. The all-French staff prides itself on serving the most authentic French experience, serving entrees such as magret de canard aux deux facons (grilled and smoked duck breasts with a plum and ginger reduction, grilled marinated zucchini and potato au gratin).
French. Lunch, dinner, Sunday brunch. Closed Tuesday. Reservations recommended. Bar. $36-85

VALLEY FORGE NATIONAL HISTORICAL PARK

See also King of Prussia, Philadelphia

Two thousand soldiers died here from hunger, disease and cold, but General George Washington and his beleaguered army ultimately triumphed over the British in 1778. Today, Valley Forge has come to symbolize American perseverance and sacrifice on a lush, hilly, 3,600-acre expanse with rich historical significance and beautiful scenery. Visitors can tour the park by car or bus and see Washington's restored stone headquarters, log soldier huts, bronze statues and monuments, and weapons and equipment used during the American Revolution. You can even learn how Washington's soldiers were taught to load and fire their muskets. The visitor's center features exhibits, artifacts, a gift shop and an 18-minute film. Choose from a 16-mile walking trail, 10-mile horse trails, a bike path or a 10-mile self-guided tour. Picnic areas are available as well.

WHAT TO SEE

NATIONAL MEMORIAL ARCH

Built in 1917 to commemorate Washington's army. Inscribed in the arch is a quote from General Washington: "Naked and starving as they are, we cannot enough admire the incomparable patience and fidelity of the soldiery."

WASHINGTON HEADQUARTERS

Park staff will provide information about the house where Washington lived for six months and which served as military headquarters for the Continental Army during that time.
Daily 9 a.m.-5 p.m.

WASHINGTON MEMORIAL CHAPEL

Highway 23, Valley Forge, 610-783-0120; www.washingtonmemorialchapel.org

This is a private property within park boundaries. Stained-glass windows depict the story of the New World, its discovery and development. There are hand-carved oak choir stalls, Pews of the Patriots and the Roof of the Republic bearing the State Seal of all the states. Also part of the chapel is the 58 cast-bell Washington Memorial National Carillon, with bells honoring states and territories.

Monday-Saturday 10 a.m.-5 p.m., Saturday 1-5 p.m.

WARREN

See also Bradford

At the junction of the Allegheny and Conewango rivers, Warren is the headquarters and gateway of the famous Allegheny National Forest. Named for General Joseph Warren, an American patriot killed in the Battle of Bunker Hill, the town was once the point where great flotillas of logs were formed for the journey to Pittsburgh or Cincinnati.

WHAT TO SEE
ALLEGHENY NATIONAL FOREST

222 Liberty St., Warren, 814-723-5150; www.fs.fed.us

This national forest is more than 510,000 acres South and East on Highways 6 and 62, located in Warren, Forest, McKean and Elk counties. You'll find black bear, whitetail deer, wild turkey, a diversity of small birds and mammals and streams and reservoirs with trout, walleye, muskellunge, northern pike and bass. There are rugged hills, quiet valleys, open meadows, and dense forest. These lures, plus swimming, boating, hiking, camping and picnicking facilities, draw more than 2 million visitors a year.

KINZUA DAM AND ALLEGHENY RESERVOIR

1205 Kinzua Road, Warren, 814-726-0661

The Kinzua Dam, at 179 feet high and 1,877 feet long has a 24-mile-long lake where visitors can enjoy swimming, fishing, boating, picnicking, and vistas from overlooks. This is a popular destination in the summertime. There are also campsites here.

Visitor center: Memorial Day-Labor Day daily; September-October, Saturday-Sunday.

WAYNE

See also Philadelphia

Originally settled by Quakers, Wayne is known as a pleasant suburb of Philadelphia with a low crime rate and top-notch education system. It's a small community with plenty to offer.

WHERE TO STAY
★★COURTYARD PHILADELPHIA VALLEY FORGE/KING OF PRUSSIA

1100 Drummers Lane, Wayne, 610-687-6700; www.courtyard.com

150 rooms. Fitness center. Pool. $61-150

★★★EMBASSY SUITES PHILADELPHIA-VALLEY FORGE

888 Chesterbrook Blvd., Wayne, 610-647-6700, 866-388-6106; www.vfsuites.com

Guest rooms here off pillow-top mattresses, a flat-screen TV, Internet access, a work desk and a Herman Miller Aeron chair. Enjoy a meal at the Town and Country Grille where you can enjoy American fare and then have a cocktail at the E Bar.

229 rooms. Restaurant, bar. Business center. Fitness center. Pool. $151-250

★★★WAYNE HOTEL

139 E. Lancaster Ave., Wayne, 610-687-5000, 800-962-5850; www.waynehotel.com

Located 18 miles west of Philadelphia, this restored property reflects the elegance of a time past with its wraparound porch and antique reproduction furnishings. Individually decorated guest rooms feature wireless Internet access, pillow-top mattresses and complimentary breakfast each morning.

38 rooms. Restaurant, bar. Complimentary breakfast. $61-150

WHERE TO EAT
★★★TAQUET

Wayne Hotel, 139 E. Lancaster Ave., Wayne, 610-687-5005; www.taquet.com

This elegant Main Line restaurant prides itself on serving local products prepared with a French sensibility. Entrees include Norwegian salmon with cucumber and black bean salad or Nebraska center-cut beef filet mignon with polenta and bordelaise sauce.

French. Lunch, dinner. Closed Sunday. Outdoor seating. Bar. $16-35

★★TOWN AND COUNTRY GRILLE

888 Chesterbrook Blvd., Wayne, 610-647-6700; www.vfsuites.com

American. Breakfast, lunch. Bar. $16-35

WEST CHESTER

See also King of Prussia, Philadelphia

In the heart of three Pennsylvania Revolutionary War historic sites—Brandywine, Paoli and Valley Forge—West Chester today is a university and residential community with fine examples of Greek Revival and Victorian architecture.

WHERE TO STAY
★★★DULING-KURTZ HOUSE & COUNTRY INN

146 S. Whitford Road, Exton, 610-524-1830; www.dulingkurtz.com

Rich in history and comfort, this small inn offers a homey, elegant atmosphere for relaxation. The Duling-Kurtz House was built in 1783 and is located within walking distance of shopping, the train station and more. Rooms are small but comfortable and cozy.

13 rooms. Complimentary breakfast. Restaurant, bar. $61-150

★★HOLIDAY INN

943 S. High St., West Chester, 610-692-1900, 800-972-2796; www.ichotelsgroup.com

141 rooms. Restaurant, bar. Business center. Fitness center. Pool. $61-150

★★INN AT CHESTER SPRINGS

815 N. Pottstown Pike, Exton, 610-363-1100, 888-253-6119;
www.innatchestersprings.com

225 rooms. Restaurant, bar. Business center. Fitness center. Pool. $61-150

★★MENDENHALL HOTEL

323 Kennett Pike, Mendenhall, 610-388-2100; www.mendenhallinn.com

70 rooms. Restaurant, bar. Complimentary breakfast. Business center. Fitness center. Pool. $151-250

WHERE TO EAT
★★DULING-KURTZ HOUSE

146 S. Whitford Road, Exton, 610-524-1830; www.dulingkurtz.com

French. Lunch, dinner. Bar. $36-85

★★GILMORE'S

133 E. Gay St., West Chester, 610-431-2800; www.gilmoresrestaurant.com

French. Dinner. Closed Sunday-Monday. Bar. $36-85

★★MENDENHALL INN

Mendenhall Hotel, Highway 52, Mendenhall, 610-388-1184; www.mendenhallinn.com

American, French. Lunch, dinner, Sunday brunch. Children's menu. Reservations recommended. Outside seating. Bar. $36-85

WILKES-BARRE

See also Hazleton, Scranton

Named in honor of two members of the British Parliament who championed individual rights and supported the colonies, Wilkes-Barre and the Wyoming Valley were settled by pioneers from Connecticut. Pennsylvania and Connecticut waged the Pennamite-Yankee War, the first phase ending in 1771 with Connecticut in control of the valley. It was later resumed until Connecticut relinquished its claims in 1800. Wilkes-Barre was burned by the Native Americans and Tories during the Revolution and again by Connecticut settlers protesting the Decree of Trenton, in which Congress favored Pennsylvania's claim to the territory. Discovery of anthracite coal in the valley sparked the town's growth after Judge Jesse Fell demonstrated that anthracite could be burned in a grate without forced draft.

WHERE TO STAY
★★BEST WESTERN EAST MOUNTAIN INN & SUITES

2400 E. End Blvd., Wilkes-Barre, 570-822-1011, 800-780-7234;
www.eastmountaininn.com

152 rooms. Restaurant, bar. Business center. Fitness center. Pool. $61-150

★HOLIDAY INN EXPRESS

1063 Highway 315, Wilkes-Barre, 570-825-3838, 888-465-4329;
www.ichotelsgroup.com

123 rooms. Restaurant, bar. Complimentary breakfast. Business center. Fitness center. $61-150

★★★THE WOODLANDS INN & RESORT
1073 Highway 315, Wilkes-Barre, 570-824-9831, 800-762-2222;
www.thewoodlandsresort.com

The Woodlands Inn & Resort offers urban warriors a chance to bask in the simple joys of nature. This wooded resort on 40 acres in the foothills of the Poconos is a perfect place to spend a vacation, a romantic getaway or even a corporate retreat. Golf and skiing are a short distance away, and the resort offers five nightclubs, bars and lounges, with live jazz and dancing.
179 rooms. Restaurant, bar. Fitness center. Pool. Tennis. $36-85

YORK
See also Gettysburg, Harrisburg, Lancaster

York claims to be the first capital of the United States. The Continental Congress met here in 1777 and adopted the Articles of Confederation, using the phrase "United States of America" for the first time. The first Pennsylvania town founded west of the Susquehanna River, York was and is still based on an agricultural and industrial economy. The city is dotted with 17 historical markers and 35 brass or bronze tablets marking historical events or places. There are more than 10 recreation areas in the county.

WHAT TO SEE
CENTRAL MARKET HOUSE
34 W. Philadelphia St., York, 717-848-2243

Opened in March 1888, this street market features more than 70 vendors who offer fresh produce, homemade baked goods, regional handcrafts and specialty items.
Tuesday, Thursday, Saturday.

COLONIAL COMPLEX GENERAL GATES HOUSE AND GOLDEN PLOUGH TAVERN
157 W. Market St., York, 717-845-2951; www.yorkheritage.org

Here, you'll find General Gates' House, where Lafayette gave a toast to Washington, marking the end of a movement to replace him. Also here is Golden Plough Tavern, one of the earliest buildings in York, which reflects the Germanic background of many of the settlers in its furnishings and half-timber architecture, and the Bobb Log House, furnished with painted and grained furniture. Also here is the York County Colonial Court House which is a replica of 1754 original. Exhibits include a multimedia presentation of Continental Congress's adoption of the Articles of Confederation, audiovisual story of 1777-1778 historic events, an original printer's copy of Articles of Confederation, historic documents and artifacts.
Admission: adults $10, students $7, children 8-18 $5. Tuesday-Saturday 10 a.m.-4 p.m.

FIRE MUSEUM OF YORK COUNTY
757 W. Market St., York, 717-846-6452; www.yorkheritage.org/fire_museum.html

This turn-of-the-century firehouse preserves two centuries of firefighting history; from leather bucket brigades to hand-drawn hose carts and pumps, horse-drawn equipment and finally to motorized equipment; artifacts and

memorabilia; fire chief's office and firefighter's sleeping quarters are re-created, complete with brass slide pole.
Admission: adults $10, children 8-18 $5, students $7. Mid-April-mid-December, Saturday 10 a.m.-4 p.m.

HARLEY-DAVIDSON U.S.A.

1425 Eden Road, York, 717-852-6590; www.harley-davidson.com
For motorcycle lovers, take a guided tour through motorcycle assembly plant and the Rodney Gott Antique Motorcycle Museum.
Tours: Monday-Friday 9 a.m.-2 p.m. Tour center and gift shop: Monday-Friday 8 a.m.-4 p.m.; also June-August, Saturday 10 a.m.-2 p.m.

HISTORICAL SOCIETY MUSEUM AND LIBRARY

250 E. Market St., York, 717-848-1587; www.yorkheritage.org
The Historical Society houses a museum and library with genealogical records. The museum features exhibits on the history of York County.
Admission: adults $10, children 8-18 $5, students $7. Museum: Tuesday-Saturday 10 a.m.-4 p.m. Library: Tuesday-Saturday 9 a.m.-5 p.m.

WHERE TO STAY
★BEST WESTERN WESTGATE INN

1415 Kenneth Road, York, 717-767-6931; www.bestwestern.com
104 rooms. Restaurant, bar. Complimentary breakfast. Business center. Fitness center. $61-150

★HAMPTON INN

1550 Mount Zion Road, York, 717-840-1500, 800-426-7866; www.hamptoninn.com
144 rooms. Complimentary breakfast. Business center. Fitness center. Pool. $61-150

★★HOLIDAY INN

2000 Loucks Road, York, 717-846-9500, 800-465-4329; www.holidayinn.com
180 rooms. Restaurant, bar. Business center. Fitness center. Pool. Pets accepted. $61-150

★★THE YORKTOWNE HOTEL

48 E. Market St., York, 717-848-1111; www.yorktowne.com
121 rooms. Restaurant, bar. Business center. Fitness center. $151-250

WHERE TO EAT
★★★ACCOMAC INN

6330 S. River Drive, York, 717-252-1521; www.accomac.com
This elegant country restaurant comes complete with white tablecloths and tableside preparation and serves delicious French fare. They also have a screened-in porch where you can enjoy a meal and enjoy a sunset.
French. Dinner, Sunday brunch. Bar. $36-85

★★SAN CARLO'S
333 Arsenal Road, U.S. 30, York, 717-854-2028; www.sancarlosrestaurant.com
American. Dinner. Children's menu. Bar. $16-35

VIRGINIA

FROM VIENNA TO VIRGINIA BEACH AND RICHMOND TO ROANOKE, VIRGINIA REALLY IS FOR lovers—of nature, history, art, fine dining and family fun. The first of the Southern states stays true to its tourism slogan, "Virginia is for lovers," four words that just might be vague enough to encapsulate all that Virginia has to offer.

The state is best known for its prominent role in U.S. history, and strong ties to the past are readily apparent. More than 1,600 historical markers dot its 55,000 miles of paved roads. And over 100 historic buildings are open all year; hundreds more welcome visitors during the statewide Historic Garden Week (usually the last week in April).

Permanent English settlement of America began in Jamestown in 1607 and started a long line of Virginia "firsts:" the first legislative assembly in the Western Hemisphere; the first armed rebellion against royal government (Bacon's Rebellion, 1676); the first stirring debates, in Williamsburg and Richmond, which left pre-Revolutionary America echoing Patrick Henry's inflammatory "Give me liberty, or give me death!" Records show that America's first Thanksgiving was held December 4, 1619, on the site of what is now Berkeley Plantation.

To Virginia the nation owes its most cherished documents: Thomas Jefferson's Declaration of Independence, George Mason's Bill of Rights and James Madison's Constitution. The Old Dominion was the birthplace of George Washington and seven other U.S. presidents.

Ironically, the state so passionately involved in creating a new nation was very nearly the means of its destruction. Virginia was the spiritual and physical capital of the Confederacy; the Army of Northern Virginia was the Confederacy's most powerful weapon, General Robert E. Lee its greatest commander. More than half the fighting of the Civil War took place in Virginia; and here, in the courthouse of the quaint little village of Appomattox, is where it finally came to an end.

When chartered in 1609, the Virginia territory included about one-tenth of what is now the United States; the present state ranks 36th in size, but the area is remarkably diverse. Tidewater Virginia—the coastal plain—is low, almost flat, arable land cut by rivers and bays into a magnificent system of natural harbors. Inland lies the gentle rolling Piedmont, Virginia's leading tobacco area, covering about half the state. The Piedmont also produces apples, corn, wheat, hay and dairy products. West of the Piedmont rise the Blue Ridge Mountains; high, rugged, upland plateaus occur to the south. Farther west is the Valley of Virginia, which is actually a series of valleys. The best known is the Shenandoah Valley, which contains some of the richest—and once bloodiest—land in the nation. Civil War fighting swept the valley for four years; Winchester changed hands 72 times. To the southwest are the Appalachian Plateaus, a rugged, forested region of coal mines.

For the vacationer today, the state offers colonial and Civil War history at every turn, seashore and mountain recreation year-round, caverns in the west, the Dismal Swamp in the southeast and the Skyline Drive, one of the loveliest scenic drives in the East.

ABINGDON

See also Bristol

Daniel Boone passed through this area in 1760 and dubbed it "Wolf Hill" after a pack of wolves from a nearby cave disturbed his dogs. Wolf Hill had long been a crossing for buffalo and Native Americans; Boone later used it for his own family's westward migration. Later, Black's Fort was built here and the community adopted that name. Now known as Abingdon, this summer resort in the Virginia Highlands just north of Tennessee is Virginia's largest burley tobacco market and a livestock auction center.

WHAT TO SEE
ABINGDON HISTORIC DISTRICT

276-676-2282, 800-435-3440; www.virginia.org

Listed on the National Register of Historic Places, this 20-block district features buildings that date from the 1700s. The historically significant structures aren't the only draw: The area has dozens of shops and galleries.

GRAYSON HIGHLANDS STATE PARK

Abingdon, 276-579-7092, 800-933-7225; www.dcr.virginia.gov

Within this 4,822-acre park are rugged peaks, some more than 5,000 feet high, you can go hiking, riding on horse trails, picnicking, and camping. There is a visitor center with interpretive programs and pioneer life displays in the summer. This state park is adjacent to Mount Rogers National Recreation Area.

Daily dawn-dusk.

RIVERSIDE CAMPGROUND

18496 N. Fork River Road, Abingdon, 276-628-5333;
www.riversidecampgroundabingdon.com

This family-owned campground is located near the Holston River. Campers will enjoy the live music, pool, bingo hall, arcade, playground, basketball courty, volleyball court and more.

April-November.

VIRGINIA CREEPER NATIONAL RECREATION TRAIL

Virginia Creeper Trail Club, Abingdon, 276-676-2282, 800-435-3440;
www.vacreepertrail.org

Hikers, bicyclists, equestrians and anyone who wants to enjoy a good hike will find one on this 34-mile scenic railroad bed converted into a recreational facility. There are numerous shuttle and bike rental facilities nearby.

WHITE'S MILL

12291 White's Mill Road, Abingdon, 276-628-2960; www.whitesmill.org

White's Mill is a still-functioning grist and flour mill built in 1790. Just 4 1/2 miles from Abingdon, this Virginia Historic Landmark is one of the only water-powered mills in existence in southwestern Virginia. Watch as corn becomes cornmeal, and don't forget to take home a sample. Nearby is a working Blacksmith Shop.

Wednesday-Sunday 10 a.m.-6 p.m.

SPECIAL EVENTS
BARTER THEATRE
127 W. Main St., Abingdon, 540-628-3991; www.bartertheatre.com
This is America's oldest and longest-running professional repertory theater. It was founded during the Depression in 1933 on the theory that residents would barter their abundant crops for first-rate professional entertainment. It was designated State Theatre of Virginia in 1946.
February-December.

VIRGINIA HIGHLANDS FESTIVAL
208 W. Main St., Abingdon, 276-623-5266; www.vahighlandsfestival.org
This festival features exhibits, demonstrations of rustic handicrafts, plays, musical entertainment, historical reenactments and house tours as well as an antique market.
Late-July-early-August.

WHERE TO STAY
★COMFORT INN
170 Old Jonesboro Road, Abingdon, 276-676-2222, 877-424-6423;
www.choicehotels.com
80 rooms. Complimentary breakfast. Pool. $61-150

★DAYS INN
887 Empire Drive Southwest, Abingdon, 276-628-7131, 800-329-7466;
www.daysinn.com
98 rooms. Restaurant, bar. Complimentary breakfast. Business center. Pool. Pets accepted. $61-150

★★★THE MARTHA WASHINGTON INN
150 W. Main St., Abingdon, 276-628-3161, 888-888-5252;
www.marthawashingtoninn.com
Experience Southern hospitality at its finest in this historic inn, built as a private residence for a Virginia general in 1832. The original architecture has been painstakingly maintained, with wood floors, crystal chandeliers and plaster detailing. Meals served in the Dining Room are innovative and well prepared.
51 rooms. Restaurant, bar. Complimentary breakfast. Business center. Fitness center. Pool. Spa. Tennis. $36-85

ALEXANDRIA
See also Arlington County, Fairfax, Falls Church, Mount Vernon
A group of English and Scottish merchants established a tobacco warehouse at the junction of Hunting Creek and the "Potowmack" River in the 1740s. The little settlement prospered, and 17 years later surveyor John West, Jr., and his young assistant, George Washington, arrived and "laid off in streets and 84 half-acre lots" the town of Alexandria. Among the first buyers on the July morning in 1749 when the lots were offered for public sale were Lawrence Washington and his brother Augustus, William Ramsay, the Honorable William Fairfax and John Carlyle. Erecting handsome town houses, these

gentlemen soon brought a lively and cosmopolitan air to Alexandria with parties, balls and horse racing. George Washington made his home here, as did George Mason and Robert E. Lee.

In 1789, Virginia ceded Alexandria to the District of Columbia, but in 1846, the still Southern-oriented citizens asked to return to the Old Dominion, which Congress allowed. During the Civil War, Alexandria was cut off from the Confederacy when Union troops occupied the town to protect Potomac River navigation. Safe behind Union lines, the city escaped the dreadful destruction experienced by many other Southern towns. Today, Alexandria has developed into a trade, commerce, transportation and science center.

WHAT TO SEE
ALEXANDRIA BLACK HISTORY MUSEUM
638 N. Alfred St., Alexandria, 703-838-4356; oha.alexandriava.gov
This museum displays photographs, letters, documents and other artifacts relating the history of African-Americans in Alexandria.
Admission: $2. Tuesday-Saturday 10 a.m.-4 p.m.

THE ATHENAEUM
201 Prince St., Alexandria, 703-548-0035; www.nvfaa.org
Located in Old Town Alexandria, this Greek Revival structure was built as a bank but now houses the Northern Virginia Fine Arts Association. They host art shows, dance performances, yoga, dance classes and other classes and events.
Thursday-Friday, Saturday noon-4 p.m., Sunday1-4 p.m.

BOYHOOD HOME OF ROBERT E. LEE
607 Oronoco St., Alexandria, 703-548-8454; www.leeboyhoodhome.com
This was the home of Robert E. Lee through most of his childhood. Famous guests included Washington and Lafayette.

CARLYLE HOUSE
121 N. Fairfax St., Alexandria, 703-549-2997; www.nvrpa.org
This 1753 stately stone mansion built in Palladian style was the site of a 1755 meeting between General Edward Braddock and five British colonial governors who planned the early campaigns of the French and Indian War.
Admission: adults $4, children 11-17 $2, children 10 and under free.
Tuesday-Saturday 10 a.m.-4 p.m., Sunday noon-4 p.m.

CHRIST CHURCH
118 N. Washington St., Alexandria, 703-549-1450; www.historicchristchurch.org
George Washington and Robert E. Lee were pewholders at his church. It has fine Palladian windows, an interior balcony, a wrought-brass and crystal chandelier brought from England. The structure has been extensively restored but has changed little since it was built. There is also a gift shop at Columbus Street entrance.
Services: Wednesday 7:15 a.m., 12:05 p.m., Sunday 8 a.m., 9 a.m., 11:15 a.m., 5 p.m. Gift shop: Tuesday-Saturday 10 a.m.-4 p.m., Sunday 8:45 a.m.-1 p.m.

FORT WARD MUSEUM AND HISTORIC SITE

4301 W. Braddock Road, Alexandria, 703-838-4848
Restored Union Fort from the Civil War contains a museum with a pristine
Civil War collection. There's also a park with picnicking areas.
Museum: April-October, Tuesday-Saturday 9 a.m.-5 p.m., Sunday noon-5
p.m.; November-March, Tuesday-Saturday 10 a.m.-5 p.m., Sunday noon-5
p.m. Park: Daily 9 a.m.-dusk.

GADSBY'S TAVERN MUSEUM

134 N. Royal St., Alexandria, 703-838-4242; www.oha.alexandriava.gov/gadsby
Gadsby's Tavern was frequented by Washington and other patriots. It com-
bines two 18th-century buildings, the tavern and an old city hotel.
Admission: adults $4, children 11-17 $2, children 10 and under free.
November-March, Wednesday-Saturday 11 a.m.-4 p.m., Sunday 1-4 p.m.;
April-October, Tuesday-Saturday 10 a.m.-5 p.m, Sunday-Monday 1-5 p.m.

GEORGE WASHINGTON MASONIC NATIONAL MEMORIAL

101 Callahan Drive, Alexandria, 703-683-2007; www.gwmemorial.org
As American Freemasons' memorial to their most prominent member, this
333-foot-tall structure houses a large collection of objects that belonged to
George Washington, which were collected by his family or the masonic lodge
where he served as the first Master. Guided tours explore a replica of Alexandria Washington Lodge's first hall, a library, museum and an observation
deck on the top floor.
Admission: Free. April-September, daily 9 a.m.-4 p.m.; October-March,
daily 10 a.m.-4 p.m.

★★★★★ VIRGINIA

KING STREET

This street is lined with trendy restaurants, shops, galleries and fine antique
stores. It's the main street in Alexandria.

237

LEE-FENDALL HOUSE

614 Oronoco St., Alexandria, 703-548-1789; www.leefendallhouse.org
This house was built by Phillip Richard Fendall in 1785 and occupied by the
Lee family for 118 years. Both George Washington and Revolutionary War
hero "Light Horse Harry" Lee were frequent visitors to the house. Remod-
eled in 1850, the house is furnished with Lee family belongings.
Admission: adults $5, children 11-17 $3, children 10 and under free.
Wednesday-Saturday10 a.m.-4 p.m., Sunday 1-4 p.m.

OLD PRESBYTERIAN MEETING HOUSE

321 S. Fairfax St., Alexandria, 703-549-6670; www.opmh.org
Founded in 1772, this meeting house provides worship services for members
and visitors alike along with Christian education for children in grade school
and middle school. There is also a historic burial in the churchyard here with
a tomb of the unknown soldier of the Revolutionary War.
Services: Sunday 8:30 a.m., 11 a.m.

SIGHTSEEING BOAT TOURS

Potomac Riverboat Company, 205 the Strand, Alexandria, 703-684-0580;
www.potomacriverboatco.com

Take a sightseeing boat tour of the Alexandria waterfront. Tickets must be purchased 24-hours in advance.
Office: Monday-Friday 9 a.m.-5 p.m. See Web site for schedules and ticket information.

STABLER-LEADBEATER APOTHECARY MUSEUM

105-107 S. Fairfax St., Alexandria, 703-838-3852; oha.alexandriava.gov/apothecary

Here, you'll find the largest collection of apothecary glass in its original setting in the country with more than 1,000 apothecary bottles. The original building is now a museum of early pharmacy with collection of old prescriptions, patent medicines, scales and other 18th-century pharmacy items. George Washington, Robert E. Lee, and John Calhoun were regular customers.
Admission: adults $4, children 11-17 $2, children 10 and under free.
April-October, Sunday-Monday 1-5 p.m., Tuesday-Saturday 10 a.m.-5 p.m.; November-March, Wednesday-Saturday 11 a.m.-4 p.m., Sunday 1-4 p.m.

TORPEDO FACTORY ART CENTER

105 N. Union St., Alexandria, 703-838-4565; www.torpedofactory.org

This renovated munitions plant houses an artists' center with more than 160 professional artists of various media. There are studios, cooperative galleries and an art school. The Alexandria Archaeology Museum is also here.
Admission: Free. Friday-Wednesday 10 a.m.-5 p.m., Thursday 10 a.m.-9 p.m.

WALKING TOUR OF HISTORIC SITES

Ramsay House, 221 King St., Alexandria, 703-838-4200; www.visitalexandriava.com

Start at the visitor center in Ramsay House, which is the oldest house in Alexandria and has been used as a tavern, grocery store and cigar factory. Here, you can obtain special events information and a free visitors' guide, and purchase block tickets good for reduced admission to three of the city's historic properties. Guided walking tours depart from here. The bureau also issues free parking permits, tour and highway maps, and hotel, dining and shopping information.
Daily 9 a.m.-8 p.m.

WOODLAWN PLANTATION

9000 Richmond Highway, Alexandria, 703-780-4000; www.woodlawn1805.org

In 1799, George Washington gave 2,000 acres of land as a wedding present to Eleanor Parke Custis, his foster daughter, who married his nephew, Major Lawrence Lewis. Dr. William Thornton, first architect of the U.S. Capitol, then designed this mansion. The Lewises entertained such notables as Andrew Jackson, Henry Clay and the Marquis de Lafayette. The house was restored in the early 1900s and later became the residence of a U.S. senator. The home has 19th-century period rooms with many original furnishings. The exterior houses formal gardens.
Admission: adults $8.50, children $4. April-December, Thursday-Monday 10 a.m.-5 p.m. Combination ticket for both houses available.

SPECIAL EVENTS
GEORGE WASHINGTON BIRTHDAY CELEBRATIONS
1108 Jefferson St., Alexandria, 703-991-4474; www.washingtonbirthday.net
Events include a race and a Revolutionary War reenactment followed by a birthday parade on the federal holiday.
February.

RED CROSS WATERFRONT FESTIVAL
123 N. Alfred St., Alexandria, 703-549-8300; www.waterfrontfestival.org
This festival commemorates Alexandria's maritime heritage. It features "tall ships," blessing of the fleet, river cruises, races, arts and crafts, exhibits, food, a variety of music and fireworks.
June.

SCOTTISH CHRISTMAS WALK
George Washington Masonic Memorial, 101 Callahan Drive, Alexandria, 703-548-0111, 800-388-9119; www.scottishchristmaswalk.com
This weekend celebration includes a parade, house tour, concerts, greens and heather sales, and a dinner/dance to emphasize the city's Scottish origins. Enjoy sounds of bagpipes through the streets of Old Town.
December.

VIRGINIA SCOTTISH GAMES
Great Meadow, the Plains, 703-912-1943; www.vascottishgames.org
This traditional Scottish even features athletic competitions, Highland dances and music, antique cars, displays and food.
September.

WHERE TO STAY
★BEST WESTERN OLD COLONY INN
1101 N. Washington St., Alexandria, 703-739-2222, 800-528-1234; www.hotel-alexandria.com
49 rooms. Complimentary breakfast. Business center. Fitness center. $61-150

★★CROWNE PLAZA HOTEL OLD TOWN ALEXANDRIA
901 N. Fairfax St., Alexandria, 703-683-6000, 800-972-3159; www.crowneplaza.com
253 rooms. Restaurant, bar. Business center. Fitness center. $61-150

★HAMPTON INN ALEXANDRIA
4800 Leesburg Pike, Alexandria, 703-671-4800; www.hamptoninn.com
130 rooms. Complimentary breakfast. Business center. Fitness center. Pool. $61-150

★★★HILTON ALEXANDRIA MARK CENTER
5000 Seminary Road, Alexandria, 703-845-1010; www.hilton.com
The lakeside Hilton Alexandria Mark Center is situated near the central business district of Washington, D.C., and the shops and galleries of Old Town. This elegant atrium hotel sits adjacent to a 43-acre botanical preserve and offers views of the Capitol. Guests looking for onsite activities can work out in

the 24-hour fitness center or take a swim in the heated indoor/outdoor pool. 496 rooms. Restaurant, bar. Complimentary breakfast. Business center. Fitness center. Pool. Pets accepted. $61-150

★★★HILTON SPRINGFIELD
6550 Loisdale Road, Springfield, 703-971-8900, 800-445-8667; www.hilton.com
The Hilton Springfield is located just 15 minutes from Washington, D.C., and offers complimentary shuttle service to the Springfield/Franconia Metro station. This modern, welcoming hotel puts every comfort at your fingertips. Accommodations are streamlined and stylish. Guest rooms feature complimentary wireless Internet access. Unwind and grab a drink and a bite at the hotel's restaurant, Houlihan's.
244 rooms. Restaurant, bar. Business center. Fitness center. Pool. Pets accepted. $61-150

★★★MORRISON HOUSE BOUTIQUE HOTEL
116 S. Alfred St., Alexandria, 703-838-8000, 866-324-6628; www.morrisonhouse.com
Just down the river from the Capitol, this Federal-style mansion presents visitors with a peaceful alternative to the bustling city. Decorative fireplaces, four-poster mahogany beds and silk sofas fill the guest rooms, all furnished in early American décor. But the amenities are decidedly 21st century, with oversized marble bathrooms and luxurious Frette linens. The Grille attracts a smart, casual set with its clubby ambience and live piano music. Don't miss the exceptional Dining Room, where menus are banished and the dishes are determined by the chef's conversations with each patron.
45 rooms. Restaurant, bar. Pets accepted. $151-250

★★★SHERATON SUITES OLD TOWN ALEXANDRIA
801 N. St. Asaph St., Alexandria, 703-836-4700, 800-325-3535; www.sheraton.com
Just steps from the Potomac River, this hotel offers an easy commute from both Ronald Reagan Washington National Airport and D.C.
247 rooms. Restaurant, bar. Business center. Fitness center. Pool. $151-250

WHERE TO EAT
★★BILBO BAGGINS
208 Queen St., Alexandria, 703-683-0300; www.bilbobaggins.net
American. Lunch, dinner, Sunday brunch. Bar. $16-35

★★BISTROT LAFAYETTE
1118 King St., Alexandria, 703-548-2525; www.bistrotlafayette.com
French. Lunch, dinner. Closed Sunday-Monday. Bar. $36-85

★★CHART HOUSE
1 Cameron St., Alexandria, 703-684-5080; www.chart-house.com
Seafood. Lunch, dinner, Sunday brunch. Children's menu. Outdoor seating. Bar. $36-85

★★★CHEZ ANDRÉE
10 E. Glebe Road, Alexandria, 703-836-1404; www.chezandree.com

Chez Andrée, family-owned for more than 40 years, offers country French cuisine in three different dining rooms. Originally a railroad bar that catered to the Potomac Yards, the restaurant now serves specials such as duck l'orange and rack of lamb to hungry diners.

French. Lunch (Monday-Friday), dinner. Closed Sunday. Reservations recommended. Bar. $16-35

★FACCIA LUNA

823 S. Washington St., Alexandria, 703-838-5998; www.faccialuna.com

American, Italian. Lunch (Tuesday-Friday), dinner. Children's menu. Outdoor seating. Bar. $15 and under.

★★FISH MARKET

105 King St., Alexandria, 703-836-5676; www.fishmarketoldtown.com

Seafood. Lunch, dinner. Children's menu. Bar. $16-35

★★GADSBY'S TAVERN

138 N. Royal St., Alexandria, 703-548-1288; www.gadsbystavernrestaurant.com

American. Lunch, dinner, Sunday brunch. Outdoor seating. Reservations recommended. Bar. $16-35

★★GERANIO

722 King St., Alexandria, 703-548-0088; www.geranio.net

Italian. Lunch (Monday-Friday), dinner. Bar. $16-35

★★★THE GRILLE

Morrison House, 116 S. Alfred St., Alexandria, 703-838-8000, 800-367-0800; www.morrisonhouse.com

The Grille in the Morrison House Boutique Hotel lets diners create their very own flight of food based on what the chef has purchased from local markets and farmers that day. Instead of a dinner menu, you'll be presented with a wine list, followed by a personal visit from the chef to discuss what you're in the mood to eat. He'll give you the list of ingredients, and you work together to develop the menu. After dinner, a butler will escort you to the parlor for an after-dinner drink or an aromatic pot of special-blend loose tea made for the Morrison House Boutique Hotel.

International. Breakfast, dinner, Sunday brunch. Bar. $36-85

★★IL PORTO

121 King St., Alexandria, 703-836-8833; www.ilportoristorante.com

Italian. Lunch, dinner. Children's menu. Bar. $16-35

★★★LA BERGERIE

218 N. Lee St., Alexandria, 703-683-1007; www.labergerie.com

In a historic brick warehouse, La Bergerie serves up French dishes, including roasted wild rockfish on mussel and salmon caviar risotto with a saffron vanilla sauce, roasted wild boar chop with kimchi cabbage, burgundy carrots and a sweet and sour sauce, along with a daily prix fixe menu.

French. Lunch (Monday-Saturday), dinner. Reservations recommended. Bar. $16-35

★★LANDINI BROTHERS
115 King St., Alexandria, 703-836-8404; www.landinibrothers.com
Italian. Lunch, dinner. Reservations recommended. Bar. $15 and under.

★★LE REFUGE
127 N. Washington St., Alexandria, 703-548-4661; www.lerefugealexandria.com
French. Lunch, dinner. Closed Sunday. Bar. $36-85

★MANGO MIKE'S
4580 Duke St., Alexandria, 703-370-3800; www.mangomikes.com
Caribbean. Lunch, dinner, Sunday brunch. Children's menu. Outdoor seating. Bar. $15 and under.

★★MONROE'S
1603 Commonwealth Ave., Alexandria, 703-548-5792; www.monroesrestaurant.com
Italian. Dinner, Sunday brunch. Outdoor seating. Bar. $16-35

★★RT'S RESTAURANT
3804 Mount Vernon Ave., Alexandria, 703-684-6010; www.rtsrestaurant.net
Cajun, Creole. Lunch (Monday-Saturday), dinner. Children's menu. Reservations recommended. Bar. $16-35

★★TEMPO
4231 Duke St., Alexandria, 703-370-7900; www.temporestaurant.com
Italian, French. Lunch (Sunday-Friday), dinner, Sunday brunch. Reservations recommended. Outdoor seating. Bar. $15 and under.

★★UNION STREET PUBLIC HOUSE
121 S. Union St., Alexandria, 703-548-1785; www.unionstreetpublichouse.com
American. Lunch, dinner, Saturday-Sunday brunch. Bar. $16-35

★★VILLA D'ESTE
818 North Saint Asaph St., Alexandria, 703-549-9477; www.villadiesterestaurant.com
Italian. Lunch, dinner. Reservations recommended. Bar. $36-85

★★THE WHARF
119 King St., Alexandria, 703-836-2836; www.wharfrestaurant.com
Seafood. Lunch (Monday-Saturday), dinner, Sunday brunch. Children's menu. Bar. $16-35

ARLINGTON COUNTY
(RONALD REAGAN/WASHINGTON-NATIONAL AIRPORT AREA)
See also Alexandria, Fairfax, Fall Church, McLean; Washington, D.C.
Arlington County is located across the Potomac River from Washington, D.C., and is a thriving metropolitan area with both a residential and commerical development. Perhaps it is best known for the Arlington National Cemetery.

WHAT TO SEE
ARLINGTON FARMERS MARKET
North Courthouse Road and North 14th Street, Arlington, 703-228-6423;
www.arlingtonfarmersmarket.com

Irresistibly fresh berries, peaches and heirloom tomatoes are just some of the pleasures available at this lively market, which has been featuring the produce of farmers within 125 miles of Arlington since 1979. Don't miss the grass-fed meats, specialty goat cheeses and unusual varieties of familiar fruits and vegetables (one longtime vendor grows 35 different types of apples). Mid-April-December, Saturday 8 a.m.-noon; January-mid-April, Saturday 9 a.m.-noon.

ARLINGTON HOUSE, THE ROBERT E. LEE MEMORIAL
Arlington National Cemetery, Arlington, 703-235-1530; www.nps.gov/arho

National memorial to Robert E. Lee. Built between 1802 and 1818 by George Washington Parke Custis, Martha Washington's grandson and step-grandson/ foster son of George Washington. In 1831 his daughter, Mary Anna Randolph Custis, married Lieutenant Robert E. Lee; six of the seven Lee children were born here. As executor of the Custis estate, Lee took extended leave from the U.S. Army and devoted his time to managing and improving the estate. It was the Lee homestead for 30 years before the Civil War. On April 20, 1861, following the secession of Virginia, Lee made his decision to stay with Virginia. Within a month, the house was vacated. Some of the family possessions were moved for safekeeping, but most were stolen or destroyed when Union troops occupied the house during the Civil War. In 1864, when Mrs. Lee could not appear personally to pay property tax, the estate was confiscated by the federal government; a 200-acre section was set aside for a national cemetery. (There is some evidence that indicates this was done to ensure the Lee family could never again live on the estate.) G. W. Custis Lee, the general's son, later regained title to the property through a Supreme Court decision and sold it to the U.S. government in 1883 for $150,000. Restoration of the house to its 1861 appearance began in 1925. The Classic Revival house is furnished with authentic pieces of the period, including some Lee family originals. From the grand portico with its six massive, faux-marble Doric columns there is a panoramic view of Washington, D.C.
Admission: Free. Daily 9:30 a.m.-4:30 p.m.

ARLINGTON NATIONAL CEMETERY
Arlington, 703-979-0690, 703-607-8000; www.arlingtoncemetery.org

The solemn grounds of Arlington National Cemetery are a profoundly stirring sight. Gentle hills are studded as far as the eye can see with white stones marking the graves of more than 300,000 Americans who served in the nation's military, from the American Revolution to more recent conflicts. Many visitors stop at the Tomb of the Unknowns, which contains the unidentified remains of servicemen killed in the world wars and the Korean War, and provides quiet tribute to anonymous sacrifice. Tomb Guard sentinels stand guard here 24 hours a day, 365 days a year. Most pay their respects at the eternal flame that marks the granite-paved gravesite of President John F. Kennedy and his wife, Jacqueline, as well as that of Robert F. Kennedy nearby.
Admission: Free. April-September, daily 8 a.m.-7 p.m.; October-March,

daily 8 a.m.-5 p.m.

CRYSTAL CITY SHOPS

Crystal Drive, Arlington, 703-922-4636; www.thecrystalcityshops.com
Crystal City, a mixed-use residential and commercial development, is a bustling downtown area with a lot of street-level activity with more than 200 stores and restaurants. Tree-lined sidewalks are filled with outdoor cafés, shops, parks, hotels and more. You will find jewelry and gift shops, men's and women's apparel, books and home furnishings, as well as a Japanese steakhouse and two American steakhouses.
Monday-Friday 10 a.m.-7 p.m., Saturday 10 a.m.-6 p.m. Shops at 2100: Monday-Saturday 10 a.m.-6 p.m.

THE FASHION CENTRE AT PENTAGON CITY

1100 S. Hayes St., Arlington, 703-415-2400; www.fashioncentrepentagon.com
The Ritz-Carlton Hotel's presence dictates a glamorous tone at this huge, glittering mall, anchored by Macy's and Nordstrom and home to more than 170 other tantalizing shops and restaurants. Women's fashion and accessories stores include Kenneth Cole and MAC Cosmetics. For home furnishings, check out Brookstone and Williams-Sonoma.
Monday-Saturday 10 a.m.-9:30 p.m., Sunday 11 a.m.-6 p.m.

IWO JIMA STATUE/MARINE CORPS WAR MEMORIAL

On Arlington Boulevard, near Arlington National Cemetery;www.nps.gov
The Marine Corps War Memorial depicts raising of the flag on Mount Suribachi, Iwo Jima, February 23, 1945; this is the largest sculpture ever cast in bronze. Attend the Sunset Parade concert with performances by the U.S. Marine Drum and Bugle Corps, U.S. Marine Corps Color Guard and the Silent Drill Team near the statue.
Admission: Free. Sunset parade: Early-June-mid-August, Tuesday 7-8 p.m. Grounds: April-September, daily 8 a.m.-7 p.m.; October-March, daily 8 a.m.-5 p.m.

SPECIAL EVENTS
ARLINGTON COUNTY FAIR

Thomas Jefferson Community Center, 351 S. Second St., Arlington, 703-228-8772
www.arlingtoncountyfair.org
This countywide fair features arts, crafts, international foods, and more. August.

MARINE CORPS MARATHON

Route 110 and Marshall Drive, Arlington, 800-786-8762; www.marinemarathon.com
Cheer on your favorite runner at the Marine Corps Marathon. The 26-mile, 385-yard route starts and ends near the Iwo Jima Memorial and winds through Arlington, Georgetown and D.C., passing the Capitol, the Pentagon and other inspiring sights along the way.
October.

MEMORIAL DAY SERVICE CEREMONY

Arlington National Cemetery, Arlington

Wreaths are placed by the President at the Tomb of the Unknown Soldier as a memorial. The National Symphony Orchestra gives a free concert later in the evening on the lawn of the Capitol.
Memorial Day.

WHERE TO STAY

★★ARLINGTON COURT HOTEL

1200 N. Courthouse Road, Arlington, 703-524-4000; www.arlingtoncourthotel.com

187 rooms. Complimentary breakfast. Business center. Fitness center. Pets accepted. $61-150

★★COURTYARD ARLINGTON CRYSTAL CITY/REAGAN NATIONAL AIRPORT

2899 Jefferson Davis Highway, Arlington, 703-549-3434; www.marriott.com

272 rooms. Restaurant, bar. Fitness center. Pool. $151-250

★★★CROWNE PLAZA WASHINGTON NATIONAL AIRPORT HOTEL

1480 Crystal Drive, Arlington, 703-416-1600, 800-227-6963;
www.cpnationalairport.com

This Crowne Plaza Hotel is conveniently located near the attractions of Washington, D.C., Ronald Reagan National Airport and many businesses. Guest rooms feature two-line phones, 25-inch TVs and work desks.
308 rooms. Restaurant, bar. Business center. Fitness center. Pool. $151-250

★★EMBASSY SUITES CRYSTAL CITY-NATIONAL AIRPORT

1300 Jefferson Davis Highway, Arlington, 703-979-9799, 800-362-2779;
www.embassysuites.com

267 rooms. Restaurant, bar. Complimentary breakfast. Business center. Fitness room. Pool. $151-250

★HAMPTON INN & SUITES REAGAN NATIONAL AIRPORT

2000 Jefferson Davis Highway, Arlington, 703-418-8181, 800-426-7866;
www.hamptoninn.com

161 rooms. Complimentary breakfast. Business center. Fitness center. Pool. $61-150

★★★HILTON ARLINGTON

950 N. Stafford St., Arlington, 703-528-6000, 800-695-7487; www.hiltonarlington.com

This centrally located hotel is connected by a skybridge to the Ballston Common Mall and National Science Foundation Office Complex. The contemporary guest rooms feature Hilton's Serenity Bed and amenities such as Crabtree & Evelyn toiletries.
209 rooms. Restaurant, bar. Complimentary breakfast. Business center. Fitness center. Pets accepted. $151-250

★★★HYATT ARLINGTON

1325 Wilson Blvd., Arlington, 703-525-1234, 800-233-1234; www.arlington.hyatt.com
This hotel is located in the Rosslyn neighborhood across the bridge from Washington, D.C., and close to the Arlington National Cemetery. Sitting among businesses, shops and restaurants, the Hyatt Arlington is within walking distance of the Metro and Georgetown.
317 rooms. Business center. Fitness center. $151-250

★★★MARRIOTT CRYSTAL CITY AT REAGAN NATIONAL AIRPORT

1999 Jefferson Davis Highway, Arlington, 703-413-5500; www.crystalcitymarriott.com
This conveniently located, boutique-style hotel has an underground walkway that gives guests access to the Metro system, the Crystal City shopping mall and the surrounding metropolitan area. A curved staircase in the lobby leads you to guest rooms that feature Revive, Marriott's new bed with 300 thread-count linens, and wireless Internet service.
343 rooms. Restaurant, bar. Fitness center. Pool. $151-250

★★★★THE RITZ-CARLTON, PENTAGON CITY

1250 S. Hayes St., Arlington, 703-415-5000, 800-241-3333; www.ritzcarlton.com
Five minutes from Washington National Airport, the Ritz-Carlton, Pentagon City offers tailored elegance with feather beds, Egyptian cotton linens, updated technology and luxurious club-level accommodations. Massages and personal fitness assessments are available at the fitness center. Enjoy afternoon tea at Fyve Restaurant Lounge or enjoy their American fare for breakfast, lunch or dinner.
366 rooms. Restaurant, bar. Complimentary breakfast. Business center. Fitness center. Pool. Pets accepted. $251-350

★★★SHERATON CRYSTAL CITY HOTEL

1800 Jefferson Davis Highway, Arlington, 703-486-1111, 800-325-3535;
www.sheraton.com/crystalcity
Just across the river from Washington, D.C., the Sheraton Crystal City Hotel offers complimentary shuttle service to and from local businesses and Ronald Reagan Washington National Airport.
217 rooms. Restaurant, bar. Business center. Fitness center. Pets accepted. $151-250

WHERE TO EAT
★★ALPINE

4770 Lee Highway, Arlington, 703-528-7600; www.arlingtonsalpinerestaurant.com
Italian. Lunch, dinner. Closed Monday. Reservations recommended. Bar. $36-85

★★BISTRO BISTRO

4021 Campbell Ave., Arlington, 703-379-0300; www.bistro-bistro.com
French. Lunch, dinner, Sunday brunch. Children's menu. Reservations recommended. Outdoor seating. Bar. $16-35

★★CARLYLE

4000 Campbell Ave., Arlington, 703-931-0777;
www.greatamericanrestaurants.com/carlyle

American. Lunch, dinner, Saturday-Sunday brunch. Children's menu. Outdoor seating. Bar. $16-35

★FACCIA LUNA

2909 Wilson Blvd., Arlington, 703-276-3099; www.faccialuna.com

Italian. Lunch, dinner. Children's menu. Outdoor seating. Bar. $16-35

★★★FYVE RESTAURANT LOUNGE

Ritz-Carlton, Pentagon City, 1250 S. Hayes St., Arlington, 703-415-5000;
www.ritzcarlton.com

Fyve Restaurant Lounge at the Ritz-Carlton Pentagon City offers upscale American classics in a warm, clubby dining room decked out in mahogany wood. The seasonal menu features dishes such as lobster, filet mignon, foie gras, caviar and oysters. On Sunday, Fyve hosts one of the best champagne brunches in the area and on weekends, afternoon tea is also offered.
American. Breakfast, lunch, dinner, brunch. Children's menu. Reservations recommended. Bar. $36-85

★★LA COTE D'OR CAFE

6876 Lee Highway, Arlington, 703-538-3033; www.lacotedorcafe.com

French. Lunch, dinner. Reservations recommended. Outdoor seating. Bar. $36-85

★MATUBA

2915 Columbia Pike, Arlington, 703-521-2811; www.matuba-sushi.com

Japanese. Lunch (Monday-Friday), dinner. $16-35

★RED HOT AND BLUE

1600 Wilson Blvd., Arlington, 703-276-7427; www.redhotandblue.com

American. Lunch, dinner. Children's menu. Bar. $16-35

★SILVER DINER

3200 Wilson Blvd., Arlington, 703-812-8600; www.silverdiner.com

American. Breakfast, lunch, dinner, late-night. Children's menu. $16-35

★VILLAGE BISTRO

1723 Wilson Blvd., Arlington, 703-522-0284; www.villagebistro.com

American, French. Lunch (Monday-Friday), dinner. Reservations recommended. Outdoor seating. Bar. $16-35

BRISTOL

See also Roanoke

Essentially a city in two states, Bristol is actually two cities—Bristol, Tenn., and Bristol, Va.—sharing the same main street and the same personality. Each has its own government and city services. Together they constitute a major shopping center. Named for the English industrial center, Bristol is an important factory town in its own right. These cities carry on the pioneer tradition of an ironworks established here about 1784, which made the first nails for use on the frontier. Bristol also has the distinction of being the "Official Birthplace of Country Music."

WHAT TO SEE
ANTIQUES
State Street and Commonwealth Avenue, Bristol
More than 20 large antiques shops are within a half-mile of these two perpendicular streets in downtown Bristol. Those searching for eclectic collectibles and furniture rave about the selection.

BIRTHPLACE OF COUNTRY MUSIC CULTURAL HERITAGE CENTER
510 Cumberland St., Bristol, 276-645-0111; www.birthplaceofcountrymusic.org
Country music pioneers like Jimmie Rodgers, the Carter Family, Jim and Jesse, and Tennessee Ernie Ford all got their starts in Bristol. The Birthplace of Country Music Alliance is in the process of building a cultural center (*510 Cumberland St.*) which is proposed to be open in 2011. They host many different country music events.

BRISTOL WHITE SOX
Devault Memorial Stadium, 1501 Euclid Ave., Bristol, 276-669-6859;
www.bristolsox.com
This minor league team is owned by and affiliated with the Chicago White Sox.

WHERE TO STAY
★COMFORT INN
2368 Lee Highway, Bristol, 276-466-3881, 877-424-6423; www.choicehotels.com
87 rooms. Complimentary breakfast. Pool. $61-150

★★HOWARD JOHNSON BRISTOL
2221 Euclid Ave., Bristol, 276-669-7171, 800-446-4656; www.hojo.com
77 rooms. Complimentary breakfast. Pool. $61-150

★LA QUINTA INN
1014 Old Airport Road, Bristol, 276-669-9353, 800-753-3757; www.laquinta.com
123 rooms. Complimentary breakfast. Pool. Pets accepted. $61-150

CHARLOTTESVILLE
See also Waynesboro
Popularly known as the number one small city in the South, Charlottesville is famous as the home of Thomas Jefferson, the third president of the United States, and the University of Virginia, which Jefferson founded and designed.

Charlottesville offers much more than history. The downtown pedestrian mall streetscape at the center of the historic district is alive with more than 120 shops and 30 restaurants, outdoor cafés, theaters, bookstores and a skating rink. Charlottesville can also brag about its beautiful parks, top-notch museums, and award-winning wineries and outstanding entertainment.

The area's historic attractions include Monticello, Michie Tavern, Ash Lawn-Highland (James Monroe's home) and Montpelier. Constructed sculptures from the Art in Place program stand along the roadways. A myriad of scenic byways, hiking trails and river paths run throughout the area, as does the Blue Ridge Parkway, considered by some to be America's most beautiful drive.

WHAT TO SEE
ALBEMARLE COUNTY COURTHOUSE
Court Square, 501 E. Jefferson St., Charlottesville, 434-972-4083;
www.courts.state.va.us
North wing was used in 1820s as a "common temple" shared by Episcopalian, Methodist, Presbyterian and Baptist sects, one Sunday a month to each but with all who wished attending each week. Jefferson, Monroe and Madison worshipped here. Now, this circuit court handles all civil cases.
Daily 8:30 a.m.-4:30 p.m.

ASH LAWN-HIGHLAND
1000 James Monroe Parkway, Charlottesville, 434-293-8000; www.ashlawnhighland.org
Built on a site personally selected by Thomas Jefferson in 1799, this 535-acre estate was the home of President James Monroe from 1799 to 1823. The estate is now owned by Monroe's alma mater, the College of William and Mary. This early 19th-century working plantation offers guided tours of the house with Monroe possessions, spinning and weaving demonstrations, old-boxwood gardens, peacocks and picnic spots.
Admission: adults $10, seniors $9, children 6-11 $5. April-October, daily 9 a.m.-6 p.m.; November-March, daily 11 a.m.-5 p.m.

HISTORIC MICHIE TAVERN
683 Thomas Jefferson Parkway, Charlottesville, 434-977-1234; www.michietavern.com
Visitors dine on hearty fare in the Tavern's Ordinary, where servers in period attire greet them. Afterwards, a tour of the original tavern features living history where guests participate in 18th-century activities, including a lively Virginia dance.
Admission: Free. Tours: Daily 9 a.m.-5 p.m. Dining room: April-October, daily 11:15 a.m.-3:30 p.m.; November-March 11:30 a.m.-3 p.m.

LEWIS, CLARK AND SACAGAWEA STATUE
Midway Park, Ridge and Main streets, 434-293-6789, Charlottesville
Memorial to Jefferson's secretary, Meriwether Lewis, who explored the Louisiana Territory with his friend William Clark and Sacagawea.

MONTICELLO
931 Thomas Jefferson Parkway, Charlottesville, 434-984-9822; www.monticello.org
Located on a mountaintop, Monticello is one of the most beautiful estates in Virginia and is considered a classic of American architecture. The house was designed by Thomas Jefferson and built over the course of 40 years, symbolizing the pleasure he found in "putting up and pulling down." Jefferson moved into the first completed outbuilding of his new home in 1771, although construction continued until 1809. Most of the interior furnishings are original. Tours of the restored orchard, vineyard, 1,000-foot-long veg-

etable garden, and Mulberry Row, once the site of plantation workshops. Jefferson died at Monticello on July 4, 1826, and was buried in the family cemetery. The Thomas Jefferson Memorial Foundation maintains the house and gardens. Also, stop in the brand new visitor center and Smith Education Center where you'll find exhibits, a film about Jefferson, a discovery room and classrooms as well as a café, and outdoor courtyard and more.

Admission: adults $15 (November-Feburary), $20 (March-October), children 6-11 $8, children 5 and under free. March-October, daily 8 a.m.-5 p.m.; November-February, daily 9 a.m.-4:30 p.m.

UNIVERSITY OF VIRGINIA

914 Emmet St. North, Charlottesville, 434-924-1019; www.virginia.edu

Founded by Thomas Jefferson and built according to his plans. Handsome red brick buildings with white trim, striking vistas, smooth lawns, and ancient trees form the grounds of Jefferson's "academical village." The serpentine walls, one brick thick, which Jefferson designed for strength and beauty, are famous. Room 13, West Range, occupied by Edgar Allan Poe as a student, is displayed for the public. Historical walking tours take place year-round except during a break in December and January and Mayand they start at the Rotunda.

Tours: Daily 10 a.m., 11 a.m., 2 p.m., 3 p.m., 4 p.m.

SPECIAL EVENTS
DOGWOOD FESTIVAL

Charlottesville, 434-961-9824; www.charlottesvilledogwoodfestival.org

The Dogwood Festival features a parade, lacrosse and golf tournaments, fireworks, a carnival and more.

Mid-April.

GARDEN WEEK

Charlottesville, 804-644-7776; www.vagardenweek.org

This week offers visitors an inside look at some of the finest private homes and gardens in the area, which are open to the public to tour.

Mid-late April.

WHERE TO STAY
★★★BOAR'S HEAD INN

200 Ednam Drive, Charlottesville, 434-296-2181, 800-476-1988;
www.boarsheadinn.com

Located in the Blue Ridge Mountains, this resort welcomes guests to visit the past and enjoy the present. Guests can visit past presidential homes (a short drive away), stroll through local wineries or enjoy a panoramic view by hot-air balloon. Enjoy the many onsite amenities including a spa, golf course, swimming pools and numerous restaurants.

170 rooms. Restaurant, bar. Fitness center. Pool. Spa. Tennis. Golf. $151-250

★CAVALIER INN

105 Emmet St., Charlottesville, 434-296-8111, 800-882-2129;
www.bestwesterncavalierinn.com

118 rooms. Complimentary breakfast. Business center. Pool. $61-150

★★DOUBLETREE HOTEL
990 Hilton Heights Road, Charlottesville, 434-973-2121, 800-222-8799;
www.charlottesville.doubletree.com
235 rooms. Restaurant, bar. Business center. Fitness center. Pool. $61-150

★ENGLISH INN OF CHARLOTTESVILLE
2000 Morton Drive, Charlottesville, 434-971-9900, 800-786-5400; www.wytestone.com
88 rooms. Complimentary breakfast. Fitness center. Pool. $61-150

★HAMPTON INN CHARLOTTESVILLE
2035 India Road, Charlottesville, 434-978-7888, 800-426-7866; www.hamptoninn.com
123 rooms. Complimentary breakfast. Business center. Pool. $61-150

★★★KESWICK HALL AT MONTICELLO
701 Club Drive, Keswick, 434-979-3440, 888-778-2565; www.keswick.com
Keswick Hall's 600-acre estate, set at the foot of the Blue Ridge Mountains, offers visitors individually designed guest rooms that reflect a modern interpretation of early American style, with overstuffed furniture, club chairs, Aubusson carpets and canopied four-poster beds. The rolling hills of the Shenandoah Valley invite exploration and the historic halls of Monticello are only minutes away, but this resort also entices its guests with a variety of recreational opportunities. The members-only Keswick Hall, adjacent to the hotel, presents an exclusive opportunity for guests to enjoy its indoor/outdoor pool, tennis courts, spa services and 18-hole Arnold Palmer golf course.
48 rooms. Restaurant, bar. Fitness center. Pool. Spa. Golf. Tennis. $351 and up.

★★★OMNI CHARLOTTESVILLE HOTEL
235 W. Main St., Charlottesville, 434-971-5500, 888-444-6664; www.omnihotels.com
Located on a downtown pedestrian mall, the Omni Charlottesville Hotel is within walking distance of the government buildings. Guest rooms offer views of the Blue Ridge Mountains and historic Charlottesville.
208 rooms. Restaurant, bar. Business center. Fitness center. Pool. Pets accepted. $61-150

★★★SILVER THATCH INN
3001 Hollymead Drive, Charlottesville, 434-978-4686, 800-261-0720;
www.silverthatch.com
Built in 1780, this clapboard home is full of history and is one of the oldest buildings in the area. Guest rooms are named for Virginia-born presidents.
7 rooms. Restaurant, bar. Complimentary breakfast. No children under 14. $151-250

WHERE TO EAT
★★ABERDEEN BARN
2018 Holiday Drive, Charlottesville, 434-296-4630; www.aberdeenbarn.com
American. Dinner. Reservations recommended. Bar. $16-35

★★C & O

515 E. Water St., Charlottesville, 434-971-7044; www.candorestaurant.com

French. Dinner, late-night. Reservations recommended. Outdoor seating. Bar. $36-85

★★★FOSSETT'S RESTAURANT

Keswick Hall at Monticello, 701 Club Drive, Keswick, 434-979-3440; www.keswick.com

"A feast for the eyes" best describes the chef's classically inspired culinary creations, most appropriate given the formal dining room's trompe l'oeil wall murals and expansive garden views. Enjoy alfresco dining when the weather is warm, and enjoy the views of the golf course.

American. Breakfast, dinner, Sunday brunch. Children's menu. Reservations recommended. Outdoor seating. Bar. $36-85

★IVY INN

2244 Old Ivy Road, Charlottesville, 434-977-1222; www.ivyinnrestaurant.com

American. Dinner. Closed Sunday. Reservations recommended. Outdoor seating. Bar. $16-35

★★MAHARAJA

139 Zan Road, Charlottesville, 434-973-1110; www.maharaja-indian-restaurant.com

Indian. Lunch, dinner. Reservations recommended. Bar. $16-35

★★★OLD MILL ROOM

Boar's Head Inn, 200 Ednam Drive, Charlottesville, 434-972-2230, 800-476-1988; www.boarsheadinn.com

This dining room is located in the Boar's Head Inn at the University of Virginia. Dishes such as pan roasted salmon with lobster hushpuppies, shaved fennel, lobster caviar butter and lobster oil and organic butter lettuce and citrus salad prepared with vegetables from the restaurant's garden.

American. Breakfast, lunch, dinner, Sunday brunch. Outdoor seating. Children's menu. Reservations recommended. Bar. $36-85

★★★OXO

215 W. Water St., Charlottesville, 434-977-8111; www.oxorestaurant.com

Chef and co-owner John Haywood reinterprets French classics inside this airy restaurant. Try items such as braised pheasant breast with potato feuillette or pan-seared halibut, and don't leave without a sweet ending like chocolate souffle.

French. Dinner, late-night. Outdoor seating. Bar. $36-85

CHESAPEAKE

See also Norfolk, Portsmouth, Virginia Beach

For beach lovers who seek a vacation off the beaten path, Chesapeake is an excellent choice. You'll be minutes away from 18th-century America, the oceanfront boardwalk of Virginia Beach, theme parks and more. The active Atlantic Intra-coastal Waterway, home to a myriad of birds and wildlife, is complemented by the 49,000-acre Great Dismal Swamp National Wildlife Refuge managed by the Nature Conservancy. Bring your binoculars, your camera and your lifelong checklist of birds.

Farther up the coast, the Back Bay National Wildlife Refuge encompasses a series of barrier islands that feature large sand dunes, maritime forests, freshwater marshes and ponds populated with large flocks of wintering waterfowl. Move through the bay on the unique trolley designed not to disturb the wildlife, kayak on the waterway itself or stroll on the more than 19 miles of hiking trails at First Landing State Park.

WHAT TO SEE
NORTHWEST RIVER PARK
1733 Indian Creek Road, Chesapeake, 757-421-3145; www.chesapeake.va.us
Approximately eight miles of hiking/nature trails wind through this 763-acre city park. There's plenty to do here including fishing, boating, canoeing, picnicking, playground, nine-hole miniature golf, camping and trailer sites. Daily 9 a.m.-dusk.

WHERE TO STAY
★COMFORT SUITES CHESAPEAKE
1550 Crossways Blvd., Chesapeake, 757-420-1600, 877-424-6423;
www.comfortsuites.com
124 rooms. Complimentary breakfast. Fitness center. Pool. $61-150

★★RED ROOF INN CHESAPEAKE CONFERENCE CENTER
724 Woodlake Drive, Chesapeake, 757-523-0123, 800-733-7663; www.redroofinn.com
229 rooms. Pets accepted. $61-150

WHERE TO EAT
★★KYOTO
1412 Greenbrier Parkway, Chesapeake, 757-420-0950; www.kyotochesapeake.com
Japanese. Lunch, dinner. Children's menu. Bar. $16-35

CHINCOTEAGUE
See also Virginia Beach; Ocean City, MD
Oysters, wild ponies and good fishing are the stock in trade of this small island, connected with Chincoteague National Wildlife Refuge by a bridge and to the mainland by 10 miles of highway. The oysters, many of them grown on the hard sand bottoms off Chincoteague from seed or small oysters brought from natural beds elsewhere, are among the best in the East. Commercial fishing has always been the main occupation of the islanders, but now catering to those who fish for fun is also economically important. Chincoteague's wild ponies are actually small horses, but when fully grown they are somewhat larger and more graceful than Shetlands. They are thought to be descended from horses that swam ashore from a wrecked Spanish galleon, their limited growth caused by generations of a marsh grass diet.

WHAT TO SEE
ASSATEAGUE ISLAND
8586 Beach Road, Chincoteague, 757-336-6577; www.nps.gov/asis
A 37-mile barrier island, Assateague has stretches of ocean and sand dunes, forest and marshes that create a natural environment unusual on the East

Coast. Sika deer, a variety of wildlife, and countless birds, including the peregrine falcon, can be found here, but wild ponies occasionally roaming the marshes offer the most exotic sight for visitors. There are nature and auto trails, interpretive programs, swimming, lifeguards in summer, surf fishing, camping, hike-in and canoe-in camp sites and day-use facilities. Picnicking is permitted in designated areas; cars are limited to designated roads. Daily.

CAPTAIN BARRY'S BACK BAY CRUISES & EXPEDITIONS

The Chincoteague Inn Restaurant, 6262 Marlin St., Chincoteague, 757-336-6508;
www.captainbarry.net

Captain Barry's features cruises including a Bird Watch Cruise, a Back Bay Expedition, a Champagne Sunset Cruise, Moonlight Excursions and a Fun Cruise. Trips vary from one to four hours. Reservations recommended.

SPECIAL EVENTS
CHINCOTEAGUE PONY SWIM

Chincoteague, 757-336-6161; www.assateagueisland.com

Since 1925, the "wild" ponies are rounded up on Assateague Island, then swim the inlet to Chincoteague, where foals are sold at auction before the ponies swim back to Assateague. There are also carnival amusements at Chincoteague after the swim.

Last Wednesday and Thursday in July.

OYSTER FESTIVAL

Maddox Family Campground, 6742 Maddox Blvd., Chincoteague,
www.chincoteaguechamber.com

This all-you-can-eat Oyster festival raises funds for the Chincoteague Chamber of Commerce. There are plenty of oysters, clam fritters, hot dogs, hush puppies, potato salad, cole slaw and much more to enjoy.

October.

WHERE TO STAY
★BEST WESTERN CHINCOTEAGUE ISLAND

7105 Maddox Blvd., Chincoteague, 757-336-6557, 800-553-6117;
www.bestwestern.com

52 rooms. Complimentary breakfast. Pool. $61-150

★COMFORT SUITES CHINCOTEAGUE

4195 Main St., Chincoteague, 757-336-3700, 877-424-6423; www.comfortsuites.com

87 rooms. Complimentary breakfast. Business center. Fitness center. Pool. $61-150

★★ISLAND MOTOR INN RESORT

4391 Main St., Chincoteague, 757-336-3141; www.islandmotorinn.com

60 rooms. Fitness center. $61-150

★REFUGE INN
7058 Maddox Blvd., Chincoteague, 757-336-5511, 800-257-0034; www.refugeinn.com
72 rooms. Complimentary breakfast. Fitness center. Pool. $61-150

WHERE TO EAT
★DON'S SEAFOOD
4113 Main St., Chincoteague Island, 757-336-5715; www.donsseafood.com
Seafood. Lunch, dinner, late-night. Children's menu. Bar. $16-35

DULLES INTERNATIONAL AIRPORT AREA
See also Fairfax
Located in Chantilly, Virginia, the Washington Dulles International Airport is only 26 miles from Washington, D.C. It serves both both domestic and international travel and due to its location, is a main hub for the mid-Atlantic.

WHAT TO SEE
RESTON TOWN CENTER
11900 Market St., Reston, 703-689-4699; www.restontowncenter.com
A 20-acre urban development incorporating elements of a traditional town square. It includes more than 50 retail shops and 30 restaurants, a movie theater complex, office space and a hotel. There arc also special events and concerts heald in the Pavilion, along with ice skating in the winter.
Hours vary; see Web site for details.

SPECIAL EVENTS
NORTHERN VIRGINIA FINE ARTS FESTIVAL
Reston Town Center, 11900 Market St., Reston, 703-471-9242;
www.restonarts.org/festival
This festival features an art sale featuring more than 200 artists, a children's art activity area, live music, food and drink.
Mid-May.

OKTOBERFEST
Reston Town Center, 11900 Market St., Reston; www.oktoberfestreston.com
This annual German festival features a biergarten with authentic German beer, food and music.
Early-October.

SUMMER CONCERTS
Reston Town Center, 11900 Market St.,703-912-4062, Reston;
www.restontowncenter.com
Saturday evenings in the summer, the Reston Town Center hosts concerts in the Pavilion.
June-August.

WHERE TO STAY
★COMFORT INN DULLES INTERNATIONAL AIRPORT
200 Elden St., Herndon, 703-437-7555, 800-228-5150; www.choicehotels.com

104 rooms. Complimentary breakfast. Business center. Fitness center. Pets accepted. $61-150

★★CROWNE PLAZA WASHINGTON, D.C. DULLES AIRPORT
2200 Centreville Road, Herndon, 703-471-6700; www.cpdulles.com/herndon.html
327 rooms. Restaurant, bar. Complimentary breakfast. Business center. Fitness center. Pool. $61-150

★★HOLIDAY INN WASHINGTON DULLES INTERNATIONAL AIRPORT
45425 Holiday Drive, Sterling, 703-471-7411, 800-465-4329; www.holidayinn.com
296 rooms. Restaurant, bar. Business center. Fitness center. Pool. $151-250

★★★HYATT REGENCY RESTON
1800 Presidents St., Reston, 703-709-1234; www.hyatt.com
Located in the heart of Fairfax County's technology hub, this property offers a resort-like ambience in a suburban setting. The oversized guest rooms offer flatscreen TVs, ergonomic desk chairs and wireless Internet access.
518 rooms. Restaurant, bar. Business center. Fitness center. Pool. $151-250

★★★SHERATON RESTON HOTEL
11810 Sunrise Valley Drive, Reston, 703-620-9000, 800-325-3535;
www.starwoodhotels.com
Located just 20 minutes from Washington, D.C., and near shopping, various corporate headquarters and Reston Town Center, this contemporary hotel is a smart choice for both business and leisure travelers. Each spacious guest room features the famous Sheraton Sweet Sleeper Bed with a pillow-top mattress, individual climate control and a large work area. Golf lovers can get a game in at the adjacent Reston National Golf Course.
301 rooms. Restaurant, bar. Business center. Fitness center. Pool. Pets accepted. $151-250

★★★WASHINGTON DULLES MARRIOTT SUITES
13101 Worldgate Drive, Herndon, 703-709-0400, 800-228-9290; www.marriott.com
This all-suite hotel located in the Dulles Technology Corridor is just minutes from the airport and corporate offices. After a long day at the office or at play, guests can relax in their spacious suites with high-speed Internet access and luxury bedding. The hotel and surrounding area offer an indoor/outdoor pool, biking and jogging trails, tennis, squash, bowling and miniature golf.
253 rooms. Restaurant, bar. Fitness center. Pool. $151-250

★★★WESTFIELDS MARRIOTT WASHINGTON DULLES
14750 Conference Center Drive, Chantilly, 703-818-0300; www.marriott.com
Located within 10 miles of the National Air and Space Museum and the Wolf Trap Center for Performing Arts, the Westfields Marriott Washington Dulles Hotel offers spacious rooms and the Signature Fred Couples Golf Club.
336 rooms. Restaurant, bar. Fitness center. Pool. $151-250

WHERE TO EAT

★★CLYDE'S

11905 Market St., Reston, 703-787-6601; www.clydes.com

American. Lunch, dinner, Sunday brunch, late-night. Outdoor seating. Reservations recommended. Bar. $16-35

★★★PALM COURT

Westfields Marriott Washington Dulles Hotel, 14750 Conference Center Drive, Chantilly, 703-818-3520; www.westfieldspalmcourt.com

In the Westfields Marriott Hotel, this restaurant offers a buffet-style Sunday brunch with tuxedo-clad waiters, mimosas and an unending array of sweets. American. Breakfast (Saturday-Sunday), lunch (Monday-Saturday), dinner (Tuesday-Saturday), Saturday-Sunday brunch. Children's menu. Reservations recommended. Bar. $16-35

★★★RUSSIA HOUSE RESTAURANT

790 Station St., Herndon, 703-787-8880; www.russiahouserestaurant.com

This contemporary restaurant features Russian artwork. The aristocratic dining experience includes dishes such as beef stroganoff or puff pastry with lamb, vegetables and tarragon sauce.
Seafood. Lunch (Tuesday-Friday), dinner. Reservations recommended. $16-35

★THE TORTILLA FACTORY

648 Elden St., Herndon, 703-471-1156; www.thetortillafactory.com

Mexican. Lunch, dinner. Children's menu. Reservations recommended. $16-35

FAIRFAX

See also Alexandria, Arlington, Falls Church, McLean

Fairfax, nestled in northern Virginia in the shadow of Washington, D.C., is a quaint, historic town, which has become a government center, home to many major corporations and a thriving technology industry.

WHAT TO SEE

ALGONKIAN REGIONAL PARK

47001 Fairway Drive, Sterling, 703-450-4655; www.nvrpa.org

This 800-acre park on the Potomac Rive features a par-72 golf course, miniature golf, swimming and an aquatics play complex, fishing, boating, picnicking areas, vacation cottages, and meeting and reception areas. The hours for the pool and golf courses vary; see Web site for information. Daily.

BULL RUN REGIONAL PARK

7700 Bull Run Drive, Centreville, 703-631-0550; www.nvrpa.org

Bull Run consists of 1,500 acres with a themed swimming pool/water park, campgrounds, picnicking areas, a playground, miniature golf, a public shooting center, and nature trail. The hours for the pool and mini golf course vary; see Web site for information. Daily.

BURKE LAKE

7315 Ox Road, Fairfax Station, 703-323-6600; www.fairfaxcounty.gov/parks/burkelake
This park features a 218 acre lake where visitors can enjoy fishing and boating (swimming is prohibited). There are also picnicking areas, a playground, a concession stand, a miniature train ride, a carousel, an 18-hole and par-three golf course, camping areas, an ice cream parlor, an amphitheater, disk golf, outdoor volleyball courts, and a new miniature golf course.
Admission: April-late-October, car/motorcycle $8, bus $40. Grounds: Daily dawn-dusk.

GEORGE MASON UNIVERSITY

4400 University Drive, Fairfax, 703-993-1000; www.gmu.edu
This state-supported university (24,000 students.) started as a branch of the University of Virginia. Performing Arts Center features concerts, theater, dance; Fenwick Library maintains largest collection anywhere of material pertaining to Federal Theatre Project of the 1930s. Research Center for Federal Theatre Project contains 7,000 scripts, including unpublished works by Arthur Miller, sets and costume designs, and oral history collection of interviews with former Federal Theatre personnel.
Tours: Monday-Friday 10:30 a.m., 1:30 p.m., Saturday 10 a.m., 11:30 a.m.

LAKE FAIRFAX PARK

1400 Lake Fairfax Drive, Reston, 703-471-5415; www.fairfaxcounty.gov
This 476 acre park features Lake Fairfax which covers 18 acres. Although swimming and windsurfing are prohibited, there's plenty to do here including swimming at a pool with a lazy river, called the Water Mine, and fishing and boating in the lake. There are also picnicking areas, a carousel and camping. Daily.

SULLY HISTORIC SITE

3601 Sully Road, Fairfax, 703-437-1794; www.fairfaxcounty.gov
This landmark is a restored 1794 house of Richard Bland Lee, brother of General "Light Horse Harry" Lee. It features some original furnishings; a kitchen washhouse, log house store and smokehouse on the grounds. Guided tours are at 11 a.m. and take place every hour.
Admission: adults $6, students $5, seniors and children 5-15 $4. Tours: adults $8, students, seniors and children 5-15 $6. March-December, Wednesday-Monday 11 a.m.-4 p.m.

SPECIAL EVENTS
FALL FESTIVAL

Old Town Fairfax, Fairfax, 703-385-7949; www.fairfaxva.gov
This fall festival features a parket with arts, foods and more from more than 400 vendors. There are also children's activities, music and Classic Car Show.
October.

WHERE TO STAY
★COMFORT INN UNIVERSITY CENTER

11180 Fairfax Blvd., Fairfax, 703-591-5900, 877-424-6423; www.comfortinn.com
205 rooms. Complimentary breakfast. Restaurant, bar. Fitness center. Pool. Pets accepted. $61-150

★★★HYATT FAIR LAKES
12777 Fair Lakes Circle, Fairfax, 703-818-1234; www.hyatt.com
Minutes from Washington Dulles Airport, this striking high-rise hotel in the wooded Fair Lakes Office Park offers large guest rooms. This property features a column-free ballroom and a towering atrium lobby.
316 rooms. Restaurant, bar. Business center. Fitness center. Pool. $151-250

WHERE TO EAT
★★ARTIE'S
3260 Old Lee Highway, Fairfax, 703-273-7600; www.greatamericanrestaurants.com
American. Lunch, dinner, late-night, Sunday brunch. Children's menu. Bar. $16-35

★BLUE OCEAN
9440 Main St., Fairfax, 703-425-7555; www.izakayablueocean.com
Japanese. Lunch, dinner. $16-35

★★BOMBAY BISTRO
3570 Chain Bridge Road, Fairfax, 703-359-5810; www.bombaybistro.com
Indian. Lunch, dinner, brunch. Children's menu. Outdoor seating. Bar. $16-35

★★★LARUE 123 AT BAILIWICK INN
4023 Chain Bridge Road, Fairfax, 703-691-2266; www.larue123.com
This Federal-style inn and restaurant, on the National Register of Historic Places, offers French-American cuisine in a quaint, romantic space. Visit for one of the seasonal wine dinners or for traditional English high tea in one of the intimate parlors.
French. Lunch (Tuesday-Friday), dinner. Reservations recommended. Outdoor seating. Bar. $36-85

★P.J. SKIDOO'S
9908 Lee Highway, Fairfax, 703-591-4515; www.pjskidoos.com
American. Lunch, dinner, Saturday-Sunday brunch. Outdoor seating. Bar. $16-35

FALLS CHURCH
See also Alexandria, Arlington County, Fairfax, McLean; Washington, D.C.
Falls Church is a pleasant, cosmopolitan suburb of Washington, D.C., just over the Arlington County line, graced with many interesting old houses. This was a crossover point between the North and the South through which pioneers, armies, adventurers and merchants passed.

WHAT TO SEE
THE FALLS CHURCH
115 E. Fairfax St., Falls Church, 703-532-7600; www.thefallschurch.org
This 1769 Episcopal building replaced the original wooden church built in 1732. Served as a recruiting station during the Revolutionary War; abandoned until 1830; used during the Civil War as a hospital and later as a stable for cavalry horses. It has been restored according to original plans with gallery additions in 1959.
Worship services: Wednesday noon, Saturday 5 p.m., and Sunday at 8 a.m., 11 a.m.

FOUNTAIN OF FAITH
7400 Lee Highway, Falls Church
Located in National Memorial Park, this memorial dedicated to the four chaplains—two Protestant, one Jewish, one Catholic—who were aboard the *USS Dorchester* when it was torpedoed off Greenland in 1943. They gave their life jackets to four soldiers on deck who had none.

WHERE TO STAY
★★★MARRIOTT FAIRVIEW PARK
3111 Fairview Park Drive, Falls Church, 703-849-9400; www.marriott.com
Sitting on a park-like setting, this property offers jogging paths through woods and around a lake. Guest rooms feature luxurious down pillows and comforters plus the Marriott's classic Revive beds.
395 rooms. Restaurant, bar. Business center. Fitness center. Pool. $151-250

WHERE TO EAT
★★BANGKOK STEAKHOUSE
926 W. Broad St., Falls Church, 703-534-0095;
www.fallschurchwebsite.com/BangkokSteakhouse.htm
Thai, Laotian. Lunch (Monday-Thursday), dinner, late-night. $16-35

★★★DUANGRAT'S
5878 Leesburg Pike, Falls Church, 703-820-5775; www.duangrats.com
This Thai restaurant has been a Virginia/Washington, D.C. area staple since its inception in 1980. Ignore its strip-mall location and dive into the vast menu; standouts include a spicy tom yum soup, flavorful bhram and the "grandma" duck dish.
Thai. Lunch, dinner. Bar. $16-35

★★★HAANDI
1222 W. Broad St., Falls Church, 703-533-3501; www.haandi.com
The accolades are plentiful for this fine dining restaurant, renowned as one of the best in the region. The depth of flavor and unique spices found in each dish are unmatched. Entrées include kesar chicken korma, barbecued chunks of boneless chicken breast marinated in saffron and cooked in a curry sauce.
Indian. Lunch, dinner. $16-35

★★PEKING GOURMET INN
6029 Leesburg Pike, Falls Church, 703-671-8088; www.pekinggourmet.com
Chinese. Lunch, dinner. Reservations recommended. $16-35

★★PILIN THAI
116 W. Broad St., Falls Church, 703-241-5850; www.pilinthairestaurant.com
Thai. Lunch (Monday-Saturday), dinner. Bar. $16-35

FREDERICKSBURG
See also Richmond, Shenandoah National Park
One of the seeds of the American Revolution was planted here when a resolution declaring independence from Great Britain was passed on April 29, 1775. George Washington went to school in Fredericksburg, his sister Betty lived here and his mother, Mary Ball Washington, lived and died here. James Monroe practiced law in town. Guns for the Revolution were manufactured here, and four of the most savage battles of the Civil War were fought nearby.

Captain John Smith visited the area in 1608 and gave glowing reports of its possibilities for settlement. In 1727, the General Assembly directed that 50 acres of "lease-land" be laid out and the town called Fredericksburg, after the Prince of Wales.

Ships from abroad sailed up the Rappahannock River to the harbor—ampler then than now—to exchange their goods for those brought from "up-country" by the great road wagons and river carriers. The town prospered.

The Civil War left Fredericksburg ravaged. Situated midway between Richmond and Washington, it was a recurring objective of both sides; the city changed hands seven times and the casualties were high.

Even so, many buildings put up before 1775 still stand. Proudly aware of their town's place in the country's history, the townspeople keep Fredericksburg inviting with fresh paint, beautiful lawns and well-kept gardens.

WHAT TO SEE
CONFEDERATE CEMETERY
Willliam Street and Washington Avenue, Fredericksburg; 540-373-6122;
www.nps.gov/frsp
There are more than 3,300 Confederate Civil War soldiers buried here, about 2,184 of the graves are marked "Unknown."

THE GARI MELCHERS HOME AND STUDIO AT BELMONT
224 Washington St., Fredericksburg, 540-654-1015; www.umw.edu
The Belmont Estate was the residence from 1916 to 1932 of American-born artist Gari Melchers (1860-1932), best known for his portraits of the famous and wealthy, including Theodore Roosevelt, William Vanderbilt and Andrew Mellon and as an important impressionist artist of the period. The artist's studio comprises the nation's largest collection of his works, housing more than 1,800 paintings and drawings. The site is a registered National and State Historic Landmark and includes a 27-acre estate, frame house built in the late 18th century and enlarged over the years, and a stone studio built by

Melchers. Owned by the state of Virginia, Belmont is administered by Mary Washington College.
Admission: adults $10, seniors $9, children 6-18 $5. Monday-Saturday 10 a.m.-5 p.m.

FREDERICKSBURG AREA MUSEUM AND CULTURAL CENTER

1001 Princess Anne St., Fredericksburg, 540-371-3037; www.famcc.org
Former 1814 Town Hall is a Museum and cultural center that interprets the history of Fredericksburg area from its first settlers to the 20th century. There are changing exhibits and children's events.
December-February, Monday-Saturday 10 a.m.-4 p.m., Sunday 1-4 p.m.; March-November, Monday-Saturday 10 a.m.-5 p.m., Sunday 1-5 p.m.

FREDERICKSBURG AND SPOTSYLVANIA NATIONAL MILTARY PARK

Fredericksburg Battlefield Visitor Center, 1013 Lafayette Blvd.,Fredericksburg,
540-373-6122; www.nps.gov/frsp
While at Fredericksburg and Spotsylvania National Military Park, you can visit many different historic spots. See the battlefield where the Battle of Fredericksburg was fought in 1862. Visit Chatham Manor (*120 Chatham Lane*), a Georgian brick manor house, owned by a wealthy planter, which was converted to Union headquarters during two of the battles of Fredericksburg. The house was eventually used as a hospital where Clara Barton and Walt Whitman nursed the wounded. Near Chatham Manor, there's the Stonewall Jackson Shrine in front of the plantation office where Confederate General Jackson, ill with pneumonia and with his shattered left arm amputated, murmured, "Let us cross over the river, and rest under the shade of the trees," and died on May 10, 1863. Visit the Fredericksburg National Cemetery where more than 15,000 are buried and almost 13,000 are unknown.
Admission (to park): Free. Visitor center: September-October, Monday-Friday 9 a.m.-5 p.m., Saturday-Sunday 9 a.m.-6 p.m.; November-mid-April, daily 9 a.m.-5 p.m.

GEORGE WASHINGTON'S HOME AT FERRY FARM

268 Kings Highway, Fredericksburg, 540-370-0732; www.kenmore.org
This is the site of George Washington's boyhood home. Once a tobacco plantation, it now serves as an archaeological dig and a nature preserve.
Admission: adults $5, students $3, children 5 and under free. March-October, daily 10 a.m-5 p.m.; November-December, daily 10 a.m.-4 p.m.

HUGH MERCER APOTHECARY SHOP

1020 Charles St., Fredericksburg, 540-373-1776; www.apva.org
This 18th-century medical office and pharmacy offers exhibits on the medicine and methods of treatment used by Dr. Hugh Mercer before he left to join the Revolutionary War as brigadier general. There are authentic herbs and period medical instruments.
 Admission: adults $5, children 6-18 $2, children 5 and under free. March-October, Monday-Saturday 9 a.m.-4 p.m., Sunday noon-4 p.m.; November-December, Monday-Saturday 10 a.m.-2 p.m., Sunday noon-4 p.m.

JAMES MONROE MUSEUM AND MEMORIAL LIBRARY

908 Charles St., Fredericksburg, 540-654-1043; www.umw.edu

As a young lawyer, James Monroe lived and worked in Fredericksburg from 1786 to 1789 and even served on Fredericksburg's City Council. This museum houses one of the nation's largest collections of Monroe memorabilia, articles and original documents. Included are the desk bought in France in 1794 during his years as ambassador and used in the White House for signing the Monroe Doctrine, formal attire worn at Court of Napoleon, and more than 40 books from Monroe's library. There is also a garden. The site is a national historic landmark owned by the Commonwealth of Virginia and administered by Mary Washington College.

Admission: adults $5, children $1. Monday-Saturday 10 a.m.-5 p.m., Sunday 1-5 p.m.

KENMORE PLANTATION

1201 Washington Ave., Fredericksburg, 540-373-3381; www.kenmore.org

Considered one of finest restorations in Virginia; former home of Colonel Fielding Lewis, commissioner of Fredericksburg gunnery, who married George Washington's only sister, Betty. On an original grant of 863 acres, Lewis built a magnificent home in 1752; three rooms have full decorative molded plaster ceilings. Diorama of 18th-century Fredericksburg.

Admission: adults $8, students $4, children 5 and under free. March-October, daily 10 a.m.-5 p.m.; November-December, daily 10 a.m.-4 p.m.

MARY WASHINGTON COLLEGE

1301 College Road, Fredericksburg, 540-654-1000, 800-468-5614; www.umw.edu

This coeducational liberal arts and sciences institution (4,000 students) offers historic preservation, computer science, and business administration. College also includes 275 acres of open and wooded campus; red brick, white-pillared buildings. President of the college occupies Brompton house built in 1830 on land sold to Fielding Lewis in 1760 and expanded by a later owner, Colonel John Lawrence Marye.

MARY WASHINGTON HOUSE

1200 Charles St., Fredericksburg, 540-373-1569; www.apva.org

This house was bought by George for his mother in 1772; she lived here until her death in 1789. Here she was visited by General Lafayette. Some original furnishings are still here as well as the boxwood garden she loved.

Admission: adults $5, children 6-18 $2, children 5 and under free. March-October, Monday-Saturday 11 a.m.-5 p.m., Sunday noon-4 p.m.; November-December, Monday-Sunday noon-4 p.m.

PRESBYTERIAN CHURCH

810 Princess Anne and George streets, Fredericksburg, 540-373-7057;
www.fredericksburgpc.org

Cannonballs in the front pillar and other damages inflicted in 1862 bombardment. Pews were torn loose and made into coffins for soldiers. Clara Barton, founder of the American Red Cross, is said to have nursed the wounded here.

Services: Sunday 8:30 a.m., 11 a.m.

RISING SUN TAVERN
1304 Caroline St., Fredericksburg, 540-371-1494; www.apva.org
Washington's youngest brother Charles built this tavern around 1760, which became a social and political center and stagecoach stop. Restored and authentically refurnished as an 18th-century tavern; costumed tavern staff, English and American pewter collection.
Admission: adults $5, children 6-18 $2, children 5 and under free. March-October, Monday-Saturday 10 a.m.-5 p.m., Sunday noon-4 p.m.; November-December, Monday-Saturday 11 a.m.-3 p.m., Sunday noon-4 p.m.

SAILOR'S CREEK BATTLEFIELD HISTORIC STATE PARK
6888 Green Bay Rd., Fredericksburg, 434-315-0349; www.dcr.virginia.gov
The site of last major battle of the Civil War on April 6, 1865, preceding Lee's surrender at Appomattox by three days. There are picnic tables and grills available here along with hiking trails, a battlefield memorial. Daily.

ST. GEORGE'S EPISCOPAL CHURCH AND CHURCHYARD
905 Princess Anne and George streets, Fredericksburg, 540-373-4133;
www.stgeorgesepiscopal.net
Patrick Henry, uncle of the orator, was the third rector. Headstones in the churchyard bear the names of illustrious Virginians.
Services: Sunday 7:45 a.m., 10 a.m., 5:30 p.m.

ST. JAMES HOUSE
1300 Charles St., Fredericksburg, 800-678-4748; www.apva.org
This frame house was built in 1760s and is furnished with antiques, porcelain and silver collections and also has a landscaped gardens. It is open to the public during Historic Garden Week in April, the first weekend in September and first week in October; call for information.
Admission: adults $3, children 6-18 $1, children 5 and under free.

STRATFORD HALL PLANTATION
Highway 3 E. and Highway 214, Montross, 804-493-8038; www.stratfordhall.org
This is the boyhood home of Richard Henry Lee and Francis Lightfoot Lee and birthplace of General Robert E. Lee. Center of restored, working plantation is a monumental Georgian house built circa 1735, famous for its uniquely grouped chimney stacks. Interiors span approximately a 100-year period and feature a Federal-era parlor and neoclassical paneling in the Great Hall. Flanking dependencies include kitchen, plantation office and gardener's house. Onsite, you'll see a boxwood garden, 18th- and 19th-century carriages, a working mill, a visitor center with museum.
Admission: adults $10, seniors and military personnel $9, children 6-11 $5, children 5 and under free. Visitor center: Daily 9:30 a.m.-4 p.m.

SPECIAL EVENTS
CHRISTMAS CANDLELIGHT TOUR
Mary Washington House, 1200 Charles St., Fredericksburg, 540-371-4504;
www.visitfred.com

The Mary Washington historic home opens to the public and there are Christmas decorations and refreshments of the Colonial period. December.

WHERE TO STAY
★★RAMADA SOUTH FREDERICKSBURG
5324 Jefferson Davis Highway, Fredericksburg, 540-898-1102, 800-272-6232; www.ramada.com
195 rooms. Restaurant, bar. Fitness center. Pool. Pets accepted. $61-150

WHERE TO EAT
★★RISTORANTE RENATO
422 William St., Fredericksburg, 540-371-8228; www.ristoranterenato.com
Italian. Lunch (Monday-Friday), dinner. Outdoor seating. $36-85

FRONT ROYAL
See also Winchester
Once known as "Hell Town" for all the wild and reckless spirits it attracted, Front Royal was a frontier stop on the way to eastern markets. The present name is supposed to have originated in the command, "Front the royal oak," given by an English officer to his untrained mountain militia recruits.

Belle Boyd, the Confederate spy, worked here extracting military secrets from Union officers. It is said that she once invited General Nathaniel Banks, whose regiment was occupying the town, and his officers to a ball. Later she raced on horseback to tell General Jackson what she had learned. The next morning (May 23, 1862), the Confederates attacked and captured nearly all of the Union troops, providing Jackson one of his early victories in the famous Valley Campaign.

Front Royal was a quiet village until the entrance to Shenandoah National Park and the beginning of Skyline Drive opened in 1935, just one mile to the south. With millions of motorists passing through every year, the town has grown rapidly. The production of automotive finishes, limestone and cement contributes to the town's economy, but the tourism industry remains one of its largest.

WHAT TO SEE
JACKSON'S CHASE GOLF COURSE
65 Jackson's Chase Drive, Front Royal, 540-635-7814; www.jacksonschase.com
Jackson's Chase is built on a tract of land that was used by Confederate General "Stonewall" Jackson to chase Union forces through the Shenandoah Valley and into the eventual first Battle of Winchester. The course itself incorporates the area's rolling terrain into plateau fairways and holes lined with water. Holes three through eight surround a small area being developed for homes with one-acre lots, for those who wish to live in full view of history and the links.
Admission: November-March, Monday-Thursday $25, Friday-Sunday $27; April-Ocobter, Monday-Friday $20-30, Saturday-Sunday $40-45.

SHENANDOAH VALLEY GOLF CLUB

134 Golf Club Circle, Front Royal, 540-636-4653; www.svgcgolf.com

Nestled into the Blue Ridge Mountains, Shenandoah Valley offers 27 holes on 250 acres and has hosted such prestigious tournaments as the PGA Tour's Kemper Open. If you want to play, make sure to reserve a tee time at least a week in advance. The course is affordable and playable for most any golfer. See Web site for schedules and green fees.

SKYLINE CAVERNS

10344 Stonewall Jackson Highway, Front Royal, 540-635-4545, 800-296-4545; www.skylinecaverns.com

Explore these caverns to see extensive, rare, intricate flowerlike formations of calcite; sound and light presentation; 37-foot waterfall; and a clear stream stocked with trout. Caverns are electrically lighted and kept at a temperature of 54 Farenheit year-round. A miniature train provides tripa through the surrounding wooded area. There's also a snack bar and gift shop here. Cavern tours start every few minutes.

Admission: adults $16, children 7-13 $8, children 5 and under free. Minitrain: adults and children 3-18 $3, children 2 and under free. Mid-March-mid-June and September-mid-November, Monday-Friday 9 a.m.-5 p.m., Saturday-Sunday 9 a.m.-6 p.m.; mid-June-September, Monday-Friday 9 a.m.-6 p.m., Saturday-Sunday 9 a.m.-6 p.m.; mid-November-mid-March, Monday-Friday 9 a.m.-4 p.m., Saturday-Sunday 9 a.m.-4 p.m.

WARREN RIFLES CONFEDERATE MUSEUM

95 Chester St., Front Royal, 540-636-6982; www.vaudc.org/museum

This museum displays historic relics and memorabilia from the Civil War. Mid-April-November, Monday-Friday 9 a.m.-4 p.m., Sunday noon-4 p.m.; rest of year, by appointment.

SPECIAL EVENTS

FESTIVAL OF LEAVES

Main and Chester streets, Front Royal, 540-636-1446; www.virginia.org

This festival features arts and crafts, demonstrations, historic exhibits, live entertainment, food, and a parade.
Second weekend in October.

WARREN COUNTY FAIR

Front Royal, 540-635-5821; www.warrencountyfair.com

This county fair features live entertainment, livestock exhibits and sales, contests, plenty of food and more.
First week in August.

WHERE TO STAY

★★QUALITY INN SKYLINE DRIVE

10 S. Commerce Ave., Front Royal, 540-635-3161, 877-424-6423; www.choicehotels.com

106 rooms. Complimentary breakfast. Pool. Pets accepted. $61-150

GEORGE WASHINGTON BIRTHPLACE
NATIONAL MONUMENT

See also Fredericksburg, Montrose

George Washington, first child of Augustine and Mary Ball Washington, was born on February 22, 1732 (on the old-style calendar, February 11) at his father's estate on Popes Creek on the south shore of the Potomac. The family moved in 1735 to Little Hunting Creek Plantation (later called Mount Vernon), then in 1738 to Ferry Farm near Fredericksburg. The 538-acre monument includes much of the old plantation land.

WHAT TO SEE
COLONIAL FARM
1732 Popes Creek Road, George Washington Birthplace National Monument,
804-224-1732; www.nps.gov/gewa

This "living" colonial farm is designed to show 18th-century Virginia plantation life with livestock and tobacco which is still grown here. There's also a colonial garden, several farm buildings, a furnished colonial kitchen, a household slave quarters and spinning and weaving room.

Admission: adults $4, children 15 and under free. Daily 9 a.m.-5 p.m.

FAMILY BURIAL GROUND
1732 Popes Creek Road, George Washington Birthplace National Monument,
804-224-1732; www.nps.gov/gewa

Site of 1664 home of Colonel John Washington, first Washington in Virginia and great-grandfather of the first president. And Washington's ancestors are buried here.

Daily 9 a.m.-5 p.m.

MEMORIAL HOUSE
1732 Popes Creek Road, George Washington Birthplace National Monument,
804-224-1732; www.nps.gov/gewa

The original house burned and was never rebuilt. The Memorial House is not a replica of the original; it represents a composite of a typical 18th-century Virginia plantation house. Bricks were handmade from nearby clay. Furnishings are typical of the time.

Admission: adults $4, children 15 and under free. Daily 9 a.m.-5 p.m.

VISITOR CENTER
1732 Popes Creek Road, George Washington Birthplace National Monument,
804-224-1732; www.nps.gov/gewa

Stop in the vistor center for information, and to watch an orientation film as well as view museum exhibits. There are also picnic areas here to sit outside while enjoying a packed lunch.

Daily 9 a.m.-5 p.m.

HAMPTON

See also Newport News, Norfolk, Portsmouth, Virginia Beach

Hampton is the oldest continuous English-speaking community in the United States (Jamestown, settled in 1607, is a national historical park, but not a town). The settlement began at a place then called Kecoughtan, with the building of Fort Algernourne as protection against the Spanish. In the late 1600s and early 1700s, pirates harassed the area. Finally in 1718, the notorious brigand Blackbeard was killed by Lieutenant Robert Maynard and organized piracy came to an end here.

Hampton was shelled in the Revolutionary War, sacked by the British in the War of 1812 and burned in 1861 by retreating Confederates to prevent its occupation by Union forces. Only the gutted walls of St. John's Church survived the fire. The town was rebuilt after the Civil War by its citizens and soldiers. Computer technology, manufacturing, aerospace research and commercial fishing are now big business here.

Langley Air Force Base, headquarters for the Air Combat Command, Fort Monroe, headquarters for the U.S. Army's Training and Doctrine Command, and the NASA Langley Research Center are all located here.

WHAT TO SEE
BLUEBIRD GAP FARM
60 Pine Chapel Road, Hampton, 757-727-6739; www.hampton.gov/bbgf
This 60-acre farm includes barnyard zoo; indigenous wildlife such as deer and wolves; antique and modern farm equipment and farmhouse artifacts. There's picnicking and a playground.
Admission: Free. Wednesday-Sunday 9 a.m.-5 p.m.

BUCKROE BEACH
22 Lincoln St., Hampton, 757-850-5134; www.hampton.gov
This sandy beach offers swimming with lifeguards on duty, a public park, outdoor movies and concerts.
Memorial Day-Labor Day, daily 8 a.m.-6 p.m.

CASEMATE MUSEUM AT FORT MONROE
20 Bernard Road, Hampton, 757-788-3391; www.virginia.org
The first fort here was a stockade called Fort Algernourne; the second, Fort George, though built of brick, was destroyed by a hurricane in 1749; the present fort was completed about 1834. The musuem provides insight on heritage of the fort, Old Point Comfort and the Army Coast Artillery Corps. It offers access to a series of casemates and a walking tour of the fort. Jefferson Davis casemate contains a cell in which the Confederacy's president was confined on false charges of plotting to kill Abraham Lincoln. Museum features Civil War exhibits, military uniforms and assorted artwork, including three original Remington drawings, along with audiovisual programs. Scale models of coast artillery guns and dioramas represent the role of the coast artillery from 1901 to 1946.
Admission: Free. Daily 10:30 a.m.-4:30 p.m.

HAMPTON CAROUSEL
602 Settlers Landing Road, Hampton, 757-727-6381; www.virginia.org
Completely restored in 1991, this antique 1920 carousel is housed in its own

pavilion and features 48 hand-carved horses.
Admission: $2. Mid-May-September, Monday-Wednesday noon-5 p.m., Thursday-Sunday noon-7 p.m.; September-December, Friday-Sunday noon-4 p.m.

HAMPTON UNIVERSITY

Cemetery Road and Frissell Avenue, Hampton, 757-727-5000; www.hamptonu.edu
Founded by Union Brigadier General Samuel Chapman Armstrong, chief of the Freedman's Bureau, to prepare the youth of the South, regardless of color, for the work of organizing and instructing schools in the Southern states; many blacks and Native Americans came to be educated. Today, it's Virginia's only coeducational, nondenominational, four-year private college with more than 5,700 students. The Hampton choir is famous. It "sang up" a building, Virginia-Cleveland Hall, in 1870 on a trip through New England and Canada, raising close to $100,000 at concerts.

ST. JOHN'S CHURCH AND PARISH MUSEUM

W. Queens Way and Franklin Street, Hampton, 757-722-2567; www.stjohnshampton.org
This is the fourth site of worship of Episcopal parish established in 1610. They have a bible dating from 1599; communion silver from 1618; a Colonial Vestry Book; and a taped historical message.
Services: Sunday 8 a.m., 9:15 a.m., 10:30 a.m., Thursday 10 a.m.

VIRGINIA AIR AND SPACE CENTER

600 Settlers Landing Road, Hampton, 757-727-0900, 800-296-0800; www.vasc.org
Exhibits show the historical link between Hampton Roads' seafaring past and spacefaring future. Exhibits include 19 full-sized air- and spacecraft, the *Apollo 12* Command Module, a moon rock and rare NASA artifacts. Films shown in 283-seat IMAX theater.
Hours vary; see Web site for schedule and ticket information.

SPECIAL EVENTS
HAMPTON BAY DAYS

Hampton, 757-727-6122; www.baydays.com
These days feature arts and crafts, rides, science exhibits and entertainment.
Mid-September.

HAMPTON CUP REGATTA

Mill Creek, Hampton, 800-800-2202; www.hamptoncupregatta.org
This event features inboard hydroplane races.
Mid-August.

HAMPTON JAZZ FESTIVAL

Hampton Coliseum, 1000 Coliseum Drive, Hampton, 757-838-4203; www.hampton.gov/coliseum
This jazz festival features jazz acts which have included Patti Labelle, Kenny "Babyface" Edmonds, the O'Jays and more.
Late June.

WHERE TO STAY
★QUALITY INN CONVENTION CENTER

1813 W. Mercury Blvd., Hampton, 757-838-8484, 877-424-6423; www.qualityinn.com

129 rooms. Complimentary breakfast. Fitness center. $61-150

★★RADISSON HOTEL HAMPTON

700 Settlers Landing Road, Hampton, 757-727-9700; www.radisson.com/hamptonva

173 rooms. Restaurant, bar. Business center. Fitness center. Pool. $61-150

★★★TIDES INN

480 King Carter Drive, Irvington, 804-438-5000, 800-843-3746; www.tidesinn.com

Water figures largely in the experience at this inn, which is Bordered by the Chesapeake Bay, Potomac River and Rappahannock River, and with views of gentle Carters Creek, a 60-slip marina is a boater's paradise. Golf, tennis, croquet, biking, pampering yourself in the spa and exploring the nearby historic sites are just some of the ways guests fill their days. Dining runs the gamut from the elegant setting at the East Room dining room to the casual atmosphere of the Chesapeake Club.

106 rooms. Closed January-mid-March. Restaurant, bar. Business center. Fitness center. Pool. Spa. Pets accepted. Golf. Tennis. $151-250

HARRISONBURG

See also Staunton

Originally named Rocktown for the limestone outcroppings prevalent in the area, Harrisonburg became the county seat of Rockingham County when Thomas Harrison won a race against Mr. Keezle of Keezletown, three miles east. They had raced on horseback to Richmond to file their respective towns for the new county seat.

Harrisonburg is noted for good hunting and fishing, recreational opportunities, beautiful scenery and turkeys. The annual production of more than five million turkeys, most of them processed and frozen, has made Rockingham County widely known. This is a college town with three four-year universities. Much of the Washington and Jefferson national forests are here.

WHAT TO SEE
GRAND CAVERNS REGIONAL PARK

Dogwood Avenue, Grottoes, 888-430-2283; www.uvrpa.org

Known for its immense underground chambers and spectacular formations, the caverns were visited by Union and Confederate troops during the Civil War. There are unique shield formations. Caverns are electrically lighted and kept at a temperature of 54 F. Park facilities include a swimming pool, tennis courts, miniature golf, picnic pavilions and hiking and bicycle trails. Guided tours are available; call for a reservation.

April-October, daily; November-March, Saturday-Sunday.

LINCOLN HOMESTEAD

Route 42, Harrisonburg;

Located just north of Harrisonburg is the Lincoln Homestead. It was in this brick house where President Lincoln's father was born. The rear wing was built by Abraham Lincoln's grandfather. Main portion of the house was built about 1800 by Captain Jacob Lincoln. This is now privately owned.

SHENANDOAH VALLEY FOLK ART AND HERITAGE CENTER

382 High St., Dayton, 540-879-2681; www.heritagecenter.com
Featured here is the Stonewall Jackson Electric Map that depicts his Valley Campaign of 1862. The 12-foot vertical relief map fills an entire wall and lets visitors see and hear the campaign, battle by battle. Also displays of Shenandoah Valley history, artifacts.
Monday-Saturday 10 a.m.-4 p.m.

SPECIAL EVENTS
NATURAL CHIMNEYS JOUSTING TOURNAMENT

Natural Chimneys Regional Park, 94 Natural Chimneys Lane, Harrisonburg;
www.uvrpa.org
America's oldest continuous sporting event, held annually since 1821. "Knights" armed with lances charge down an 80-yard track and attempt to spear three small rings suspended from posts. Each knight is allowed three rides at the rings, thus a perfect score is nine rings. Ties are run off using successively smaller rings.
Third Saturday in June and August.

WHERE TO STAY
★COMFORT INN

1440 E. Market St., Harrisonburg, 540-433-6066, 800-424-6423;
www.choicehotels.com
102 rooms. Complimentary breakfast. Fitness center. Pool. Pets accepted. $61-150

★HAMPTON INN

85 University Blvd., Harrisonburg, 540-432-1111, 800-426-7866; www.hamptoninn.com
163 rooms. Complimentary breakfast. Business center. Fitness center. Pool. $61-150

★★THE VILLAGE INN

4979 S. Valley Pike, Harrisonburg, 540-434-7355, 800-736-7355; www.thevillageinn.info
37 rooms. Restaurant, bar. Pool. $61-150

WHERE TO EAT
★★VILLAGE INN RESTAURANT

4979 South Valley Pike, Harrisonburg, 800-736-7355; www.thevillageinn.travel
American. Breakfast, lunch (Monday-Friday), dinner. Closed Sunday. Children's menu. $16-35

HOT SPRINGS

See also Warm Springs
A Ranger District office of the Washington and Jefferson national forests is located here.

WHAT TO SEE
THE HOMESTEAD SKI AREA
Highway 220, Hot Springs, 540-839-3860, 866-354-4653; www.thehomestead.com
The ski area offers 45 acres to ski and snowboard with a double chairlift, T-bar, J-bar, baby rope tow; patrol, school, rentals, snowmaking; cafeteria, and bar. There's also an ice skating rink.
Late-November-March, daily 10 a.m.-5 p.m.

WHERE TO STAY
★★★THE HOMESTEAD
Highway 220, Hot Springs, 540-839-1766, 866-354-4653; www.thehomestead.com
Founded 10 years before the American Revolution, The Homestead is one of America's finest resorts. For more than two centuries, presidents and other notables have flocked to this idyllic mountain resort on 15,000 acres in the scenic Allegheny Mountains. From the fresh mountain air and natural hot springs to the legendary championship golf, this Georgian-style resort is the embodiment of a restorative retreat. A leading golf academy sharpens skills, while three courses challenge players. America's oldest continuously played tee is located here at the Old Course. Guests take to the waters as they have done for 200 years, while the spa incorporates advanced therapies for relaxation and rejuvenation.
483 rooms. Restaurant, bar. Fitness center. Pool. Spa. Golf. Tennis. $151-250

WHERE TO EAT
★★SAM SNEAD'S TAVERN
The Homestead, 220 Main St., Hot Springs, 540-839-7666; www.thehomestead.com
American. Dinner. Children's menu. Reservations recommended. Bar. $36-85

SPAS
★★★THE HOMESTEAD SPA

Highway 220, Hot Springs, 540-839-1766; www.thehomestead.com
The Homestead Spa at the Homestead Resort grows out of a healing tradition nearly as old as the Allegheny Mountains themselves: taking the waters that bubble up from the ground in Hot Springs, Va. For thousands of years, natives and the Europeans who came later them have soaked in these mineral-rich waters, to ease aches and ailments. The Homestead is a National Historic Landmark, a spa since 1766. The octagonal wooden building atop the Hot Springs is even older, built in 1761 and essentially unchanged. Thomas Jefferson came to the Gentleman's Pool House to soak several times a day during his Homestead visit in 1818. Today, men can still retreat to the Jefferson Pools, while women have their own Ladies' Pool House atop another spring. Treatments have become more exotic over time, encompassing reflexology and Ayurvedic head massage, alpha-beta skin peels and banana-and-coconut hair therapy. The spa still values the time-tested mineral baths and salt scrubs of the past, often combined with fresh-picked flowers and herbs from the mountains that hug the Homestead.

JAMESTOWN COLONIAL NATIONAL HISTORICAL PARK

On May 13, 1607, in this unpromising setting, the first permanent English settlement in the New World was founded. From the beginning, characteristics of the early United States were established: self-government, industry, commerce, the plantation system and a diverse populace, originally made up of men of English, German, African, French, Italian, Polish and Irish descent.

Nothing of the 17th-century settlement remains above ground on Jamestown island except the Old Church Tower. Since 1934, however, archaeological exploration by the National Park Service has made the outline of the town clear. Cooperative efforts by the Park Service and the Association for the Preservation of Virginia Antiquities (which owns 22 1/2 acres of the island, including the Old Church Tower) have exposed foundations and restored streets, property ditches, hedgerows, fences and the James Fort site from 1607. Markers, recorded messages, paintings and monuments are everywhere. The gates of the park open daily at 8:30 a.m. and then close at 4:30 p.m. but visitors may remain in the actual park until dusk.

WHAT TO SEE
GLASSHOUSE
Colonial National Historic Parkway and Jamestown Road,
Jamestown Colonial National Historical Park; www.nps.gov/jame
Colonists produced glass here in 1608, and attempted again in 1622. Here you can see the remains of furnaces used for glassblowing and you can watch demonstrations of glassblowing as it's done today. There is also a gift shop here where you can purchase glass.
Daily 8:30 a.m.-5 p.m.

JAMESTOWN MEMORIAL CHURCH
Colonial National Historic Parkway and Jamestown Road,
Jamestown Colonial National Historical Park; www.historicjamestowne.org
The brick church that stands here was built in 1907 by the National Society of the Colonial Dames of America over the foundations of the original church built in 1639. Only a brick tower is left (built in 1690) and stands behind the church.

NEW TOWNE
1367 Colonial Parkway, Jamestown Colonial National Historical Park;
www.nps.gov/jame
This is the area where Jamestown expanded around 1620 may be toured along "Back Streete" and other original streets. Section includes reconstructed foundations indicating sites of Country House, Governor's House, homes of Richard Kemp, builder of one of the first brick houses in America, Henry Hartwell, a founder of the College of William & Mary, and Dr. John Pott and William Pierce, who led the "thrusting out" of Governor John Harvey in 1635.
Daily 8:30 a.m.-4:30 p.m.

VISITOR CENTER

Colonial National Historic Parkway and Jamestown Road,
Jamestown Colonial National Historical Park; www.historicjamestowne.org
Stop here to pick up guide leaflets, watch an introductory film and check out exhibits. While there are only vending machines at the visitor center, nearby the Dale House Café provides snacks and lunch for visitors.
Daily 9 a.m.-5 p.m. Admission (to park): adults $10, children 15 and under free. Café: Daily 9 a.m.-5 p.m.

SPECIAL EVENTS
JAMESTOWN DAY

1368 Colonial Parkway, Jamestown, 757-229-1733; www.historicjamestowne.org
This event commemorates the arrival of first settlers in 1607 with special tours and activities including trade demonstrations, a commemorative ceremony, music from that time period and more.
Mid-May.

LEESBURG

See also Arlington County, McLean; also see Washington, D.C.
Originally named Georgetown for King George II of England, this town was later renamed Leesburg, probably after Francis Lightfoot Lee, a signer of the Declaration of Independence and a local landowner. Leesburg is located in a scenic area of rolling hills, picturesque rural towns and thoroughbred horse farms, where point-to-point racing and steeplechases are popular. There are also plenty of vineyards to visit and enjoy.

WHAT TO SEE
BALL'S BLUFF BATTLEFIELD

Ball Bluff Road, Leesburg, 703-737-7800; www.nvrpa.org
One of the smallest national cemeteries in the U.S. marks the site of the third armed engagement of the Civil War. On October 21, 1861, four Union regiments suffered catastrophic losses while surrounded by Confederate forces; the Union commander, a U.S. senator and presidential confidant, was killed here along with half his troops, while attempting to recross the Potomac River. Oliver Wendell Holmes, Jr., later to become a U.S. Supreme Court justice, was wounded here.
Daily dawn-dusk. Tours: April-October, Saturday-Sunday 11 a.m.-1 p.m.

LOUDOUN MUSEUM

16 Loudoun St. S.W., Leesburg, 703-777-7427; www.loudounmuseum.org
This century-old restored building contains exhibits and memorabilia of the area and an audiovisual presentation "A Special Look at Loudoun." You can also obtain brochures amd information about Loudoun County or take a walking tour, or get self-guided tour booklets to do it at your own pace.
Admission: adults $3, seniors, students and teachers $1, children 4 and under free. Monday, Wednesday-Saturday 10 a.m.-5 p.m., Sunday 1-5 p.m.

MORVEN PARK

17263 Southern Planter Lane, Leesburg, 703-777-2414; www.morvenpark.org

Originally the residence of Thomas Swann, an early Maryland governor, the estate was expanded by Westmoreland Davis, governor of Virginia from 1918 to 1922. The 1,200-acre park includes a 28-room mansion, boxwood gardens, Winmill Carriage Museum with more than 70 horse-drawn vehicles, Museum of Hounds and Hunting with video presentation and artifacts depicting the history of fox hunting, and Morven Park International Equestrian Center.

Admission: Free. April-November, Friday-Monday afternoons. Grounds: Daily 7 a.m.-6 p.m. Tours: Friday-Monday 11 a.m.-4 p.m., Sunday 1-4 p.m.

OATLANDS

20850 Oatlands Plantation Lane, Leesburg, 703-777-3174; www.oatlands.org

On this 261-acre estate a Classical Revival mansion, built by George Carter, was the center of a 5,000-acre plantation. The house was partially remodeled in 1827, which was when the front portico was added. Most of the building materials, including bricks and wood, came from or were made on the estate. Interior furnished with American, English and French antiques; reflects period between 1897 and 1965 when the house was owned by Mr. and Mrs. William Corcoran Eustis, prominent Washingtonians. Formal garden has some of the finest boxwood in U.S. Farm fields provide equestrian area for races and horse shows.

Admission: adults $10, seniors and children 6-16 $9, children 5 and younger free. Admission (to garden and grounds only): $7. April-December, Monday-Saturday 10 a.m.-5 p.m., Sunday 1-5 p.m. Tours: on the hour.

VINEYARD AND WINERY TOURS

Loudon County Visitor Center, 112-G South St. S.E., Leesburg, 703-771-2617,
800-752-6118; www.visitloudoun.org

Stop into the Loudon County Visitor Center to get information on the surrounding wineries to plan a tour of your own. You can take part in a winery and vineyard tour chauffeured by a limousine. In Leesburg alone, there are numerous wineries to visit including Casanel Vineyards, Dry Mill Vineyard and Winery, Fabbioli Cellars and more.

Visitor center: Daily 9 a.m.-5 p.m.

WATERFORD

15609 High St., Waterford, 504-882-3018; www.waterfordva.org

This eighteenth-century Quaker village, designated a National Historic Landmark, has been restored as a residential community. An annual homes tour (first full weekend in October) has craft demonstrations, exhibits and traditional music. The Waterford Foundation has brochures outlining self-guided walking tours. If the Waterford Foundation is closed, visit the Waterford Market (*15487 Second St.*) where you can also grab a bite to eat as there are no restaurants in Waterford.

Waterford Foundation: Monday-Friday 10 a.m.-3 p.m. Waterford Market: Monday-Friday 10 a.m.-7 p.m., Saturday 10 a.m.-5 p.m.

WHERE TO STAY

★DAYS INN

721 E. Market St., Leesburg, 703-777-6622, 800-329-7466; www.daysinn.com
81 rooms. Complimentary breakfast. Pets accepted. $61-150

★★HOLIDAY INN LEESBURG AT CARRADOC HALL

1500 E. Market St., Leesburg, 703-771-9200, 877-834-3613; www.holidayinn.com
122 rooms. Restaurant, bar. Business center. Fitness center. Pool. Pets accepted. $61-150

★★★LANSDOWNE RESORT

44050 Woodridge Parkway, Leesburg, 703-729-8400, 877-509-8400;
www.lansdowneresort.com
The stylishly streamlined Lansdowne Resort, which comprises a nine-story tower and two five-story wings, underwent a $55 million renovation. Guest rooms are reminiscent of a country manor, elegant but casual, with lush woodland views.
296 rooms. Restaurant, bar. Fitness center. Pool. Spa. Golf. Tennis. $151-250

★★★LEESBURG COLONIAL INN

19 S. King St., Leesburg, 703-777-5000, 800-392-1332;
www.theleesburgcolonialinn.com
Bordered by the majestic Blue Ridge Mountains and the Potomac River, this circa 1830 inn is located in the heart of historic Leesburg (just 25 miles from Washington, D.C.) The inn is decorated in 18th-century American style. Each guest room features individual climate controls, antique poster beds, hardwood floors, fine rugs and period pieces. Some rooms also have whirlpool tubs and fireplaces. A complimentary full gourmet breakfast is offered each morning in the dining room.
10 rooms. Restaurant. $61-150

LEXINGTON

See also Charlottesville, Richmond
Lexington was home to two of the greatest Confederate heroes: Robert E. Lee and Thomas J. "Stonewall" Jackson. Both are buried here. Sam Houston, Cyrus McCormick and James Gibbs (inventor of the sewing machine) were born nearby.

Set in rolling country between the Blue Ridge and Allegheny mountains, this town is the seat of Rockbridge County. Lexington is known for attractive homes, trim farms, fine old mansions and two of the leading educational institutions in the Commonwealth: Washington and Lee University and Virginia Military Institute.

WHAT TO SEE

GEORGE C. MARSHALL MUSEUM

Virginia Military Institute Parade Ground, Lexington, 540-463-7103;
www.marshallfoundation.org
This museum features isplays on the life and career of George C. Marshall, the illustrious military figure and statesman (1880-1959). Exhibits include

a World War I electric map and recorded narration of World War II; a gold medallion awarded with his Nobel Prize for Peace in 1953.

Admission: adults $5, seniors $3, children 13-18 $2, children 12 and under and military personnel free. Tuesday-Saturday 9 a.m.-5 p.m.

GOSHEN PASS

Route 39, Lexington; www.lexingtonvirginia.com

This scenic mountain gorge was formed by Maury River. There is a memorial to "the father of modern oceanography," Matthew Fontaine Maury is here. Stop and picnic here or take a hike near the river.

LEE CHAPEL AND MUSEUM

Washington and Lee University campus, Lexington, 540-458-8768; www.leechapel.wlu.edu

Robert E. Lee is entombed here. Also houses Lee family crypt and museum, marble "recumbent statue" of Lee, portions of art collection of Washington and Lee families. Lee's office remains as he left it.

April-October, Monday-Saturday 9 a.m.-5 p.m., Sunday 1-5 p.m.; November-March, Monday-Saturday 9 a.m.-4 p.m., Sunday 1-4 p.m.

LEXINGTON CARRIAGE COMPANY

106 E. Washington St., Lexington, 540-463-5647; www.lexcarriage.com

These narrated horse-drawn carriage tours take you through historic Lexington for approximately 45 minutes. The hitching post is located across from the Visitor center. Groups of 10 or more are by appointment only.

Admission: adults $16, seniors $14, children 7-13 $7, children 6 and under free. April-October, daily 11 a.m.-5 p.m.; June-August, daily 10 a.m.-6 p.m.

STONEWALL JACKSON HOUSE

8 E. Washington St., Lexington, 540-463-2552; www.stonewalljackson.org

This is the only home owned by Confederate General Thomas J. "Stonewall" Jackson, restored to its appearance in 1859-1861. Many of the furnishings were once owned by Jackson. There's an interpretive slide presentation, guided tours, restored gardens and a gift shop.

Admission: adults $6, children 6-17 $3, children 5 and under free. Monday-Saturday 9 a.m.-5 p.m., Sunday 1-5 p.m.

STONEWALL JACKSON MEMORIAL CEMETERY

White and Main streets, Lexington; www.lexingtonvirginia.com

General Jackson and more than 100 Confederate soldiers are buried here. Admission: Free. Daily dawn-dusk.

VIRGINIA MILITARY INSTITUTE

Letcher Avenue, Lexington, 540-464-7207; www.vmi.edu

Founded in 1839, this state military, engineering, sciences and arts college has 1,300 cadets. It was the first state military college in the nation and became coeducational in 1997. Stonewall Jackson taught here, as did Matthew Fontaine Maury, famed naval explorer and inventor. George Catlett Marshall, a general of the army and author of the Marshall Plan, was a graduate. Me-

mentos of these men on display in VMI museum.
Tours: Daily noon. Museum: Daily 9 a.m.-5 p.m.

WASHINGTON AND LEE UNIVERSITY

West Washington Street, Lexington, 540-463-8400; www.wlu.edu
This liberal arts university with 2,189 students is situated on an attractive
campus with white colonnaded buildings and also includes Washington and
Lee Law School. Founded as Augusta Academy in 1749, it became Liberty
Hall in 1776 and then the name changed to Washington Academy in 1798
after receiving 200 shares of James River Canal Company stock from George
Washington, and then to Washington College. General Robert E. Lee served
as president from 1865-1870. Soon after Lee's death in 1870, it became
Washington and Lee University.

SPECIAL EVENTS
GARDEN WEEK IN HISTORIC LEXINGTON

106 E. Washington St., Lexington, 804-644-7776; www.vagardenweek.org
Tour of gardens in the Lexington and the Rockbridge County area.
Mid-late April.

LIME KILN ARTS THEATER

14 S. Randolph St., Lexington, 540-463-7088; www.theateratlimekiln.com
The Lime Kiln Theater produces professional theatrical productions and
concerts in outdoor theater, natural amphitheater and tent (when weather
isn't cooperating).
April-September, December.

WHERE TO STAY
★★BEST WESTERN INN AT HUNT RIDGE

25 Willow Springs Road, Lexington, 540-464-1500, 800-780-7234;
www.bestwestern.com
100 rooms. Restaurant, bar. Pool. Pets accepted. $61-150

★COMFORT INN VIRGINIA HORSE CENTERS

62 Comfort Way, Lexington, 540-463-7311, 877-424-6423; www.choicehotels.com
80 rooms. Complimentary breakfast. Pool. Pets accepted. $61-150

★HOLIDAY INN EXPRESS LEXINGTON

880 N. Lee Highway, Lexington, 540-463-7351, 877-834-3613 www.ichotelsgroup.com
72 rooms. Complimentary breakfast. Business center. Pets accepted. $61-
150

★★MAPLE HALL COUNTRY INN

3111 N. Lee Higway, Lexington, 540-463-6693, 877-463-2044;
www.lexingtonhistoricinns.com
43 rooms. Complimentary breakfast. Pool. Tennis. $61-150

WHERE TO EAT
★REDWOOD FAMILY RESTAURANT
898 N. Lee Highway, Lexington, 540-463-2168
American. Breakfast, lunch, dinner, Sunday brunch. Children's menu. $15 and under.

LURAY

See also Front Royal, Harrisonburg, New Market
This town's name is of French origin, and its fame comes from the caverns discovered here in 1878. Situated at the junction of Highways 211 and 340, Luray is nine miles away from—and within sight of—Shenandoah National Park and Skyline Drive. Park headquarters are located here. There are three developed recreation areas north and west of town in Washington and Jefferson national forests.

WHAT TO SEE
LURAY CAVERNS
970 Highway 211 W., Luray, 540-743-6551; www.luraycaverns.com
One of the largest caverns in the East. Huge underground rooms (one is 300-feet wide, 500-feet long, with a 140-foot ceiling) connected by natural corridors and paved walkways are encrusted with colorful rock formations, some delicate as lace, others massive. In one chamber is the world's only "stalacpipe" organ, which produces music of symphonic quality from stone formations. Indirect lighting permits taking of color photos within caverns. The temperature in the caverns is 54 F. One-hour guided tours start about every 20 minutes.
Admission: adults $21, seniors $18, children 6-12 $10.

LURAY SINGING TOWER
970 Highway 211/340 W., Luray, 540-743-6551; www.luraycaverns.com
Officially known as the Belle Brown Northcott Memorial, the tower houses a 47-bell carillon with the largest bell weighing 7,640 pounds. Features 45-minute recitals by celebrated carillonneur. The tower is in the park adjacent to caverns.
April-May, Saturday-Sunday 2 p.m.; June-August, Tuesday, Thursday, Saturday-Sunday 8 p.m.; September-October, Sunday 2 p.m.

LURAY ZOO
1087 Highway 211 W., Luray, 540-743-4113; www.lurayzoo.com
The Luray Zoo features large reptile collection, exotic animals and tropical birds as well as a petting zoo, live animal shows and life-sized dinosaur reproductions. There's also a gift shop.
Admission: adults $10, children 3-12 $5, children 2 and under free. Daily 10 a.m.-5 p.m.; hours may vary seasonally so call ahead.

WHERE TO STAY
★★BIG MEADOWS LODGE
Skyline Drive, Mile 51, Luray, 540-999-2221, 800-999-4714; www.visitshenandaoh.com
97 rooms. Restaurant, bar. Pets accepted. Closed November-mid-May. $61-150

★★DAYS INN LURAY SHENANDOAH

138 Whispering Hill Road, Luray, 540-743-4521, 800-329-7466; www.daysinn-luray.com
100 rooms. Complimentary breakfast. Fitness center. Pool. Pets accepted.
$61-150

★★SKYLAND RESORT

Skyline Drive, Luray, 540-999-2211, 800-999-4714; www.visitshenandoah.com
177 rooms. Restaurant, bar. Closed December-March. Pets accepted. $61-150

LYNCHBURG

See also Roanoke
Lynchburg is perched on hills overlooking the James River, which was for
many years the city's means of growth. Today, Lynchburg is home to more
than 3,000 businesses and diversified industries. Educational institutions located here include Lynchburg College, Randolph-Macon Women's College
and Liberty University.

One of the first buildings in the town was a ferry house built by John
Lynch. The same enterprising young man later built a tobacco warehouse,
probably the first one in the country. During the Civil War, Lynchburg was
important as a supply base and hospital town. In June 1864, General Jubal A.
Early successfully defended the town from an attack by Union forces. More
than 2,200 Confederates are buried in the Confederate Cemetery, located
within the Old City Cemetery.

WHAT TO SEE
ANNE SPENCER HOUSE

1313 Pierce St., Lynchburg, 434-845-1313; www.annespencermuseum.com
House of the noted poet, the only black woman and only Virginian to be
included in the Norton Anthology of Modern American and British Poetry.
On grounds is Spencer's writing cottage Edan Kraal. Many dignitaries have
visited here. The museum is filled with artifacts, memorabilia, period antique
furnishings; there is also a formal garden.
Admission: adults $5, seniors $4, children 13-18 $3, children 12 and under
$2. Gardens: Daily dawn-dusk. House: by appointment.

APPOMATTOX COURT HOUSE NATIONAL HISTORICAL PARK

Highway 24, Appomattox, 434-352-8987; www.nps.gov/apco
The series of clashes between General Ulysses S. Grant and General Robert
E. Lee that started with the Battle of the Wilderness May 5, 1864 finally ended here on Palm Sunday, April 9, 1865, in the little village of Appomattox.
A week earlier, Lee had evacuated besieged Petersburg and headed west in
a desperate attempt to join forces with General Johnston in North Carolina.
Ragged and exhausted, decimated by desertions, without supplies and beset
by Union forces at every turn, the once-great Army of Northern Virginia
launched its last attack April 9 at dawn. By 10 a.m., it was clear that further
bloodshed was futile; after some difficulty in getting a message to Grant,
the two met in the parlor of the McLean House. By 3 p.m., the generous
surrender terms had been drafted and signed. The war was over. Three days
later, 28,231 Confederate soldiers received their parole here The 1,743-acre

park includes the village of Appomattox, restored and reconstructed to appear much as it did in 1865. Uniformed park rangers or interpreters in period dress answer questions about the residents and events.

Admission: Memorial Day-Labor Day, $4 ($10 maximum per vehicle), children 15 and under free; Labor Day-Memorial Day, $3 ($5 maximum per vehicle), children 15 and under free. Visitor center: Daily 8:30 a.m.-5 p.m.

FORT EARLY

Memorial and Fort avenues, Lynchburg, 434-847-1811; www.discoverlynchburg.org

Defense earthwork for Lynchburg's closest battle during the Civil War. Confederates under General Jubal A. Early turned back forces under General David Hunter in 1864.

Daily dawn-dusk.

MAIER MUSEUM OF ART AT RANDOLPH COLLEGE

2500 Rivermont Ave., Lynchburg, 434-947-8136; www.randolphcollege.edu

Collection is representative of 19th- and 20th-century American painting. Artists include Thomas Hart Benton, Edward Hicks, Winslow Homer, James McNeil Whistler, Mary Cassatt and Georgia O'Keeffe.

Admission: Free. Late-August-late-May, Tuesday-Sunday 1-5 p.m.; late-May-August, Wednesday-Sunday 1-4 p.m.

OLD COURT HOUSE MUSEUM

901 Court St., Lynchburg, 434-455-6226; www.lynchburgmuseum.org

This museum has been restored to original 1855 Greek Revival appearance. Three galleries have exhibits on early history of the area, highlighting Quaker settlement and role of tobacco.

Admission: adults $6, seniors and students $5, children 6-17 $3, children 5 and under free. Monday-Saturday 10 a.m.-4 p.m., Sunday noon-4 p.m.

THE PEST HOUSE MEDICAL MUSEUM

Old City Cemetery, Fourth and Taylor streets, Lynchburg, 434-847-1465;
www.gravegarden.org/pesthouse.htm

The 1840s white-frame medical office of Quaker physician Dr. John Jay Terrell has been joined with Pest House quarantine hospital to typify the standard of medicine during the late 1800s. Original medical instruments include operating table, hypodermic needle, clinical thermometer and chloroform mask. Period furnishings on one side duplicate Dr. Terrell's office during the Civil War; other side represents a quarantine hospital for Confederate soldiers in which Dr. Terrell volunteered to assume responsibility. Window displays with audio description.

Admission (tours): adults $5, children $2. Tours (by appointment).

Grounds: Daily dawn-dusk. Museum: March-October, Daily 11 a.m.-3 p.m.; November-February, Monday-Saturday 11 a.m.-3 p.m.

POINT OF HONOR

112 Cabell St., Lynchburg, 434-455-6226; www.pointofhonor.org

This restored mansion on Daniel's Hill above the James River, was built by Dr. George Cabel in 1815, Sr., physician to Patrick Henry. It's a Federalist style home with octagon bay façade and finely crafted interior woodwork with period furnishings and gardens.

Admission: adults $6, seniors and students $5, children 6-17 $3, children 5 and under free. Monday-Saturday 10 a.m.-4 p.m., Sunday noon-4 p.m.

RANDOLPH-MACON WOMEN'S COLLEGE

2500 Rivermont Ave., Lynchburg, 434-947-8000; www.rmc.edu

Founded in 1891, this 100-acre campus is located on historic Rivermont Avenue near James River with an enrollment of 1,175. This was the first college for women in the South that was granted a Phi Beta Kappa chapter. The campus has interesting mixture of architecture, including Vincent Kling design for Houston Chapel.

RIVERSIDE PARK

2270 Rivermont Ave., Lynchburg

This 47 acres park has basketball courts, a playground and a trail that leands toward the James River where you'll be surrounded by trees and wildlife. Daily dawn-dusk.

SOUTH RIVER MEETING HOUSE

5810 Fort Ave., Lynchburg, 434-239-2548; www.qmpc.org

Completed in 1798, the stone building remained the site of Quaker worship and activity until the 1840s. John Lynch, founder of Lynchburg, and other early leaders of community are buried in adjacent historic cemetery. Daily 9 a.m.-3 p.m.

WHERE TO STAY

★HOLIDAY INN EXPRESS LYNCHBURG

5600 Seminole Ave., Lynchburg, 434-237-7771, 877-834-3613; www.hiexpress.com

102 rooms. Complimentary breakfast. Fitness center. Pool. Pets accepted. $61-150

★★HOLIDAY INN SELECT LYNCHBURG

601 Main St., Lynchburg, 434-528-2500, 877-834-3613; www.hiselect.com/lynchburgva

241 rooms. Restaurant, bar. Business center. Fitness center. Pool. Pets accepted. $61-150

★★★KIRKLEY HOTEL AND CONFERENCE CENTER

2900 Candler's Mountain Road, Lynchburg, 434-237-6333, 866-510-6333;
www.kirkleyhotel.com

Located at the foot of the Blue Ridge Mountains, this hotel sits on a unique, 10-acre, landscaped and wooded spread. The Natural Bridge, which some say is one of the seven natural wonders of the world, is easily accessible. 168 rooms. Restaurant, bar. Business center. $61-150

WHERE TO EAT

★★★PORTERHOUSE RESTAURANT AND LOUNGE

126 Old Graves Mill Road, Lynchburg, 434-237-5655;
www.theporterhouserestaurant.com

The Porterhouse has been in business for 25 years, serving beef, lamb, chicken and seafood dishes, as well as pastries fresh from their in-house bakery. American. Dinner. Closed Sunday. Reservations recommended. Bar. $16-35

MANASSAS

See also Arlington County, Fairfax, Falls Church; also see Washington, D.C.

The Native Americans who had occupied this area for thousands of years were driven out under a treaty in 1722. Afterwards, settlement remained concentrated along the Potomac River until the coming of the railroad in 1858. The Manassas rail junction was vital to the South, and many troops were stationed along this line of communication. Control of this junction led to two major battles nearby.

WHAT TO SEE
THE MANASSAS MUSEUM

9101 Prince William St., Manassas, 703-368-1873; www.manassascity.org

This museum features collections dealing with Northern Virginia Piedmont history from prehistoric to modern times, with emphasis on Civil War. Admission: adults $4, seniors and children $3, children 5 and under free. Tuesday-Sunday 10 a.m.-5 p.m.

MANASSAS (BULL RUN) NATIONAL BATTLEFIELD PARK

6511 Sudley Road, Manassas (Bull Run) National Battlefield Park, 703-361-1339; www.nps.gov/mana

This 5,000-acre park was the scene of two major Civil War battles. More than 26,000 men were killed or wounded here in struggles for control of a strategically important railroad junction. The war's first major land battle was fought here on July 21, 1861, between poorly trained volunteer troops from both the North and South. The battle finally evolved into a struggle for Henry Hill, where "Stonewall" Jackson earned his nickname. With the outcome in doubt, Confederate reinforcements arrived by railroad from the Shenandoah Valley and turned the battle into a rout. Thirteen months later (August 28-30, 1862) in the second battle of Manassas, General Robert E. Lee outmaneuvered and defeated Union General John Pope and cleared the way for a Confederate invasion of Maryland. While here, be sure to check out the Battlefield Musuem, which has exhibits that reflect incidents of battles. The Chin House Ruins was where the house served as a field hospital in both engagements and marked the left of the Confederate line at First Manassas; it was also the scene of Longstreet's counterattack at Second Manassas. The Stone Bridge is where Union artillery opened the Battle of First Manassas; it afforded an avenue of escape for the Union troops after both First and Second Manassas. Stop in the Visitor Center to pick up information on self-guided tours and more.

Park: Daily dawn-dusk. Visitor center: Daily 8:30 a.m.-5 p.m.

SPECIAL EVENT
PRINCE WILLIAM COUNTY FAIR
9101 Prince William St., Manassas, 703-368-0173; www.pwcfair.com
This annual fair features a carnival, entertainment, tractor pull, exhibits, contests, food and much more.
Mid-August.

WHERE TO STAY
★★FOUR POINTS BY SHERATON MANASSAS BATTLEFIELD
10800 Vandor Lane, Manassas, 703-335-0000; www.starwoodhotels.com
158 rooms. Restaurant, bar. Complimentary breakfast. Business center. Fitness center. Pool. $61-150

★★★POPLAR SPRINGS
9245 Rogues Road, Casanova, 540-788-4600, 800-490-7747;
www.poplarspringsinn.com
This pretty inn is a lovely country getaway. Rooms are kitted out in colonial-style fur-nishings, but in case you don't want to enjoy lounging around in plush robes or sleeping under luxe duvets, then take a calming walk around the 200 acres.
21 rooms. Complimentary breakfast. Restaurant, bar. Fitness center. Pool. Spa. Tennis. $251-350

WHERE TO EAT
★★★CARMELLO'S AND LITTLE PORTUGAL
9108 Center St., Manassas, 703-368-5522; www.carmellos.com
At Carmello's and Little Portugal, Italian and Portuguese cuisines are beautifully combined to create generous contemporary dishes. The restaurant's intimate atmosphere makes it a popular spot to celebrate special occasions.
Italian, Spanish. Lunch (Monday-Friday), dinner. Bar. $16-35

★★MACKEY'S AMERICAN PUB
9412 Main St., Manassas, 703-330-1534; www.jakesofmanassas.com
American. Lunch, dinner. Outdoor seating. Bar. $16-35

★★★PALM COURT
Marriott Westfields Washington Dulles, 14750 Conference Center Drive, Chantilly,
703-818-3520; www.westfieldspalmcourt.com
Housed in the Marriott Westfields Resort, this restaurant's menu is a throwback to the days of tableside dining. The buffet-style Sunday brunch is an extravaganza with tuxedo-clad waiters, mimosas and an array of sweets.
American. Breakfast (Saturday-Sunday), lunch (Monday-Saturday), dinner (Tuesday-Saturday), Sunday brunch. Children's menu. Reservations recommended. Bar. $36-85

★★★PANINO
9116 Mathis Ave., Manassas, 703-335-2566
Although off the beaten path, this chef-owned and operated restaurant has for the past decade offered perhaps the best regional Italian cuisine outside the Beltway. Only the freshest ingredients are used.

Italian. Lunch (Monday-Friday), dinner. Closed Sunday. Reservations recommended. $16-35

MCLEAN

See also Arlington County, Fairfax, Falls Church; also see Washington, D.C. and Rockville, MD

Located in Fairfax County, McLean was named after John Roll McLean, who once was the publisher and owner of *The Washington Post*. Other important political figures and large companies are located here. Also near Great Falls, you'll find natural beauty and plenty of attractions.

WHAT TO SEE
CLAUDE MOORE COLONIAL FARM

6310 Georgetown Pike, McLean, 703-442-7557; www.1771.org

This colonial farm features demonstrations of a 1770s low-income working farm as costumed interpreters work with crops and animals using 18th-century techniques.

Admission: adults $3, seniors and children 3-12 $2.

April-mid-December, Wednesday-Sunday 10 a.m.-4.30 p.m.

COLVIN RUN MILL HISTORIC SITE

10017 Colvin Run Road, Great Falls, 703-759-2771; www.fairfaxcounty.gov

Take a tour of this historical gristmill as it operated in the 19th century. There's also the Colvin Run Mill General Store, which still operates today, selling old-fashioned items including penny candy. Miller's House also displays an exhibit about milling, and there's a barn and grounds to explore.

Admission (to park): Free. March-December, Wednesday-Monday 11 a.m.-5 p.m.; January-February, Wednesday-Monday 11 a.m.-4 p.m. Tours: adults $6, students $5, seniors and children 15 and under $4

GREAT FALLS PARK

George Washington Memorial Parkway, McLean, 703-285-2965, 703-285-2513; www.nps.gov/grfa

Spectacular natural beauty only 15 miles from the nation's capital at Great Falls Park, where the usually peaceful Potomac River narrows into a series of dramatically cascading rapids and 20-foot waterfalls before heading through Mather Gorge. Enjoy the view from a scenic overlook and then explore some of the park's 15 miles of trails, which take you past the remains of the Patowmack Canal, part of an 18th-century engineering project backed by George Washington, among others.

Park: Daily 7 a.m.-dusk. Visitor center: Daily 10 a.m.-4 p.m.

TYSONS CORNER CENTER

1961 Chain Bridge Road, McLean, 703-893-9400; www.shoptysons.com

Tyson Corners features more than 300 stores and restaurants, including Nordstrom, Bloomingdale's and Lord & Taylor.

Monday-Saturday 10 a.m.-9:30 p.m., Sunday 11 a.m.-7 p.m.

WHERE TO STAY
★★CROWNE PLAZA
1960 Chain Bridge Road, McLean, 703-893-2100; www.cptysonscorner.com
312 rooms. Restaurant, bar. Business center. Fitness center. Pool. $151-250

★★★HILTON MCLEAN TYSONS CORNER
7920 Jones Branch Drive, McLean, 703-847-5000, 800-445-8667;
www.mclean.hilton.com
Located close to the famous shopping area of Tyson Corners, this atrium-style hotel offers comfortable rooms, local shuttle service, a gift shop and live jazz Thursday-Saturday evenings.
458 rooms. Restaurant, bar. Business center. Fitness center. Pool. Pets accepted. $151-250

★★★★THE RITZ-CARLTON, TYSONS CORNER
1700 Tysons Blvd., McLean, 703-506-4300, 800-241-3333; www.ritzcarlton.com
Only 15 miles from Washington, D.C., this northern Virginia hotel is a luxurious retreat from the bustle of the city center. Guest rooms feature luxurious fabrics, flatscreen TVs and down duvet-covered beds. The Ritz-Carlton Day Spa offers unique treatments such as coffee anti-cellulite wrap—you'll get a buzz just thinking about it—and the bamboo lemongrass body scrub. Opt for a Club Level room for extra amenities including a private lounge with complimentary snacks throughout the day and concierge service. The adjacent Tysons Galleria and Tysons Mall have more than 300 shops and a movie theater.
398 rooms. Restaurant, bar. Business center. Fitness center. Pool. Spa. Pets accepted. $351 and up.

WHERE TO EAT
★★CAFÉ OGGI
6671 Old Dominion Drive, McLean, 703-442-7360; www.cafeoggi.com
Italian. Lunch, dinner. Reservations recommended. $16-35

★★CAFÉ TAJ
1379 Beverly Road, McLean, 703-827-0444; www.mycafetaj.com
Indian. Lunch (Monday-Saturday), dinner Outdoor seating. $16-35

★★DA DOMENICO
1992 Chain Bridge Road, McLean, 703-790-9000; www.da-domenico.com
Italian. Lunch (Monday-Sunday), dinner. Closed Sunday. Reservations recommended. Bar. $16-35

★★★DANTE RISTORANTE
1148 Walker Road, Great Falls, 703-759-3131; www.danterestaurant.com
A historic Victorian home (previously a dairy farm and "lying-in" hospital) is the setting for this romantic restaurant. There are several small dining areas, each with its own unique décor, but all are charming—one room even has an entire wall displaying wine bottles. The authentic northern Italian menu offers items such as rabbit legs, osso buco and homemade ravioli. Don't leave

without trying the layered chocolate cake (filled with a chocolate mousse) with a cup of espresso.

Italian. Lunch (Monday-Friday), dinner. Closed Sunday. Reservations recommended. Outdoor seating. Bar. $36-85

★★★FIORE DI LUNA
1025-I Seneca Road, Great Falls, 703-444-4060; www.fiorediluna.com

Fiore di Luna is a simple but elegant Northern Italian restaurant, serving dishes such as butternut squash gnocchi with a robiola cheese sauce, julienne celery, amaretti cookies and parmesan cheese or Grimaud farm-raised Muscovy duck breast with baby green and red Brussels sprouts, white polenta timbale and parsley purée.

Italian. Lunch (Tuesday-Friday), dinner. Closed Monday. Reservations recommended. Outdoor seating. Bar. $36-85

★★J GILBERT'S STEAKHOUSE
6930 Old Dominion Drive, McLean, 703-893-1034; www.jgilberts.com

American. Lunch (Monday-Saturday), dinner, Sunday brunch. Outdoor seating. Bar. $16-35

★★J.R.'S STOCKYARDS INN
8130 Watson St., McLean, 703-893-3390, 703-893-0546; www.jrsbeef.com

American. Lunch (Monday-Friday), dinner. Reservations recommended. Bar. $16-35

★★KAZAN
6813 Redmond Drive, McLean, 703-734-1960; www.kazanrestaurant.com

Middle Eastern. Lunch (Monday-Friday), dinner. Closed Sunday. $16-35

★★★L'AUBERGE CHEZ FRANCOIS
332 Springvale Road, Great Falls, 703-759-3800; www.laubergechezfrancois.com

Rich, hearty dishes at this Alsatian-themed restaurant are served by dirndl-clad waitresses and waiters in red vests with gold buttons. Located outside the Great Falls area, this charming farmhouse restaurant is set along a winding, two-lane road. Outside, it is surrounded by flowers and an herb garden, a gazebo and fountains on the terrace. The inside is cozy with wood beams, wood burning fireplaces and stained glass panels. The Haeringer family focuses on traditional Alsatian French cuisine and offers a prix fixe menu.

French. Lunch (Tuesday-Friday), dinner. Closed Monday. Children's menu. Reservations recommended. Outdoor seating. $36-85

★★PULCINELLA
6852 Old Dominion Drive, McLean, 703-893-7777; www.pulcinellarestaurant.com

Italian. Lunch, dinner. Bar. $16-35

★★★SERBIAN CROWN
1141 Walker Road, Great Falls, 703-759-4150; www.serbiancrown.com

Russian and French cuisines are fearlessly combined to create an elegant menu at this special-occasion restaurant. Beef stroganoff, stuffed cabbage rolls, marinated wild boar, and duck braised in sauerkraut are just a few of the items that keep diners coming back for more. Various live entertainments such as a violinist, Gypsy music and a piano bar add to the ambience. French, Russian. Lunch (Wednesday-Friday), dinner, late-night. Closed Monday. Reservations recommended. Bar. $36-85

★★TACHIBANA
6715 Lowell Ave., McLean, 703-847-1771; www.j-netusa.com/com/tachibana
Japanese. Lunch, dinner. $36-85

MOUNT VERNON
See also Alexandria, Fairfax, Springfield; also see Washington, D.C.
This historic state is open 365 days a year and is the most popular historic estate in the U.S. as it was once the home of George and Martha Washington.

WHAT TO SEE
FRANK LLOYD WRIGHT'S POPE-LEIGHEY HOUSE
9000 Richmond Highway, Mount Vernon, 703-780-4000;
www.nationaltrust.org/woodlawn
Erected in Falls Church in 1940, the house was disassembled due to the construction of a new highway and rebuilt at the present site in 1964, at Woodlawn. Built of cypress, brick and glass, the house is an example of Wright's "Usonian" structures, which he proposed as a prototype of affordable housing for Depression-era middle-income families. .
Admission: adults $8.50, children $4. April-December, Thursday-Monday 10 a.m.-5 p.m. Combination ticket for both houses available.

MOUNT VERNON
George Washington Parkway, Mount Vernon, 703-780-2000; www.mountvernon.org
Touring Mount Vernon, George Washington's home for more than 45 years, gives visitors a fascinating glimpse of the world of landed gentry in 18th-century America, as well as the personal vision of the first U.S. president. Washington designed sections of the beautifully landscaped grounds himself, incorporating woods, meadows and serpentine walkways. He also added the red-roofed mansion's cupola, weathervane and two-story piazza, from which guests can enjoy an awe-inspiring view of the Potomac River. Explore the working areas of the estate, an audio tour describes the lives of some of the more than 300 slaves who lived and worked there. Also, visit the gristmill which was reconstructed in 1930 on the original foundation of a mill George Washington operated on the Dogue Run. The house has been restored to its appearance in 1799, the year Washington died. He is buried on the estate with his wife, Martha.
Admission: adults $15, seniors $14, children 6-11 $7, children 5 and under free. April-August, Daily 8 a.m.-5 p.m.; March, September-October, Daily 9 a.m.-5 p.m.; November-February, Daily 9 a.m.-4 p.m.

WHERE TO EAT
★★MOUNT VERNON INN RESTAURANT
On the Grounds of Mount Vernon, Mount Vernon, 703-780-0011;
www.mountvernon.org
American. Lunch, dinner. Children's menu. Bar. $16-35

NEW MARKET

See also Harrisonburg

New Market, situated in the Shenandoah Valley, gained its niche in Virginia history on May 15, 1864, when, in desperation, Confederate General Breckinridge ordered the cadets from Lexington's Virginia Military Institute to join the battle against the forces of General Franz Sigel. The oldest was just 20, but they entered the fray fearlessly, taking prisoners and capturing a battery. Their heroism inspired the Confederate defeat of Sigel's seasoned troops.

WHAT TO SEE

ENDLESS CAVERNS

1800 Endless Caverns Road, New Market, 540-896-2283, 800-544-2283;
www.endlesscaverns.com

Visit these caverns to see lighted display of unusual rock formations including stalagmites and stalactites, columns, shields, flowstone and limestone pendants, all presented in natural color. The temperature remains at 55 F in the caves in the summer and winter. Camping is available abone their year round campground.

Admission: adults $16, children 4-12 $8. Daily.

HALL OF VALOR MUSEUM AT NEW MARKET BATTLEFIELD STATE HISTORICAL PARK

9500 George R. Collins Drive, New Market, 540-740-3101; www.vmi.edu/newmarket

Located on actual site of Battle of New Market, the museum houses a private collection of more than 2,000 military artifacts and genuine, personal artifacts of the American soldier from 1776 to the present. It includes uniforms, weapons, battlefield diaries, medals, mementos and a film. The museum shop has more than 500 titles, some antique among other things. Union and Confederate troop position markers are on museum grounds.

Admission: adults $10, seniors $9, children 6-12 $6, children 5 and under free. Daily 9 a.m.-5 p.m.

NEW MARKET BATTLEFIELD STATE HISTORICAL PARK

8895 Collins Drive, New Market, 540-740-3101, 866-515-1864;
www.vmi.edu/newmarket

Site of Civil War Battle of New Market (May 15, 1864), in which 257 Virginia Military Institute cadets played a decisive role. The original Bushong farmhouse and outbuildings have been restored and they have period furnishings. The Hall of Valor Civil War Museum is also here with exhibits and films. There are also scenic overlooks and walking tours.

Admission: adults $10, seniors $9, children 6-17 $6, children 5 and under free. Daily 9 a.m.-5 p.m.

SHENANDOAH CAVERNS

261 Caverns Road, New Market, 540-477-3115, 888-422-8376;
www.shenandoahcaverns.com

An elevator lowers visitors 60 feet underground to large subterranean rooms filled with fascinating rock formations. The caverns stay at a constant 54° F (so bring a sweatshirt to stay warm). There's also a café here with an original 1957 soda fountain. So you can grab a burger and a milkshake or homemade cherry coke after exploring the caverns.

Admission: adults $22, seniors $20, children 6-14 $10, children 5 and under free. Tour times vary; see Web site for information.

WHERE TO STAY
★★SHENVALEE GOLF RESORT
9660 Fairway Drive, New Market, 540-740-3181, 888-339-3181; www.shenvalee.com
42 rooms. Restaurant. Pool. Golf. $61-150

NEWPORT NEWS
See also Hampton, Jamestown, Portsmouth, Virginia Beach, Yorktown
One of the three cities that make up the Port of Hampton Roads, Newport News has the world's largest shipbuilding company, Newport News Shipbuilding. During the two World Wars it was a vitally important point of embarkation and supply. The area still has many important defense establishments.

Newport News is located on the historic Virginia Peninsula between Williamsburg and Virginia Beach. The peninsula also contains Hampton, Yorktown and Jamestown, and it hosted some of the earliest landings in this country. The name "Newport News" is said to derive from the good "news" of the arrival of Captain Christopher Newport, who brought supplies and additional colonists to the settlement at Jamestown.

WHAT TO SEE
HISTORIC HILTON VILLAGE
Warwick Boulevard and Main Street, Newport News; www.shophiltonvillage.com
Listed on the National Register of Historic Places, this village was built between 1918 and 1920 as a way to house workers during wartime at Newport News Shipbuilding. This architecturally significant neighborhood features 500 English cottage-style homes, restaurants and antique and specialty shops.

MARINERS' MUSEUM
100 Museum Drive, Newport News, 757-596-2222; www.mariner.org
Exhibits and displays represent international nautical history; ship models, figureheads, scrimshaw, paintings, decorative arts and small craft. The Age of Exploration Gallery chronicles advancements in shipbuilding, ocean navigation and cartography that led to early transoceanic exploration. The Chesapeake Bay Gallery exhibits Native American artifacts, workboats, racing shells, multimedia exhibits, a working steam engine and hundreds of artifacts and photos that tell the story of this body of water. There are also historical interpreters, a research library and a museum shop. A 550-acre park on the James River features five-mile Noland Trail with 14 pedestrian bridges and a picnic area.

Admission: adults $14, students and military personnel $13, seniors $12, children 6-12 $8, children 5 and under free. Monday-Saturday 10 a.m.-5 p.m., Sunday noon-5 p.m.

NEWPORT NEWS PARK

13564 Jefferson Ave., Newport News, 757-886-7912, 800-203-8322;
www.nnparks.com

Facilities in this 8,000-acre park include freshwater fishing, canoes and paddleboats rentals along with roaming wildlife including deer, fox and raccoons to otters and beavers. There are history and nature trails, bicycle paths (along with bicycle rentals), archery range, playgrounds, an arboretum, disc golf course, a discovery center, picnicking areas, and 188 campsites.
Daily dawn-dusk.

PENINSULA FINE ARTS CENTER

101 Museum Drive, Newport News, 757-596-8175; www.pfac-va.org

Changing bimonthly exhibits ranging from national traveling exhibitions to regional artists at this arts center. There are also classes, workshops and special events. And there's a children's hands-on activity area as well as a museum shop.
Admission: adults $7.50, seniors, military personnel, students and teachers $6, children 6-12 $4, children 5 and under free. Tuesday-Saturday 10 a.m.-5 p.m. Sunday 1-5 p.m. Tuesday 5:30-8 p.m. free.

US ARMY TRANSPORTATION MUSEUM

300 Washington Blvd., Besson Hall, Fort Eustis, 757-878-1115, 888-493-7386;
www.transchool.eustis.army.mil/museum

This museum has displays that depicts development of Army transportation from 1776 to the present including amphibious vehicles, trucks, helicopters and more. There is also a gift shop onsite.
Admission: Free. Tuesday-Sunday 9 a.m.-4:30 p.m.

VIRGINIA LIVING MUSEUM

524 J. Clyde Morris Blvd., Newport News, 757-595-1900; www.thevlm.org

This museum features exhibits on natural science from native Virginia including wildlife living in natural habitats, indoor and outdoor aviaries, aquariums and wildflower gardens. Also here is the Abbit Planetarium and Observatory, a children's hands-on Discovery Center, and a café to grab a bite after exploring exhibits.
Admission: adults $15, children $12. Memorial Day-Labor Day, daily 9 a.m.-5 p.m.; Labor Day to Memorial Day, Monday-Saturday 9 a.m.-5 p.m., Sunday noon-5 p.m.

VIRGINIA WAR MUSEUM

9285 Warwick Blvd., Newport News, 757-247-8523; www.warmuseum.org

More than 60,000 artifacts, including weapons, uniforms, vehicles, posters, insignias and accoutrements relating to every major U.S. military involvement from the Revolutionary War to the Vietnam War. Military history library and film collection. Tours and educational programs are available.
Admission: adults $6, seniors $5, children $4, children under 3 and under free. Monday-Saturday 9 a.m.-5 p.m., Sunday 1-5 p.m.

WHERE TO STAY
★COMFORT INN
12330 Jefferson Ave., Newport News, 757-249-0200, 877-424-6423;
www.newportnewscomfort.com
124 rooms. Complimentary breakfast. Pool. Pets accepted. $61-150

★HAMPTON INN & SUITES NEWPORT NEWS
12251 Jefferson Ave., Newport News, 757-249-0001, 800-426-7866;
www.hamptoninn.com
120 rooms. Complimentary breakfast. Business center. Fitness center. Pool.
$61-150

★★★OMNI NEWPORT NEWS HOTEL
1000 Omni Blvd., Newport News, 757-873-6664, 800-843-6664; www.omnihotels.com
Located minutes from historic Williamsburg, this upscale suburban hotel is
located in the Newport News central business district. Relax in comfortable guest rooms which feature luxurious bedding, wireless Internet access,
a complimentary newpaper and a coffeemaker. There are numerous dining
options including Mitty's Ristorante which serves seafood and Italian fare.
182 rooms. Restaurant, bar. Business center. Fitness center. Pool. $61-150

WHERE TO EAT
★★AL FRESCO
11710 Jefferson Ave., Newport News, 757-873-0644;
www.alfrescoitalianrestaurant.com
Italian. Lunch (Monday-Friday), dinner. Closed Sunday. Children's menu.
Reservations recommended. Outdoor seating. Bar. $151-250

★★DAS WALDCAFE
12529 Warwick Blvd., Newport News, 757-930-1781
German. Lunch, dinner. Closed Monday-Tuesday. Reservations recommended. Bar. $61-150

★★PORT ARTHUR
11137 Warwick Blvd., Newport News, 757-599-6474
Chinese. Lunch, dinner. Children's menu. $61-150

NORFOLK
See also Chesapeake, Hampton, Newport News
This city is part of the Port of Hampton Roads, with a bustling trade center
and many historic, cultural and resort areas nearby. Harbor tours depart from
Norfolk's downtown waterfront.

In 1682, the General Assembly purchased 50 acres on the Elizabeth River
from Nicholas Wise for "ten thousand pounds of tobacco and caske." By
1736, the town that developed was the largest in Virginia. On January 1,
1776, Norfolk was shelled by the British and later burned by the colonists to
prevent a British takeover. The battle between the Merrimac and the Monitor
in Hampton Roads in March 1862 was followed by the city's fall to Union
forces in May of that year. In 1883, the first shipment of coal to the port by

the Norfolk and Western Railway (now Norfolk Southern) began a new era of prosperity for the city.

Norfolk houses the largest naval facility in the world, and is headquarters for the United States Navy's Atlantic Fleet and NATO's Allied Command Atlantic. Norfolk has shipbuilding and ship-repair companies, consumer and industrial equipment manufacturers and food-processing plants. The city ships coal, tobacco, grain, seafood and vegetables. It is also the region's cultural center, home to the Virginia Opera, Virginia Symphony, Virginia Waterfront International Arts Festival and Virginia Stage Company.

Old Dominion University, Virginia Wesleyan College, Norfolk State University and Eastern Virginia Medical School are all located in Norfolk. Within a 50-mile radius are ocean, bay, river and marsh fishing, as well as hunting. Nearby, there are 25 miles of beaches. The 17.6-mile-long Chesapeake Bay Bridge-Tunnel between Norfolk and the Delmarva Peninsula opened in 1964.

WHAT TO SEE
AMERICAN ROVER
Norfolk, 757-627-7245; www.americanrover.com
This 135-foot, three-masted topsail passenger schooner cruises the "smooth waters" of Hampton Roads historical harbor; spacious sun decks, below-deck lounges, and concessions. The tour passes historic forts, merchant and U.S. Navy ships. Some tours pass the naval base.
Mid-April-October, 1 1/2- and 2-hour tours daily; see Web site for schedule and pricing.

CHRYSLER MUSEUM OF ART
245 W. Olney Road, Norfolk, 757-664-6200; www.chrysler.org
Art treasures representing nearly every important culture, civilization and historical period of the past 4,000 years can be found at this museum. There's a photography gallery, a fine collection of Tiffany decorative arts and glass, which includes the 8,000-piece Chrysler Institute of Glass.
Admission: adults $7, seniors, military personnel $5, children $18 and under free. Wednesday 10 a.m.-9 p.m., Thursday-Saturday 10 a.m.-5 p.m., Sunday 1-5 p.m.

GENERAL DOUGLAS MACARTHUR MEMORIAL
City Hall Avenue and Bank Street, Norfolk, 757-441-2965; www.macarthurmemorial.org
The museum is housed in the restored former city hall where MacArthur is buried in a large rotunda with his wife, which is surrounded by inscriptions banners, flags and more. Nine galleries contain memorabilia of his life and military career. There are three other buildings on MacArthur Square: a theater where a film biography is shown, a gift shop and the library/archives.
Admission: Free. Monday-Saturday 10 a.m.-5 p.m., Sunday 11 a.m.-5 p.m.

HAMPTON ROADS NAVAL MUSEUM
1 Waterside Drive, Norfolk, 757-322-2987; www.hrnm.navy.mil
This naval museum interprets the extensive naval history of the Hampton Roads area, including detailed ship models, period photographs, archaeo-

logical artifacts, and a superior collection of naval prints and artwork. Admission: Free. Memorial Day-Labor Day, daily 10 a.m.-5 p.m.; Labor Day-Memorial Day, Tuesday-Saturday 10 a.m.-5 p.m., Sunday noon-5 p.m.

HERMITAGE FOUNDATION MUSEUM

7637 N. Shore Road, Norfolk, 757-423-2052; www.hermitagefoundation.org
Take a guided tour of this fine arts museum located within a Tudor-style mansion. They have collections of tapestries, Chinese bronzes and jade and ancient glass.
Admission: adults $5, students, $4, children 6-18 $2, children 5 and under free. Monday-Tuesday, Thursday-Saturday 10 a.m.-5 p.m., Sunday 1-5 p.m.

HUNTER HOUSE VICTORIAN MUSEUM

240 W. Freemason St., Norfolk, 757-623-9814; www.hunterhousemuseum.org
Built in 1894 and rich in architectural details, the house contains the Hunter family's collection of Victorian furnishings and decorative pieces, including a Renaissance Revival bedchamber suite, a nursery with children's playthings, an inglenook, and stained-glass windows; lavish period reproduction floor and wall coverings, lighting fixtures and drapery. Also exhibited is a collection of early-20th-century medical memorabilia.
Tours begin every 30 minutes. April-December, Wednesday-Sunday 12:30-3:30 p.m. Admission: adults $5, seniors $4, children $1.

NAUTICUS-THE NATIONAL MARITIME CENTER

1 Waterside Drive, Norfolk, 757-664-1000, 800-664-1080; www.nauticus.org
This center interprets aspects from marine biology and ecology to exploration, trade and shipbuilding. Interactive computer exhibits allow visitors to navigate a simulated ocean voyage, design a model ship, pilot a virtual reality submarine, and view actual researchers at work in two working marine laboratories. Active U.S. Navy ships and scientific research vessels periodically moor at Nauticus and open to visitors. Also 350-seat, 70 mm widescreen theater; shark petting tank.
Admission: adult $10.95, seniors and military personnel $9.95, children 4-12 $8.50, children 3 and under free. Memorial Day-Labor Day, daily 10 a.m.-5 p.m.; Labor Day-Memorial Day, Tuesday-Saturday 10 a.m.-5 p.m.; Sunday noon-5 p.m.

NORFOLK BOTANICAL GARDEN

6700 Azalea Garden Road, Norfolk, 757-441-5830; www.norfolkbotanicalgarden.org
Azaleas, camellias, rhododendrons, roses (May-October), dogwoods and hollies on 155 acres. Japanese, Colonial, perennial and rose gardens; flowering arboretum; fragrance garden for the visually impaired; picnicking, restaurant and gift shop; tropical pavilion.
Admission: adults $7, seniors and military personnel $6, children 3-18 $5, children 2 and under free. April-mid-October, daily 9 a.m.-7 p.m.; mid-October-March, daily 9 a.m.-5 p.m. Children's Garden: mid-October-March, daily 9:30 a.m.-4:30 p.m.; April-mid-October, daily 9:30 a.m.-6:30 p.m.

SPIRIT OF NORFOLK

109 E. Main Road, Norfolk, 757-625-1748, 866-304-2469, 866-451-3866;
www.spiritofnorfolk.com

Enjoy a harbor cruise aboard a 600-passenger cruise ship. The captain's narration highlights the harbor's famous landmarks, including Waterside Festival Marketplace, Portsmouth Naval Hospital, Old Fort Norfolk, Blackbeard's hiding place, Norfolk Naval Base, and downtown area's dynamic skyline. There are lunch, midday and dinner cruises to choose from; see Web site for schedules and ticket information.

ST. PAUL'S EPISCOPAL CHURCH

201 St. Paul's Blvd., Norfolk, 757-627-4353; www.saintpaulsnorfolk.com

This is the only building to survive the burning of Norfolk in 1776.
Monday-Friday 9 a.m.-4 p.m. Services: Sunday 8 a.m., 10:30 a.m.

TOWN POINT PARK

120 W. Main St., Norfolk, 757-441-2345; www.festeventsva.org

Town Point Park is the home to Norfolk Festevents and hosts more than 100 free outdoor concerts, parties, dances, movies and festivals each year. The park covers seven acres and is located on the Elizabeth River making it the perfect spot to enjoy a lovely spring or summer evening.
April-October; see Web site for schedules and ticket information.

VIRGINIA ZOOLOGICAL PARK

3500 Granby St., Norfolk, 757-441-2374; www.virginiazoo.org

This combination of a zoo, park and conservatory features plenty of fun things to do for the whole family. The zoo houses more than 350 animals ranging from lion cubs to red pandas to meerkats. There's a zoo train, which takes you around the property and is narrated by the engineer. There's a playground, tennis courts, basketball courts, picnic areas, and concessions within the park.
Admission: adults $7, children 2-11 $5, seniors $6, children 2 and under free. Train rides: $2. Daily 10 a.m.-5 p.m.

WATERSIDE FESTIVAL MARKETPLACE

333 Waterside Drive, Norfolk, 757-627-3300; www.watersidemarketplace.com

A waterfront pavilion with more than 90 shops, restaurants, and bars. Bordering the Waterside are the city's marina and dock areas, where harbor tour vessels take on passengers.
Food Court: Monday-Saturday 11 a.m.-9 p.m., Sunday noon-6 p.m. Shops: Monday-Saturday 10 a.m.-9 p.m., Sunday noon-6 p.m.

SPECIAL EVENTS
HARBORFEST

Town Point Park, 120 W. Main St., Norfolk, 757-441-2345; www.festeventsva.org

This annual festival features sailboat and speedboat races, tall ships, ship tours, waterskiing, military demonstrations, live entertainment, wine tastings, fireworks and delicious seafood, corn on the cob, barbecue, and more. Fourth of July weekend.

NORFOLK INTERNATIONAL AZALEA FESTIVAL
220 Boush St., Downtown and Norfolk Botanical Garden, Norfolk, 757-282-2801; www.azaleafestival.org
This festival is a salute to NATO and includes a parade, coronation ceremony, air show (held at Norfolk Naval Air Station), events, concerts, a fair, a ball and live entertainment. Each year, they focus on one specific nation to celebrate. Late April-early May.

VIRGINIA ARTS FESTIVAL
220 Boush St., Norfolk, 757-282-2800; www.virginiaartsfest.com
This festival spans eighteen days of classical and contemporary music, dance, visual arts and theater performances.
Late April-mid-May.

VIRGINIA CHILDREN'S FESTIVAL
Town Point Park, 120 W. Main St., Norfolk, 757-441-2345; www.festeventsva.org
This festival benefits Sain Jude Children's Research Hospital with more than 200 educational, creative and interactive activities, entertainment and more. Early October.

WHERE TO STAY
★★BEST WESTERN CENTER INN
235 N. Military Highway, Norfolk, 757-461-6600, 800-237-5517; www.norfolkabvi.com
152 rooms. Restaurant, bar. Complimentary breakfast. Business center. Pool. $61-150

★BEST WESTERN HOLIDAY SANDS INN & SUITES
1330 E. Oceanview Ave., Norfolk, 757-583-2621, 800-525-5156; www.bestwestern.com
90 rooms. Complimentary breakfast. Business center. Fitness center. Pool. $61-150

★★★HILTON NORFOLK AIRPORT
1500 N. Military Highway, Norfolk, 757-466-8000, 800-445-8667; www.hilton.com
Conveniently located two miles from Norfolk International Airport, this hotel is ideal for those visiting the business district or military installations. 254 rooms. Restaurant, bar. Business center. Fitness center. Pool. Pets accepted. $151-250

★★★NORFOLK WATERSIDE MARRIOTT
235 E. Main St., Norfolk, 757-627-4200, 888-236-2427; www.marriott.com
In Norfolk's historic district, the Marriott Norfolk Waterside offers well-appointed guest rooms and dining options such as Shula's 347 Steakhouse.

405 rooms. Restaurant, bar. Fitness center. Pool. $151-250

★QUALITY INN NORFOLK NAVAL BASE
8051 Hampton Blvd., Norfolk, 757-451-0000, 877-424-6423; www.qualityinn.com
119 rooms. Complimentary breakfast. Pool. $61-150

★RAMADA NORFOLK AIRPORT
1450 N. Military Highway, Norfolk, 757-466-7474; www.ramada.com
130 rooms. Complimentary breakfast. Pool. $61-150

★★★SHERATON NORFOLK WATERSIDE HOTEL
777 Waterside Drive, Norfolk, 757-622-6664, 800-325-3535; www.sheraton.com
Adjacent to Waterside Marketplace on the Elizabeth River, this landmark hotel affords great views of the harbor and downtown skyline. 468 rooms. Restaurant, bar. Fitness center. Pool. $61-150

WHERE TO EAT
★★BAKER'S CRUST
330 W. 21st St., Norfolk, 757-625-3600; www.bakerscrust.com
American. Lunch, dinner. Children's menu. Outdoor seating. Bar. $16-35

★THE BANQUE
1849 E. Little Creek Road, Norfolk, 757-480-3600; www.thebanque.com
American. Dinner. Closed Sunday-Tuesday. Bar. $16-35

★FREEMASON ABBEY
209 W. Freemason St., Norfolk, 757-622-3966; www.freemasonabbey.com
American, seafood. Lunch (Monday-Saturday), dinner, Sunday brunch. Children's menu. Bar. $16-35

★★MONASTERY
443 Granby St., Norfolk, 757-625-8193
Czech, Eastern European. Dinner. Closed Monday. Bar. Reservations recommended. $16-35

PETERSBURG
See also Petersburg National Battlefield, Richmond
This city, Lee's last stand before Appomattox (1864-1865), was settled in 1645 when the General Assembly authorized construction of Fort Henry at the falls of the Appomattox River. In 1784, three separate towns united to become the single city of Petersburg. Between the Revolutionary War and Civil War, the town was a popular stopping place with a social life that for a time eclipsed that of Richmond.

Physically untouched during the early years of the Civil War (though the town sent 17 companies to the front), Petersburg in 1864 was the scene of Lee's final struggle against Grant. In April 1865, when Lee's supply routes were finally cut and he was forced to evacuate the city, the Confederacy collapsed. A week later Lee surrendered at Appomattox.

The shattered city made a new start after the war, showing amazing recuperative powers. Petersburg added 20 more industries in 20 years, between 1850 and 1870. Today, besides being a storehouse of colonial and Civil War history, Petersburg is a thriving industrial city.

WHAT TO SEE
BLANDFORD CHURCH AND CEMETERY
111 Rochelle Lane, Petersburg, 804-733-2396; www.petersburg-va.org/tourism
The church was built in 1735 and was left abandoned in 1806. In 1901, it was restored as a memorial to the Confederacy and has 15 Tiffany stained-glass windows. The oldest marked grave in the adjacent cemetery is from 1702. Admission: adults $5, seniors, military personnel, children 7-12 $4, children 6 and under free. Daily 10 a.m.-5 p.m.

CENTRE HILL MANSION
1 Centre Hill Court, Petersburg, 804-733-2401; www.petersburg-va.org/tourism
Built in 1823, this Federalist mansion was visited by Presidents Tyler, Lincoln and Taft. It's furnished with chandeliers, finely detailed carvings, antiques, and an 1886 Knabe Art grand piano with hollywood inlaid on rosewood. Admission: adults $5, seniors, military personnel and children 7-12 $4, children 6 and under free. Daily 10 a.m.-5 p.m.

FORT LEE
This was the army training center in World War I and World War II. It is now the site of the Quartermaster Corps, U.S. Army Quartermaster Museum and the U.S. Army Women's Museum.

LEE MEMORIAL PARK
1832 Johnson Road, Petersburg, 804-733-2394
Facilities of this 864-acre park include a lake where visitors can go fishing; game fields and courts and a picnic area.
Daily; lake facilities closed mid-October-mid-April.

LEE'S RETREAT
Petersburg Visitors Center, 425 Cockade Alley, Petersburg, 800-673-8732;
www.varetreat.com
This 98-mile driving tour follows the route of General Robert E. Lee's retreat from Petersburg to Appomattox. There are roadside pull-overs, signs and audio interpretation at important Civil War sites.
Visitor center: Daily 9 a.m.-5 p.m.

NATIONAL MUSEUM OF THE CIVIL WAR SOLDIER
6125 Boydton Plank Road, Petersburg, 804-861-2408, 877-726-7546;
www.pamplinpark.org
With an exhibit on the Civil War's common soldier, this is one of the country's largest Civil War bookshops. There is also a restaurant.

PAMPLIN PARK CIVIL WAR SITE
6125 Boydton Plank Road, Petersburg, 804-861-2408; www.pamplinpark.org
This is the site of General Ulysses S. Grant's decisive victory over Confederate forces in 1865. This 422-acre park includes battle trails, reconstructed sol-

dier huts, and a plantation home. There is an interpretive Center and museum. Admission: adults $10, children 6-12 $5, children 5 and under free. Daily 9 a.m.-5 p.m.

PETERSBURG NATIONAL BATTLEFIELD

5001 Siege Road, Petersburg, 804-732-3531; www.nps.gov/pete

At the price of 70,000 Union and Confederate casualties, the campaign that spelled doom for the Confederacy occurred in a huge, 40-mile semicircle around Richmond and Petersburg. After his unsuccessful attempt to take Richmond by frontal assault (at Cold Harbor, June 3, 1864), General Grant withdrew and attacked Petersburg. After four days of fighting and failing to capture the city, Grant decided to lay siege. Petersburg was the rail center that funneled supplies to Lee and Richmond. The siege lasted 10 months, from June 15, 1864, to April 2, 1865, with the two armies in almost constant contact. When Petersburg finally fell, Lee's surrender was only a week away. The park, at more than 2,700 acres, preserves Union and Confederate fortifications, trenches and gun pits. See the Crater, a hole remaining after Union troops tunneled beneath Confederate artillery position and exploded four tons of powder in 1864.

Daily 9 am.-5 p.m.

SIEGE MUSEUM

15 W. Bank St., Petersburg, 804-733-2404; www.petersburg-va.org/tourism

This Greek Revival building houses exhibits describing the 10-month Civil War siege of Petersburg. The film *The Echoes Still Remain*, with Joseph Cotten, is shown every hour on the hour.

Admission: adults $5, seniors, military personnel and children 7-12 $4, children 6 and under free. Daily 10 a.m.-5 p.m.

★★★★★ VIRGINIA

TRAPEZIUM HOUSE

299

Market and High Street, Petersburg, 804-733-2400; www.virginia.org

This house was built in 1817 by eccentric Irish bachelor Charles O'Hara in the form of a trapezium with no right angles and no parallel sides. O'Hara is said to have believed the superstitions of his West Indian servant, who thought that ghosts and evil spirits inhabited right angles. Because this house is privately owned, it is only open during events.

U.S. ARMY QUARTERMASTER MUSEUM

1201 22nd St., Fort Lee, 804-734-4203; www.qmmuseum.lee.army.mil

This museum displays uniforms, flags, weapons and equestrian equipment from 200 years of military service.

Admission: Free. Tuesday-Friday 10 a.m.-5 p.m., Saturday-Sunday 11 a.m.-5 p.m.

WHERE TO STAY

★★COMFORT INN PRINCE GEORGE

5380 Oaklawn Blvd., Prince George, 804-452-0022; www.comfortinn.com

190 rooms. Restaurant, bar. Complimentary breakfast. Fitness center. Pool. $151-250

★DAYS INN PETERSBURG-FORT LEE/SOUTH

12208 S. Crater Road, Petersburg, 804-733-4400, 800-329-7466; www.daysinn.com
155 rooms. Complimentary breakfast. Restaurant. Fitness center. Pool. Pets accepted. $61-150

★★HOWARD JOHNSON INN PETERSBURG

12205 S. Crater Road, Petersburg, 804-733-0600, 800-446-4656; www.hojo.com
137 rooms. Complimentary breakfast. Pool. -Pets accepted. Tennis. $61-150

WHERE TO EAT
★ALEXANDER'S

101 W. Bank St., Petersburg, 804-733-7134
Greek, Italian. Breakfast, lunch, dinner. Closed Saturday. Children's menu. $16-35

PORTSMOUTH

See also Chesapeake, Hampton, Newport News, Norfolk, Virginia Beach
Connected to Norfolk by two bridge tunnels and a pedestrian ferry that cross the Elizabeth River, Portsmouth is part of the great Hampton Roads port, unrivaled for commercial shipping and shipbuilding activity. It is also the headquarters of the United States Coast Guard Atlantic Fleet.

In Gosport, long a part of Portsmouth, Scotsman Andrew Sprowle built a marine yard in 1767 that became a British naval repair station and after the Revolutionary War, a federal navy yard. Now called the Norfolk Naval Shipyard, it is the largest naval shipyard in the world. The *Chesapeake*, sister of the *USS Constitution* and one of the U.S. Navy's first warships, was built here. So was the *Merrimac*, which was seized by the Confederates, changed into an ironclad in 1861, and rechristened the *CSS Virginia*. The oldest dry dock here is still in use.

WHAT TO SEE
CHILDREN'S MUSEUM OF VIRGINIA

221 High St., Portsmouth, 757-393-5258; www.childrensmuseumva.com
This museum for children features more than 60 interactive activities in 15 areas including a planetarium.
Admission: adults and children 2-18 $6, children under 2 free. Tuesday-Saturday 9 a.m.-5 p.m., Sunday 11 a.m.-5 p.m.

COURTHOUSE GALLERIES

420 High St., Portsmouth, 757-393-8543; www.courthousegalleries.com
These galleries feature changing exhibits as well as provide lectures, classes, performances and other special events within an 1846 courthouse.
Admission: adults $5, children 2-17 $2, children under 2 free. Memorial Day-Labor Day, Tuesday-Saturday 10 a.m.-5 p.m., Sunday 1-5 p.m.; Labor Day-Memorial Day, Wednesday-Saturday 10 a.m.-5 p.m., Sunday 1-5 p.m.

HILL HOUSE

221 N. St., Portsmouth, 757-393-0241; www.portsmouthva.gov
Headquarters of the Portsmouth Historical Association. Built in early 1820s,

this four-story English basement-style (with a raised basement) house contains original furnishings collected by generations of the Hill family. In near-original condition, the house has undergone only limited renovation through the years. and the garden has been restored.
April-December, Wednesday 12:30-4:30 p.m., Sunday 1-5 p.m.

HISTORIC HOUSES
6 Crawford Parkway, Portsmouth, 757-393-5111
Portsmouth has over 300 years of history represented by more than 20 examples of colonial, Federal-style and antebellum houses. Among them is the circa 1730-50 Nivison-Ball House, 417 Middle St., where Andrew Jackson and General Lafayette were entertained. These houses are private and may be viewed only from the exterior. Obtain Olde Towne Portsmouth walking tour brochures with map and descriptions of churches, homes and old buildings from the Visitor Center (*6 Crawford Parkway; 757-393-5111*).

LIGHTSHIP PORTSMOUTH MUSEUM
London Slip and Water Street, Portsmouth, 757-393-8591;
www.portsnavalmuseums.com
Built in 1915, commissioned in 1916 as "Lightship 101," it served 48 years in Virginia, Delaware and Massachusetts. It was retired in 1964 and renamed *Portsmouth*. See artifacts and more aboard this ship which is now a museum.
Admission: adults $3, children 2-17 $1, children under 2 free. Memorial Day-Labor Day, Saturday 10 a.m.-5 p.m., Sunday 1-5 p.m.; Labor Day-Memorial Day, Wednesday-Saturday 10 a.m.-5 p.m., Sunday 1-5 p.m.

★★★★★ **VIRGINIA**

NAVAL SHIPYARD MUSEUM
Second High St., Portsmouth, 757-393-8591; www.portsnavalmuseums.com
This shipyard museum features thousands of items of naval equipment, plus flags, uniforms, prints, maps and models, including models of the *CSS Virginia*; the U.S. Ship-of-the-line *Delaware*, which was built in Portsmouth; and the first ship drydocked in the U.S.

301

Admission: adults $3, children 2-17 $1, children under 2 free. Memorial Day-Labor Day, Saturday 10 a.m.-5 p.m., Sunday 1-5 p.m.; Labor Day-Memorial Day, Wednesday-Saturday 10 a.m.-5 p.m., Sunday 1-5 p.m.

TRINITY CHURCH
500 Court St., Portsmouth, 757-393-0431; www.trinityportsmouth.org
This is the oldest church building and parish in Portsmouth. Legend has it that the church bell cracked while ringing out news of Cornwallis' surrender; it was later recast. Many colonial patriots are buried here.
Monday-Friday, on request. Services: Sunday 8 a.m., 10:30 a.m., Tuesday 12:05 p.m.

WHERE TO STAY
★★★RENAISSANCE PORTSMOUTH HOTEL & WATERFRONT CONFERENCE CENTER
425 Water St., Portsmouth, 757-673-3000, 888-839-1775; www.marriott.com
249 rooms. Restaurant, bar. Business center. Fitness center. Pool. $61-150

WHERE TO EAT
★★CAFÉ EUROPA
319 High St., Portsmouth, 757-399-6652; www.portsmouthva.gov
Mediterranean. Lunch (Tuesday-Friday), dinner. Closed Sunday-Monday.
Reservations recommended. Outdoor seating. Bar. $36-85

RICHMOND
See also Petersburg, Tappahannock
Located at the falls of the James River, Richmond had to wait 170 years
before becoming the state capital. Four hundred years later, with a history
almost as old as Jamestown, the city blends its heritage with vibrant, contemporary commerce and trade. Its location, equidistant from the plantations
of Tidewater Virginia and the Piedmont of central Virginia, gives the city a
unique mix of heritage, culture and geography.

There have been few dull moments in Richmond's history. Native Americans and settlers fought over the ground on which it now stands. In 1775, Patrick Henry made his famous "liberty or death" speech in St. John's Church,
and in 1780, the city was named capital of the state. British soldiers plundered
it brutally during the Revolutionary War. And as the capital of the Confederacy from 1861 to 1865, it was constantly in danger. Finally, in 1865, the city
was evacuated and retreating Confederate soldiers burned the government
warehouse. A portion of the rest of the city also went up in flames. Richmond
survived, and it now proudly exemplifies the modern South: industrially ag-
gressive yet culturally aware, respectful of its own historical background yet
receptive to new trends in architecture and modes of living.

Tobacco, paper, aluminum, chemicals, textiles, printing, publishing and machinery contribute to the city's economy. Richmond is also an educational
hub; Virginia Commonwealth University, Virginia Union University and the
University of Richmond are based here.

WHAT TO SEE
17TH STREET FARMERS' MARKET
17th and Main Street, Richmond, 804-646-0477; www.17thstreetfarmersmarket.com
This farmers' market is built at the site of a Native American trading village
and features seasonal local produce, baked goods and homemade products.
April-early-December, Thursday 8:30 a.m.-4 p.m., Saturday-Sunday 9
a.m.-4 p.m.; also late May-early September, Friday 4-8 p.m.

AGECROFT HALL
4305 Sulgrave Road, Richmond, 804-353-4241; www.agecrofthall.com
This half-timbered Tudor manor built in the late 15th century near Man-
chester, England was disassembled, brought here and rebuilt during the late
1920s in a spacious setting of formal gardens and grassy terraces overlooking
the James River. It has English furnishings from 16th and 17th centuries.
Tuesday-Saturday, 10 a.m.-4 p.m., Sunday 12:30-5 p.m.

BILL "BOJANGLES" ROBINSON STATUE
Leigh and Adams streets, Richmond
This is a memorial to the famous dancer who was born at 915 N. Third St.

BLACK HISTORY MUSEUM AND CULTURAL CENTER

3 E. Clay St., Richmond, 804-780-9093; www.blackhistorymuseum.org

Founded in 1981, this museum is dedicated to commemorating the lives and accomplishments of Blacks in Virginia through displaying exhibits featuring limited editions, prints, art, photographs, memorabilia and more. There are collections from artists such as Sam Gilliam, John Biggers and P.H. Polk. Admission: adults $5, seniors, students and teachers $4, children 12 and under free. Tuesday-Saturday 10 a.m.-5 p.m.

CANAL CLUB

1545 E. Cary St., Richmond, 804-643-2582; www.thecanalclub.com

Catch live music, especially blues and rock, or shoot a game of pool in Shockoe Bottom. A bonus: there's an interesting menu at The Downstairs Lounge, which is the smaller room below the Canal Club upstairs. See Web site for schedules and tickets.

Downstairs Lounge: Wednesday-Sunday.

CANAL WALK

Enter at S. Fifth, Seventh, 14th, 15th, or 17th streets; 804-788-6466

The Canal Walk will take you 1 1/4 miles through downtown and features a pedestrian bridge to Brown's Island. You'll see historic monuments and more on your walk. If you want to take a canal boat ride or head to Brown's Island, Richmond Canal Cruisers (*804-649-2800; www.venturerichmond.com*) depart on the hour from noon to 7 p.m. Wednesday to Saturday and from noon to 5 p.m. on Sunday from the Turning Basin between 14th and Virginia streets. The schedule varies by season so call or visit the Web site for a complete schedule.

Brown's Island: Daily dawn-dusk.

CARYTOWN

West Cary Street, between Boulevard Street an Thompson Street, Richmond, 804-422-2279; www.carytown.org

More than 300 shops and restaurants in this area include quirky clothing boutiques, antique shops, the city's best music store and collectibles ranging from Christmas decorations to glass and dolls. It covers nine blocks so you'll find plenty of fun things to buy.

Monday-Saturday 10 a.m.-6 p.m.; some shops open on Sunday.

CHILDREN'S MUSEUM OF RICHMOND

2626 W. Broad St., Richmond, 804-474-7000, 877-295-2667; www.c-mor.org

A fun place for children to play and explore, this museum has a nice range of hands-on exhibits including the interactive James River Waterplay, which explores the hydrology and history of the James River.

Admission: adults $8, children under 1 free. Daily after 4 p.m. $4. Labor Day-Memorial Day, Tuesday-Saturday 9:30 a.m.-5 p.m., Sunday noon-5 p.m.; Memorial Day-Labor Day, Monday-Saturday 9:30 a.m.-5 p.m., Sunday noon-5 p.m.

CHURCH HILL HISTORIC AREA

Main and 21st streets, bounded by Broad, 29th, Main, and 21st streets,
East of Capitol Square, Richmond

This neighborhood is filled with 19th-century houses, more than 70 of which predate Civil War. Some Church Hill houses are open for viewing during Historic Garden Week. You'll also find Chimborazo Park, which is the site of the largest military hospital in the Civil War.

CITY HALL OBSERVATION DECK

901 E. Broad St., Richmond, 804-646-7000; www.richmondgov.com

The eighteenth-floor observation deck at city hall offers a panoramic view of the city, including the Capitol grounds, James River and Revolutionary and Civil War-era buildings contrasted with modern skyscrapers.
Admission: Free. Monday-Friday 8 a.m.-5 p.m.

CIVIL WAR VISITOR CENTER

490 Tredegar St., Richmond, 804-780-1865; www.tredegar.org

Begin your exploration of Richmond's Civil War heritage at the National Park Service Center at the restored Tredegar Iron Works near the James River. On the bottom floor, a continuously running film orients you to the 12 battlefields in the area. Park Service guides explain to kids how to fire the kind of cannon that Tredgar Iron Works made for the war.
Admission: adults $8, seniors and students $6, children 7-12 $2, children 6 and under free. Daily 9 a.m.-5 p.m.

EDGAR ALLAN POE MUSEUM

1914-1916 E. Main St., Richmond, 804-648-5523, 888-213-2763;
www.poemuseum.org

The Old Stone House portion is thought to be oldest structure in Richmond dating back to 1737. Three additional buildings house Poe mementos; James Carling illustrations of "The Raven;" and a scale model of the Richmond of Poe's time.
Admission: adults $6, seniors and students $5. Tuesday-Saturday 10 a.m.-5 p.m., Sunday 11 a.m.-5 p.m.

EQUESTRIAN STATUE OF WASHINGTON

Ninth and Grace streets, Richmond

Created by Thomas Crawford, this statue was cast in Munich over an 18-year period. The base features allegorical representations of six famous Revolutionary War figures from Virginia.

THE FAN DISTRICT AND MONUMENT AVENUE

Main and Belvidere streets, Richmond; www.fandistrict.org

Named for the layout of streets that fan out from Monroe Park toward the western part of town, this historic neighborhood has restored antebellum and turn-of-the-century houses, museums, shops, restaurants and famed Monument Avenue. The fashionable Boulevard, between Lombard and Belmont streets, is dotted with imposing statues of Generals Lee, Stuart and Jackson.

GOVERNOR'S MANSION

Ninth and Grace streets, Richmond, 804-371-8687; www.virginia.org

This two-story Federal-style house was built after the capital was moved from Williamsburg in 1813. It is the oldest governor's mansion in the U.S. still in use as a governor's residence.

Tours by appointment.

HISTORIC RICHMOND TOURS

1015 E. Clay St., Richmond, 804-649-0711; www.richmondhistorycenter.com

The Valentine Richmond History Center offers guided bus tours with pickup at the Visitor Center and major hotels; reservations required. They also provide guided walking tours.

Admission: bus tour, adults $23, children 6-18 $10, children 5 and under free; walking tour, $10. Walking tour: April-October. Bus tour: Monday-Saturday; see Web site for schedule.

HOLLYWOOD CEMETERY

412 S. Cherry St., Richmond, 804-648-8501; www.hollywoodcemetery.org

James Monroe, John Tyler, Jefferson Davis, and other notables and 18,000 Confederate soldiers are buried here. They offer an audiovisual program.

Daily 8 a.m.-5 p.m. Walking tour: April-October, Monday-Saturday 10 a.m.

JACKSON WARD

Broad and Belvidere streets, Richmond; www.richmondgov.com

This historic downtown neighborhood was home to many famous black Richmonders, including Bill "Bojangles" Robinson, Duke Ellington and others. Also, the Maggie Walker House is located here. It's where Maggie Walker, the nation's first woman bank president lived. The area has numerous 19th-century, Greek Revival and Victorian buildings with ornamental ironwork that rivals the wrought iron of New Orleans.

JAMES RIVER PARK

West 22nd Street and Riverside Drive, Richmond, 804-646-8911;
www.jamesriverpark.org

This urban park offers fishing, canoeing, swimming, rock-climbing, biking, walking and more. The James River also creates whitewater rapids, some safe enough for canoeing and rafting through the city. Daily.

JOHN MARSHALL HOUSE

818 E. Marshall St., Richmond, 804-648-7998; www.apva.org/marshall

The restored 1790 house of famous Supreme Court justice features original woodwork and paneling, family furnishings and mementos. There is a combination ticket available for Marshall House, Valentine Richmond History Center, Wickham House, and Monumental Church.

Admission: adults $8, seniors $7, students $6, children 6 and under free. March-October, Wednesday-Friday 11 a.m.-3 p.m., Saturday 10 a.m.-5 p.m., Sunday noon-5 p.m.; November-February, by appointment only.

JOSEPH BRYAN PARK

Bellevue Avenue and Hermitage Road, Richmond

A 279-acre park, 20 acres of which are an azalea garden with more than 55,000 plants is best viewed late April-mid-May. Picnic facilities and tennis courts are available as well as soccer fields, a fishing lake and more. Daily.

KANAWHA CANAL LOCKS

14th Street and Virginia Street, Richmond, 804-649-2800; www.venturerichmond.com

These impressive stone locks were part of the nation's first canal system, planned by George Washington.

MAGGIE L. WALKER NATIONAL HISTORIC SITE

110 1/2 E. Leigh St., Richmond, 804-771-2017; www.nps.gov/malw

This site commemorates the life and career of Maggie L. Walker, daughter of former slaves, who overcame great hardships to become successful in banking and insurance and was an early advocate for women's rights and racial equality. This two-story, red brick house was home to her family from 1904 to 1934. Head to the visitor center first (*600 N. Second St.*) and watch a film on Walker's life and take a guided tour (leaving from the visitor center). Monday-Saturday 9 a.m.-5 p.m.

MAYMONT

1700 Hampton St., Richmond, 804-358-7166; www.maymont.org

The Dooley mansion, late Victorian in style, houses an art collection and decorative arts exhibits. Also here are formal Japanese and Italian gardens, an arboretum, a nature center with a wildlife habitat for native species, an aviary, a children's farm and a working carriage collection.

Admission: $5 (suggested donation). Grounds: Daily 10 a.m.-5 p.m. Mansion: Tuesday-Sunday noon-5 p.m. Visitor center: Tuesday-Sunday noon-5 p.m.

MEADOW FARM MUSEUM

General Sheppard Crump Memorial Park, 3400 Mountain Road, Glen Allen,
804-501-5520; www.co.henrico.va.us

This is a living history farm museum depicting rural life in the 1860s, including an orientation center, farmhouse, barn, outbuildings, crop demonstration fields and 1860s doctor's office. There is also a 150-acre park with picnic shelters and a playground.

Admission: Free. March-November, Tuesday-Sunday noon-4 p.m.; December-February, Saturday-Sunday noon-4 p.m.

MONTPELIER

11407 Constitution Highway, Montpelier Station, 540-672-2728; www.montpelier.org

The former residence of James Madison, fourth president of the United States. Madison was the third generation of his family to live on this extensive plantation. He inherited Montpelier and expanded it twice. After his presidency, he and Dolley Madison retired to the estate, which Mrs. Madison sold after the president's death to pay off her son's gambling debts. In 1901, the estate was bought by William du Pont, who enlarged the house, added many outbuildings, including a private railroad station, built greenhouses and planted gardens. Today, under the stewardship of the National Trust for Historic Preservation, a long-term research and preservation project has begun. Self-guided tours of the arboretum, nature trails and formal garden. Admission: adults $14, children 6-14 $7, children 5 and under free. April-October, daily 9:30 a.m.-5:30 p.m.; November-March, daily 9:30 a.m.-4:30 p.m.; closed first Saturday in November.

MONUMENTAL CHURCH
1224 E. Broad St., Richmond
Located on the Medical College of Virginia campus of Virginia Commonwealth University, this octagonal domed building was designed by Robert Mills, the architect of the Washington Monument. This commemorative structure was built in 1812 on the site where many prominent people, including the governor, perished in a theater fire in 1811. The interior is closed; behind the church is the distinctive Egyptian Building.

MUSEUM OF THE CONFEDERACY
1201 E. Clay St., Richmond, 804-649-1861; www.moc.org
The museum features the world's largest collection of Confederate artifacts: uniforms, weapons, tattered flags and daguerreotypes. Exhibits feature artifacts from Confederate officers with descriptions of their demise.
Admission: adults $8, seniors $7, children 7-13 $6, children 6 and under free. Monday-Saturday 10 a.m.-5 p.m., Sunday noon-5 p.m.

PLANTATIONS
Visitor Center, 405 N. Third St., Richmond, 804-783-7450; www.visitrichmondva.com
The Richmond-Petersburg-Williamsburg area has many fine old mansions and estates. Some are open most of the year; others only during Historic Garden Week.

RICHMOND NATIONAL BATTLEFIELD PARK
Civil War Visitor Center, 470 Tredegar St., Richmond, 804-226-1981; www.nps.gov/rich
The Union made a total of seven drives on Richmond, the symbol of secession, during the Civil War. Richmond National Battlefield Park, 770 acres in 10 different units, preserves sites of the two efforts that came close to success: McClellan's Peninsula Campaign of 1862 and Grant's attack in 1864. Of McClellan's campaign, the park includes sites of the Seven Days' Battles at Chickahominy Bluffs, Beaver Dam Creek, Gaines' Mill (Watt House) and Malvern Hill. Grant's campaign is represented by the battlefield at Cold Harbor, where on June 3, 1864, Grant hurled his army at fortified Confederate positions, resulting in 7,000 casualties in less than one hour. Confederate Fort Harrison, Parker's Battery, Drewry's Bluff (Fort Darling) and Union-built Fort Brady are also included. Stop by the Civil War Visitor Center at Tredegar Iron Works first to pick up a park map. They also offer audio-visual programs and other information.

Admission: Free. Daily 9 a.m.-5 p.m.

SCIENCE MUSEUM OF VIRGINIA
2500 W. Broad St., Richmond, 804-864-1400; www.smv.org
Located in the historic Broad Street Station (train tracks are still on the ground floor), this engaging museum will appeal to children with exhibits about space, flight, electricity, physics and the atom. Be sure to check out the laboratories and animal exhibits on the second floor.
Admission: adults $10, children 4-12 $9, children 3 and under free.
Monday-Saturday 9:30 a.m.-5 p.m., Sunday 11:30 a.m.-5 p.m.

SHOCKOE SLIP DISTRICT
11 S. 12th St., Richmond; www.ci.richmond.va.us
This restored area of historic buildings and gas-lit cobblestone streets includes shopping, restaurants and galleries.

STATE CAPITOL
Ninth and Grace streets, Richmond, 804-698-1788; www.virginiacapitol.gov
Modeled after La Maison Carre, an ancient Roman temple at Némes, France, the Capitol was designed by Thomas Jefferson. In this building, where America's oldest continuous English-speaking legislative bodies still meet, is the famous Houdon statue of Washington. The rotunda features the first interior dome in the United States.
Admission: Free. Monday-Saturday 9 a.m.-4 p.m., Sunday 1-4 p.m. Tours: 9 a.m.-4 p.m.

ST. JOHN'S EPISCOPAL CHURCH
2401 E. Broad St., at 24th St., Richmond, 804-648-5015, 877-915-1775;
www.historicstjohnschurch.org
This is where Patrick Henry delivered his stirring "liberty or death" speech. The reenactment of the Second Virginia Convention occurs in late May-early September every Sunday; see Web site for schedule.
Admission: adults $6, seniors $5, students 7-18 $4, children 6 and under free. Tours: Monday-Saturday 10 a.m.-4 p.m., Sunday 1-4 p.m. (last tour leaves at 3:30 p.m.)

ST. PAUL'S CHURCH
815 E. Grace St., Richmond, 804-643-3589; www.stpauls-episcopal.org
Established in 1843, the Episcopal church survived the Civil War intact. It was here that Jefferson Davis received news of Robert E. Lee's retreat from Petersburg to Appomattox. Beginning in 1890, the church added many fine stained-glass windows, including eight from the Tiffany studios. Sanctuary ceiling features decorative plasterwork interweaving Greek, Hebrew and Christian motifs around a central panel. A Tiffany mosaic of da Vinci's "Last Supper" surmounts the altar.
Services: 7:45 a.m., 9 a.m., 11:15 a.m.

VALENTINE RICHMOND HISTORY CENTER

1015 E. Clay St., Richmond, 804-649-0711; www.valentinemuseum.com

Tracing the history of Richmond, exhibits focus on city life, decorative arts, costumes and textiles and industrial and social history; and tours are offered of restored 1812 Wickham House. Enjoy lunch in the garden at Café Richmond, behind the history center.

Admission: adults $8, seniors, students and children 7-18 $7, children 6 and under free. Tuesday-Saturday 10 a.m.-5 p.m., Sunday noon-5 p.m.

VIRGINIA AVIATION MUSEUM

5701 Huntsman Road, Richmond, 804-236-3622; www.vam.smv.org

This museum offers exhibits and artifacts on the history of aviation, with an emphasis on Virginia pioneers.

Admission: adults $6, seniors and children 4-12 $5, military personnel $5.50, children 3 and under free. Tuesday-Sunday 9:30 a.m.-5 p.m., Sunday noon-5 p.m.

VIRGINIA HISTORICAL SOCIETY

428 N. Boulevard St., Richmond, 804-358-4901; www.vahistorical.org

The society has a comprehensive collection of Virginia history housed in its museum with permanent and changing exhibits, and the Library of Virginia History with historical and genealogical research facilities.

Admission: adults $5, seniors $4, students $3, children 18 and under free. Free Sunday. Tuesday-Sunday 10 a.m.-5 p.m., Sunday 1-5 p.m.

VIRGINIA MUSEUM OF FINE ARTS

200 N. Blvd., Richmond, 804-340-1400; www.vmfa.state.va.us

America's first state-supported museum of art has collections of paintings, prints and sculpture from major world cultures; Russian Imperial Easter eggs and jewels by Fabergé; decorative arts of the Art Nouveau and Art Deco movements; and a sculpture garden.

Wednesday-Sunday 11 a.m.-5 p.m.

VIRGINIA WAR MEMORIAL

621 S. Belvidere St., Richmond, 804-786-2060; www.vawarmemorial.org

The Virginia War Memorial honors Virginians who died in World War II and the Korean and Vietnam wars. There are also mementos of battles, an eternal flame and more than 12,000 names engraved on glass and marble walls.

Admission: Free. Monday-Friday 9 a.m.-4 p.m., Saturday 9 a.m.-4 p.m., Sunday noon-4 p.m.

WHITE HOUSE OF THE CONFEDERACY

1201 E. Clay St., Richmond, 804-649-1861; www.moc.org

Next door to the Museum of the Confederacy downtown, this Classical Revival house was used by Jefferson Davis as his official residence during the period when Richmond was the capital of the Confederacy. Abraham Lincoln met with troops here during the Union occupation of the city. A National Historic Landmark, it has been restored to its prewar appearance with many of its original furnishings.

Admission: adults $8, seniors $7, children 7-13 $4, children 6 and under free. (A combination ticket with the Confederacy Museum is available.) Monday-Saturday 10 a.m.-5 p.m., Sunday noon-5 p.m.

WILLIAM BYRD PARK

0 South Boulevard, Richmond, 804-646-5733; www.ci.richmond.va.us
This park includes 287 acres of groves, three lakes, picnic areas, tennis courts, softball fields and a fitness course. There is also the Carillon bell tower and an amphitheater that hosts summer concerts and plays. Daily.

WILTON HOUSE MUSEUM

215 S. Wilton Road, Richmond, 804-282-5936; www.wiltonhousemuseum.org
This Georgian mansion was built in 1753 by William Randolph III. It has fully paneled, authentic 18th-century furnishings and is the headquarters of the National Society of Colonial Dames in Virginia.
Admission: adults $10, seniors $8, children 6 and under free. Tuesday-Saturday 10 a.m.-4:30 p.m., Sunday 1:30-4:30 p.m.

SPECIAL EVENTS
HISTORIC GARDEN WEEK IN VIRGINIA

12 E. Franklin St., Richmond, 804-643-4137; www.vagardenweek.org
Many private houses and gardens of historic or artistic interest are opened for this event, which includes more than 200 houses and gardens throughout the state.
Mid-late April.

VIRGINIA STATE FAIR

600 E. Laburnum Ave., Richmond, 804-228-3200; www.statefairva.org
Virginia's annual state fair is fun for all with animal and 4-H contests, music, a horse show, carnival, a tasty variety of food and more.
Late September-early October.

WHERE TO STAY
★★★THE BERKELEY HOTEL

1200 E. Cary St., Richmond, 804-780-1300, 888-780-4422; www.berkeleyhotel.com
This hotel opened in 1988 but its stylish look seems much more historic. The Berkeley Hotel is located at the crossroads of the business district and Historic Shockoe Slip. Dark wood paneling adorns the lobby and dining room. Dramatic windows to the ceiling give the hotel a European appearance. Diners at the hotel's restaurant get a view of the Slip's cobblestones and lamplights.
55 rooms. Restaurant, bar. $151-250

★★COURTYARD RICHMOND WEST

6400 W. Broad St., Richmond, 804-282-1881; www.marriott.com
145 rooms. Business center. Fitness center. Pool. $61-150

★★★CROWNE PLAZA

555 E. Canal St., Richmond, 804-788-0900, 888-444-0401; www.crowneplaza.com

Just nine miles from Richmond International Airport, this hotel is situated in the heart of the historic district on the Canal Walk. Its higher floors have a spectacular view of the James River. The hotel is located minutes from area attractions such as Shockoe Slip, Sixth Street Market Place, museums, theaters and fine dining. Brown's Island, a concert and special-events venue, is located behind the hotel. Richmond Ballet is adjacent to the hotel, and ballet packages are available.

298 rooms. Restaurant, bar. Business center. Fitness Center. Pool. $61-150

★DAYS INN

6910 Midlothian Turnpike, Richmond, 804-745-7100; www.daysinnrichmond.com

115 rooms. Complimentary breakfast. Pool. Pets acccpted. $61-150

★★DOUBLETREE HOTEL RICHMOND AIRPORT

5501 Eubank Road, Sandston, 804-226-6400, 800-222-8733; www.doubletree.com

160 rooms. Restaurant, bar. Business center. Fitness center. Pool. $61-150

★★EMBASSY SUITES HOTEL RICHMOND-THE COMMERCE CENTER

2925 Emerywood Parkway, Richmond, 804-672-8585, 800-362-2779; www.embassysuites.com

226 rooms. Restaurant, bar. Complimentary breakfast. Business center. Fitness center. Pool. $151-250

★★★★★THE JEFFERSON HOTEL

101 W. Franklin St., Richmond, 804-788-8000, 800-424-8014; www.jeffersonhotel.com

The Jefferson Hotel is an institution in the heart of Richmond. A historic Beaux-Arts landmark dating back to 1895, the hotel offers elegant guest rooms furnished in a traditional style with antique reproductions and fine art. Pedigreed residents take afternoon tea here. TJ's provides a casual setting for fine dining with local dishes like oyster chowder and peanut soup, while the hotel's newly revamped star restaurant, Lemaire, offers a new bar, sparkling ambience and a farm-to-table inspired menu. The hotel's location is ideal, putting you in close proximity to the city's financial district, museums and shopping. If you don't feel like walking, a complimentary car service will transport you to these and other destinations within a three-mile radius.

262 rooms. Restaurant, bar. Business center. Fitness center. Pool. Pets accepted. $251-350

★★LINDEN ROW INN

100 E. Franklin St., Richmond, 804-783-7000, 800-348-7424; www.lindenrowinn.com

70 rooms. Complimentary breakfast. $61-150

★★★MARRIOTT RICHMOND

500 E. Broad St., Richmond, 804-643-3400, 800-228-9290; www.marriott.com/ricdt

Attached to the Convention Center via skybridge, this high-rise hotel in the heart of the city is close to the Coliseum and both the historic and river districts. Business travelers will appreciate high-speed Internet access in their rooms, while families will love the spacious rooms, indoor pool and downtown location. The hotel offers complimentary shuttle service to Shockoe Slip, as well as to all major businesses within 3 miles.

410 rooms. Restaurant, bar. Business center. Fitness center. Pool. $151-250

★★★OMNI RICHMOND HOTEL

100 S. 12th St., Richmond, 804-344-7000, 888-444-6664; www.omnihotels.com

This contemporary hotel is conveniently located in the center of the financial and historic districts in the James Center and features scenic river views. It's across the street from the famous Tobacco Company restaurant, and a great place to stay if you intend to explore Shockoe Slip and Shockoe Bottom.

361 rooms. Restaurant, bar. Business center. Pool. Pets accepted. $61-150

★QUALITY INN

8008 W. Broad St., Richmond, 804-346-0000, 877-424-6423; www.qualityinn.com

190 rooms. Complimentary breakfast. Business center. Pool. Pets accepted. $61-150

★★★SHERATON RICHMOND WEST HOTEL

6624 W. Broad St., Richmond, 804-285-2000, 800-325-3535;
www.starwoodhotels.com

With luxurious furnishings such as plush pillows and duvets on Sweet Sleeper beds, this upscale hotel offers its guests comfortable accommodations set in a richly landscaped business park just off the highway. With oversize writing desks and in-room wireless Internet access, the hotel is geared toward the business traveler, but tourists and families will be just as comfortable here.

372 rooms. Restaurant, bar. Business center. Fitness center. Pool. Pets accepted. $61-150

WHERE TO EAT

★★ACACIA

2601 W. Cary St., Richmond, 804-354-6060; www.acaciarestaurant.com

American. Dinner. Closed Sunday. Reservations recommended. Outdoor seating. Bar. $36-85

★★AMICI RISTORANTE

3343 W. Cary St., Richmond, 804-353-4700; www.amiciristorante.net

Italian. Lunch, dinner. Closed Sunday. Reservations recommended. Outdoor seating. Bar. $36-85

★★BYRAM'S LOBSTER HOUSE

3215 W. Broad St., Richmond, 804-355-9193; www.byrams.com

American, seafood. Lunch, dinner. Bar. $16-35

★★★THE DINING ROOM AT THE BERKELEY HOTEL

The Berkeley Hotel, 1200 E. Cary St., Richmond, 804-225-5105, 888-780-4422;
www.berkeleyhotel.com

Located in a European-style hotel, this handsomely decorated dining room serves elegant, impeccably prepared meals in a sophisticated and tranquil atmosphere. Entrée selections include pan seared scallops, spinach and tomatoes with homemade fettuccine with bacon cream sauce; and aged New York strip steak with parmesan butter with broccolini and mashed potatoes. American. Breakfast, lunch (Monday-Saturday), dinner, Sunday brunch. Reservations recommended. Bar. $36-85

★★HALF WAY HOUSE
10301 Jefferson Davis Highway, Richmond, 804-275-1760, 800-897-0848; www. halfwayhouserestaurant.com
American. Lunch, dinner. Reservations recommended. $36-85

★★HELEN'S
2527 W. Main St., Richmond, 804-358-4370
International. Dinner. Closed Monday. Reservations recommended. Bar. $16-35

★★KABUTO JAPANESE HOUSE OF STEAK
8052 W. Broad St., Richmond, 804-747-9573
Japanese. Lunch, dinner. Reservations recommended. Bar. $16-35

★★★LEMAIRE
The Jefferson Hotel, 101 W. Franklin, Richmond, 804-788-8000, 800-424-8014; www.jeffersonhotel.com
Located in the historic Jefferson Hotel, the newly revamped Lemaire has evolved from its Old World fine dining, as it had previously been known for, to a more casual atmosphere serving innovative cuisine, but still with it's rich history intact. The restaurant is named for Etienne Lemaire, who served as maître d' to President Jefferson and was widely credited for introducing the fine art of cooking with wines to America. His love of food and wine is continued at Lemaire, where local seasonal ingredients are used by chef Walter Bundy, inspired by the farm-to-table philosophy. Enjoy small plates, wine and cocktails in the new bar and lounge.
American. Breakfast, lunch, dinner. Reservations recommended. Bar. $36-85

★★★THE OLD ORIGINAL BOOKBINDER'S
2306 E. Cary St., Richmond, 804-643-6900; www.bookbindersrichmond.com
The first Bookbinder's to open outside of Philadelphia, this restaurant is located in a historic building that was once a Philip Morris manufacturing plant. Menu selections include high-quality seafood and homemade desserts. There is an outdoor courtyard area for alfresco dining.
Seafood. Dinner. Reservations recommended. Outdoor seating. Bar. $36-85

★O'TOOLES
4800 Forest Hill Ave., Richmond, 804-233-1781; www.otoolesrestaurant.com
American Lunch, dinner, brunch. Children's menu. Bar. $16-35

★★SAM MILLER'S RESTAURANT
1210 E. Cary St., Richmond, 804-644-5465; www.sammillers.com
Seafood. Lunch (Monday-Saturday), dinner (Monday-Saturday), Sunday brunch. Bar. $36-85

★STRAWBERRY STREET CAFÉ

421 N. Strawberry St., Richmond, 804-353-6860; www.strawberrystreetcafe.com

American. Lunch, dinner, Saturday-Sunday brunch. Reservations recommended. Bar. $16-35

★★★THE TOBACCO COMPANY

1201 E. Cary St., Richmond, 804-782-9555; www.thetobaccocompany.com

The Tobacco Company, the restaurant that helped pioneer the renaissance of Richmond's Shockoe Slip neighborhood, is carved from a former tobacco warehouse. Its centerpiece is a dramatic, skylit atrium with an antique cage elevator servicing three floors of dining. The menu is extensive if not inventive: steaks, prime rib, lobster, veal, shrimp, scallops, salmon, rainbow trout, chicken, crab, Virginia ham and pasta. Enjoy live music every Friday and Saturday night and cigars in the bar.

American. Lunch, dinner, Sunday brunch. Reservations recommended. Bar. $36-85

ROANOKE

See also Harrisonburg

The view from the top of Mill Mountain standing under the famous Roanoke Star (the world's largest man-made star) reveals the spectacular beauty and vastness of the Roanoke Valley, which seems to go on forever in every direction.

Tucked in the valley's center, the city itself evolved from a thriving, industrial railroading nexus in the late 1800s to a state-of-the-art destination. Over the years, Roanoke has become a sophisticated place, with a thriving arts community, a wealth of museums, and varied entertainment and theater offerings, which now share the stage with several world-class educational institutions. The hustle and bustle of the Norfolk and Southern Railroad has given way to health care, education, travel, conventions, industry and trade.

WHAT TO SEE
CENTER IN THE SQUARE

1 Market Square, Roanoke, 540-342-5700; www.centerinthesquare.org

A restored 20th-century furniture warehouse, now houses independent cultural and science organizations including The Arts Council of the Blue Ridge, Historical Society of Western Virginia, Mill Mountain Theatre, and the Science Musuem of Western Virginia. See Web site for special event information and hours for each organization.

GEORGE WASHINGTON AND JEFFERSON NATIONAL FORESTS

5162 Valleypointe Parkway, Roanoke, 540-265-5100; www.southernregion.fs.fed.us/gwj

The forests consist of approximately two million acres which offer many different outdoor activities including swimming; fishing, hunting, riding trails, camping and picnicking. There are scenic drives past Crabtree Falls, hardwood forests and unusual geologic features. Be sure to check out the beautiful overlooks of the Shenandoah Valley. There are also trails for the visually impaired. Beach: Daily 6 a.m.-8 p.m.

HISTORY MUSEUM OF WESTERN VIRGINIA

1 Market Square S.E., Roanoke, 540-342-5760; www.history-museum.org

Permanent exhibits here deal with Roanoke history from days of Native Americans to the present. There are archives and a library available by appointment.

Admission: adults $3, seniors, students and children $2, children 5 and under free. Tuesday-Friday 10 a.m.-4 p.m., Saturday 10 a.m.-5 p.m., Sunday 1-5 p.m.

MILL MOUNTAIN ZOOLOGICAL PARK

Highway 220/I-581 and Blue Ridge Parkway, Roanoke, 540-343-3241; www.mmzoo.org

This zoo sits atop Mill Mountain and offers picnic areas with magnificent views of city and valley. They house 16 different species of mammals, 36 species of birds, 12 of reptiles, 7 of amphibians and 3 of invertebrates. Animals include the snow leopard, red panda, red wolf, crested wood partridge, dart frog, crested porcupine, wolverine and many others.

Admission: adults $7.50, children 3-11 $5, children 2 and under free. Daily 10 a.m.-4:30 p.m.

SCIENCE MUSEUM OF WESTERN VIRGINIA & HOPKINS PLANETARIUM

1 Market Square, Roanoke, 540-342-5710; www.smwv.org

This museum contains hands-on exhibits in the natural and physical sciences: animals of land and ocean, computers, and a TV weather station. Enjoy workshops, programs and classes for children and adults as well as many special exhibits. Hopkins Planetarium shows IMAX films in their Mega-Dome Theater.

Admission: adults $8, seniors $7, children 3-12 $6, children 2 and under free. Tuesday-Saturday 10 a.m.-5 p.m., Sunday 1-5 p.m.

VIRGINIA MUSEUM OF TRANSPORTATION

303 Norfolk Ave., Roanoke, 540-342-5670; www.vmt.org

Vehicles from the past and present are displayed here. For those interested in trains, there is a large steam, diesel and electric locomotive collection. There are hands-on exhibits.

Admission: adults $8, seniors $7, children 3-11 $6, children 2 and under free. Monday-Saturday 10 a.m.-5 p.m., Sunday 1 p.m.-5 p.m.

SPECIAL EVENTS
VIRGINIA STATE CHAMPIONSHIP CHILI COOK-OFF

19 West Salem Ave., Roanoke, 540-342-4716; www.greenvale-school.org

Teams compete to win the state title in this chili cook-off. There is alos a beer garden, live entertainment, a jalepeno eating contest, arts and crats vendors and more.

First Saturday in May.

WHERE TO STAY
★★HOLIDAY INN ROANOKE-VALLEY VIEW

3315 Ordway Drive N.W., Roanoke, 540-362-4500, 877-834-3613;

153 rooms. Restaurant, bar. Business center. Fitness center. Pool. Pets accepted. $61-150

★★HOLIDAY INN ROANOKE-TANGLEWOOD
4468 Starkey Road, Roanoke, 540-774-4400, 800-282-0244; www.holidayinn.com

190 rooms. Restaurant, bar. Business center. Fitness Center. Pool. Pets accepted. $61-150

★★THE HOTEL ROANOKE & CONFERENCE CENTER,
A DOUBLETREE HOTEL
110 Shenandoah Ave., Roanoke, 540-985-5900; www.hotelroanoke.com

332 rooms. Restaurant, bar. Business center. Fitness center. Pool. $61-150

WHERE TO EAT
★★KABUKI JAPANESE STEAK HOUSE
3503 Franklin Road S.W., Roanoke, 540-981-0222; www.kabukiva.com

Japanese. Dinner. Reservations recommended. Bar. $16-35

★★★LIBRARY
3117 Franklin Road, Roanoke, 540-985-0811

Not only is this 1785 New England-style mansion a historic landmark, but it has served the likes of George Washington and a host of other presidents. French, American. Dinner. Closed Monday-Sunday. Reservations recommended. $36-85

SHENANDOAH NATIONAL PARK
See also Front Royal, Harrisonburg

About 450 million years ago, the Blue Ridge was at the bottom of a sea. Today, it averages 2,000 feet above sea level, and some 300 square miles of the loveliest Blue Ridge area are included in Shenandoah National Park.

The park is 80 miles long and 2-13 miles wide. Running its full length is the 105-mile Skyline Drive. Main entrances are the North Entrance, from I-66, Highways 340, 522 and 55; Thornton Gap Entrance, from Highway 211; Swift Run Gap Entrance, from Highway 33; and the South Entrance, from I-64, Highway 250, and the Blue Ridge Parkway. The drive, twisting and turning along the crest of the Blue Ridge, is one of the finest scenic trips in the East. Approximately 70 overlooks give views of the Blue Ridge, the Piedmont and to the west, the Shenandoah Valley and the Alleghenies. Also, driving along Skyline Drive, you'll go through Marys Rock Tunnel, 600 feet of granite rock, and be sure your vehicle will clear it as it's at not quiet 13 feet.

The drive offers much, but the park offers more. Thousands of visitors explore the 500 miles of trails (101 miles are of the Appalachian Trail) on foot or on horseback. Most of the area is wooded, predominantly in white, red and chestnut oak, with hickory, birch, maple, hemlock, tulip poplar and nearly 100 other species. At the head of Whiteoak Canyon are 300-year-old hemlocks. The park, a sanctuary for deer, bears, foxes and bobcats, along with more than 200 varieties of birds, bursts with color in the fall, which makes this season particularly popular with visitors.

The park is open all year; campgrounds, lodge and cabin accommodations and picnic grounds vary, but usually are open March through the end of November; call or see Web site for information (*540-999-3500; www.nps.gov/shen*). Also, Skyline Drive is occasionally closed for short periods during November-March.

WHAT TO SEE
BLUE RIDGE PARKWAY
828-298-0398; www.nps.gov/blri
Winding 469 mountainous miles between the Shenandoah and Great Smoky Mountains national parks (about 217 miles are in Virginia), the Blue Ridge Parkway represents a different concept in highway travel. It is not an express highway but a road intended for leisurely travel. Travelers in a hurry would be wise to take state and U.S. routes, where speed limits are higher.The parkway follows the Blue Ridge Mountains for about 355 miles, then winds through the Craggies, Pisgahs and Balsams to the Great Smokies. Overlooks, picnic and camp sites, visitor centers, nature trails, fishing streams and lakes, and points of interest are numerous and well-marked. Accommodations are plentiful in cities and towns along the way. Food availability is limited on the parkway.The parkway is open all year, but the best time to drive it is between April and November. Some sections are closed by ice and snow for periods in winter and early spring. Fog may be present during wet weather. The higher sections west of Asheville to Great Smoky Mountains National Park and north of Asheville to Mount Mitchell may be closed January through March due to hazardous driving conditions.

BYRD VISITOR CENTER
Mile 51 on Skyline Drive, Shenandoah; www.nps.gov/shen
The Byrd visitor center offers restrooms, an information desk with informaton, maps, brochures, permits and first aid. There are also exhibits, a bookstore, orientation programs, videos and ranger programs.
April-November, daily 8:30 a.m.-6 p.m..

DICKEY RIDGE VISITOR CENTER
Mile 4.7 on Skyline Drive, Shenandoah; www.nps.gov/shen
Dickey Ridge visitor center offers restrooms, and an information desk with maps, permits, first aid and information. They also have exhibits, a bookstore, and an orientation movie.
April-November, daily 8:30 a.m.-5 p.m.

WHERE TO STAY
★★★L'AUBERGE PROVENÇAL BED AND BREAKFAST
13630 Lord Fairfax Highway, Boyce, 540-837-1375, 800-638-1702;
www.laubergeprovencale.com
This French-style inn, decorated with Victorian and European antiques, is located in the heart of Virginia's wine country and Shenandoah Valley.
11 rooms. No children under 10. Complimentary breakfast. Restaurant.
$151-250

WHERE TO EAT
★★★L'AUBERGE PROVENÇAL
13630 Lord Fairfax Highway, Boyce, 540-837-1375, 800-638-1702;
www.laubergeprovencale.com
This country inn has earned a reputation for fine cuisine served with detailed, personal attention. Innkeeper/chef Alain Borel, from Avignon, and his wife, Celeste, provide an authentic, garden-inspired menu.
French. Lunch (Sunday), dinner. Closed Tuesday. Outdoor seating. Reservations recommended. Bar. $36-85

STAUNTON
See also Harrisonburg
To historians, Staunton is known as the birthplace of Woodrow Wilson, and to students of government it is the place where the City Manager plan was first conceived and adopted. Set in fertile Shenandoah Valley fields and orchards between the Blue Ridge and Allegheny mountain ranges, the area around Staunton produces poultry, livestock and wool. Manufacturing firms in the city make air conditioners, razors, candy and clothing. A Ranger District office of the George Washington and Jefferson national forests is located here.

WHAT TO SEE
FRONTIER CULTURE MUSEUM
1290 Richmond Road, Staunton, 540-332-7850; www.frontiermuseum.org
Living history museum consists of working farms brought together from England, Germany, Northern Ireland and an American farm. The European farms represent what America's early settlers left; the American farm, from the Valley of Virginia, reflects the blend of the various European influences. Visitors are able to see and take part in life as it was lived on these 17th-, 18th- and 19th-century farmsteads. Costumed interpreters demonstrate daily life at all four sites.
Admission: adults $10, seniors $9.50, students $9, children 6-12 $6, children 5 and under free. Regular hours: mid-March through December 1, 9 a.m.-5 p.m. Mid-March-November, daily 9 a.m.-5 p.m., December-mid-March, daily 10 a.m.-4 p.m.

GYPSY HILL PARK
Churchville and Thornrose avenues, Staunton, 540-332-3945; www.staunton.va.us
This 214 acre park is located in the center of Staunton. There's plenty to do here including a lake stocked with fish, swimming (late May-Labor Day); a lighted softball field with a concession stand, outdoor basketball courts, tennis, 18-hole golf, picnicking, horseshoe pits, the Duck Pond, a miniature train ride, playground, a bandstand and fairgrounds.
Admission: Free. Daily 4 a.m.-11 p.m.

WOODROW WILSON BIRTHPLACE AND PRESIDENTIAL MUSEUM
24 N. Coalter St., Staunton, 540-885-0897; www.woodrowwilson.org
This restored Greek Revival manse has period furnishings and Wilson family mementos from the 1850s. The museum building on the grounds houses a

seven-gallery presidential exhibit, "The Life and Times of Woodrow Wilson," and his 1919 Pierce-Arrow limousine. Also onsite are Victorian gardens. Admission: adults $12, seniors, military personnel $10, students $5, children 6-12 $3, children 5 and under free. November-February, Monday-Saturday 10 a.m.-4 p.m., Sunday, noon-4 p.m.; March-October, Monday-Saturday 9 a.m.-5 p.m., Sunday noon-5 p.m.

SPECIAL EVENT
JAZZ IN THE PARK
Gypsy Hill Park, 1000 Montgomery Ave., Staunton, 540-337-6944; www.staunton.va.us
This series of free concerts take place over the summer on Thursday night. It brings out jazz musicians from all over the country.
July-August, Thursday.

WHERE TO STAY
★★★BELLE GRAE INN
515 W. Frederick St., Staunton, 540-886-5151, 888-541-5151; www.bellegrae.com
This century-old bed and breakfast offers carefully restored Victorian accommodations in four buildings. Enjoy a meal in their dining room which features fresh organic produce and homemade soups, breads and salads.
14 rooms. Restaurant, bar. Complimentary breakfast. $151-250

★BEST WESTERN STAUNTON INN
92 Rowe Road, Staunton, 540-885-1112, 800-752-9471; www.bestwestern.com
80 rooms. Complimentary breakfast. Pool. Pets accepted. $61-150

★COMFORT INN
1302 Richmond Ave., Staunton, 540-886-5000, 877-424-6423; www.comfortinn.com
97 rooms. Complimentary breakfast. Pool. Pets accepted. $61-150

★★★FREDERICK HOUSE
28 N. New St., Staunton, 540-885-4220, 800-334-5575; www.frederickhouse.com
Built in 1809, the Frederick House's five restored buildings offer spacious rooms furnished with antiques and period furniture.
23 rooms. Complimentary breakfast. $61-150

★★HOLIDAY INN GOLF & CONFERENCE CENTER
I-81, Highway 275, Staunton, 540-248-6020, 800-932-9061; www.histaunton.com
114 rooms. Restaurant, bar. Fitness center. Pool. $61-150

WHERE TO EAT
★MRS. ROWE'S RESTAURANT & BAKERY
74 Rowe Road, Staunton, 540-886-1833; www.mrsrowes.com
American. Breakfast, lunch, dinner. $15 and under

STRASBURG
See also Front Royal, Winchester
Lying at the base of Massanutten Mountain and on the north fork of the

Shenandoah River, Strasburg was founded in 1761 by German settlers. Prospering in the early 19th century as a center of trade and flour milling, the village later became identified with the manufacturing of high-quality pottery, earning the nickname "Pottown" after the Civil War. Strasburg played a pivotal role in Stonewall Jackson's Campaign of 1862 because of its location on the Manassas Gap Railroad and the Shenandoah Valley Turnpike. The first western Virginia town to be served by two railroads, Strasburg became a prominent railroad town, manufacturing center, and home of printing and publishing businesses after 1890.

Today Strasburg is located near the entrance to the Skyline Drive, attracting visitors with its antebellum and Victorian architecture and its burgeoning art community. The town calls itself the "antique capital of Virginia."

WHAT TO SEE
BELLE GROVE PLANTATION
336 Belle Grove Road, Strasburg, 540-869-2028; www.bellegrove.org
This 1794 limestone mansion's design reflects Thomas Jefferson's influence. It was used as Union headquarters during the Battle of Cedar Creek, October 19, 1864. You'll see unusual interior woodwork and a herb garden in rear. Guided tours: April-October, Monday-Saturday 10:15 a.m.-3:15 p.m., Sunday 1:15-4:15 p.m. (depart 15 minutes after each hour). Self-guided tours: Late March-December, Monday-Friday 10 a.m.-4 p.m., Saturday 10:15 a.m.-3:15 p.m., Sunday 1:15-4:15 p.m.

STONEWALL JACKSON MUSUEM AT HUPP'S HILL
33229 Old Valley Pike, Strasburg, 540-465-5884; www.stonewalljacksonmuseum.org
The former campsite for six different Civil War generals' troops, is now a museum and hands-on interpretive center with artifacts and exhibits. Admission: adults $5, seniors, students, military personnel and children 6-18 $4, children 4 and under free. April-October, daily 10 a.m.-5 p.m.; November-March, daily 10 a.m.-4 p.m.

STRASBURG MUSEUM
440 E. King St., Strasburg, 540-465-3175
Situated in a building built in 1890 as a pottery and then became the Southern Railway Depot, the museum now has displays of blacksmith, cooper and potter shop collections; displays from colonial homes; relics from Civil War and railroad eras; and Native American artifacts.
May-October, daily 10 a.m.-4 p.m.

WHERE TO STAY
★★HOTEL STRASBURG
213 S. Holliday St., Strasburg, 540-465-9191, 800-348-8327; www.hotelstrasburg.com
29 rooms. Complimentary breakfast. Reservations recommended. $61-150

WHERE TO EAT
★★★HOTEL STRASBURG
213 S. Holliday St., Strasburg, 540-465-9191, 800-348-8327; www.hotelstrasburg.com
The inn's ornate Victorian lobby gives way to an invitingly cozy country

restaurant, where locals and travelers alike dine on fine wines and elegant cuisine, including seasonal seafood dishes.
Mediterranean. Lunch, dinner. Reservations recommended. Bar. $61-150

VIENNA

See also Front Royal, Winchester

Just fifteen miles from Washington, D.C., Vienna has a small town feel to it with a Historic District with architecturally significant houses and historic sites. Maple Avenue has plenty of shops and restaurants to peruse and the nearby Wolf Trap Foundation for the Performing Arts is a popular destination for those interested in art, theater and music.

WHAT TO SEE
BARNS OF WOLF TRAP
1645 Trap Road, Vienna, 703-938-8463; www.wolf-trap.org

This intimate 350-seat theater, set in an old barn, features different types of performances including chamber music, recitals, mime, jazz, folk, theater and children's programs. There is also lighter fare served here and a bar. See Web site for schedules and ticket information.

FILENE CENTER AT WOLF TRAP PARK FOR THE PERFORMING ARTS
1624 Trap Road, Vienna, 703-255-1900; www.wolf-trap.org

This performance venue was aimed for Catherine Filene Shouse who donated 100 acres of farmland to the U.S. Govenrnment. In warmer weather, varied concerts and programs include ballet, musicals, opera, classical, jazz and folk music among others. Filene Center has an open theater seats, 3,800 under cover and 3,000 on the lawn. For those with lawn seats, you can picnic on the grounds, all year. Past performers include Diana Krall, Huey Lewis & the News, Buddy Guy, Michael McDonald and more.
Late May-September.

MEADOWLARK BOTANICAL GARDENS
9750 Meadowlark Gardens Court, Vienna, 703-255-3631;
www.nvrpa.org/parks/meadowlark

Lilac, wildflower, herb, native plants, and landscaped gardens are abloom on 95 acres. The garden includes three ponds, a water garden, gazebos, trails and a visitor center.
Admission: adults $5, seniors and children 7-17 $2.50, children 6 and under free. May, daily 10 a.m.-7:30 p.m.; June-August, daily 10 a.m.-8 p.m.; September, April, daily 10 a.m-7 p.m.; October, March, daily 10 a.m.-6 p.m.; November-February, daily 10 a.m.-5 p.m.

WHERE TO STAY
★★★MARRIOTT TYSONS CORNER
8028 Leesburg Pike, Vienna, 703-734-3200, 800-228-9790; www.marriott.com

This property is located in the heart of Tysons corner, next to a major shopping mall. You don't have to miss your workout while you're on vacation, the Marriott offers a 24 hour fitness center and indoor pool. Grab a bite to eat and

relax with a cocktail at Shula's Steak House.
396 rooms. Restaurant, bar. Fitness center. Pool. $151-250

WHERE TO EAT
★★BONAROTI
428 Maple Ave. East, Vienna, 703-281-7550; www.bonarotirestaurant.com
Italian. Lunch (Monday-Friday), dinner. Closed Sunday. Reservations recommended. Bar. $16-35

★★CLYDE'S
8332 Leesburg Pike, Vienna, 703-734-1901; www.clydes.com
American. Lunch, dinner, Sunday brunch, late-night. Bar. $16-35

★★HUNAN LION
2070 Chain Bridge Road, Vienna, 703-734-9828; www.hunanlion.com
Chinese. Lunch (Monday-Saturday), dinner. Reservations recommended. Bar. $15 and under.

★★MARCO POLO
245 Maple Ave. West, Vienna, 703-281-3922; www.marcopolorestaurant.com
Italian, seafood. Lunch, dinner, Sunday brunch. Closed Monday-Tuesday. Bar. $16-35

★★★MORTON'S, THE STEAKHOUSE
8075 Leesburg Pike, Vienna, 703-883-0800; www.mortons.com
Consistent with expectations, this outlet serves the same famed entrées as its sister restaurants. The tableside menu presentation reveals generous portions and high-quality ingredients in the restaurant's warm, club-like atmosphere. Steak. Dinner. Reservations recommended. Bar. $36-85

★★★NIZAM'S
523 Maple Ave. West, Vienna, 703-938-8948
Doner kebob, a forebear of the gyro, is the legendary mainstay of this refined Turkish restaurant. Thin, tender slices of marinated, spit-roasted lamb nestle inside soft pita bread in a dish that rivals anything Istanbul could turn out. Service is polished and attentive.
Turkish. Dinner. Closed Monday. Reservations recommended. Bar. $16-35

★★PANJSHIR II
224 W. Maple Ave., Vienna, 703-281-4183
Middle Eastern. Lunch, dinner. Closed Monday. Bar. $16-35

★★TARA THAI
226 Maple Ave. West, Vienna, 703-255-2467; www.tarathairichmond.com
Thai. Lunch, dinner. Reservations recommended. Bar. $16-35

VIRGINIA BEACH
See also Chesapeake, Hampton, Newport News, Norfolk, Portsmouth
Strolling down the expanded boardwalk, you can relive the pleasures of your youth and enjoy the buzz of entertainment, good food and people-watching

at its finest.

The area's historical sites tie Virginia Beach to the first permanent English settlement over 400 years ago. In fact, First Landing State Park is where John Smith alighted before he went on to Jamestown. There are museums too, including the Virginia Marine Science Museum, voted one of the top ten marine science aquariums/museums in the United States.

Virginia Beach is also home to more than 106 square miles of wetlands and water, a 3,000-acre state park and two wildlife refuges. Amazingly, being this close to Virginia's largest city, the natural ecological areas surrounding Virginia Beach are among the most pristine and undiscovered areas along the mid-Atlantic. Even on a rainy day, the wildlife—native birds, whales and dolphins—are close enough for you to get a good look.

WHAT TO SEE
ADAM THOROUGHGOOD HOUSE
1636 Parish Road, Virginia Beach, 757-460-7588; www.virginiabeachhistory.org
This National Historic Landmark, built circa 1680, is one of the oldest remaining brick houses in U.S. The house and its gardens have been restored. Admission: adults $4, seniors $3, students $2, children 5 and under free. Tuesday-Saturday 9 a.m.-5 p.m., Sunday 11 a.m.-5 p.m..

ASSOCIATION FOR RESEARCH AND ENLIGHTENMENT
67th Street and Atlantic Avenue, Virginia Beach, 757-428-3588; www.are-cayce.com
The headquarters for psychic Egar Cayce's studies and research on transpersonal subjects are located here. His studies have included work on dreams, intuition, philosophy, reincarnation, ancient mysteries, holistic health and more. The visitor center has a bookstore, a library, displays, an ESP-testing machine, movies and daily lectures.
Visitor center: Monday-Saturday 10 a.m.-8 p.m., Sunday noon-6 p.m.

CONTEMPORARY ART CENTER OF VIRGINIA
2200 Parks Ave., Virginia Beach, 757-425-0000; www.cacv.org
This 32,000-square-foot facility is devoted to the presentation of 20th-century art through exhibitions, education, performing arts and special events. Admission: adults $7, seniors, students and military personnel $5, children 17 and under free. Tuesday 10 a.m.- 9 p.m., Wednesday-Friday 10 a.m.-5 p.m., Saturday 10 a.m.-4 p.m., Sunday noon-4 p.m.; see Web site for seasonal hours. Museum shop: Monday-Friday 9 a.m.-5 p.m., Saturday 10 a.m.-4 p.m., Sunday noon-4 p.m.

FIRST LANDING STATE PARK
2500 Shore, Virginia Beach, 757-412-2300; www.dcr.virginia.gov
Covering more than 2,800 acres, First Landing State Park has lagoons, cypress trees and sand dunes. There are campsites with electric hook-ups, restrooms and showers, trailer sites and picnic areas. Visitors can go swimming at own risk, fishing, boating, hiking, bicycling and hike the many nature trails. Daily.

FISHING

Linkhorn Bay and Rudee Inlet, Virginia Beach

In the Lynnhaven and Rudee Inlets, look for channel bass, speckled trout, spots, croakers, flounder and whiting in season. Go pier fishing and surf casting from four piers jutting into the Atlantic and piers in the Chesapeake Bay. You don't need a permit, and rod and reel rentals and bait is usually available at the piers. Hop aboard a charter boat to go reef, deep-sea and Gulf Stream fishing for sea bass, flounder, tuna, marlin, false albacore and others. You can head to Lake Smith, Lake Christine and the inland waterways of the Chesapeake and Albemarle Canal for lake and stream fishing. If you're looking for crabs, go crabbing for blue crabs in Lynnhaven waters, Linkhorn Bay and Rudee Inlet. For surf fishing, you do need a saltwater fishing license and to bring your own gear.

FRANCIS LAND HOUSE HISTORIC SITE AND GARDENS

3131 Virginia Beach Blvd., Virginia Beach, 757-431-4000; www.virginiabeachhistory.org

A late 18th-century plantation home features period rooms, special exhibits, gardens and museum gift shop.

Admission: adults $4, seniors $3, students $2, children 5 and under free. Tuesday-Saturday 9 a.m.-5 p.m., Sunday 11 a.m.-5 p.m.

LYNNHAVEN HOUSE

4405 Wishart Road, Virginia Beach, 757-431-4000; www.virginiabeachhistory.org

This stately story-and-a-half masonry structure is a well-preserved example of 18th-century architecture and decorative arts.

Admission: adults $4, seniors $3, children 6-18 $2, children 5 and under free. Tuesday-Saturday 10 a.m.-4 p.m., Sunday noon-4 p.m..

MOTOR WORLD

700 S. Birdneck Road, Virginia Beach, 757-422-6419; www.vbmotorworld.com

This amusement park includes go-karts, mini-golf, bumper boats, rides and paintball. There's a lot more here for kids and parents to enjoy.

Admission and hours vary; see Web site for information.

NORWEGIAN LADY STATUE

25th Street and Boardwalk, Virginia Beach; www.virginia.org

A gift to Virginia Beach from the people of Moss, Norway, the statue commemorates the tragic wreck of the Norwegian bark Dictator off the shores of Virginia Beach in 1891.

OCEAN BREEZE WATER PARK

849 General Booth Blvd., Virginia Beach, 757-422-4444;
www.oceanbreezewaterpark.com

This water park features a cool break from the hot sun with waterslides, a wave pool, rapids and children's water amusements.

Admission: adults $23.99, seniors and children 3-9 $16.99, children 2 and under free. Memorial Day-Labor day, Daily; hours vary.

OLD CAPE HENRY LIGHTHOUSE AND MEMORIAL PARK

583 Atlantic Ave., Fort Story, Virginia Beach, 757-422-9421; www.apva.org/capehenry
On Fort Story sits an active army base and the first U.S. government-built lighthouse (circa 1791).
Admission: adults $4, children 3-12 $2, children 2 and under free.
November-mid-March, daily 10 a.m.-4 p.m.; mid-March-October, daily 10 a.m.-5 p.m.

OLD COAST GUARD STATION

24th Street and Atlantic Avenue, Virginia Beach, 757-422-1587;
www.oldcoastguardstation.com
This former Coast Guard Station displays visual exhibits of numerous ship-wrecks along the Virginia coastline tell of past bravery and disaster. "The War Years" exhibit relates United States Coast Guard efforts during World War I and World War II. There are photographs, ship models and artifacts.
Admission: adults $4, seniors and military personnel $3, children 6-18 $2, children 5 and under free. Monday-Saturday 10 a.m.-5 p.m., Sunday noon-5 p.m.

VIRGINIA AQUARIUM, A MARINE SCIENCE CENTER

717 General Booth Blvd., Virginia Beach, 757-385-3474; www.vmsm.com
Head to the aquarium to see live animals, interactive exhibits, a 300-seat IMAX 3-D theater and more. Exhibits include an ocean aquarium with sharks, large fish; a sea turtle aquarium; seals and other habitats; an aviary; a salt marsh preserve; a touch tank; a river room; and a garden.
Admission: adults $11.95, seniors $10.95, children 3-11 $7.95, children 2 and under free. Memorial Day-Labor Day, Daily 9 a.m.-6 p.m.; Labor Day-Memorial Day, Daily 9 a.m.-5 p.m.

SPECIAL EVENTS
NEPTUNE FESTIVAL'S BOARDWALK WEEKEND

Virginia Beach Oceanfront, Virginia Beach, 757-498-0215, 866-637-3378;
www.neptunefestival.com
Neptune Festival puts on events from March-September with the end of summer bash, Boardwalk Weekend, being the biggest as it covers 30 blocks of the oceanfront and boardwalk. Friday, attend the Endless Summer Beach Bash on the beach with endless food, drinks and music. The rest of the weekend is filled with a parade, music, food, drinks, a sand-sculpting competition, an arts and crafts show, a regatta, an 8K and 5K run, a surfing competition, volleyball tournament and more.
Last weekend in September.

PUNGO STRAWBERRY FESTIVAL

1776 Princess Anne Road, Virginia Beach, 771-721-6001;
www.pungostrawberryfestival.info
Virginia Beach's miles of farmland is referred to as Pungo and this weekend, 120,000 people come out to eat strawberries, compete in bake-offs and pie eating contests, take part in pig races, watch a livestock show and an arts and crafts show and more.
Memorial Day weekend.

WHERE TO STAY

★★★CROWNE PLAZA HOTEL VIRGINIA BEACH-NORFOLK

4453 Bonney Road, Virginia Beach, 757-473-1700, 877-834-3613;
www.cpvabeach.com

Just off Interstate 264, this traditional hotel is conveniently located in the Town Center Business District with easy access to downtown Virginia Beach, Norfolk, Chesapeake and many corporate offices. Guests are treated to comfortable rooms, a 24-hour fitness center, indoor pool and whirlpool and sauna. Golf courses and tennis courts are nearby.

149 rooms. Restaurant, bar. Business center. Fitness center. Pool. $151-250

★★DOUBLETREE HOTEL

1900 Pavilion Drive, Virginia Beach, 757-422-8900, 800-222-8733;
www.doubletree.com

292 rooms. Restaurant, bar. Business center. Fitness center. Pool. Pets accepted. $151-250

★★★FOUNDERS INN

5641 Indian River Road, Virginia Beach, 757-424-5511, 800-926-4466;
www.foundersinn.com

Sitting on 26 beautifully manicured acres, this Georgian-style inn has a southern-colonial décor and a unique combination of intimate charm and extensive meeting space. Unwind by the pool while your children enjoy the waterslide. Or head to the jacuzzi which overlooks the lake. Pamper yourself at the Flowering Almond Spa with a hot stone massage or a caviar facial. Then head to the Swan Terrace Restaurant for fresh seafood at this fine dining spot or choose The Hunt Room, a more casual spot where you can also catch up on sports or shoot some pool.

240 rooms. Restaurant, bar. Business center. Fitness center. Pool. Spa. Pets accepted. Tennis. $61-150

★★HOLIDAY INN

2607 Atlantic Ave., Virginia Beach, 757-491-6900, 877-834-3613;
www.ichotelsgroup.com

143 rooms. Complimentary breakfast. Fitness center. Pool. $151-250

★LA QUINTA INN AND SUITES

2800 Pacific Ave., Virginia Beach, 757-428-2203; www.laquinta.com

137 rooms. Complimentary breakfast. Fitness center. Pool. Pets accepted. $61-150

★★WYNDHAM VIRGINIA BEACH OCEANFRONT

5700 Atlantic Ave., Virginia Beach, 757-428-7025, 877-999-3223; www.wyndham.com

243 rooms. Restaurant, bar. Business center. Fitness center. Pool. Pets accepted. Beach. $151-250

WHERE TO EAT

★★ALDO'S
1860 Laskin Road, Virginia Beach, 757-491-1111; www.aldosvb.com
Italian. Lunch (Monday-Saturday), dinner. Reservations recommended. Outdoor seating. Bar. $16-35

★★COASTAL GRILL
1427 N. Great Neck Road, Virginia Beach, 757-496-3348; www.coastalgrill.com
American. Dinner, late-night. Reservations recommended. Outdoor seating. Bar. $16-35

★★IL GIARDINO
910 Atlantic Ave., Virginia Beach, 757-422-6464; www.ilgiardino.com
Italian. Dinner. Children's menu. Outdoor seating. Bar. $16-35

★★LYNNHAVEN FISH HOUSE
2350 Starfish Road, Virginia Beach, 757-481-0003; www.lynnhavenfishhouse.net
Seafood. Lunch, dinner, Saturday-Sunday brunch. Children's menu. Bar. $16-35

★★RUDEE'S RESTAURANT AND RAW BAR
227 Mediterranean Ave., Virginia Beach, 757-425-1777, 800-883-0850;
www.rudees.com
Seafood, steak. Lunch, dinner, Sunday brunch. Outdoor seating. Bar. $16-35

WARM SPRINGS

See also Hot Springs
Nestled at the foot of Little Mountain, the spring wildflowers and groves of fall foliage make Warm Springs a very scenic spot for sightseeing, hiking and water activities. There are also walking tours to view the many historic buildings.

WHERE TO STAY

★★★INN AT GRISTMILL SQUARE
Highway 619, Warm Springs, 540-839-2231; www.gristmillsquare.com
Wake up to the smell of fresh-baked muffins every morning at the Inn at Gristmill Square, a village-like collection of restored 19th-century buildings. Tucked into picturesque Warm Springs, the inn offers 19 guest rooms with comfortable, country décor. After exploring the area, end your day with a dinner of fresh local trout at the inn's restaurant in a converted mill.
19 rooms. Restaurant, bar. Complimentary breakfast. $61-150

WHERE TO EAT

★★THE WATERWHEEL RESTAURANT
Route 619, Warm Springs, 540-839-2231; www.gristmillsquare.com
American. Dinner, Sunday brunch. Reservations recommended. Outdoor seating. Bar. $16-35

WASHINGTON

See also Front Royal, Shenandoah National Park

The oldest of more than 25 American towns to be named after the first president, this town was surveyed in 1749 by none other than George Washington himself. The streets remain laid out exactly as surveyed and still bear the names of families who owned the land on which the town was founded. It is rumored that Gay Street was named by the 17-year-old Washington after the lovely Gay Fairfax. The town is situated in the foothills of the Blue Ridge Mountains, which dominate the western horizon.

WHERE TO STAY
★★★BLUE ROCK INN

12567 Lee Highway, Washington, 540-987-3190; www.thebluerockinn.com
The Blue Rock Inn, a turn-of-the-century restored farmhouse that now holds a dining room, a pub and five guest rooms, sits on 80 rolling acres, which guests can enjoy from their private balconies.
5 rooms. Complimentary breakfast. $151-250

★★★★★THE INN AT LITTLE WASHINGTON

309 Main St., Washington, 540-675-3800; www.theinnatlittlewashington.com
Savvy epicureans book a room—and a table—at the Inn at Little Washington. Tucked away in the foothills of the Blue Ridge Mountains, the inn offers visitors a taste of the good life, complete with afternoon tea with scones and tartlets. Tempting as it may be to indulge, guests save their appetites for the evening's cuisine. Many make special trips just for the talented chef's award-winning meals, though lucky guests recount their memorable feasts while ensconcing themselves in one of the inn's lovely guest rooms. The surrounding area provides opportunities for hiking, fly-fishing, hot air ballooning, antiquing and wine tasting.
18 rooms. Restaurant, bar. Complimentary breakfast. Closed Tuesday in January-March and July. $351 and up.

WHERE TO EAT
★★★BLUE ROCK INN

12567 Lee Highway, Washington, 540-987-3190; www.thebluerockinn.com
This country-inn farmhouse is located on 80 acres of rolling hillside overlooking the Blue Ridge Mountains and adjoining vineyards. It is a great place to stop between Harrisonburg and Washington, D.C. Enjoy seared duck breast with a port cherry reduction, grilled pork loin with mango chutney or thai-style scallops with thai green chili sauce. For dessert, try the homemade pumpkin pie.
French. Dinner, Sunday brunch. Closed Monday-Tuesday. Reservations recommended. Outdoor seating. Bar. $36-85

★★★★★THE INN AT LITTLE WASHINGTON

309 Main St., Washington, 540-675-3800; www.theinnatlittlewashington.com
Chef Patrick O'Connell has amassed almost every culinary award in ex-

istence. Seasonal dishes include a crab cake "sandwich" with fried green tomatoes and tomato vinaigrette; prosciutto-wrapped pan roasted veal loin with spinach raviolini and parmesan broth; salmon in lemon butter sauce with spring vegetables and Louisiana crawfish tails; and for dessert, a southern butter pecan ice cream sandwich with hot caramel sauce. The atmosphere is no less enticing with rose-colored lampshades, high-backed chairs and gilted mirrors.

American. Dinner. Closed Tuesday. Reservations recommended. Bar. $86 and up.

WILLIAMSBURG

See also Jamestown, Newport News, Yorktown

After the Native American massacre of 1622, this Virginia colony built a palisade across the peninsula between the James and York rivers. The settlement that grew up around it was called Middle Plantation, now the site of Colonial Williamsburg.

Middle Plantation figured prominently in Bacon's Rebellion against Governor Berkeley. Renamed in honor of William III of England, the new capital gradually became a town of about 200 houses and 1,500 residents. For 81 years, Williamsburg was the political, social and cultural capital of Virginia.

The colony's first successful printing press was established here by William Parks, and in 1736 he published Virginia's first newspaper. Williamsburg's capitol was the scene of stirring colonial events such as Patrick Henry's Stamp Act speech.

The First Continental Congress was called from here by the dissolved House of Burgesses in 1774. Two years later, the Second Continental Congress was boldly led by delegates from Virginia to declare independence; George Mason's Declaration of Rights, which became the basis for the Bill of Rights, was adopted here.

Williamsburg's exciting days came to an end in 1780 when the capital was moved to Richmond for greater safety and convenience during the Revolutionary War. For a century and a half it continued as a quiet college town, its tranquility interrupted briefly by the Civil War. In 1917, when a munitions factory was built near the town and cheap housing for the factory's 15,000 workers was hastily erected, Williamsburg seemed destined to blandly live out its days.

In 1926, however, John D. Rockefeller, Jr., and Dr. W.A.R. Goodwin, rector of Bruton Parish Church, who saw the town as a potential treasure-house of colonial history, joined forces for Williamsburg's restoration. For more than 30 years, Rockefeller devoted personal attention to the project and contributed funds to accomplish this nonprofit undertaking.

Today, after many years of archaeological and historical research, the project is near completion. The Historic Area, approximately a mile long and a half-mile wide, encompasses most of the 18th-century capital. Eighty-eight of the original buildings have been restored; 50 major buildings, houses and shops and many smaller outbuildings have been reconstructed on their original sites; 45 of the more historically significant buildings contain more than 200 exhibition rooms, furnished either with original pieces or reproductions, and are open to the public on regular seasonal schedules.

Visitors stroll Duke of Gloucester Street and mingle with people in 18th-century attire. Craftsmen at shops ply trades such as wig-making and black-smithing, using materials, tools and techniques of pre-Revolutionary times. The Historic Area is closed to private motor vehicles 8 a.m.-10 p.m.

WHAT TO SEE
1700S SHOPPING
Superior wares typical of the 18th century are offered in nine restored or reconstructed stores and shops; items include silver, jewelry, herbs, candles, hats and books. Two craft houses sell approved reproductions of the antiques on display in the houses and museums.

ABBY ALDRICH ROCKEFELLER FOLK ART CENTER
307 S. England St., Williamsburg, 757-229-1000; www.colonialwilliamsburg.org
This art center has an outstanding collection of American folk art. Items in this collection were created by artists not trained in studio techniques, but who faithfully recorded aspects of everyday life in paintings, sculpture, needlework, ceramics, toys and other media.
Mid-March-early January, daily 10 a.m.-7 p.m.; early January-mid-March 10 a.m.-5 p.m

BRUTON PARISH EPISCOPAL CHURCH
331 Duke of Gloucester St., Williamsburg, 757-229-2891; www.brutonparish.org
This is one of America's oldest Episcopalian churches, in continuous use since 1715.
Monday-Saturday 10 a.m.-4 p.m., Sunday 12:30 p.m.-4:30 p.m.

BUSCH GARDENS WILLIAMSBURG
1 Busch Gardens Blvd., Williamsburg, 757-253-3000, 800-343-7946;
www.buschgardens.com
This European-style theme park on 360 acres features recreated 17th-century German, English, French, Italian, Scottish and Canadian villages. Attractions include more than 50 thrill rides, attractions and shows, including the Alpengeist roller coaster, one of the fastest and tallest in the world; Sesame Street: Forest of Fun attractions for kids; live shows, an antique carousel, celebrity concerts, and rides for small children. There are theme restaurants and shops. Transportation around the grounds by sky ride or steam train. A computer-operated monorail links the park with the Anheuser-Busch Hospitality Center, where visitors can take a brewery tour.
Admission: adults $59.95, children 3-9 $49.95, children 2 and under free.
Mid-April-August, daily; late March-mid-April and September-December, hours vary; see Web site for schedule.

THE COLLEGE OF WILLIAM & MARY
Richmond Road, Williamsburg, 757-221-4000; www.wm.edu
Established in 1693, William & Mary is America's second-oldest college (only Harvard is older). It initiated an honor system, an elective system of studies, and schools of law and modern languages; it was the second to have a school of medicine (all in 1779). The prestigious Phi Beta Kappa Society was founded here in 1776. Today, there are more than 7,500 students.

Tours: Late May-early September, hours vary; see Web site for information.

COLONIAL WILLIAMSBURG

Visitor Center, 102 Information Center Drive, Williamsburg, 757-229-1000,

800-441-8679; www.colonialwilliamsburg.com

There is so much to see and do in Colonial Williamsburg, so your best bet is to go to the visitor center first where you can get information, make your selections, and purchase tickets. An admission ticket is necessary to enjoy the full scope of Colonial Williamsburg and there are different ones to choose from, depending upon what you want to see and how long you want to spend here. Some things not to miss while you're visiting: the Courthouse, where county and city business was conducted from 1770 to 1932; the Magazine, an arsenal and military storehouse of the Virginia Colony where authentic arms are exhibited; the Capitol where the House of Burgesses met and the scene of Patrick Henry's speech against the stamp act; Raleigh Tavern which was frequented by Jefferson, Henry and other Revolutionary patriots; the Wren Building, the oldest academic building in America, was designed by the great English architect Sir Christopher Wren; the Wythe House which was the home of George Wythe, America's first law professor, teacher of Jefferson, Clay and Marshall; the Peyton Randolph House, which was the home of the president of the First Continental Congress; the Public Gaol, where debtors, criminals and pirates (including Blackbeard's crew) were imprisoned; and the Public Hospital which was the first public institution in the English colonies devoted exclusively to treatment of mental illness.

Visitor center: Daily 8:45 a.m.-5 p.m.

DEWITT WALLACE DECORATIVE ARTS MUSEUM

Henry and Francis streets, Williamsburg, 757-220-7724, 800-447-8679

This modern museum adjoining the Public Hospital, features exhibits, lectures, films and related programs centering on British and American decorative arts of the 17th to early 19th centuries.

Mid-March-early January, daily 10 a.m.-7 p.m.; early January-mid-March, daily 10 a.m.-5 p.m.

EVENING ENTERTAINMENT

Williamsburg; www.colonialwilliamsburg.com

Colonial Williamsburg presents "rollicking 18th-century plays" throughout the year; wide variety of cultural events, concerts and historical reenactments. Chowning's Tavern offers colonial "gambols" (games), music, entertainment and light food and drink.

See Web site for schedules and ticket information.

FORD'S COLONY WILLIAMSBURG

1 Ford's Colony Drive, Williamsburg, 800-334-6033; www.fordscolony.com

This acclaimed Dan Maples-designed golf course features 54 holes, comprising the par-72 Marsh Hawk Course, the par-71 Blackheath Course, and the par-72 Blue Heron Course. The course touts itself as a "player's course" that appeals to golfers of all levels There's a Dining Room and Country Club

where you can relax after a round of golf.
See Web site for schedule and pricing information.

GO-KARTS PLUS
6910 Richmond Road, Highway 60 W., Williamsburg, 757-564-7600;
www.gokartsplus.com
This eight-acre park has four go-kart tracks that appeal to various ages and driving skills, as well as bumper cars and boats, rides, a miniature golf course and an arcade. While admission is free, tickets must be purchased for activities and rides.
Admission: Free. June-August, daily 11 a.m.-10 p.m.; April-May, September-October, hours vary; call for information.

MUSCARELLE MUSEUM OF ART
The College of William and Mary, Jamestown Road and Phi Beta Kappa Circle,
Williamsburg, 757-221-2700; www.wm.edu/muscarelle
Located on the campus of the College of William and Mary, this museum features traveling displays and exhibitions from an extensive collection.
Admission: $5, students, children 11 and under free; special exhibits additional $5. Tuesday-Friday 10 a.m.-5 p.m., Saturday-Sunday noon-4 p.m.

SHIRLEY PEWTER SHOP
417 Duke of Gloucester St., Williamsburg, 757-229-5356, 800-550-5356;
www.shirleypewter.com
This shop features Williamsburg's own brand of pewter, Shirley Pewter. Items available include dinnerware, oil lamps and tableware. Many items can be engraved.
Monday-Saturday 10 a.m.-6 p.m., Sunday 10:30 a.m.-6 p.m.

WATER COUNTRY USA
176 Water Country Parkway, Williamsburg, 757-253-3350, 800-343-7946;
www.watercountryusa.com
This park, the mid-Atlantic's largest water park, features water slides, thrill rides and live entertainment. If you're interested in visiting Busch Gardens as well, which is three miles from Water Country USA, a Bounce Pass gives admission to both parks.
Admission: adults $41.95, children 3-9 $34.95, children 2 and under free.
Mid May-early September, hours vary; see Web site for schedule.

WILLIAMSBURG NATIONAL GOLF COURSE
3700 Centerville, Williamsburg, 757-258-9738, 800-859-9182; www.wngc.com
Williamsburg National features the Jamestown Course, an 18-hole, par-72 public course, which is the only Jack Nicklaus-designed course in Virginia; and the Yorktown Course, a new 7,000 yard championship course designed by Tom Clark.
See Web site for schedules and rates.

WILLIAMSBURG WINERY
5810 Wessex Hundred, Williamsburg, 757-229-0999; www.williamsburgwinery.com

Founded in 1985, the winery carries on a Virginia tradition that began with the Jamestown settlers in 1607. Located two miles from the Historic Area, it has 50 acres of vineyards. Visitors can take 30-45 minute guided walking tours, and tastings are available after the tour.

Admission (tour and tasting): $8. April-October, Monday-Saturday 10 a.m.-6 p.m., Sunday 11 a.m.-6 p.m.; November-March, Monday-Saturday 10 a.m.-5 p.m., Sunday 11 a.m.-5 p.m. Tours: Daily 11 a.m.-4 p.m. (every half hour).

YORK RIVER STATE PARK
5526 Riverview Road, Williamsburg, 757-566-3036; www.dcr.virginia.gov
A 2,550-acre park along the York River and its related marshes. It includes the Taskinas Creek National Estuarine Research Reserve. Enjoy fishing, boating, hiking and bridle trails, picnicking, programs, and nature walks. Daily.

SPECIAL EVENTS
FIFE AND DRUM PERFORMANCES
Williamsburg General Store and Wallace's Trading Post, Williamsburg, 757-253-1796; www.fifedrum.org
The Williamsburg Fifes and Drums perform 18th century fife and drum music in front of Williamsburg General Store on Thursday and Saturday evenings and at Wallace's Trading Post on Wednesday and Friday evenings. Mid-June-August.

INDEPENDENCE DAY CELEBRATION
102 Information Center Drive, Williamsburg, 800-447-8679
This celebration takes place in Colonial Williamsburg's historic area with fifes and drums, militia parades, and fireworks. Head to Market Square for the parade and where you can also view the fireworks. Mid-May.

TRADITIONAL CHRISTMAS ACTIVITIES
102 Information Center Drive, Williamsburg, 800-447-8679
Witness this magical seasons in Colonial Williamsburg featuring a grand illumination, which is a display of fireworks with holiday music and glowing candles. The town is filled with decorations, carolers, frost covered windows, cobblestone lanes, fresh pines and lampposts. There's a Christmas homes gour, a community Christmas tree lighting in Market Square and more. December.

WHERE TO STAY
★★CROWNE PLAZA
6945 Pocahontas Trail, Williamsburg, 757-220-2250, 877-424-4225; www.cpwilliamsburghotel.com
303 rooms. Restaurant, bar. Business center. Fitness center. Pool. Pets accepted. Tennis. $61-150

★★★KINGSMILL RESORT & SPA

1010 Kingsmill Road, Williamsburg, 757-253-1703, 800-832-2665; www.kingsmill.com
This playground for adults attracts golfers, tennis players and those seeking rest and relaxation to its 2,900 manicured acres along the James River. Three 18-hole golf courses and a nine-hole par-three course challenge players while the Golf Academy provides clinics and individual instruction. Tennis players take their pick from fast-drying clay, Deco-Turf and hydro courts at the state-of-the-art facility, while other racquet sports and a fitness center are available at the Sports Club. After a day filled with activities, hearty appetites are always satisfied at the resort's six restaurants and lounges.
425 rooms. Restaurant, bar. Complimentary breakfast. Business center. Fitness center. Pool. Spa. Tennis. Golf. Beach. $251-350

★★★MARRIOTT WILLIAMSBURG
50 Kingsmill Road, Williamsburg, 757-220-2500; www.williamsburgmarriott.com
The closest hotel to Busch Gardens, the Marriott Williamsburg is also conveniently located near Colonial Williamsburg, Jamestown and Yorktown, as well as shopping and outlet centers. After a busy day spent sightseeing, relax in the well-appointed guest rooms.
295 rooms. Restaurant, bar. Business center. Fitness center. Pool. Tennis. $61-150

★★★★WILLIAMSBURG INN
136 E. Francis St., Williamsburg, 757-253-2277, 800-447-8679;
www.colonialwilliamsburg.com
Furnished in English Regency style, the guest rooms have just the right amount of sophistication to appeal to adults while keeping children comfortable and satisfied. Blessed with a central location in the heart of this re-created 18th-century village, the inn is within a leisurely stroll of the blacksmith's shop, candle-maker and cobbler. After reliving history, guests reap the rewards of the inn's plentiful activities and play a round of golf, dive into the spring-fed pool, rally on the clay tennis courts, head to the fitness center to keep in shape, or spoil themselves at the spa or gourmet restaurant.
62 rooms. Restaurant, bar. Business center. Fitness center. Pool. Golf. Tennis. $351 and up.

★★WILLIAMSBURG LODGE
310 S. England St., Williamsburg, 757-253-2277, 800-447-8679;
www.colonialwilliamsburg.com
323 rooms. Restaurant, bar. Business center. Fitness center. Pool. Tennis. $151-250

★★★WILLIAMSBURG WOODLANDS HOTEL AND SUITES
105 Visitor Center Drive, Williamsburg, 757-253-2277, 800-447-8679;
www.colonialwilliamsburg.org
One of Colonial Williamsburg's five resorts and inns, Woodlands Hotel and Suites is located on the grounds of the visitor center at the edge of a 40-acre pine forest.
300 rooms. Restaurant. Complimentary breakfast. Business center. Fitness

center. Pool. Tennis. $61-150

WHERE TO EAT

★★BERRET'S SEAFOOD RESTAURANT AND TAPHOUSE GRILL
199 S. Boundary St., Williamsburg, 757-253-1847; www.berrets.com
American. Lunch, dinner, late-night, Sunday brunch. Closed Monday, January-February. Reservations recommended. Outdoor seating. Bar. $16-35

★★★THE DINING ROOM AT FORD'S COLONY
240 Ford's Colony Drive, Williamsburg, 757-258-4107; www.fordscolony.com
Rich, imaginative American and European dishes are served in a quiet, elegant dining room.
American. Dinner. Closed Sunday-Wednesday. Reservations recommended. Outdoor seating. Bar. $36-85

★★KING'S ARMS TAVERN
416 E. Duke of Glouchester St., Williamsburg, 757-229-2141, 800-447-8679; www.colonialwilliamsburg.com
American. Lunch, dinner. Children's menu. Reservations recommended. Outdoor seating. Bar. $36-85

★★LE YACA
1915 Pocahontas Trail No. C10, Williamsburg, 757-220-3616; www.leyacawilliamsburg.com
French. Lunch (Monday-Friday), dinner. Closed Sunday. Children's menu. Reservations recommended. Bar. $36-85

★OLD CHICKAHOMINY HOUSE
1211 Jamestown Road, Williamsburg, 757-229-4689; www.oldchickahominy.com
American. Breakfast, lunch. $15 and under.

★PIERCE'S PITT BAR-B-QUE
447 E. Rochambeau Drive, Williamsburg, 757-565-2955; www.pierces.com
American. Lunch, dinner. Children's menu. $15 and under.

★★★REGENCY DINING ROOM
136 E. Francis St., Williamsburg, 757-229-2141, 800-447-8679; www.colonialwilliamsburg.com
Set in the charming Williamsburg Inn, the Regency Dining Room offers diners a graceful setting in which to enjoy a leisurely dinner of contemporary Southern fare. The menu runs the gamut from dishes like citrus-glazed scallops and herbed prawns with butternut squash and Yukon Gold potatoes; salmon filet with crabmeat and corn risotto; and Berkshire pork tenderloin with almond bread pudding and braised cabbage. Live music and dancing are offered on Friday and Saturday night.
American. Breakfast, dinner, Sunday brunch. Bar. $36-85

★★RIVER'S INN RESTAURANT & CRAB DECK
8109 Yacht Haven Drive, Gloucester Point, 804-642-9942, 888-780-2722;

www.riversinnrestaurant.com
Seafood. Lunch, dinner. Closed Monday. Outdoor seating. Bar. $16-35

★★SEASONS CAFÉ
110 S. Henry, Williamsburg, 757-259-0018; www.seasonsofwilliamsburg.com
International. Lunch, dinner, Sunday brunch. Children's menu. Bar. $16-35

★★★THE TRELLIS
403 Duke of Gloucester St., Williamsburg, 757-229-8610; www.thetrellis.com
Entrées include deep-dried catfish with sweet corn, black beans, summer savory, confetti rice and Trellis barbecue sauce; and grilled pork tenderloin medallions with grits cake, black-eyed peas, oven-roasted Roma tomatoes and steamed spinach.
American. Lunch, dinner. Outdoor seating. Bar. $36-85

★★THE WHALING COMPANY
494 McLaw Circle, Williamsburg, 757-229-0275; www.thewhalingcompany.com
Seafood. Dinner. Bar. $16-35

★★YORKSHIRE STEAK AND SEAFOOD HOUSE
700 York St., Williamsburg, 757-229-9790; www.theyorkshirerestaurant.com
American. Dinner. Children's menu. Reservations recommended. $16-35

WINCHESTER

See also Front Royal, Strasburg

Winchester is the oldest colonial city west of the Blue Ridge, a Civil War prize that changed hands 72 times (including 13 times in one day). Sometimes called the "apple capital of the world," it is located at the northern approach to the Shenandoah Valley.

George Washington, as a red-haired 16-year-old, headed for Winchester and his first surveying job in 1748, and began a decade of apprenticeship for the military and political responsibilities he would later assume as a national leader. During the French and Indian Wars, Colonel Washington made the city his defense headquarters while he built Fort Loudoun in Winchester. Washington was elected to his first political office as a representative from Frederick County to the House of Burgesses.

At the intersection of travel routes, both east-west and north-south, Winchester grew and prospered. By the time of the Civil War it was a major transportation and supply center, strategically located to control both Union approaches to Washington and Confederate supply lines through the Shenandoah Valley. More than 100 minor engagements and six battles took place in the vicinity. General Stonewall Jackson had his headquarters here during the winter of 1861-1862. From his headquarters in Winchester, Union General Philip Sheridan started his famous ride to rally his troops at Cedar Creek, 11 miles away, and turn a Confederate victory into a Union rout.

Approximately 3.5 million bushels of apples are harvested annually in Frederick County and are one of Winchester's economic mainstays. The world's largest apple cold storage plant and one of the world's largest apple processing plants are here.

WHAT TO SEE
ABRAM'S DELIGHT AND LOG CABIN
1340 S. Pleasant Valley Ave., Winchester, 540-662-6519
The oldest house in city, was built in 1754 and then restored. It's furnished in
18th-century style with a boxwood garden and a log cabin.
Admission: adults $5, seniors $4.50, students 7-15 $2.50, children 6 and under
free. April-October, Monday-Saturday 10 a.m.-4 p.m., Sunday noon-4 p.m.

FIRST PRESBYTERIAN CHURCH OF WINCHESTER
116 S. Loudoun St., Winchester, 540-662-3824; www.firstchurch-winchester.org
This building has been used as a church, a stable by Union troops in Civil
War, a public school, and an armory. It was restored in 1941.
Services: Sunday 7:30 a.m., 8:30 a.m., 11 a.m.

HANDLEY LIBRARY AND ARCHIVES
100 W. Piccadilly St., Winchester, 540-662-9041; www.hrl.lib.state.va.us/handley
Completed in 1913, the public library was designed in Beaux-Arts style. The
rotunda is crowned on the outside with a copper-covered dome and on the
inside by a dome of stained glass. The interesting interior features include
wrought-iron staircases and glass floors. Historical archives are housed on
the lower level.
Admission: Free. Tuesday-Wednesday 1-8 p.m., Thursday-Saturday 10
a.m. 5 p.m.

STONEWALL JACKSON'S HEADQUARTERS
415 N. Braddock St., Winchester, 540-667-3242; www.winchesterhistory.org
This was Jackson's headquarters from November 1861 through March 1862.
It now serves as a museum housing Jackson memorabilia and other Confederate items of the war years.
Admission: adults $5, seniors $4.50, children 7-15 $2.50, children 6 and
under free. April-October, Monday-Saturday 10 a.m.-4 p.m., Sunday
noon-4 p.m.

WASHINGTON'S OFFICE-MUSEUM
Cork and Braddock streets, Winchester, 540-662-4412; www.fortedwards.org
This building was used by George Washington in 1755-1756 during the con-
struction of Fort Loudoun. Housed in this museum are French and Indian,
Revolutionary and Civil War relics.
Admission: adults $5, seniors $4.50, children 7-15 $2.50, children 6 and
under free. April-October, Monday-Saturday 10 a.m.-4 p.m., Sunday
noon-4 p.m.

SPECIAL EVENTS
SHENANDOAH APPLE BLOSSOM FESTIVAL
135 N. Cameron St., Winchester, 540-662-3863; www.thebloom.com
This festival features the coronation of the Apple Blossom Queen, parades,

arts and crafts, band contests, music, food and attractions. Late-April-early May.

WHERE TO STAY
★HAMPTON INN
1655 Apple Blossom Drive, Winchester, 540-667-8011, 800-426-7866;
www.hamptoninn.com
100 rooms. Complimentary breakfast. Business center. Fitness center. Pool. $61-150

★★HOLIDAY INN
333 Front Royal Pike, Winchester, 540-667-3300, 877-834-3613;
www.holidayinn.com/winchesterva
130 rooms. Restaurant, bar. Business center. Fitness center. Pool. $61-150

YORKTOWN
See also Jamestown, Newport News, Williamsburg
Free land offered in 1630 to those adventurous enough "to sate and inhabit" the 50-foot bluffs on the south side of the York River brought about the beginning of settlement. When the Assembly authorized a port, started in 1691, the town slowly expanded and in the following years became a busy shipping center, its prosperity peaking around 1750. From then on, the port declined along with the Tidewater Virginia tobacco trade.

Yorktown's moment in history came in 1781. After raiding up and down Virginia with minimal resistance from the Marquis de Lafayette, British commander Cornwallis was sent here to establish a naval base in which supplies and reinforcements could be shipped to him. The Comte de Grasse's French fleet effectively blockaded the British, however, by controlling the mouth of the Chesapeake Bay. At the Battle of the Capes on September 5, 1781, a British fleet sent to investigate the French presence was defeated by the French. Cornwallis found himself bottled up in Yorktown by combined American and French forces under Washington, which arrived on September 28.

Shelling began October 9. The siege of Yorktown ended on October 17 with Cornwallis requesting terms of capitulation. On October 19, Cornwallis' troops marched out with flags and arms cased, their bands playing. Then they laid down their arms, bringing the last major battle of the Revolutionary War to a close.

Yorktown Battlefield, part of Colonial National Historical Park, surrounds the village. Though Yorktown itself is still an active community, many surviving and reconstructed colonial structures supply an 18th-century atmosphere.

WHAT TO SEE
MOORE HOUSE
Yorktown Battlefield, 224 Ballard St., Yorktown, 757-898-3400; www.nps.gov/york
In this 18th-century house, the "Articles of Capitulation" were drafted, marking the surrender of Cornwallis's British army. These were signed by General Washington on October 19, 1781, which ended the last battle in the Revolu-

tionary War.
Daily 9 a.m.-5 p.m.

NELSON HOUSE

Yorktown Battlefield, Nelson and Main streets, Yorktown, 757-898-3400;
www.nps.gov/york
Part of Colonial National Historic Park, the original mansion was built by
"Scotch Tom" Nelson in the early 1700s and since then has been restored. It
was the home of his grandson, Thomas Nelson, Jr., a signer of the Declaration of Independence. It is an impressive example of Georgian architecture.
Daily 9 a.m.-5 p.m.

YORKTOWN BATTLEFIELD IN COLONIAL NATIONAL
HISTORIC PARK

Colonial Parkway and Yorktown Visitor Center, Yorktown, 757-898-3400;
www.nps.gov/york
The Battlefield surrounds and includes part of town. It is the remains of 1781
British fortifications, modified and strengthened by Confederate forces in
Civil War. Reconstructed American and French lines lie beyond. While here,
see the Yorktown National Civil War Cemetery, which has 2,204 burials,
1,436 of which are unknown. Stop by the Visitor Center located at the Battlefield to pay the park admission fee which includes access to the visitor center,
battlefield tour, the Moore House and the Nelson House.
Admission: adults $10, children 15 and under free. Grounds: Daily dawn-dusk. Visitor center: Daily 9 a.m.-5 p.m.

YORKTOWN VICTORY CENTER

Route 1020, Williamsburg, 757-253-4838; www.historyisfun.org
This museum of the Revolutionary War chronicles the struggle for independence from the beginning of colonial unrest to the new nation's formation.
There are exhibit galleries, a living history Continental Army encampment
and late-18th-century farm. See Web site for a combination ticket with Jamestown Settlement available.
Admission: adults $9.25, children 6-12 $6.50, children 5 and under free.
Daily 9 a.m.-5 p.m.

SPECIAL EVENTS
YORKTOWN VICTORY CELEBRATION

Yorktown Battlefield, 757-898-2410; www.nps.gov/york
This fest is an observance of America's Revolutionary War victory at Yorktown on October 19, 1781. The celebration includes a parade and more.
Mid-October.

WHERE TO STAY
★DUKE OF YORK HOTEL

508 Water St., Yorktown, 757-898-3232; www.dukeofyorkmotel.com
57 rooms. Pool. $61-150

WASHINGTON, D.C.

WHEREVER YOU'RE STANDING IN DOWNTOWN D.C., CHANCES ARE THE WASHINGTON MONU-ment is within sight. By law, no building may be taller than the 12-story monument—but regardless of their physical stature, the rest of D.C.'s buildings cannot be overshadowed. There are world-renowned museums and monuments, first-rate restaurants and shops within quaint neighborhoods, grassy parks and tree-lined streets. And all are just a short ride away on the city's efficient mass-transit system.

Washington was not the first capital of the United States. The city didn't even exist at the time the nation gained its independence in 1789. For a year, the nation's new government met in New York City before relocating to Philadelphia. In 1790, President Washington selected a site for the nation's capital at the junction of the Potomac and Anacostia rivers, 14 miles north of his home in Mount Vernon. Andrew Ellicott surveyed the area, aided by Benjamin Banneker, a free black from Maryland. Using celestial calculations, Banneker, a self-taught astronomer and mathematician, laid out 40 boundary stones at one-mile intervals to mark the city's borders.

President Washington chose Pierre-Charles L'Enfant to plan the new capital. L'Enfant, a French-born architect and urban designer who served in the American Revolutionary Army, created a bold and original plan, one that called for a grid pattern of streets intersected by wide, diagonal avenues. The diagonal avenues would meet at circles, which would anchor the residential neighborhoods. Today, Logan Circle is a clear example where four different thoroughfares converge, including Rhode Island and Vermont avenues. The large open circle sits at the core of a beautiful neighborhood, with many of its residences building up the area soon after the Civil War.

L'Enfant envisioned the Congress House (now the Capitol) situated atop Jenkins Hill, which offered sweeping views of the Potomac River. To the west of Jenkins Hill, L'Enfant planned a 400-foot-wide avenue (now the National Mall) bordered by embassies and cultural institutions. Not everyone was pleased with his plan. Though he had the president's support, L'Enfant faced opposition from some of the district commissioners who had been appointed to oversee the capital city's development. Secretary of State Thomas Jefferson, a noted architect in his own right, disapproved of the plan, but L'Enfant refused to compromise his vision. In 1792, Washington dismissed the genius planner whom he had appointed only a year earlier. In L'Enfant's place, Washington appointed Andrew Ellicott to prepare a map of the city. Along with Benjamin Banneker, Ellicott produced a map of the city that adhered closely to L'Enfant's plan.

L'Enfant sought $95,500 for his services but received less than $4,000. He died in 1825, financially destitute and never having received acclaim for his work in planning Washington. He was buried in Maryland, then disinterred and reburied at Arlington National Cemetery in 1909. A marble monument marks the site of his grave.

L'Enfant's visionary plan fostered the growth of the city's eclectic mix of neighborhoods: Capitol Hill, with its 19th-century row houses and brick-lined streets; the National Mall's massive stone monuments, museums and government buildings; Georgetown's quaint shops and restaurants; cosmopolitan Dupont Circle; Adams Morgan, with its bustling nightlife; and Woodley Park's leaf-shaded residential streets.

Thanks to L'Enfant's plan, which identified parks and open spaces as essential elements in urban design, D.C. possesses the sorts of places, as L'Enfant wrote, that may be attractive to the learned and afford diversion to the idle. Pulitzer Prize-winning-historian David McCullough has expressed his appreciation of the capital's natural beauty. "In many ways it is our most civilized city," McCullough wrote of Washington. "It accommodates its river, accommodates trees and grass, makes room for nature as other cities don't."

All three branches of the U.S. federal government are based in Washington, D.C., and the number of federal employees commuting into downtown has grown significantly over the years. In 1800, there were 130 federal workers; at the end of the Civil War, there were 7,000; and now there are well over half a million. From politicians on the Hill to lobbyists on K Street to visiting dignitaries, D.C. hosts some of the nation's busiest movers and shakers.

Tourists, too, flock to the nation's capital, visiting their senators and representatives on Capitol Hill, touring the Smithsonian museums along the National Mall, and posing for pictures in front of the Washington Monument and the Lincoln and Jefferson memorials. Sightseeing opportunities abound in this picturesque city. Dining and nightlife options are just as plentiful in neighborhoods such as Georgetown, Dupont Circle, Adams Morgan and the U Street Corridor.

WHAT TO SEE
AFRICAN AMERICAN CIVIL WAR MEMORIAL
1200 U St. N.W., Washington D.C., 202-667-2667; www.afroamcivilwar.org
This sculpture pays tribute to the more than 200,000 African-American soldiers who fought in the Civil War. There are permanent exhibits that give visitors insight into African Americans' struggle for freedom. There is a registry for visitors to find information on their descendants.
Monday-Friday 10 a.m.-5 p.m., Saturday 10 a.m.-2 p.m.

AMERICAN RED CROSS MUSEUM
430 17th St., Washington D.C., 202-303-7066; www.redcross.org/museum
The American Red Cross national headquarters is made up of three buildings bounded by 17th, 18th, D and E streets N.W. The 17th St. building includes marble busts Faith, Hope and Charity by sculptor Hiram Powers and three original Tiffany stained-glass windows. Tours must be scheduled 72 hours in advance.
Wednesday, Friday 10 a.m., 2 p.m., Saturday noon, 2 p.m.

ANACOSTIA MUSEUM

1901 Fort Place S.E., Washington D.C., 202-633-4820; www.anacosta.si.edu
This exhibition and research center by the Smithsonian focuses on African American heritage in the historic Anacostia section of southeast Washington. There are ongoing changing exhibits and lecture series.
Daily 10 a.m.-5 p.m.

ANDERSON HOUSE MUSEUM
2118 Massachusetts Ave. N.W., Washington D.C., 202-785-2040;
www.societyofthecincinnati.org
This Revolutionary War museum and national headquarters of the Society of the Cincinnati has portraits by early American artists; 18th-century paintings; 17th-century tapestries; decorative arts of Europe and Asia; displays of books, medals, swords, silver, glass and china.
Admission: Free. Tuesday-Saturday 1-4 p.m.

ARLINGTON NATIONAL CEMETERY
Arlington, VA, 703-607-8000; www.arlingtoncemetery.org
This famous cemetery was originally designed to be a military cemetery

when it was created in 1864. Today, more than 300,000 people are buried here, including veterans from every war the U.S. has been involved including the American Revolution and the Iraq wars. One of the most famous and most-visited gravesites is that of President John F. Kennedy whose grave has an eternal flame at it's head. Next to him, Jacqueline Bouvier Kennedy Onassis is buried. There is also a memorial here for his brother, Robert F. Kennedy. Also here is the Tomb of the Unknowns (or the Tomb of the Unknown Soldier), which is the resting place for three unknown veterans, guarded 24 hours a day, 365 days a year by the U.S. Army.

Admission: Free. April-September, daily 8 a.m.-5 p.m.; October-March, daily 8 a.m.-7 p.m.

ARTHUR M. SACKLER GALLERY

1050 Independence Ave. S.W., Washington D.C., 202-357-2700; www.asia.si.edu
This gallery, opened in 1987 by the Smithsonian Institution, holds changing exhibitions of Asian art, both near- and far-Eastern, from major national and international collections. Permanent collection includes Chinese and South and Southeast Asian art objects presented by Arthur Sackler.

Admission: Free. Daily 10 a.m.-5:30 p.m.

BASILICA OF THE NATIONAL SHRINE OF THE IMMACULATE CONCEPTION

400 Michigan Ave. N.E., Washington D.C., 202-526-8300; www.nationalshrine.com
This is the largest Roman Catholic church in the U.S. and one of the largest in the world. Architecturally, this Basilica is of the Byzantine-Romanesque style with an extensive and elaborate collection of mosaics and artwork.

Guided tours: Monday-Saturday 9 a.m., 10 a.m., 11 a.m., 1 p.m., 2 p.m., 3 p.m., Sunday 1:30 p.m., 2:30 p.m., 3:30 p.m.

BLAIR-LEE HOUSE

1651 Pennsylvania Ave. N.W., Washington D.C.; www.blairhouse.org
The Blair House has served as a guest house for heads of government and state visiting the U.S. as guests of the president, which dates back to 1824. Such notables to have stayed here are General Charles de Gaulle, Margaret Thatcher, Boris Yeltsin, President Ronald Reagan and Nancy Reagan, and Vladimir Putin among many others. Although the house is not open to the public, its worth taking a look of the exterior.

BLUES ALLEY

1073 Wisconsin Ave. N.W., Washington D.C., 202-337-4141; www.bluesalley.com
For nearly 40 years, serious jazz lovers have flocked to this intimate club to hear Dizzy Gillespie, Sarah Vaughan and Maynard Ferguson, among others. Nightly shows run the gamut from vocal and instrumental sounds to solo performers and larger ensembles. Located in an 18th-century brick carriage house in Georgetown, the club has a sophisticated ambience and a Creole-themed-dinner menu.

Ticket prices vary. Daily 6 p.m.-12:30 a.m.

BUREAU OF ENGRAVING AND PRINTING

14th and C St. S.W., Washington D.C., 202-874-2330, 866-874-2330;
www.bep.treas.gov

The tour here allows visitors to watch currency being printed. Learn about the latest high-tech steps the Bureau has taken to thwart counterfeiting. You can buy uncut sheets of bills in different denominations as well as shredded cash at the BEP store.

Tours: September-March, Monday-Friday 9 a.m.-10:45 a.m., 12:30-2 p.m. (every 15 minutes); April-August, Monday-Friday 9 a.m.-10:45 a.m., 12:30-3:45 p.m., 5-7 p.m. (every 15 minutes). Visitor center: Monday-Friday 8:30 a.m.-3:30 p.m.

THE CAPITOL

Capitol Hill, Washington D.C., 202-225-6827; www.visitthecapitol.gov

The Capitol has been home to the legislative branch of the U.S. government for more than 200 years. Visitors can take guided tours of several sections, including the beautifully restored Old Supreme Court Chamber and the Old Senate Chamber. The Rotunda, a ceremonial space beneath the soaring dome, is a gallery for paintings and sculptures of historic significance. Below it is the Crypt, built for the remains of George Washington (who asked to be buried at Mount Vernon instead), which is now used for exhibits. Don't miss the National Statuary Hall, where statues of prominent citizens have been donated by all 50 states, and the ornate Brumidi Corridors, named for the Italian artist who designed their murals and many other decorative elements in the Capitol. Along the Capitol's west front are terraces, gardens and lawns designed by Frederick Law Olmsted. Halfway down the hill are the Peace Monument (on the north) and the Garfield Monument (on the south). At the foot of Capitol Hill is Union Square with a Reflecting Pool and the Grant Monument. A state-of-the-art visitor center has exhibitions, a store and restaurant for visitors. See Web site for booking tours.

Monday-Saturday 8:30 a.m.-4:30 p.m. Tours: Monday-Saturday 8:50 a.m.-3:20 p.m.

CAPITOL CITY BREWING COMPANY

2 Massachusetts Ave. N.E., Washington D.C., 202-842-2337; www.capcitybrew.com

Shiny copper vats and a large, oval copper bar are the centerpieces of this huge—and hugely popular—brewpub in the beautifully restored 1911 Postal Square Building. Hill staffers and tourists crowd in for made-on-the-premises ales, lagers and pilsners that go down well with warm pretzels and mustard or with whole meals.

Monday-Saturday 11 a.m.-midnight, Sunday 10 a.m.-midnight.

CHESAPEAKE & OHIO CANAL NATIONAL HISTORIC PARK

1057 Thomas Jefferson St. N.W., Washington D.C., 202-653-5190; www.nps.gov/choh

Biking or strolling along the Chesapeake & Ohio Canal towpath is a great way to immerse yourself in history and nature. The canal, which runs 184 1/2 miles between Georgetown and Cumberland, Md., was completed in 1850. Locks, lock houses, aqueducts and other original structures remain. Expect spectacular scenery and all manner of wildlife along the way, including deer, fox and woodpeckers. Take a narrated one-hour, round-trip canal tour led by park rangers in period clothing aboard mule-drawn boats.

Boat Rides: adults $5, children 3 and under free. April-October, Wednesday-Sunday.

CHINATOWN

Between 6th and 8th streets and H and I streets, Washington D.C.

Once populated by German immigrants, Chinatown became a popular location for Chinese immigrants to live in the 1930's. Marked by the Chinatown Friendship Archway at 7th and H streets, which is decorated in Chinese architectural styles of Qing and Ming dynasties and is topped with nearly 300 painted dragons. It was built by not only Washington D.C., but also with help from its sister city, Beijing. The neighborhood is filled with Chinese restaurants and shops.

CONSTITUTION GARDENS

900 Ohio Drive S.W., Washington D.C., 202-426-6841; www.nps.gov/coga

This 50-acre park, with a manmade lake, is also the site of the Signers of the Declaration of Independence Memorial, which has the names and signatures of the 56 men who signed this landmark document. Daily.

CORCORAN GALLERY OF ART

500 17th St. N.W., Washington D.C., 202-639-1700; www.corcoran.org

The city's oldest art museum and the largest non-federal one, this gallery is known for its strong collection of 19th-century American art (don't miss John Singer Sargent's luminous *Oyster Gatherers of Cancale*) and its support for local artists. The museum also shows important European pieces and contemporary works, including photography, performance art and new media.

Admission: adults $10, students, seniors and military personnel $8, children 6 and under free. Wednesday, Friday-Sunday 10 a.m.-5 p.m., Thursday 10 a.m.-9 p.m.

DAR HEADQUARTERS

1776 D St. N.W., Washington D.C., 202-628-1776; www.dar.org

The Daughters of the American Revolution (DAR) National Society, founded in 1890, promotes patriotism through this non-profit organization that has more than 165,000 members and over 3,000 chapters throughout the U.S. and beyond. The national headquarters located here includes Memorial Continental Hall and Constitution Hall; the DAR Museum Gallery, located in the administration building, which has 33 state period rooms; and an outstanding genealogical research library.

DAR Museum & Shop: Monday-Friday 9:30 a.m.-4 p.m., Saturday 9 a.m.-5 p.m. DAR Library: Monday-Friday 8:30 a.m.-4 p.m., Saturday 9 a.m.-5 p.m.

DECATUR HOUSE MUSEUM

1610 H St. N.W., Washington D.C., 202-842-0920; www.decaturhouse.org

This Federal townhouse was built for naval hero Commodore Stephen Decatur by Benjamin H. Latrobe, second architect of the Capitol. After Decatur's death in 1820, the house was occupied by a succession of American and foreign statesmen, and was a center of political and social life in the city. The ground floor family rooms reflect Decatur's Federal-period lifestyle. The house is now operated by the National Trust for Historic Preservation. Gallery Admission: $5, children 12 and under free. Gallery: Monday-Saturday 10 a.m.-5 p.m., Sunday noon-4 p.m. Tour Admission: $5. Tours: Friday-Saturday 10 a.m-4 p.m., Sunday noon-3 p.m.

DEPARTMENT OF THE TREASURY

1500 Pennsylvania Ave. N.W., Washington D.C., 202-622-0896; www.treasury.gov
According to legend, this Greek Revival building, one of the oldest (built in the mid-1800s) in the city, was built in the middle of Pennsylvania Avenue because Andrew Jackson was tired of endless wrangling over the location and walked out of the White House, planted his cane in the mud and said, "Here." The building has been extensively restored. Take a guided one-hour tour of the main building including the Andrew Johnson Suites, the newly restored West dome and blobby and the Cash Room and more; advanced reservations are required.
Admission: Free. Tours: Saturday 9 a.m., 9:45 a.m., 10:30 a.m., 11:15 a.m.

DUMBARTON OAKS

1703 32nd St. N.W., Washington D.C., 202-339-6401; www.doaks.org
These formal, romantic gardens span 16 acres. The Museum has antiques and European art, including El Greco's "The Visitation," galleries of Byzantine art, and a library of rare books on gardening and horticulture. The Philip Johnson Pavillion holds Pre-Columbian art in eight domed galleries.
Garden admission: adults $8; seniors, students and children 2-12 $5; Harvard students, faculty, staff free; November-March 14 free. Museum admission: Free. Gardens: Mid-March-October, Tuesday-Sunday 2-6 p.m. November-March 14, Tuesday-Sunday 2-5 p.m.

EASTERN MARKET

225 Seventh St. S.E., Washington D.C.; www.easternmarket.net
The oldest of Washington's 19th century markets, Eastern Market was built in 1873 and has been in continuous operation since then. In the Capitol Hill neighborhood, meander through fresh meat, fish, bread, cheese and produce vendors. The South Hall Market has a butcher, seafood merchants, dairy, bakery, flower shop, and produce vendors. Weekends provide the Farmers' Line where you can pick up fresh produce, flowers and breads. There are also arts and crafts booths. The Flea Market at Eastern Market runs every Sunday.
South Hall: Tuesday-Friday 7 a.m.-7 p.m., Saturday 7 a.m.-6 p.m., Sunday 9 a.m.-5 p.m. Flea Market: Saturday-Sunday 9 a.m.-6 p.m. Farmers' Line: Saturday-Sunday 7 a.m.-4 p.m.

EMANCIPATION STATUE

Lincoln Park, 11th and E. Capitol streets N.E., Washington D.C.
This bronze work of Thomas Ball depicting Lincoln presenting the Emancipation Proclamation was paid for by voluntary subscriptions from emancipated slaves. It was dedicated on April 14, 1876, the 11th anniversary of

Lincoln's assassination and Frederick Douglass was in attendance.

EMBASSY ROW
Massachusetts Avenue and 23rd Street N.W., Washington D.C.
This neighborhood within the city's northwest quadrant is centered around Sheridan Circle and is home to dozens of foreign legations (about 170) which are found on Massachusetts Avenue. Walk along and see each embassy, along with the Vice President's house, located on Observatory Circle, which will take about three hours.

FEDERAL TRIANGLE
Pennsylvania Avenue and 13th Street N.W., Washington D.C.
The Triangle holds a group of government buildings, nine of which were built for $78 million in the 1930s in modern classic design. The "crown jewel" of the triangle is the Ronald Reagan International Trade Center, located on Pennsylvania Avenue at 13th Street N.W.

FOLGER SHAKESPEARE LIBRARY
201 E. Capitol St. S.E., Washington D.C., 202-544-4600; www.folger.edu
This library, erected in 1932, houses the finest collections of Shakespearean materials in the world, including the 1623 *First Folio* edition and large holdings of rare books and manuscripts of the English and continental Renaissance. The Great Hall offers year-round exhibits from the Folgers' extensive collection. The Elizabethan Theatre, which was designed to resemble a theater in Shakespeare's day, is the site of the Folger Shakespeare Library's series of museum and performing arts programs, which include literary readings, drama, lectures and education and family programs.
Public Library: Monday-Saturday 10 a.m.-5 p.m. Reading room: Monday-Friday 8:45 a.m.-4:45 p.m., Saturday 9 a.m.-4:30 p.m. Free tours: Monday-Friday 11 a.m., 3 p.m., Saturday 11 a.m., 1 p.m.

FONDO DEL SOL VISUAL ARTS CENTER
2112 R St. N.W., Washington D.C., 202-483-2777; www.dkmuseums.com
Dedicated to presenting, promoting and preserving cultures of Latinos, the museum presents exhibitions of contemporary artists and crafters, holds special events and hosts traveling exhibits for museums and other institutions.
Tuesday-Saturday 12:30-5:30 p.m.

FORD'S THEATRE, LINCOLN MUSEUM AND PETERESEN HOUSE
511 10th St. N.W., Washington D.C., 202-426-6924; www.fordstheatre.org
This is the site of Abraham Lincoln's assassination in 1865. Ford's became a working theater again in 1968; recent productions have included the play *Inherit the Wind* and a one-man show about George Gershwin. The newly renovated theater recently reopened in February 2009 with new seats, renovated restrooms, upgraded sound and lighting systems and more. The museum was also recently renovated, reopening in the summer of 2009. After Lincoln was shot at Ford's Theatre, he was taken to the Petersen House, where he died the following morning. It is open to the public and appears the way it did then. Admission and tours of the theatre, museum and Petersen House are free but

require a ticket which you can reserve on the Web site.
Admission: Free. Tours: Daily 9 a.m.-5 p.m. Petersen House: Daily 9:30 a.m.-5:30 p.m.

FORT DUPONT PARK
1900 Anacostia Drive S.E., Washington D.C., 202-426-7723; www.nps.gov/fodu
Visitors to Dumont Park can picnic, hike and bicycle in hilly terrain; and in the summer, there is a concert series featuring different musical performers. Also films, slides and activities involving natural science; environmental education programs, nature discovery room, Junior Ranger program; garden workshops and programmed activities take place by reservation. Daily.

FRANCISCAN MONASTERY
1400 Quincy St. N.E., Washington D.C., 202-526-6800; www.myfranciscan.org
Within the church and grounds is the "Holy Land of America"; replicas of sacred Holy Land shrines including the Manger at Bethlehem, the Garden of Gethsemane and the Holy Sepulcher. Also included are the Grotto at Lourdes and Roman catacombs. Guided tours are given by the friars.
Daily 10 a.m.-5 p.m.

FRANKLIN DELANO ROOSEVELT MEMORIAL
West Basin Drive, Washington D.C., 202-426-6841; www.nps.gov/fdrm
This newer memorial, dedicated in 1997, features a series of sculptures depicting the 32nd U.S. President and his wife, Eleanor. Four outdoor rooms represent each of FDR's four presidential terms, which began in the Great Depression and ended at the close of World War II. His "fireside chats" are broadcast throughout the exhibits. Daily.

FREDERICK DOUGLASS NATIONAL HISTORIC SITE
1411 W. St. S.E., Washington D.C., 202-426-5961, 800-967-2283; www.nps.gov/frdo
This 21-room house on nine acres is where Douglass, a former slave who became minister to Haiti and a leading black spokesman, lived from 1877 until his death in 1895. There is a visitor center with film and other memorabilia.
Mid-April-mid-October, 9 a.m.-5 p.m.; mid-October-mid-April, 9 a.m.-4 p.m.

FREER GALLERY
Jefferson Drive at 12th St. S.W., Washington D.C., 202-633-1000; www.asia.si.edu
The Freer Gallery holds Asian art with objects dating from Neolithic period to the early 20th century. There are also works by late 19th- and early 20th-century American artists, including a major collection of James McNeill Whistler's work, highlighted by the famous Peacock Room. Next to the Freer is the Smithsonian Institution Building, or "the Castle."
Admission: Free. Daily 10 a.m.-5:30 p.m.

FRESHFARM MARKETS
20th St. N.W., Washington D.C., 202-362-8889; www.freshfarmmarket.org
Located in Dupont Circle, Freshfarm Market features more than 30 local farmers selling seasonal fruits, vegetables, artisanal cheeses, breads, meat,

poultry, and organic offerings every week throughout the year. There are other Freshfarm Market locations in the D.C. area.

April 5-December 27, Sunday 9 a.m.-1 p.m.; January 3-March 28, Sunday 10 a.m.-1 p.m.

GEORGETOWN FLEA MARKET

1819 35th St. N.W., Washington D.C., 202-775-3532; www.georgetownfleamarket.com

The famous Georgetown Flea Market offers antique furniture, jewelry, books, rugs, toys, linens and other vintage treasures on Sundays since 1973. More than 100 dealers set up booths year-round; come early for the biggest selection or late for the best bargains. Saturday also features a farmer's market and Sunday focuses on vintage and antique furnishings.

Saturday-Sunday 8 a.m.-4 p.m.

GEORGETOWN UNIVERSITY

37th and O streets N.W., Washington D.C., 202-687-0100; www.georgetown.edu

The famous Georgetown University is the oldest Catholic and Jesuit college in the U.S., established in 1789. The school colors are blue and gray which they adopted in 1876 as a symbol of the union between the north and the south after the Civil War. A liberal arts school, it gives students the opportunity to learn about themselves and others in a diverse setting.

Campus tours: Monday-Saturday, by reservation.

GRAY LINE BUS TOURS

50 Massachusetts Ave. N.E., Washington D.C., 301-386-8300, 800-862-1400;
www.graylinedc.com

Since Gray Line bus tours have been around for more than 100 years, then they must be the best way to see the D.C. area. Offering tours of city and area attractions, you can choose whether you want to take a full- or half-day which include sites such as the Capitol building, the White House visitor center, FBI Building, Tidal Basin, the Washington Monument and more. Tours depart from Union Station. See Web site for tour schedules and pricing.

HIRSHHORN MUSEUM AND SCULPTURE GARDEN

Independence Avenue and Seventh Street S.W., Washington D.C., 202-633-4674;
www.hirshhorn.si.edu

The modernity of the paintings and sculptures here—and of the curvy building itself—are a respite for history-sated visitors. Inside is some of the most interesting art produced in the last 100 years: everything from Constantin Brancusi's egg-like Sleeping Muse I to Nam June Paik's Video Flag made with 70 video monitors. The lush plaza and sculpture garden make this an inviting spot to relax.

Admission: Free. Museum: Daily 10 a.m.-5:30 p.m. Sculpture garden: 7:30 a.m.-dusk. Plaza: 7:30 a.m.-5:30 p.m.

HOWARD UNIVERSITY

2400 Sixth St. N.W., Washington D.C., 202-806-6100; www.howard.edu

This university dates back to 1867 and has three other campuses in the area. The main campus has a Gallery of Fine Art with a permanent Alain Locke

African Collection and changing exhibits. Howard has produced more African-American Ph.D.s than at any other university in the world and boasts honorable alumni such as the late U.S. Supreme Court Justice Thurgood Marshall, author Toni Morrison, and actress Phylicia Rashad, among many others. Daily.

HR-57

1610 14th St. N.W., Washington D.C., 202-667-3700; www.hr57.org
This ultra-friendly, bare-bones spot is the performance arm of the Center for the Preservation of Jazz and Blues, a not-for-profit cultural center that named its club after a 1987 House Resolution designating jazz as a rare and valuable national American treasure. Expect to hear well-known and lesser-known artists at the top of their game.
Admission: $8. Wednesday-Thursday 8:30 p.m.-midnight, Sunday 7-11 p.m.

INTERNATIONAL SPY MUSEUM

800 F St. N.W., Washington D.C., 202-393-7798, 866-779-6873; www.spymuseum.org
Opened in 2002, this museum sheds light on the world of international espionage with artifacts including invisible ink, high-tech eavesdropping devices, a through-the-wall camera and a KGB lipstick pistol. Find out how codes were made and broken throughout history, how successful disguises are created and what real-life James Bonds think of the high-stakes game of spying.
Admission: adults $18, seniors and military $17, children 5-11 $15, children under 5 free. Hours vary; see Web site for details.

THE MARINE CORPS WAR MEMORIAL - IWO JIMA STATUE

Arlington, Virginia; www.mbw.usmc.mil
This famous statue depicts an iconic photograph of U.S. Marines raising the American Flag at Mount Suribachi in 1945 during the Battle of Iwo Jima in World War II. It's located Across Theodore Roosevelt Bridge on Arlington Boulevard. In summer months, you can see the Sunset Parade on Memorial grounds when the Marine Corps Drum and Bugle Corps perform.

JOHN F. KENNEDY CENTER FOR THE PERFORMING ARTS

2700 F St. N.W., Washington D.C., 202-416-8340, 800-444-1324;
www.kennedy-center.org
The home of the National Symphony Orchestra and Washington Opera hosts an impressive array of internationally known artists in dance, theater and music. Opened in 1971 as a living memorial to John F. Kennedy, a large bronze bust of the former president graces the Grand Foyer, and paintings, sculptures and other artwork presented by foreign governments are also displayed. See Web site for schedule and pricing.
Tours: Monday-Friday 10 a.m.-5 p.m., Saturday-Sunday 10 a.m.-1 p.m.

KENILWORTH PARK AND AQUATIC GARDENS

1900 Anacostia Ave. S.E., Washington D.C., 202-426-6905; www.nps.gov/keaq
These historic water gardens are filled with water lilies, lotuses and other water plants which bloom from mid-May until the frost. What was once a land

used for clean water, food, medicine and shelter, is now a park and garden for us to enjoy and explore. Guided walks are available from Memorial Day-Labor Day, on Saturday-Sunday and holidays, or by appointment.
Gardens: Daily 7 a.m.-4 p.m.

KOREAN WAR VETERANS MEMORIAL
French Drive S.W. and Independence Avenue, Washington D.C., 202-426-6841; www.nps.gov/kwvm
This massive sculpture honors the Americans who served in the Korean War, showing 19 soldiers dressed and armed for battle heading toward the American flag. The adjacent wall features etched photographs that pay tribute to military support personnel.
Admission: Free. Daily 8 a.m.-11:45 p.m.

LAFAYETTE SQUARE
Pennsylvania Avenue and Jackson Place N.W., Washington D.C.
On the National Register of Historic Places, Lafayette Square hosts the statue of Andrew Jackson on horseback in the center, which was the first Equestrian figure in Washington. One of the park benches is dedicated to political advisor Bernard Baruch as it was known as his "office" in the 1930s. It's located directly across from the White House on Pennsylvania Avenue.
Admission: Free. Daily.

LIBRARY OF CONGRESS
101 Independence Ave. S.E., Washington D.C., 202-707-6400; www.loc.gov
Treasures include a Gutenberg Bible, the first great book printed with movable metal type, and the Giant Bible of Mainz, a 500-year-old illuminated manuscript. Collection includes manuscripts, newspapers, maps, recordings, prints, photographs, posters and more than 30 million books and pamphlets in 60 languages. In the elaborate Jefferson Building is the Great Hall, decorated with murals, mosaics and marble carvings; exhibition halls. In the Madison Building, a 22-minute audiovisual presentation, America's Library, provides a good introduction to the library and its facilities.
Thomas Jefferson Building: Monday-Saturday 8:30 a.m.-4:30 p.m. Madison Memorial Building: Monday-Friday 8:30 a.m.-9:30 p.m., Saturday 8:30 a.m.-5 p.m.

LINCOLN MEMORIAL
23rd St. N.W., Washington D.C., 202-426-6841; www.nps.gov/linc
Dedicated in 1922, Daniel Chester French's Abraham Lincoln looks across a reflecting pool to the Washington Monument and the Capitol. Lincoln's Gettysburg Address and Second Inaugural Address are inscribed on the walls of the temple-like structure, which is particularly impressive at night. The 36 columns represent the 36 states in the Union in existence at the time of Lincoln's death.
Rangers are available from 9:30 a.m. to 11:30 p.m. to answer visitors' questions. Daily.

MARINE BARRACKS

Eighth and First streets S.E., Washington D.C., 202-433-6060; www.mbw.usmc.mil

The parade ground, more than two centuries old, is surrounded by handsome and historic structures, including the Commandant's House facing G Street, which is said to be the oldest continuously occupied public building in the city. These barracks were established in 1801 and is the "oldest post of the corps." The parade is open to the public on Friday evenings in summer. The parade was first conducted in 1957.

Evening Parade: May 8-August 28, Friday 8 p.m.

MARTIN LUTHER KING, JR. MEMORIAL LIBRARY
901 G St. N.W., Washington D.C., 202-727-0321; www.dclibrary.org

This main branch of the D.C. public libraries was designed by architect Mies van der Rohe in 1972. The King Mural, located in the lobby of the library, tells the story of Dr. Martin Luther King Jr.'s life and struggle for social justice. Books, periodicals, photographs, films, videocassettes, recordings, microfilms, Washingtonian and the "Washington Star" collection are located here. There is a library for the visually impaired; a librarian for the hearing impaired; a black studies division; and a community information service. Underground parking is also available making this library accessible. There is also the Library Store located in the lobby where you can pick up gifts and memorabilia.

Admission: Free. Monday-Tuesday 9:30 a.m.-9 p.m., Wednesday-Saturday 9:30 a.m.-5:30 p.m.; September 7-May 24, Sunday 1-5 p.m.

NATIONAL AIR AND SPACE MUSEUM
600 Independence Ave. S.W., Washington D.C., 202-633-2563; www.nasm.si.edu

View the Wright brothers' 1903 *Kitty Hawk Flyer*, Charles Lindbergh's *Spirit of St. Louis* and the command module *Columbia*, which carried the first men to walk on the moon. In the Apollo to the Moon exhibit, you'll see lunar rocks, spacesuits and John Glenn's squeeze-tube beef stew, among other artifacts. An IMAX theater enables you to view on a huge, five-story-high screen Earth as seen from the space shuttle. And don't miss the high-tech shows at the Albert Einstein Planetarium.

Admission: Free. September 8-March 27, daily 10 a.m.-5:30 p.m. March 28-September 7, daily 10 a.m.-7:30 p.m.

NATIONAL AQUARIUM
Department of Commerce Building, 14th St. and Constitution Ave. N.W., Washington D.C., 202-482-2825; www.nationalaquarium.com

The nation's oldest public aquarium was established in 1873. It now exhibits more than 1,500 specimens representing approximately 250 species, both freshwater and saltwater. Exhibits include a National Marine Sanctuaries and National Parks Gallery which increases public awareness and gives information about such places as the Florida Everglades. There's the Amphibians Gallery where you can learn about amphibians and the Amazon River Basin Gallery where you can learn about what dwells in the river. If you want to witness sharks, alligators or piranhas feasting, you can do so here.

Admission: adults $7, seniors and military personnel $6, children 2-10 $3, children under 2 free. Daily 9 a.m.-5 p.m.

NATIONAL ARCHIVES

Constitution Avenue, Washington D.C., 202-501-5205; www.archives.gov

The original Declaration of Independence, Bill of Rights and the Constitution are all guarded here. The National Archives were established by President Franklin D. Roosevelt in 1934 and since then visitors have come to view these important historical documents. Also located here are a 1297 version of the Magna Carta and other historic documents, maps and photographs. Guided tours take place by appointment only; check out the Web site for details. Archives are also available to the public for genealogical and historical research Monday through Saturday.

Admission: Free. Mid-March-Labor Day, daily 10 a.m.-7 p.m.; Labor Day-mid-March, daily 10 a.m.-5:30 p.m.

NATIONAL BUILDING MUSEUM

401 F St. N.W., Washington D.C., 202-272-2448; www.nbm.org

This museum was created in 1980 through an act of Congress to exchange ideas about architecture, design, engineering and construction. Permanent exhibits include drawings, blueprints, models, photographs, artifacts and the architectural evolution of Washington's buildings and monuments. You can check out exhibits focusing on building sustainable residences and affordable housing of the future. The museum's enormous Great Hall is supported by eight of the world's largest Corinthian columns.

Admission: Free; suggested donation $5. Monday-Saturday 10 a.m.-5 p.m., Sunday 11 a.m.-5 p.m.

NATIONAL GALLERY OF ART

Fourth and Constitution avenues N.W., Washington D.C., 202-737-4215; www.nga.gov

The West Building, designed by John Russell Pope, contains Western European and American art spanning periods between the 13th and 20th centuries: Highlights include the only Leonardo da Vinci painting on display outside of Europe, *Ginevra de' Benci*; a comprehensive collection of Italian paintings and sculpture; major French Impressionists; numerous Rembrandts and examples of the Dutch school; masterpieces from the Mellon, Widener, Kress, Dale and Rosenwald collections; and special exhibitions. Adjacent to the West Building is the Sculpture Garden, which features a large fountain (which turns into an ice rink in the winter), trees, shrubs, and flowers as well as works of art from Claes Oldenburg and Joan Miró. The East Building, designed by architect I.M. Pei, houses the gallery's growing collection of 20th-century art, including Picasso's *Family of Saltimbanques* and Jackson Pollock's *Lavender Mist*.

Admission: Free. Monday-Saturday 10 a.m.-5 p.m., Sunday 11 a.m.-6 p.m.

NATIONAL GEOGRAPHIC MUSEUM AT EXPLORERS HALL

1145 17th St. N.W., Washington D.C., 202-857-7588; www.nationalgeographic.com

This museum is filled with ongoing and changing exhibits and photographs of past and present expeditions, adventures and scientific research that has been done for National Geographic. The ongoing exhibit, Lions & Leopards, is a look at footage and prints of these wild animals from explorers Dereck

and Beverly Joubert. It's also the National Geographic Society headquarters.
Admission: Free. Monday-Saturday 9 a.m.-5 p.m., Sunday 10 a.m.-5 p.m.

NATIONAL MUSEUM OF AFRICAN ART

950 Independence Ave. S.W., Washington D.C., 202-633-4600; www.nmafa.si.edu

This Smithsonian Museum houses permanent exhibits which display masks, musical instruments, sacred objects, ceramics, textiles, household tools and the visual arts of the sub-Sahara. Traveling shows cover even more ground; recent ones have featured colonial-era photography and Ethiopian religious icons. Also here is the Warren M. Robbins Library, which holds more than 32,000 volumes about African art, history and culture. A full schedule of films, musical presentations, lectures and children's events keeps things lively.
Admission: Free. Daily 10 a.m.-5:30 p.m. Library: Monday-Friday 8:45 a.m.-5:15 p.m.

NATIONAL MUSEUM OF AMERICAN HISTORY

14th St. and Constitution Ave. N.W., Washington D.C., 202-633-1000; www.americanhistory.si.edu

More than 17 million artifacts cover aspects of American cultural heritage at this Smithsonian museum. Check out Julia Child's cheerful and organized kitchen from the famous chef's longtime home in Cambridge, Mass., reassembled here in 2001. Or watch textile conservators take painstaking steps to restore the fragile Star-Spangled Banner, the actual flag that inspired Francis Scott Key in 1814 to write the poem that became America's national anthem. The museum's collections include the lap desk at which Thomas Jefferson drafted the Declaration of Independence, Henry Ford's 1913 Model-T, first ladies' inaugural gowns and Dorothy's ruby slippers from *The Wizard of Oz*. Children will especially enjoy the Hands-On History Room, where they can harness a life-size model of a mule or tap out a telegraph message in Morse code.
Admission: Free. September 7-April 19, daily 10 a.m.-5:30 p.m.; April 20-September 6, daily 10 a.m.-6:30 p.m.

NATIONAL MUSEUM OF HEALTH AND MEDICINE

Walter Reed Army Medical Center, Building No. 54, 6900 Georgia Avenue and Elder Street, Washington D.C., 202-782-2200; www.nmhm.washingtondc.museum

One of the most important medical collections in America is located here. This mueum began during the Civil war as an Army Medical Museum to collect specimens for research. Exhibits include interpretations of the link between history and technology; AIDS education; an interactive exhibit on human anatomy and lifestyle choices; and a collection of microscopes, medical teaching aids, tools and instruments (dating from 1862-1965) and famous historical icons exhibits. You can also see specimens and historical artifacts related to President Abraham Lincoln including the bullet that killed him along with the probe used to remove the bullet and even bone fragments and hair from his skull.
Admission: Free. Daily 10 a.m.-5:30 p.m.

NATIONAL MUSEUM OF NATURAL HISTORY

Constitution Avenue and 10th Street N.W., Washington D.C., 202-633-1000;
www.mnh.si.edu

Before you enter this museum, stop on the Ninth Street-side of the building to see the mesmerizing Butterfly Garden with four different habitats. The National Museum of Natural History holds more than 124 million artifacts and specimens dating back to the Ice Age. Museum exhibits include an insect zoo with thousands of live specimens, a section on gems (including the 45.52-carat, billion-year-old Hope Diamond), dinosaur skeletons, a live coral reef, and botanical, zoological and geological materials.

Admission: Free. Daily 10 a.m.-5:30 p.m.

NATIONAL MUSEUM OF WOMEN IN THE ARTS

1250 New York Ave. N.W., Washington D.C., 202-783-5000, 800-222-7270;
www.nmwa.org

More than 3,000 works by female artists from the Renaissance to the present are on display at this museum. Collections include paintings, drawings, sculpture, pottery and prints, and even silver from female silversmiths from the 18th and 19th centuries in Ireland and England. There is a library holds more than 18,500 books and other resources as well as a research center for researchers available by appointment only. There are also literary events, lectures, films and music performances.

Admission: adults $10, seniors and students $8, children 18 and under free. First Sunday of every month free. Monday-Saturday 10 a.m.-5 p.m., Sunday noon-5 p.m.

NATIONAL THEATRE

1321 Pennsylvania Ave. N.W., Washington D.C., 202-628-6161, 800-447-7400;
www.nationaltheatre.org

Theatrical luminaries such as Sarah Bernhardt, Laurence Olivier and the Barrymores have performed at this historic playhouse, which is said to be haunted by the ghost of murdered actor, John McCullough. But, don't be scared if you see his apparition; it's been said that he's a friendly ghost. These days, you'll see touring productions of shows such as *Mamma Mia*, *Jersey Boys* or Disney's *High School Musical*. On Monday nights, there are free films shown in the summer and performances drawing on local talent the rest of the year. Saturday mornings feature free children's shows.

Tours: Monday-Friday 11 a.m.-3 p.m.

NATIONAL ZOO

3001 Connecticut Ave. N.W., Washington D.C., 202-633-4800; www.nationalzoo.si.edu

A branch of the Smithsonian Institution, the National Zoo, located in Rock Creek Park, features 2,000 animals of 400 species. Visit the newborn baby gorilla, Kibibi, or the popular giant pandas Tian Tian, Mei Xiang and Tai Shan (come when the zoo first opens or after 2 p.m. if you want to see them without waiting in long lines).

Admission: Free. April-October, daily 10 a.m.-6 p.m.; November-March, daily 10 a.m.-5 p.m.

NAVY YARD

901 M St. S.E., Washington D.C., 202-433-4882

Founded in 1799 along the Anacostia River at a location chosen by George Washington, the yard was nearly destroyed during the War of 1812. Within the yard, you can visit the Navy Art Gallery, Future Cold War Gallery, the Navy Museum, and more. Outside the yard at 636 G St. S.E. is the John Philip Sousa house, where the "March King" wrote many of his famous compositions.

Admission: Free. Monday-Friday 9 a.m.-5 p.m., Saturday-Sunday 10 a.m.-5 p.m.

THE NEW YORK AVENUE PRESBYTERIAN CHURCH

1313 New York Ave. N.W., Washington D.C., 202-393-3700; www.nyapc.org

President Abraham Lincoln and his family worshipped here during the Civil War. Martin Luther King, Jr. preached here during the Civil Rights movement. While the church was rebuilt in 1950-1951, the pew in which Lincoln and his family sat in regularly is still there for visitors to use. Bells chime before services from the Lincoln Memorial Tower, which was from the Robert Todd Lincoln family and the chimes were given to the church from Lincoln's granddaughter, Mary Lincoln Isham. Mementos on display include the first draft of the Emancipation Proclamation, which is located in the Lincoln Parlor on the first floor.

Tuesday-Friday. Worship Services: Sunday 8:45 a.m. and 11 a.m.

NEWSEUM

555 Pennsylvania Ave., Washington, D.C., 888-639-7386; www.newseum.org

This 250,000-square-foot interactive museum of news takes visitors behind the scenes to see and experience how and why news is made. There are seven different levels, which feature galleries, theaters, retail and visitor centers. Be a reporter or newscaster; relive great news stories through multimedia exhibits; see today's news as it happens on a block-long video wall. The Journalists Memorial is also located here (it used to be located at Freedom Park in Arlington, Virginia).

Daily 9 a.m.-5 p.m.

OLD STONE HOUSE

3051 M St. N.W., Washington D.C., 202-426-6851; www.nps.gov/olst

Believed to be the oldest pre-Revolutionary building in Washington, dating back to 1765. Constructed on parcel No. 3 of the original tract of land that was then Georgetown, the house was used as both a residence and a place of business; five rooms are furnished with household items that reflect a middle-class residence of the late 18th century. Located within Rock Creek Park, the grounds are lush with fruit trees and seasonal blooms.

Admission: Free. Wednesday-Sunday noon-5 p.m.

THE OLD POST OFFICE PAVILION

1100 Pennsylvania Ave. N.W., Washington D.C., 202-289-4224;
www.oldpostofficedc.com

This romanesque structure from 1899 was for years the headquarters of the U.S. Postal Service. The building has been remodeled into a marketplace with 100 shops and restaurants and daily entertainment. In the 315-foot tower are replicas of the bells of Westminster Abbey, a bicentennial gift from Great Britain. The tower is the second-highest point in D.C. and offers spectacular views from an open-air observation deck. Above the Pavilion shops are headquarters for the National Endowment for the Arts.

March-April, Monday-Saturday 10 a.m.-8p.m., Sunday noon-7 p.m.; September-February, Monday-Saturday 10 a.m.-7 p.m., Sunday noon-6 p.m.

THE PENTAGON

1400 Defense Pentagon, Washington, D.C., 703-697-1776; pentagon.afis.osd.mil

With some 6 million square feet of floor area, this is one of the largest office buildings in the world. It houses the offices of the Department of Defense. It was part of the September 11, 2001 attacks when terrorists hijacked an American Airlines flight 77 and crashed it into the Pentagon. Damaging the structure and killing 125 people in the building and all 64 onboard the airplane, the attack is now remembered as a memorial inside the building where there is also a chapel. The outdoor Pentagon Memorial, opened in 2008, memorializes the victims with a park and 184 benches.

Tours: Monday-Friday 9 a.m.-3 p.m.; reservations required.

THE PHILLIPS COLLECTION

1600 21st St. N.W., Washington D.C., 202-387-2151; www.phillipscollection.org

Built as a memorial for Duncan Phillips's brother and father, this was the first museum of modern art in the nation. Founded in 1918 and opened to the public in 1921, the museum continues to emphasize the work of emerging as well as established international artists. The permanent collection includes 19th- and 20th-century Impressionist, Post-Impressionist and modern painting and sculpture including artists such as Mark Rothko, Pablo Picasso, Georgia O'Keeffe, and many more. From October through May, every Sunday evening you can enjoy a concert (they are free with admission) featuring pianists, harpists and more. Every first Thursday of the month, Phillips After 5 takes place featuring jazz performances, food, drinks, gallery talks and more.

Tuesday-Saturday 10 a.m.-5 p.m., Thursday 10 a.m.-8:30 p.m., Sunday 11 a.m.-6 p.m. Concerts: October-May, Sunday.

POTOMAC PARK (EAST AND WEST)

1100 Ohio St. S.W., Washington D.C., 202-619-7222; www.nps.gov/ncro

These 720 riverfront acres are divided by Washington's famous Tidal Basin into East and West Potomac parks. East Potomac Park has three golf courses, a large swimming pool, picnic grounds, tennis courts and biking and hiking paths. Pedal boats can be rented at the Tidal Basin. At West Potomac Park, you'll find the Vietnam, Korean, Lincoln, Jefferson and FDR memorials; Constitution gardens; and the Reflecting Pool. This is also the site of the famous D.C. cherry trees. You can enjoy the two-week burst of pink and white cherry blossoms from more than 3,000 trees, a 1912 gift of friendship from Japan, in late March/early April. The Cherry Blossom Festival begins each year with the lighting of the 300-year-old Japanese Stone Lantern, presented by the governor of Tokyo in 1954.

ROCK CREEK PARK

3545 Williamsburg Lane N.W., Washington D.C., 202-895-6070; www.nps.gov/rocr

Just five miles from the White House are dozens of miles of clearly marked, well-maintained, easy and moderately hard hiking trails through the park's 1,754 acres of meadows and woodlands. There's also a gentle walk along Beach Drive that takes you through dramatic Rock Creek Gorge; on weekends and holidays, cars are prohibited, making it even more peaceful. The public Rock Creek Golf Course offers 18-holes of golf. There is a boat center where you can rent bicycles, kayaks, canoes and sailboats. There are also tennis courts, a playground and picnic areas. The Nature Center offers information, hands-on activities, guided nature walks and more. Within the Nature Center is the Planetarium, where you can learn about astronomy and view the sky above (pick up free tickets for the Planetarium at the Nature Center). The Carter Barron Amphitheater is also located here, where you can see outdoor musical and theater performances during the summer.

Nature Center, Planetarium and Old Stone House: Wednesday-Sunday 9 a.m-5 p.m.

SEWALL-BELMONT HOUSE AND MUSEUM

144 Constitution Ave. N.E., Washington D.C., 202-546-1210; www.sewallbelmont.org

The Sewall-Belmont House is a monument to Alice Paul, the author of the Equal Rights Amendment. From this house, she spearheaded the fight for the passage of the amendment. Now a national landmark, the house contains portraits and sculptures of women from the beginning of the suffrage movement; extensive collection of artifacts of the suffrage and equal rights movement. It is also the historic headquarters of the National Woman's Party. They host many educational programs for all ages as well as private events.

Admission: $5 (suggested donation). Wednesday-Saturday noon-4 p.m.

Tours: noon-3 p.m.

SHAKESPEARE THEATRE COMPANY AT THE LANSBURGH

Lansburgh Theatre, 450 Seventh St. N.W., Washington D.C., 202-547-1122,

877-487-8849; www.shakespearedc.org

This theatre company was founded in 1985 and features the Bard's classics as well as more modern work by playwrights such as Oscar Wilde, Eugene O'Neill and Tennessee Williams. Most recently, *Twelfth Night*, *King Lear* and *Romeo and Juliet* have been performed. Other plays have included *Ion* by Euripides and *Design for Living* by Noël Coward. Plays take place at either the Lansburgh Theatre or at the Sidney Harman Hall (*610 F. Street N.W.*).

See Web site for schedules and ticket information.

SHOPS AT GEORGETOWN PARK

3222 M St. N.W., Washington D.C., 202-342-8190; www.shopsatgeorgetownpark.com

This stylish urban mall has four levels of upscale shops and restaurants to explore and is especially strong in apparel. Stores include Anthropology, Ann Taylor, H&M, Intermix, and Victoria's Secret. There is a concierge center.

Monday-Saturday 10 a.m.-8 p.m., Sunday noon-6 p.m.

THE SHOPS AT NATIONAL PLACE

1331 Pennsylvania Ave. N.W., Washington D.C., 202-662-1250;
www.downtowndc.org/visit/go/shops-at-national-place-the
This three-level marketplace features more than 100 specialty shops and restaurants including Filene's Basement, Corner Bakery Cafe, and a pretty big food court, where you'll find plenty of workers lunching during the workday.
Monday-Saturday 10 a.m.-7 p.m., Sunday noon-5 p.m.

SMITHSONIAN AMERICAN ART MUSEUM

8th and F streets, N.W., Washington D.C., 202-633-7970; www.americanart.si.edu
Located in the Penn Quarter, the American Art Museum holds the first collection of American art in the U.S. On display, you'll find more than 7,000 artist's work including Mary Cassatt, Georgia O'Keeffe, Edward Hopper, and John Singleton Copley. There are collections including folk art, African American and Latino artists, and art covering the Gilded Age to the 20th century. There are also changing exhibits, which have featured art from the Great Depression in 1934.
Admission: Free. Daily 11:30 a.m.-7 p.m.

SMITHSONIAN INSTITUTION

1000 Jefferson Drive S.W., Washington D.C., 202-633-1000; www.si.edu
There are 19 museums that are part of the Smithsonian Institution, with 9 research centers; 17 of these museums along with the National Zoo are located here in D.C. Two other museums are in New York City. The majority of Smithsonian museums are located on the National Mall. Most of the museums are open daily from 10 a.m.-5:30 p.m., except December 25. Admission to all museums is free. Before heading to museums, stop at the Smithsonian Information Center (also known as the Castle) to pick up information.
Daily 8:30 a.m.-5:30 p.m.

ST. JOHN'S CHURCH GEORGETOWN PARISH

3240 O St. N.W., Washington D.C., 202-338-1796; www.stjohnsgeorgetown.org
St. John's is the oldest Episcopal congregation in Georgetown, established in 1796 by notable founding members including Thomas Jefferson and Francis Scott Key. It was originally designed by Dr. William Thornton, the architect of the Capitol. Many presidents since Madison have worshiped here.
Worship Services: Sunday 9 a.m., 11 a.m.

SUPREME COURT OF THE UNITED STATES

First Street N.E. and Maryland Avenue, Washington D.C., 202-479-3211;
www.supremecourtus.gov
This Neoclassical-style building was designed by Cass Gilbert. Court is in session October-April (Monday-Wednesday, at two-week intervals from the first Monday in October) and on the first workday of each week in May and June; court sessions are open to the public (10 a.m. and 1 p.m.), on a first-come, first-served basis; lectures are offered in the courtroom (Monday-Friday except when court is in session; 20-minute lectures hourly on half

hour); on the ground floor are exhibits and a short film, cafeteria, snack bar and gift shop. On the third floor is the Library, which has more than 450,000 volumes.
Monday-Friday 9 a.m.-4:30 p.m.

TEXTILE MUSEUM
2320 S. St. N.W., Washington D.C., 202-667-0441; www.textilemuseum.org
Founded in 1925 with the collection of George Hewitt Myers, the museum features changing exhibits of non-Western textiles, Oriental rugs and other handmade textile art from all over the world including Asia, Persia, Turkey, Africa and Greece. Guided tours daily. Changing exhibits have included Common Threads, which displays textiles that examine the similarities between cultures and how their textiles reflect their lives.
Admission: Free (there is a suggested donation of $5).Tuesday-Saturday 10 a.m.-5 p.m., Sunday 1-5 p.m.

THOMAS JEFFERSON MEMORIAL
National Mall, East Basin Drive S.W., Washington D.C., 202-426-6841;
www.nps.gov/thje
This memorial, dedicated in 1943, honors the third president and author of both the Declaration of Independence and the Bill of Rights. The white-marble dome surrounded by columns, representing the classic style that Jefferson introduced to the U.S., is quite beautiful when lit up at night. In the basement, you'll find a museum and the plaster statue from which the 19-foot bronze one in the center of the monument was created. Rangers are on duty daily from 9:30 a.m.-11:30 p.m. if you have any questions.
Admission: Free. Daily.

TOURMOBILE SIGHTSEEING
1000 Ohio Drive S.W., Washington D.C., 202-554-5100; www.tourmobile.com
These narrated shuttle tours take you to 18 historic sites on the National Mall and to Arlington National Cemetery (this tour is called the American Heritage Tour). They offer unlimited re-boarding throughout day, so you can hop off and have lunch or do some shopping and then, hop back on to move onto the next stop. You can take additional tours separately or in combinations, including a tour of Arlington National Cemetery, Mount Vernon and Frederick Douglass Home. You can pick up your tickets from the driver at any of the Tourmobile stops or at the ticket-booths located at Arlington National Cemetery and Union Station.
Tour: adults $27, children 3-11 $13. Daily 9:30 a.m.-4:30 p.m.

TUDOR PLACE HISTORIC HOUSE AND GARDEN
1644 31st St. N.W., Washington D.C., 202-965-0400; www.tudorplace.org
This 12-room neoclassical mansion was designed by Dr. William Thornton, architect of the Capitol, and built in 1805 for Martha Custis Peter, granddaughter of Martha Washington. The Peter family lived in the house for 180 year and all furnishings and objects d'art are original. There are also more than five acres of gardens which are filled with a Japanese Tea House, ponds, sculptures, and beautiful flowers, shrubs and trees. The original plot of land

had orchards, vegetable gardens, a stable and an area for cows and horses to graze.

Admission: adults $8, seniors and military personnel $6, students 7-18 $3, children 6 and under free. Tours: Tuesday-Saturday 10-11 a.m., noon-3 p.m., Sunday noon-3 p.m. Garden: Monday-Saturday 10 a.m.-4 p.m., Sunday noon-4 p.m.

UNION STATION

50 Massachusetts Ave. N.E., Washington D.C., 202-289-1908;
www.unionstationdc.com

Archiet Daniel Burnham designed Union Station in 1907. It was restored (costing $160 million) and reopened in 1988. The white granite Beaux Arts masterpiece is still a functioning train station and is now home to more than 130 restaurants and shops, many of them catering to the special needs of travelers. But many locals patronize the shops, too (including former President Bill Clinton, who regularly bought holiday presents here). Also located within the station are the Amtrak depot and Gray Line and Tourmobile Sightseeing operators. It's also home to Amtrak's headquarters and executive offices. Monday-Saturday 10 a.m.-9 p.m., Sunday noon-6 p.m.

U.S. BOTANIC GARDEN

100 Maryland Ave. S.W., Washington D.C., 202-225-8333; www.usbg.gov

The Botanic Garden, one of the oldest in the country, was established by Congress in 1820 for public education and exhibition. It features plants collected by the famous Wilkes Expedition of the South Seas. The Conservatory has tropical, subtropical and desert plants as well as seasonal displays. Exterior gardens are planted for seasonal blooming where you'll also find the Bartholdi Fountain, designed by the sculptor of the Statue of Liberty, Frederic Auguste Bartholdi.

Admission: Free. Daily 10 a.m.-5 p.m.

U.S. HOLOCAUST MEMORIAL MUSEUM

100 Raoul Wallenberg Plaza S.W., Washington D.C., 202-488-0400; www.ushmm.org

Opened in 1993, this privately funded museum hosts temporary exhibits that cover everything from the diary of Anne Frank to the role of Oskar Schindler in saving the lives of hundreds of Jews. At the heart of the museum is its self-guided Permanent Exhibition, The Holocaust, which includes powerful photos, film footage, eyewitness testimonies, clothing, children's drawings and other victims' belongings, as well as reconstructions of concentration camp buildings. The Hall of Remembrance is designed for visitors to quietly reflect and light a candle as a symbol of remembrance. Timed daily-use passes are necessary for visiting the museum's permanent exhibition during March through August and can be obtained each day at the museum or in advance.

Admission: Free. Mid-June-March, daily 10 a.m.-5:30 p.m.; April-mid-June, daily 10 a.m.-6:30 p.m.

U.S. NATIONAL ARBORETUM

3501 New York Ave. N.E., Washington D.C., 202-245-2726; www.usna.usda.gov

Established in 1927 by Congress, the Arboretum is run by the U.S. Depart-

ment of Agriculture. There are floral displays in spring, summer, fall and winter on 446 acres. There is a Japanese garden, a National Bonsai and Penjing Museum which has one of the largest collections of Bonsai trees in North America; a National Herb Garden; major collections of azaleas, wildflowers, ferns, magnolias, crabapples, cherries and dogwoods; aquatic plantings, including water lilies and lotus flowers; and dwarf conifers (the world's largest evergreen collection).
Admission: Free. Daily 8 a.m.-5 p.m.

U.S. NAVY MEMORIAL

701 Pennsylvania Ave. N.W., Washington D.C., 202-737-2300; www.lonesailor.org
This U.S. Navy Memorial is dedicated to those who have served in the Navy in war and in peacetime. A 100-foot-diameter granite world map dominates the Plaza, where the Lone Sailor, a seven-foot bronze sculpture, stands to represent all that Navy sailors stands for. The U.S. Navy Band performs free concerts on Tuesday nights during the summer outside. The visitor center features electronic kiosks with interactive video displays on naval history and the Navy Memorial Log Room with information about past veterans and U.S. Presidents' Room which features portraits of presidents who were active in the Navy.
Admission: Free. Daily 9:30 a.m.-5 p.m.

U.S. NAVY MUSEUM

805 Kidder Breese S.E., Washington D.C., 202-433-6897; www.history.navy.mil
This museum covers the history of the U.S. Navy from the Revolutionary War to the space age. Located within the museum are dioramas depicting achievements of early naval heroes; displays featuring development of naval weapons; and a fully rigged foremast fighting top and gun deck from frigate *USS Constitution* on display. There's also guns from World War II and a submarine room that has operating periscopes. Approximately 5,000 objects are on display including paintings, ship models, flags, uniforms, naval decorations and the bathyscaphe Trieste. A two-acre outdoor park displays 19th- and 20th-century guns, cannon, other naval artifacts along with the U.S. Navy destroyer *Barry* located on the waterfront. If you're planning a visit, you now must call ahead to make an appointment. If you're planning to go on the weekend, be sure to call before noon on Friday.
Admission: Free. Monday-Friday 9 a.m.-5 p.m., Saturday-Sunday 10 a.m.-5 p.m. Tours: Monday-Friday 10 a.m.-2 p.m., Saturday-Sunday 10 a.m.-3 p.m.; reservations required.

VERIZON CENTER

601 F St. N.W., Washington D.C., 202-628-3200; www.verizoncenter.com
This 20,000-seat, state-of-the-art arena, home to the NBA's Washington Wizards, the WNBA's Washington Mystics, the NHL's Washington Capitals and Georgetown Hoyas basketball, is also a popular venue for concerts and other events, from Bruce Springsteen to Beyonce. Even when nothing is scheduled, you can check out The Greene Turtle Sports Bar and Grille for burgers and beer.
See Web site for schedule and prices.

VIETNAM VETERANS MEMORIAL

900 Ohio Drive S.W., Washington D.C., 202-426-6841; www.nps.gov/vive

Designed by Maya Lin and funded by private citizens' contributions, this memorial's polished black granite walls are inscribed with the names of the 58,260 U.S. servicemen who died in or remain missing from the Vietnam War (a large directory helps visitors locate specific names). Deliberately apolitical, the memorial aims to foster reconciliation and healing given the divisiveness the war caused in American society; and more importantly, to honor those who sacrificed their lives for the Nation. Also onsite are the Three Servicemen Statue and Flagpole and the Vietnam Women's Memorial. Rangers are onsite to help answer any questions you have. Daily.

WARNER THEATRE

13th and E. Street N.W., Washington D.C., 202-783-4000; www.warnertheatre.com

Originally opened in 1924 as the Earle Theatre showing vaudeville and silent movies, the Warner Theatre has presented it all, from movies to concerts to theater. A major renovation restored this theatre with more than 1,800 seats, a sparkling chandelier, stained-glass lamps and Portuguese draperies, it reflects what it was in the 1920s. The Warner is host to many performances, including comedies, musicals, an annual *Nutcracker* performance and movie premieres from time to time.

See Web site for schedule and prices. Box Office: Opens two hours prior to shows.

WASHINGTON CONVENTION CENTER

801 Mount Vernon Place N.W., Washington D.C., 202-249-3000, 800-368-9000; www.dcconvention.com

Washington's biggest building is also one of its newest. Opened in 2003, the Washington Convention Center occupies six city blocks, housing 700,000 square feet of exhibit space and 125,000 square feet of meeting space. The roof of the structure alone covers 17 acres. It houses more than 120 pieces of art from sculptures to paintings, photography and more. The Shaw Wall features art from artists in the Shaw community where the center is located. The Washington Convention Center is located immediately north of Mount Vernon Square, offering convenient access to some of the city's finest hotels and restaurants. Many other attractions can be found nearby, including Chinatown, the National Portrait Gallery, Ford's Theatre and the Verizon Center.

WASHINGTON HARBOUR

3000 K St. N.W., Washington D.C.

In Georgetown, walk along the boardwalk along the Potomac River where you'll find dining and shopping which features plazas and lavish fountains. Some restaurants feature outdoor seating so you can relax, and enjoy the atmosphere. Tony and Joe's is a popular seafood restaurant where you can dine outside and enjoy the waterfront.

WASHINGTON MONUMENT

15th St. S.W., Washington D.C., 202-426-6841; www.nps.gov/wamo

This obelisk, the tallest masonry structure in the world, at more than 555 feet, was dedicated in 1885 to the memory of the first U.S. president. Before its dedication, it had been under construction for almost 40 years, as a lack of funds and the Civil War interrupted its progress. You can see where construction resumed after a 28-year delay about a quarter of the way up the monument, where two different shades of marble meet. From the top, you can view over 30 miles of the city. Views of the majestic structure can be enjoyed anytime, but to enter, you must have a free ticket. Tickets are distributed at the kiosk at 15th and Madison starting at 8:30 a.m. for same-day entrance or you can reserve tickets for a small fee by calling 877-444-6777 (in warmer months, people line up early to get tickets, so get there early). There is an elevator to the observation room at the 500-foot level. To take the 898 steps up or down, arrangements must be made in advance.
Admission: Free. Daily 9 a.m.-5 p.m.

WASHINGTON NATIONAL CATHEDRAL
3101 Wisconsin Ave. N.W., Washington D.C., 202-537-6207;
www.cathedral.org/cathedral
This edifice, 83 years in the making, was completed in 1990, its $65 million cost covered by private donations. Graced with intricate carvings inside and out, it has a 30-story central tower and 215 stained-glass windows, including one that contains a piece of lunar rock presented by the astronauts of *Apollo 11*. Bring binoculars if you want to see close-up the more than 100 gargoyles, which depict not just dragons but also a child with his hand in a cookie jar and *Star Wars* villain Darth Vader. Worshippers of all faiths are welcome at services held daily. There are also frequent musical events, including recitals given on the magnificent pipe organ, which consists of 10,646 pipes. Famous Americans interred at the cathedral include President Woodrow Wilson and Helen Keller.
Admission: adults $5, seniors, students and military personnel $3. Monday-Friday 10 a.m.-5:30 p.m., Saturday 10 a.m.-4:30 p.m., Sunday 8 a.m.-4 p.m.

WASHINGTON WALKS
819 G St. S.W., Washington D.C., 202-484-1565; www.washingtonwalks.com
These guided tours sponsored by Washington Walks are a great way to see the city and get some exercise. There are plenty of different tours to choose from. If you're interested in ghosts and haunted houses, take the Most Haunted Houses tour where you'll learn about all that's haunted in D.C. The group (along with Children's Concierge) runs two tours that kids will especially enjoy: for "Goodnight Mr. Lincoln," children can show up in pajamas at the Lincoln Memorial for stories, games and music about Honest Abe. The White House Un-Tour offers role-playing (you might be asked to impersonate the president who loved bowling) and fun facts about the executive mansion.
Admission: adults and children 4-18 $10, children 3 and under free. April-October, days vary; rest of year by appointment.

THE WHITE HOUSE
1600 Pennsylvania Ave. N.W., Washington D.C., 202-456-7041; www.whitehouse.gov
Constructed in 1800 under George Washington's supervision, the house has hosted every U.S. president since John Adams. The British burned it dur-

ing the War of 1812, and it was reconstructed under the guidance of James Monroe (from 1817-1825). The West Wing, which includes the Oval Office, the president's private office, which was ordered by President Taft; before its construction, executive offices shared the second floor with the president's private quarters. The interior of the White House was gutted and rebuilt using modern construction techniques during the Truman administration, so the Trumans lived at the Blair House. The Library and the Vermeil Room (on the Ground Floor); the East, Green, Blue and Red Rooms, and the State Dining Room (on the State Floor) are accessible to groups of 10 for tours. In this era of heightened security, you'll find Secret Service agents in every room, doubling as tour guides. Obtain tickets through your congressperson or senator. Tuesday-Saturday 7:30 a.m.-10 a.m.

WOODROW WILSON HOUSE
2340 S. St. N.W., Washington D.C., 202-387-4062; www.woodrowwilsonhouse.org
A National Historic Landmark, this red brick Georgian Revival townhouse was built in 1915 for President Wilson to retire after leaving office. Located in the Kalorama area of D.C., this house is furnished as it was when Wilson lived there. You'll see memorabilia and gifts-of-state on display to get an idea of what life was like in the 1920s.
Admission: adults $7.50, seniors $6.50, students $3, children under 7 free.
Tuesday-Sunday 10 a.m.-4 p.m.

WORLD WAR II MEMORIAL
National Mall, 17th St., Washington D.C., 202-426-6841; www.nps.gov/nwwm
The World War II Memorial honors America's Greatest Generation, the men and women who emerged from the Depression to serve in a hard-fought war that took the lives of 50 million people worldwide. Situated on the National Mall between the Lincoln Memorial and the Washington Monument, this memorial opened to visitors in spring 2004. Twin Atlantic and Pacific pavilions are divided by an oval-shaped pool, symbolizing a war fought across two oceans. Fifty-six wreath-adorned stone pillars—each representing a U.S. state or territory—form semicircles on the memorial's north and south sides. To the west, the Reflecting Pool cascades over twin waterfalls that bookend the Freedom Wall, which glitters with 4,000 gold stars (one-tenth the number of Americans who lost their lives in the war). National park rangers staff an information station south of the memorial, answering questions and providing brochures. Daily.

SPECIAL EVENTS
CARTER BARRON AMPHITHEATRE SUMMER CONCERTS
Rock Creek Park, 16 St. and Colorado Ave. N.W., Washington D.C., 202-426-0486; www.nps.gov/rocr/cbarron
This 4,200-seat outdoor theater located in Rock Creek Park in a wooded area is the setting for summer performances of symphonic, folk, pop and jazz music and Shakespearean theater. Such notables of the past who have performed here include Nat King Cole, Ella Fitzgerald, Stevie Wonder, Ray Charles, Bruce Springsteen and many others. Mid-June-August.

CHERRY BLOSSOM FESTIVAL

Tidal Basin and Ohio Drive N.W., Washington D.C., 202-789-7000;
www.nationalcherryblossomfestival.org

About 150 trees remain from the original 1912 gift of 3,000 from the city of Tokyo, but thousands of others have been planted in parks along the Tidal Basin, and for two weeks each year their lush pink and white blooms transform the cityscape. The festival celebrates this annual event with activities that appeal to visitors of all ages such as the Smithsonian's Kite Festival on the National Mall and the rousing parade or Sakura Matsuri, a day-long Japanese street festival. Visitors can enjoy drummers, traditional dancers and musical performances; demonstrations of flower arranging, calligraphy and martial arts; a Taste of Japan food fair; and the bustling Ginza Arcade, with shops selling everything from origami paper to antique kimonos.
Late March-early April.

DUPONT-KALORAMA MUSEUM WALK

Washington D.C., 202-387-4062; www.dkmuseums.com

Nine museums (Anderson House, Fondo del Sol, Mary McLeod Bethune Council House, The Phillips Collection, The Woodrow Wilson House, Dumbarton House, General Federations of Women's Clubs, National Museum of American Jewish Military History, and the Textile Museum) joined forces to create an awareness of the Dupont-Kaloram area and to celebrate its art, history and culture. You can visit each museum for free and there are special activities over the weekend at each, including live music, food, quilt making, walking tours and more.
First weekend in June.

EASTER EGG ROLL

White House Lawn, 1600 Pennsylvania Ave. N.W., Washington D.C., 202-456-2200;
www.whitehouse.gov/eastereggroll

First introduced to Washington by Dolley Madison in 1878, this public event is held at the White House on the South Lawn. Each year, there is a special theme assigned to the day and included in events are live music and activities including an Easter egg hunt and Easter egg roll contest. The 2009 Easter Egg Roll with President Obama and First Lady Michelle Obama featured Ziggy Marley, Fergie and the D.C. Youth orchestra performing among others.
Monday after Easter.

EVENING PARADE AT MARINE BARRACKS

Eighth and First streets S.E., Washington D.C., 202-433-6060; www.mbw.usmc.mil

Enjoy a spectacular parade with the U.S. Marine Band, U.S. Marine Drum and Bugle Corps, Color Guard, Silent Drill Team and marching companies. It last for an hour and fifteen minutes and takes place Friday evenings from May through August. The first parade took place in 1957. To attend, fill out a reservation request online and you will receive an email with information.
Early May-late August.

FESTIVAL OF AMERICAN FOLKLIFE

National Mall, Constitution Ave., Washington D.C., 202-357-2700;

www.folklife.si.edu/center/festival.html

Held on the National Mall outside during summer months, the free Smithsonian Folk-life Festival features folk-life traditions from America and abroad, including music, dance, storytelling and more. There are workshops and performances focused on children, including musician Ella Jenkins.
Late June-early July.

FORT DUPONT SUMMER CONCERT SERIES

Fort Dupont Park, Minnesota Avenue and Randle Circle, Washington D.C.

This series of summer concerts features different types of music in the park on Saturday evenings. This year, it features R&B and Jazz. You can relax in the park and take in the music and enjoy your summer evening.
Early July-late August.

THE GEORGETOWN HOUSE TOUR

3240 O St. N.W., Washington D.C., 202-338-1796; www.georgetownhousetour.com

Held since 1927, participants take a walking tour, viewing 10-12 houses and gardens in Georgetown. St. John's Episcopal Church members serve as hosts and guides, and serve tea in the parish's Blake Hall in the afternoon to enjoy sandwiches and treats along with your tea. Tickets can be ordered online.
Late April.

MILLENNIUM STAGE FREE CONCERT SERIES

Millenium Stage, The Kennedy Center, 2700 F St.,, Washington D.C., 202-467-4600; www.nps.gov/ncro

This free concert series offers free performances nightly at 6 p.m., at the Millennium Stage at the Kennedy Center. The series includes the Washington National Opera, Los Gringos, a National Symphony Orchestra prelude, the Rapppahannock Youth Orchestra and others.
Mid-April-Early May.

NATIONAL CHRISTMAS TREE PROGRAM

Ellipse, South of White House,15th and E. streets N.W., Washington D.C., 202-619-7222; www.nps.gov/whho

This free annual event takes place through the month of December near the White House. It includes the National Christmas tree lighting ceremony in which the President addresses the nation with a message of peace and lights the tree. The "Christmas Pathway of Peace" includes the National Christmas Tree along with 56 smaller ones, which symbolize each state and the five territories and the District of Columbia. There is seasonal musical entertainment and performances along with carolers.
December.

NATIONAL INDEPENDENCE DAY PARADE AND FIREWORKS

Constitution Avenue and Seventh Street, Washington D.C., 800-215-6405; www.july4thparade.com

This annual parade on the 4th of July takes place along Constitution Avenue from 7th to 17th Street. There are marching bands, pipe and drum corps, floats, military units marching, drill teams, celebrities, political figures and more. Later that night, a huge fireworks display is presented over the monuments on the National Mall during which a PBS concert takes place featuring the National Symphony Orchestra. One of the best viewing spots is the Capitol, where you can get a good view of both the concerts and fireworks. July 4.

WHERE TO STAY

★★★THE FAIRFAX AT EMBASSY ROW

2100 Massachusetts Ave. N.W., Washington D.C., 8202-293-2100, 800-434-9990; www.starwoodhotels.com

Since 1927, this Embassy Row property has welcomed guests with turn-of-the-century style. All rooms and suites are decorated with Federal and Empire furnishings, including rich fabrics and antique reproductions, and boast beautiful views of Washington National Cathedral and historic Georgetown. Join the distinguished political and social crowd at the Jockey Club for innovative American cuisine.

259 rooms. Restaurant, bar. Business center. Fitness center. $251-350

★★★THE FAIRMONT WASHINGTON D.C.

2401 M St. N.W., Washington D.C., 202-429-2400, 800-257-7544; www.fairmont.com

Located in the West End, this hotel is an ideal base for corporate travelers or vacationers. The well-appointed rooms and suites are comfortable and spacious, and guests on the Gold Floor level are treated to additional perks, such as private check-in and dedicated concierge service. Hotel guests and local denizens celebrate the weekend at the Colonnade's special brunch, while the Juniper is an informal spot for contemporary American fare.

415 rooms. Restaurant. Business center. Pets accepted. $251-350

★★★★★FOUR SEASONS HOTEL, WASHINGTON D.C.

2800 Pennsylvania Ave. N.W., Washington D.C., 202-342-0444, 800-332-3442; www.fourseasons.com

This Four Seasons, located in Washington's historic Georgetown neighborhood, delivers a refined, residential experience that extends from your first step in the modern, sophisticated lobby to lights out in one of the luxuriously appointed guest rooms. Yoga classes, a lap pool and cutting-edge equipment are found in the well-equipped fitness center, while the seven spa treatment rooms are a quiet spot for indulging in signature services like the cherry blossom champagne body treatment. The hotel boasts two restaurants: Seasons, which offers a menu with a focus on fresh, regional ingredients, and Bourbon Steak, created by Michael Mina, which features fine meats and seafood. The Garden Terrace Lounge is the capital's top spot for afternoon tea.

211 rooms. Restaurant, bar. Fitness center. Pool. Spa. Pets accepted. $350 and up.

★★★GEORGETOWN INN

1310 Wisconsin Ave. N.W., Washington D.C., 202-333-8900, 800-368-5922; www.georgetowncollection.com

This hotel, located in the heart of historic Georgetown, puts travelers close to the eclectic and charming shops and restaurants for which this neighbor-

hood is known. Rooms come equipped with marble bathrooms, pillow-top beds, luxurious linens, fluffy bathrobes, Internet access, a complimentary daily newspaper and complimentary turndown service. The inn's restaurant, the Daily Grill, serves classic American fare in a casual setting.
96 rooms. Fitness center. $151-250

★★★GRAND HYATT WASHINGTON
1000 H St. N.W., Washington D.C., 202-582-1234, 800-633-7313;
www.grandwashington.hyatt.com
The Grand Hyatt Washington, D.C., is situated in Penn Quarter, a newly revitalized shopping and dining district, and is close to attractions such as the Verizon Center, the Spy Museum, Ford's Theater and the U.S. Capitol. Talk about convenient—there's Metro Center access in the lobby. Guest rooms feature plush beds with luxurious linens, marble baths and Internet access with warm décor throughout. The Cure Bar & Bistro serves family-style French bistro fare along with a large wine, beer and cocktail list.
888 rooms. Restaurant, bar. Business center. Fitness center. Pool. $350 and up.

★★THE HAMILTON CROWNE PLAZA
14th and K streets N.W., Washington D.C., 202-682-0111, 800-263-9802;
www.hamiltonhoteldc.com
301 rooms. Restaurant, bar. Business center. Fitness center. $61-150

★★★★THE HAY-ADAMS
1800 16th St. N.W., Washington D.C., 202-638-6600, 800-424-5054;
www.hayadams.com
Set on Lafayette Square across from the White House, this hotel has welcomed notables since the 1920s, including the Obamas before they moved into the White House. The guest rooms are a happy marriage of historic preservation and 21st-century conveniences—intricately carved plaster ceilings and ornamental fireplaces reside alongside high-speed Internet access and CD players. Windows frame views of the White House, St. John's Church and Lafayette Square. All-day dining is available at the Lafayette Room, while the Off the Record Bar is a popular watering hole for politicians and hotel guests.
145 rooms. Restaurant, bar. Business center. $351 and up.

★★★HILTON WASHINGTON EMBASSY ROW
2015 Massachusetts Ave. N.W., Washington D.C., 202-265-1600, 800-445-8661;
www.hilton.com
This elegant hotel is in the heart of D.C.'s international business community and is conveniently located half a block from the Metro transit system. In the evening, you can relax with drinks and hors d'oeuvres in the lobby lounge or take in the fabulous view of D.C. from the seasonal rooftop pool. The International Marketplace restaurant features a casual environment serving American cuisine.
193 rooms. Restaurant, bar. Business center. Fitness center. Pool. $151-250

★★HOLIDAY INN GEORGETOWN

2101 Wisconsin Ave. N.W., Washington D.C., 202-338-2120, 800-465-4329;
www.higeorgetown.com

285 rooms. Restaurant, bar. Business center. Fitness center. Pool. $61-150

★★★THE HOTEL GEORGE

15 E. St. N.W., Washington D.C., 202-347-4200, 800-576-8331; www.hotelgeorge.com
Travelers book this boutique hotel for its dynamic interiors and central Capitol Hill location. The rooms offer bold artwork, monochromatic tones, clean lines and high-tech amenities. You'll note the many contemporary portraits of George Washington. The hotel's restaurant, Bistro Bis, is often considered one of the top tables in town and its French bistro fare is a favorite of politicos and celebrities. Those traveling with pets will appreciate the hotel's "Pet Amenity Program," which includes water and food dish, dog mat and special treats.

139 rooms. Restaurant, bar. Business center. Fitness center. Pets accepted. $251-350

★★★HOTEL MONACO

700 F St. N.W., Washington D.C., 202-628-7177; www.monaco-dc.com
Conveniently located near the Washington Convention Center and Verizon Center, Monaco is a funky alternative to the traditional hotel experience. Housed within the D.C.'s former General Post Office (which was built in 1839 by Robert Mills, who designed the Washington Monument), the all-marble building is fronted by soaring columns—a example of quintessential Washington architecture. Inside, however, a bright palate of colors from the walls to floors to furnishings is a delight for the senses for travelers looking for something out-of-the-ordinary. Uniqueness follows through to things like in-room extras (check out the Nintendos) and services (you can get a temporary pet goldfish delivered to your room, if you start feeling lonely).

184 rooms. Business center. Pets accepted. $251-350

★★★HOTEL PALOMAR

2121 P St. N.W., Washington D.C., 202-448-1800; www.hotelpalomar-dc.com
The rather bland beige brick exterior belies the trendy style within this art-centric boutique hotel. The marble-floored lobby is filled with striking sculptures and bold, colorful artwork. Art receptions are hosted regularly in a partnership with the Smithsonian and Phillips Collection. And to create a perception of art in motion, the staff has been trained by the Washington, D.C. ballet. The 520-square-foot rooms highlight contemporary design concepts, with zebrawood furnishings, Italian marble floors in the bathrooms, L'Occitane bath amenities, and a Frette duvet and linens on the bed. The hotel's popular restaurant, Urbana, serves up Western Mediterranean cuisine.

335 rooms. Restaurant, bar. Business center. Fitness room. Pool. Pets accepted. $251-350

★★★J.W. MARRIOTT HOTEL ON PENNSYLVANIA AVENUE

1331 Pennsylvania Ave. N.W., Washington D.C., 202-393-2000;
www.marriotthotels.com/wasjw

Just two blocks from the White House, the J.W. Marriott Hotel offers well-appointed and spacious guest rooms with luxurious bedding, flat-screen TVs and unique black-and-white art. Two restaurants allow guests to enjoy a meal on the property—1331 Bar & Lounge serves International cuisine and unique cocktails in a contemporary setting and Avenue Grill features fine dining specializing in fresh seafood and steaks. Centrally located to theaters, shops, and some famous landmarks, this hotel has something for everyone. 738 rooms. Restaurant, bar. Business center. Fitness center. Spa. Pool. $251-350

★★★THE JEFFERSON

1200 16th St. N.W., Washington D.C., 202-347-2200;
www.thejeffersonwashingtondc.com

With a recent full renovation (completed in summer 2009), The Jefferson, features a luxurious and personalized hotel stay. Built in 1923 and just four blocks from the White House, this Beaux Arts hotel is a stylish and centrally located retreat, with antique-filled public rooms and a museum-quality collection of artwork and original documents signed by Thomas Jefferson. Upon arrival, you'll be greeted with a personal butler who will assist you during your stay. Guest rooms feature elegant designs with soothing color palettes, luxurious bedding, oversized showers, Italian stonework in the bathroom and walk-in closets. The hotel's restaurant, Plume, serve artistic cuisine by chef Damon Gordon and Quill, the hotel's lounge offers creative cocktails. Pamper yourself in the new Spa, which features treatments based on herbs grown on Thomas Jefferson's farm.

119 rooms. Restaurant, bar. Fitness center. Pool. Spa. Pets accepted. $151-250

★★★L'ENFANT PLAZA HOTEL

480 L' Enfant Plaza, S.W., Washington D.C., 202-484-1000, 800-636-5065;
www.lenfantplazahotel.com

L'Enfant Plaza Hotel offers spacious and bright rooms with pillow-top mattresses, luxurious linens, Internet access and terry cloth robes. There's a heated rooftop pool to enjoy year-round with a large sundeck. The American Grill serves fresh steaks and seafood in a contemporary setting. The hotel is only steps away from the Air and Space Museum, the National Mall, Smithsonian Museums and the Holocaust Museum. Conveniently, a Metro Subway station is underneath the hotel so you can easily explore the city. 370 rooms. Restaurant, bar. Fitness center. Pool. Spa. $151-250

★★★LATHAM HOTEL

3000 M St. N.W., Washington D.C., 202-339-6318, 888-587-2377; www.thelatham.com

This European-style boutique hotel is located in the heart of Georgetown, where shopping and dining options abound. But when your stomach growls, you might not want to leave the Latham. Michele Richard, a high-profile local chef with an international reputation, owns and operates the onsite Citronelle, where diners savor award-winning French and American cuisine. Well-appointed guest rooms offer marble showers, terry cloth robes, luxurious bedding and high-speed Internet access. In summer, cool off in the rooftop swimming pool.

133 rooms. Restaurant, bar. Business center. Fitness center. Pool. $61-150

★★★THE MADISON

1177 15th St. N.W., Washington D.C., 202-862-1600, 800-424-8577;
www.loewshotels.com

The beautiful Georgian architecture and clock tower cupola distinguish this hotel, as does the hospitable staff. Rooms are simple yet stylishly decorated and feature cotton bed linens, plush robes and expanded showers. The elegant atmosphere is enhanced by contemporary amenities such as a fitness center and pool. The popular Palette Restaurant and Bar shows off changing art exhibits in this modern designed space, serving creative cuisine and inventive cocktails. After dinner, enjoy a glass of Scotch from their long list in Postscript, a relaxed lounge.

353 rooms. Restaurant, bar. Fitness center. Pool. Pets accepted. $151-250

★★★★MANDARIN ORIENTAL, WASHINGTON D.C.

1330 Maryland Ave. S.W., Washington D.C., 202-554-8588, 888-888-1778;
www.mandarinoriental.com

Overlooking the Tidal Basin with views of the Jefferson Memorial, this Washington outpost of the Asian hotel brand delivers a scenic and central location on the Potomac River. Guest rooms mix an Eastern sensibility with East Coast style (think preppy plaids and toiles alongside clean-lined furniture and fresh-clipped orchids). Contemporary Asian-influenced American cuisine pleases palates in two restaurants, CityZen and Café Mozu, while the Empress Lounge offers a casual alternative with cocktails and small plates like the lobster salad BLT and live jazz vocalists on the weekend. A more than 10,000-square-foot spa, fitness center and indoor pool offer waterfront views, a full spa menu and on-call personal trainers to make your stay here as pampering as possible.

400 rooms. Restaurant, bar. Fitness center. Spa. Pool. Pets accepted. $351 and up.

★★★WASHINGTON MARRIOTT WARDMAN PARK HOTEL

2660 Woodley Road, N.W., Washington D.C., 202-328-2000, 888-733-3222;
www.marriotthotels.com/wasdt

This hotel gracefully combines historic charm, beauty and convenience. Its Wardman Tower, built in 1928, is listed on the National Register of Historic Places. The award-winning gardens have been featured on the *NBC Nightly News* and boast nearly 100,000 seasonal flowers. Guest rooms are spacious with bright colors and feature Marriott's new Revive bedding, Internet access and Bath and Body Works bath amenities. With the Lobby Bar, Harry's Pub serving and Old English menu, Stone's Throw Restaurant and Bar serving steaks and seafood, an in-house gourmet market, and the full service Cafe Illy, you can easily make this your home away from home.

1,316 rooms. Restaurant, bar. Business center. Fitness center. Pool. Pets accepted. $151-250

★★★OMNI SHOREHAM HOTEL

2500 Calvert St. N.W., Washington D.C., 202-234-0700, 800-444-6664;
www.omnihotels.com

Omni Shoreham Hotel's Woodley Park location puts you close to attractions and restaurants, and the eclectic Adams Morgan neighborhood is only minutes away. This urban resort is also located near Rock Creek Park where you can hike, bike, jog or horseback ride through the scenic trails. The guest rooms are elegantly appointed and lavishly decorated with extra pillows, plush robes, and marble bathrooms. Its full-service spa and fitness center are state-of-the-art with dry saunas and a heated outdoor pool. Enjoy American Continental cuisine in an elegant setting at Robert's Restaurant.

834 rooms. Restaurant, bar. Business center. Fitness center. Pool. Spa. Pets accepted. $251-350

★★★RENAISSANCE MAYFLOWER HOTEL

1127 Connecticut Ave. N.W., Washington D.C., 202-347-3000;

www.renaissancehotels.com

Built in 1925 for Calvin Coolidge's inauguration, this hotel has played host to the likes of Franklin Delano Roosevelt and J. Edgar Hoover. The block-long lobby features gilded trim, crystal chandeliers and Oriental rugs, but the guest rooms are quite homey with luxurious bedding and bright colors. Enjoy a meal at the hotel's Fifteen Squares Restaurant, the Lobby Bistro and Lounge, Liberty Market or the President's Sports Bar. For groups, the Mayflower offers state-of-the-art meeting facilities and it's near the Convention Center and just blocks from the Verizon Center, Chinatown and the National Portrait Gallery.

657 rooms. Business center. Fitness center. Pets accepted. $61-150

★★★★THE RITZ-CARLTON, GEORGETOWN

3100 South St. N.W., Washington D.C., 202-912-4100, 800-241-3333;

www.ritzcarlton.com

Embassy delegations often stay at the Ritz-Carlton, Georgetown, with its contemporary décor and historic setting (it is housed in a National Historic Landmark). Many of the hotel's guest rooms offer views of the Potomac River, along with feather duvets, Egyptian cotton linen, goose-down pillows, plush robes, and marble deep soaking baths. Sip one of the fire-red martinis in the 40s-vibe of Degrees Bar and Lounge, then dine on fire-inspired American cuisine in Fahrenheit Restaurant. Spend a day pampering yourself in The Boutique Spa, where you can choose from a menu of facials, massages, body treatments, and relax in the steam room and sauna.

86 rooms. Restaurant, bar. Business center. Fitness center. Spa. Pets accepted. $351 and up.

★★★★THE RITZ-CARLTON, WASHINGTON D.C.

1150 22nd St. N.W., Washington D.C., 202-835-0500, 800-241-3333;

www.ritzcarlton.com

The Ritz-Carlton, Washington D.C. offers noteworthy attention to detail along with innovative amenities in this central location near Georgetown, the White House and the Smithsonian museums. Rooms are elegantly decorated and feature Egyptian cotton linen, feather beds, down comforters, Bulgari bath products and plush robes. On-call technology butlers can assist with computer woes, while the Luggage-less Travel program allows frequent visitors to leave items behind for their next stay. All guests are granted access to the Sports Club/LA fitness complex next door, which has a state-of-the-art facility, fitness classes and a full spa and salon. You won't have to leave the hotel for a fabulous meal, with chef Eric Ripert's Westend Bistro, which serves casual American cuisine using fresh local produce.

300 rooms. Restaurant, bar. Business center. Pets accepted. $351 and up.

★★RIVER INN

924 25th St. N.W., Washington D.C., 202-337-7600, 888-874-0100; www.theriverinn.com

126 rooms. Restaurant, bar. Fitness room. Pets accepted. $151-250

★★★SOFITEL WASHINGTON D.C. LAFAYETTE SQUARE

806 15th St. N.W., Washington D.C., 202-730-8800; www.sofitelwashingtondc.com

Just a short walk from the White House, the National Mall and the Metro, this historic hotel is located in a downtown business area. Its décor is 1930s Art Deco with a contemporary edge. With gold-leaf crown molding, marble and velvet furniture, the Sofitel Lafayette Square has earned a spot on the National Register of Historic Places. Pets receive a welcome bag, silver bowls and a small version of Sofitel's guest bed with goose-down bedding. Enjoy a fresh take on French bistro cuisine at ICI Urban Bistro.

237 rooms. Restaurant, bar. Business center. Fitness center. $251-350

★★★★THE ST. REGIS WASHINGTON, D.C.

923 16th St. N.W., Washington D.C., 202-638-2626; www.stregis.com/washingtondc

Built in 1926, this grand hotel has hosted world leaders for more than 80 years—after all, it is only two blocks from the White House. Renovated in 2008, rooms and suites include wireless Internet access, iPod docking stations on Bose clock radios, 32-inch flat-screen TVs, luxurious robes, Remède bathroom amenities and electric mirrors in the bathrooms, with television screens imbedded within the reflective surface of the mirror. Elegant and tasteful furnishings and décor provide a seamless feeling of classic luxury throughout the common areas and the beautiful rooms including Palladian windows and Italian Renaissance chandeliers. Their signature Bespoke Service offers St. Regis butlers to assist guests with all of their needs. When it's time for dinner, be sure to enjoy French American cuisine from Alain Ducasse's Adour and then sip on a cocktail in the lavish St. Regis Bar.

150 rooms. Restaurant, bar. Business center. Fitness center. $351 and up.

★★TOPAZ HOTEL

1733 North St. N.W., Washington D.C., 202-393-3000, 800-775-1202; www.topazhotel.com

99 rooms. Restaurant, bar. Complimentary breakfast. Business center. Pets accepted. $151-250

★★★THE WESTIN GRAND, WASHINGTON D.C.

2350 M St. N.W., Washington D.C., 202-429-0100, 888-627-8406; www.westin.com

Not as glitzy as many of the other top D.C. hotels, the Westin offers attentive service and a more low-key environment. The stylish rooms offer ultra-comfortable beds, sizable bathrooms, leather furniture and CD players. Suites go the extra mile with wood-burning fireplaces and three telephone lines.

Westin Doggie Beds offer the same plush sleep experience to four-legged friends. The hotel's location is within walking distance of Georgetown and many waterfront restaurants along the Potomac. Enjoy American cuisine at one of two restaurants here, Café on M or the M Street Grill.

263 rooms. Restaurant, bar. Business center. Fitness center. Pool. Pets accepted. $251-350

★★★THE WESTIN WASHINGTON, D.C. CITY CENTER

1400 M St. N.W., Washington D.C., 202-429-1700; www.starwoodhotels.com/westin

Conveniently located near both Georgetown and Dupont Circle, this hotel offers comfortable rooms that feature Herman Miller Aeron ergonomic desk chairs and flat-screen TVs. Rooms are spacious and simple, yet comfortable. Enjoy a meal at the hotel's contemporary restaurant, 1400 North, which overlooks the main lobby. Get your workout in at the 24-hour fitness facility and book an in-room massage. Bring along your dog, they'll be treated to the good life with a dog bed, food and water bowls, a floor mat, a "dog in room" sign and a welcome kit!

406 rooms. Restaurant, bar. Business center. Fitness center. Pets accepted. $151-250

★★★WILLARD INTERCONTINENTAL, WASHINGTON D.C.

1401 Pennsylvania Ave. N.W., Washington D.C., 202-628-9100, 877-424-4225; www.washington.interconti.com

Only two blocks from the White House, this legendary Beaux Arts hotel has been at the center of Washington's political scene since 1850. In the Willard's lobby, Lincoln held fireside staff meetings, Grant escaped the rigors of the White House to enjoy brandy and cigars, and the term "lobbyist" was coined. The guest rooms and suites are a traditional blend of Edwardian and Victorian styles furnished in deep jewel tones. The Jenny Lind suite is perfect for honeymooners, with its mansard roof and canopy bed, while the Oval suite, inspired by the Oval Office, makes guests feel quite presidential indeed. Head to the Elizabeth Arden Red Door Spa to get pampered like the politicos and then, dine at the famous Round Robin Bar where you can enjoy a cocktail and a cigar.

332 rooms. Restaurant, bar. Business center. Fitness center. Spa. $351 and up.

WHERE TO EAT

★★★701 RESTAURANT

701 Pennsylvania Ave. N.W., Washington D.C., 202-393-0701; www.701restaurant.com

Overlooking the Navy Memorial fountains and just steps from the Washington National Mall, this fine-dining restaurant features a diverse menu and a caviar bar. The roomy tables, comfortable chairs and live piano music provide a nice atmosphere. And the lounge, which features a sunken bar, is the perfect place to meet friends for a drink. Live music is played in the evenings, so try to grab a table on the exterior patio for a great view.

American. Lunch (Monday-Friday), dinner. Bar. Reservations recommended. Outdoor seating. $36-85

★★★1789 RESTAURANT

1226 36th St. N.W., Washington D.C., 202-965-1789; www.1789restaurant.com

Located in a restored Federal mansion just on the edge of Georgetown University's campus, this restaurant is a top destination for students with visiting relatives or diners celebrating a special occasion. The restaurant features Victorian decor with fine china, Civil War pictures and artifacts, antiques and a gas fireplace. The menu changes seasonally, but the popular rack of lamb is always available. A chef's tasting menu is offered, as well as a pre/post-theater menu.

American. Dinner. Bar. Children's menu. Reservations recommended. $36-85

★★★★ADOUR

The St. Regis Washington D.C., 923 16th St. N.W., Washington D.C., 202-509-8000; www.adour-washingtondc.com

Adour's executive chef Julien Jouhannaud takes the best of local ingredients, such as Maryland blue crab, Amish chicken breast and quail eggs from Virginia, and infuses them with the charm of southwestern French cooking. Located within the St. Regis hotel, the ultra-contemporary and elegant setting matches that of the hotel showcasing black walls with accenting hues of brown, gold, silver and cream; white seating and chrome galore. A backdrop of a floor-to-ceiling, temperature-controlled wine vault serves as a reminder that French fare always goes down better with wine, especially when there is a selection more than 400 deep.

French, American. Breakfast, dinner. $86 and up.

★BILLY MARTIN'S TAVERN

1264 Wisconsin Ave. N.W., Washington D.C., 202-333-7370; www.billymartinstavern.com

American. Lunch, dinner, late-night, Saturday-Sunday brunch. Bar. $16-35

★★★BISTRO BIS

The Hotel George, 15 E. St. N.W., Washington D.C., 202-661-2700; www.bistrobis.com

This popular French restaurant is located in the contemporary Hotel George on Capitol Hill. Its sleek, modern interior features a zinc bar, cherry wood accents, an open kitchen, leather banquettes, pendant lamps and high ceilings. The menu features dishes like the lamb shank with tomatoes, flageolets, garlic, rosemary and creamy goat cheese polenta; veal sweetbreads with parmesan polenta cake, fava beans, morels, crawfish tails and crawfish-tarragon cream; and pan roasted sirloin strip with pommes frites, mesclun salad and red wine shallot butter. Bistro Bis offers an extensive wine list. This popular spot attracts celebrities and politicians, so be on the lookout for famous faces.

French. Breakfast, lunch (Monday-Friday), dinner, Saturday-Sunday brunch. Bar. Reservations recommended. Outdoor seating. $36-85

★★BISTRO FRANÇAIS

3128 M St. N.W., Washington D.C., 202-338-3830; www.bistrofrancaisdc.com

French. Lunch, dinner, Saturday-Sunday brunch, late-night. $16-35

★★BISTROT LEPIC & WINE BAR

1736 Wisconsin Ave. N.W., Washington D.C., 202-333-0111; www.bistrotlepic.com
French. Lunch, dinner. Bar. Reservations recommended. $16-35

★★★THE BOMBAY CLUB

815 Connecticut Ave. N.W., Washington D.C., 202-659-3727; www.bombayclubdc.com
One of the most respected Indian restaurants in the area, the Bombay Club has served plenty of famous politicians and celebrities including President Clinton, President Nelson Mandela, Former Secretary of State Madeleine Albright, Dr. Deepak Chopra and Harrison Ford. Their extensive menu blends Parsi fare, Goan specialties, Moghlai specialties and coastal cuisine. The Sunday buffet brunch features seven entree dishes, desserts and fruit, all for $20 per person (or for $25, you'll also get plenty of champagne) plus live piano music playing in the background. The elegant dining room is bright and cheery but the large seasonal outdoor patio also gives you a view of Lafayette Park.
Indian. Lunch (Monday-Friday), dinner, Sunday brunch. Bar. Outdoor seating. $16-35

★★★BRASSERIE BECK

1101 K St. N.W., Washington D.C., 202-408-1717; www.beckdc.com
Belgium boldly comes to the U.S. capital with this ultra-modern bistro that still manages to feel down-to-earth. The atmosphere of the main dining room is inspired by rail travel with train station clocks, and with an exhibition kitchen, you can watch as the chefs do their thing. The French-Belgian dishes are heavy and filling, and best complemented by a crisp glass of beer. The bistro serves nine draught beers and over 100 varieties by bottle—Belgian, of course. The Chef's Table dinner features five courses with optional wine or beer pairings. And it would be a sin to leave without with a Belgian waffle for dessert; or enjoy a coffee at the coffee bar.
Belgian. Lunch (Monday-Friday), dinner, Sunday brunch. $16-35

★★★CAFÉ ATLÁNTICO

405 Eighth St. N.W., Washington D.C., 202-393-0812; www.cafeatlantico.com
One of celebrity chef Jose Andres' restaurants, Cafe Atlantico is known for having one of the best cocktail lists in D.C. The caipirinhas and mojitos are delicious, as are the aguas frescas. The menu offers a mix of everything, from strip loin with a plantain puree to a daily fish served Veracruz-style and guacamole made tableside. Or try the chef's tasting menu to get a taste of it all. For brunch, the restaurant offers Latino Dim Sum which you either à la carte or from a tasting menu.
Latin American. Lunch, dinner, brunch. Closed Monday. Bar. Reservations recommended. Outdoor seating. $36-85

★★★CAFÉ DU PARC

Willard InterContinental Washington, 1401 Pennsylvania Ave. N.W., Washington D.C., 202-942-7000; www.washington.intercontinental.com
Located in the Willard InterContinental Washington hotel, this Parisian bistro-like spot, overlooking Pershing Park, provides a delightful spot to dine. With a large outdoor seating area, you'll feel as though you're on the streets of Paris. Chef Antoine Westermann's menu includes French favorites includ-

ing mussels, roasted chicken and veal, pork and foie gras terrine wrapped in a house-made pastry, which is served in the upstairs restaurant. The downstairs café by day is more relaxed and serves freshly baked croissants and other pastries, which are available for take-away. By night, the café turns into a wine bar, with plenty of wines to choose from.

American, French. Breakfast, lunch, dinner. Bar. Reservations recommended. $36-85

★★CAFE MILANO

3251 Prospect St. N.W., Washington D.C., 202-333-6183; www.cafemilano.net

Italian. Lunch, dinner, late-night. Bar. Reservations recommended. Outdoor seating. $36-85

★★★THE CAPITAL GRILLE

601 Pennsylvania Ave. N.W., Washington D.C., 202-737-6200; www.thecapitalgrille.com

Dark, polished wood accents and dark leather chairs and booths may be reminiscent of a "boys' club" steakhouse, but everyone flocks here for the fresh seafood and signature dry-aged steaks. For dinner, start with fresh New England oysters or lobster and crab cakes and then, try the seared tenderloin with fresh butter poached lobster; or the grilled swordfish with lemon shallot relish. The restaurant offers an impressive wine list with more than 5,000 bottles. House-made ice cream and sorbet make for a refreshing dessert or try the chocolate hazelnut cake.

American. Lunch, dinner. Bar. Reservations recommended. $36-85

★★CASHION'S EAT PLACE

1819 Columbia Road, N.W., Washington D.C., 202-797-1819;
www.cashionseatplace.com

International. Dinner, Sunday brunch. Closed Monday. Bar. Reservations recommended. Outdoor seating. $36-85

★★★CENTRAL MICHEL RICHARD

1001 Pennsylvania Ave. N.W., Washington D.C., 202-626-0015;
www.centralmichelrichard.com

This restaurant won a 2008 James Beard Award for Best New Restaurant, and we can see why. With its warm atmosphere, Central is devoted to good, old-fashioned American selections, including macaroni and cheese, burgers, fried chicken with mashed potatoes and gastro-pub fare such as fish and chips, bangers and mash, and onion soup. Richard's French background, of course, sneaks into dishes like the country pate and ratatouille. Even the desserts carry this traditional vibe with a banana split, bread and butter pudding, and cheesecake with raspberry sauce. Everything is prepared with a sharp focus on bettering the basics.

American. Lunch (Monday-Friday), dinner. Bar. $36-85

★★★★CITYZEN

Mandarin Oriental, Washington D.C., 1330 Maryland Ave. S.W., Washington D.C.,
202-787-6006; www.mandarinoriental.com

Under chef Eric Ziebold, CityZen serves modern American-French cuisine. Ziebold offers a new three-course prix fixe menu monthly, including an appe-

tizer such as purée of cardoon soup with grated potato and Périgord truffles; and an entrée such as pan-seared scallops with roasted celery branch, black pepper brioche, horseradish bavarois and bloody Mary consommé. Desserts include smore soufflé (a chocolate and marshmallow soufflé with graham cracker ice cream), a CityZen sacher tort or an apple cobbler. Ziebold also offers a six-course tasting menu, with a vegetarian option. The restaurant and the lounge, designed by the acclaimed Tony Chi, feel intimate despite the large space and vaulted ceilings.
American, French. Dinner. Closed Sunday-Monday. Bar. Reservations recommended. $86 and up.

★★CLYDE'S OF GEORGETOWN
3236 M St. N.W., Washington D.C., 202-333-9180; www.clydes.com
American. Lunch, dinner, Saturday-Sunday brunch. Bar. Children's menu. $16-35

★★★DC COAST
1401 K St. N.W., Washington D.C., 202-216-5988; www.dccoast.com
This restaurant, housed in a Beaux Arts-style building popular in the city, offers a menu heavy on seafood dishes. Chef Jeff Tunks shines with dishes such as seared Atlantic salmon with wild mushrooms, lettuce and truffle vinaigrette; iced Blue point oysters; and Tahitian-style tuna tartare. The wine list pleases with the many choices, and there are plenty of specialty cocktails and beer to choose from to accompany your meal.
Seafood. Lunch, dinner. Closed Sunday. Bar. $36-85

★★DISTRICT CHOPHOUSE & BREWERY
509 Seventh St. N.W., Washington D.C., 202-347-3434; www.districtchophouse.com
American. Lunch, dinner, late-night, Saturday-Sunday brunch. Bar. Children's menu. $36-85

★★★GALILEO
1110 21st St. N.W., Washington D.C., 202-293-7191;
www.robertodonna.com/restaurants
This is the flagship enterprise of Roberto Donna, the celebrity chef behind Bebo Trattoria and many others. In keeping with the cutting-edge, there's a much-sought-after kitchen table, called Laboratorio del Galileo, where he creates special menus for small groups a few times during the week. The European country décor features terra-cotta floors, small alcoves in the dining room and a mural of Galileo. The casual and relaxed bar and lounge is a perfect spot to end the night with an after dinner drink. There's also a wine cellar and outdoor terrace to enjoy in the warmer months.
Italian. Lunch, dinner. Bar. Reservations recommended. Outdoor seating. $36-85

★★★GEORGIA BROWN'S
950 15th St. N.W., Washington D.C., 202-393-4499; www.gbrowns.com
At this popular McPherson Square spot, diners have trouble choosing from among the many creative, modern dishes, such as fried green tomatoes stuffed with herbed cream cheese and served on a bed of green tomato relish

with lemon-cayenne mayonnaise and watercress; and cornmeal-crusted catfish fingers served with red grape and blue cheese slaw and corn tartar sauce. The Sunday brunch menu features a large buffet of tasty dishes you can fill your plate with, then you can choose an entrée, and after that a dessert. The dining room features blonde wood and a bronzed ceiling scroll.
American. Lunch, dinner, Sunday brunch. Bar. Reservations recommended. $16-35

★★★GERARD'S PLACE
915 15th St. N.W., Washington D.C., 202-737-4445; www.gerardsplacedc.net
Gerard's Place is an intimate hideaway near the White House with high-back chairs, sheaths draped overhead, vibrant colors and a large glass chandelier with amber-colored tones. Two menus are offered nightly: a five-course chef's tasting menu as well as an à la carte menu. Expect classic French dishes with refined twists, such as foie gras confit, organic greens and olive oil vinaigrette; poached lobster with sauternes sauce, fresh mango, avocado, spinach and piquillo peppers and lime; and a soup of rhubarb and strawberry, perfumed with vanilla and citrus. If you want, bring your own wine on Monday as there isn't a corkage fee then.
French. Lunch, dinner. Closed Sunday. Outdoor seating. $36-85

★★GRILL FROM IPANEMA
1858 Columbia Road, N.W., Washington D.C., 202-986-0757;
www.thegrillfromipanema.com
Brazilian. Lunch, dinner. Bar. Outdoor seating. $16-35

★★★ICI URBAN BISTRO
Sofitel Lafayette Square Hotel, 806 15th St. N.W., Washington D.C., 202-730-8700;
www.iciurbanbistro.com
Nobody does pastry better than the French. And this is certainly true of the creations of pastry chef Jerome Colin, who grew up in Roanne, France, and began his career in pastries at age 14. If you really want to go all out, skip dinner completely and get the sweet Dessert Sampler. But if you feel compelled to exercise restraint, the international-inflected French cuisine and the trendy, modern setting here don't disappoint. Be sure to start with the Cajun pommes frites with Louisiana rémoulade.
French. Breakfast, lunch, dinner. $36-85

★★JALEO
480 Seventh St. N.W., Washington D.C., 202-628-7949; www.jaleo.com
Spanish. Lunch, dinner, Saturday-Sunday brunch. Bar. Outdoor seating. $16-35

★★★★THE JOCKEY CLUB
The Fairfax at Embassy Row, 2100 Massachusetts Ave. N.W., Washington D.C., 202-835-2100; www.thejockeyclub-dc.com
A Washington D.C. mainstay for nearly four decades, The Jockey Club underwent a major renovation in 2008, but has retained much of its history—even the maitre d' from 1978 has returned to the front of the house. Chef Levi Meznik has created a classic American menu, churning out dishes such as steak tartare and Maine lobster thermidor with aplomb. The three-course

pre-theater menu is a nice way to sample Meznik's culinary talents, which include a divine rhubarb and ginger cobbler with Alpine flower ice cream. Lunch is slightly more casual, but chances are the bar will still be stocked with politicos and power suits.

American. Lunch, dinner. Reservations recommended. Bar. $36-85

★★★KINKEAD'S
2000 Pennsylvania Ave. N.W., Washington D.C., 202-296-7700; www.kinkead.com
Senators, journalists, models, financiers and media moguls rub elbows at chef/owner Bob Kinkead's spot for distinctive global fare. The deep, cherry wood-paneled dining room has an intimate, clubby feel to it, with low lighting, vintage wrought-iron staircases and elegant table settings. The menu, which changes daily and draws influences from Spain, France, Italy, Morocco and Asia, offers a terrific selection of appetizers, soups, salads, chops and seafood. To complement the menu, the user-friendly wine list is color-coded from light to dark according to nose, weight, body and flavor. Kinkead's hosts live jazz in the evenings.

Seafood. Lunch (Monday-Friday), dinner. Bar. Outdoor seating. $36-85

★★LA CHAUMIÈRE
2813 M St. N.W., Washington D.C., 202-338-1784; www.lachaumieredc.com
French. Lunch (Monday-Friday), dinner. Closed Sunday. $16-35

★★LAURIOL PLAZA
1835 18th St. N.W., Washington D.C., 202-387-0035; www.lauriolplaza.com
Latin American, Mexican. Lunch, dinner, Sunday brunch. Bar. Outdoor seating. $16-35

★★★MENDOCINO GRILL AND WINE BAR
2917 M St. N.W., Washington D.C., 202-333-2912; www.mendocinodc.com
Located in Georgetown, the most impressive feature of this restaurant is of course its excellent, all-American award-winning wine list, with wines from California, Washington state and Oregon. The menu, full of seasonal produce and naturally-raised meats and seafood, is designed to complement the wine. Entreés include mushroom bread pudding; housemade spinach gnocchi with ham, pecorino tartufo, rapini and pesto; and pork chop with cranberry bean ragout and housemade apple mustard. There is a thoughtful cheese menu along with cheese flights and even a beer and cheese flight, which includes three artisinal cheeses with three microbrews. Wood and slate dominate the décor, accented with wall mirrors.

American. Dinner. Bar. Reservations recommended. $36-85

★★★★MICHEL RICHARD CITRONELLE
3000 M St. N.W., Washington D.C., 202-625-2150; www.citronelledc.com
Like chef Michel Richard's food, the restaurant is stylish and elegant. Filled with fresh flowers and lit in a creamy, golden glow, the room has a chic vibe and a glass-enclosed open kitchen for a bird's-eye view of the cooks. Ingredients are the stars here; the chef manages to wow diners by highlighting the simple flavors of each dish's main component. Choose from a multi-course tasting menu or from the à la carte menu. Dishes may include chestnut soup,

a lobster burger or squab and duck with apple risotto and apricot sauce. Desserts include house-made ice cream and sorbets and blueberry cheesecake with dulce de leche sauce, among others. Nabbing a seat at one of Richard's coveted tables is like winning the lottery.

French. Dinner. Bar. Outdoor seating. $86 and up.

★★★MIO

1110 Vermont Ave. N.W., Washington D.C., 202-955-0075; www.miorestaurant.com

Enjoy sounds of live music from the grand piano in a crisp atmosphere in this two-story bistro. An open kitchen allows diners to take in the action as the chef's staff creates American-style offerings, such as roasted lamb and pan-seared Alaska salmon. Chef Nicholas Stefanelli follows through on his belief of a sustainable approach to cuisine by using local produce and meats, including whole fish and whole animals. There is a four- or six-course tasting menu offered in which you might find dishes such as crispy smelts with persevered lemon slush; duck with celery root, clementine, cardamom and almonds; and brown butter panna cotta and clementine tangelo. For a change of pace, ask for beer pairings with each course.

American. Lunch (Monday-Friday), dinner. Closed Sunday. $36-85

★★MORRISON-CLARK

1015 L St. N.W., Washington D.C., 202-898-1200; www.morrisonclark.com

American. Dinner. Closed Monday. Bar. Outdoor seating. $36-85

★★★NAGE

Courtyard Embassy Row, 1600 Rhode Island Ave. N.W., Washington D.C., 202-448-8005; www.nage.bz

Tucked off to one side of the Courtyard Embassy Row Hotel, American and French cuisines find a home in a setting that resembles the Far East, with hanging lamps and hues of red. The D.C. location is the second Nage in the mid-Atlantic region, the first being just to the east, in the seashore town of Rehoboth Beach, Delaware. Like its beachside counterpart, the menu features numerous seafood options, such as crab cakes and baked oysters, sea scallops and striped bass. Desserts include banana toffee roulade, hot buttered rum custard and warm vanilla risotto rice pudding. Be sure to check the chalkboard for the chef's specials of the day.

American, French. Breakfast, lunch, dinner, Sunday brunch. $16-35

★★OCCIDENTAL GRILL

1475 Pennsylvania Ave. N.W., Washington D.C., 202-783-1475; www.occidentaldc.com

American. Lunch, dinner. Closed Sunday. Bar. $36-85

★★OLD EBBITT GRILL

675 15th St. N.W., Washington D.C., 202-347-4800; www.ebbitt.com

American. Breakfast, lunch, dinner, late-night, Saturday-Sunday brunch. Bar. $16-35

★★OVAL ROOM

800 Connecticut Ave. N.W., Washington D.C., 202-463-8700; www.ovalroom.com

American, Mediterranean. Lunch, dinner. Closed Sunday. Bar. $36-85

★★★★PALENA
3529 Connecticut Ave. N.W., Washington D.C., 202-537-9250;
www.palenarestaurant.com

Executive chef Frank Ruta and pastry chef Ann Amernick met while work-ing in the White House kitchen in the 1980s and decided to open a restaurant together in 2000. They now offer a seasonal menu of French- and Italian-influenced fare—such as sea scallops with chestnut purée or gnocchi with roasted endive, turnips, black truffle and shaved pecorino—complimented by comforting desserts including a chocolate-toffee torte and a lime tartlet. The décor is simple and understated with buttercream colored walls and a large picture window, and the waitstaff is attentive.

American. Dinner. Closed Sunday. Bar. Reservations recommended. $36-85

★★THE PALM
1225 19th St. N.W., Washington D.C., 202-293-9091; www.thepalm.com

Steak. Lunch, dinner. Bar. $36-85

★★PAOLO'S
1303 Wisconsin Ave. N.W., Washington D.C., 202-333-7353; www.paolosristorante.com

Italian. Lunch, dinner, late-night, Saturday-Sunday brunch. Bar. Children's menu. Outdoor seating. $16-35

★★PESCE
2016 P St. N.W., Washington D.C., 202-466-3474; www.pescebistro.com

Seafood. Lunch, dinner. $16-35

★PIZZERIA PARADISO
2029 P St. N.W., Washington D.C., 202-223-1245; www.eatyourpizza.com

Pizza. Lunch, dinner. $16-35

★★★PLUME
The Jefferson Hotel, 1200 16th St. N.W., Washington D.C., 202-833-6206;
www.thejeffersonwashingtondc.com

This new restaurant at the recently renovated (Summer 2009) Jefferson Ho-tel, is elegantly designed with a lavish chandelier, sconces, a fireplace and a skylight allowing light to shine in during the day. Executive chef Damon Gordon provides the creative cuisine that focuses on seasonal local organ-ic ingredients. A chef's table in the kitchen allows guests to experience a French country kitchen. After dinner, you can enjoy a cocktail at Quill, the hotel's bar and lounge.

American. Breakfast, lunch, dinner, Sunday brunch. Bar. $36-85

★★★PRIME RIB
2020 K St. N.W., Washington D.C., 202-466-8811; www.theprimerib.com

This K Street business spot features the décor of a 1940s New York supper club. With leopard print carpeting, black and gold colors, and piano music, you'll feel as if you've been transported back in time to a more elegant era. It remains one of the best steakhouses inside the Beltway with fresh seafood and prime quality meats. The wait-staff are decked out in tuxedos and take care of your every need. Choose from prime rib, New York strip, filet mignon, chopped sirloin, veal chop, lamb chops, chicken, shrimp, crab, halibut and more.

Steak. Lunch, dinner. Closed Sunday. Bar. $36-85

★★★PROOF
775 G St. N.W., Washington, D.C., 202-737-7663; www.proofdc.com

Wine lovers, rejoice! The 65-page wine menu includes nearly 1,200 bottle selections and 40 choices by glass—the largest wine list in the D.C. area. Sommeliers help match to a dynamic assortment of more than 20 artisanal cheeses and a diverse menu that ranges from Mediterranean- to Asian-inspired dishes. Choose from the à la carte menu or from the four-course tasting menu. You might enjoy dishes like miso glazed Alaskan sablefish with buckwheat noodles, baby bok choy and toasted sesame; or roasted organic chicken breast with oyster mushrooms and goat cheese stuffing, creamy polenta and sautéed rapini. An eclectic style mixes old and new with antiques, walnut floors, a French pewter bar and four flat-screen televisions displaying images from the collection at the Smithsonian American Art Museum.

Contemporary American. Lunch, dinner, late night. $36-85

★★★RESTAURANT NORA
2132 Florida Ave. N.W., Washington D.C., 202-462-5143; www.noras.com

In this 19th-century grocery store-turned-organic American eatery, seasonal ingredients are the focus. Chef/owner Nora Pouillon is a pioneer in the organic movement; Restaurant Nora was the first certified organic restaurant in the country (95 percent of the products used are organic). Pouillon integrates flavors from the American South to Spain and from Latin America to Asia and India, and the menu changes daily. Or you can also choose to order the tasting menu, which includes options such as wild mushroom soup, crab salad, herb crusted rack of lamb, and Amish yogurt panna cotta. The rustic dining room is decorated with dried flowers and museum-quality antique Mennonite and Amish quilts.

American, Mediterranean. Dinner, late-night. Closed Sunday. Bar. Reservations recommended. $36-85

★★★SAM AND HARRY'S
1200 19th St. N.W., Washington D.C., 202-296-4333; www.samandharrys.com

This upscale steakhouse in downtown D.C. is decorated with jazz-themed artwork, green leather booths and dark wood accents. Along with prime aged center New York strip steak, center cut filet mignon and rack of lamb, a number of fresh seafood options are available, from whole Maine lobster to jumbo lump crab cakes. And the seafood is so fresh it's flown in daily. A full bar features a wide selection of liquors and spirits, and the extensive wine list features 25 selections available by the glass.

Steak. Lunch (Monday-Friday), dinner. Closed Sunday. Bar. Reservations recommended. $36-85

★★★SEASONS
2800 Pennsylvania Ave. N.W., Washington D.C., 202-944-2026; www.fourseasons.com

With deep upholstered armchairs, dark wood and fresh flowers, Seasons is the flagship restaurant of the Four Seasons Hotel. The sophisticated American-French menu offers simple, elegant fare and an extensive wine list. For an afternoon delight, stop by the Garden Terrace for tea service with all the trimmings—scones with clotted cream, cucumber and watercress sandwiches with the crusts cut off, petits fours, chocolate-dipped strawberries and assorted butter cookies. The Sunday brunch should not be missed—with plenty of stations to fill up your plate including a bagel bar, carving station, crepe station, an Asian station, salad bars, seafood station, cheese station, dessert and beverages.

American, French. Breakfast, lunch, dinner, Sunday brunch. Bar. Children's menu. Reservations recommended. Outdoor seating. $36-85

★★★TABERNA DEL ALABARDERO

1776 First St. N.W., Washington D.C., 202-429-2200; www.alabardero.com

For 16 years, Taberna del Alabardero has served classic Spanish cuisine such as chorizo paella with chicken or gazpacho Andaluz to D.C. diners. Executive chef Santi Zabaleta also uses locally grown produce to enhance seasonal menu selections. The à la carte lunch and dinner menu features dishes like strip loin paella with fresh herbs and ali oli crust; braised boneless beef oxtail with wild rice; and grilled monkfish with sweet cream of carrot and French beans. There are also tapas and vegetarian menus. Executives can enjoy a three-course menu here during the week.

Spanish. Lunch (Monday-Friday), dinner. Closed Sunday. Bar. Outdoor seating. $36-85

★★★TEATRO GOLDONI

1909 K St. N.W., Washington D.C., 202-955-9494; www.teatrogoldoni.com

Named after a famous Venetian playwright from the 1800s, this downtown restaurant is decorated like a Venetian theater during the carnival, with a wall of masks, velvet curtains, blown-glass pendant lights and harlequin and striped patterns. Innovative but simple Venetian dishes are served, and a pianist performs on weekends. Dishes include risotto with Fontina cheese, with roasted cardoons and fresh black truffle; and braised lamb shank with roasted artichoke, flan of corn, black olives and roasted sweet garlic potatoes. The restaurant also serves a prix fixe theater menu and offers wine dinners and cooking classes.

Italian. Lunch (Monday-Friday), dinner. Closed Sunday. Bar. Reservations recommended. $36-85

★★★VIDALIA

1990 M St. N.W., Washington D.C., 202-659-1990; www.vidaliadc.com

Taking his lead from the South and the Chesapeake Bay area, chef/owner Jeffrey Buben serves up inventive appetizers such as warm crayfish and sweet corn ragout with crispy plantain, piquillo pepper purée, catfish boudin blanc and rich crayfish consommé. Entrées include gulf shrimp with yellow grits, shellfish cream, spring garlic, vidalia onions, and ragout of andouille; and chicken breast, liver, leg croquette, morels and green beans. Decadent desserts are to die for. A tasting menu is also available for you to create with your entire party. Vidalia is also the sister restaurant of Bistro Bis.

American. Lunch (Monday-Friday), dinner. Closed Sunday in July-August.

Bar. Children's menu. $36-85

★★★WESTEND BISTRO BY ERIC RIPERT
The Ritz-Carlton, Washigton D.C., 1190 22nd St. N.W., Washington D.C.,
202-974-4900; www.westendbistrodc.com
Founded by French chef Eric Ripert, one of New York City's top culinary masters, this airy and fun bistro in The Ritz-Carlton, Washington D.C. is yet another example of his tasteful marriage of French and American cuisines. Ripert's vision is carried out by hand-picked protégés and the menu leans toward seafood and beef. For a quirky touch not found at most gourmet eateries, try the fries and fish burger topped with roasted tomato, saffron aioli and fennel. Other tasty options include grilled truffled ham with tasty gruyere cheese; salmon with lentil, pickled mushrooms and black truffle butter.
French, American. Lunch, dinner. $36-85

SPAS

★★★★THE SPA AT THE MANDARIN ORIENTAL, WASHINGTON, D.C.
1330 Maryland Ave. S.W., Washington D.C., 202-787-6100; www.mandarinoriental.com
This Spa creates a calming retreat for the overworked city-goers. The staff at the Spa promotes the Time Ritual concept, a customized two- or three-hour experience during which clients receive a one-on-one consultation with a therapist to determine which treatments are best suited to the clients' needs. Clients can also book specific treatments such as facials, massages and body therapies, each enhanced with Eastern philosophies and techniques. In the Spa's signature Cherry Blossom Ritual, the staff starts with a scrub using cherry tea leaves, sugar and nourishing oils to strengthen the immune system and remove dead skin cells; then, they move on to a massage using hot stones; and to end, you'll enjoy a cup of Cherry Tea. Before or after your treatment, enjoy the vitality pools, showers, steam room and sauna. There are personal trainers available and private yoga sessions in the state-of-the-art fitness center.

WEST VIRGINIA

JOHN DENVER SAID IT BEST: WEST VIRGINIA IS ALMOST HEAVEN. FOR NATURE LOVERS AND outdoor sports enthusiasts, the Mountain State is a natural paradise of rugged mountains and lush, lyric-inspiring countryside. With the highest total altitude of any state east of the Mississippi River, West Virginia's ski industry has opened several Alpine and Nordic ski areas. Outfitters offer excellent whitewater rafting on the state's many turbulent rivers. Rock climbing, caving and hiking are popular in the Monongahela National Forest. And West Virginia's state parks and areas for hunting and fishing are plentiful.

West Virginia is also a land of proud traditions, with many festivals held throughout the year as tributes to the state's rich heritage. These events include celebrations honoring the state's stern-wheel riverboat legacy, its spectacular autumn foliage and even its strawberries, apples and black walnuts.

Archaeological evidence indicates that some of the area's very first settlers were the Mound Builders, a prehistoric Ohio Valley culture that left behind at least 300 conical earth mounds. Many have been worn away by erosion, but excavations in some have revealed elaborately adorned human skeletons and artifacts of amazing beauty and utility.

Centuries later, pioneers who ventured into western Virginia in the 18th century (West Virginia did not break away from Virginia until the Civil War) found fine vistas and forests, curative springs and beautiful rivers. George Washington and his family frequented the soothing mineral waters of Berkeley Springs, and White Sulfur Springs later became a popular resort among the colonists. But much of this area was still considered "the wild West" in those days, and life here was not easy.

The Commonwealth of Virginia largely ignored its western citizens—only one governor was elected from the western counties before 1860. When the western counties formed their own state during the Civil War, it was the result of many years of strained relations with the parent state. The war finally provided the opportunity the counties needed to break away. Although many sentiments in the new state remained pro-South, West Virginia's interests were best served by staying with the Union.

The war left West Virginia a new state, but like other war-ravaged areas, it had suffered heavy losses of life and property and the recovery took many years. West-Virginians eventually rebuilt their state. New industry was developed, railroads were built and resources like coal, oil and natural gas brought relative prosperity.

West Virginia continues to be an important source of bituminous coal and a major producer of building stone, timber, glass and chemicals. The state is also home to technological wonders such as the National Radio Astronomy Observatory, where scientists study the universe via radio telescopes, and the New River Gorge Bridge, the world's longest steel span bridge.

BERKELEY SPRINGS

See also Charles Town

Popularized by George Washington, who surveyed the area for Lord Fairfax in 1748, Berkeley Springs is the oldest spa in the nation. Fairfax later

GEORGE WASHINGTON'S SPA AND BERKELEY SPRINGS

Tucked in a narrow, rock-shadowed valley along the Cacapon River, the little mountain community of Berkeley Springs has transformed itself into "Spa Town USA." A total of five separate spas employ more than 40 massage therapists—three times the number of practicing lawyers, town officials claim.

The town's clustering of so many spas is relatively new, but Berkeley Springs has a long heritage as a spa destination. Well before white settlers arrived, Native Americans sought out the warm, 74.3 degree mineral springs. Still bubbling forth from the base of Warm Springs Ridge at 2,000 gallons per minute, the water was believed to have curative powers. George Washington, who first visited the springs in 1748 as a 16-year-old surveyor, returned nearly a dozen times in later years seeking health benefits. In 1776, he and his prominent friends and family established the Town of Bath, intent on making it a popular spa, and the first bathhouses were built. Thus, Berkeley Springs claims to be "the country's first spa."

You can explore the town's spa heritage in a 30-minute, half-mile stroll in Berkeley Springs State Park, which doubles as the community's town square. One of America's most curious public parklands, the seven-acre Berkeley Springs State Park operates year-round as a very affordable, government-run spa. Begin a loop around the park at the large public swimming pool, which is fed by spring waters. Heading clockwise, take a peek inside the Main Bath House, where you can enjoy a private hot-tub soak and Swedish-style massage. Continue on to a stone-lined natural pool of flowing spring water, dubbed "George Washington's Bath Tub" in his honor. Move on to the Gentlemen's Spring House, where you are welcome to draw jugs of the famed drinking water for free. Conclude this plunge into historic bathing with a look into the Roman Bath House, where you can indulge in a private hot-tub soak without an accompanying massage.

granted the land around the springs to Virginia. The town is officially named Bath, for the famous watering place in England, but the post office is Berkeley Springs. The waters, which are piped throughout the town, are fresh and slightly sweet, without the medicinal flavor of most mineral springs. Washington and his family returned again and again.

The resort's popularity peaked after the Revolutionary War, becoming something of a summer capital for Washingtonians in the 1830s. But like all resort towns, Berkeley Springs declined as newer, more fashionable spas came into vogue. The Civil War completely destroyed the town's economy. Today, the town is again visited for its healthful waters, spas and charming downtown.

WHAT TO SEE
BERKELEY SPRINGS STATE PARK

2 S. Washington St., Berkeley Springs, 304-258-2711; www.berkeleyspringssp.com
This famous resort features health baths and five warm springs. There are Roman baths with mineral water heated to 102 Farenheit. You can also enjoy a relaxing bath or a Swedish massage. There are also steam cabinets heated to 124 F Farenheit, which can be included with a bath or massage treatment. Daily 10 a.m.-6 p.m. (last appointment at 4:30 p.m.); April-October, Friday 10 a.m.-9 p.m. See Web site for rates.

CACAPON RESORT STATE PARK

818 Cacapon Lodge Drive, Berkeley Springs, 304-258-1022, 800-225-5328;
www.cacaponresort.com

More than 6,000 acres with swimming, a sand beach, fishing, boating (row-boat and paddleboat rentals); hiking and bridle trails, horseback riding, 18-hole golf course, tennis, game courts, cross-country skiing, picnicking, playground and concessions are available on site. Also located here is the Cacapon Lodge which features 48 rooms and modern cabins available for rental. There is also a restaurant located within the lodge. A Nature Center offers programs year-round.

See Web site for schedules and rates.

PROSPECT PEAK

Highway 9, Berkeley Springs

The Potomac River winds through what the National Geographic Society has called one of the nation's outstanding vistas.

WHERE TO STAY

★★CACAPON RESORT STATE PARK

818 Cacapon Lodge Drive, Berkeley Springs, 304-258-1022, 800-225-5982;
www.cacaponresort.com

48 rooms. Restaurant. Golf. Beach. $61-150

★★THE COUNTRY INN AT BERKELEY SPRINGS

110 S. Washington St., Berkeley Springs, 304-258-2210, 866-458-2210;
www.thecountryinnatberkeleysprings.com

68 rooms. Restaurant, bar. Complimentary breakfast. Business center. Fitness center. Spa. $61-150

CHARLES TOWN

See also Harpers Ferry

Charles Town is serene, aristocratic and full of tradition, with orderly, tree-shaded streets and 18th-century houses. It was named for George Washington's youngest brother, Charles, who laid out the town and named most of the streets after members of his family. Charles Washington's family lived here for many years. Charles Town is also known as the place where John Brown was jailed, tried and hanged in 1859 after his antislavery raid on Harpers Ferry.

WHAT TO SEE

CHARLES TOWN RACES AND SLOTS

Flowing Springs Road, Route 340 North, Charles Town, 304-725-7001, 800-795-7001;
www.ctownraces.com

Head to the Charles Town Races and Slots for a day full of fun. You can enjoy thoroughbred racing year round. There are over 5,000 slot machines here and plenty of other machines to play (players must be 18 years or older to gamble). There are also numerous restaurants to where you can dine.

Slots: Daily 7 a.m.-4 a.m. racing: Wednesday-Sunday.

JEFFERSON COUNTY COURTHOUSE

100 E. Washington, Charles Town, 304-728-7713; www.nps.gov

This red brick, Georgian colonial structure (1836) was the scene of John Brown's trial, one of three treason trials held in the U.S. before World War II. The courthouse was shelled during the Civil War but was later rebuilt; the original courtroom survived both the shelling and fires and is open to the public. In 1922, leaders of the miners' armed march on Logan City were tried here; one, Walter Allen, was convicted and sentenced to 10 years.

Tours: April-November; call for schedule.

JEFFERSON COUNTY MUSEUM

200 E. Washington, Charles Town, 304-725-8628; www.jeffctywvmuseum.org

Visit the Jefferson County Museum, which houses John Brown memorabilia, old guns, Civil War artifacts and documents and more.

Admission: adults $3, children 17 and under free. Mid-March-mid-December, Tuesday-Saturday 11 a.m.-4 p.m..

SITE OF JOHN BROWN GALLOWS

S. Samuel and Hunter streets, Charles Town

Marked by a pyramid of three stones supposedly taken from Brown's cell in Charles Town jail. At the execution, 1,500 troops were massed around the scaffold. Some were commanded by Thomas "Stonewall" Jackson; among them was John Wilkes Booth, Virginia militiaman.

ZION EPISCOPAL CHURCH

300 E. Congress St., Charles Town, 304-725-5312; www.zionepiscopal.net

This church was built in 1815. Buried in the cemetery around the church are about 75 members of the Washington family, as well as many Revolutionary War and Confederate soldiers.

Interior, by appointment. Services: Sunday 8 a.m., 9:15 a.m., 11 a.m.

CHARLESTON

See also Parkersburg

Charleston, the state capital, is the trading hub for the Great Kanawha Valley, where deposits of coal, oil, natural gas and brine have greatly contributed to this region's national importance as a production center for chemicals and glass. Two institutions of higher learning, West Virginia State College and the University of Charleston, are located in the metropolitan area. Charleston is also the northern terminus of the spectacular West Virginia Turnpike.

Daniel Boone lived around Charleston until 1795. In 1789, during his residence in Charleston, he was appointed a lieutenant colonel in the county militia and was elected to the Virginia assembly. The area became important as a center of salt production in 1824, when steam engines were used to operate brine pumps. After Charleston became the capital of West Virginia in 1885, following a dispute with Wheeling, the town came into its own. During World War I, an increased demand for plate and bottle glass, as well as for high explosives, made Charleston and the nearby town of Nitro boom.

CANYON COUNTRY-AROUND NEW RIVER GORGE

The New River has cut a deep and narrow gorge for more than 50 miles through the rugged mountains of southeastern West Virginia. Rafting enthusiasts consider this to be one of the best whitewater rivers in the nation. It's also very pretty to look at while standing on dry ground—albeit on a cliff's edge high above.

This two-day, 300-mile drive out of Charleston, which circles the gorge, provides plenty of scenic viewing opportunities. At the same time, the tour offers a look at the state's coal-mining heritage. At the turn of the century King Coal ruled the gorge, and at one time two dozen coal-mining towns prospered on the banks of the New River. Now, much of the gorge is protected as the New River Gorge National River.

From Charleston, head east on Highway 60, following the old Midland Trail up the Kanawha River. In the first few miles, the highway winds past industrial plants. The mountain scenery begins after about 30 miles at Gauley Bridge, where the New River flows into the Kanawha. Here, as the New River begins to display whitewater turbulence, the road climbs steeply and you spot the first of many waterfalls. One of finest gorge views is just ahead at Hawk's Nest State Park, which has a 31-room lodge at cliff's edge. A steep hiking trail down to the river provides a chance to stretch your legs.

About 25 minutes on, detour south on Highway 19 to the Canyon rim Visitor Center, which provides information about the park and the region. You also get a good look at the New River Gorge Bridge, one of the highest bridges in the country. Linking the north and south rims of the gorge, it has become famous for its once-a-year parachute jumps in October. Dozens of parachutists leap from its concrete safety barriers and float 876 feet to the river sandbar below. A stairway takes you partway down the cliff for more river and bridge views.

Continue east on Highway 60 to Route 41, where you again detour south (right) to Babcock State Park to see its old stone gristmill and to try its hiking trails. Back on Highway 60, head east to Route 20 south to Hinton, a picturesque riverfront town. A river-level road leads to a view of Sandstone Falls on the New River. You can stay in Hinton or continue south on Route 20 to Pipestem Resort State Park, a 4,000-acre preserve with a 113-room lodge and an 18-hole golf course.

From Pipestem, double back on Route 20 to Route 3 west to Highway 19 north to Beckley. Here you can ride a coal car deep into the Beckley Exhibition Coal Mine. From Beckley, take Route 61 north to Glen Jean and then head east on Route 25 to Thurmond, a former riverside mining boomtown. The still-active train tracks run down the main street next to the sidewalk. An Amtrak station doubles as a railroad museum. Return to Route 61 north to Interstate 64/Interstate 77 and back to Charleston. Approximately 300 miles.

WHAT TO SEE
CULTURAL CENTER

1900 E. Kanawha Blvd., Charleston, 304-558-0220;
www.wvculture.org/agency/cultcenter.html

The Center houses the Commission on Arts, the State Historic Museum and the State Archives. There are also changing exhibits and special events. Monday-Thursday 9 a.m.-8 p.m., Friday-Saturday 9 a.m.-6 p.m., Sunday noon-6 p.m.

ELK RIVER SCENIC DRIVE

Charleston

Along the Elk River, you can take a beautiful drive from Charleston northeast to Sutton (approximately 60 miles). The drive begins just north of town; take

Highway 119 northeast to Clendenin, then Highway 4 northeast to Highway 19 in Sutton.

PEARL S. BUCK BIRTHPLACE MUSEUM

Route 219, Hillsboro, 304-653-4430; www.pearlsbuckbirthplace.com

The Stulting House is the birthplace of the Pulitzer and Nobel Prize-winning novelist, restored to its 1892 appearance with original and period furniture and memorabilia displayed inside. Sydenstricker House, the birthplace and home of Buck's father and his ancestors, was moved 40 miles from its original site and restored here and now serves as a cultural center.

Admission: adults $6, seniors $5. May-November, Monday-Saturday 9 a.m.-4 p.m.

STATE CAPITOL

1900 E. Kanawha Blvd., Charleston, 304-558-4839, 800-225-5982

One of America's most beautiful state capitols, the building was designed by Cass Gilbert in Italian Renaissance style and built in 1932. Within the gold-leaf dome, which rises nearly 300 feet above the street, hangs a 10,080-piece, hand-cut imported chandelier weighing more than two tons. Nearby is the Governor's Mansion.

WHITEWATER RAFTING

90 MacCorkle Ave. S.W., Charleston, 304-558-2200, 800-225-5982; www.wvriversports.com

Many outfitters offer guided whitewater rafting, canoeing and fishing trips on the New and Gauley rivers. You can choose between an intense adventure or a more tame trip. For a listing of rafting companies and other information, visit the Web site.

WHERE TO STAY

★★EMBASSY SUITES CHARLESTON

300 Court St., Charleston, 304-347-8700; www.embassysuites.com

253 rooms. Restaurant, bar. Complimentary breakfast. Business center. Fitness center. Pool. $61-150

★HAMPTON INN CHARLESTON-SOUTHRIDGE

1 Preferred Place, Charleston, 304-746-4646, 800-426-7866; www.hamptoninn.com

104 rooms. Complimentary breakfast. Business center. Pool. $61-150

★★★MARRIOTT CHARLESTON TOWN CENTER

200 Lee St. East, Charleston, 304-345-6500, 800-228-9290; www.charlestonmarriott.com

This hotel, which is conveniently located just off the Interstate 77 and Interstate 64 interchange, sits adjacent to the Charleston Town Center and Civic Center in the heart of downtown. Many services and amenities are offered here, and there are plenty of recreational activities, restaurants and shops in the immediate area. Guest rooms are attractively decorated in hues of green and terra-cotta.

352 rooms. Restaurant, bar. Business center. Fitness center. Pool. $61-150

WHERE TO EAT

★★★LAURY'S

350 MacCorkle Ave. Southeast, Charleston, 304-343-0055
Located downtown near the Kanawha River in the old C&O Railroad Depot, this French-American Continental restaurant has welcomed diners since 1979. The dining room is an elegant space with dramatic high ceilings, floor-to-ceiling windows, oil paintings, crystal chandeliers and fresh flowers. American, French. Dinner. Closed Sunday. Reservations recommended. Bar. $16-35

HARPERS FERRY

See also Charles Town, Shepherdstown
Scene of abolitionist John Brown's raid in 1859, Harpers Ferry is at the junction of the Shenandoah and Potomac rivers, where West Virginia, Virginia and Maryland meet. A U.S. armory and rifle factory made this an important town in early Virginia, and John Brown had this in mind when he began his insurrection. He and 16 other men seized the armory and arsenal the night of October 16 and took refuge in the engine house when attacked by local militia. On the morning of October 18, the engine house was stormed, and Brown was captured by 90 marines from Washington under Brevet Colonel Robert E. Lee and Lt. J.E.B. Stuart. Ten of Brown's men were killed, including two of his sons. He was hanged in nearby Charles Town for treason, murder and inciting slaves to rebellion.When war broke out, Harpers Ferry was a strategic objective for the Confederacy, which considered it the key to Washington. The town changed hands many times in the war, during which many buildings were damaged. In 1944, Congress authorized a national monument here, setting aside 1,500 acres for that purpose. In 1963, the same area was designated a National Historical Park.

WHAT TO SEE

HARPERS FERRY NATIONAL HISTORICAL PARK

Shenandoah and High streets, Harpers Ferry, 304-535-6029; www.nps.gov/hafe
The old town has been restored to its 19th-century appearance; exhibits and interpretive presentations explore the park's relation to the Civil War, abolitionist John Brown and Storer College, a school established for freed slaves after the war. The visitor center is located off Highway 340 at 171 Shoreline Drive. From there, a bus will take visitors to Lower Town. There is also a shop for books and gifts. Admission: vehicle $6, individual (on foot or bicycle) $4. Park: Daily 8 a.m.-5 p.m. Store: Daily 9 a.m.-5 p.m.

HARPER HOUSE

Shenandoah and High streets, Harpers Ferry
This three-story stone house was built between 1775 and 1782 by the founder of the town; both George Washington and Thomas Jefferson were entertained as overnight guests. Harper House has been restored and furnished with period pieces.

JEFFERSON ROCK

Harpers Ferry; www.nps.gov/hafe
In 1783, it was from this rock that Thomas Jefferson pronounced the view to

be "one of the most stupendous scenes in nature." Hike up to the Jefferson Rock where you'll enjoy a beautiful vista where the Potomac and Shenandoah Rivers connect. Stone steps lead up to the rock.

JOHN BROWN WAX MUSEUM
168 High St., Harpers Ferry, 304-535-6342; www.johnbrownwaxmuseum.com
This museum contains an exhibit and film on John Brown. To the right of the museum is High Street, which has two Civil War museums and two black history museums.
Admission: adults $7, seniors $6, children 6-12 $5, children 5 and under free. Mid-March-mid-December, Daily 9 a.m.-5 p.m.

JOHN BROWN'S FORT
Shenandoah and High streets, Harpers Ferry; www.nps.gov/hafe
Originally erected in 1848, this fort is where John Brown made his last stand; it was rebuilt and moved nearer the original site.

LOCKWOOD HOUSE
Harpers Ferry; www.nps.gov/hafe
This Greek Revival house built in 1848 was used as headquarters, barracks and a stable during Civil War and was later used as a classroom building by Storer College, which was founded to educate freed men after the war. It is located at the crest of Camp Hill and sits on seven acres of property.

THE POINT
Shenandoah and High streets, Harpers Ferry;www.nps.gov/hafe
In Lower Town, three states (West Virginia, Virginia and Maryland) and two rivers, the Shenandoah and Potomac, meet at the Blue Ridge Mountains.

RUINS OF ST. JOHN'S EPISCOPAL CHURCH
Harpers Ferry; www.nps.gov/hafe
St. John's Episcopal Church was built in 1852 and used as a guardhouse and hospital during the Civil War and then was abandoned in 1895. You can view these stone ruins which overlook the town.

WHITEWATER RAFTING
Harpers Ferry, 800-225-5982; www.wvriversports.com
Many outfitters offer guided trips on the Shenandoah and Potomac rivers.

SPECIAL EVENTS
MOUNTAIN HERITAGE ARTS AND CRAFTS FESTIVAL
102 Frontage Road, Harpers Ferry, 304-725-2055, 800-624-0577;
www.jeffersoncountywvchamber.org
More than 200 craftspeople and artisans demonstrate quilting, wool spinning, pottery throwing, vegetable dyeing and other crafts. There are also bluegrass music concerts and food.
Second weekend in June and last weekend in September.

WHERE TO STAY
★COMFORT INN
25 Union St., Harpers Ferry, 304-535-6391, 877-424-6423; www.comfortinn.com
50 rooms. Complimentary breakfast. $61-150

LEWISBURG
See also White Sulphur Springs
At the junction of two important Native American trails, the Seneca (now Highway 219) and the Kanawha (now Highway 60), Lewisburg was the site of colonial forts as well as a Civil War battle. The town's 236-acre historic district has more than 60 buildings from the 18th and 19th centuries in a variety of architectural styles.

WHAT TO SEE
NORTH HOUSE MUSEUM
301 W. Washington St., Lewisburg, 304-645-3398
The North House Museum, which was built in 1820, holds colonial and 19th-century objects and artifacts. Previous exhibits have included antique bridal gowns and teddy bears
Admission: adults $5, seniors $4.50, children 6-18 $2, children 5 and under free. Monday-Saturday 10 a.m.-4 p.m.

WHERE TO STAY
★★★GENERAL LEWIS INN
301 E. Washington St., Lewisburg, 304-645-2600, 800-628-4454;
www.generallewisinn.com
Operating as a guest house since 1928, this bed and breakfast was built in the early 1800s. It is surrounded by flower gardens and lawns with a lily pond. Every room is furnished with antiques and crafts made by early settlers.
25 rooms. Restaurant. $61-150

MORGANTOWN
See also Charleston
Morgantown is both an educational and an industrial center. West Virginia University was founded here in 1867, and the Morgantown Female Collegiate Institute in 1839. Known internationally for its glass, Morgantown is home to a number of glass plants, which produce wares ranging from lamp parts to decorative paper-weights and crystal tableware. The town is also home to a number of research laboratories maintained by the federal government.

WHAT TO SEE
COOPERS ROCK STATE FOREST
Route 1, Morgantown, 304-594-1561; www.coopersrockstateforest.com
Just 13 miles east of Morgantown, Coopers Rock State Forest covers more than 12,700 acres. Offered here is trout fishing, hunting and hiking trails to historical sites, including the Henry Clay Iron Furnace trail, which takes you by a large stone structure. There are also cross-country ski trails, picnicking, a playground, concessions, and tent and trailer camping.
Campgrounds: April-November.

PERSONAL RAPID TRANSIT SYSTEM
88 Beechhurst Ave., Morgantown, 304-293-5011; www.wvu.edu
A pioneering transit system, the PRT is the world's first totally automated system. Operating without conductors or ticket takers, computer-directed cars travel between university campuses and downtown Morgantown. Admission: $.50. Monday-Saturday; may not operate holidays and university breaks.

WEST VIRGINIA UNIVERSITY
Visitors Resource Center, 1 Waterfront Place, Morgantown, 304-293-0111;
www.wvu.edu
The university, which was founded in 1867, has more than 28,000 students attending its 15 college and 185 degree programs. The Visitors Center in the Communications Building on Patterson Drive has touch-screen monitors and video presentations about the university and upcoming special events. Of special interest on the downtown campus are Stewart Hall and the university's original buildings, located on Woodburn Circle. In the Evansdale area of Morgantown are the Creative Arts Center, the 75-acre Core Arboretum and the 63,500-seat Coliseum.
Tours: Monday-Saturday; for reservations, call 304-293-3489.

SPECIAL EVENTS
MASON-DIXON FESTIVAL
Morgantown Riverfront Park, Morgantown, 304-599-1104; www.masondixonfestival.org
This free festival features a river parade, talent shows, pageants, kid's activities, free concerts, boat races, arts and crafts, concessions and more.
Early September.

WHERE TO STAY
★★★LAKEVIEW GOLF RESORT & SPA
1 Lakeview Drive, Morgantown, 304-594-1111, 800-624-8300; www.lakeviewresort.com
The Lakeview Golf Resort & Spa offers more than just driving ranges and putting greens. Located in the foothills of the Allegheny Mountains, this resort offers comfortable and well-sized guest rooms, conference and meeting space, a fitness center, pool, and several dining and recreation options. There's also a spa on the premises.
187 rooms. Restaurant, bar. Fitness center. Pool. Spa. Golf. $61-150

WHERE TO EAT
★PUGLIONI'S PASTA & PIZZA
1137 Van Voorhis Road, Morgantown, 304-599-7521
Italian. Lunch, dinner. Children's menu. Bar. $16-35

PARKERSBURG
See also Clarksburg
After the Revolutionary War, Blennerhassett Island, in the Ohio River west of Parkersburg, was the scene of the alleged Burr-Blennerhassett plot. Harman Blennerhassett, a wealthy Irishman, built a lavish mansion on this island. After killing Alexander Hamilton in a duel, Aaron Burr came to the island,

allegedly to seize the Southwest and set up an empire; Blennerhassett may have agreed to join him. On December 10, 1806, the plot was uncovered. Both men were acquitted of treason but ruined financially in the process. The Blennerhassett mansion burned in 1811 but was later rebuilt.

WHAT TO SEE
BLENNERHASSETT ISLAND HISTORICAL STATE PARK
137 Juliana St., Parkersburg, 304-420-4800, 800-225-5982;
www.blennerhassettstatepark.com
This 500-acre island accessible is only by taking a sternwheeler over. There are self-guided walking tours of the island, horse-drawn wagon rides and tours of the Blennerhassett mansion. Tickets are available for the boat ride at the Blennerhassett Museum in Parkersburg.
Sternwheeler: adults $8, children 3-12 $7. Tour: adults $4, children $2. Island: May-October; see Web site for hours.

BLENNERHASSETT MUSEUM
Second and Juliana streets, Parkersburg, 304-420-4840;
www.blennerhassettislandpark.com
This museum features archaeological and other exhibits relating to history of Blennerhassett Island and Parkersburg area, including artifacts dating back 12,000 years. You can purchase tickets here for the sternwheeler, which will take you to Blennerhassett Island Historical State Park.
Admission: adults $4, children 3-12 $2. Hours vary.

NORTH BEND STATE PARK
Route 1, Parkersburg, 304-643-2931, 800-225-5982; www.northbendsp.com
With approximately 1,400 acres, North Bend State Park is located in the wide valley of the North Fork of the Hughes River with scenic overlooks of famous horseshoe bend. There is a large swimming pool, miniature golf course, tennis courts and other game courts here. There is also the 72-mile North Bend Rail Trail for hiking, biking and walking and includes 13 tunnels to pass through. There is also the 305 acre North Bend Lake for fishing, canoeing, kayaking and more. There are picnicking areas, a playground, concessions, restaurants, a lodge, tent and trailer camping, and eight cabins.
Pool: Memorial Day-Labor Day, Tuesday-Thursday noon-6 p.m., Friday-Saturday noon-7 p.m., Sunday 1-6 p.m.

PARKERSBURG ART CENTER
725 Market St., Parkersburg, 304-485-3859; parkersburgartcenter.org
This art center features changing exhibits, offers classes and workshops for children and adults and rents out the property for special events.
Admission: $2. Wednesday-Saturday 10 a.m.-5 p.m.

RUBLE'S STERNWHEELERS RIVERBOAT CRUISES
Second and Ann streets, Parkersburg, 740-423-7268; www.rublessternwheelers.com
Ruble's offers public and private riverboat cruises, from weekend sightseeing tours to Friday night dances to Sunday night Bluegrass jam sessions.
May-October, daily.

WHERE TO STAY
★★★THE BLENNERHASSETT HOTEL
320 Market St., Parkersburg, 304-422-3131, 800-262-2536;
www.theblennerhassett.com

This landmark hotel was built before the turn of the century in the "gaslight era" and was fully restored in 1986. The hotel's Victorian style is evident in the rich crown molding, authentic English doors, brass and leaded-glass chandeliers and antiques.

94 rooms. Restaurant, bar. Business center. Fitness center. Pool. Pets accepted. $61-150

WHERE TO EAT
★★★SPATS AT THE BLENNERHASSETT
320 Market St., Parkersburg, 304-422-3131, 800-262-2536;
www.theblennerhassett.com

Its downtown location makes Blennerhassett a great place to stop for a lunch break, and its continental menu makes it easy for everyone to find something to eat. The restaurant features dark wood ceilings, crown molding, wainscoting and leather armchairs. A charming garden patio area includes a bar, a dining area, a music stage and a large screen for sporting events. The restaurant also features a martini night, wine tastings and live music.

Continental. Breakfast, lunch, dinner, Sunday brunch. Reservations recommended. Outdoor seating. Bar. $36-85

SHEPHERDSTOWN
See also Charles Town, Harpers Ferry

In 1787, Shepherdstown was the site of the first successful public launching of a steamboat. However, James Rumsey, inventor of the craft, died before he could exploit his success. Rival claims by John Fitch and Robert Fulton's commercial success with the "Clermont" 20 years later, have clouded Rumsey's achievement.

The state's first newspaper was published here in 1790, and Shepherdstown almost became the national capital. (George Washington considered it as a possible site, according to letters in the Library of Congress.) Shepherdstown is also the location of one of the early gristmills, which was most likely constructed around 1739. It finally ceased production in 1939. This is the oldest continuously settled town in the state.

WHAT TO SEE
GUIDED WALKING TOURS
Visitor Center, 136 1/2 E. German St., Shepherdstown, 304-876-2786

Take a walking tour of the historic sites in Shepherdstown. Most of the town is part of the Historic District on the National Register of Historic Places. Visitor center: Daily 10 a.m.-4 p.m.

HISTORIC SHEPHERDSTOWN MUSEUM
129 E. German St., Shepherdstown, 304-876-0910;
www.historicshepherdstown.com/museum.htm

Artifacts dating to the 1700s, including many items concerning the founding of the town, are on display here. Guided tours are by appointment. Admission: Free. Tours: $4. April-October, Saturday 11 a.m.-5 p.m., Sunday 1 p.m.-4 p.m.

WHERE TO STAY
★★★BAVARIAN INN & LODGE
164 Shepherd Grade Road, Shepherdstown, 304-876-2551; www.bavarianinnwv.com
This inn is decorated with Federal period reproductions and provides European-style hospitality. Four-poster mahogany beds, brass chandeliers and bathrooms with imported marble grace each room.
72 rooms. Restaurant, bar. Business center. Fitness center. Pool. Tennis. $151-250

WHERE TO EAT
★★★BAVARIAN INN AND LODGE
164 Shepherd Grade Road, Shepherdstown, 304-876-2551; www.bavarianinnwv.com
Few places serve such authentic German fare. Seasonal dishes include pork tenderloin picatta on sautéed spatzle, wilted spinach and a Dijon mustard sauce. Stone fireplaces and dark woods create a rustic yet elegant ambience. German. Breakfast, lunch (Monday-Saturday), dinner, Sunday brunch. Children's menu. Bar. $36-85

★★★YELLOW BRICK BANK RESTAURANT
201 E. German St., Shepherdstown, 304-876-2208; www.yellowbrickbank.com
Housed in a restored 19th-century bank building in a rural town near the upper Potomac, this surprisingly inventive restaurant serves creative cuisine in an airy, high-ceilinged dining room.

SENECA ROCKS
Serious rock climbers rate West Virginia's massive Seneca Rocks as one of the top East Coast destinations for their sport. More than 375 major mapped climbing routes ascend the sheer, slender rocks that thrust 900 feet above the North Fork River. On any nice day you are apt to see a half-dozen or more climbers laboriously pulling themselves, hand over hand, slowly up the wall. It might take them hours to get to the top. You can enjoy the same view from the summit, but without the effort.

A 1½ mile foot trail—rated only moderately difficult—zig-zags to the top. Heavily traveled and well-marked, it is a non-climber's introduction to West Virginia's panoramic vistas. A notable West Virginia landmark, the dramatic rock formation is worth a visit simply as a scenic attraction. From the edge of the river, which tumbles in a fury of white water, a thickly forested ridge forms an imposing pedestal for the rocks. From this base, the twin towers form a rough, craggy wall with a knife's-edge point barely 15 feet wide.

Begin your ascent near the foot of the rocks at Seneca Rocks Discovery Center, a beautiful structure of stone and glass. Inside, exhibits detail the natural history of the rocks; outside, the deck is positioned for great views of the climbers. The hiker's trail to the top begins just across the river from the Discovery Center. It climbs steadily through shady woods. Sturdy benches are placed along the way if you need to rest. At several especially steep points, stone steps seem to stretch endlessly above, but that's only your imagination. From the summit overlooks, the view of the river-traced valley below is a generous reward for your pains. Give yourself an hour to reach the top and another 30 minutes for the much easier descent.

Contemporary American. Lunch (Tuesday-Saturday), dinner (Tuesday-Saturday), Sunday brunch. Closed Monday. Bar. $16-35

WHEELING
See also Clarksburg, Parkersburg

Wheeling stands on the site of Fort Henry, built in 1774 by Colonel Ebenezer Zane and his two brothers, who named the fort for Virginia's Governor Patrick Henry. In 1782 the fort was the scene of the Revolutionary War's final battle, a battle in which the valiant young pioneer Betty Zane was a heroine. The fort had withstood several Native American and British sieges during the war. However, during the last siege (after the war had officially ended), the fort's defenders ran out of powder. Betty Zane, sister of the colonel, volunteered to run through the gunfire to the outlying Zane cabin for more. With the powder gathered in her apron, she made the 150-yard trek back to the fort and saved the garrison. Today, Wheeling is home to many industries, including producers of steel, iron, pottery, glass, paper and coal.

WHAT TO SEE
ARTISAN CENTER
1400 Main St., Wheeling, 304-232-1810; www.artisancenter.com
This restored 1860s Victorian warehouse houses River City Restaurant, plenty of shopping and a market. You'll also find "Made in Wheeling" crafts and exhibits and artisan demonstrations here.
Monday-Thursday 11 a.m.-5 p.m., Friday-Saturday 11 a.m.-6 p.m.

KRUGER STREET TOY & TRAIN MUSEUM
144 Kruger St., Wheeling, 304-242-8133, 877-242-8133; www.toyandtrain.com
This collection of antique toys, games and playthings is located within a restored Victorian-era schoolhouse.
Admission: adults $9, seniors $7.50, students 6-17 $5, children 5 and under free. January-Memorial Day, Saturday-Sunday 9 a.m.-5 p.m.; Memorial Day-December, Daily 9 a.m.-5 p.m.

WEST VIRGINIA INDEPENDENCE HALL
1528 Market St., Wheeling, 304-238-1300; www.wvculture.org
This is the site of the 1859 meeting at which Virginia's secession from the Union was declared unlawful, and the independent state of West Virginia was created. The building, used as a post office, custom office and federal court until 1912, has been restored. It now houses exhibits relating to the state's cultural heritage, including an interpretive film and rooms with period furniture.
Admission: Free. Monday-Saturday 10 a.m.-4 p.m.

WHEELING PARK
1801 National Road, Wheeling, 304-243-4085; www.wheeling-park.com
Opened in 1925 and covering more than 400 acres, Wheeling Park is a popular spot to visit and has both recreational activities and historic points of interest. There is an Olympic-sized swimming pool with a waterslide, boating on Good Lake golf, tennis, ice skating rink and more.

WHERE TO STAY
★HAMPTON INN
795 National Road, Wheeling, 304-233-0440, 800-426-7866; www.hamptoninn.com
104 rooms. Complimentary breakfast. Fitness center. $61-150

WHERE TO EAT
★★★ERNIE'S ESQUIRE
1015 E. Bethlehem Blvd., Wheeling, 304-242-2800
A local landmark for nearly 50 years, this fine-dining restaurant serves a wide variety of options to suit any palate. Diners can enjoy the likes of tableside cooking and steaks cut to order.
American. Lunch, dinner, late-night, Sunday brunch. Children's menu. Bar. $36-85

WHITE SULPHUR SPRINGS
See also Lewisburg
In the 18th century, White Sulphur Springs became a fashionable destination for rich and famous colonists who came for the "curative" powers of the mineral waters. It has, for the most part, remained a popular resort ever since. A number of U.S. presidents summered in the town in the days before air-conditioning made Washington habitable in hot weather. The Tylers spent their honeymoon at the famous "Old White" Hotel. In 1913, the Old White Hotel gave way to the present Greenbrier Hotel, where President Wilson honeymooned with the second Mrs. Wilson. During World War II the hotel served as an internment camp for German and Japanese diplomats and later, as a hospital.

The first golf course in America was laid out near the town in 1884, but the first game was delayed when golf clubs, imported from Scotland, were held for three weeks by customs men who were suspicious of a game played with "such elongated blackjacks or implements of murder."

WHERE TO STAY
★★★★THE GREENBRIER
300 W. Main St., White Sulphur Springs, 304-536-1110, 800-453-4858;
www.greenbrier.com
Resting on a 6,500-acre estate in the picturesque Allegheny Mountains, The Greenbrier is one of America's oldest and finest resorts. The resort offers more than 50 recreational activities on its sprawling grounds. In addition to the three championship golf courses, the highly acclaimed *Golf Digest* Academy, tennis courts and fitness and spa facilities, guests are invited to partake in unique adventures like falconry, sporting clays and trap and skeet shooting. Consisting of rooms, suites, guest and estate houses, the accommodations reflect the resort's renowned tradition. Enjoy a delicious meal at the Main Dining Room where classic American cuisine is served.
635 rooms. Restaurant, bar. Fitness center. Pool. Spa. Golf. Tennis. $251-350

WHERE TO EAT
★★★THE GREENBRIER MAIN DINING ROOM
300 W. Main St., White Sulphur Springs, 24986, 304-536-1110; 800-453-4858; www.greenbrier.com

The breakfast menu changes with the seasons and the dinner menu changes daily at this elegant yet family-friendly resort, where diners can expect contemporary riffs on classic American dishes along with a Southern-influenced continental style. The dinner menu offers lighter meals for those watching their intake, as well as a tempting dessert menu for those who are not.
American. Breakfast, dinner. Children's menu. Reservations recommended. Bar. $36-85

SPAS
★★★★THE GREENBRIER SPA
300 W. Main St., White Sulphur Springs, 800-453-4858; www.greenbrier.com

White Sulphur Springs has long drawn visitors to its waters for its purported healing powers. Modern-day wellness seekers visit the Greenbrier for its state-of-the-art spa facility. The spa's treatment menu draws on the history of the mineral springs, and guests are encouraged to enjoy one of the spa's famous hydrotherapy treatments, from mountain rain showers and sulphur soaks to detoxifying marine baths and mineral mountain baths. Mud, rose petal, mineral and marine wraps release toxins and revitalize skin, whereas black walnut and aromatherapy salt glows exfoliate and polish skin. Treatments designed for men, pregnant women and teenagers round out this spa's comprehensive approach to well-being.

INDEX

★★★★★ **INDEX**

403

E

★★★
★★★★
★★
INDEX

421

R

W

★ ★ ★ ★ ★ **INDEX**

429

430

DELAWARE

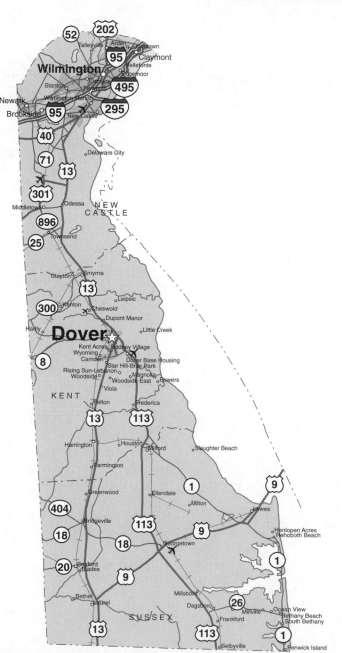

MARYLAND

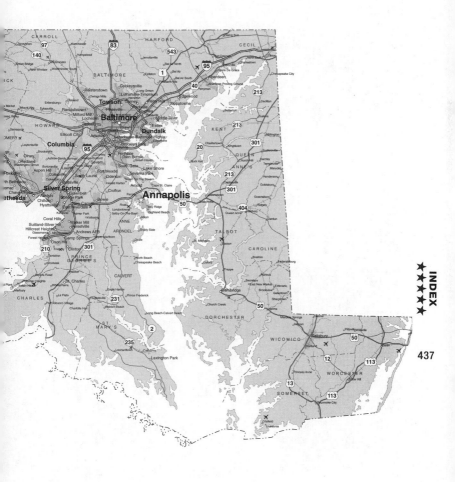

PENNSYLVANIA

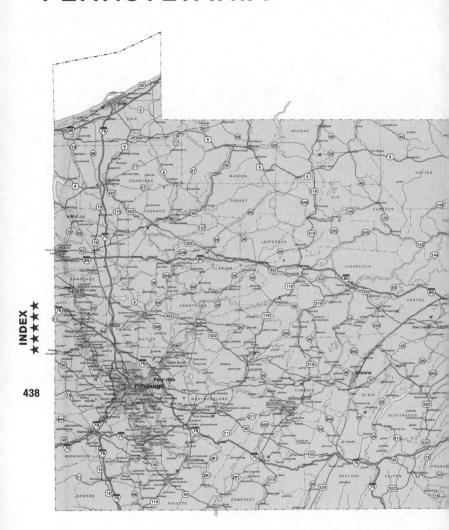

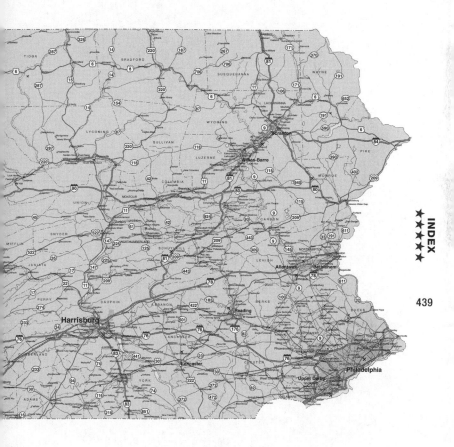

NEW JERSEY

WASHINGTON, D.C.

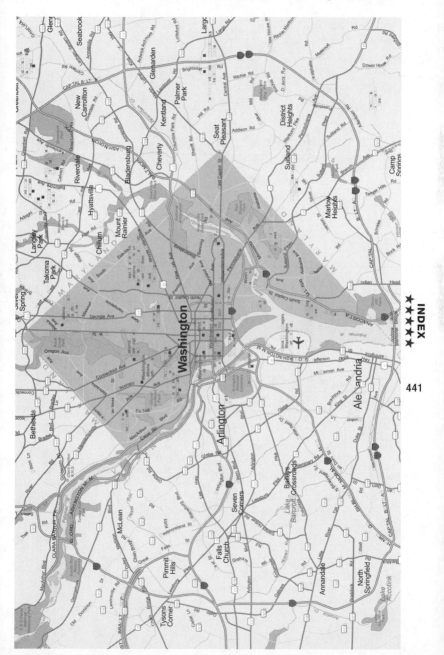

VIRGINIA

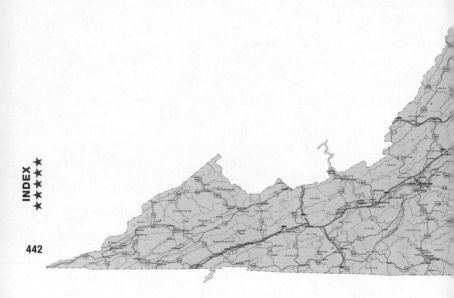

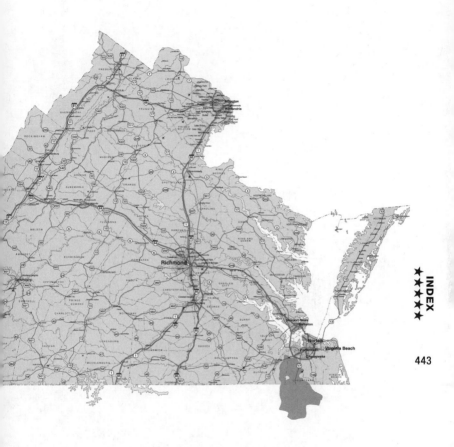

WEST VIRGINIA

444

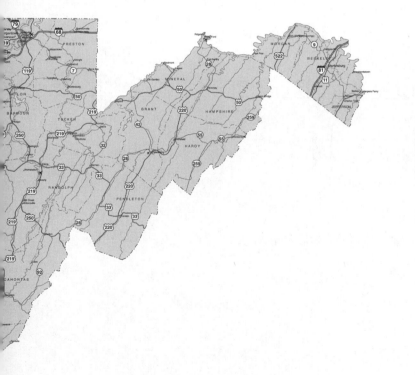

NOTES

NOTES

NOTES